FRANKLIN PIERCE

FRANKLIN PIERCE

YOUNG HICKORY
OF THE GRANITE HILLS

By

ROY FRANKLIN NICHOLS

PHILADELPHIA

UNIVERSITY OF PENNSYLVANIA PRESS

To

ANNA S. NICHOLS

and

to the memory

of

FRANKLIN C. NICHOLS

PREFACE TO REVISED EDITION

THE occasion of a new printing of this biography allows a second look and a fresh judgment. This opportunity is a welcome one, for new sources and new studies have become available. Also, much further thinking on the problem of the antebellum years on my part has suggested certain lines of reappraisal. I have scattered a number of changes over the pages and have included a selective bibliographical addendum. Finally, I have written an entirely new final chapter in which I set forth a revised concept of the meaning of Pierce's life and its historical significance.

In rethinking this life, I have been helped most by the late Professor William Appleton Aiken of Lehigh University, kinsman of Mrs. Pierce. He loaned me Mrs. Means' Diary and gave me a new insight into the personal tragedy of Franklin and Jane Pierce. Professor Ivor D. Spencer of Kalamazoo College gave me the privilege of reading his perceptive biography of William L. Marcy before its publication. Professor William E. Parrish of Westminster College likewise permitted me to read portions of his study of David R. Atchison. I am deeply obligated to these gentlemen.

My thanks are also gratefully tendered to William S. Ewing, of the Clements Library at the University of Michigan, to Francis L. Berkeley, Curator of Manuscripts at the University of Virginia, and to his associate, William H. Runge, to Professor James C. Malin of the University of Kansas, to Professor Thomas D. Clark of the University of Kentucky, to Professors E. Merton Coulter and Horace Montgomery of the University of Georgia, to Miss Mary Verhoeff and Miss Mabel C. Weaks of The Filson Club, to Julien C. Yonge of the Florida Historical Society and Professor Arthur W. Thompson of the University of Florida, to Professor James Z. Rabun of Emory University, to Leslie E. Bliss, Librarian, and his associate, Miss Helen S. Mangold, of the Henry E. Huntington Library, to Philip N. Guyol, Director, and Miss Charlotte D. Conover, Librarian of the New Hampshire Historical Society, to Edward B. Holloway, and to R. W. Hunt, Keeper of the Western Manuscripts, Bodleian Library, Oxford, and his associate, W. O. Hassall, all of whom have helped me to consult new material. I am particularly indebted to the Earl of Clarendon for his gracious permission to me to use the Clarendon MSS deposited in the Bodleian. The staffs of the Library of Congress, the University of Pennsylvania and the Historical Society of Pennsylvania have performed innumerable services and extended numerous courtesies.

ROY F. NICHOLS

PREFACE TO FIRST EDITION

ONE of the adventures in freedom vouchsafed to a wanderer in the White Hills is the ascent of Mt. Washington from Crawford's by the sky-line trail. On the upward path, if he is at all wont to think on things historical, he may have an interesting opportunity to ponder on the mutability of human existence. As he passes over that bare and lofty trail from summit to summit with the world seemingly at his feet he comes to the height for years known as Mt. Clinton, but since 1913, so the trail guide tells him, called Mt. Pierce. Vague reminiscences of a long-lost history may call to mind the name of Franklin Pierce, who once in an enthusiasm of temporary popularity was introduced to the people of the United States as the Young Hickory of the Granite Hills in happy reminiscence of the days when Andrew Jackson, as Old Hickory, had made the Democratic party invincible. This Young Hickory also became President and was to be New Hampshire's only son so favored. Why then, may come the question, did the state refuse to honor this distinguished citizen until sixty years had passed? The answer to the query is found in the bitterness of that troubled period of the nation's history when a large group of people in its northern states, conscientiously and patriotically laboring for what they considered to be the best means of preserving the Union, so lost caste in the community that their names became bywords of reproach for more than a generation. Such a one was Franklin Pierce, and to explain him not only as himself but as a type, this biography is written.

The course of this project has been aided very materially by many individuals and institutions. To mention all of them would be impossible and to select a few seems hardly gracious to many others. However, certain aid has been so very material that I wish to make specific acknowledgment.

I found New Hampshire a very congenial atmosphere in which to work. Mr. Otis G. Hammond, Director of the New Hampshire Historical Society, coöperated in this project from its start to its conclusion. He went out of his way to get special

material and to introduce me to people who could help, besides
making life pleasant for me in and out of his well-managed
organization. He gave me valuable advice about New Hampshire people and ways, and finally read and criticized the
manuscript. To his associates, Miss Edith S. Freeman, Mrs.
Agnes Horwood-Martin, Miss 'Florence E. Fulford, and Miss
Rachel Sanborn, I am also under special obligations, for their
aid in the handling of material and for many pleasant courtesies. Mr. Hammond introduced me to the grandnieces of
President Pierce, Miss Susan H. and Miss Mary K. Pierce of
Hillsborough, who immediately and unreservedly placed valuable data at my disposal and gave me the opportunity to become
acquainted with Pierce's Hillsborough environment.

Officials of the Library of Congress, the State Department, the
University of Pennsylvania Library, the Historical Society of
Pennsylvania, and the Massachusetts Historical Society have
been uniformly coöperative, giving much valuable assistance.
The American Council of Learned Societies favored me with
two grants-in-aid for research assistance and photostats. Dr.
Grace Lee Nute and Dr. Newton D. Mereness were at great
pains to find material in the Minnesota Historical Department
and in the Interior Department archives; and in the latter
connection Mr. Alban W. Hoopes gave me the benefit of some
of his research. Mr. Gerald G. Wilder, librarian of the Bowdoin Library, searched the records there and checked the account of Pierce's college days.

Miss Louise Guyol and Mr. William P. Fowler gave access to
valuable private collections of Pierce material. Mr. John A.
Dix and Mr. Gist Blair permitted me to examine manuscripts in
their possession. In this connection I am also much indebted
to Mrs. Gordon Woodbury, to Dr. H. Adye Prichard and to
Mr. Herbert B. Howe.

Just as I was finishing the volume Mr. George Fort Milton,
who is preparing a biography of Stephen A. Douglas, discovered a large mass of Douglas correspondence which he with
exceptional generosity immediately invited me to examine,
thereby providing the historical guild with a noteworthy example of coöperation.

When the book was first drafted my friends proved themselves generous both of time and constructive criticism. Dr. H. Barrett Learned and my colleagues, Professors St. George L. Sioussat, Herman V. Ames, and Albert E. McKinley gave the manuscript careful reading and suggested many improvements. I am greatly indebted to Dr. Josiah H. Penniman, Provost of the University of Pennsylvania, for sympathetic and helpful interest. However, for all errors of fact or judgment I alone am responsible.

To Miss Elizabeth Calhoun and Miss Margaret Macfeat I am indebted for much typing and retyping.

I am forbidden to make the most deserved acknowledgment of all, by stern domestic edict.

ROY F. NICHOLS

CONCORD, NEW HAMPSHIRE,
   June 17, 1931.

THE POLITICAL CREDO OF FRANKLIN PIERCE

"OUR forefathers of the thirteen united colonies in acquiring their independence and in founding this Republic of the United States of America, have devolved upon us, their descendants, the greatest and the most noble trust ever committed to the hands of man, imposing upon all, and especially such as the public will may have invested for the time being with political functions, the most sacred obligations. We have to maintain inviolate the great doctrine of the inherent right of popular self-government; . . . to render cheerful obedience to the laws of the land, to unite in enforcing their execution, and to frown indignantly on all combinations to resist them; to harmonize a sincere and ardent devotion to the institutions of religious faith with the most universal religious toleration; . . . to carry forward every social improvement to the uttermost limit of human perfectibility, by the free action of mind upon mind, not by the obtrusive intervention of misapplied force; . . . to preserve sacred from all touch of usurpation, as the very palladium of our political salvation, the reserved rights and powers of the several States and of the people; to cherish with loyal fealty and devoted affection this Union, as the only sure foundation on which the hopes of civil liberty rest." (*Second Annual Message.*)

CONTENTS

xiii

CONTENTS

ILLUSTRATIONS

INTRODUCTION

I

AN INHERITANCE [1]

*Being an account of the life and adventures of
Gen. Benjamin Pierce in his own words such
as was oft told to his son Franklin in his earli-
est years.*

I WAS born in the town of Chelmsford, Mass. in the year
1757 Dec. 25th. At the age of six years, my father Benjamin Pierce,[2] deceased, leaving a family of ten children, of
which I was the seventh. Upon the death of my father, I
was immediately placed under the care of my uncle, Robert
Pierce, with whom I remained till the 19th of April 1775,
the (day) on which the British marched out of Boston to
take possession of the stores and arms at Concord. I was
ploughing in the field when the news first came that the
British had fired upon the Americans at Lexington and
killed eight men. I stepped between the cattle, dropped
the chains from the plough, and without any further ceremony, shouldered my uncle's fowling piece, swung the
bullet-pouch and powder-horn and hastened to the place
where the first blood had been spilled, but finding the
enemy had retired, I pursued my way towards Boston, but
was not able to overtake them till they had effected their
retreat to the garrison. Next morning, I enlisted in Capt.
John Ford's company, which was stationed at Cambridge
for eight months. June 17th I was at the battle on Breed's
Hill, and upon the retreat of the Americans retired to Cambridge. At the expiration of my enlistment, I enlisted in
Capt. William Bullard's company for one year. I was at
Dorchester Heights, when the British evacuated Boston,
and entered the city with the American army. There I
remained till June, when the regiment to which I belonged
was ordered to Ticonderoga. At the expiration of the year
for which I had enlisted, I returned to Chelmsford and immediately enlisted again for three years in Capt. James
Farnum's company. In the spring of 1777, (made a Sergeant) our company was ordered to march to Albany, and
upon Gen. Herkimer's defeat in attempting to drive away
the Tories and Indians that had besieged Fort Stanwix, I
was in the regiment of Col. John Brooks who was detached
under Arnold to retain the fort, in which he finally suc-

3

ceeded. The garrison was removed, and the Fort demol-
ished, when I returned with Gen. Arnold's detachment to
Bemis's heights, when the American army lay watching
the movements of Burgoyne. There I remained during the
summer, was present in the several engagements that preceded the surrender of the British army.[3] When Burgoyne
had signed the articles of capitulation and laid down his
arms, I marched under General Patterson to Valley Forge,
and was quartered for the winter with the continental
army. In the spring of 1778, I joined the army at White
Plains. At the close of the campaign, I was quartered at
Westpoint. During the remainder of the war, I was stationed along the Hudson and in New Jersey; [4] in 1780 was
made a Lieutenant. When the army was disbanded, I was
retained in the regiments that went with Gen. Washington
to take possession of New York. I was dismissed Feb. 5,
1784, after I had removed with the company of which I
had the command to Westpoint; and returned to my native
town, Chelmsford. Here I stayed among my early friends
and acquaintances till the year 1785, and on account of the
depreciation of the continental money, finding myself without funds, as I had received nothing from my father, I was
solicited and accepted the appointment of agent to explore
the lands owned by Col. Stoddard in New Hampshire.[5]
Destitute of money, and without any learning except what
I had gathered up before I entered the Army by attending
school from the age of ten to the sixteen years, three weeks
in each year, I came to New Hampshire, and did the business for which I had been appointed. When I had finished
my business, passing from Stoddard through Hillsboro, I
called at a log-hut, and after a few words, asked how he
lived? As other farmers. Where do you get your meat?
In yonder brooks. Where your meal—At Litchfield—I
asked him if he would sell—he replied that he would. I
told him to go along with me to a Justice of the Peace, and
I would purchase his farm, which was about fifty acres.
After the deed was executed I continued my journey to
Chelmsford and the spring following, 1786, in company
with a soldier, my companion in the army, I came to Hillsboro, and took up my residence in the log-hut I had lately
purchased. Here I commenced cutting and clearing away
the trees, lying on a blanket with my companion, and living
as best we could.[6] During the summer I was appointed
Brigade Major and Inspector for the county. Estimating
the time I held this office, and subsequently that of Aidde-
camp to Gov. Sullivan, Col. of a regiment, and Brigadier
Gen.[7] I served in the militia twenty-one years, resigning the

GENERAL BENJAMIN PIERCE

last office in the year 1807. In the year 1789, I was elected
a representative for the town of Hillsborough, and continued to be re-elected, thirteen years in succession. I was a
member of the Convention to revise the constitution in
1791. In 1803 I was elected to the Council for the county
of Hillsboro. This office I filled six years successively till
1809, when I was appointed Sheriff for the county of Hillsboro for five years.

During this period a new danger threatened the country; the
partisanship that developed under Washington's administration
caused General Pierce much trouble. As he described it:

I remained in the Army during the war. I enjoyed it
much. I had the blessing of fine health returned home
full of joyfull feelings that we had driven the enemy into
their wooden walls and left the soil of our Country for
peaceful enjoyment of a most happy and free government
during the first eight years under Gen. Washington. Mr.
Adams followed and about this time to many of the old
Tories by their false profession had got into Congress and
by their sophistry and deceit had so much power that they
passed just such laws as we had fought against. These
laws being published the republicans began to complain
and said these are like the laws which we have been fighting against upon this the Tories said we will let you know
about that and to be sure to preserve their laws they raised
a standing army and placed it in the heart of the Country
to give aid to the support of these laws. The Tories then
with all their followers mounted the black cockade in imi-
tation of their friends the british and then called all that
would not join their ranks plough joggers and poor spruce
shingle folks unworthy the character of men but thank kind
providence the republicans took the hint and did their duty
at the ballot box and soon laid their standing army and
tyrannical laws prostrate by the election of Thomas Jefferson.[6]
In 1798—if I recollect—when the standing army was
raised by President Adams, a message was received through
William Gordon a representative in Congress from N.
Hampshire, informing me that an appointment to the command of a regiment was ready for my acceptance. Gordon
was an old acquaintance of mine. I invited him to stop
with me through the night, and I would give him my answer in the morning. In the morning I told him that I
had matured the subject; and that although arms was my
profession, I could not consistently accept of an appoint-

ment in an army which appeared to me to have been raised to subvert those principles for which I had fought in the revolution; that I was forbidden by the duty I owed to myself my country and my God; and that although I was poor rather than be instrumental in rivetting upon the necks of my countrymen the chains which had been forged for them, I would retire to a cave and eat potatoes to the last day of my life.[9]

YOUTH
1804-1829

II

A BOY IN THE LAND OF HILLS

It was Sunday morning at the Hancock Academy and one of the new boys was homesick. Higher education, he concluded, had few charms equal to those of his father's "elegant mansion"; besides, he was twelve years old and had had enough schooling. Firm, or at least trying to be firm, in his faith, this undisciplined soul started back afoot to his native hills. No one was there to greet him; they were all at church so he had more time to prepare for the expected argument with his father. But when at length his parent came home, he evinced no surprise; he heard his son's story and without comment invited him to dinner. Frank was rather nonplussed at so easy a victory, a feeling which presumably did not destroy his appetite. But the incident was not over. After dinner his father had the chaise hitched and with no explanations drove his son back toward Hancock. In a stretch of wood-girt road, he ordered Frank to alight and turned the horse's head toward home. His son had nothing left to do but to continue on to school on foot and as a shower came up he arrived at his quarters drenched as well as impressed. This, he said in after life, was a turning point in his career; his father had not been a military officer most of his life in vain.

The youth thus disciplined was Franklin Pierce, son of General Benjamin Pierce, one of the pioneer settlers in Hillsborough County, New Hampshire. While his parents still lived in a log house on the "Branch" of the Contoocook he had been born, November 23, 1804. His father was the personage of the community, politically active, usually in office, a militia general and Revolutionary veteran. He was a typical back country leader who, though rough in manners and lacking in education and culture, had a vivid personality with much native force and strength which made him a domineering yet generous "squire." He enjoyed the respect of the community and greatly impressed his young son. He had aided in bringing about the political overturn which had brought the democratic

9

disciples of Jefferson into control of New Hampshire the year
Franklin was born and Federalists to the Pierce children were
little better than the hated British whom their father had
helped to vanquish.

Of his mother, Frank later wrote: " She was a most affectionate and tender mother, strong in many points and weak in some
but always weak on the side of kindness and deep affection . . .
when others chided and reproached she never failed to interpose excuse and justification." Local tradition has it that she
was vivacious, fond of show and of an effervescing, mercurial
temperament which occasionally sought refuge in alcoholic
stimulant. These parents were not an ideal couple to discipline
a pranky boy, for between his father's strictness and his
mother's easy-going ways there was sure to be a chance for the
quick-witted to escape many of the consequences of boyish disobedience.

Shortly after Frank's birth the family had moved into a new
and impressive home in Hillsborough Lower Village. It was
an active household; five brothers and three sisters, the last
born in 1812, made it a center of noisy life. Besides, their
home was on the highway, the general's hospitality was far-
famed, and since he had a liquor license at various times, his
house was a tavern. Their little community might be isolated
but an artery ran through it, Turnpike No. 2, and the stage
coach from Keene and Dunstable or from Concord brought
them news from a world which to the lad must have seemed
far away and legendary.

For Hillsborough was in the New Hampshire back-country, a
land of hills and hollows, brief summers and long winters. To
reach this township from the state capital, Concord, the traveller had to make a retreat into the hills. He jogged along the
winding Contoocook, which so sleepily lazied its way between
its green banks or crawled under its ice blanket until perchance
spring made a freshet of it. After a good six hours' ride the
wayfarer reached Hillsborough Bridge and three miles farther
on came to Lower Village. Very close to this little cluster in
1804 General Pierce had built his new home.

He and his neighbors on this spur of the frontier had developed a cluster of farmsteads not long since by hewing their
acres out of the forest. Here Puritan dwelt with Yorkshire

yeoman and Scotch-Irish farmer and their thrifty, hard-working lives were spiced by a dash of homely joy and recreation which gave an air of social freedom. Calvinism was combined with shivery superstitions and God must share his sway with shadowy beings, witches and fairies. In this hunting and fishing community, Frank had found a fair field for sports. The winding Contoocook and Loon and Contention ponds were the scenes of many a fishing, swimming or skating expedition. The fields of the village, the gentle slopes of Bible Hill, the highway and the by-roads, the steeps of Gibson and McClintock, the depths of the pine forest with the clustering legends of witches and Indians, all afforded him and his companions an extensive playfield by day; and at night at his fireside the old general was ever ready to relate his many experiences in the glorious struggle for liberty. Frank was an eager listener and was sure that the only life for him was that of a soldier. How thrilling it would be if he could see his father start out as in the days of yore in his full military panoply to review the militia on Amherst plain.

Into this peaceful environment when Franklin was eight had come the clamor of war and partizan strife. With the outbreak of the War of 1812 the Federalists who heretofore, according to General Pierce, had " become pale and shamed and drawed in their heads apparently " now took heart and sought to regain power by strenuous opposition to the unpopular war. For three years, 1813, 1814, 1815, John T. Gilman, Federalist, was elected governor of New Hampshire and there began a " reign of terror." No effort was spared by the Federalists to ruin prominent Republicans that dared oppose them. The general was sheriff of Hillsborough County and his Federalist opponents sought his disgrace. After some preliminary legal proceedings based on fraudulent evidence, the legislature removed him. Suits then were instituted which would have ruined the erstwhile sheriff had he not been saved by the fortunate appointment of a judge favorable to him. In 1814 he was vindicated by election to the governor's council and was thus placed in a position to serve as a thorn in that executive's flesh.

Of the political strife Franklin presumably understood but little, but the war was real. New Hampshire was near the border and Portsmouth was a seaport open to attack and invasion; detachments of soldiers marched by on the highroad and often stopped for refreshment at the general's establishment; each soldier was to the worshipping lad a hero, going north to fame or to Valhalla. But the war was even nearer home; no sons of the general who were of age could possibly escape the contagion of his enthusiasm, and Benjamin, a student at Dartmouth, enlisted while Betsey's husband, the gigantic John McNeil, raised a company in Hillsborough and marched it to the front. The general himself as member of the council in the trying year 1814, frequently was absent at the capital and incessantly active against the Tory-Federalists. Eagerly did Franklin, Harriet and Charles await the news, and Franklin, as he recalled after he became President, regularly went to the post-office down the road for letters and papers and burned with impatience when the mail was delayed. In the summer of 1814, he was especially excited for McNeil was twice promoted for heroism at Chippewa and Lundy's Lane and severely wounded during the latter engagement. Then he saw his brother John, not yet eighteen, go off to join the forces at Plattsburgh just in time for the battle, and he shared in the general fear of an attack at Portsmouth. These were days that left deep impressions. Soon thereafter came peace but not forgetfulness; Federalist treason and military glory had stamped an indelible impress upon the mind of the ten-year-old. He and Charles could hardly wait until their beau-ideal, McNeil, and their brothers came back to tell them of the battles, the red-coats, the Indians and the heroes.

While war's alarms were sounding there was school to be thought about, and Frank was sent to the brick schoolhouse over in Hillsborough Center, a mile and a half away. There were some twenty other scholars, and two legends, perhaps apocryphal because so usual, have emerged. One is that he excelled in his studies and would occasionally spend his recess generously aiding the more backward; the other that a speaker talking to the children one day urged them to aim high for under the free political system of America a future President might be among them. School facilities in Hillsborough were limited in their extent, and General Pierce, having the unlettered man's faith in education, was determined his sons should have the best. In Hancock, a town not far off, was an academy of some reputation to which Frank was sent, and it was from thence he sought to retreat on that historic Sunday morning.

* * *

One day in September, 1852, a woman far away from her girlhood home laboriously wrote a letter to an old playmate. She had been reminded of him frequently during the summer just passed because his name was much in the public prints and the fact that she had known him when they were children had given her no little prestige among her neighbors. Her flood of recollections could be dammed up no longer, she must share them with him who, it seemed, was probably to be the next President of the United States. Writing wasn't very easy and spelling was even more difficult but pride was greater than these obstacles, and so on her ruled blue paper she regaled him and herself with the cherished treasures of her memory.

> Neither have I forget (*sic*) when you was a boy you meet (*sic*) with a little misfortune by falling into the River one Lexion Day you came to my mother and she dried your clothes and ironed them and you did not wish to let your mother no (*sic*) your misfortune, my Mother said you was so agreeable in conversation that day she almost fell in love with you.

Mrs. Fanny Currier had drawn a curiously revealing portrait of her quondam schoolmate as she had known him nearly forty years before in the Land of Hills.

III

SCIENTIA SUOS CULTORES CORONAT

GENERAL PIERCE had chosen his sons Benjamin and Franklin to receive the benefits of higher education. Benjamin matriculated at Dartmouth but politics intervened to convince the general that Franklin had better go to a less Federalistic institution in as much as Webster's eloquence before the Supreme Court had defeated the attempt of the New Hampshire Republicans to gain permanent control of Dartmouth. Dr. William Allen, who had been president during the brief period of Republican ascendancy, was ousted by the court decision and became president of Bowdoin College, a thoroughly democratic seat of learning. The boy's studies at Hancock Academy had not been sufficiently advanced so he was sent to Francestown Academy to obtain final preparation for college entrance. Here in the spring term of 1820 he lived with his father's friend, Peter Woodbury, and enjoyed the care and comfort of Mrs. Woodbury's motherly housekeeping. In the academy his education was presided over by the youthful Simeon Ingersoll Bard, a walking dictionary and a strong disciplinarian, who, tradition has it, used to double up one leg under him and then tilt his chair back against the wall; while thus enthroned he put his scholars through a rigid drill in the elements and in Latin and Greek. Life in Francestown was not all discipline by any means. Frank was inclined to " rough-house " and used to delight, so the story goes, in calling on his fellows, starting a scrap and usually damaging the furniture, a fact which did not make him especially popular with those sober townspeople who boarded the school-boys. One irate individual, Captain William Bixby, is recorded as having lain in wait for him the better part of an evening under the front stairs, only to learn that the prankster had slipped out the back way. Happy-go-lucky, he finished at the academy and left his place at the feet of Simeon Bard. Presently in September, 1820, General and Mrs. Pierce started out in their chaise with Franklin between them to settle him at Bowdoin.

14

Brunswick, in the new state of Maine, was just another village but its atmosphere and surroundings were not those of Hillsborough. Here were no hills but miles of flat sandy plain covered with pine forest, where instead of the slumbering Contoocook there was the rushing, noisy Androscoggin which fell two score feet in three tumultuous plunges within sight of the village:

> O ye familiar scenes,—ye groves of pine,
> That once were mine and are no longer mine,—
> Thou river, widening through the meadows green
> To the vast sea, so near and yet unseen,—

A little clearing in the pine woods by the river, this was the seat of Bowdoin, and pine and river clung to the memories of her sons of this early day, an impression ineffaceable.

Wedged in the family chaise between his mother and father, Franklin had his first view of the campus as they jogged along Maine Street. This acreage was a gap in the pine forest, rather bare of shade in those days. The activities of the college were housed in three buildings, two rectangular brick halls, Massachusetts and Maine, and an unpainted wooden chapel. Massachusetts Hall, the original building, housed Professor Cleaveland's renowned activities in natural science and the Bowdoin art collection. Maine Hall was the student center where the boys lived and recited. The chapel was entirely innocent of heating apparatus and in winter provided a fittingly rugged setting for the warming Calvinism of the preachers. The library was also housed in the chapel and was open one hour daily from 12 to 1; no student could borrow more than once in three weeks and freshmen were limited to one book at a time. On the borders of the campus were the Presidential mansion, a church and a tavern, while off along Maine Street stretched the little lumber town. Here Franklin Pierce was to be initiated into the arts.

President Allen's home was the first objective, for Frank must be matriculated and he must satisfy the authorities of his ability to write Latin grammatically and to translate Cicero's *Orations*, the *Bucolics, Georgics* and the *Aeneid* of Virgil, Sallust, the Greek *Testament* and selections from the *Collectanea Graeca Minora*; he must also show familiarity with geography

and Walsh's *Arithmetic*. Simeon Bard's work had been sufficiently well done to satisfy the requirements, and so after presenting evidence of his good moral character, Frank was admitted to the class of 1824, one of nineteen in an entering group
that was small even for Bowdoin. His parents placed him at
Mr. Grows's boarding house and left him with the usual ad-
monitions. As a lone freshman in the house with five sopho-
mores, he settled down, as he described himself, " being then
a very small, slight and apparently frail boy of 16. My spirits
were exuberant. I was far from my home without restraint
except such as the government of a college imposed."

When the bell called the students to chapel at eight-thirty
on the morning of October 4, 1820, the college career of Freshman Pierce officially began. He heard the opening greeting of
President Allen and then at nine o'clock went to his first recitation. There followed an hour for study, another recitation and
at noon two hours for dinner and exercise. After two, the
afternoon, except on Saturday, was presumably devoted to
study and the day closed with a third recitation toward twilight
and evening prayer which was held according to the season at
hours ranging from seven to nine. Most of his day was supposed to be dedicated to Xenophon, Livy and Webber's *Arithmetic*, the first to be conned from the formidable *Collectanea
Graeca Majora*, elaborately equipped with notes—in Latin.
Instead of reciting in regular classrooms, Pierce, '24, and his
fellows went to recitations in the rooms of those who lived in
Maine Hall where they gathered in a semi-circle facing the
teacher; in winter there was a race to see who would get the
coveted seats on the ends near the fire. Professor Newman
assisted by Tutor Packard, Pierce's future brother-in-law, heard
the classics as the students parsed them word by word with nary
a thought of connected translation, while Tutor Hale had charge
of the arithmetic. Wednesday afternoon was the occasion for
the weekly exercises in forensics at which all students, in alpha-
betical rotation, declaimed set pieces. President Allen presided at morning and evening prayers and at the Sunday evening Bible recitations where his frequent polemics filled his
youthful charges with an awful sense of religion. Many rules
also were laid down and published in a little book, *Laws of
Bowdoin*. Said these commandments:

No student shall eat or drink in any tavern unless in company with his parent or guardian, nor attend any theatrical entertainment or any idle show in Brunswick or Topsham, nor frequent any tavern nor any house or shop after being forbidden by the President or other Instructor . . . nor play at cards, billiards, or any game of hazard nor at any game whatever for money or other things of value nor without permission keep a gun or pistol, nor discharge one nor go shooting or fishing.

No student shall be concerned in loud and disorderly singing in College, in shouting or clapping of hands, nor in any Bacchanalian conduct disturbing the quietness and dishonorable to the character of a literary institution.

No student may go out of town except into Topsham nor be absent a night except by leave—upon request of parent or guardian.

Students must be in their rooms Saturday and Sunday evenings and abstain from diversions of every kind. They who profane the Sabbath by unnecessary business, visiting or receiving visits, or by walking abroad, or by any amusement, or in other ways, may be admonished or suspended.

For this instruction and this regime General Pierce paid $8.00 a term for the three terms each year, various small fees for damages, library, monitor, catalogues, and bell ringing amounting to about $1.50 and such fines ranging from ten cents to a dollar for neglect of forensics, absence from recitations, absence from prayers, including one of fifty cents for " sitting in an improper posture in chapel," as Franklin's youthful ideas of propriety might make necessary. Board and room at Grows's were probably about $2.00 a week. In other words his expenses were in the neighborhood of $200 a year, a sum which was supposed to purchase the magic touch of higher learning.

In the midst of these homesick days came his first letter from home. It was a sort of round robin from his father and his sisters Betsey and Harriet. Sister Harriet was filled with the gravity of the situation and she gave her brother her very best advice. " May you continue, Franklin, throughout life, to conduct in a manner to meet that, let you be where you may and merit the friendship and praise of all wise and virtuous people." But that was not exactly what Franklin was doing. To be sure the location of the little lumber town was remote and the opportunities for " life " seemingly few, but in spite of the strict paternal government of the college youth had its day. The boy was revelling in a new-found freedom and the classics were not all absorbing nor the president's Calvinism sufficiently gripping. He was cultivating a talent for discovering exactly how many times he could cut recitations and prayers without suffering a disconnection from his Alma Mater.

For no matter where a college may be, whether in the heart of life or upon its remote borders youth creates a pleasure world of its own in which to take its ease. Franklin had soon discovered his. There was the forest with its sweet-smelling shade, its miles of winding paths, its whispering pines with all that charm and mystery which have ever called men to the groves. There was the river with its moods. In the spring it was a furious freshet, often carrying giant tree trunks in its swift course and tossing them like chips over the falls. Always it was fascinating by day and filled the nights with a slow continuous roar which gradually sank into silence in the last few seconds before the boy was completely lost to the world in sleep. Those who knew early Bowdoin were wont to describe also the shadowy stream which flowed into the Androscoggin and below the college afforded " along its wood-fringed banks, many shady retreats, where even study [was] pleasant and idleness delicious . . . with wild calla, pogonia, and calopogon along its sides." This brook was reached through the intervale, and near it was a forest fountain known as Paradise spring which the students had converted into a lounging place and out-door meeting ground. In the woods, along the banks of the streams and on the campus the boys found the thousand and one substitutes for study which only students can find. Exploring the forest, shooting pigeons and gray squirrels, picking blueberries, fishing at the river side, by the old oak with the trout pool beneath its roots, swimming, and just dreaming the dreams of youth to the tune of the varying cadences of the moving water, or " batfowling in the summer twilight," so the hours went. Then down the road was Maquoit Bay, an arm of Casco, where the water was salt, and farther on near the Bath Turnpike was New Meadows River. When the tide was high, here was the place to swim and the exhilaration of the cold salt water paid for the long tramp.

There were attractions on the campus and in the town as well

as in the woods.   Occasionally there might be seen a venerable
man with a wheel-barrow; old Uncle Trench with his gingerbread, plain or sugared, and his root beer, was a popular figure.
Down by the river in an old shack lived a dingy sybil who told
many a student's future with tea leaves or a greasy pack of
cards; always the future promised much wealth and beautiful
women.   Then there was the tavern where the students were
not supposed to go and did, where many a long game and empty
bottle gave evidence of a none too fervent respect for the *Laws
of Bowdoin*, while often a student might be seen crossing the
campus from the grocery with an oil can which had never contained a drop of oil but was by no means innocent of liquid.
So the three terms came and went and Franklin became more
skilled in the arts not found on the pages of the *Graeca Majora*,
nor in Murray's *English Grammar:* the year closed in September with a grand commencement graced by the presence of the
governor and his military escort.   Then it was home to Hillsborough for the four weeks' vacation.

In his freshman year he had found chums, especially two
Castine lads, Little and Mason; but in his sophomore year he
made friendships that were to become historic.   Travelling by
stage back to Bowdoin for his second year's work he fell in
with three freshmen who boarded the same vehicle.   One of
these was a shy and retiring youth with a far-away air whose
name was Hathorne and the others were more assertive chaps,
Jonathan Cilley from New Hampshire and Horatio Bridge of
Maine.   The sophomore there made an acquaintance which
ripened into friendship and which resulted in insuring for himself his own greatest monument; for the mutual attachment
between him and Nathaniel Hawthorne was life-long and led
the latter to record a phase of Pierce's personality which otherwise might never have survived.   Presumably the freshmen
learned much, wise and otherwise, from the engaging, yet
superior, sophomore.   Upon arrival at Bowdoin in this company Pierce changed his quarters; he joined his classmate
Moody and a varying number of others from all classes at the
home of Hon. B. Orr, Esq., one of the local dignitaries.   He
observed, curiously, no doubt, with the rest of " '24 " a newcomer, a tall, narrow-chested, mature young man whose peculiarities of manner and action, to say nothing of digestion, became

matters of much remark; Zenas Caldwell had joined the class.

The change of quarters and the opening of the year were not long in taking place and soon thereafter '24 and the rest of the college settled down to routine. To Latin and Greek were added Hedge's *Logic,* but the most important advance was in " math ": algebra and geometry, mensuration of superfices, solids, heights, and distances, navigation. Franklin applied himself no more diligently than the year before; in fact he was better versed than ever in " beating the system." Carefree and irresponsible, he trailed along, getting his work from others if he couldn't do it himself. An episode which his tutor recorded demonstrates not only his irresponsibility but also a certain disarming frankness which was one of his leading characteristics. One day much to Packard's surprise Pierce, when called upon, had a difficult algebra problem correctly solved. Packard, rather non-plussed, asked his none-too-diligent student how he had arrived at this solution. Without hesitation came the reply " From Stowe's slate." And so the year passed, with the varying excitements of student life heightened in March when a serious fire damaged Maine Hall and somewhat disrupted the college program.

When he returned at the beginning of his Junior year it was to changed surroundings. Maine Hall was repaired and New College was approaching completion. Methods had been changed, regular class rooms had been fitted upon the ground floor of " Maine " and the course of study mapped out for the " Junior Sophisters " was quite different from that of the two earlier years. Also he again changed his residence. He and Moody moved over into 26 Maine Hall and he was to have his first taste of dormitory experience. The luxuries of life were here non-existent, no carpet, no wall-paper, no paint. The heat came from an open fireplace kept burning by wood which they got from the woodsled after the usual dicker, and dumped in their wood closet. Light was supplied by oil lamps for which they must purchase oil from the grocery. Other conveniences were even more primitive. In summer the small study, or closet, in each room could be used, but not in a Maine winter. These environmental changes were slight as compared with the personal crisis about to manifest itself.

Soon after the beginning of his third year the relative stand-

ings of the men were announced.   Pierce went to scan the list
and found that his was the lowest in his class.   This was too
much for his pride and bitterly he decided never to attend another recitation.   This resolution he proceeded to carry out
and for several days he moped.   But such conduct caused his
friend Little much concern and he labored with him, aided by
Caldwell, a serious fellow of two and twenty whose life was
deeply immersed in an earnest and unflagging Methodism.   Together these two prevailed upon their chum to " come back "
and he pitched headlong into the solution of his problem.   It
was no easy matter, for lack of practice made concentration
extremely difficult and stern measures were necessary.   So for
three months he rose at four and retired at twelve, devoting
unceasing labor to repairing the inroads of idleness.   What the
long-suffering Moody endured during the strenuous reaction
history does not relate.   Still Pierce continued with the inevitable *Graeca*; Horace sang—we hope sweetly; conic sections and
mechanics were to be mastered; and in addition Locke's *Essay
on the Human Understanding* and Paley's *Evidences of Christianity* were followed in the spring by Henry's *Chemistry* and
Priestley's *Lectures on History*.   By dint of heroic measures
Pierce achieved a mastery of Locke which left a profound impression upon his memory and modes of expression.   In this
much-conned work he sought to discover the limits of that
understanding which Locke pointed out God had thought fit
for him, and which would prove sufficient for " conveniences of
life and information of virtue."   Thereby he would know his
strength and be able to " find out those measures whereby a
rational creature, put in that state in which man is in this
world, may, and ought to govern his opinions, and actions de-
pending thereon."   Herein, too, he might read the riddle of
the universe, namely, that he lived in a rational world, the
processes of which were all logical and necessary.   In this study
he gained a lasting reverence for, and belief in, the rational,
which was to prove quite at variance with his own emotional
and illogical methods of action.

In this campaign for reconstruction he had the continuous
aid of Caldwell whose burning eyes and feverish earnestness
considerably influenced him.   In order to help in the struggle
for discipline, Caldwell turned over to him his duties as chapel

monitor, and thus put him on the road to regular chapel attendance. So successful was this campaign, Hawthorne could write many years later, that Pierce never again missed a class or an exercise (with two exceptions) nor went to a class unprepared.

Naturally, after such a strenuous term Franklin anticipated a vacation in January, with a return home and a pleasant season of idleness at Hillsborough. Zenas, however, had other plans for him. He proposed that Franklin go home with him and teach there in the district school. This was too much—a vacation was a vacation and Franklin was going home; Col. McNeil was there and he was anxious to see him. But when the wills clashed the stronger dominated; and so, thirty miles back into the Maine woods, the two wended their way to Hebron. There on the side of a hill perched the little schoolhouse whence he could look south down the valley of the Androscoggin stretching into the dim distance and west toward his beloved White Hills, which spoke eloquently of home and New Hampshire.

At Hebron he was welcomed into the Caldwell home and entered upon a new experience. They gave him their best room and plenty to eat but, what was more, absorbed him into their atmosphere. They were devout Methodists and such was their piety and religious devotion that the home was " a perpetual Bethel, where, morning and evening, the incense of prayer and praise ascended to God." Twenty rods away was the schoolhouse and here daily for six weeks Pierce, the eighteen year old pedagogue, met the motley little throng struggling through the rudiments of learning: evenings he spent tutoring Zenas' brother Merritt who was preparing for college; Sallust, Livy, Xenophon and Herodotus were conned over again—perhaps this time with more enthusiasm than before. On the whole it was a very pleasant experience for he enjoyed the warm welcome and interest of the Caldwells and he was succeeding in a new work. " To think . . . that I am by my own exertions obtaining a little cash and at the same time gaining some useful lessons of instruction is to me no small source of satisfaction." So with the six weeks soon past and his wages of $14 a month in his possession, he and Zenas hied them back to Bowdoin in the middle of February.

The spring term was a memorable one. In the first place

there was the spring exhibition and for this Pierce had the pleasure of preparing a " dissertation in Latin " entitled " De triumphis Romanorum." Just what he did or how he did it must remain an interesting puzzle; judging by the usual accompanying emotions he was greatly relieved when it was over. But other activities were in order. Of sport and athletics there were very little; rules were strict and there was undoubtedly much energy to spare. Pierce and some of his associates were very enthusiastic friends of the Greeks in their struggle against the Holy Alliance and felt quite Byronic. " And indeed, what spectacle is better calculated to excite a deep interest than a nation whose noble and patriotic spirit ages of suffering has not been able to subdue, struggling for civil liberty against their cruel and tiranical oppressors. Americans ought certainly to assist and encourage the Greeks in their glorious conflict, if for no other purpose than to stifle the hopes and frustrate the wicked designs of the Holy Alliance, improperly so-called." In this enthusiastic season, as Franklin put it, to kill two or three birds with one stone and have exercise, amusement and instruction, a military company called the Bowdoin Cadets was formed and Pierce elected captain. Pierce naturally had a military bent and felt the full glow of military enthusiasm. He plunged into this work with all his energy and his drilling zeal was infectious. Up and down the bare flat campus the cadets marched and one of their favorite parades was quite near President Allen's. The " Praeses " stood this awhile but evidently the drill bothered him and finally he ordered the cadets to detour around his grounds. But it was an unruly spring and the cadets and their captain resented this order. Consequently the very next day they filed by in usual formation. This defiance brought irate authority out of his house with a demand upon the debonair cadet for the meaning of this insubordination. The leader replied that the order was unjust inasmuch as their march put the president to no inconvenience while a change of route would injure the method of their evolutions. The president retired threatening punishment and the story hath it that he attempted unsuccessfully to discipline the captain. The company marched on with Captain Pierce at the head and in the rear rank a curiously unwarlike high private, Hathorne.

As has been said it was an unruly spring. In the midst of ramblings among "the classic shades of Greece" and Delphic woods, and while contemplating the "immortal mind of Bacon" and basking in the "glorious light of the 16th century" there was trouble stirring in the Junior class. For some reason not recorded, perhaps because of this cadet incident, rebellion broke out. The class "went out in the forty-five," they held a meeting, voted to be "free, sovereign and independent," threw themselves on their "reserved rights" and seceded from the recitation room. Once again was "Praeses" wroth and his mind fixed upon Pierce. He attempted to prove that the Junior Sophister had put the question at the meeting but failed. Somehow the matter was settled and without resort to discipline.

Even so glorious a season could not last indefinitely and the third Wednesday in May brought the usual three weeks respite. Instead of going home Frank decided to stay in Brunswick and study. Of this fact he duly informed his father who replied in one of his nearly illegible letters which contained much good advice couched in indifferent English. In this epistle he hoped his son would "improve" his time "to good advantage" and not waste in "march or merriment" time which could be better used. Language he should especially cultivate, and careful and correct "habbitts," "manly and gentlemanlike deportment"; avoid vice, no vice should be indulged in the least "as vices kreep in unexpectedly and become confirmed when there is no such thing as aradacating them," avoid all "uncouth jesting, treat all men with becoming sivility." This unlettered Chesterfield ended with the comment "money seems to be getting scarce tell me by letter what I must send to close your private Bills." This latter advice his son hastened to follow, asking for $86.35 which included $16 for books for the coming year, $8 for two pairs of pantaloons and $10 for a frock coat and vest, not forgetting $3 "for oil etc."

When the class of 1824 returned for its last year there were but fourteen remaining to seek the goal. The final touches were applied to their erudition. They listened to the eloquent lectures of the great Cleaveland on chemistry and mineralogy and to the learned discourses of "Praeses" Allen on Butler's *Analogy* and the evidences of Christianity. They read Stewart's *Philosophy of the Mind*, which, like Locke's work, impressed

SENIOR AT BOWDOIN

him greatly, and Burlamaqui on natural law.   Naturally Caldwell and Pierce each decided to cast his lot with the other, and
they shared 13 Maine.   The senior year marked the climax of
one of Pierce's most valuable activities.   Though it was before
the day of fraternities, the Bowdoinites revelled in the rivalry
of the two literary societies, the Athenæan and the Peucinian.
These societies represented two opposite poles of temper, the
former being radical and democratic while the latter was conservative.   Pierce had early joined the radical Athenæans and
in this final year he was the executive, chairman of the standing
committee, upon which body " Hath " bore him company.   The
debates and discussions of the organization as well as the plans
for successful rivalry with Peucinian were matters of active interest; so also was politics, for Pierce and the Athenæans were
Jacksonians.

But the most vivid experience of his closing months at Bowdoin was life with Zenas.   This latter was a personality, six
feet in his stockings, square-shouldered, pale-faced, hollow-
chested with " a fine forehead and a large development of
hair."   He was not without his peculiarities; his earnestness
and his brilliance took eccentric turns as once when, to use the
words of a classmate, he " caught poetry and had to take saffron
tea for a fortnight to keep it from striking to his stomach " during which attack he composed some lines which became a by-
word with '24 and which started " I'm not a poet nor a poet's
son."   But Zenas was not ridiculous to Franklin—far from it.
As Pierce wrote in later life he was " a man of well-considered
and firmly established religious opinions and . . . one of the
truest and most consistent followers of the Blessed Redeemer "
whom he was ever to meet.   They became roommates, so
Pierce wrote, " from the power of attraction not from any
outside force or suggestion. . . . While we occupied the same
room he was on his knees every night and I by his side praying
for himself and me.   He conquered me by his faith and Christian life."   Such a moving experience he treasured throughout
his life and while it did not impel him to make open profession
of religion it made a lasting impression.

Science, politics, religion, friendship; in the midst of them
the Senior year wore away and early in the summer the necessary preparations for commencement began to be made.   The

announcement of the commencement honors was a high reward
to Pierce, for they indicated that since the beginning of his
Junior year he had risen from last place to fifth in his class.
As he wrote " Stow has the Valedictory oration, Deane the
intermediate English oration, Caldwell the Salutatory oration,
these three parts rank first. Burk has a Disquisition of seven
minutes. I also have a Disquisition of seven minutes, these two
hold the next rank. . . . The subject of my part is " the influence of circumstances on the intellectual character "; a subject
which permitted him plenty of opportunity to display his mastery of Locke. He wrote to his father July 22 to know if he
and Benjamin were coming to commencement, desiring to be
informed immediately so that he might secure accommodations
before the " crowd " came. Taking advantage of a Senior's
privilege he was going to spend August in Castine with Little
and Mason, driving down behind his own horse, a luxury his
father had permitted him to keep at Brunswick in his senior
year.

The commencement exercises began August 31 with orations
before the societies, Dr. Shaw of Wiscasset serving as orator
for the Athenæans. Next day was the great day. Brunswick
was temporarily transformed.

> Stage coaches and extras came crowded to the great festal
> day. Visitors, however, came for the most part in private
> conveyances. Wagons were not then known. . . . Booths
> were erected at available points for pies, gingerbread and
> small and stronger drinks. There was a noticeable differ-
> ence in costume. The aristocracy of knee-breeches and silk
> hose had not given place to what Jefferson had styled the
> democracy of pantaloons. The graduating class appeared
> in . . . silk robes borrowed from neighboring clergy, presi-
> dent and professors in like array, with the addition of the
> Oxford cap. The Commencement platform showed an im-
> posing array of personages of distinction.

A slight shade of disappointment was present because Lafayette,
then in New England, had been invited to receive an LL.D. but
had been unable to come. This disappointment was especially
keen to Franklin, for as a reception was being tendered Lafayette that day in Portsmouth, his father with the other Revolutionary survivors were at the metropolis, and the young orator
must perforce deliver his disquisition without the approving

glance of the old general. He and his twelve associates gravely did their best and sat down for a final admonition. President Allen waxed eloquent on the subject of the " Knowledge of Man "; he described its extent and its wonders and solemnly exhorted the graduates to go forth feeling " a sacred thirst for truth . . . to seek for knowledge rather than for choice gold . . . to rise high, and rise rapidly forever in the knowledge of that only which is good." These words were the final " wreath " with which " knowledge crowned " her young disciples but it may be doubted whether the laurel crown of knowledge was the chief of Bowdoin's gifts to Franklin. Those he was to use and cherish were friendship, the mystery of religion and the consciousness of victory snatched from defeat; these Bowdoin had given him in generous measure.

The exercises over, the graduates held their final meeting in Pierce's room. With the deep feeling which is so strong on commencement day, they swore eternal friendship and parted each registering a vow of constant and continuous correspondence.

> How beautiful is youth! how bright its gleams
> With its illusions, aspirations, dreams!
> Book of beginnings, story without end,
> Each maid a heroine, and each man a friend!
> Aladdin's Lamp, and Fortunatus' Purse
> That holds the treasures of the universe!
> All possibilities are in its hands,
> No danger daunts it, and no foe withstands;
> In its sublime audacity of faith,
> " Be thou removed " it to the mountain saith,
> And with ambitious feet, secure and proud,
> Ascends the ladder leaning on the cloud!
> —Longfellow (Bowdoin, '25)

IV

INITIATION OF ESQUIRE PIERCE INTO LAW AND POLITICS

THERE was a profession peculiar to the early days of American Democracy which played no small part in the development of the nation. Technically this profession was that of the law, but it was marked by much wider activity than practice before the courts. Its followers studied Blackstone and the Federal and State Constitutions; they became intrigued by the new American political machine and wished to guide and regulate it by trying new duties and holding a variety of offices; lastly, they were artists and made themselves practised in oratory that they might sway human emotions by the voice and personality. Flowery, fiery, rhetorical, flowing, flamboyant, their speech drew a pleasure-starved people out of themselves, stimulated their imaginations and roused their feelings. To address the audiences of the shire towns and villages was to play the keys and stops of their emotions by means of the cadence of the voice, by commanding gesture and flashing eye. To their fellow-townsmen they were leaders in public affairs. To themselves, they were laborers for the welfare of the community. In actuality, they were eager for places in the local limelight, that they might have the knowledge of power and reap the fruits of leadership. The members of this profession were products of towns and villages where all men were known of their neighbors. Their calling might be termed politics, but that term has become so restricted in its meaning in these later years that it gives a false view of the interests and motives of these public mentors. In many respects, they were like the ancient tribunes of the people.

For such a profession Franklin Pierce was preparing. Bowdoin had given him her classical blessing; now he must delve into the technicalities of the law. Before commencement his father who had lately become postmaster of the village, had offered to turn over the duties of the office to his son while he was studying law. So back to Hillsborough he went in the fall

of 1824 and settled down to distribute the mail and con Blackstone under the tutelage of the local legal light, John Burnham.
He kept in touch with the outside world to some extent by
correspondence with his classmates as they had agreed. In
the months that followed Commencement, he wrote some four
or five letters to each. The first were " quite sentimental and
full of poetic recollections of old Bowdoin," while those that
followed were " far more brief, matter of fact and material in
style and matter."

Franklin found the mansion more cheerful that winter than
it had been before he entered Bowdoin. His father had pros-
pered, new furniture and decorations, including a wonderful
scenic wall paper in the parlor, graced the homestead and
hospitality reigned. The tedium of the winter was broken by
the Christmas dinner that the old general gave to the score
of revolutionary veterans living in the vicinity. The ancients
gathered in the large upper room and ate and drank to by-gone
glory, a glory not all departed, by any means, for this dinner
was to be politically useful to the host as later events proved.
Political excitement also stirred popular interest, the result of
the presidential election of 1824 being very uncertain and long
in doubt. The final announcement of Adams's triumph over
Jackson could be only a disappointment to Franklin who had
made Old Hickory his political patron saint at Bowdoin.
Meanwhile March town meetings demonstrated that some few
people were thinking of his father for governor. These various
happenings were all ominous of future political events.

One winter in the land of hills demonstrated that the homestead was not the best environment for law study, so in the
spring Franklin went to Portsmouth and made a more serious
start in the law office of Levi Woodbury at whose mother's
home he had boarded while at Francestown Academy. In this
delightful old seaport he settled down in very business-like and
sober fashion, as he wrote his sister Betsey:

> I have done nothing as yet in the visiting line. While I
> remain as I now am I shall feel perfectly independent,
> whereas if I were to form an extensive acquaintance it
> would be rather necessary to spend one or two evenings in
> the week abroad. I make it my rule to retire about 11
> o'clock and rise about 5 or ½ past 5. Being pretty closely

engaged in study and enjoying fine health and a full flow of spirits I hardly notice the flight of time.

To Zenas he defended himself against the charge of religious scepticism, but confessed he had not been able to experience rebirth, though few days passed without some serious reflection on the subject. As summer approached he made record of a cough which he first thought to be " the chin cough " and which was often to trouble him.

Politically his interest was active. National politics presented much uncertainty, party lines were nowhere clearly drawn and no one knew what form organization would take. Pierce was an enthusiastic supporter of Jackson, and with his friends longed to punish the perpetrators of the " corrupt bargain." But friends of Adams were seeking to maintain that there were no parties, that all groups had amalgamated and were rallying behind Adams. This idea must be crushed and made to fall " before the light of reason." For Pierce believed that " a Republic without parties is a complete anomaly. The history of all popular Governments show how absurd is the idea of their attempting to exist without parties and the experience of these latter times has I suspect convinced the immortal Daniel [Webster] and his coadjutors that with all their powers, they cannot accomplish impossibilities. The citizens are convinced that Jeffersonian principles are the principles for a free people, and I trust they have no notion of renouncing their faith, and that they have too much good sense to change their position or break down those landmarks which have remained unshaken amid the hardest storms." This is his first recorded political statement, and on his deathbed forty-four years later he would have subscribed to its principles, perhaps without expressing its hope. Tradition has it that at the Fourth of July banquet he had the temerity to propose a Jackson toast —in Federalist Portsmouth of all places.

New Hampshire was by no means unaffected by this situation. On the surface in this state, too, there was but one party, presumably all were Democratic-Republicans. However, things are seldom what they seem and there were many who had once been Federalists. Federalism was a state of mind and though the ex-Federalists may have joined the party of Jefferson it was with numerous mental reservations. In New Hampshire these ancient foes were objects of suspicion to some of the original Jeffersonians who were much disturbed during Adams's administration because they thought they saw efforts on the part of their quondam enemies to gain control of the Democratic Republican party. There were other antagonisms, too; the agricultural communities of the state often resented the dominance of Rockingham County where commercial Portsmouth and its interests predominated. Such opposition was capitalized by that powerful personality, Isaac Hill, editor of the *New Hampshire Patriot*, who dwelt, wrote and aspired at Concord. He became the leader of the "fundamentalist" Jeffersonians who feared Federalist revival and he led the yeomen in their opposition to the domination of Portsmouth and the eastern towns; the seat of power, he felt, should be in Concord, not Portsmouth.

In January, 1826, after several years of maneuvering, lines were beginning to form in opposition to President Adams and in preparation for 1828. This was the month when the voters prepared for the March elections by choosing candidates for the governor's council. There were five councillors, and there were five councillor districts each holding a convention. Two of these conventions passed resolutions proposing General Benjamin Pierce for governor in opposition to the ex-Federalist, David L. Morril. Today in reading the press of that time it seems clear that Isaac Hill and his followers were bringing forth the popular old general to build up their strength. The general's revolutionary record, his antagonism to Federalists in 1798 and 1812, the semi-centennial anniversary enthusiasm for the Declaration of Independence, Lafayette's recent visit to Concord, at which the general had been a prominent figure, and the general's Christmas dinner were discussed and utilized. All the opposition could do was to point to Pierce's age and his lack of education and to claim pretty openly that he would be only a tool of Hill. As a result, although in 1825 Morril had been elected almost unanimously, only 194 votes being cast for General Pierce, in 1826 he defeated Pierce by but 5,000 votes (17,538 to 12,287) in an election at which Franklin presumably cast his first vote. Partisanship in New Hampshire was reviving, the "era of good (?) feeling" was over.

Shortly after this illuminating political activity, Franklin

once more changed his residence. His preceptor, Judge Woodbury, had been elected United States Senator and in November,
1825, left Portsmouth for Washington. For this reason, perhaps, or possibly because he was just twenty-one and restless,
he decided to go to Northampton, Massachusetts, and try the
law school of Judge Howe, whither he departed in May. Here
he roomed with one of his Bowdoin friends, also named Pierce.
He reported to his sister in July that his health was much as it
had been the previous summer, " rather feeble."

Just how long he remained at Northampton is a matter of
doubt, but 1827 found him back home. The previous June the
Democratic-Republican members of the legislature had held a
caucus and had nominated General Pierce for governor, ignoring Morril. The general had accepted and as no candidate
appeared against him, the March election of 1827 saw him
chosen for the office. Now the Hillsborough homestead was
all agog, for " Pa " must be made ready for his triumph. Betsey was especially concerned as to his costume, and at her
instigation he got a three-cornered cocked hat in which he
entered Concord in triumph for the June inauguration. The
hat came to be a familiar sight at the state capital whenever
its wearer came to perform the rather limited duties of New
Hampshire's chief executive, duties which permitted him to
spend most of his year term at Hillsborough. In the midst of
these unusual happenings Franklin completed his law studies
under Edmund Parker at Amherst, Hillsborough's shire town,
and at the September, 1827, term of the Court of Common Pleas
was admitted to practice as an attorney. His old mentor at
Hillsborough, Burnham, was dead, and as his successor, Tim-
othy Darling, was leaving town, Governor Pierce built his son
an office across the road from his mansion and aided him in
purchasing Darling's law library at $50.75 by paying half the
cost. So in his new office, with his seventy-five volumes of
texts, digests, reports and commentaries, to say nothing of Bacon, Smith's *Wealth of Nations*, Montesquieu and the *New
Hampshire Gazetteer*, he settled down to earn his living from
the legal needs of his fellow townsmen.

Hard upon his induction into the legal fraternity came his
political baptism. His initiation into politics took place amid
unusual circumstances. In the first place his father's political

fortunes were so involved as to call forth all his ardent loyalty, and in addition the country itself was in the midst of a political revival which quickened popular interest and stirred enthusiasm as it had not been stirred in many years. Under such conditions politics was to prove a strenuous contender with the law for the attention of the new attorney.

The political year of 1828 was the occasion for the friends of Andrew Jackson to rally in an enthusiastic attempt to avenge the defeat of 1824. Young Esquire Pierce was ardent in this cause and entered into the local fray with zeal. The contest opened with a glorification on January 8 to celebrate the anniversary of the hero's victory at New Orleans. At Hillsborough the affair surpassed the " most sanguine expectations," for in spite of bad roads some four or five hundred marched in the procession and sat down to dinner at Putnam's tavern. The Rev. Joseph Allen made an address and after dinner the toastmasters, Sam Dutton and Frank Pierce, performed their duties through thirteen regular and twenty-eight or more volunteer toasts. Afterwards a group gathered at Hillsborough Bridge and Pierce made an impromptu speech which he declined to have published.

This rally was but one of many strenuous exertions made on both sides throughout the state. The Governor was meeting stiff opposition. He ran afoul of the sectional and national issues of the presidential campaign. New Hampshire was a New England state and Adams was a New England President. The administration group in New Hampshire made the most of this. On the other hand, Isaac Hill had been a Crawford man in 1824; he had always been covertly or openly unfriendly to Adams, and was now actively pressing Jackson's claims. Governor Pierce had endeavored not to take sides; in 1826 he had publicly avowed support of the administration, but in 1827 and 1828 he did not commit himself, and he endeavored to stand for re-election on state issues. The Adams men, many of whom were ex-Federalists, had never liked him and in this campaign they sought to defeat him. Senator Bell, ex-Governor Morril, the Plumers, father and son, and their friends organized a convention in Hillsborough, the Governor's own county, and nominated John Bell (December 12) to oppose him. They were carrying on a bitter campaign against the governor who they charged was opposed to Adams, a tool of Hill, and a decrepit old man with an impaired memory, incapable of carrying on the duties of the office. So effective were these attacks that two weeks before the March town meetings Franklin was doubtful of his father's success.

The votes for governor and legislature were cast in the various towns throughout the state at their annual meetings held the second Tuesday in March. New Hampshire was laid out in large towns several miles square and local government was carried on by means of these annual meetings at which all the freemen interested assembled and participated in the town's management. The meeting at Hillsborough Center in March, 1828, was of more than common importance, not only because the chief citizen was running for governor, but also because there was an unusual undercurrent of protest manifested by the citizens as they came in from all parts of the wide-spread town to the church at the Center where the assembly was wont to deliberate and vote. A group of insurgents was challenging the authority of "King" Healy and the town meeting ring. For some time Healy and his friends, by no means sympathetic to the new tendencies, had controlled the town, but now the old order was attacked by the Jacksonians. The key maneuver in town meeting was to elect a moderator to preside over the day's proceedings. Healy and his group had fixed upon Dr. Hatch as the proper presiding officer, but the Jacksonians had been actively working for a candidate, and when the balloting was finished it was found that the doctor had been defeated 178–96 by an attractive young fellow named Franklin Pierce. So the youthful lawyer with his ready smile and gravely ministerial manner ascended the pulpit to preside over the deliberations of that eventful day; he was also presiding over the inauguration of a new order. As the new moderator wrote:

> The election is over and the federalists have prevailed in New Hampshire. . . . The contest has been as distinctly between the friends of Mr. Jackson and those of Mr. Adams. . . . The most unparalleled exertions and unfair means have been resorted to by federalists and Amalgams. . . . The King (Joseph Healy) Doctor Hatch etc. have said that Adams' party would carry 130 votes . . . and they entertained strong hopes of obtaining a majority. They numbered among the Adams men—Deacon Stowe, David Fuller,

James Butler, Doctor Bard and some others. . . . To show you how far the influence of these men extended.   In the first place the Adams men made their *mightiest* effort to elect Dr. Hatch Moderator but failed. . . .

You never knew the Republicans in this town so zealous and so active. . . . The King (with whom I have had no kind of intercourse for more than six weeks) with all his friends old and new probably felt more mortified and chagrined at my being elected Moderator than they would at anything else that could have happened.

For six successive years he was to preside over Hillsborough's annual political congregation until called to a " higher sphere of usefulness."   On this eventful day the governor was less fortunate than his son; in spite of the *Patriot's* charges that the Federalist, pro-British aristocrats who made up the Adams party wanted to destroy the Union, the governor went down to defeat by twenty-five hundred votes.   This disaster made the success of Jackson in the November election, as far as New Hampshire was concerned, doubtful, but there were seven months in which to work and the Jacksonians went at it with a will, the defeated governor now openly with them.

The spring term of the court of common pleas soon followed the March meetings and for a young lawyer his first term of court is no small event.   This court sat in the various counties and the term which was to be most familiar to Pierce during the succeeding years was the Hillsborough term held in Amherst. In April, therefore, he went to Amherst to try his first case.   Of this experience Hawthorne writes:

His first case was a failure, and perhaps a somewhat marked one.   But it is remembered that this defeat, however mortifying at the moment, did but serve to make him aware of the latent resources of his mind, the full command of which he was far from having yet attained.   To a friend, an older practitioner, who addressed him with some expression of condolence and encouragement, Pierce replied, . . . " I do not need that.   I will try nine hundred and ninety-nine cases, if clients will continue to trust me, and if I fail just as I have today, will try the thousandth.   I shall live to argue cases in this court house in a manner that will mortify neither myself nor my friends."

In September he resumed his legal work with the lesson of the spring fresh in his mind.   His principal interest was a case which he finally won for one McClintock against his brother-in-law, Solomon McNeil. As Hawthorne says, however,

> Pierce's distinction at the bar . . . did not immediately follow; nor did he acquire what we may designate as positive eminence until some years after this period. The enticements of political life—so especially fascinating to a young lawyer, but so irregular in its tendencies, and so inimical to steady professional labor—had begun to operate upon him. . . . I remember meeting Pierce, about this period, and catching from him some faint reflection of the zeal with which he was now stepping into the political arena.

So back to politics he went.

The summer had been sadly initiated by the death of his brother, Charles, at Utica, New York. Word had come in June that Charles was dangerously ill and Frank, though he left immediately, arrived too late. He came home by way of New York where he visited his oldest brother " B. K." and returned to Hillsborough with very little time to prepare his first oration. He was to be the speaker of the day at the Fourth of July celebration at the Center and delivered what was described as " an appropriate and eloquent address," although the reporter failed to note down the subject.

While Frank toiled in his office or in his father's hay field that summer the Jacksonians rallied their forces. As they had lost control of the legislature they called a mass convention to meet in Concord and select candidates. General Pierce they renominated for governor and placed upon the electoral ticket for Jackson, which latter honor he declined on the ground that he could not run for two offices at once. Also they issued a long address supporting Jackson and Calhoun and charging that Adams and his administration were extravagant, Federalistic, loose-constructionists—that the treasonable Federalists were using the idea of no parties as a blind to control the government and remain in power. This address Hill presented to the people in the *Patriot* with a long editorial embracing his interpretation of American political history. There were always two parties, said Hill, might *vs.* right. The administration of the first Adams had been a reign of terror dominated by the Tories, whereupon " the sovereign people arose in the majesty of their strength and expelled from office the men who had abused their trust," by electing Jefferson. In the glorious years that followed the debt was decreased, the standing army abolished, office holders reduced in numbers and liberty restored. But the aristocrats continued their devious plotting and in the War of 1812 were traitors. When James Monroe became President and came north the Federalists hastened to welcome him and in many places crowded out the more humble Republicans. Monroe was flattered and partially caught. Whereupon there was an amalgamation of Federalists and Republicans and the second Adams restored the party of his father. He had been extravagant, instituted new foreign missions, put the tariff to political use, destroyed trade with English colonies, revived the slavery contest and interfered with local elections. The country, therefore, needed Jackson now as it needed Jefferson in 1800. This was the ammunition for the campaign.

In the face of these charges, counter-charges were made by the "Ebonies," as the Adams men were called by Hill because Adams had once likened the British troops and the Republican militia of the War of 1812 to Ebony and Topaz, spirits of darkness and light. The "Ebonies" called Jackson unfit. They quoted Hill to that effect digging up something he had written when supporting Crawford in 1824. They circulated hand bills with representations of coffins on them, referring to Jackson's execution of six militia men for insubordination, and finally they slandered Mrs. Jackson. To this Hill, very unfortunately for him, replied in bad taste with references to Mrs. Adams. Thus the campaign proceeded; by September Franklin was none too hopeful for the result in New Hampshire but expected victory in the country at large. His forecast was correct. The "Ebonies" carried their "coffin-hand-bill" ticket in New Hampshire by three thousand votes but lost the election generally. Jackson had at length triumphed and when the result was known General Pierce sat down and wrote congratulations to Hill.

The defeat of the party in the state made political rivalry even more intense. The old general was again a candidate for governor, and there was talk of sending his son from Hillsborough as her representative in the Great and General Court, as the New Hampshire legislature was called. Frank kept him-

self before the public eye by acting as orator of the day at the
Jackson Day celebration at Henniker, the halfway stop between
Concord and Hillsborough.   His office business took a sudden
spurt and in January amounted to as much as he had obtained
in the previous six months.   The winter was further broken by
a trip to Boston to visit his sister, Elizabeth McNeil, and concluded with a very successful town meeting.   On that great day
he was again chosen moderator, without opposition he was sent
to the legislature and his father for a second time was elected
governor.   In May his honors were further increased by an
appointment as justice of the peace.   He was now fully
launched in his new profession and looked forward with interest to going to Concord to represent his 2000 Hillsborough
neighbors at the capitol.

He had found career and preferment easily, one is inclined
to say too easily.   But there had been some elements of struggle
—not so much with the world as with himself.   Therein is
found the key to the secret of Pierce's development.   Too little
of his life was taken by struggle with outward circumstance;
too much, by fighting or more often regretting personal weakness.   So far, at Bowdoin and in starting his law career, he
was determined to conquer himself.

LOCAL POLITICIAN
1829-1833

V

THE GOVERNOR'S SON

A YOUNG country attorney of twenty-four coming to the capital for his first term in the state legislature would ordinarily find himself rather lost and unnoticed, but not so Pierce. He entered Concord life as the governor's son and suffered none of the usual oblivion. Not at all submerged, he engaged upon his new duties.

The first week of the legislative session was known as " Election " week and was the gala period in the Concord year. The town, ordinarily a quiet little capital with less than four thousand population, was transformed in June for the coming of the new governor and the meeting of the legislature. The General Court with its 239 members must be accommodated and proper respect shown to the new executive; so for days Concord was in the hands of vigorous housewives, householders and hired men. Homes were swept and garnished, lawns and hedges were put in order, and occasionally the sight and odor of fresh paint were noticeable. On Monday the stages brought in some of the legislators, the hotels began to bustle and spare rooms were aired for their annual use; many of the thrifty legislators did not stop at the hotels, and " court boarders " were a source of revenue to numerous households. Franklin Pierce and his father were to stay at John George's house near the North Church, where board was to be had for 3 shillings (50 cents) a day. The old general was to come in state later in the week, but Franklin arrived early to take his seat at the opening of the General Court.

Wednesday forenoon the new solon entered the little granite capitol with its great gilt eagle atop the cupola, and climbed the stairs to the Hall of Representatives. Here gradually assembled the members, more of them than usual beginning their first term. Governor Bell and his council soon came in and, having examined their credentials and found them in due form, withdrew. Thornton of Merrimack was elected speaker, 124–103, proof that the new Jacksonian party was in the majority. Having chosen a clerk and an assistant the house adjourned until three. Meanwhile the town had become more noisy, visitors were abroad along Main Street. Booths had been erected and all sorts of refreshments were on display; gingerbread and multifarious cakes, early apples, candy, ginger-beer, decanters of wine, whiskey, and New England rum, were laid out in the shade of the bough-covered shelters. Various pedlars and showmen were seeking to attract by their wares or their agility the attention of townsman and rustic, legislator and yeoman. The pleasures of the evening, however, were disturbed by the discovery that the vote for governor had not been canvassed, and opponents were darkly prophesying that this invalidated General Pierce's election. The Jacksonians did not know just what to do; they assembled a quorum and tried to get the governor and council to call a special session, but as those worthies had adjourned there was nothing to do but wait and discount any difficulties that might be said to arise from the oversight. Meantime the rest of Concord was making merry; a strolling circus was giving a performance in a tent.

Thursday was "Election Day," the great day of the year. From early morning visitors came riding into the capital, many of whom had risen before dawn to accomplish the journey. The local militia began to appear on the streets in their show uniforms; stray sounds of various instruments being tried out penetrated the atmosphere; the whole town was going to march in the parade or watch state officialdom as it went to the North Church to hear the election sermon. The legislature met briefly and then adjourned to the capitol yard for the procession. The musicians were booming drums and shrilling fifes, Captain Pecker and his resplendent Columbian Artillery, Governor Bell and his military aides, even more resplendent, the council, the twelve gentlemen of the senate and the horde of 227 members of the house, all took their places. After the usual restless delays and the nervous fussing of the marshals the music started, the procession moved and Concord street was treated to its annual display as the visual representation of the state marched to the North Meeting House.

Before its portals the military halted and through files of militia Franklin Pierce and his associates passed into the sanctuary. Rev. Humphrey Moore of Milford presided, the order of exercises advanced and then came the election sermon. " And the eye cannot say unto the hand I have no need of thee, nor again the head to the feet, I have no need of you." Knowledge, religion and civil freedom were the reciprocal aids necessary for the support of the Union and the promotion of the interest of the body politick,—all three were indispensable. So the clergyman unfolded his theme and closed with an appeal for the perpetuity of the Union, expressing his hope that the time might never come in our wide-extended and highly favored country when the South should say to the North or the North to the South, the West to the East or the East to the West " I have no need of thee." It was an able and restrained sermon, but long, and no doubt many were quite ready to partake of the invariable election dinners of salmon and plum pudding.

There were numerous other preliminaries of vote canvassing and notification but finally Friday afternoon brought word that the governor-elect was approaching Concord escorted by the committee of notification. Numerous citizens hurried out to the Hopkinton line and accompanied him triumphantly into town, as he rode along peering out from under his cocked-hat—truly he was the last of the old order. So accoutered and accompanied he went to John George's where lodgings were prepared for him. The next morning at 10:30 he was inaugurated. The message was received and the council organized—election week was over.

After these elaborate preliminaries the legislature settled down to its thirty-day task. The old governor had set forth the problems in his message in such " chaste and elegant " English that the opposition refused to believe that he could have written it himself. Better roads were necessary if the New Hampshire farmers were going to be able to compete with the new western agriculture. There was the question of the educational tax or literary fund; the opposition had voted to distribute it among the towns to aid local education, but the governor recommended that it be used for its original purpose, to establish a state university which should be more truly the people's university than aristocratic Dartmouth. He reported that the militia needed reorganization. These questions were discussed and some legislation passed but they were not the matters of greatest importance that session either to Pierce or to the state.

A young man serving his first term in so unwieldy a legislative body, even though he were the governor's son, would scarcely take a very prominent part in legislation, nor did Pierce. His interests were confined chiefly to the educational problems of the state. So many of the representatives were serving their first terms that several of the committee chairmanships had to go to new men. Consequently, having had the benefit of a college education, Pierce was looked upon as fitted to be chairman of the committee on education. This committee was charged with investigating the management of primary education by the towns and with considering whether such management should be exercised by a general committee for each town or by committees in the school districts into which each town was divided. The committee decided in favor of the latter scheme, and the bill which Pierce reported and managed was passed without a record vote. The question of the disposition of the " literary fund " was not referred to his committee but to a " select committee," and when the question of the establishment of a university came to the committee on education in the final days of the session, Pierce reported a resolution to postpone consideration until the next session.

To Pierce presumably the most important legislative question was that which permitted him to make his maiden speech in the midst of an exciting debate. The particular issue before the legislature involved the fundamentally important political agent—the press. Heretofore, the laws had been published by all the papers in the state, but since the greater number of the papers were not Jacksonian, the majority soon discovered that the system in vogue was too expensive. As they were earnest champions of reform and economy, a less costly mode must be found. What could be better than to have the laws published by Jackson papers only; as a measure of " economy " state patronage was to be confined to Jacksonian editors. But to put this into effect was not easy, even though the caucus had accepted it and a very mild partisan had been selected to introduce the bill. The initial moves did not work out as expected and, according to a local journalist, the leaders " took alarm." Claggett looked confused and the speaker sat " like Augustus consulting Horace " until a motion to lay on the table prevailed and the house recessed for dinner. A caucus was held hurriedly and the party decided to stick to their plan—but would the cohorts stand firm?

When the house met that afternoon, the vote stood 106–102— a close squeeze—party lines were not holding very well. The minority attempted to have the bill indefinitely postponed but were snowed under 117–89 and the house adjourned. It had been an exciting midsummer's day but the partisans were triumphant and among them Pierce.

Another caucus of a rather disciplinary nature was held that evening to prepare for the morrow, the stragglers were whipped in and when the house met next morning the party showed itself better drilled.

After proceedings had advanced several days with various expedients and no progress Franklin Pierce obtained the floor for his maiden speech. He had prepared it, had been awaiting his opportunity, and now, speech in hand, he rose to the occasion. He was getting weary, he said, of continually voting on the same question. The printing of the laws obviously had cost too much. By the Jacksonian scheme the number of papers was reduced one-half while two-thirds of the circulation was retained. Thus the information would be adequately distributed while economy was practised. Economy was necessary. The legislature had found the treasury in a deplorable condition, a condition never before experienced. But now the minority captiously was resisting this measure of necessary economy by delay, amendment and every other expedient. It had been considered now for some days and while no man regretted more deeply than himself delay in the orderly progress of business, he believed a principle was at stake, an honest and just and economical principle. "Full in this faith, sir, I am prepared to sit here two days longer before I will yield such principle." This was as far as the prepared speech went but as a point which Wilson, the opposition leader, had attempted to make, had been left unanswered he essayed to reply extemporaneously. Of what he said there is no record. It drew from the opposition press the comment that answering Wilson was "a task for which the member from Hillsborough never was born." Nevertheless, Pierce had made his debut and the bill was ordered to a third reading on the morrow. Biographically the speech is of interest because it shows, as his speeches did so many times, his predilection for the assumption of a principle as the motive for his very human actions. The next day the bill passed and after one last exhibition of partisanship in changing the name of the town of Adams to Jackson, on July 4, the legislature adjourned. Partisan supremacy had been maintained, and Pierce had been an active and enthusiastic helper in that work.

The reawakening of partisanship was in fact the feature of this session. The name of New Hampshire, as time went on, was to become a by-word in political history for thoroughness of party organization, for the efficiency of its machine, the firm control which its "bosses" maintained over legislation and for many other political devices. At an early day these tendencies had begun to manifest themselves. They may be said to have been born in the session of 1804, when the Jeffersonians obtained control of the legislature for the first time and instituted new methods; but the decline of active partisanship in the miscalled "era of good feeling" had made the new methods more or less unnecessary and they had been generally abandoned. Now in 1829, they were revived and much amplified by the Jacksonians; from that time they never again fell into disuse. At his first session, therefore, Pierce had witnessed the reorganization upon a permanent basis of a system of politics which in time was to bask in the spotlight of nation-wide attention because of its particularly notorious character. The center and soul of this politics was the caucus. Pierce's first legislative experience had been his attendance at a meeting of his Jacksonian associates in election week to nominate candidates for speaker and the state offices. Thereafter in the ensuing month these Jacksonian Republicans, or Democrats as they may now be called, met each night at the Eagle Coffee House or at the "Dictator's Palace" to determine what their joint action should be on the various measures before the legislature.

New Hampshire, so the "Ebony" press said, had a dictator as well as a caucus. Isaac Hill had been an active figure politically for twenty years as editor of the *Patriot* but he had never come into the full power of his leadership until the advent of Jackson. He had become the recognized confidant of "Old Hickory" in the state, and Jacksonian editors throughout the nation had quoted extensively from the *Patriot*. Upon his

inauguration Jackson had appointed Hill second comptroller
of the treasury and he was recognized as the President's principal New England adviser.   Many also held him responsible
for Benjamin Pierce's election and conduct in office.   There is
very little evidence upon this latter point; certainly there appear times when Hill was none too well in accord with the old
general, and Pierce undoubtedly had a popular strength of his
own which Hill realized and attempted to use, perhaps without
as much influence over the governor as their enemies charged.
The charge is scarcely important because the governor had
such slight power and really counted for little as a force in state
legislation.   The important fact is that the meeting of the
legislature brought Hill back from Washington on " private
business," and the caucus often thereafter convened in a room
next to the *Patriot* office known to the opposition as the " Dictator's Palace," situated on Main Street just south of the state
house yard.   The extent of Hill's influence is not apparent in
any record; whether he dominated his party as completely as
his enemies charged is a problem still unsolved.

It was in the caucus that Pierce received his first legislative
training.   Just as his first campaigns, so closely entwined with
his father's success, had made politics very personal and called
out family loyalty, so this first legislative experience, set as it
was in a background of earnest and enthusiastic party organization, made public service and party loyalty almost synonymous.
To understand Pierce as a politician and public man we cannot,
therefore, consider too closely these years 1827 to 1829 which
marked his entrance into politics.   These months made the New
Hampshire Democracy an organization which called forth the
deep loyalties which men have for their families and their fraternal associates.   The Democratic party was to become for
Pierce his family, his fraternity, his church and his country.
But of these things presumably Pierce and his father thought
little as they returned to Hillsborough " well satisfied with the
proceedings of the session."

VI

MOODS AND MUSINGS OF THE GENTLEMAN FROM HILLSBOROUGH

THE return to Hillsborough brought a distinct and unpleasant reaction. After the experiences at the capital life in the village was tame and monotonous. By temperament Pierce was not well equipped to protect himself against depression. The common necessities confronting young men which compel them to go and make a place by their own efforts did not particularly affect him. He lived at home and profited by his father's prominence. So instead of matching his wits with the world he gave himself over to his moods and took an intensive course in self study seeking to gain a comfortable knowledge of his own personality in order to find self confidence and nerve control, that coördination so necessary for happiness.

Politics served periodically as an antidote but regularly the moods, the sentimental melancholy born of an abundance of energy and a too commonplace existence would return and the young lawyer alone in his office would sigh for the moon, for worlds to conquer and fair ladies to dazzle. This effectually prevented, for those few minutes at least, other thought or any work. So upon his return from the June session he settled down to banish these moods with the reflection:

> It is a fact that so far as our happiness is concerned it matters not much where we are, so that we are satisfied with our situation and whether we will be satisfied or not depends upon ourselves. There is nothing which so certainly establishes our prosperity as constant industry and a spirit of stern self-relying perseverence, which quails not before adversity nor is elated by good fortune and nothing surely contributes so much to our happiness as a fixed determination to be satisfied with the lot fortune has cast for us. You know my doctrine is that almost everything depends upon ourselves. We can be satisfied if we will.

So fortified by philosophy he had scarcely arrived home before he set forth upon another journey. Nearly ten years before, his brother Sullivan, then stationed far up in the northwest

48

at Mackinac Island, had married the daughter of the Indian
agent.   Sullivan had died in 1824 and his wife with their two
children settled finally in Detroit.   She outlived her husband
less than five years and now it was necessary for Franklin to
go west and bring the little girls of eight and four to their
grandfather's.   Late in July Pierce began his journey.   He
went by land to Saratoga, revisited Utica and passed on through
Auburn, Geneva and Rochester to Buffalo.   From there, he
went to Niagara and marvelled at its grandeur.   He visited
Lewiston and Queenstown with their historic memories and
then on to Detroit.   Here his stay was brief; he learned what
he could from Colonel Biddle and others who had known his
brother and his wife and then started with Mary and Anne
upon the homeward journey.   Whatever his impressions of the
West, he left them unrecorded, but they were the only ones he
ever received at first hand during the period of his active life.
He returned to Hillsborough with his nieces within less than
six weeks from the time he left it.   Here he found his business
needed his attention and he started in to apply himself " very
closely."

A journey to Boston in September to visit his sisters caused
him further reflection.   His two brothers-in-law, McNeil and
Jameson, with their families had moved to the " Hub," and
were soon to receive appointments in the custom house.   Harmony, however, had not gone with them, so their brother felt
called upon to admonish his sisters.   " I hope you and Harriet
make your sojourn together as agreeable as possible, *tho I very
much doubt the disposition of either of you to do so.*   There
seems to be a strange fatality attending the existence of some
persons which pushes them forward continuously to take steps
that must make themselves and those who are about them
miserable.   Such I hope are neither of you.   You may both be
comfortable and happy if you will.   If you elect otherwise I
know not where you will look for sympathy."   Whether this
wise letter had the desired effect is doubtful but the half-sisters
united in agreeing that Franklin was less ministerial in his carriage than formerly.

Hillsborough winters begin early and long is their duration.
When the birds fly south and the first snow falls life becomes a
monotonous struggle with cold and bad roads.   There was in

those days a minimum temptation or indeed possibility of seeking the outer world; life centered in the community and there
was little to distract. Small things assumed large proportions,
interests became petty. With Pierce energy and interest were
dammed up only to overflow in moods and melancholy. New
Year's day, 1830, he sat down and wrote Betsey:

> I am here and doing just business enough to live. My
> prospects are Heaven knows what. I dare not look upon
> them with much confidence since it has been with me thus
> far pretty much as with the polished philosopher, who de-
> clared that in his life he had never met with but two things
> that equalled his anticipations, sunrise from a mountain
> and a draught of water when he was dry. My purposes
> for the future are quite as unsettled as they were three
> years ago. If they were ever fixed at all, they are now
> afloat. In every change that may be suggested to our
> minds, in almost every step we take there are a thousand
> considerations to be weighed and when our inclination
> might most decidedly lead us, precisely then, some interest
> some circumstance we cannot control intervenes and as we
> regard our own happiness or the happiness of those we love
> dearly as ourselves forbids us to go. I fear tis so in every-
> thing, a curse we cannot escape.
>
> > Circumstance that unspiritual God
> > And miscreator makes and helps along
> > Our coming evils with a crutch-like rod
> > Whose touch *turns hope to dust—the dust we all have trod*
>
> But I am getting out of my usual strain and must for
> consistency's sake either stop or change. By way of im-
> provement therefore I would just remark that this is un-
> questionably " a funny old world " and further that there
> is no other way but to " push along keep moving " as other
> people do. While [here is] not a sylable as to what I
> shall do, there are [some things] I certainly shall not do.
> I shall not drag [out the] life of an old bachelor in Hills-
> borough and [yet the] circumstances and prospects are
> such as to render every thought of my giving up the
> " pleasures of single blessedness in the highest degree
> ridiculous."

He had previously written to McNeil: " I want something in
an hour of relaxation besides trudging from house to office and
back again. I should like some society which might keep off
that *ennui* so sure to punish a moment of idleness—something

to break the dull monotony, which in such a place as this, hangs about human existence." Especially did this mood strike him because he was "full in the faith" that he was "to know whatever of joy there is, in a life of single blessedness." Just why is a question. Perhaps a mysterious Miss C. was not favorable to his advances.

But no winter, however long, does not give way to spring; and as all life takes on new lease with the equinox so Pierce's spirits rose in tune with budding nature. The mountains turned green, the forest trees began to leaf, gone was the melancholy of the ice-bound winter and he could say "I am at ease; the best that can happen will not much elate me and the worst that may befall *shall not overwhelm.*" Then, too, politics had again come into action, and the spring sessions of the courts.

Town meeting day found Pierce in the moderator's chair for the third time and his townsmen sent him again to the legislature as their spokesman. Jacksonians were all excitement because Isaac Hill had been rejected by the Senate and many felt that the honor of the state had been directly attacked, although the ostensible reason for the rejection was Hill's unfortunate reference to Mrs. Adams. On the eve of the meeting of the legislature Pierce wrote his brother-in-law in a manner which showed concern over the possibility of Calhoun causing a split in the party.

> The present appears to me to be a very important crisis in politicks. Calhoun I apprehend is determined to take the field at all hazards, and there seem to be good reasons for fearing a division of the present dominant party . . . one can hardly avoid laughing in anticipation, to think, if it should be so, what a hell of a scrambling there would be among our *eleventh hour* Jackson men. . . . We deem it prudence here to say as little as possible of the politicks of the day and to speak not a word of the signs which some may have discovered of an approaching scism (*sic*) because it is by no means certain what course it will be for the interest of the Republican party to pursue. This alone ought to be regarded and it would be extreme folly for one individual to work himself into a fever about the future fortunes of another. "Sufficient for the day is the evil thereof."

A few days later he rode off to Concord to attend the June session. This year he went to live at Mrs. Dearborn's and fared well for sixty cents a day, washing extra.

Election week with its festivities again held all attention. Old General Pierce in his cocked hat and blue and buff led the procession to the election sermon and thereafter delivered his last message. After he had welcomed Matthew Harvey, the new governor, he retired to Hillsborough, full of years and honors. His son found himself again one of a well organized majority, and the legislative activity moved on apace. Pierce, as chairman of the committee on towns and parishes, was prominent in the chief event, namely, a lively gerrymandering squabble. Some years before the legislature had created the town of Franklin. The Democrats declared it had been done by those in sympathy with Adams to increase their strength in the legislature. In doing this the legislature had deprived the town of Northfield of its most valuable taxable assets and the Jacksonians now desired to do justice to Northfield and perhaps make Franklin Democratic. Down in room 13 Pierce's committee outvoted him and brought in a report against the partition. A lively series of legislative maneuvers followed which finally resulted in the passage of a bill to restore to Northfield its lost taxables, the bill passing only by the casting vote of the speaker; party lines had barely held in spite of the caucus. In this scrimmage Pierce was quite active and as chairman of the committee was called upon to speak in explanation several times. Besides passing this partisan legislation, the Democrats went further and rebuked the United States Senate for refusing to confirm Hill, passing resolutions to that effect and, as Woodbury's term was expiring, making Hill a member of the body that had rejected him.

As in the previous session, the outside activities of the Jacksonian legislators were noteworthy; this year the legislative caucus for nominating a state ticket increased its interests. A platform was drawn up protesting against internal improvements at national expense, calling for low taxes and distribution of the surplus revenue, and renominating Jackson for the presidency. The convention sought to increase the solidity of the state organization by a central committee of four, and a general committee of correspondence composed of one man from

each county; C. G. Atherton was to represent Pierce's county.
Having done what they could in these ways, the Democrats
adjourned the legislature after a session of thirty-three days,
marked by a minimum of legislation; or, as the opposition papers had it, the caucus closed its session of twenty-five nights.

The year intervening between the legislative sessions of 1830
and 1831 seems to have been a more active and less moody
sequence of seasons. Rather than the usual winter melancholy,
there was " fine health " and he found himself " very happy " in
pursuing his profession, success in which he " esteemed more
important . . . than politicks or anything else." This, too, on
St. Valentine's Day. Pierce's law practice was growing and as
usual there was McNeil vs. McClintock to be looked after.
Then there were a trip to Boston, a brief period of illness and
more politics than usual. Gov. Harvey had been appointed
to the federal bench. Consequently he had withdrawn as candidate for re-election. This situation called for a state convention to provide a new candidate. January, therefore, found
Concord temporarily aroused from its winter quiet while
warming pans and hot bricks struggled with the icy sheets for
a night or two. On the thirteenth the convention assembled,
and among them Pierce. He was made one of the committee
on address and resolutions and that afternoon, while Samuel
Dinsmoor was being nominated, they labored to produce an
elaborate series of resolutions. They hailed Jackson and
lauded his achievements. The Adams dynasty had been com-
parable to the Stuarts. Both had been harmful to American
liberty. Jackson's election, therefore, had been a veritable
revolution and they hoped he would run again. They declared
themselves opposed to internal improvements, upheld states'
rights as the bulwark of liberty, and condemned the protective
tariff. In private Pierce expressed his tariff views in somewhat indefinite fashion, " it appears to me that a tariff upon
proper articles properly graduated is desirable and consistent
with the most enlarged and liberal policy, but it should as far
as practicable be equal in its operations, and never be so extended as to throw the current of capital into one particular
channel or to enable the manufacturer to fatten upon the hard
and scanty earnings of the consumer."

This platform was evidently attractive to New Hampshire

voters, for Dinsmoor was elected and Pierce sent to the legislature at the March town meetings. In fact this election sealed
the Democratic triumph and their power was not menaced at
the annual election for the next seven years.

When Pierce went to Concord in June for his third session
he settled down with Arlond Carroll for roommate. At the
first meeting of the caucus he was nominated for speaker. During election week he was duly chosen and assumed his station
as presiding officer with considerable temerity; he felt rather
strange, at twenty-six, to be presiding over two hundred and
twenty-nine legislators in the intricacies of parliamentary procedure. Nothing daunted, however, he purchased a frock coat
and proceeded to make what his friend Ben French called " a
devilish fine speaker" whom everyone liked. His arduous
duties required some relaxation, so he went with Ben French
on the first weekend over to Chester. Here he was introduced
to French's sisters-in-law, the daughters of Chief Justice Richardson. They had a capital time and Pierce fell in love with
all three girls, Mary, Ann and Louise. He perhaps fancied
Ann the most and escorted her on a jaunt to the " great rock."
Returning to Concord he confided to his friend that he never
had seen young ladies who filled his ideas of perfection so
well, and if he were able he would be married in six months.
A few days later the " Dictator " gave a reception at his home,
and after experiencing the delights of this jam, Pierce and
French went to the speaker's lodging and there indulged in
trials of strength which drew from French the comment that
" he is the most powerful man of his size I know of." The
session thus passed pleasantly enough, a whole army of bills was
passed under the speaker's amiable presiding, a number of
bank and manufacturing corporations were chartered, and aid
was given poor debtors; the session adjourned at the usual time
and the speaker laid down his gavel.

Pierce's trip this year was again on an errand of consolation.
His brother Benjamin had lost his second wife that winter and
had recently met with a serious accident, so Franklin went
south to visit him at his post in New Castle, Delaware, where
he tried to cheer him up and made the acquaintance of his little
nephew Benjamin, Jr., whose few months of life had not given
him the experience necessary to appreciate his uncle.

Speaker, traveller, responsible uncle, life still had experiences in store for Pierce of a nature especially pleasing. He was to become what he had often desired to be, a military man. Governor Dinsmoor had appointed him his aide and it was hereafter " Col. Pierce." His great delight in this honor was so spontaneous that he must be permitted to record it himself.

There was a volunteer muster of the independent companies in the different Regts. of the County. I arrived at Keene on Thursday afternoon and during the whole of that beautiful night companies were coming in from all directions and pitching their tents in true military style. Four of His Excellency's aids-de camp were present. The next forenoon . . . (You will remember there was never a more splendid day for a military display) His excellency reviewed 16 companies of light troops elegantly equipped and well disciplined. The whole corpse (*sic*) dined at the same table prepared with good taste in the open field.

After dinner His Excellency addressed the troops through his aid-de camp Col. Pierce who came off much better than Anderson at the Park Theatre. . . . I never enjoyed myself more highly on any occasion. Such a concourse of people were probably never before assembled in this state excepting perhaps the day on which LaFayette was received at Concord. . . . The idea that I was soon to make a *devil of a display* in chapeau buffs and military boots has reigned so perfectly triumphant in my cranium that any other subject during the last ten days was almost certain to plead in vain for consideration.

The glories of this splendid event, however, could not carry him through the dullness of his final Hillsborough winter. By Christmastide melancholy reigned supreme.

How fortunate it is that however worthless the present may appear, there is always something cheering before, indeed anticipation of good is all or nearly all that makes life tolerable. It is not the present that we cling to but something that sparkles in the distance and beckons us on—to find what? disappointment. Silver spoons at the termination of the rainbow: But of him whom I was speaking [Kimball who was going to be married] If man must run risques, I think he has made a judicious selection—but he will find (—is my opinion) that matrimony has at this moment slipped on her prettiest dress and presents a much more *taking mien* than she will some ten years hence when the hallucination of earlier days shall have passed away and half a dozen little total depravities shall be springing up about him. Will he not then find that "there is a vast difference between a horse chestnut and a chestnut horse?" Well, if he does! What's that to me aye or you either. What foundation there may be for the "brisk report," I neither know or care disavowing at the same time all want of due respect. Fate has hewn out for me perhaps a rougher but I believe a happier course than to barter my independence perhaps my peace for "the sheen of beautys cheek" or the more sordid consideration of this worlds lucre. But if I were not wedded to a "life of single blessedness." The Genl says I am fastidious. I acknowledge it and what is worse I have little hope of being less so. If my whole life is a lonely one, be it so, if it cannot be otherwise but with the certainty of binding myself indisolubly and fatally to one to whom I cannot pour forth the tribute of my whole soul, with its highest noblest admiration. But what am I talking about? If not an old bachelor certainly I am no rhapsodist.

From these depths not even the approach of town meeting could arouse him, and in the spring he was slow to revive. However, he did not shirk his responsibilities and wrote some sage advice to Benjamin's fourteen year old daughter Harriet at school in Boston. He advised her to get up early and be careful of her diet for her health was delicate. "As you now commence taking lessons in some of the fashionable accomplishments you should study the graces—whatever you do, let it be done gracefully and with ease. Observe this alike at all times and in all situations, whether at home or abroad in the presence of your instructress or alone in your [room] Among your studies neglect not that best . . . [the] Bible . . . let it be opened before you in the [morning] and at evening."

Meantime the political world was interested in the approaching presidential election and Jackson's bank and tariff struggles. In May Jackson was renominated at Baltimore. Whereupon Pierce and some of his cronies got a four-pounder and took it up Meeting House hill to the liberty pole. Having no carriage it was mounted on cart wheels and chained fast, with the result that when fired the ancient artillery exploded. Hard upon the heels of this escapade came the legislature. As the members assembled at Concord they talked much of the election, but as far as legislative politics were concerned the opposition to the

Jacksonians had practically disappeared; Pierce was re-elected Speaker with but three votes opposed. This triumph added to his credit, Mr. Speaker with his salary of $2.50 *per diem* settled down in state at the Eagle, where he lived extravagantly at a dollar a day. During the seventeen-day session his expenses were further augmented by seven bottles of wine at a dollar a bottle, numerous segars at three cents straight and in addition 50c for having his boots blacked. He was charged for " keeping hoss 17 knights at 20c and 3 bushels of oats," $4.90. His old friend " Hath " rejoiced in his election and wrote him a letter acknowledging receipt of the *Patriot* containing his speech of acceptance. Hawthorne, especially amused at the anti-temperance activity of their Bowdoin mate, John P. Hale, who was now in the legislature, was moved to comment " he seems to have taken quite a characteristic and consistent course in this respect, and I presume he gives the retail dealers as much of his personal patronage as ever." Temperance activity was typical of the times for this legislature had much social legislation before it. The condition of the poor, the insane, the debtors, the deaf and the dumb all demanded attention and many were calling upon the state to assume obligations for their better care. As these new duties would involve considerable expense, the cautious legislators would not be hurried. Little was accomplished that session but the preparatory work was going on.

The phase of the June work which presumably interested the speaker most was the state convention. It was time for the nomination of the congressional ticket, and there was war in the Jacksonian ranks. It is evident that a number wanted to postpone the nomination until fall although the situation is not clear. Finally the decision was reached to nominate at once; and next day, after considerable political maneuvering, nature unknown, Pierce was designated with four others to form the general ticket to be presented to the state electorate.

Clothed with this new honor the candidate went to Hillsborough for the Fourth, where he again was to deliver the oration of the day. It was a gala occasion. His father was there as chairman of the meeting with his Revolutionary chapeau that had made him famous as the " last of the cocked hats," and before fully fifteen hundred people Pierce thrilled them with the old, old story: the Revolution, its heroism and suffering and the great glory of the achievement. The day's enthusiasm gained for him the following significant newspaper comment:

Frank Pierce is the most popular man of his age that I know of in N. H.—praises in every one's mouth. Every circumstance connected with him seems to contribute to his popularity. In the first place he has the advantage of his fathers' well earned reputation to bring him forward, and there is aristocracy enough, even in a community democratic as our own, to make this of no trifling importance to a young man just starting in life. In the next place he has a handsome person, bland and agreeable manners, a prompt and off-hand manner of saying and doing things, and talents competent to sustain himself in any station.

His congressional nomination, plus the fact that it was presidential year, meant that the next nine months would be pretty well taken up with politics. He campaigned actively for Jackson, not only in New Hampshire, but also in Massachusetts. The November election was a triumph and the old general was chosen a Jacksonian elector. Another incident of the presidential year was the quadrennial winter session of the legislature to reapportion the taxes. This December sojourn in Concord was made exciting by the nullification controversy with South Carolina and the passage by the legislature of resolutions endorsing Jackson's stand. But otherwise politics lacked the zest of conflict. The bored speaker reported that the legislature was tame enough as there was "no longer any opposition." For local excitement the legislators must content themselves with card games and sleigh riding. There is evidence of keen rivalry around the card table, and something similar out on the snowy highways. Else why should the *Patriot* feel called upon to caution the townspeople about reckless driving and frequent accidents? Adjournment finally was had early in January. Town meeting day in March found Pierce moderator for the last time and the incoming returns showed that he was to be one of New Hampshire's five congressmen.*

* There had been no regularly nominated ticket in opposition to the Democratic general congressional ticket but several newspapers had placed five anti-Jacksonians before the people. There was no real contest, the Jacksonians averaged 23,000 votes each while the highest opponent received only 6688.

This honor its recipient seemed not to view very enthusiastically.

I am gratified tho' certainly not elated. Three or four years ago I should have viewed the prospect of an election to Congress at this time as the most bright and dazzling that could possibly be presented to my ambition—still it may well be doubted whether it would not ultimately have been better for me had my whole attention been devoted to my profession, besides I find that the remark that "Tis distance lends enchantment to the view " is no less true of the political than of the natural world. I saw Mr. Hill the other day at Concord and conversed with him some time. I ought to be thankful for the kind interest he would seem to take in my well-being. However *unfortunate* it may be to be *young* I trust he will admit it is not criminal.

REPRESENTING NEW HAMPSHIRE IN WASHINGTON

1833-1842

VII

A FITTING PRELUDE

TRIUMPHANT rulers have ever celebrated their victories by royal progresses through their domains. Andrew Jackson having overcome Carolina nullification and having been re-elected in spite of all that the bank could do, set out upon a triumphal journey. To be sure he could not exhibit Nick Biddle in chains at his chariot wheel, nor to use an American figure, could he carry the scalps of Clay and Calhoun at his belt, but the absence of these trophies in no wise lessened the plaudits of his admirers as he made a tour of the northern states in the early summer of 1833. Concord made elaborate plans to receive him and when he arrived accompanied by Van Buren and New Hampshire's two sons, Woodbury and Cass, enthusiasm ran high. For three days he was feted and lionized. Congressman-elect Pierce, protégé of the President's intimate friend, Isaac Hill, law student of Woodbury and brother of one of Gen. Cass's officers in his famous exploit at the Saulte Ste. Marie in 1820, could not fail to be admitted to the inner circle of the illustrious guests; and at one of the dinners he had an opportunity to become acquainted with Van Buren. These three days so filled with ceremony and the companionship of the most distinguished Democrats in state and nation, especially his hero, Old Hickory, were an auspicious introduction to his new dignity.

VIII

A JACKSONIAN CONGRESSMAN

THE cholera played havoc in the United States in the summer of 1833 and Pierce not only gave up plans for an extended trip on that account but succumbed to a serious illness while on a visit at the McNeil's in Boston. So violent was this "bilious attack" that his life was despaired of and when he recovered he was in no particularly enthusiastic state of mind about his winter away from home at Washington. But there was no shirking the duty and he set out from Boston about the 21st of November for the capital. The journey in those days was tedious and marked by many changes. From Boston his route lay by stage to one of the Sound ports whence he went by boat to New York. Here he trans-shipped to another boat which took him to Amboy, New Jersey, where a train then whizzed through space to Bordentown at the rate of 18 miles an hour. From here a small steamer brought the adventurer to Philadelphia for his third night's rest. Early next morning another vessel took him to New Castle, Delaware, a second long railroad journey of sixteen miles to Frenchtown followed, then a boat trip to Baltimore, and finally after a stage ride of forty miles in seven hours, lo! the capitol appeared on the horizon and the interminable journey was over.

"I arrived here Thursday night [Nov. 28] in good health, took quarters at Gadsby's and remained there till this morning [Saturday] when I moved to the other side of the Avenue [Pennsylvania], at Mr. Hill's where I now write. The location is convenient, rooms pleasant and company agreeable." Thus New Hampshire's youngest representative described his lodgings on the south side of the capital's wide and dusty thoroughfare just west of Third Street. Mrs. Hill's four-story brick boarding house was one of the many congressional "messes" managed in true southern style with a profusion of negro servants. There were a dozen or more negro slaves, male and female, and all properly married, we are told, neatly dressed and continually singing. They acted as body servants to the

64

guests, starting the day by building fires in each room before the occupants arose and then making themselves generally useful; besides, they served the meals in the dining room. To the New Hampshire people not used to such attendance, for which they paid $10 a week, the new life was strange and a matter of much comment. In this house besides Pierce were Senator and Mrs. Hill of New Hampshire, the Maine Senators, White of Tennessee, Wilkins of Pennsylvania and a group of congressmen all but one from either Maine or New York; several of them were accompanied by their wives. This group was soon joined by Pierce's friend and erstwhile colleague in the New Hampshire legislature, Benjamin B. French, and these two young men found much solace in each other's company. Of his " mess " Pierce wrote that they were " all men of industrious habits and correct political principles." All told he could look forward to " an agreeable and profitable winter."

At noon, Monday, December 2, Pierce was sworn in and with his two hundred and forty associates proceeded to the organization of the House. The Jacksonians were in a generous majority and easily re-elected Andrew Stevenson, speaker. The following Monday the committees were announced and Pierce found himself last on the judiciary committee. Congress thereupon considered itself organized and began to function.

Meanwhile Pierce and French had been exploring their new environment under the guidance of Henry Hubbard, New Hampshire's most influential congressman. They discovered that their new abiding place was a curious city. Pierce's experiences to be sure were not those of his predecessors a generation before, when Congress first established itself upon the banks of the Potomac, but Washington was still none too sightly or comfortable. The plan of greatness and beauty was there, but the wide avenues were unpaved and the small houses looked lost on the broad thoroughfares. Here were clerks, tradespeople, members of Congress, cabinet officers, foreign diplomats, claim agents, lobbyists, all the flotsam and jetsam of the hangers-on clinging to the fringe of the government, here they all lived as best they might. Some existed in hotels and boarding places while others dwelt more comfortably in the small brick and frame houses with their dormer windows, gracefully curved iron railings, and white, brass-fitted doorways, or in the few more pretentious houses such as those on Lafayette Square.

One New Englander who visited Pierce that winter confided his thoughts on Washington to his father in the following strain:

> . . . there is too much roaring, swearing, lying and fawn-
> ing to please decent folks. . . . The better sort of people
> here, the senators and some of the representatives and of-
> ficers are very polite, but the great throng taking men as we
> meet them are low and vulgar enough. They are from all
> parts of the country and come here from interest or for
> pleasure. So that they are generally rough unfeeling and
> unmannered or rakish, brandy-drinking fellows with their
> hats cocked, a sword cane in hand and a quid of tobacco in
> their mouths. . . . There are a great many merely fashion-
> able folks here. . . . Even those who support the most ex-
> pensive establishments are deficient in keeping them in
> good order, so that sometimes they almost make a burlesque
> of dignity. For instance it would not be at all strange to
> see servants in livery with ragged stockings and big dirty
> shoes; a liveried footman and driver on a rickety carriage,
> or a handsome carriage (not very handsome neither for
> there are none) with mean horses. Everybody is careless
> of external appearance.

In this atmosphere the government had at length become rather comfortably located after the initial confusions and the demoralization of the British invasion. The President's palace was practically completed, the east room was furnished, the north portico was in use and a number of conveniences which the elder Adams never dreamed possible had been established for the comfort of the Presidential menage. Around the execu-tive mansion were the four white-painted, brick buildings in its yard, housing the state, treasury, war and navy departments. Here daily from 9 to 3 the government clerks did what they conceived to be their duty. To the north was an unkempt vacant space with St. John's on the other side and to the south a malarial swamp in the hollow; beyond was the Potomac with its malodorous flats, especially noxious when the tide was out. To the east several squares away were the old Patent Office with its two halls filled with models, and the Post Office, two tolerably handsome connecting brick buildings; farther eastward was the incomplete city hall.

The crowning glory of the city was the capitol building itself.

Down Pennsylvania Avenue from the Treasury, across the melli-
fluous Tiber, on an eminence in the distance stood a domed
building. Tramping down Pennsylvania Avenue through horrible dust, which, if the wind blew, resembled a sandstorm on
the Arabian desert, or through bottomless mud if it were rainy,
the pedestrian crossed the nasty Tiber and arrived at the foot
of capitol hill. If he entered the grounds, trudged up the hill
and mounted the first flight of steps, he could rest and contemplate the monument erected to those fallen in the Barbary
war; and if he persisted up another flight of steps he was on
the capitol level. Passing around to the front he beheld the
seat of government, still innocent of some of the decoration
since bestowed upon it; its entrance was yet unadorned by
the " triumphs " of Persico and Greenough which now excite
various emotions in the breast of the visitor. Within, was the
rotunda, rather bare because but four of the panels designed
for historical paintings were thus decorated; four large spaces
gaped and would gape until congressional wisdom could decide
what additional episodes in the history of the Republic were
glorious enough for such honor. The dome in those days was
a squat affair called the " iron pot " and did not add the lofty
grandeur to the rotunda which that structure has today.

In the north wing the Senate was housed in a handsome, ill-
ventilated room; and in the basement, sat the Supreme Court
where John Marshall had been presiding since the days before
Pierce was born. On the west front was the Library of Congress; but the center of attraction for Pierce and French, who
was an assistant to the clerk of the House, was in the south wing.
Here was the semi-circular Hall of Representatives presided
over by a loftily placed figure of Liberty attended by one eagle
and a serpent, while just below her was another eagle with out-
spread wings about to take flight. The room was surrounded
on all sides by immense dark marble pillars. However, it had
never been a success acoustically, so during the last recess the
floor had been raised; the speaker's throne had been moved
from the south to the north side of the room and the members
faced about, toward the circular rather than toward the straight
end. Also heavy curtains had been introduced to deaden some
of the queer echoes and these hangings added a certain sombre
dimness to the hall. All told, it gave a feeling of grandeur, so

one of Pierce's visitors confided to his journal " until you see
the members." Pierce's colleagues were a miscellaneous lot,
many uncouth, some dirty, a number were hard drinkers, and
a considerable proportion often sat through sessions with their
hats on. Of this conglomerate group Pierce was one and with
them he set himself to solve the legislative problems of the
nation.

The President's message, read to the members by the clerk,
dealt largely with the status of Jackson's war upon the bank
and reported the removal of the " deposites " from that institution; the President's emphasis upon this matter was ominous
of the session's debates. Not a week elapsed before the oratorical guns began to boom and the war on the bank reopened to
continue with hardly a pause for the next six months. Much
was at stake, for 1834 was a year of congressional elections, and
panic and distress were too apparent in the economic life of
the people.

The bank question, so engrossing of congressional attention
during Pierce's first session, presented no problems for him.
He was in entire accord with the Jacksonian policies and ever
ready to cast his vote to uphold the President's action in removing the deposits. This he was called upon to do often.
Scarcely a day went by without debate on the subject. In
fact, after January 14, under agreement, only the first hour
of each day was put aside for general business and the entire
remainder of the time was given over to financial speeches.
At the end of January Pierce wrote: " The debate upon the
deposite question seems to be interminable. At least it appears
likely to continue for weeks to come. The Secy will finally be
sustained in the House by a very respectable majority." He
was confident moreover that the deposit question was only a
cloak to hide the real question, namely, the recharter of the
bank. On the first of February he wrote that: " There is now
at the close of each speech as general a rush for the floor as
there was three weeks since. The subject it is true is quite
threadbare and very little attention is given to those who speak
but since speeches are not intended for effect here, but for
home consumption it matters little whether Gentlemen have
listeners or not." Finally upon February 18 the majority acted.
Under the spur of the previous question, after a series of four

exciting roll calls, the report of the secretary of the treasury on the removal was at length referred to the committee on ways and means. Pierce voted on all four roll calls with the administration and presumably rejoiced at the result; at any rate, the next morning he awoke with a "most violent billious attack" similar to that of the last summer in Boston. "The question for some time was to faint or not to faint" but he at length reached the bell rope—a servant—a physician—and "a very favourable opperation (*sic*) of calomel" whereby the cause was "quite removed."

This illness had rather disarranged Pierce's plans. While the deposit question was being debated he had been preparing to make his maiden speech. His military interest was always apparent and the type of legislation which seems first to have attracted him was the question of Revolutionary pensions. Such bills long had been pressed upon Congress by Revolutionary officers and their relatives trying to obtain the five years half pay granted them under resolution of Congress of March 22, 1783, for which they had not applied before the expiration of the period set by law. In order to do away with this mass of private legislation, the committee on Revolutionary pensions introduced a bill to turn over these claims to the treasury to be settled according to certain rules laid down in the proposed law. This bill had been brought in on January 30 and by February 14 had advanced to the third reading when Pierce asked that it be laid over so that he might examine the subject more carefully. His request was granted and he was to have spoken on the bill the morning of his sickness when upon motion of his messmate, F. O. J. Smith, it was further postponed.

February 27, therefore, was the occasion of Pierce's first speech. He opposed the bill on the ground that all such claims that were just must have been settled long ago, and that because of the great loss of records sustained by the government the contemplated action would fasten upon the treasury a system which would permit much fraud to be committed. He stuck strictly to his subject and avoided the least reference to sectionalism. He urged a policy that would save the government money and make fraud less easy. It was a business speech with little of the politician in it—rather a contrast to the quantities of buncombe poured forth over the bank. The speech was delivered in three-quarters of an hour, in Pierce's pleasing manner to " an attentive House " and earned for the speaker a number of compliments, even the hypercritical J. Q. Adams confiding to his diary that he spoke " very handsomely against it." It is notable that of the number who came and congratulated Pierce for making as his first, a " sensible " speech, the ones he appreciated most were three southerners, W. R. Davis of South Carolina and Gilmer and Clayton of Georgia. He found early the key to southern sympathy and friendship and for weal or woe he was never to lose it. Pierce was well satisfied with his debut. He had made a pleasant impression on various types and he had succeeded in killing the bill.

The most time-consuming activity of the new congressman at the capitol was his service on the judiciary committee; to this body was referred a most miscellaneous group of bills, for report as to the legality and justice of the claims or immunities asked. Pierce reported to the House a number of measures releasing bondsmen from further liability, renewing patents and granting petitioners their due shares of fees, and also made adverse reports on a number of petitions for financial relief. This sort of work if taken seriously, and Pierce did take it seriously, was laborious but neither demanded nor inspired broad statesmanship. Besides these committee duties there were many things to be looked after. Claims of constituents must be pressed before the departments, petitions presented to Congress, private bills introduced and followed through committees. Also much information of a heterogeneous and often puzzling character was requested by constituents, and all told the office involved a good deal of correspondence. As this was the day before typewriters and private offices, Pierce had to do his writing at his desk in the Hall of Representatives or in his room at the boarding house, often he " wrote under debate."

Outside the capitol his regimen was the usual pointless miscellany of boarding house life. Breakfast was served at nine at Mrs. Hill's, heavy and nourishing, for it must sustain until late afternoon. Pierce then spent his mornings on business before the departments, in committee, or at his desk in the House chamber. The House went into session at twelve and transacted business until three or four. Unless the debate was interesting or exciting many of the members utilized the session hours to their own advantage. Pierce once wrote " A few are attending to the bills in which they are particularly interested but the great mass are engaged in reading newspapers, writing letters et cet. and I go with the majority." Dinner was served after the house adjourned and at Mrs. Hill's was very substantial, a fact which congressmen who had eaten nothing since breakfast could appreciate, although the lunch counter or oyster bar in the House basement may have helped during the course of the day. Roast beef, boiled turkey, boiled ham and roast duck are recorded as on one menu with soup and various heavy desserts. At the beginning of the session each member of the mess was taxed $10 and the fund turned over to a treasurer who kept the table supplied with wine. Congressman Fairfield thought the meals too " fleshy " with too little salt, but Mrs. Hill was an Englishwoman with her native ideas of correct diet. To cap this digestive experience another meal was served in the form of supper shortly after nightfall. How congressional digestions survived is a matter of wonder.

From this boarding routine there was a small variety of diversions. The social season began at New Year's with the President's levee, and the festivities on the 8th of January, New Orleans Day. Numerous parties were given by the cabinet and permanent residents, and Pierce was duly invited with the other congressmen. That winter Fanny Kemble, whose husband, Pierce Butler, was to become an intimate of Pierce's in later days appeared on the Washington stage, and after witnessing her interpretation of the rôle of " Julia " in the " Hunchback " Pierce went home in raptures. In spite of these diversions Pierce lived what he called an " industrious " but rather tame life, mingling little in the gaieties of the fashionable world, or at least so he wrote his sister, and by February he was longing for New England. There was a girl back in Amherst who presumably contributed to that longing.

Mrs. Hill's boarders were not without their own diversions. Pierce found much in common with his messmates Mr. and Mrs. F. O. J. Smith from Maine and Mr. and Mrs. French. When Sunday afternoons hung heavy on their hands they " cut up." On one occasion they got so gay over crackers and cheese that their messmates began to inquire the reason for the noise only to find that French had locked Pierce and Mrs. French in while he went down to invite Mrs. Smith to the repast and when he returned found the prisoners had fastened the door on the inside. The hilarity was ended by Pierce who carried some of the refreshment down to Mr. Smith. Sometimes these friends were less jovial, as when Pierce and French discussed " Misserrimus " and debated the question of free will, Pierce arguing against it on the ground that man could not control his own happiness.

In May the races added their attractions and official and unofficial Washington rode out to the course. Here the races started daily at noon for about a week and " Tyrant " and " Busiris " and other nags caused much money to change hands. Pierce went out with the rest and was perhaps, like French, reminded of an old-fashioned New England muster. Gambling booths attracted all classes and there was gaming " in all its moods and tenses." Senators and negroes wagered anything from a thousand dollars to a " fip " and drank julep or raw whiskey according to taste and purse. The races were another example of the straggling cosmopolitanism of the unkempt capital.

The end of May brought hot weather and very opportunely the Chesapeake and Ohio Canal Company provided an excursion for the members of Congress to inspect their work. Pierce in company with a large party took advantage of this hospitality and set out from Georgetown on two canal boats accompanied by the marine band. All day long they crawled through the thirty-four locks whiling away the hours with two meals accompanied by the drinking of wine, which as J. Q. Adams said " made some of the company loquacious and some drowsy." Harper's Ferry which they reached at nine in the evening was their destination. Next day there were excursions up and down the river and visits to the armory. Some clambered up to Jefferson's rock, watched the meeting of the Potomac and the Shenandoah, and looked off to the blue hills. None thought that day of John Brown. The evening witnessed a party at the armory superintendent's home which presumably did not contribute much to the delight of a five o'clock start the next morning. The return journey took place on a day as hot as only the Potomac valley can produce. The stifling hours were

enlivened by Representative Hawes of Kentucky who entertained with "facetious humors and coarse jokes and a very
frequent and copious consumption of whiskey drams." He was
alternately a delight and a tedious bore. A heavy shower late
in the afternoon sent the ladies to the cabin where they sang
"with great facility a variety of Methodistical hymns." Damp
and tired the party arrived at Georgetown past midnight.

During this round of congressional life the mills of Congress
had been grinding rather listlessly, but the approach of hot
weather reminded all that the session must soon come to an
end. As the conditions most unfavorable for hard work became more prevalent, need for it became greater. Such is
our congressional system. So the House dropped a Kentucky
election case which had been dragging along, to buckle on its
armor for a new outbreak of the bank war. The Senate had
sent over resolutions disapproving Jackson's removal of the
deposits and ordering them replaced in the Bank. These resolutions the Jacksonian majority laid on the House table and
settled down to its final grind. During these June days and
nights Pierce gave a number of significant votes forecasting a
future all too consistent. He voted against the bill to grant
pre-emption rights to settlers on the public lands (act of June
25, 1834), standing alone of all the New Hampshire delegation
and with a small minority of fifty-three against this measure.
He opposed internal improvements on various occasions, finally
voting against the general bill which Jackson signed June 28;
the federal government was one of limited powers and among
them Pierce never found any to help the West. Just before
adjournment, the New Hampshire legislature sent down resolutions approving the course of Hill and the congressmen, and
the state convention nominated Pierce for a second term.

His first session in Congress, like his first session in the New
Hampshire legislature, had been completely permeated with
partisanship. Jackson's war against the bank, carried on with
all the power of his leadership, made a great impression upon
his followers and especially upon Pierce who was a devout hero-
worshipper. Opposition to Jackson had come to be resented
by his partisans with an intensity hardly understandable in
this present day. A new political group had been forming
which purposed to destroy Jacksonian power. In New York

that spring a strange standard had been unfurled by an alignment of forces called " Whigs."

Well-groomed capitalists and their editorial sympathizers
called upon the voters to overthrow the tyranny of this " King
Andrew " and restore individual rights and liberty. Jackson's
opponents were attempting to meet the " Democracy " on their
own ground. Congress had shared this excitement, feeling had
mounted, the lie was passed, duels threatened; but whenever
necessary, James K. Polk and his associates had been able to
muster a majority vote or two-thirds if a suspension of rules
was necessary. Finally the permanence and solidarity of the
Jacksonian party had been demonstrated. On April 4, the
House had sustained Jackson's removal of the deposits and had
voted that the bank ought not to be rechartered. Thus in
Washington as in New Hampshire, Pierce had appeared on the
scene during a tense period of renewed partisan strife and his
feeling of loyalty to party was now more firmly entrenched than
ever.

IX

A POLITICAL HONEYMOON

SOME time or other Pierce had lost his once strong conviction that he was destined to go through life alone. He had fallen in love with a charming but "delicate" young lady of the neighboring town of Amherst, sister-in-law of his Bowdoin teacher, Packard, and daughter of the late President Appleton of the same college. Jane Means Appleton * and her widowed mother were living with her grandmother, the formidable Madame Means, in the Means mansion on Amherst plain and were obviously of the local aristocracy. The suit of the young rural Democrat had been frowned on by the stiff-necked Federal ladies, but Jane too was in love and in revolt against this matriarchal repression. So love had conquered a reluctant consent and the young swain was going to be married on the eve of the next session of Congress and take his bride back to Washington. On the morning of November 19, 1834, a small party of the Means-Appleton family gathered with only old General Pierce of that connection in the Means parlor. Jane was escorted by her brother, Robert Appleton, and, attired in traveling dress, was married to Franklin by the Reverend Silas Aiken, her brother-in-law. There were brief congratulations and farewells, a few tears from the nervous bride, and they were off.

* Born at Hampton, N. H., March 12, 1806. She was the third of six children, two of whom were then dead. Her father had died in 1819 and Mrs. Appleton had taken her family back to her home at Amherst. Mrs. Pierce's eldest sister Mary had just married John Aiken who was a manufacturer at Lowell and with their family Mrs. Pierce spent a great deal of her life. Her sister Elizabeth had married Pierce's teacher Alpheus S. Packard of Bowdoin and her brother Robert, who had married a cousin, Rebecca Means, was in business in Boston. One of Mrs. Pierce's aunts, Mary, had married Jeremiah Mason and another, Nancy, was the second wife of Amos Lawrence, two wealthy men who led in their professions, the one in law and the other in business. The hospitable Lawrence mansion in Boston was a frequent stopping place for the Pierces, quite different from the humbler quarters of the McNeils. Three weeks previously Jane's uncle, Robert Means, Jr., had married her intimate friend, Abigail Atherton Kent. Jane had visited her and her own sister, Mary, at Lowell on the eve of her marriage. The fate of these three women was to be tragically intertwined.

Jane Appleton Pierce was shy, retiring, frail and tubercular, well-bred in the straightest sect of New England theocracy with a host of substantial and aristocratic connections and very strict ideas of propriety. Her husband presented quite a contrast, buoyant, vain, social, at home in political caucus and tavern, a son of the frontier. They were ill-mated; but for thirty years they lived together, he dividing himself between politics and law, giving her a very real affection and love which made her the center of his thoughtful attention: she shyly appreciative but unresponsive, often oppressed by ill-health and melancholy, hating politics and public life and sorely troubled by her husband's social weaknesses. They represented two different strata of New England society and he must now assume the responsibility of his new connections. The Masons of Portsmouth and the Lawrences of Boston, cultured aristocrats, were seemingly far removed from the bluff gaucheries of Hillsborough farm houses, but Pierce set himself to bridge the gulf and his success was a tribute to his adaptability and his sensitiveness to environment.

Shortly after the ceremony the two set out together and three days later arrived somewhere in the vicinity of Washington, perhaps Baltimore, where they stayed six days at the boarding house of Sophia Southurt. On November 28 they registered at Brown's Indian Queen Inn at the capital and the next day went to Birth's on 3d Street, north of the Avenue, where they settled for the winter. Not many congressmen lived there, Beardsley of New York, Dickerson and Parker of New Jersey, with Pierce, made up the contingent; Beardsley and Dickerson had lived at Hills's last session. Mrs. Pierce would appreciate the comparative quiet of this new boarding place where the charges were still $10 a week and in addition the Pierces paid $1.50 (per session) for the luxury of a rocking chair. Mrs. Pierce had not stood the journey very well. French reported she looked miserable upon arrival though a week or so later a colleague recorded that she was in much better health and that Pierce was "well, in firm spirits and apparently as happy as a man should be during the first month of the honeymoon."

The lady herself is perhaps an interesting commentator, as she wrote to her father-in-law:

I received your letter my dear father with very sincere pleasure and (as you were not aware at the time of writing that I had already sent you a few lines at the end of a note of Frank's) I shall consider it the *true* and *gentlemanlike* beginning of the correspondence, and proceed accordingly—for to say truth, my dear sir, I consider it not a *little favor* that at your time of life and with many cares you are willing to devote your time and thoughts to me in this way occasionally. . . .

We still continue to be pleased with our accommodation here and are in fact as comfortably situated as we could be —have both generally been very well and not very unhappy. Frank does very well thus far, sir, and is as you say a *pretty good boy*—it is to be sure rather *soon* to judge but I hope I shall have no reason to alter my opinion—in *such* a *case*, I shall appeal to you, who I am sure will lend me your *countenance*. I find Washington very much as I expected both in appearance and climate—as to the former, my expectations were not very highly raised, and the latter has realized the favorable impression I had of it. Today however is so excessively windy that I am disappointed in my wish of going to church which is a deprivation to which I hope I shall not often be subjected—these high winds are common here, and exceedingly disagreeable. I have been out very frequently and intend to take your advice my dear sir, to exercise as much as possible in the open air. I have not yet seen the President. . . . We have an invitation to dinner to Gov Cass' on Wednesday which is accepted notwithstanding my predilections for a quiet dinner at home. The gentlemen and ladies of our family are quite social and pleasant and we are on a very easy footing as we should be to live so long together.

Pray my dear Father whenever you feel like scribbling a few lines remember your affectionate daughter

Jane

This session of Congress was not to prove legislatively productive as the only interest of the leaders seemed to be the passage of the necessary appropriation bills by the fourth of March. During its brief course Col. Pierce had an opportunity to ride one of his hobbies. His father and he entertained the militia officer's dislike for West Point and in Congress that distrust had become so widespread, especially because so many cadets resigned just as soon as they had been educated at public expense, that a select committee of investigation was ordered consisting of one member from each state; Pierce became the

New Hampshire member.   F. O. J. Smith, Pierce's former messmate, was delegated with Pierce to prepare the committee's report after the deliberations were concluded, and their work
was adopted and presented in February.   The minority, however, blocked the printing of the document and the House, itself, refused to consider it.

This committee was not so absorbing but that Pierce could
fully enjoy his honeymoon, and what would have been a dull
winter was much lightened by the companionship of his wife.
Her delicate health and retiring disposition made her an appealing object for his solicitude and gave him much strength
in resisting boisterous temptations which he could ill withstand.
He reported home:

> . . . I have been leading, I need not say, a very *agree-
> able* life—it has also been very quiet.   Jane's health has
> prevented her from mingling as much in gay society as
> we might otherwise have done, but we have been to several
> large parties in the evening and she is now enjoying better
> health.   I think she has hardly been better since I have
> known her.   Last night the anniversary of the victory of
> New Orleans and at the same time the extinguishment of
> the National Debt were celebrated at Brown's Hotel.
> Great numbers and uncommon glee marked the festivities
> of the evening or rather night—for we sat down at 7 o'clock
> and I believe many remained till 12.   I left the table at
> ½ past nine and lost I understand a good deal, that was
> amusing by coming away so early. . . . Judging from the
> appearance of most of my friends today I believe I gain
> in the feelings of today what I lost by leaving early last
> night.

Further excitement was provided at the end of the month by
an attempt to assassinate Jackson.   Also there were some difficulties at home, and Pierce lent his good offices to healing a
party breach by bringing two papers, the *Argus* and the *Spectator*, together and thus ending a press rivalry harmful to the
party.   These negotiations produced a political friendship with
Edmund Burke of the *Argus* which was to have fateful consequences.

Congress was not to be permitted to adjourn without some
unusual activity.   The prevailing calm was but the precursor
of a violent storm.   Late in February came the news that what

had been suspected was true. France was not going to meet her obligations under the treaty of 1831. For nearly two years negotiations had been hanging fire but heretofore there had been reassuring promises. A report of the diplomatic rupture was officially communicated to Congress February 26, just six days before adjournment; resolutions denouncing the French position were introduced and in order to prepare for a possible contingency a $3,000,000 item was inserted in an appropriation bill to provide for increased fortifications. The final days witnessed much exciting debate but the climax came on the last night. The Senate would not accept the $3,000,000 item and the House would not recede. A conference committee worked without avail and midnight approached. Pierce had voted three times with the majority to adhere to the amendment and finally, as the House was passing a bill to carry on the Cumberland Road which Pierce voted against as usual, twelve o'clock struck. To a number this meant that Congress was over, though the majority considered twelve noon next day as the hour of termination; many, Pierce presumably among them, retired and when Cambreleng finally came back after one o'clock with a $800,000 compromise, there was no quorum and one could not be obtained. The oldest members said they had never witnessed such a scene. Many were "very essentially corned . . . there was laughing and scolding, swearing and joking, hissing and cheering and all sort of things. . . . There seemed to be two determinations running counter to each other —one that there *should* be something done and other that there should not and the latter party by leaving their seats, whenever a count was called for, prevented there being a quorum and carried their object into effect."

As a matter of fact the trouble was the result of a long drawn out contested election case from Kentucky which had split the House, and partisans of one of the contestants were determined that the other should not be paid. Finally at three in the morning this disgraceful scene was brought to a close and the congressmen made their way home as best they could.

X

HOME-MAKING

THE close of the session found Washington ice-bound. So severe had been the winter that the rivers were frozen and the homeward journey had to be postponed. In the capital city therefore Col. and Mrs. Pierce lingered and sought to while away the time; one day they went out to Georgetown with Mr. and Mrs. French and visited the college and nunnery there. Meanwhile in New Hampshire the town meetings came and went; the newly organized Whigs had put a congressional ticket in the field but it had attracted only 14,000 supporters and Pierce, as high man on the Democratic ticket, found himself elected by a vote ten thousand greater. At length transportation opened and the colonel and his bride went back to New Hampshire full of the pleasant anticipations of setting up house-keeping.

Two years before, Pierce had bought Gen. McNeil's house at Hillsborough and his father had enlarged it for his son's first home. The old general was pleased with his new daughter-in-law and was anxious to do what he could to make her comfortable. Pierce left his wife with relatives at Lowell and went on to Hillsborough to make ready the new abode. Mr. and Mrs. Francis E. Pearsons had been living in the house during the winter and they were to stay on, tend to the place and provide the meals as Mrs. Pierce was not able to bear the burden of the housekeeping. During the latter part of April and early May, Pierce was busy ordering wallpaper from Boston, making gravel walks, new fences, transplanting trees, white-washing and doing numerous other odd jobs. Then he went to Amherst to get Mrs. Pierce's belongings from her old home and on May 27 she arrived " to make everything that is agreeable, doubly so."

Having settled his home, the colonel went back to his law office. Here he was assisted by a young man from Bow in whom his father and he had been much interested. Albert Baker was the son of Mark Baker, an old friend of the general's and while he was at Dartmouth the Pierces had become interested in the boy and had helped him. They invited him, when he graduated in 1834, to live at the homestead and study law with Franklin, the general paying his expenses during his novitiate. This association had rather far reaching influence; the polish and learning of Franklin Pierce and his protégé, Albert Baker, so impressed the latter's little sister that she too became anxious for the advantages of education. Later when she had become Mrs. Mary Baker Eddy and had successfully founded the First Church of Christ, Scientist, she attributed her initial intellectual stimulus to the example and tutoring of her brother during his vacations from Dartmouth and his visits home from Hillsborough.

After a summer's work at the law, Col. Pierce arranged with Baker to look after his father and his business while he was in Washington and hired Dyer Cilley to work his farm the next spring. Mrs. Pierce would not be able to go to Washington with him and her health was so frail as to cause him a great deal of anxiety. She went with him as far as Boston where she visited her relatives, the Lawrences, and then went back to spend the winter with her mother at Amherst. Her husband joined the New Hampshire delegation and went on to the capital writing his wife daily letters which reached her irregularly according to the caprices of winter mail service.

XI

THE WINTER OF HIS DISCONTENT

At Washington Pierce found that the city was now rejoicing in railroad service, and the noise of the trains as they rattled and coughed in and out twice a day was adding a new note to the otherwise rather pastoral symphony of the capital. For living quarters Pierce chose a famous mess and joined Senator Benton's coterie at Dowson's, No. 1 Capitol Hill, right under the eaves of the Capitol building itself. He was now close to the center of things and was ready for the opening of what was destined to be a memorable session.

Pierce's first satisfaction came from the election of his friend James K. Polk as speaker. Polk re-appointed him to the judiciary committee, and a few days later placed him upon a select committee to consider the boundary dispute between Ohio and Michigan, headed by J. Q. Adams. While this group was soon discontinued Pierce was still concerned with the question because it was referred to the judiciary committee. On December 30 Polk again singled him out and placed him upon a second select committee, this time to consider the recharter of banks in the District of Columbia. As Pierce wrote, " If we had nothing else to do this Bank investigation would occupy 6 weeks or two months." In fact the committee was not a great success and its report was much criticized for its incompleteness. The only excuse its members had to offer was the difficulty of the subject and the burden of other business. There was more to Pierce's service this session than committee work, however. It may be truly said that this was the most important session of his nine years in Congress. He was frequently on the floor and had to encounter personal and political problems which were to trouble him as long as he lived.

In this session Pierce was called upon for the first time to face the political question of slavery. Since the controversy of 1820 Congress had not concerned itself particularly with the problem as no new states were ready for admission and there was no question of acquiring new territory. During the last five years, however, the opposition to slavery had become more militant and on December 16, 1835, it reached Congress once more. From this date until 1861, there was to be little relief from debate on some phase or other of this subject. The first attack was to be made on the question of the abolition of slavery in the District of Columbia.

When Fairfield of Maine presented that innocent looking petition of 172 ladies residing in his district praying that slavery be abolished at the capital, he precipitated a war of words and parliamentary maneuvers which became increasingly menacing to the peace of the nation. This petition and others soon brought the whole question of the congressional attitude toward these prayers before the House. The summer of 1835 had witnessed much agitation on the subject of abolition and even in quiet Concord some of the inhabitants had endeavored to " rotten egg " the famous English abolitionist, George Thompson, who had been invited there to lecture. The question, therefore, was one of keen interest throughout the country and in Pierce's own locality. Some wished to reject these petitions outright, others followed the move of John Y. Mason who wished simply to lay them on the table.

Among the latter Pierce took his stand and so stated in a speech on December 18. During the summer he had watched the rising tide of " abolitionism " with disgust. He had written Polk in October that in New Hampshire, " there can hardly be said to be two parties upon this embarassing question. I do not believe there is one person out of a hundred who does not wholly reprobate the course of the few reckless fanatics who are only able to disturb occasionally the quiet of a village, without producing any general impression." These views he elaborated in his December speech. He defended northern members from the charge of wishing to dodge the issue. With a fulsome compliment to Mason of Virginia he praised his understanding of the true northern temper. He was unwilling that any imputation should rest upon the North, in consequence of the misguided and fanatical zeal of a few—comparatively very few—who however honest might have been their purposes, he believed had done incalculable mischief, and whose movements he knew received no more sanction among the great mass of the people of the North, than they did at the South. In New Hamp-

shire there was " not one in a hundred who does not entertain
the most sacred regard for the rights of their Southern brethren
—nay not one in five hundred who would not have those rights
protected at any and every hazard. There is not the slightest
disposition to interfere with any rights secured by the constitution, which binds together and which I humbly hope ever will
bind together this great and glorious confederacy as one family."
On the twenty-first Owens offered a gag resolution to prevent
further discussion of the question; Pierce voted unsuccessfully
but in a very large minority, 100 to 115, to have it considered
immediately.

The debate continued until February 8 when the House voted
to constitute a select committee to consider the whole question
of congressional relation to slavery. The House instructed the
committee to report that Congress had no power to interfere
with slavery in the states; that it *ought* not to interfere with it
in the District of Columbia because it would be a violation of
public faith, unwise, impolitic and dangerous to the Union.
For these propositions the committee was instructed to formu-
late such reasons as would best tend to repress agitation and re-
establish harmony and tranquility amongst various sections of
the Union. To this committee of nine Pierce of New Hampshire received appointment, but before anything could be done
by the group, the whole matter became very personal to the
New Hampshire member.

On February 12 the Senate presented a scene not unusual.
Senator Hubbard was in the chair and Senator Hill was speaking. He was condemning Calhoun and his supporters for their
violent attacks upon the North because of the activities of " a
few misguided fanatics " and was boasting of New Hampshire's
abhorrence of fanaticism. Calhoun immediately rose to sub-
stantiate his accusation by sending a clipping from a New
Hampshire paper up to the clerk's desk to be read. Now it
happened that this article was from the *Herald of Freedom,* the
New Hampshire abolition organ recently established in Concord, and it was charged therein that when Pierce had declared
recently that not one in five hundred in New Hampshire approved of abolition doctrines, he had falsified. The editor
endeavored to prove his charge by printing petitions signed by
local people numbering more than one in five hundred. As

the clerk's voice was droning over this article Pierce himself
appeared in the Senate, just in time to hear his name and the
charge against him made by no less a personage than the great
Calhoun. He turned pale and hurried to his friend Benton
for counsel. This august personage sympathized deeply with
the young congressman. While they were talking Hill and
Hubbard both rebuked Calhoun and after the latter had disclaimed any intention of disrespect to Pierce, Benton rose
majestically to defend his young friend with whom he declared
himself to have "the pleasure of an intimate acquaintance."
Pierce had used the term "one in five hundred" loosely and
although he knew nothing of these petitions cited in the *Herald
of Freedom* he remained convinced that abolitionists in New
Hampshire were negligible in numbers. He concluded with a
dig at Calhoun, requesting the reporters not to print the *Herald's* article in the account of the debate as it might inflame
the South; with this request the reporters complied. A few
days later Senator King of Georgia also condemned Calhoun's
action in having the article read, whereupon the latter once
more explained he had meant no disrespect. All this did not
satisfy Pierce and although he was sick with a cold and could
scarcely speak, he arose in the House February 15 and answered
the charges.

To be singled out by so renowned an antagonist and held up
before the country as unreliable and unmindful of the truth
had stung him to the quick and he could not rest without justifying himself. He bitterly attacked the writer, whom Calhoun
had cited, as a "worthless editor of an incendiary abolition
publication." He showed that when he had said one in five
hundred he had meant sturdy yeomen, legal voters, not women
and children. These multi-signatured petitions which this
editor so confidently listed, to prove one in thirty-three were
abolitionists, had been largely signed by women and children.
"Children who knew not what they did," ladies, who, "in their
proper sphere" had his "highest respect and veneration." As
Fairfield reported the affair, "Pierce replied with a good deal
of feeling and vindicated himself from the charge of having
stated what was not true, and as he had been called 'a dough
face' in the article alluded to, he took occasion to say that if
any gentleman was disposed to take that statement for truth,

he would then inform him that ' he was ready at any time, and in any way, to test it with him.' And I presume there is no doubt but that he would make his declaration good and fight if any one should challenge him."

Calhoun's attack had struck Pierce at a time when he was suffering from severe mental and physical shock, for while this slavery debate had been going on Pierce's personal problems had been increasing in difficulty. The last part of January had been a very anxious time, made more so because communication with home was of necessity so slow. Letters at their quickest could not pass between Washington and New Hampshire in less than two days. Finally the suspense was broken by a brief note from Mrs. Appleton telling him of the birth upon February 2 of Franklin, Jr. This joy did not last very long for Mrs. Appleton's first letter was soon followed by another with the news that the little boy had died three days later. " He who has lived thirty years in this world of ours, seen its vanity, aye its inanity and felt its miseries ought not to repine at or weep over the demise of an infant but alas! what has our experience or what has philosophy to do with the feelings of a father." His sadness was deepened by anxiety for his wife whose feeble constitution did not rally easily. To add to his unhappiness his own weaknesses were troubling him.

Pierce was not very well fitted for certain aspects of congressional life. The term of the average congressman was short and few of them established homes in the capital city. Life in the numerous hotels and boarding houses was free and easy and many of the congressmen pursued freedom strenuously. There was a great deal of drinking, and roistering was common. Pierce had the misfortune to be unable to carry liquor, and at the same time he was of a social nature quite unable, without great effort, to refrain from participating in prevailing social customs. So when companions whose heads were harder than his started in, he tried to keep up, but was soon in a hilarious state while they were hardly conscious of having taken anything. Pierce's resistance was all the weaker because his mother was inclined to the same tendency and he believed he had inherited it. At this particular time his sorrow and a bad cold made him drift into carelessness and a life by no means regular. The climax came one evening late in February when he and Wise of

Virginia and Hannegan of Indiana, one of his messmates, drank too much and then decided to go to the theatre. They found themselves in the same box with an army officer with whom Hannegan recently had had a difficulty. It wasn't long before a fight ensued. Hannegan drew a pistol while his intoxicated companions added to the noise. The theatre was soon in an uproar, and when Pierce finally shook off the effects of the spree he was in bed with the pleurisy. Doctor Sewall came in and "took about 16 oz. of blood" from him and afforded him "immediate relief"; the next day he lost 10 or 12 more ounces by the cupping of his side and shoulder. This vigorous treatment brought him around gradually but unpleasant weather kept him indoors. The tedium of the illness was broken, however, by good news from Jeanie in the shape of a pencil note from her own hand, his first since her confinement.

Gradually the dark cloud of illness, grief and depression began to lift and his spirits revived, but the scars of February, 1836, remained permanently. This conjunction of strains and tensions accounts largely for the intensity of his feeling on the slavery question and his hatred of abolitionism, because a man of Pierce's emotional and irrational character could never analyze the causes of his complexes. It never occurred to him or to any one else, in all probability, that the chief reason for the deepseated convictions which were to color his future career was this month of "sturm und drang," with its feverish anxiety to justify himself before Calhoun and the southern leaders. All the experiences and impressions of those weeks were out of their true proportion in their strength and effect upon his character. What he thought he had achieved by the strength of his reason, had been crystallized in the test tube of his wayward emotions.

By the second week in March he was able to return to his round of congressional duties and found the House in a tangle of appropriation bills, financial debates and President-making. The conflict with France which had threatened earlier in the session seemed now unlikely but the Seminoles were making war in Florida and political warfare was incessant. The Whigs were trying to prevent Democratic success in the next Presidential election and were taking advantage of the country's unstable financial condition to further their campaign ends;

Henry A. Wise was making Polk's life miserable in the House, and bloodshed nearly resulted on more than one occasion.

The high point in the session occurred in May. On the sixteenth news arrived that Texas had defeated Mexico and become free while two days later the report of the Pinckney Committee was submitted to the House. This lengthy document discussed the relation of Congress to the slavery question. The committee found they could rejoice that the great body of the people of the non-slaveholding states had come forward " in the true spirit of American patriotism to sustain their constitutional obligations to their southern brethren and to arrest the disturbance of the public peace. . . . As moderation is essential to the discovery of truth, your committee will carefully abstain from everything that may cause offence, or inflame excitement in any section of the Union. But while they would make every allowance for the motives of individuals, where the objects contemplated are utterly destructive to society they cannot too strongly express their condemnation of the conduct of the abolitionists, and their utter abhorrence of the consequences to which, if persisted in, it must inevitably lead." A political crisis had come to the country because of this agitation, they reported, and in this crisis neutrality would be criminal, a choice must be made between the suppression of abolitionism and the destruction of the Union.

Congress had only done its duty in declaring that it had no authority to interfere with slavery in the states; and the committee piled up voluminous reasons, legal and otherwise, to show how undesirable interference with slavery in the District of Columbia would be. The committee emphasized the patriotism of the South, the injustice done that section by this mistaken agitation, and the great disasters which would follow if the horde of Negroes were loosed all unprepared for freedom upon the southern people. In fine the committee refused to advert to the horrors or depict the consequences of that most awful of days, " when the sun of American freedom shall go down in blood, and nothing remain of this glorious Republic but the bleeding scattered and dishonored fragments. It would indeed be the extinction of the world's last hope, and the jubilee of tyranny over all the earth! " They concluded by appealing to the good sense and patriotism of the abolitionists, hoping they would cease the dangerous agitation, and to aid this hope they proposed a resolution that all papers referring to slavery or abolition, " shall, without being either printed or referred, be laid upon the table, and that no further action whatever shall be had thereon." Petitions might be received but Congress would ignore them; there was to be no more wrangling over the subject. This report the House accepted. Pierce was in hearty agreement with its content and made it a part of his political creed. He hated abolitionists with all the zeal of orthodox bitterness towards " come-outers," with all the intensity of the conservative and law-abiding toward disturbers of public security and the rights of property. The country was peaceful and prosperous, destined for great things if this little group of trouble makers could be stopped from agitation which threatened the safety of the Union. In this manner were formulated opinions which had been firmly set in the foundation laid by his February demoralization.

The last week of the session continued to be filled with the extraordinary. The Pinckney report as might be expected unloosed the wrath of the anti-slavery people upon the heads of its supporters and under the leadership of John Q. Adams strenuous protests were raised. The question was further complicated by Texan independence, because the freedom of that area meant probable annexation, a project to which Jackson was favorable. But Texas permitted slavery and the newly awakened anti-slavery conscience would not submit to this great increase in slave area. Already the country was being heard from and calls were made on the President for information. On May 25 and 26 two significant events occurred. Adams in a long speech began to make war upon the annexation of Texas, and the House, 117–68, adopted the gag resolution. For the next nine years one or the other of these questions was to be the excuse for much angry debate which was to widen the breach between the sections.

As the end of the session approached, the question of new states was debated once again after an interval of fifteen years. Bills for the admission of Michigan and Arkansas had the floor and riotous scenes ensued. A rough and tumble fight in the press gallery enlivened the situation and after a five day debate which was concluded by a twenty-five hour session and marred

by drunkenness and disorder, the House passed these bills and
necessary accompanying legislation on June 13 and 14; part
of the time Pierce was in the chair.

Close on the heels of these bills came the disputed financial
legislation for the regulation of the deposit banks and the
distribution of the surplus revenue. After much parliamentary
maneuvering in which Pierce participated it was found that
the only way to pass any distribution scheme was to do it under
the guise of calling the distribution of the surplus, " depositing "
government funds with the states; in this guise a bill passed on
June 21. Benton was bitterly opposed to this bill and Pierce
loyally followed him as did three others of the New Hampshire
congressmen in that small minority of twenty-eight which Benton described as " courageous as well as meritorious, and deserving to be held in honorable remembrance." When the
rivers and harbors bill and a bill to extend the Cumberland
Road came up Pierce voted against both of them as was his
consistent practise; New Hampshire yeomen were not anxious
to have the tax money spent upon measures of doubtful constitutionality, beneficial to other sections only.

With these questions under debate the session crept nearer
its close; business was prolonged now into the hot nights and
tempers were more than ever ragged, and nerves on edge. During one of these evening meetings Pierce seized an opportunity
he had long sought. Back in January he had started to make a
speech against the West Point Academy for the purpose of
having the report of last session's investigating committee considered, but parliamentary order had intervened and the speech
was still only partially delivered. On the evening of June 30,
just after the death of James Madison was announced, the House
took up the West Point appropriation bill and this was Pierce's
opportunity. He launched forth a bitter attack upon the institution and tried to force the House to publish the report made
during the last session, threatening that if this report was not
published he would not vote a dollar for its support. He proceeded to give the main points which the committee had discussed. This institution educated at public expense young men
who had no intention of going into the army. Such a practice
under the " general welfare " clause like many others, he
warned, would even in his lifetime leave " little ground to

boast of a government of limited powers." The academy was an anomaly among the institutions of this country at variance with the spirit if not the letter of the Constitution. In spite of this appeal the report was not printed and the appropriation bill was passed.

In the last hours Texas was disposed of by resolutions to the effect that as soon as practicable the new republic ought to be recognized as independent and that the House approved the President's action in investigating the condition of Texas. These resolutions, in spite of Adams's protests, were passed by large votes, with Pierce in the affirmative. Without much more ado the House adjourned. Few sessions had been more filled with dangerous questions, and afar off on the horizon the dark cloud of sectionalism was lowering; two warning peals of thunder, the gag resolution and Adams's speech against annexation, had been heard. But to Pierce and his fellow Jacksonians as they left for their homes, these rumblings seemed only the necessary noise of a summer shower.

XII

SENATOR-ELECT

NEW HAMPSHIRE Democrats believed in rotation in office and no man was permitted to hold any office very long. While their party was in the ascendancy no United States senator ever succeeded himself and very rarely did a congressman serve more than two terms. Late in May, 1836, Isaac Hill had resigned his seat in the Senate to become governor, and the June legislative session had been faced with the problem of his successor for the balance of the term which ended March 4, 1837, and for the next six years. When the caucus met it appeared that there were six candidates with sizable followings. Ex-Congressman Harvey who had been passed over once or twice before led with forty-two, and Pierce came next with thirty-four; besides these leaders John Page had twenty-eight and young Charles G. Atherton who had succeeded Pierce as speaker of the house came fourth with twenty-six. Two others had twenty-one each. With the vote so scattered, there was a clear field for combination. After the second ballot the Atherton strength disappeared and on the fourth ballot the Pierce votes dropped, the bulk of his supporters seemingly going to Page who was nominated on the fifth ballot and elected next day for the short term only. As the state convention met the day following and nominated Atherton for Congress in Pierce's place, the whole matter gave rise to newspaper comment to the effect that Atherton got the congressional nomination as a reward for withdrawal and that an arrangement had been made whereby Page was to serve the short term and at the winter session of the legislature Pierce was to be chosen for the long term, 1837–1843. Just how much of this was true does not appear. As Barton, editor of the *Patriot,* was not friendly to Pierce's advancement, Pierce assumed, so others said, that Hill who owned the paper was opposed to him, especially as their relations had become none too friendly. The future congressman, John Wentworth, assured Baker, however, that Hill had not been unfriendly but that Atherton had been the real oppo-

nent and that he had used Barton. Pierce himself has left no
reference in his correspondence on the subject. All of this
maneuvering had occurred while he was in Washington, and
when he returned to Hillsborough in the middle of July it
was to pitch into the hayfield and his law practice rather than
into politics.

In the course of the summer he began to perfect plans which
he had long been contemplating. Since his marriage, life in
Hillsborough had become increasingly unattractive. His law
practice was limited to the small business which this agricultural environment could produce and his income did not satisfy
him. We have reason to believe also that Mrs. Pierce did not
like the village and its people. Pierce therefore decided to
move to Concord where conditions for happiness and prosperity
were more favorable. Albert Baker would go to Boston for the
winter to complete his law studies and take over Pierce's practice on his return, or at least so Pierce hoped. In the meantime
Mrs. Pierce remained at Lowell for the summer trying leeches
as a means of restoring her health, and her husband sought
unsuccessfully to sell their home.

In spite of the fact that it was a presidential year there was
little politics that summer, and soon after winter sent its first
heralds in October with two snowfalls the apathetic campaign
came to a close with the election of Van Buren. Then, with
his house unsold because of the increasing hard times, Pierce
was forced to borrow $500 to meet his bills before he set out
for Lowell. There Mrs. Pierce and he were to meet for their
journey to Washington.

Shortly after their departure for the south the legislature met
and with some obscure preliminary maneuvering elected him
senator for the term beginning March 4, 1837. The *Statesman*
took occasion to remark that Pierce's election was " a triumph
over his enemies in which he and his friends may well exult.
No man has been so strongly and so ungenerously opposed by
professed political friends, the inventions of malice never urged
slander more assiduously than have his rivals and personal enemies—men who now control the political affairs of the state.''
We have some reason to believe that the *Statesman* referred to
opposition from the *Patriot*. Pierce's old friend Bridge wrote
to Hawthorne that this election was " an instance of what a

man can do by trying. With no very remarkable talents, he at the age of 34 fills one of the highest stations in the nation." Scarcely, therefore, had the Pierces settled at a fourth boarding house, Mrs. C. A. Pitman's on Third Street, when they learned that after March 4 they would be Senator and Mrs. Pierce. Their new boarding place was very comfortable, even elegant, and very reasonable. Mrs. Pitman was an " excellent motherly sort of a woman, and disposed to make . . . all as comfortable as possible." The board was the usual heavy fare of the messes but there was no wine. As Fairfield wrote home, " There is not a wine drinker among us, even Frank Pierce has left off." Mrs. Pierce upon her arrival immediately retired to her room with a bad cold and was not very often seen by the rest: she seemed to be " in very delicate health and wanting in cheerfulness." She was not very much impressed by her husband's promotion.

Before Pierce could cross the rotunda the short session must be reckoned with. Its deliberations were not started under auspicious circumstances. Jackson was so ill that the New Year's reception had to be canceled, and a disastrous fire similar to that which had destroyed the Treasury some years before laid the old Patent Office and Post Office in ashes. In Congress much of the session was devoted to angry quarrels, the most menacing being the renewal of the struggle over the question of slavery petitions. Pierce voted for a gag resolution even more obnoxious to its opponents than the one he had helped draw up last session, but otherwise he did not participate; as usual, he was engrossed in committee work. He was still on the judiciary committee, and the speaker appointed him to one select committee to investigate the abuses alleged to exist at West Point, and to another to investigate the relations of the treasury and the deposit banks. Service on the former was not laborious as the members of the committee took the report Pierce and Smith had written in 1835 and, with few changes, presented it to the House on March 1. They succeeded in getting it printed, although their principal recommendation involving the abolition of the cadet system and the substitution therefor of a technical curriculum for army officers with no academic departments was not considered. The work of the other select committee, however, absorbed practically all of Pierce's legislative energy.

The Reuben M. Whitney investigation, so called because that individual was supposed to be an agent whose business it was to conduct clandestine negotiations between the treasury and the " pet " banks, was in reality a long and heated battle day by day and often night by night between the Whig and Democratic members of the committee. The Whigs wished to prove that Democratic banks were favored and that if they hired Reuben M. Whitney as their Washington agent they received special privileges and advance information. Pierce and the Democrats sought to prevent the investigation from going too far afield into the political activities of their party. At length after much that resembled *opera bouffe* Pierce prepared a set of resolutions exonerating the accused banks and Whitney. The minority could only report that Whitney was an agent of some of the banks, which all admitted, and charge that an obscurely worded letter from Woodbury had been influential in getting him certain of his agencies. They stated their belief, however, that much of the business of the deposit banks was transacted through Whitney and that he handed on to them much valuable information. Pierce and his party friends considered the whole affair an example of rank partisanship, and he with Fairfield and Hamer even went so far as to vote against permitting the minority to report; but in this they were overruled by their committee associates. This attempt to use a congressional investigation for partisan ends had wasted a great deal of the time of those serving on the select committee.

Pierce's exit from the lower house was a stormy one. In the first place, family troubles seemed to be increasing. Mrs. Pierce had been sick much of the winter. Then news came that his sister Harriet was seriously ill, and finally that his father had suffered a stroke. Added to these domestic afflictions were the gruelling experiences always attendant upon the last days and nights of a short session. Much legislation was crowded into the last hours. February 27 the House was in committee of the whole on the rivers and harbors bill. Pierce was called to the chair and all that day the debate dragged. Hour after hour Pierce held the chair—most of the time until six in the morning, when the twenty-hour session was brought to a close. Such sessions were no small drain upon the vitality, though this one, so the *Globe* said, was " marked throughout with the usual courtesy of the body, and the best feelings generally prevailed among the members."

During the next two days Pierce voted against the rivers and harbors bill, against the Cumberland road bill, and against the law repealing the specie circular; but in vain, as they all passed. Much of March 3 was spent in a contest between the Senate and the House over the fortifications bill. This bill contained a rider inserted by the House continuing the distribution of the surplus, against which Pierce had fruitlessly voted. Now on the last day the Senate refused to concur in this amendment and Cambreleng, the chairman of the ways and means committee, helplessly struggled to convince the House that it ought to recede. Pierce joined with a number in favor of recession but not even the fact that the administration favored it could induce the majority of the House to give in, and after much debate, needless confusion, and many roll calls the bill was lost.

During this excitement, Pierce and his friend F. O. J. Smith shared the chair with Polk, and their difficulties were exasperating. Pierce had an encounter with the redoubtable John Quincy Adams who made a point of order which Pierce refused to entertain. Adams attempted to push his point of order by charging that Cambreling was attempting to intimidate the House. Pierce denied this contention and Adams was at length compelled to sit down. To add to the confusion, there was an unusual problem. On the last night a mob invaded the House, a mob of beautiful ladies who supplied sufficient hubbub to hamper effectually much of the business before the House. The presiding officers were helpless against the fair invaders as most of them stayed until nearly midnight. " The confusion was like that of a town meeting, and the sound of voices like that of many waters drowning even the powerful voice and distinct enunciation of the clerk." After such a contest the House adjourned at two in the morning and hurried home to get a little sleep in preparation for the festivities of inauguration day.

* * *

That winter a young planter from Mississippi had visited Washington, hoping that the gay life of the capital might divert his flagging spirits and shaken health. He mingled with the coterie at Dowson's and met many of the congressmen. A number of pleasant acquaintanceships were formed in that convivial atmosphere, among them one that was to become historic, for it was during this winter that Jefferson Davis and Franklin Pierce became friends.

XIII

THE YOUNGEST SENATOR

PIERCE'S career in the House had not been spectacular. He had acted uniformly as a loyal Jacksonian, and his vote had been ever at his party's disposal on the financial questions uppermost during the last four years. He had even out-Jacksoned Jackson in his relentless opposition to internal improvements. His greatest labors had been confined to committee rooms, where he had faithfully performed numerous assignments. At no time had he emerged from the mass of congressmen and his name was connected with no legislation or policy. His elevation to the Senate brought him upon a much smaller but more important stage with fewer fellow actors. Here there might be opportunity to come forth and display powers of statesmanship ripened by his House experience. Militating against such emergence was a primary disadvantage: Pierce found himself in point of age the youngest senator.

As Pierce was sworn in, just before the inauguration of Martin Van Buren, and joined Henry Hubbard in representing New Hampshire's interests, he found himself in august company. Here were Henry Clay, Crittenden, Webster, Calhoun, Benton, William R. King, Buchanan, R. J. Walker, Hugh L. White, Silas Wright; never was there a stronger Senate. Pierce was to be among the giants. With such colleagues, he whose most successful rôle had ever been that of the protégé of older men could only continue to be the industrious and loyal young man whose chief pleasure it was to be thought well of by his elders. In this environment he was very content to be a follower; there was little stimulus for original action.

The few days of the extra session of the Senate were quiet and pleasant and there was little evidence of the dangers ahead for either the party or the young senator. It did not take long to confirm Van Buren's chief appointments, and then Senator and Mrs. Pierce were free to turn their faces northward. Spring was slow in arriving that year in New Hampshire, so Mrs. Pierce lingered at Lowell and Amherst while her husband proceeded homeward. It was dismal at the homestead. His father was partially paralyzed and very feeble, his mother had fallen into hopeless senility, his sister Nancy was gradually sinking. The snow clung to the hills until May and the countryside dreaded another cool summer and poor harvest. Troubles did not come singly that year, for shortly the business structure of the country broke down and panic was abroad in the land. Local business men were going to the wall, near home several extensive shoe dealers at Keene failed in one day, and Pierce could philosophize. " I never exactly understood before the force of the expression ' blessed be nothing ' but it is now made plain for those who have large sums due to them have quite as much cause for anxiety as those who are in debt; perhaps more in as much as we prefer the losses of others to our own." He analyzed the chief causes of these difficulties as the monstrous increase of banking without capital, and speculation; to this situation the United States Bank had contributed by attempting to tighten the money market for its own purposes and had overplayed its hand.

The financial stringency soon created a demand for a special session of Congress which Van Buren heeded. He summoned the national legislature to meet September 4. This call was unwelcome to the new senator, for it came just as the fall court terms were opening. He was able to attend one week of court at Amherst, and then planned to leave his practice with Albert Baker, now a full-fledged lawyer.

Upon arrival at Washington, Pierce established himself once more at Birth's, where Senators Wall of New Jersey and Williams of Maine were stopping; here too lived his old Bowdoin friend, Jonathan Cilley, now one of the Maine representatives, and the new senator was to have good reason long to remember this " mess." The session itself was short and business-like, the Senate passed the bills reported by the finance committee and adjourned with the majority rather self-satisfied, confident that the administration now stood " upon firm and impregnable ground." Even this short session, however, was not without its blight, for word came that his nephew Scott McNeil, whose education he had watched with so much interest, had been killed in the faraway everglades of Florida fighting the Seminoles.

At Washington the December reunion of the politicians, at

least on the Democratic side, was not very joyful. The panic
hung over their party fortunes like a pall. But in spite of the
fall elections they did their best to put on a brave front " not
doubting in the least the ultimate triumph of correct principles." Soon other menacing questions were to appear, but
before the full danger became apparent Pierce had time to
consider the novelty of his position.

Senator and Mrs. Pierce settled at Birth's which she, at least,
thought had deteriorated somewhat since her first winter there,
and found themselves exalted personages, who must not call
first upon any one but the President. At the capitol as well as
in social circles a senator was of much consequence. There
were but fifty-two senators, and compared with the House the
Senate was a much more dignified, intimate and powerful body.
Its chamber was architecturally excellent and handsomely furnished. The Vice President sat under a crimson canopy sur-
mounted by an eagle in flight, the senators had their comfortable desks each with his name written on a white wood strip,
and were supplied each morning with a quire of paper and two
pens, the unused portion of which the members prudently carried away each night. The senators debated under the enormous gilt chandelier with its thirty-two lamps. There were
usually many interested onlookers, the ladies in a gallery in
the rear, raised about a foot above the Senate floor, and the
gentlemen in one directly above, where those sitting in the
front row were admonished by the following sign: " You are
requested not to put your feet through the railing, as the dirt
falls on the members' heads." Washington mud was proverbial.
Over this body presided the careless and inefficient Richard M.
Johnson, who left the chair just as often as he could to lounge
around or stand before one of the four fireplaces which heated
the room. As in the House, Pierce found himself immediately
engrossed in committee work, and his chief activity was hard
labor on the pension committee presided over by Morris of
Ohio with Roane of Virginia and Williams of Maine (his messmate) as Democratic associates and Prentiss of Vermont as
Whig member. This service, like much of his House committee
work, was laborious but required no special breadth of vision
or statesmanship; his assignment to the committee on manufactures was purely a sinecure.

The Senate had scarcely undertaken the renewed consideration of the financial policy of the Democratic party, when the
slavery issue arose. As Pierce had passed through Boston he
had found considerable excitement over the murder of the
abolitionist editor, Lovejoy, at Alton, Illinois, by a pro-slavery
mob. This example of violence stirred up the agitation once
more and Congress could hardly expect to remain free from
the subject. Pierce was immediately involved. His messmate,
Wall, presented a petition for the abolition of slavery in the
District of Columbia and moved to receive it by laying it on
the table. His colleague, Hubbard, who had just presented
resolutions from the New Hampshire legislature advising Congress to leave the question of slavery strictly alone, moved that
Wall's motion be tabled, an action tantamount to refusing to
receive the petition. To this motion Pierce objected. He had
learned since he signed the Pinckney report that the " gag "
resolution had proved a double-edged sword. The abolitionists
at home had been making capital by declaring that he had
been one who had originated a scheme for the denial of the
constitutional right of petition. Pierce protested against Hubbard's motion. He was willing to deny boldly the plea contained in this petition, lay the document on the table, or take
any action which would silence agitators and tranquilize public
opinion, but voting not to receive the petition was playing directly into the hands of the abolitionists and presenting them
with an issue. His objection was unheeded by his party, and
he voted in the minority with the Whigs. This independent
action he repeated in January on a similar resolution.

Closely allied with these abolition issues was the question of
the annexation of Texas. In 1836 Adams had served notice
that such a proposition would be opposed by the opponents of
slavery, and now it arose to plague the Senate. Shortly after
the debate on the petition from New Jersey, Swift of Vermont
presented a memorial and resolutions from the legislature of
his state protesting against acquiring Texas and petitioning the
abolition of slavery in the District. Calhoun and his southern
friends were much disturbed; prior to this time petitions on
this subject had been received from private individuals, but
here was a sovereign state officially taking action upon a subject
involving the rights and institutions of other sovereign states.

Such conduct could only mean danger. Consequently Calhoun drew up six resolutions and presented them to the Senate; in them he set forth the states rights theory of slavery as an institution subject only to state control, and declared that any attempt to abolish slavery in the territories or the District of Columbia would be a dangerous attack on the institutions of the slaveholding states; it was the duty of Congress to maintain the equal rights of all the states.

Pierce decided to vote for these resolutions and made an extended speech in explanation. He had discovered that a change had taken place in the situation. Three years before he had thought the apprehensions of Southern gentlemen to a great extent had their origin in a morbid sensibility upon this subject. But now conditions were different. The abolitionists, who had been relatively small and harmless by themselves, had gained allies. Designing politicians had taken up the cause. He had noted a very fortuitous agreement between the editorials in Whig and in abolition papers in Connecticut and New Hampshire, not upon abolition but upon the charge that the action of the Senate and House in refusing to print, read or refer petitions was a denial of a sacred right. Pierce denied that the right of petition had been impaired, for, as he explained it, these petitions had been received, considered, reported upon and disposed of so often that their constant submission amounted to an abuse of privilege, since their frequent consideration blocked the wheels of legislation and promoted ill-feeling. This alliance of fanatic and politician in an attack upon the constitutional rights of certain of the states was fraught with great danger, he declared, and would lead to a dissolution of the Union. He would vote for Calhoun's resolutions " to preserve inviolate the public faith and the provisions of the Constitution under which we have so long lived in prosperity." The implication was that a vote for these resolutions was a vote against a Whig conspiracy to make political capital in New England.

In this fashion he concluded his thinking on the slavery question. His antipathy to abolitionists so deeply set in his bitter experience of February, 1836, now had been bolstered by his partisan animosity toward the Whigs. Hereafter to his mind the slavery controversy was the work of a few misguided fanatics joined by political schemers who sought to overthrow the Democratic party. Controversy engineered by such an alliance was always pernicious and must be fought to the last ditch. Only thus could a patriot serve his country and preserve the Union.

With this question disposed of by the adoption of the resolutions the Senate went into extended discussions of border difficulties with Great Britain, public land pre-emption, and the independent treasury. While these were being thrashed out, Birth's mess suffered a senseless tragedy. Both parties had been badgered in the debates, and Cilley had adopted a peculiarly infuriating manner of baiting the Whigs. When he repeated press charges that the notorious Whig editor, J. Watson Webb, had received a bribe to support the re-charter of the bank, the Whigs decided to call a halt. One of Clay's Kentucky delegation, Graves, carried a note to Cilley which Webb had written. When Cilley refused to receive this note Graves was insulted and challenged the Maine representative to a duel. Cilley advised with Pierce, who roomed next to him, and a correspondence ensued, but as Cilley would not give Webb a certificate of character Graves demanded satisfaction. The challenge was a perplexing problem; but rather than submit to a public assault Cilley concluded to accept, and Pierce, with Benton and Linn of Missouri, decided that rifles at eighty paces would be the proper arrangements. On the Saturday afternoon of the duel Pierce anxiously awaited news, and toward nightfall went out to the corner of Pennsylvania Avenue to watch for the returning party. A horseman soon dashed up with the news that Cilley had been killed. For many years thereafter Pierce harbored only bitterness for those Whigs, especially Henry A. Wise, whom he held most responsible for this tragedy. He himself was blamed as one of the chief promoters of the affair, and he published a long letter showing how hard they had all worked to prevent the affray. The next number of the *Patriot* bore headlines on its black-bordered sheet, " Bank Ruffians Hired to Murder Cilley."

The tragedy and its excitement bore heavily upon Mrs. Pierce and the senator, and their spirits were further oppressed by trouble and illness. The McNeils were in financial difficulties and Mrs. McNeil was suffering from melancholia. Mrs. Pierce was ill, and deaths in her family made her even more downcast.

Their own prospects were not very encouraging. Together they puzzled over their situation and reconsidered the plan of moving to Concord. Perhaps it would be better to go west where opportunities were greater. Small wonder Pierce spent a miserable spring. His whole system lagged. He had lost his "usual elasticity of spirits and capability for business." Mrs. Pierce was almost desperate. "Oh, how I wish he was out of political life! How much better it would be for him on every account!" To cap the climax the month of June was terribly hot, the hottest they had experienced, and in this torrid atmosphere Mrs. Pierce wilted and took to her bed. Dr. Sewall did his best, but she and her husband would find no help until they reached the refuge of the New Hampshire hills. Those cool slopes were very far away and the House would debate the independent treasury scheme indefinitely. When it became very hot there was some hope of adjournment, but a delightful shower cooled the air a little and the congressmen kept on speaking. As Pierce well knew, "in a body where there are more than one hundred talking lawyers . . . you can make no calculation upon the termination of any debate and frequently the more trifling the subject the more animated and protracted the discussion."

In spite of these torments of body and spirit, the work in committee room and on the floor had to go on; there were many important measures to be settled. Pierce spoke little, contenting himself with voting for the Democratic financial program, including the independent treasury. He supported the land measures which Benton had so much at heart, the pre-emption and graduation bills, but when it came to internal improvements he pursued a curiously consistent course which threw him in a minority. His scruples and his interests prevented him from supporting such subsidies. He voted against appropriations to continue the Cumberland road, against a bill for the benefit of the Alabama, Florida and Georgia Railroad and against the rivers and harbors bill—all of which passed; and on the other hand he voted for a bill to complete roads in Michigan which had been started while it was a territory, and his vote carried the bill. Congress might constitutionally aid the territories and presumably should complete what it had begun. As to the annexation of Texas, he voted to lay that question on the table in a majority of twenty-four to fourteen. He concluded his labors of the session with numerous reports from the pension committee and a speech on the Fourth of July in behalf of the line officers of the army who were discriminated against in salary and opportunity. No adjournment was ever more welcome than that which finally came July 9.

Sometime during these months it was definitely decided to give up the western experiment, and Pierce returned to his plan of moving to Concord, where he would find a wider opportunity to engage in the practice of law. He formed a partnership with a good business man, Asa Fowler, and thither in August, 1838, they moved; this town was to be their principal residence for the rest of their lives. Pierce and Fowler began a successful partnership for the two made a decided contrast. Fowler was cautious and hard-working where Pierce was careless and easy-going. Fowler preferred office work to trials and often provided the sound knowledge upon which Pierce made an eloquent pleading. There was a suggestion of incompatibility, however, which was to increase in the next few years until politics broke up the firm.

Preparatory to this move, Pierce had left his Hillsborough practice in the hands of Albert Baker who, much to his sister Mary's delight, gave up the idea of going west and settled down to law and politics in Hillsborough. Baker also kept oversight of the aged general and his wife who were pitiable in their helplessness. Unhampered, Senator Pierce could actively enter his new environment and lay plans to leave Congress.

XIV

RETIREMENT FROM PUBLIC LIFE

PIERCE had not profited by Congressional service and the disadvantage became insistently apparent during his senatorship. In September, 1839, Frank Robert was born, and the coming of the child impressed upon his parents some hard facts. In the years since 1833 Pierce had been master of little time to devote to his law practice and he was accumulating little money. Neither did he have a home. In Washington he was too easily a prey to the jovial and reckless life of the politicians, and his sojourns there were also made uncomfortable by frequent illness. Mrs. Pierce hated the capital and it is difficult to discover which was harder for her to bear, going to Washington with her husband or being separated from him by remaining in New England. She was insistent that he leave politics and in her insistence she had family allies. Another contributing factor was New Hampshire custom, which among the Democrats at least did not permit a re-election to the Senate. In 1843, therefore, Pierce would have to retire, and as early as 1838 he began to consider resigning to return to his law practice. It was to take him four years to make up his mind.

The period of indecision is of little interest or importance biographically. The outstanding changes in his life were the breaking of the old home ties by the death of his mother and father in 1838 and 1839, and the birth of his son. Frank Robert gave his father a new purpose in life and a new reason for greater care in his own living. His Washington sojourns were no longer spent in the somewhat careless atmosphere of mess surroundings. During the twenty-sixth Congress, in the absence of his wife, he lived in a private family as their only boarder. He adopted a stern and regular regimen and fortified himself to battle with temptation, loneliness, ill-health and religious doubt. As he wrote his partner during the winter of 1839, " I have dwelt somewhat more this winter upon the truths of Divine revelation than usual and perhaps have struggled somewhat harder to think and act in conformity with the precepts

and commandments of the New Testament than ever before—
but with indifferent success as every man must who is not a
humble and devoted Christian to which character I can, I
regret to say, make no pretension." He had no doubts as to
the fundamental truths which could be revealed only through
the Gospel, but the consciousness of salvation did not come to
him, invite it as he would. Amid these none too pleasant experiences, he continually heard the insistent call from home to
leave politics.

His public life was still largely a matter of pensions. He
was trying to get John McNeil a pension, but the administration was unwilling, since the giant veteran held public office,
to grant him an allowance as well. Pierce finally carried the
matter to Van Buren and when the latter refused to overrule his
subordinates, Pierce had some " words " with the executive and
broke off relations with him. More important was his service
in committee. At the opening of the twenty-sixth Congress he
became chairman of the Senate pension committee and spent
much of his time in sifting the numerous private bills which
were introduced so frequently in both houses. During one
session he made nearly one hundred reports which, he wrote,
" will find a place among the documents of this session but
will not be known beyond those who have occasion to refer to
the public documents; not very flattering to a man's pride but
must be done in the performance of his duty." Even to him
it seemed a rather futile public service.

His pension experience was not without some effort at constructive legislation. He endeavored to secure a law to prevent
agents from collecting exorbitant fees for their routine services
and he sought to weed out numerous doubtful claims by urging
the passage of a statute of limitations which would prevent
Revolutionary claims at this late date. However, he was unsuccessful nor was he any more fortunate with a measure to
provide for the equalization of the pay of staff and line officers
in the army.

The most exciting experience of the period was the election
of 1840 which was to prove, in Pierce's mind at least, a serious
disaster. He did what he could to prevent the calamity. Never
did he work harder politcially than during the late summer
and fall of that year. When Maine went Whig, " hell-bent for

Governor Kent" in September, the Democrats were admonished; Pierce wrote that they had "much to do" in New Hampshire. His party planned to organize and stump the state as never before. True, they had not lost an election in ten years, but no one could feel sure of anything in 1840. Pierce's fame as a winning and effective speaker was widespread and he was much in demand. The north country chiefs sent down for him, but his time was too much taken in the southern counties. A special messenger came over the mountains from Claremont for him to rally the Democrats in Sullivan County and he went back to join Hubbard and others in a rousing meeting which lasted from ten in the morning on into the evening; fifteen hundred were present filling the largest church to overflowing. "I was amply repaid," commented Pierce, "it was a glorious meeting and evinced a spirit in Sullivan County that will ensure them at least our usual majority."

After a week of New Hampshire meetings, early in October he made a trip into Massachusetts to aid the Democrats there. In the meantime all details of organization were carefully watched. Arrangements so perfect were planned, that not a single Democrat in any township in the state who could be carried to the polls would fail to vote; there must be "thorough minute school district organization." More spectacular and perhaps less effective were the rallies that continued to be held. The "federalists" must be overcome, the aristocratic few could not be permitted once more to rule the democratic many. If the Whigs won, the speculators would fasten upon the people of New Hampshire a portion of the debts of the states amounting to millions of dollars, a telling argument to the thrifty yeomen of a state which kept itself very largely free from debt. Moreover, the opposition candidate, Harrison, was not suitable, his military achievements were questionable. He was so ignorant he could not answer his own letters. In Ohio he had favored a law whereby a poor man might be sold into temporary slavery. As Governor of Indiana he had signed a law whereby a man so bound out might be whipped with thirty-nine lashes. He had approved a law requiring property qualifications for voting. In fine, a vote for him would be a vote for Webster, Clay, Biddle and Wise, once the friends of Adams and Hamilton. The election of Harrison would mean the return of Federalism, traitorous, aristocratic, Tory Federalism.

The spiritual successors of the Federalists had joined with the anti-Masons and abolitionists in a drunken, licentious campaign marked and marred by excess at the debauched, hard-cider and log-cabin meetings. Such behavior was corrupting democracy and Pierce was in arms. He continued his speaking through the final week at Hopkinton, Manchester, Goffstown, Francestown and Boscawen. He defended Van Buren and preached his doctrines with " frankness, candor and fervid eloquence," and as the campaign drew to a close he was " truly thankful for the strength and energy which seems to be so necessary in this crisis." November 3 was a day generally disastrous but in Democracy's crown there was one bright and radiant star. Van Buren had carried New Hampshire by 6,000 in the largest vote ever polled in the commonwealth. Pierce never felt prouder of his native state; but the country had " disgraced itself by electing a mere man of straw to the highest office in the world."

As he was leaving for Congress after this campaign, Pierce finally made up his mind to resign: the immediate cause of this determination was the anticipation of the birth of another child. However, although Benjamin arrived safely April 13, 1841, his father waited almost a year before carrying his resolution into effect. The election of 1840 had put Pierce in a new position.

In his more than ten years of legislative service he had always been in the majority group; now for the first time he found conditions reversed. When the special session met in May, 1841, the majority, according to Pierce, was a " brindled heterogeneous party " with no coherence, and the Democrats thought they saw an opportunity. Pierce and his friends foresaw the break between Clay and Tyler over the bank veto, and as the split became wider the Democrats redoubled their efforts to increase the demoralization. Pierce took great pride in their program. " Our discussion upon the Bank bill has been one of the most remarkable and able on this side of the Chamber that was ever listened to. The whole of this most corrupt and corrupting of systems has been and is in process of being probed to the very core. We shall do nothing this session but expose fraud and corruption. . . . We have made a mere *anvil* of the administration in the Senate from the beginning of the session to this moment and we intend to *hammer* them to the end of it. . . . We are making a glorious fight here from day to day. One sun goes down only to see another dawn upon a more animated renewal of the contest. Our men are all on the spot from 10 in the morning until 4 or 5 in the evening." Pierce wrote his partner making excuse for delay in attending to some matter at one of the departments, because of his constant attendance upon the daily sessions. Each night, as well, the Democrats caucused, sometimes at Boulanger's, and mapped out their tactics for the morrow. Pierce was in the midst of this partisan strife: he was back in Dowson's, No. 1 Capitol Hill.

As a minority Senator, Pierce spent his last two sessions in Congress. He undertook the strict regimen which he had prescribed for himself in previous winters. He had plenty of exercise, gave up alcohol and tobacco. He worked on the pension committee, now as a minority member, and endeavored to persuade Tyler to reappoint McNeil as surveyor of the port of Boston. In this matter he had the exasperating experience of seeing the reappointment sent to the Senate and then recalled, never to be sent back.

It was not until the month of January, 1842, that Pierce made his final preparations for leaving public life. He settled various matters for his constituents and made some provision for the future by arranging for the appointment of his partner as a commissioner in bankruptcy under the act passed by the special session, making this arrangement while the repeal of the act was pending. He voted for the repeal, but, as he had predicted, the rescinding measure did not pass. At length his business was finished and on February 16, 1842, he sent Governor Page his resignation, to take effect on the 28th. After a farewell party at Dr. Heiskel's he left Washington the 26th, not waiting for Leonard Wilcox to take his place.

His departure caused some regret among many of his colleagues. He had been a pleasant and obliging companion. He had never been afraid of hard work and had been ever a loyal party man. Commentators on his departure could say little else. His activities had been restricted to the field of military affairs and the reward and care of Revolutionary veterans, interests which it is easily seen he acquired directly from his father and his early experiences. In the pursuit of these interests he had realized that problems existed. He called the pension system of the United States the worst on the face of the earth and warned the Senate that the army and navy needed reform. Nevertheless he seemed unable to do anything effective toward bettering these services. He was too amiable and obliging, too much the follower, the willing young man eager to be thought well of by his elders. His lack of imagination and originality prevented any divergence from the paths laid down by the great leaders of the Senate. As a legislator he had been ineffective because he lacked the ruthlessness or the daring to use his position. As chairman of the pension committee by a judicious granting of favors and making of bargains he could have gained power; but Pierce did favors instead of making bargains and so could not even put through his brother-in-law's pension bill. The few desirable reforms in the pension system and army organization that he did father fell by the wayside. He left as his sole legislative monument several hundred reports on individual pension cases.

CIRCUIT LAWYER
1842-1847

XV

IN CONCORD

In March, 1842, Pierce began a new and distinctly different way of life. He was no longer in public office. He was really settling down to his law practice. He and Mrs. Pierce were to establish their first real home and to enter a different environment. Most important, Pierce had reached maturity. His life heretofore had been lived largely under the patronage of his elders as a party follower. His father had been a dominating influence in his career, and the Hillsborough and congressional environments, so unpleasant to Mrs. Pierce, had not stimulated independent action in her husband. Now this was all past and upon a new stage Pierce could cast a new part for himself. He had purchased a house on Montgomery Street not far from the law office and court house, and that spring they moved in. Even Mrs. Pierce was hopeful; and the parents, happy in their children, their new home and new environment, looked forward to a more satisfying and coherent life in Concord.

Concord itself was a little town of some five thousand inhabitants, though perhaps the term "little" is a misnomer, for the town was seven miles square and embraced a number of settlements from Mast Yard to the Ironworks and from Dimond Hill to Soucook River. Large as it was in size, its importance lay in its center of gravity, which was the main street. Here the world as Concord knew it passed by, and its length from Horse Shoe Pond to Bowline was all the world many of its inhabitants knew. At the north and south ends of this street and on the few streets up the hill parallel to it were the varied dwellings of the townspeople. Some of these houses were old enough to be relics of the fortifications against the Indians in the old "Pennycook" days. In the outlying districts were a few industries and down by the Merrimack, as it twisted its way through the intervale, were a distillery and slaughter houses. Business Concord sat squarely in the center of the town with its grasp firmly on both sides of Main Street. Physically this section was nondescript in appearance. Most imposing in architecture was the Merrimack Bank where Pierce had his office and the brick " blocks " such as Low's, Stickney's and Hill's, and the hotels.   Among these more pretentious structures were the many one- and two-story wooden buildings with their high false fronts and weatherbeaten clapboards.   Here business went on in its leisurely fashion and in the " cellars " were several gin mills, one of which offered the enticement of a bowling alley.   So Concord supplied its material needs.

If Concord economic was nondescript, Concord spiritual was imposing.   First among the churches stood the old North Church, proud reminder of the day when church and state were one, presided over by Rev. Nathaniel Bouton.   Chief for the interest of Franklin Pierce was the South Congregational, newly established and presided over by Rev. Daniel J. Noyes. Here rather than at North Church, for reasons now unknown, Mrs. Pierce became a member in 1842 and her husband accompanied her and contributed to the support of the establishment as long as she lived.   Near the capitol was St. Paul's, later to be closely associated with Pierce.   Other churches there were of most varied denominations, and the cause of religion flourished.

The crowning glory of Concord, however, was political.   The granite capitol with its golden eagle commanded the statehouse yard, with St. Paul's Episcopal Church and the American House on its north hand, and stables, blacksmith's shop and Hill's block on its south.   For Pierce the capitol was no longer the object of interest it had been in those June days of his legislative career.   Up the street a little way to the north was a less pretentious structure which was to be his center of activity, a plain and somewhat timeworn building which served the dual purpose of town house and Merrimack County court house, commonly known as the " Ark."   In the large bare room on the first floor, each second Tuesday in March gathered the citizens from the seven-mile radius to attend town meeting, and among them and active was always Col. Pierce.   On the second floor was the court room, and here the superior court and the common pleas held their sessions, the one in the second week of July and the other in the third weeks of March and September; before the bar of these courts no lawyer was a more frequent advocate in the next ten years than Pierce of Pierce and Fowler.   Politically important too were the hotels and the

Patriot office.   The American House was the seat of the Democratic power, and at the Phoenix the Whigs congregated, for the political day of the Eagle was not yet, and would not be until a power undreamed of had arisen; its " Grecian Hall," however, was often in demand for meetings.   The *Patriot* office where Henry H. Carroll and Nathaniel B. Baker, formerly law students in the offices of Pierce and Fowler, edited the paper, the Franklin Bookstore and Franklin Hall were also important rallying places for Pierce and his associates.   In fact, there were times and seasons when the town seemed wholly given over to the fascinating game of politics.

Such, then, was Concord, but it was a changing Concord; there was unwonted activity in 1842, new faces were appearing on the streets, new houses were going up and to the eastward offices and shops and railroad tracks were sure signs that soon the noise of bell and whistle would be heard through the intervale: the railroad was a transforming fact.

Upon such a stage, during the years that followed, Pierce stuck to his resolve to devote himself to the law and followed his profession literally as well as figuratively, for the courts met in various parts of the state and his practice called him to follow them.   He was an effective jury lawyer, therefore successful; and with the birth of his son, Benjamin, he had even more incentive to succeed.   The personal weaknesses of his congressional days seem to have been easier to control.   But biographically, in the light of future events, these years are important only as they picture Pierce's new political interest. He was to become a party " boss."   For four years he was to increase in power as party organizer and leader, and as such was called upon to deal with three questions which were of great moment in the Forties, not only in New Hampshire but in many communities throughout the United States—railroads, temperance, and slavery.

XVI
PUNISHING ISAAC HILL

ALTHOUGH ex-Senator Pierce came home to Concord with his public career, as he thought, behind him, he did not reckon with the qualities of attraction possessed by the political game; few senators retire permanently at thirty-eight. In fact, hardly had he returned before he re-entered the arena. A few hours after his arrival in Concord, he made a speech at the court house, and his remarks were deemed important enough to demand a special edition of one of the opposition papers. He had returned to find the annual election at hand and his party in confusion. Pierce and the railroad had arrived in Concord at the same time.

The New Hampshire farmers did not like the new railroads, especially as they wanted the right to take the farmers' lands by condemnation regardless of the owners' wishes. In June, 1840, the farm interest had been strong enough to secure the repeal of the acts of 1836 and 1837 granting condemnation rights. However, the repeal did not interfere with this right if work upon the road in question had already begun. In the winter session friends of the railroads succeeded in having the exception extended to such roads as had been surveyed. Such action the farmers felt nullified the effect of the " repealer," so they renewed the battle.

Isaac Hill complicated matters. He had been losing ground as younger men came forward and his enemies grew stronger and more numerous. But retirement did not suit his temperament and he sought to return to power via the railroad route. The new leaders among whom Albert Baker was prominent and outspoken were friends of the farmer and " radical " in their determination to protect his rights. Hill had sold his *Patriot* conditionally and now failed in an attempt to get it back. Therefore, he established a rival known as *Hill's Patriot* and endeavored to gain patronage from Tyler and fight the " radicals " on behalf of the railroads. Beaten in the convention of 1841, he organized a third or " Conservative party " friendly to the new transportation interest, and John H. White, recently defeated for the regular nomination, was made the gubernatorial candidate of Hill's new party.

Pierce by natural tendency supported Hubbard, the regular candidate, not so much because he was opposed to railroads but rather because he was opposed to bolters. He had watched carefully the rise of his protégé, Albert Baker, and Baker's untimely death the preceding October left him with a sentimental interest in the anti-railroad movement to which Baker had contributed so much enthusiasm. Besides, he and Hill had been getting into deep water. There is evidence that Hill had attempted to patronize Pierce when the latter first entered Congress. As to Pierce's attitude toward Hill, there is that significant line to McNeil: " however unfortunate it may be to be young I trust he [Hill] will admit it is not criminal." Pierce's friends at least suspected that Hill had opposed his election to the Senate. Open hostility had not broken out until 1840, when Pierce had appeared for the Merrimack County Bank as counsel in a suit against Hill. Pierce had won the case and Hill had spoken disparagingly of him in the columns of his *Patriot*. The breach of course widened when Pierce appeared against Hill before arbitrators in a dispute over the sale of the *Patriot*. Then came Pierce's speech at the court house hard on his return. Therein he denounced bolters at the same time that he endorsed the " radical " platform. Hill broke out again. He devoted an " extra " to Pierce, branding him as a trimmer who chose a course only because it seemed the more popular. The election returns showed that Hill's ticket was decisively defeated, but there remained the important fact that he and his followers had ventured an alliance with the Whigs in order to control the town meeting at Concord. Hill was determined to push the railroad issue further, and Pierce and his friends girded themselves to punish the old deserter.

Politics in New Hampshire was like intermittent fever: no one infected with it was ever long without it. The political year began and ended in June because that was the month the state officers were inaugurated, and a nominating convention was held to designate certain candidates from whom the voters would make their choices the next March. To select delegates for this June convention primary meetings were held in May. The month of June was dedicated chiefly to the meeting of the legislature, with one day, at least, devoted to the state convention. During the summer there was a lull, and the fall was not very active unless there happened to be an October state convention or a December meeting of the legislature. Winter, however, brought renewed activity; the time had come to prepare for the spring elections. Although candidates for the governorship and the state offices had been chosen, nominations for the legislature and county offices had not been made.

Late December and early January, then, were the periods for primary meetings of each party to choose candidates for the lower house of the legislature and more delegates, for in January were held three types of conventions. The state was districted into five councilor districts and twelve senatorial districts, and in addition there were, after 1840 when Carroll and Belknap were established, ten counties. Each councilor district, each senatorial district and each county, therefore, must have a convention of each party to nominate councilor, senatorial, and county-office candidates. When these nominations had been made, and until after the town meetings on the second Tuesday of March, when the votes were cast, there was little else but politics. Each party was organized to the extent of the ability of the leaders, meetings were held, and the voters harangued by speakers who grew constantly hoarser as the nights wore on. The period of active interest ended with the town meetings, but only for a few weeks, for the May primaries were soon at hand and the year started all over again. The politicians must devote from a fourth to a half of their time to this absorbing enterprise, and among these Pierce soon found himself.

Before he resigned from the Senate he had participated but little in local politics; but now he was free to be more active and when June, 1842, brought the legislature he accepted a new responsibility. The annual convention made Pierce chairman of the state central committee in spite of his reluctance, and charged him with destroying Hill's faction permanently. This disappointed and embittered old man was once more out after the scalp of his old enemy, Hubbard, and the railroad interest was by no means idle. The " conservatives " once again nominated White, and, as the anti-slavery group were running a ticket for the third year in succession, there were four slates in the field. Pierce inaugurated the conflict by a speech at the January convention of his senatorial district at Canterbury, and shortly planned a mass meeting and rally to organize Concord on January 25. He wrote to Congressman Burke for information as to Hill's connections with the Tyler administration, and called the state committee together. He addressed the mass meeting in " his peculiarly fervid and eloquent manner," denouncing the Hill people for bringing in the " Federalists " (Whigs) to determine disputes in the Democratic family. At the committee conclave the state was organized, county committees were appointed and a circular was sent out calling upon the people in the towns to organize and put down the pestiferous faction. Also he and other " radicals " noted that Hill's convention had nominated Woodbury for Vice President in 1844 in an effort to gain his support. Therefore Pierce headed a group who wrote to Woodbury asking his opinion of the " conservative " policy. Woodbury replied, taking decided " radical " ground.

Pierce had not planned to be so active or to neglect his law business; but as the campaign warmed up and the personal attacks upon him grew more bitter he decided to go on the stump. *Hill's Patriot* had been continually firing at him. He was charged with being opposed to the " radical " program until he had been retained as counsel by land owners fighting railroad advance. He was charged with having connived at the passage of the bankrupt law while voting against it, and then resigning in the midst of his term. He had cost the government thereby $500 in extra mileage just to hurry home and reap the benefit of the law by acting with his partner as attorney for bankrupts. Also Hill charged that in spite of his resignation he was still franking mail, and that, while senator, he had influenced the first comptroller to allow the excessive accounts of John P. Hale as district attorney. Pierce denied the last charge and ignored the others.

The last week in February, 1843, and the first in March, he was actively engaged, speaking almost every night in the manner of his famous campaign of 1840, at Portsmouth, Candia, Deerfield, Nashua, Manchester, Andover, Pembroke, and elsewhere. He defended his party's stand on corporations, declaring Hill and his following to be upholding the federalist doctrines of Hamilton. He showed how the Whigs had nearly ruined the treasury, how business was almost at a standstill, and how that venal party was attempting to saddle the national government with state debts amounting to two hundred millions. In preparation for this they had distributed some of the surplus as a bribe. He gloried in the fact that New Hampshire had refused that bribe and had declined for $3\frac{1}{4}$ cents a head to saddle itself with the burden of an enormous annual tax. " The man does not live who can answer these questions," he thundered. He called Hill and his followers hungry office-seekers who for contracts for paper and twine with the post office department had sold out to Tyler and were trying to wreck the party. This latter statement made Hill furious, and for six months he headed his paper with the caption: " Keep it before the people. Frank Pierce's Grand Radical Electioneering Lie." It was a typical campaign of personalities, charge and countercharge, without any very vigorous effort to prove or disprove.

The excitement culminated with another tumultuous town meeting. For four days the citizens wrangled. At first there was no choice for moderator. Pierce was the " radical " candidate, Robert Davis, Tyler postmaster, the " conservative," and General Low, the Whig. After three ballots Low was chosen. No choice at all was reached for members of the legislature, and a second time Concord was without representation. However, throughout the state the " radicals " were triumphant, and the proportion of the votes was about the same as the year before. Pierce had demonstrated his leadership in party councils in the state. Isaac Hill had been severely punished; Pierce and a younger generation were in control.

XVII

TEMPERANCE CRUSADER

REFORM was in the air in the Forties, and of the many improvements which were agitated in New England communities, the question of temperance was by no means the least in importance. During the political year of 1843–44 the chief topic of public interest in Concord was the proper regulation of the liquor traffic. Such an issue was one which Pierce could appreciate. One of the hidden phases of his career was his struggle with an alcoholic craving. It had marred his congressional experience and had caused him considerable uneasiness when at home, though his struggles, his victories, and his defeats went unrecorded. Sometime before he died, his father had set him an example by giving up his moderate drinking, and now that there was increasing agitation on the subject Pierce joined the cause with intense enthusiasm. The rollicking campaign of the Whigs in 1840 had made it a token of Democratic partisan loyalty to preach and practice temperance, and soon thereafter the evangelism of John B. Gough and the Washingtonian Total Abstinence Societies aroused much popular interest. Dr. Bouton and his fellow clergymen had been working since 1827, and when Gough came to Concord to speak in 1841 their efforts became the center of public attention. Washingtonian societies were established, and a paper, *The White Mountain Torrent*, was issued; Pierce was in the front rank as chairman of the state temperance society.

After a period of agitation and public discussion a mass meeting was called for April 29, 1843, to take measures which would lead to the suppression of the liquor traffic. A throng gathered at the court house and Pierce was appointed chairman of a committee to prepare a plan. A few days later he reported from his committee a pledge which 1760 people signed, promising to use their " best exertions " to put a stop to the using and vending of liquor within the town limits. He followed this up with a long and ardent temperance address delivered at the North Church, and he served on a committee which sought to persuade the hotel keepers and merchants to stop selling by mutual agreement. The committee discovered that there was a combination among some dealers not to make such an agreement. Towns all around Concord were going " dry " so that the trade of many visitors had become profitable to the merchants of the capital. With the failure of this effort Pierce thereupon became active in prosecuting those who were selling liquor without a permit, and an increasing number of citizens became advocates of " no license." Evidently one of the questions for the town meeting of 1844 was going to be whether Concord would become " dry."

In connection with this question Pierce received some unpleasant notoriety when he ran afoul of Isaac Hill during the fall term of the court of common pleas. Pierce appeared for a client in a suit against Hill, in the course of which this embittered editor made an unpleasant scene and permitted Pierce to put him in a very uncomfortable position. This so infuriated Hill that he printed an attack upon Pierce, and accused him of having disgraced himself by drunkenness. Pierce's situation as a temperance advocate was not easy.

November brought a sad interruption to Colonel Pierce's temperance crusade. Sickness and death seemed never very far away from his fireside, and that fall both the little boys were taken ill. Frank soon developed typhus fever and after two weeks of losing struggle, on November 14, 1843, he died. Just before the shadow crossed the threshold, Pierce recorded his philosophy of sorrow.

> The chastisement is a fearful one but I know that it originates in perfect wisdom and I desire to feel that it is sent in mercy. It was doubtless needed. We are commanded to set up no idol in our hearts and I am conscious that within the last two years particularly my prevailing feeling has been that we were living for our children. In all my labors, plans and exertions in them was the center of all my hopes, they were in all my thoughts. We should have lived for God and have left the dear ones to the care of Him who is alone able to take care of them and us. I think I have experienced as thoroughly as most men the unsatisfying character of the mere things of this world. My mind has long been impressed with the fact that if our present life is not probationary in its character, if we are not placed here, as the blessed word of God teaches, to

prepare for another and more exalted state of being, we are
destined to waste our energies upon things that are unsub-
stantial, fleeting, passing away and that can bring no permanent peace—can give no calm hope that is as an anchor
to the soul. And yet with that conviction constantly re-
curring few have been more entirely absorbed in the whirl
of business and cares purely of a worldly character than I
have.

Over the grave they inscribed in the fashion of the day: " A
loved and precious treasure lost to us here but safe in the Redeemer's care."

In the midst of the sorrow intruded the need of preparation
for the political year. Pierce was especially anxious to carry
Concord for the Democrats; Whig ascendancy still was unbroken. It was apparent that the temperance question was
going to play some part in the town election, but it is doubtful
if Pierce or anyone else foresaw the unusual proceedings that
were to mark the town meeting of 1844.

Pierce was active in making plans for the annual event. He
attended a mass meeting of the " radicals " which was held at
the Washington hotel Saturday afternoon, three weeks beforehand, to take the last measures necessary to carry the town,
and as chairman of the resolutions committee he brought in a
proposition to appoint a vigilance committee to ensure an honest election. Such action was taken and the last-minute work
was put under full steam. The vigilantes kept busy, another
mass meeting was held the Saturday before the town meeting,
and on Friday, Saturday, Monday, and even on Tuesday until
9 A.M., the selectmen were in session to make any necessary
corrections to the check list, for none but those on that list
could vote. Concord must go Democratic this spring; but
temperance was to present a complicating issue.

On the second Monday of March there was unwonted activity
around the court house. This building was located well back
from the road on a slight eminence, and bordering the path
that led up to the door stands were set up where on the morrow
cakes and ale, gingerbread and molasses candy, pictures and
knicknacks would be on display. Local merchants and itin-
erant peddlers were preparing to satisfy hunger and thirst and
tempt the pocket books of the citizens as they came to participate in the town's business or to loaf around between excite-

ments. The younger fry, who had been storing up their animal spirits against this great week, were eager to vent their excess in all sorts of antics and stunts to the amusement and more often the exasperation of their elders. Supplies were being made ready in the cellars along Main Street where those who desired the " ardent " must go to quench their thirst. Many a housewife was glad when town meeting week was over and the smell of tobacco and rum had left the garments of the head of the house.

On the morning of March 12 the throng of citizens gathered early. They were to meet within the bare hall, with its benches arranged lengthwise parallel to the length rather than the width of the room, where the participants sat facing each other. At the west end a platform had been erected whereon the moderator's broad desk was located, and between it and the door was a wide vacant space. High up on the south wall was what purported to be a clock, but it was a clock that told no time. Around the door that Tuesday morning the crowd began to gather: General Low, leading Whig, General Charles H. Peaslee, Democratic candidate for moderator, Richard Bradley, Ira Perley, Joseph Robinson, Carroll and Baker of the *Patriot*, the Hills and Peverly of *Hill's Patriot*, John R. French of the *Herald of Freedom*, N. P. Rogers, Asa Fowler, and young Sylvester Dana, law student of Pierce and Fowler, were all there. When it was time to begin, the chairman of the selectmen stationed himself at the door to receive the ballots of the citizens for moderator. The Whigs were for General Low, the " radical " Democrats for Charles H. Peaslee, chosen by the caucus Saturday night, the Hillites or " conservatives " for William Walker, Jr., and the abolitionists for Cyrus Robinson. So the voters marched in and the ballots were counted, but no one had a majority. Another ballot and then another, all that day and the next and no election; this prolonged balloting meant that no votes could be cast for the state ticket, as Tuesday had gone by without organization, so Concord was to be unrepresented in the legislature once again.

There was a variety of reasons for the deadlock. Not only was there the hostility of those interested in railroads, which caused a majority to oppose the " radical " candidate, but the temperance question contributed to the difficulty. The clergy had aided in bringing the matter to a focus at this town meeting over the question of refusing to license the sale of liquor. As the "radical" Democrats had nominated as candidates for selectmen two men who were not opposed to licensing, they were looked upon as a "wet" party in spite of Pierce's public "dry" activities. Many "drys" voted against the "radical" candidate for moderator for this reason. After two days of excitement the Whigs, "conservatives," and abolitionists finally united on a "conservative," and Dr. Ezra Carter was elected on Thursday morning. Next in order was the election of selectmen. An arrangement was made whereby a "radical," a "conservative," and a Whig, on a combination "dry" ticket were elected, all of them pledged not to license. This ticket Pierce had opposed, maintaining that all "radicals," wet or dry, should support their ticket in spite of its "dampness," and then pass a resolution which would instruct the selectmen not to license. Such an arrangement would accomplish the desired end but permit party regularity, for party success was to Pierce the fundamental need. Having settled their second important problem, the town meeting adjourned for the night.

As far as Pierce was concerned Friday was the most important day. He and his "radical" associates were so far a badly defeated party. They joined with the rest in appointing fence viewers, cullers of staves, surveyors of lumber, corders of wood, weighers of hay, sealers of leather, sealers of weights and measures, pound keepers, hog reeves, hayward, firewards, clerk of the market, highway surveyors, auditors of accounts, and constables. This done and the town reports heard, the voters who had remained through it all began to consider the items of business enumerated in the selectmen's warrant for calling the meeting. Then excitement blazed up again.

Seventeen items in the warrant were disposed of; Pierce had been appointed on several committees and afternoon shadows were lengthening; town meeting was presumably nearly over. But no sooner was the eighteenth article regarding liquor licensing announced than Pierce arose to speak. As "no-license" selectmen had been chosen, action on this item was unnecessary, but Pierce felt the need of speaking. His position on the temperance question had involved him in difficulties. In the first place his activities in furthering the cause had not been

pleasing to the very considerable " wet " element among the
" radicals," a displeasure which he had felt. To make matters
even more uncomfortable, his plan to elect " license " men, and
then instruct them not to license in order to ensure Democratic
selectmen, had of course caused him to part company with the
temperance men who were running the amalgamation ticket.
As a result he found himself charged with treachery to the
cause of temperance, with hypocrisy and want of constancy.
He was angry and excited and burst forth in a heated declama-
tion which one *Patriot* praised extravagantly and the other
ridiculed. This for an ordinary town meeting might have been
enough, but not for such an extraordinary session.

The changes had been rung on radicalism and conservatism,
Whiggery and Democracy, and then on temperance; only one
more question was needed to bring the maximum amount of
ill-feeling, and that was slavery. It was forthcoming; for the
twenty-third item in the warrant read: " To see if the town will
take measures disapproving the course pursued by John R.
Reding, Edmund Burke and Moses Norris, Jr., members of
Congress from New Hampshire, in denying to the people the
free enjoyment of their inalienable Right of Petition." These
three gentlemen had recently voted for " gag " resolutions in
Congress. A motion to postpone this item indefinitely was
vigorously debated and Pierce was finally drawn into it. He
scolded the citizens for taking the town's time by debating a
political question brought forward for political purposes. His
remarks drew upon him personal attacks wherein his congressional record was brought forth and his " gag " resolution
votes presented. Also one young speaker pointed to the love
of liberty displayed by the Revolutionary fathers, and regretted
the degeneracy of their descendants. Pierce grew angry thereupon and defended himself and his record; then he dwelt at
length upon the helpless condition of the South, unable to rid
itself of slavery, and concluded with the taunt that abolition
agitation had set back the cause of emancipation many years.

After this flurry the excitement was increased further by the
Democrats. They charged the Whigs with playing politics in
the hope of censuring Democratic congressmen. After much
jockeying, which Pierce attempted to stop by motions to post-

pone and adjourn, the moderator finally carried a motion to adjourn by asking all in favor to vote " no." Out in the cold March night the excited citizens cleansed their lungs of the pestilential air of the smoke-filled meeting room, and went home to muse on the glorious privilege of self government and partisanship. Concord had gone dry, but the distressing question of slavery had once again entered Pierce's life.

XVIII
MAINTAINING PARTY ORTHODOXY

THE conflicting issues and the unsettled state of party loyalty which the March town meeting forced upon the attention of the political leaders were indications of the uncertain temper of the times. The spring of 1844 counted within the events of its lengthening days much that was prophetic. The season was rather depressing to Pierce and his fellow Democrats. As he followed the courts that term, lingered with the loungers in the hotels and with the lawyers in the court rooms of the shire towns, he found his usually enthusiastic party associates approaching the campaign for the Presidency without vital interest. It seemed that there was to be little of novelty and faint hope of victory. Van Buren would be nominated, that was his due, he was entitled to vindication for the turbulent disaster of 1840, but he was not a compelling candidate and the brilliant Clay was to be his opponent. When the conventions were less than a month away, about May day, the situation changed; both Clay and Van Buren came out publicly against the annexation of Texas. With Clay committed, this was too great an opportunity to be missed. Some Democrats began to consider the possibility of shelving Van Buren for a candidate who would capitalize the annexation issue presented by Calhoun and Tyler.

Pierce was not a delegate to the Baltimore convention, and his state of mind in regard to Texas at the moment was not recorded. In fact, other political matters were attracting his attention. Early in May a series of riots between "native" Americans and foreigners, mostly Irish, had disturbed the peace of Philadelphia, and these riots, like the burning of the convent in Boston some ten years previous, had brought forward the anti-Catholic issue. As the Democrats in general prided themselves upon their religious tolerance, and as in New Hampshire they were agitating the removal of the religious "test" from the state constitution, it seemed a fitting occasion for a mass meeting. Pierce and his associates, Fowler, Carroll, N. B.

Baker, Gass, Peaslee, and others, joined in issuing a call to the " friends of democratic equality and religious tolerance " to meet at the town hall May 15. As this call was signed exclusively by Democrats it occasioned some comment, and Whigs and " conservatives " came to find out why they had not been included. Pierce was appointed chairman of a committee on resolutions which at first was entirely Democratic; but after protest Whigs and " conservatives " were placed thereon, while a scheme of the Whigs to postpone action was defeated. When the resolutions were reported by Pierce the Whigs made determined efforts to modify them but without much success; they were not so friendly to the " foreign element." The meeting adjourned at 1 A.M., and the partisan nature of Concord public life had been demonstrated again.

A few days later came the surprising news from Baltimore: James K. Polk had received the Democratic nomination. This outcome, while unexpected to Pierce, was a pleasant turn of fortune, and as far as New Hampshire enthusiasm was concerned " changed the aspect of things entirely." He was confident that Polk was a candidate upon whom both the " radical " and " conservative " elements of the party could unite. So a grand ratification meeting was planned and Bancroft promised to sound the keynote. On June 6, therefore, Pierce called to order a large gathering in State House yard. Bancroft was late, so Hubbard filled in until he arrived. When the historian finally stood before the cheering throng he did his best to advertise the merits of Polk and Dallas, but his main task was to make Texas palatable to the New England conscience. The annexation of this area, he maintained, would not aid the cause of slavery, would make no new slaves, but would carry the Negro population farther south where they would find " a way open to them for their escape into the Central regions of America." Then he scored his big point: if the United States did not annex Texas Great Britain would. After Bancroft's lengthy effort Pierce came forward with the ratification resolutions which he presented in one of those speeches " so peculiar to himself, delighting with his inspiriting eloquence and enlivening with his happy hits—but he was too hoarse and unwell to gratify his hearers but a short time." A few days later the convention chose him once more as state chairman.

As far as the state chairman was concerned there was nothing unusual about the campaign. The intense period of the contest came in October when he made a series of speeches arousing the farmers. He wrote Polk that the Democrats would carry New Hampshire by from 6,000 to 10,000 votes. "The party is thoroughly organized and we are to have mass meetings in every county before the election." He toured the state, went down into Massachusetts to speak at Lowell, and finally wound up at Concord, exhausted, with his voice a ruin. Polk carried the state by nearly 10,000 plurality and the Democrats carried Concord.

In December came the usual quadrennial winter session of the legislature to apportion the taxes. Pierce was representing Concord unofficially, since the town had been unable to elect legislators in March. As the politicians gathered in the capitol, around the fire at the American House, and in private conference, uneasy rumors began to be afloat. The Polk victory was not an unmixed blessing. The Democrats had been out of power four years and the question of appointments was looming up. Who would be most influential with Polk in New Hampshire? Pierce had known him well, and he was favored with new importance. But disquieting notes of discord were faintly audible in party circles. Rumor had it that some of the leaders were not in accord with him; Burke and Hubbard, it was said, were not in harmony with Pierce, Atherton, and Woodbury; and both groups were attempting to gain a controlling voice in the distribution of the patronage. These rumors caused Pierce much anxiety, and well might he be concerned over party division. The legislature that winter session sowed seeds of discord. It passed a railroad law which admitted the "conservative" contention that the railroads were public service corporations and permitted the advance of railroad construction, under what were termed proper safeguards of individual property rights, by providing a railroad commission to settle disputes. This measure thus drew the "conservative" sting; but a number of the "radicals," especially among the poorer people, felt that the legislative leaders of the party had betrayed them by passing this "backing out" law. Dissatisfaction lurked hidden, though the issue was now dead. Moreover the legislature passed resolutions instructing the senators and requesting the representatives to aid in acquiring Texas and Oregon.   The cloud no larger than a man's hand at the previous spring town meeting was perhaps a trifle larger now.   Then came a thunderclap.

When Pierce opened his afternoon mail January 12 he found therein a letter from Burke containing the disquieting news that John P. Hale, of the New Hampshire delegation, had kicked over the traces.   Although the December session of the legislature just adjourned had passed resolutions favoring the acquisition of Texas, on January 7 Hale had written an open letter to his constituents declaring himself conscientiously opposed to annexing Texas, as an unconstitutional act in the interest of slavery.   He therefore requested his constituents to sustain him in his dissent from the resolutions of the legislature, or to nominate someone else; this last in spite of the fact that he already had been renominated by the last June convention, and there would be no other convention until after the election. A letter from Woodbury also bore this news and he agreed with Burke that Hale's move was a challenge which must be met; such party insubordination could not be tolerated.   Burke urgently, and Woodbury, as usual, tentatively, urged Pierce as state chairman to action.   His reaction to these letters was instantaneous.   Hale must be disciplined, no local leader could be permitted to defy the will of the party as expressed in state convention.   Hale was too ambitious and was trying to climb to higher place by capitalizing the anti-slavery issue; in fact at the last session of Congress he had deserted his New Hampshire colleagues and voted against the gag resolution.

Pierce acted immediately.   He went to the *Patriot* office and wrote an article denouncing Hale and accusing him of starting up the abolition issue for schismatic purposes.   He wrote letters calling the state committee together the following week to arrange a program for a special state convention.   These matters attended to, he set out on a tour through Hale's section to find out how strong a backing Hale could count on, and to instruct the faithful.   It was then five o'clock and a storm was brewing in the January twilight, but nothing daunted he drove to Dover that night.   In Hale's own town he found sentiment none too favorable to the local chieftain, and thus encouraged he went on to Portsmouth in one of the " severest New England snow storms." He did his work there and went back to Exeter, Nashua, Manchester, and so to Concord. His theme during this trip was "We must throw Hale overboard"; the latter's letter was "arrogant and presumptuous," for to sustain Hale would be to pass condemnation upon all the other members of the New Hampshire delegation. Pierce returned to meet the state committee determined to drop the rebel; Atherton's cautious doubts did not shake his resolution. The committee thereupon summoned the Democratic party to Concord in state convention extraordinary; Hale's challenge was to be met.

Caucuses now began to be held throughout the state to choose delegates. The one in Concord was particularly notable. It was scheduled for February 1 up at Moore's Washington Hotel in the north end. It was a horribly cold night when only the most hardy or those warmed by the fire of ambition or the flame of indignation would stir abroad. Only a few were there and they were not the right few; when Pierce arrived he looked at the little company and was nonplussed. "By G—, we are voted down two to one," he exclaimed; but almost as he said it a coach came up from the American House with the state officers and a few hopefuls, numbering about fifteen. No time was to be lost, the meeting was organized, a delegation chosen without instructions and the meeting adjourned, all in less than ten minutes. No opportunity had been given any one to present or debate resolutions, and it was all over before the delegates from West Parish arrived. Some of the late arrivals expressed themselves freely; if Hale was going to be cast out because of treason on Texas, why not cast out those who had betrayed the people on the railroad issue. The state-house ring was carrying things with too high a hand.

The decisive action of the state committee succeeded temporarily; Hale's supporters were disorganized and scattered. The state convention over which Pierce presided on February 12 erased Hale's name from the state ticket, substituted that of John Woodbury and adopted resolutions calling for the immediate annexation of Texas. The next three weeks witnessed a sharp campaign with the full political machinery of the state going at top speed. The methods of Pierce and his collaborators were described by one of Hale's friends:

They [the anti-Hale men] were denouncing everybody, who had a vote for you without mercy. There were two good fellows who distributed votes in defiance of them all, but not without the greatest abuse. Baker and others stood at the outside door denouncing them as they handed out their votes, Allen and Carroll stood at the inside door to see that no man had a vote for you. Pierce stood at the point where the line formed to go up and vote, and Robinson stood close by the place where the ballots were taken. You will see by this what a man had to go through to be voted against dictation.

When the votes were counted it was found that neither Hale nor Woodbury had a majority; so there was no election. A similar result attended the elections in September and November so one seat remained vacant in the House of Representatives from 1845 to 1847. The rest of the Democratic ticket was successful. New Hampshire Democracy had been purified of free soil, and Woodbury, Atherton, and Burke could stand before Polk with hands clean, ready for the patronage.

While New Hampshire Democracy was asserting itself in the spring elections James K. Polk was settling himself in the White House and beginning his distribution of the patronage. His old friendship for Pierce bore fruit; he appointed him district attorney for New Hampshire, and John McNeil was restored to his position as surveyor in the Boston custom house. This new dignity added somewhat to Pierce's legal labors at a time when he was making a change of partners. Fowler had sided with Hale, and presumably political differences led to a dissolution of the partnership. A new firm was established; Pierce and Josiah Minot, a shrewd and extremely non-political lawyer of talent, joined forces and established offices in Ayer's Block, once Hill's, over the Franklin Bookshop, right on Main street under the eaves of the capitol.

With these adjustments made, Pierce settled down in his new environment. June brought the legislature and the state convention as usual, but it also brought John P. Hale to Concord. The latter arrived in the course of a stumping tour he was making over the state, and at the North Church he made a speech defending himself and denouncing the state central committee for attempting to behead him. He spoke for a long while and upon concluding Pierce sprang to his feet and asked

for an opportunity to reply. He waxed eloquent and denounced Hale as an artful schemer promoting party schism for
his own benefit. He charged Hale with attempting to detach
enough Democrats from the regular ranks on the issue of slavery to give him the balance of power in the legislature. He
accused him of planning a bargain with the Whigs and Abolitionists which should make him senator and the leader of a
great new party. Whether Hale then entertained such an idea
or not, Pierce unwittingly prophesied the course of events correctly. Pierce's rejoinder also embraced an elaborate defense
of the annexation of Texas. He had attracted a great deal of
attention and had brought himself much public notice—more
important when it came to be remembered later.

Shortly after this brush came the state convention. Over
that body Pierce once more presided and had the further satisfaction of receiving endorsement in two forms. One took the
guise of the adoption of the following Texas resolution:

> That the annexation of Texas, by widely extending the
> domain of this republic—by strengthening our means of
> defence in war, and greatly increasing our resources in
> peace—without adding to the numbers of the enslaved—
> without increasing the relative political powers of the
> slaveholding interest of our country—will guaranty the
> blessings of a republican government to millions of patri-
> otic and kindred beings who might otherwise be reduced
> to become the oppressed and unprivileged subjects of Euro-
> pean despotism.

The other endorsement consisted of an official expression of
approval of the work of his extraordinary convention in February. Having thus received his crown of laurel, he refused
longer to serve as state chairman, for the strain was too great;
and, exhausted, he laid down the responsibility which he had
borne for three years. He had done his work, the " conservative " bolters and the free soil schismatics had been disciplined,
and his party had remained triumphant through all these difficulties. But the fruits of his leadership were not all gathered.

XIX

BATTLE WITH THE " ALLIES "

HALE was not the man to bow before defeat. Straightway he organized his supporters and gathered together those with grievances against Pierce and the " state house ring." The Free Soil party, which since 1841 had been running Daniel Hoit for governor annually, took on new life; they nominated Nathaniel L. Berry and preached the martyrdom of Hale. There was much at stake in 1846 because the next legislature would choose a senator. Woodbury had been appointed to fill Judge Story's seat on the national supreme bench, and in October, 1845, Colonel Pierce had declined Governor Steele's invitation to take the Senate vacancy. Although Pierce no longer bore the responsibility for the campaign, he could not resist the call to take the stump. In the last weeks of February he even went up into the north country to harangue the faithful, to defend his action in throwing Hale overboard, and to charge Hale with that worst of all crimes—bargaining with the Whigs. Town-meeting day brought ten thousand more voters to the polls than had come out the previous year. By this increase the Democratic candidate and the Whig profited to some extent, but the significant fact was that the Free Soil vote had nearly doubled, and had now become large enough (10,379) to prevent any candidate receiving the majority necessary for election; the governor evidently must be chosen by the legislature. And here the blow had fallen, the Democrats had lost the legislature and no one knew who had gained it. Only in Concord was there consolation: a Democrat, N. B. Baker, had been chosen moderator.

Such a result caused the Quaker poet Whittier, himself no mean politician, to chuckle quietly and reach for his pen. Shortly there appeared in a Boston paper a letter in verse purporting to have been written by the chairman of the " Central Clique " at Concord, Frank Pierce, himself, to Moses Norris in Washington:

'Tis over, Moses!   All is lost!
  I hear the bells a ringing;
Of Pharaoh and his Red Sea host
  I hear the Free-Wills singing.
We're routed,—Moses, horse and foot,
  If there be truth in figures,
With Federal Whigs in hot pursuit
  And Hale, and all the "niggers."

Party lines were truly in confusion and the confusion was
heightened by strange sounds, for the drums of war were
rolling.

The *Patriot,* as it was distributed from door to door on May
14, brought to every home the news that American soldiers
had been killed on American soil by Mexican invaders.   In
the days that followed came Polk's message, the declaration of
war, and the call to arms.   Secretary Marcy made requisition
upon Governor Steele for an infantry battalion of five companies, and May 25 Adjutant General Peaslee began enlisting
volunteers.   Saturday night the Concord Light Infantry volunteered, Fire Engine Company No. 2 offered their services, and
some score citizens signed a volunteering agreement drawn up
by Peaslee; among these was Franklin Pierce.   The call of
war was native to him; besides, party and sectional loyalty demanded his enlistment.   New England might not respond to
the call of a southern president to engage in a slave-holders'
war; therefore loyal Democrats must set the example.

Volunteering did not mean immediate service; Marcy wisely
accepted troops from more enthusiastic regions nearer the seat
of conflict.   Just then Pierce faced pressing difficulties closer
at hand.   To the Democrats it was a sorry June; for the first
time in almost twenty years they were not in comfortable control of the state, and the progress of events was peculiarly
distasteful to them.   On June 5 Anthony Colby, Whig, was
elected governor by the legislature, and four days later John
P. Hale, Free Soiler, was sent to the Senate of the United States
for a term of six years.   This result had been accomplished, as
Pierce had warned, by an alliance—an unholy alliance so
the Democrats felt—of Whigs and renegade Free Soil Democrats.   Here were the first fruits of Pierce's political funda-
mentalism, here in 1846 and in New Hampshire was sown the

seed which a decade later was to produce the Republican party. If Pierce on that ninth of June, when the news buzzed along Main street, could have looked into the future to see the careers of Franklin Pierce and John P. Hale, he would have been astounded and dismayed; but, as it was, presumably he looked upon this accident of politics as a temporary error which he hoped might be eradicated by renewed and tireless efforts on the part of himself and his fellow Democrats. The party must be reanimated and the people warned of the danger to the Union from the unpatriotic " alliance."

Two days later, as a member of the resolutions committee of the state convention, he aided in drawing up a new article in the creed of New Hampshire Democrats. For years there had been no need to speak of slavery officially but now in 1846 it had intruded itself into local politics and presented an issue which could not be ignored. So Pierce and his fellow Democrats resolved:

> That we reaffirm the sentiments and opinions of the democratic party and democratic statesmen of the north entertained from 1776 to the present day, in relation to slavery—that we deplore its existence, and regard it as a great moral and social evil, but with this conviction, we do not deem ourselves more wise than Washington, Franklin, and their associates, and that patriotism, common honesty and religious principle alike bind us to a sacred observance of the compact made by those wise men.
>
> That the policy to be pursued in reference to slavery rests with the States and Territories within which it exists —that whatever parties may *profess*, it is only as citizens of such States and Territories that the members of those parties can efficiently influence that policy—and that angry external agitation, by exciting the prejudices of the slaveholding communities, while it may endanger the Union tends rather to fasten than to destroy the bonds of the enslaved.

This last paragraph is extremely significant—for here in 1846 in New Hampshire was another sign of the times. As Hale's election foreshadowed the organization of the Republican party so this resolution was a pre-statement of the doctrine of " squatter sovereignty " to be later the famous slogan of Stephen A. Douglas.

The resolutions concluded with a new call to arms. They
invoked " fidelity to the constitution, earned by the blood and
consecrated by the prayers of our Revolutionary Fathers."
1775, 1812, 1846 had been the years of crisis. There should
be " millions for defence but not one cent for tribute, either
to buy our peace with foes from abroad or to conciliate their
allies ' on our own soil.' " It was another call for patriots, as
the Whigs, like the Federalists and Tories of old, were proving
traitors.

The summer's lull was broken by a disquieting letter from
the President. On August 27 Polk had written him an invitation to come to Washington as attorney-general. Pierce took
a week to think it over and in the end declined. Perhaps
thoughts of Washington were tempting to him; we do not
know; but they certainly were not to Mrs. Pierce, and she was
in worse health than she had been when he left public life.
So his decision was made; family responsibilities and business
matters were given as the reasons for declining public office,
with the saving clause inserted, " except at the call of my
country in time of war."

With this temptation put behind him he set himself again
to the task of political reorganization. First the old breach
with Hill was healed. The two *Patriots* were to be combined
and there was need for an editor. Edmund Burke was thought
of, but he wanted to go to Washington, so William Butterfield
was chosen, and for many years his peculiar personality remained an important factor in local politics. As a second step
a fervent call for a mass meeting was issued: " Treason is rife
in the land," the broadside echoed. At the gathering in October Pierce made another " one of the most able and eloquent
speeches to which we have ever listened. The effect was truly
electric." The *Patriot* charged the air with more electricity by
editorials attacking the " alliance "; " Political Abolitionism in
New Hampshire. Its object a Dissolution of the Union," this
was their text. A campaign paper, *Rough and Ready,* was established and Pierce reported to Burke:

Unless I entirely mistake the signs of the times, the " Independent Abolition " tornado has spent itself. Whig and
Abolition orators have talked too flippantly and recklessly

of a dissolution of the Union, and honest, but misguided men, instead of consulting their passions and their prejudices, have been led to pause and weigh this treasonable language. They have been recalled, as it were, from a frensy, calmly to calculate the value of our glorious union. I think we shall triumph over the " allied forces " in March, but it will be a hard battle, requiring great effort and unremitted exertion from this time forward.

His indignation against the " Allies " became more intense. They were denouncing the war as " impolitic, unwise, uncalled for, cruel and awful." Worse still, the commander of the state's quota was none other than James H. Wilson, ancient foe of the Democrats, and he was doing nothing to fill the ranks. Pierce feared that only by resort to a draft could the necessary men be supplied. He chafed under the delay and wrote to Burke to find out whether Marcy was going to order the state's quota under arms. " If a call shall be made, nothing short of a want of health will prevent me from responding to it, but what number of those men who enrolled their names would actually go, it is impossible to say under existing circumstances. Most of those who volunteered are excellent men, and influential, thoroughgoing democrats, whose absence from the state would be most seriously felt." Pierce's call was not to come until the campaign at home was nearly finished.

When Congress assembled in December Secretary Marcy asked for more men for the regular army. In response a bill providing for ten regiments was introduced and Pierce was informed that he was slated as colonel of one of them. Here at length was his chance—the military career of which he had always dreamed. On February 15, 1847, he was appointed colonel of infantry in the regular army for the period of the war, charged with recruiting a regiment from New England. But higher rank was in store for him. The Act of February 11 had failed to provide general officers to organize the new regiments into brigades; consequently a supplementary bill designed to provide such officers and incidentally to make a place for Benton was introduced. Imagine Pierce's elation when ten days later he received a letter from Attorney-General Clifford, urging him to accept the commission as colonel and assuring him that if the new bill passed he would be appointed brigadier general. Nothing was more to Pierce's liking; he accepted the colonelcy in high hope, as he wrote Burke:

> I earnestly desire the command of a Brigade, and if Col. Benton's Bill passes, I trust the President may deem me worthy of it. There will, however, doubtless be great exertions on the part of others, and I shall never cease to be grateful to you and my other friends for your kind offices. The sudden closing of my business and breaking up here will be a painful task, but although I have not yet broached the subject to my wife, my purpose is fixed. . . . Pray write me and let me know if you can what I may expect in relation to the situation upon which, as I am at all events to be in the service, my heart is fixed. I think Judge Woodbury would cheerfully interest himself in the matter with you, Atherton, Clifford and our delegation in the House. My acquaintance with the Secretary of War is slight, but I cannot doubt that the Secretaries of State, Treasury, Navy, and the Post Master General would all favor my appointment, but after all the President will do what he thinks best for the service and that will satisfy me.

So he waited, although the thought of what a blow the news would be to his wife worried him. He could sense her anxious disapproval of the idea; but he fortified his will with thoughts of patriotism, the need of his country, and the cowardly nature of the opposition to the war at home, thus satisfying his conscience that he was properly weighing loyalties.

While events were taking their slow course in Washington, Pierce walked dazedly through a maze of legal, military and political activities. He carried a heavy court schedule, he helped raise money to aid New Hampshire men already enlisted, he addressed meetings almost nightly. In these speeches, which reporters found eloquent but of which little substance has been preserved, Pierce was chiefly concerned in stimulating patriotism; he painted the needs of the country at war, called upon patriots to vote the Democratic ticket, and branded the " allies " as traitors. He had to resist the inflammatory appeals of the latter on the slave issue, and was hard put to it sometimes to defend the national administration from the charge of southern sympathy, especially when at Canterbury Mrs. Abby Kelly heckled him. Another measure difficult to defend was the tariff of 1846, for New Hampshire was becoming

increasingly industrial.   But his heart was in it, he always had
rhetoric to answer argument, and patriotism and the Union
locked horns with the sin of slavery in many an oratorical battle, imposing considerable wear and tear upon his throat.

The meeting at Franklin on the twenty-sixth was a great
success.   Pierce spoke for three hours and tired himself out.
While he was speaking a storm came up; but in spite of this,
he was driven to Concord in an open sleigh, for it was Saturday
night and he was anxious to be home.   The exposure, added to
his fatigue, proved more than he could stand and he was forced
to take to his bed with the campaign still unfinished and military responsibilities piling up.   The enforced idleness gave him
time to think about his regimental plans.   His friend Major
Truman B. Ransom of Vermont, who was his principal military
adviser, had come to Concord, and in Pierce's sick room they
outlined the recruiting of their regiment.   They had been ordered to establish regimental headquarters at Portsmouth and
Pierce hoped that Ransom might be his lieutenant-colonel; he
wrote urgently to Burke to fix it.   The possibility of the brigadier generalship prevented Pierce from entering into too definite plans; therefore he and Ransom contented themselves with
making out a list of minor regimental officers to send to Washington.   While thus engaged word came that the "Benton Bill"
had passed March 3, and that Pierce had been appointed and
confirmed as brigadier general on the same day.

Friday before election found him able to be out again to do
what he could to combat the "bitterness, recklessness and violence" of the "allies."   Butterfield was away and Pierce stayed
up all that night to prepare an "extra" of the *Patriot*.   Next
day he was "pretty seriously indisposed but able to sit up all
night for the cause."   His efforts were rewarded and his hopes
justified on Tuesday when, with the largest vote their ticket had
ever polled, the Democrats regained the state government.   The
disaster of 1846 had been repaired and Pierce could report to
Polk:

Glory enough!   There was never fought such a political
battle in New England, in any one of our states, as that
through which we have just passed.   Gallantly fought and
most gallantly won.   Portsmouth has just sent in the *crown-*

ing results. . . . The " allies " made the war issue and we met it everywhere upon the stump. I fear my health is somewhat impaired by exposure and almost constant speaking to immense gatherings of the people. We shall raise the New England Regiment promptly and prepare for the field with all practicable despatch.

There was one flaw, however; the Democrats had lost Concord and Asa Fowler had been elected moderator.

MEXICAN WAR
1847-1848

XX

THE POLITICIAN GOES FORTH TO WAR

BRIGADIER GENERAL FRANKLIN PIERCE he was, and for some time thereafter few sounds but the trumpets of war gained any attention from his ears. He was full of plans, for campaigns must be followed, men stirred to join the colors, mobilization perfected, and a brigadier general's equipment, including an elaborate uniform, provided. Shortly he left on his first military expedition, a trip to Washington to complete arrangements. He found the capital a scene of unwonted activity and his conferences with Polk and Marcy filled him with even greater enthusiasm for this war to vindicate American spirit and the Polk administration.

Hardly had he returned to Concord, March 20, when the news came that Taylor was in danger, and orders arrived from Marcy to hasten preparation for embarking. The news and the orders caused Pierce much apprehension. He ordered his officers in Maine and Connecticut, Lieutenant-Colonel Abner B. Thompson and Major Thomas H. Seymour, both of the Ninth or New England regiment, to fill their contingents and get ready for early departure. His friend Ransom had secured the colonelcy of the Ninth and came on from Vermont to aid in the preparations, for Pierce was greatly concerned with the difficulties of enlistment. The war was not popular in New England, and recruiting was neither fast nor enthusiastic. First of all there was the fact that labor was in demand and wages were high; men who could easily earn three dollars a day did not go gladly into the army at seven dollars a month, at least not for economic reasons. Also it was a southern war, a Democratic party war; many in New England could not be counted on to support such an activity. Pierce was convinced that enlistments could not be made in the ordinary way. "Men in any great numbers can only be obtained," he wrote, "by proper and stirring appeals to the patriotism of our people, not through the press alone, but at public meetings." He established brigade headquarters at

Concord, and began to stimulate the enlistment of the two companies which were the New Hampshire quota.

Extraordinary exertions were necessary in spite of the news from Taylor's army. Spring, too, came late; it was almost the first of April and sleighing was still possible, sunrise found the windows still frosted and the few spring birds that had ventured north lived people knew not how. The lingering of winter did not hasten to unlock men's enthusiasm for adventure and wandering. The war department further complicated matters by ordering part of one company, Captain Pitman's, to depart before the rest. The order dismayed Pierce and Ransom, for it gave the anti-war men fresh arguments with which to discourage enlistment. For, said they, New Englanders who enlist will be sent forward in small detachments and scattered over Mexico, there will be no New England regiment. Furthermore, they contended, warm weather in Mexico is approaching and the deadly *vomito* will play havoc among the northern men. These were not easy arguments to answer.

While Pierce was in Boston early in April making arrangements and buying equipment, word came that Vera Cruz had been captured. These tidings made him wonder whether he would be able to get his men under arms before the war was over. Recruiting was so slow; fifteen recruits in ten days were all that the records showed. He could easily have obtained two hundred officers, but few seemed willing to enlist as privates. Funds and clothing were slow in arriving, and the new general in his eagerness to be off made advances from his own pocket.

Matters more personal to himself crowded his attention. He must provide an aide de camp; his first choice, Charles B. Fletcher of Nashua, for some reason was not available, and an army engineer, Lieutenant George Thom, at length was selected. Pierce's local affairs had to be arranged; he finally settled his old partnership with Fowler and put his business, including the district-attorneyship, in the hands of his partner, Minot. Most difficult of all was the proper care of Mrs. Pierce, whose melancholy because of his impending departure was pervasive. He finally arranged for Miss Caroline E. Carroll to stay with her, and his Concord friends, especially Minot and young John H. George, promised to take general oversight of her welfare. Later on when the summer advanced she could visit her sister,

BRIGADIER GENERAL PIERCE

Mary Aiken, at Lowell or her brother Robert at Boston. As the preparations neared completion she grew more reconciled, but her gloomy forebodings were a continual damper upon his patriotic conscience.

Public notice was taken of Pierce's new honors. Friends had been at work raising money to provide part of his equipment. The ladies of Concord presented him with a handsome sword at a gathering in Grecian Hall May 10, and his political associates provided a fine black horse. When he left three days later a great crowd came to the depot to cheer his departure. He set forth with high purpose. "I shall carry to the service upon which I now enter the same rigid personal discipline which I have found indispensable in my laborious practice at the Bar for the last five years. The profession is new to me. I have much, I might say almost everything to learn, but if labor, vigilance, and self-denying devotion to the duties and responsibilities of my position will fit me for the command . . . my friends will not be disappointed. It is my fixed purpose to enforce by example whatever I require of others; and to do nothing myself that I would not commend in the lowest commission." The only shadow was his wife's sorrow and the thought of leaving her and his son. "I can not trust myself to talk of this departure," he wrote her from Boston. "My heart is with my own dear wife and boy, and will be wherever duty may lead my steps."

Ransom had preceded him to Newport, Rhode Island, and had already dispatched Major Lally with three companies when Pierce arrived at Fort Adams to assume command. In a fortnight all was ready, the men were put aboard the barque *Kepler*, and on May 27 the vessel weighed anchor for Vera Cruz.

The novelty of the first days of the voyage is described to his wife:

Barque Kepler
At Sea, May 31, 1847.
Dearest Jeanie:
We are 400 or 500 miles on our passage—prosperous voyage thus far I have not been sick a moment altho' there has been scarcely another exception. I was never better —my horses are getting along nicely. James has been very sick. The command generally well. Yesterday my first sabbath at sea—a great and solemn day—service morning

and evening—excellent sacred music by the troops all most
solemn and impressive. It is said that we are about to
meet a Brig inward bound and I seize the moment to send
back a line to those who are ever in my thought and who
are enshrined in my heart of hearts. The motion of the
Barque is such that I can hardly write. Love to Miss Carroll. Kiss dear Benny. I am in good health and spirits
with a heart for the service before me. I shall omit no
opportunity to write. All the men from Concord are well
with the exception of seasickness. . . . It is so warm that
their thin clothes are generally in requisition. The effect
of the voyage upon me is almost magical. My appetite,
strength and robustness is a subject of general remark
among the officers. God grant that my dear ones may be
preserved from sickness and all harm and that I may again
meet them the honored husband and father.

> Yr own affectionate Frank

And so for day after day the expected three weeks drew themselves out into four. Calm seas and slow sailing, that was the
order of monotonous days and dragging nights. Down the coast
the barque gradually pushed into the tropics across the gulf.
The days became hotter, the nights more stifling, morning and
afternoon the merciless sun, at evening the glorious southern
heavens; but each brilliant star was a dart of fire and the heat
of the display destroyed its beauty, while never a ship appeared with news from the army. Worst of all, the water ran
short. Many of the men were sick, and Pierce kept his days
busy attempting with his own buoyant spirits to hearten the
men, as he had been wont to arouse his party and awaken his
juries. Down into the stifling cabins he went with what refreshment he could find, and better still, his own infectious
optimism. He had a hard task. But even voyages on becalmed
seas must end, and on Sunday, June 27, Vera Cruz finally was
sighted. There was the mighty fortress of San Juan and over
it, as a sign of past and future victory, lazily flapped the Stars
and Stripes.

XXI
MARCH TO PUEBLA

PIERCE'S immediate tasks upon landing were all incident to leading his detachment of 2,500 men and a long wagon train into the interior to join Scott, who was awaiting his arrival at Puebla before setting out on his campaign against Mexico City. There was every inducement for haste but exasperating circumstances united to prevent it. It was midsummer and the march for seventy miles at least must be made through a veritable *tierra caliente*, where the heat made life a burden, and the *vomito*, a disease with a graphically descriptive title, overtook many who were not acclimated. No transportation was ready; a herd of some two thousand wild mules had been gathered, and they were handled badly by a set of disreputable herders. Through their carelessness a stampede occurred the day after the general's arrival during which most of the animals bolted. Without wagons and draught animals, advance was wholly out of the question, so Pierce had to make camp and wait until the necessary means of transportation were collected or could arrive from the United States.

Pierce was not long in deciding that disease-infested Vera Cruz was no place for locating a camp. Two and one-half miles to the northwest, upon the beach at Vergara, Major Lally had established himself with his command, and to that place Pierce and Ransom led the remainder of the brigade then in Mexico. Here camp was made and here the men were kept free from the entanglements of Vera Cruz. Almost within the shower of the surf the general had his tent pitched, and hither after busy days of preparation at Vera Cruz he came, glad that he might spend the nights by the sea and let the noise of the waves on the hard sand remind him of less responsible days at Lynn and Hampton.

The principal reason for the transportation delay, Pierce soon discovered, arose from the chaos in the quartermaster's department. Major Hetzel, who was nominally in charge, had broken under the strain and was about to return home, leaving his

affairs in considerable disorder. Consequently Pierce and the
new quartermaster, Major Smith, who shortly arrived, had to
straighten out the confusion in what should have been a well-
organized department. Also there was fear of the dreaded
vomito which lurked in the sizzling heat of the overpowering
noonday or in the heavy dampness of the dew-laden nights.
Discipline, too, under these circumstances was no easy problem.
To these duties Pierce brought his irresistible enthusiasm; daily
he rode back and forth between Vergara and Vera Cruz, living
in his saddle and becoming well-acquainted with the ins and
outs of that well-fortified city, with its streets of high white
houses and its alameda sparkling in the tropical sunshine. His
duties were lightened by an efficient staff of trained soldiers
from whom he willingly learned many lessons, realizing his own
ignorance. Major Woods of the Fifteenth Infantry, a graduate
of West Point, was his adjutant general; Lieutenants Caldwell
and Van Bocklin of the Marine Corps and the Seventh Infantry
served as his brigade commissary and quartermaster, while
Lieutenant George Thom of the Topographical Engineers was
his personal aide. Sergeant O'Neil served indefatigably as his
mounted orderly. With this staff he established very pleasant
relations, and they saved him many a blunder.

It was not until July 12 that horses arrived from New Orleans
and definite plans for moving could be made; at once Pierce
issued general orders for the army to start on the fourteenth.
When the necessary supplies and munitions, together with
$85,000 worth of uncashable drafts, had been loaded into army
wagons, camp was struck. Early on the appointed morning
Colonel Ransom set off with the first detachment and eight
wagons; next morning a second division moved off, and on the
third day (July 16), "After much perplexity and delay on
account of the unbroken and untractable trains," Pierce left
the camp at five o'clock in the afternoon with the remainder of
the command and forty wagons. It was bad going, the road
was sandy, the wagons sank almost up to their bodies, and
worst of all were the fractious, unbroken mules. For five hours
they struggled with those miserable animals along the sandy
road until at ten that evening the general ordered a bivouac.
Only three miles had been covered but those three miles marked
an advance.

ROUTE FROM VERA CRUZ TO MEXICO.

GOLFO DE MEXICO.

Next morning at four the general was at the head of his contingent once more and after four hours of hard going over another heavy sandy road and up and down short, steep hills, they had proceeded five miles. Thereupon they encamped and shortly thereafter experienced their first alarm, albeit a false one. The three contingents which had gone to join Scott before Pierce landed had all been attacked, and of course the general naturally expected a surprise at any time. But as this alarm turned out to be the fiction of a frightened muleteer, the baptism of fire was not yet.

When the column reached the famous national highway which led from the coast to the capital the character of the march changed. Instead of ploughing through sand they could now advance over a " spacious, comfortably graded cement avenue, carried over the streams by handsome bridges of cut-stone, and flanked on both sides by the estates of Santa Anna. . . . Now it penetrated a dark forest of palms, cactus, limes and countless other trees festooned with vines, and now it crossed rolling prairies. Here it was cut through solid rock; there it skirted a beautiful hill, with a charming vista of leafy glades; and presently it was clinging as if in terror to the face of a cliff. Bowers carpeted with many soft hues and perfumed with heliotrope recalled ideas of Eden, while marshes full of strange bloated growths, bluish-green pools rimmed with flowers of a suspicious brilliancy, and thick clumps of dagger plants tipped with crimson, offered suggestions of a different sort.

" Matted tangles of leafage spattered with gold, big tulipans gleaming in the shadows like a red rose in the hair of a Spanish dancer, blossoms like scarlet hornets that almost flew at one's eyes, and blooms like red-hot hair-brushes, the sight of which made the scalp tingle, were balanced with big, close masses of white throats and purple mouths, and with banks of the greenish-white cuatismilla, discharging invisible clouds of a fragrance that seemed to be locust blended with lily of the valley. Trees with tops like balloons, like corkscrews and like tables, trees drained almost dry by starry parasites that swung from their branches, trees covered with strawberry blossoms— or what appeared to be strawberry blossoms—that were to graduate into coffee beans, trees bare of everything except great yellow suns, the Flower of God, that fascinated one's gaze—these and countless other surprises followed one another; and then would come a whole grove netted over with morning glories in full bloom." * Besides there was chaparral and every kind of thorn. The chaparral grown to the height of sixteen or twenty feet had leaves like hemlock, was thickly covered with thorns like cow's horns, and now presented the appearance of an old peach orchard. Everything was mingled with cactus of at least six or seven different species, some of them at least fifty feet in height. There were some prairies covered with herds of cattle, wild horses, asses and mules. Green corn and sweet potatoes were abundant. Parrots and all kinds of birds with beautiful plumage decorated the landscape.

Through this strange and shifting scene Pierce and his column advanced, extended along two miles of road. Marching was possible only in the early morning and the later afternoon, and there was the constant apprehension of an attack; also the rain was a disagreeable accompaniment. Finally on the nineteenth the expected materialized. As the march was being resumed toward evening, the train was fired upon, but a detachment easily drove off the few Mexicans who were sniping from a hilltop, and the march proceeded. About a mile further on they arrived at the point where McIntosh's train had been under attack. Here Pierce took great precaution, and true to expectation was met by a brisk fire. However, short and sharp return was all that seemed necessary to drive the enemy off, although a number of Mexicans were killed and several of the Americans wounded. It was Pierce's first engagement and he was pleased to be able to record that he saw nothing but coolness and courage on the part of both officers and men.

The march proceeded, with a stop at Paso de Ovejas, until the 21st when the train approached the National Bridge, one of the various bridges which spanned streams crossed by the national highway. Here further difficulty was advisedly anticipated, for a force of Mexicans was posted in the village beyond the bridge. Pierce advanced carefully and surveyed the situation from the top of a hill which overlooked the fork of the Antigua River, the bridge, and the village. Most of the Mexicans were behind a breastwork on a bluff some hundred and fifty feet high commanding the barricaded bridge. As the

* Smith, *War with Mexico*, II, 46–47.

breastwork was so situated that it could not be cleared off from a distance, Pierce decided to send Colonel Bonham and his command over the bridge and up this bluff. He planted artillery to cover the bridge and clear the village. The breastworks on the bluff unfortunately were beyond the range of the guns, but the battery served to distract the fire of the men on the bluff so that Bonham's command could dash over the bridge and leap the barricade. It was only a matter of minutes before the Mexicans were in full flight, the flag was on the breastworks and Pierce's force in possession of the situation. Although there had been a sharp fire from 200 or 300 Mexicans, the casualties were limited to five wounded. For Pierce it had been a brief but eventful few minutes; he had directed a second military operation and had been a second time under fire. A ball went through the brim of his "Quaker" hat uncomfortably near his face; but, as the men had now grown accustomed to saying, "the nearer you get to the Mexicans in a fight, the safer you are."

After some further difficulties, within a few days the command arrived at Jalapa where Pierce had his first real contact with Mexican citizens. Leaving his command at the outskirts he took a detachment of twenty dragoons and entered the town to arrange for needed supplies. He rode to the principal hotel, which was kept by a Frenchman. Here he dined and rested, and while the train of wagons passed he conversed with the hotel keeper and a number of local gentry by means of an interpreter, as he spoke no Spanish or French. He was quite astonished at the compliments and friendly expressions used to him, but could not see fit to establish his headquarters there; their friendliness seemed too smooth. His apprehensions were aroused and he returned to his command, which was encamping outside the city. As he confided to his diary: "I hardly know why that amid pleasant conversation, this feeling came over me. It was instinct, rather than any legitimate deduction from what I either saw or heard; but it was on the present occasion better than reason, for when I returned to the main road, I found the extreme rear halted, and no little sensation because a colored servant of Lieutenant Welsh who had been sent by his master to water a horse, . . . had been stabbed, and the horse stolen."

That night he confided to his diary some of his confused reactions to his rôle as invading general.

No trust is to be placed in this people. I have learned, beyond a doubt, that Jalapa is filled daily with guerillas, and that many of these bravos were about the fonda while we were there. My tent is almost upon the margin of a narrow canal, that drives Don Garcias Spindles—My Commissary buys of him cattle, My Quartermaster forage &c., &c. And altho' he is said to be one of Santa Anna's most staunch friends, he has every appearance of an honest man & a Gentleman. Has this the appearance of War? *Our* Govt. does not comprehend *this* Govt. . . . *War* has been *declared,* but with all our battles, all our brilliant victories, and the loss of all the valuable lives *war* has not yet been *prosecuted* I could desire that it may not be, but from the little I have observed I believe, that it *must* be before a peace can be "*conquered.*" I mean war as it has been recognized for 200 years in the most civilized nations. No, not as it has been recognized, but *war* as it has actually been carried on, with its fruits and its results—*War,* that actually carries wide spread woe and dessolation [*sic*] to the *conquered* and tacitly at least, allows pillage and plunder with accompanyments not to be named during a campaign like this even in a private journal—Perhaps a peace can be conquered by our present system of operations and policy. If so, we have made a grand leap in civilization, we will astonish the world—nay more, we will make wars to *cease,* a desideratum to every philanthropic heart, of all others, the most desirable because if we can conquer a peace in this way we can conquer it better without arms than with them. I hope I am mistaken, I hope I have an incorrect view of things when I am so foolish as to think that in this 19th Century *war* to be effectual must be *war* not a mission of civilization and humanity. If my boy should ever read this daily journal I desire that he may not misunderstand his father—I hate war in all its aspects, I deem it unworthy of the age in which I live & of the Govt. in which I have borne some part—All I mean to say is, that there can be no such thing as a profound sense of justice, the sacredness of individual rights and the value of human life connected with human butchery, and all men, who think and feel as I think and feel, and yet are found on fields of slaughter are in a false position from education and the force of circumstances. If you must have war the answer of Palifox—" War to the knife and the knife to the hilt " is the true sentiment, No, sentiment is not the word the true import of *sentiment* knows no such application, but it is expressive of the most emphatic and elevated tone of *war*—

The next day Pierce took alarm at what he had written the night before, and scolded himself for his efforts at self-expression.

> I see that the last two or three pages written last night are in no way consonant with the objects of this daily journal, which are simply to state facts as I *know* them without a deduction or speculation, to refresh my own recollection in years to come should I [be] permitted to return to New England and if not, for the satisfaction of my wife and boy —I see, that, one would think, that while I was writing upon this chest last night I was animated by the spirit of an early and dear friend Saml. E. Coues of Portsmouth.* Not at all, because since I am in this *war* I desire to see war prosecuted believing, that such a course would the more speedily lead to peace, which when consummated, is not likely to be broken in his day or mine. But I would extend this daily journal without limit were I not to confine myself to transactions within my personal knowledge and observation, which is its sole purpose. Hereafter let there be no digressions—

Nor were there. He turned to other difficulties of a more immediate and simpler nature. There were troubles about the supplies. Pierce had made a demand upon the Corporation of Jalapa to furnish provisions at reasonable prices, and had threatened that if they were not forthcoming he would send the municipal officials to Perote as prisoners. This the corporation answered with a high sounding manifesto but, as Pierce endorsed on the back of it, " The supplies were furnished before 3 o'clock P.M. as required." The soldiers were themselves doing some commandeering in this luxuriant environment. They found an abundance of native fruit and also some strange liquor from which many began to suffer. Pierce, being much disturbed by the guerillas, lack of supplies and the growing sick list, broke camp hastily at four on the morning of the 29th.

Their onward march brought them into the mountains, and the new scenes made a deep impression upon Pierce.

---

* In 1840 Pierce had presented a memorial to the Senate signed by Coues and others calling for a Congress of Nations to outlaw war. *Globe,* 26: 1, 198.

[We] were enveloped in driving clouds as we wound round the mountain until we reached a short turn, where there is a table land of small extent, at which point, the sun breaking through the mist and the clouds rolling partially away toward the Southeast, such a scene was revealed to our vision, hitherto hemmed in by a narrow precipitous road and dense fog, as I do not even hope ever again to witness. The guide, who was by and who had driven a stage on the route 12 years said he had never seen the striking objects stand out so boldly and distinctly before. On the left, rising above the dark precipitous mountains by the base of which we passed, was visible so much of Orisaba as is covered with eternal snow. On the right and a few miles distant the finest cascade probably in this land of mountains. It looked, in the sunlight, with a rough somber background, like a silver thread dropped down a perpendicular descent of more than two hundred feet. Beyond, lay the Ocean in plain full view, upon it, we all cast a longing lingering glance. The illusion as to distances in the clear, rare atmosphere of this elevated region, 5757 feet above the ocean and the extent to which the unaided vision reaches embracing objects with distinctness have been a matter of surprise to all. It seemed on this morning at San Miguel that one might almost lay his hand upon the perpetual snow of Orisaba and that with an inclined plane provided for him, he might in an hour's gallop bathe his charger's feet in the surf of the Gulf.

As the command came up and we moved forward Col. Ransom waved his hand with a quotation from Byron and an adieu to " Old Ocean." I fancy there was a tinge of sadness on our faces. It was our last view of this rare combination of the most sublime objects of nature, at least for months, [our] final adieu to the broad pathway to our New England homes.

Eyes were soon turned westward, for the dreaded La Hoya must be encountered. Due precautions were taken, the heights were occupied while the trains went through this dreaded pass; they were unmolested, and late on the 30th they arrived at the castle of Perote where the valorous Colonel Wynkoop held sway. Here a halt of several days was necessary, as the sick list continued large and the supplies were running low. Shortly a cavalry detachment from General P. F. Smith arrived bearing the news that Scott had heard of the attacks on the train and had sent Smith forward to lend any aid necessary. Pierce was proud to be able to send back word to his commander that he was bringing his train through practically unscathed. He left Perote August 2 and as he had promised Scott arrived at Puebla four days later.

He had achieved his first military duty; he had led 2,500 men through 150 miles of hostile country in twenty-one days, through six attacks and the dangers of disease, with the loss of hardly a man. He had conducted a heavy siege battery, a long train of wagons, and had safely transported $85,000 worth of uncashable drafts. But there was little time for satisfaction even with one's self. Scott had decided to march on immediately; Twiggs got off on the seventh, two divisions followed, and on the tenth Pillow's division, which consisted of Cadwalader's and Pierce's brigades, was marching. It was " On to Mexico City."

XXII
ELUSIVE GLORY

No longer burdened with complete responsibility, Pierce led his brigade under orders from Scott and Pillow towards the enemy's capital. Day by day the little army of less than 11,000 men penetrated deeper into the heart of the hostile country. Slowly the miles were left behind, gradually the army ascended the grades that led to the divide. Popocatepetl and Iztaccihuatl, clad in everlasting snows, seemed so close and yet were still so far away. After the first twenty miles, the ascent had become more difficult, the surroundings appeared to be almost Alpine, sixteen miles farther and they had passed Tesmalucan over the aerial bridge and had come to the Cold River which rushed straight from the snowy crevasses of the mountains. Five more miles of dragging climb and they stood upon the broad plateau 10,500 feet above the sea. Shortly thereafter the descent into the Valley of Mexico became steep and rapid, and Pierce and his army were within sight of the coveted prize, the promised land, for in this luxuriant valley with its age-old volcanoes and reflecting lakes lay the City of Mexico, seemingly as oblivious to the marching hosts as the old city of the Aztecs had been those centuries long ago when Cortez and his conquistadores first looked upon their mysterious goal.

Twiggs had been clearing away the futile barricades, but finding armed forces in his path had stopped about twenty miles from the city, and Quitman, Worth, and finally Pillow on August 14 came up and encamped at Chimalpa near the margin of Lake Chalco. After Scott had reconnoitered, he determined to approach Mexico City from the south, skirting Lake Xochimilco, and on the fifteenth he resumed the march along the marshy shore of the lake, to the annoying accompaniment of the mud which the hard rains renewed each afternoon. To these inconveniences of the advance were added the dangers of the proximity of the Mexicans. No one knew when an attack might be launched, and watchfulness was continuous. Within two days the village of San Agustin was reached and

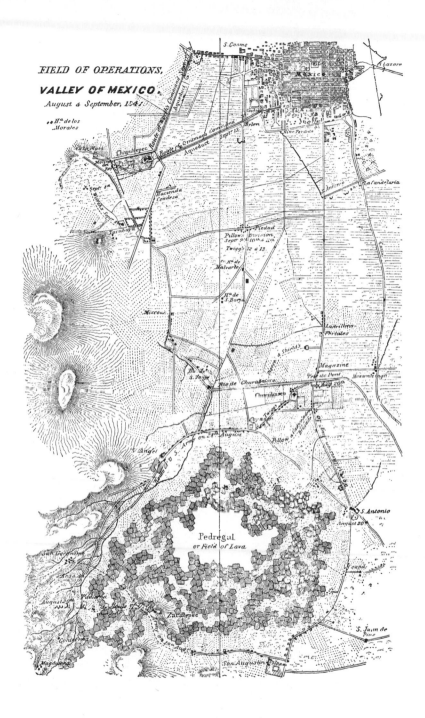

FIELD OF OPERATIONS,

VALLEY OF MEXICO.

August & September, 1847.

here again arose the problem of the proper road to take. The reconnoitering force found San Antonio too well fortified, so after some hesitation, on the eighteenth, Scott decided to make a circuit by the San Angel road and thus avoid San Antonio. To reach this road, however, a connecting path had to be made. Pillow was given the task of using his own division and that of Twiggs for this purpose. On the next day, therefore, Pierce and his brigade with the rest of the division pushed forward more than a mile and built a road to the summit of the ridge. Arriving there they found part of the Mexican army under Valencia encamped on the plain near Contreras. Pillow decided to make an assault. Pierce's brigade, with Smith's was ordered to attack the camp from the front, while a flank movement was to be undertaken at the same time. The latter did not materialize and the frontal attack was the main operation.

Here was a new experience. Pierce on horseback led his men into a brisk artillery fire, which fortunately was aimed too high, and from an eminence he urged his soldiers on, making a speech to them as they passed by—pointing the way to honor and glory. The artillery though badly aimed was noisy, and Pierce's mount was not used to such din. A sudden salvo caused the great black to jump, throwing the general forward against the high pommel of his saddle in such manner that he received an excruciating and sense-taking though hardly permanent injury. His horse stumbled in the pedragal and went down, the world went round, everything turned green and black, the general had fainted. O'Neil got to him immediately, saw he was unconscious, and called to Ransom that he must take charge of the brigade. Ransom was a little too far off to understand and he asked what was the matter. Morgan of the Fifteenth, who was not going forward, yelled out in a carrying voice, "Take command of the brigade, General Pierce is a damned coward." Many heard this canard who had no opportunity to verify it but nevertheless accepted it for all time as a fact.

Pierce soon regained consciousness, but when O'Neill helped him up he found that besides his pelvic injury his left knee had been severely wrenched and his horse had broken a leg. With difficulty the general was assisted to shelter under a projecting rock, and was covered with earth by an exploding shell.

"A lucky miss," remarked Pierce. O'Neil left him and went for help. He soon fell in with Dr. Ritchie of the brigade and when the doctor had applied hasty first aid Pierce started on, against all remonstrances, toward the battle. He hobbled to Magruder's battery where he found a horse and got himself hoisted into the saddle. In spite of his injuries he remained in the saddle until late that night, and saw the failure of Pillow's attempt to dislodge Valencia. At nine he found himself the senior officer on the field and withdrew the forces to a more sheltered area. Finally at eleven, almost spent with fatigue, he realized he must take some rest. That, however, was to be no easy matter. It was raining; he was separated from his servants, his tent, and his baggage. But he could no longer stay in the saddle, so he made the best bivouac he could in an ammunition wagon, and tried to sleep. Such was the day of Contreras—surely an unfortunate one for the general.

Sleep was not to be a very successful venture that night—for at one o'clock in the morning Twiggs and Captain R. E. Lee came to his bivouac with orders from Scott to create a diversion in favor of Brigadier General Smith, who was to attack the enemy at dawn. As Pierce was unable to move about very much, he turned the command over to Ransom. At daylight Smith finally cleaned out Valencia's camp in seventeen minutes whereupon Pierce's brigade joined in the pursuit. Meanwhile Scott was concentrating at Coyoacán for an attack on the convent at Churubusco held by the Mexicans. During the course of the day the commander decided to send Pierce's brigade north from Coyoacán across the Churubusco River toward Santa Anna's rear, in order to protect the American flank and rear as they attacked. Colonel Noah E. Smith, an American resident in Mexico, was to act as guide, and Pierce was summoned to the churchyard at Coyoacán where Scott was established, for final orders. After a sleepless night in the rain, with one foot in the stirrup and one hanging limp, he presented himself to his commander, a sorry-looking figure. Scott realized his condition and was about to send him back to the base at San Agustín, whereupon the dilapidated general was dismayed and protested vigorously. "For God's sake, General, this is the last great battle, and I must lead my brigade."

Scott yielded and Pierce was once more in pursuit of glory.

The way took them through thick standing corn, and over marshy ground intersected with ditches, many slimy with stagnant water. At first the general leaped his horse over these obstructions, but after advancing a mile or so they came to a ditch too wide for jumping; so he had himself lifted from his saddle and crawled through the water. His command was now under fire, but in the excitement of the advance the general suddenly twisted his injured knee so that the pain overcame him; he fell faint in full range of the enemy's fire. As some of his men started to carry him to shelter, he roused and ordered them to leave him there exposed as he was. He had fainted and been called a coward the day before, better to die than let that happen again. During the remainder of the battle of Churubusco he remained in that spot, with an obligato of Mexican bullets punctuating his bitter and pain-ridden thoughts. Probably the last battle—and glory was such an elusive jade. While he lay there his men did him no honor. As the authority on the Mexican War writes, " Precisely what occurred now cannot be stated, for apparently most of the reporting officers were more anxious to conceal than to disclose facts; but it seems clear that Shields handled the men clumsily, that his own regiments fell into disorder when charging and shrank from the devouring Mexican fire [behind a wall] and that Pierce's brigade, composed of excellent material but officered to a large extent with political favorites, actually skulked." * But other divisions triumphed, and the battle was won elsewhere. This was the day of Churubusco.

After the battle the crippled general again sought rest. But Santa Anna had asked for an armistice and Scott, yielding to pressure from those who wanted to avoid further bloodshed and destruction of property, had finally consented, instead of marching into Mexico City as he might well have done. He appointed Persifor F. Smith, Quitman, and Pierce, the latter two of whom had had little opportunity to distinguish themselves as commanders, to arrange the terms. Thus Pierce again was hoisted into the saddle, and he rode to Tacubaya two and a half miles away. There at the British Consul's house, he and his fellow

* Smith, *War with Mexico*, II, 116.

commissioners wrestled with terms until four o'clock in the morning. Then he felt free to seek Worth's quarters and sleep.

When he awoke it was to find that the army was bitterly disappointed at the armistice, for the men had hoped to pillage the capital. Pierce defended the armistice to his wife: " If we had marched into the city on the evening of the 20th, peace, in my judgment, would have [been] postponed indefinitely. I, for one, came here not to riot in the destruction of human life; not to destroy a city; not to subjugate a nation, but to ' conquer a peace.' I have acted from beginning to end with a sole view to this object; . . . and I felt no disposition to consult the pride or ambition of the army, flushed with triumph and eager to enter, with little possibility of restraint, a great, magnificent, subjugated city. From the beginning to the end of that conference my attention was directed solely to the great object of an honorable peace, and all the denunciations the next day of men and officers, whose thoughts seemed to have been fixed upon a ' revel in the halls,' produced no more effect upon my feelings than has sometimes an outbreak of undeserved praise." Simultaneously he found his own reputation under fire. That fatal shout of Morgan's had been heard by many, others had been told of it, and his action in pushing the armistice added to the flame. Morgan publicly retracted, when he learned the circumstances, but suspicion clung to the minds of some, and although the incident seemed soon forgotten, it was to come up again most inopportunely.

Scott's peace negotiations failed, and by September 1 Pierce was ordered to hold his men in readiness for action; but nothing happened. He and his troops had been quartered at Mixcoac and gradually his wrenched knee was improving. He was in the saddle a great deal, too; but tropical difficulties at length overtook him and he had to resort to medicine. Like the rest he could only wait, and occasionally contemplate the prize, for they were in full view of the city and Pierce gazed with wonder upon " its cathedrals and gorgeous porcelain domes and towers; the unrivalled valley, with its lakes, all in a basin skirted by bold and majestic mountains." The center of all attention was the castle of Chapultepec " with its white embattlements perched upon a lofty and almost inaccessible rock [overlooking] the

city as it were with pride," and surrounded by "lovely and en-
chanting" grounds now rather neglected, in the midst of which
Montezuma's Cypress, forty-two feet in circumference, stood
surrounded by many others almost as large covered with green
moss. Then action was renewed. Before attacking the city
Scott had become convinced he ought to capture Molina del
Rey, which he understood Santa Anna was using as a foundry
for cannon balls. Worth was sent against it September 8 and
had an exceedingly hard day. So difficult was it, that at length
Scott ordered Pierce to take his brigade in to help him. Pierce
hurried up, and arriving just as the battle was over, he put his
fresh men between Worth and the enemy, rather near the guns
of the fortress of Chapultepec. During this operation a shell
burst within a few feet of his horse and that frightened animal
nearly jumped over a precipice. Pierce aided in caring for the
wounded and led his men in driving off Mexican skirmishers,
but he had arrived too late for real fighting. Thus glory eluded
him the third time—at this, the battle of Molina del Rey. Scott
tried to do what he could for Pierce by writing in his report of
the battle, "But the battle was won just as Brigadier Gen.
Pierce interposed his corps between Garland's brigade (Worth's
division) and the retreating enemy." This disgruntled Worth,
who interpreted it to mean that he would not have won the
battle without Pierce. Generals were very touchy in the Mexican War.

Now came the final military event, the storming of the city
itself. Just how to do it presented a question. In order to
determine this Scott called a council of generals and engineers
at La Piedad, September 11. They must decide between storming Chapultepec or crossing the marshes from the south. Scott
was in favor of the first, but wanted it debated. Four of
the engineers, especially Robert E. Lee, were in favor of the
marsh route; Quitman, Shields, Cadwalader, and Pierce as well
as Pillow took the same ground. Only Twiggs and Riley
favored Chapultepec. Then another engineer, Beauregard,
gave a lengthy opinion in favor of it, whereupon Pierce
changed his mind and said so. Nobody else seemed impressed;
but Scott then announced that the assault would take place at
Chapultepec and gave the orders. Next day Pierce took up his
station at Molina del Rey. Towards noon, however, it became

certain that there would be no fighting in that area. He returned to Worth's headquarters where he collapsed; weariness and a bad case of diarrhea made it necessary for him to retire, and he had to resort to the most decided remedies. There he lay on his back for thirty-six hours, and during this period occurred the storming of Chapultepec. The knowledge that this last important battle was being fought without him was maddening, and the desire to get up somehow and join his brigade was defeated only by an absolute lack of strength. The height was stormed and his friend and mainstay, Ransom, was killed.

The night of the thirteenth brought a lull and next morning was to witness the final assault, so all believed. Pierce could not harbor the thought of not being there to enter Mexico City with his troops; therefore, early on the fourteenth, before dawn, he dressed and rode to join the Ninth before the anticipated assault. It was a gruesome ride, his horse was constantly shying at dead bodies strewn along the road. He was not quite sure of the way and asked a soldier lying in a causeway; as the man did not reply his orderly shook him, and then turned to Pierce, " He will never answer, sir, except at the call of the last trump." Pierce reported to Quitman at the Balen gateway just as that general was preparing for the final attack. He joined part of his brigade temporarily detached from Worth, and steeled himself for the last effort. But it was never made; a white flag appeared and without further opposition the American troops marched into the city. The little army had penetrated the heart of the enemy's country and was in control of the capital. But the loss had been heavy; in Pierce's beloved Ninth Regiment there were scarce three hundred effectives, and Ransom was dead. As for Pierce, he had missed his last chance for glory.

In other respects the final victory was a great relief to the general. It brought the possibility of returning to his family so much nearer. To tell the truth, he had never been quite sure that his course in leaving them was entirely justifiable, although he had convinced himself that it was his duty, and family and party pride had been able helpers. Now he had performed his service; and just as soon as it was certain that peace was assured he could plan to resign, for he had not the least intention of remaining in the army as a garrison officer.

It took time to arrange to go home. The situation in Mexico was very uncertain, and as the Mexican government was in a very chaotic state, peace negotiations lagged. For three months Pierce carried on the duties of a rather galling routine, sometimes despairing of peace. During part of this time he had command of the third division while the wounded Pillow was recuperating. He had his headquarters in the Calle de Cadena and had frequent opportunities to observe and moralize, to enjoy the comradeship of his fellow officers in their clubs, and occasionally to engage in hilarity. One incident was to loom up in later times, for several remembered the evening when Magruder, not at all himself, attempted to start a dispute with Pierce over a card game. So the time passed until arrangements for his return were completed. As a farewell, General Scott gave Generals Twiggs and Pierce a dinner on December 8 which had the double purpose of speeding the parting generals and welcoming some who had just arrived, including Caleb Cushing. That same night there was a parting jollification with the officers of the Ninth—Seymour, Lally, Clemens and the rest —and the next day he started for the coast, retracing his famous march.

Pierce had made many friends among rank and file. His fellow officers and he had come into contact especially close and intimate; during the months after the capture of the capital they had been much in each others' society; they had formed a club and found much pleasure and recreation together. Pierce had made a number of friendships which were to bear fruit in later years—Pillow, Beauregard, Claiborne, Bonham, Shields, and Quitman; and his relations with Cushing, Lally, and Seymour were strengthened and deepened. His genial personality and his solicitude for his men as he led them and shared their hardships, made many an obscure soldier an ardent friend of General Pierce, and left among the men recollections of admiration and gratitude which did not die. Pierce was also able to keep clear of the barrack-room disputes of the generals, which plagued the army and caused the famous Scott-Pillow quarrel. All told, it had been a valuable experience in spite of its hardships, and while Pierce had earned no particular military glory he had shown himself resourceful and determined, able to bear hardship and to keep up his spirits in difficulty; his constitution had proved itself elastic and able quickly to recuperate from strains and fatigue. But it was pleasanter to have the experience in retrospect than in prospect, and now he could have the anticipation of seeing Jeanie and little Ben once more, and enjoy the triumphs of a victorious military leader. His voyage on the good ship *New Orleans* across the gulf from Vera Cruz was very smooth and pleasant, and on December 28, 1847, Pierce was back in his native land.

Northward he traveled, stopping at Washington where he reported to Polk and Marcy. He wished to resign, but Polk wasn't sure the war was over, so he took a leave of absence instead. Then for Lowell, as fast as he could, to the joyous reunion with his family. Late in January Concord gave her hero a royal welcome and the following year the legislature presented him with a sword. When Polk sent the treaty of peace to the Senate on Washington's birthday, the general was free to resign; and he went back to Washington to arrange for surrendering his commission. His great ambition had been realized, he had served his country on the field in time of war, and while glory had not perched upon his standard he had done his duty. He had shown himself the old General's son.

YEARS OF GREATEST EFFECTIVENESS
1848-1851

XXIII
ZENITH

THE four years after Pierce's return from the Mexican War were to be the most satisfying of his life. During these years he achieved his greatest self-satisfaction and prosperity. Honored by the community, successful in his profession, leader of his party, happy in his home life, he reached his zenith.

Once again he and Mrs. Pierce changed their mode of living. During his service in Mexico their home had been sold, and for several months after his return Mrs. Pierce and Bennie remained at Lowell. After another period of boarding they finally entered into an arrangement which was to be lasting. They went to live with Mr. and Mrs. Willard Williams in a pleasant white cottage on South Main Street, corner of Thorndike. Mrs. Williams, whose husband was foreman in Abbott's carriage works, was to board them, and they assumed a sort of financial oversight of the establishment.

During these years Mrs. Pierce, too, spent the happiest days of her married life. She was in better health and she was devoted to Bennie, who presented all the interesting traits of a growing boy approaching his tenth birthday. She occupied herself in hovering around her child with doting fondness and set herself to give him a strict evangelical training. In this plan his father dutifully coöperated; his hopes, too, were centered on the boy. Each morning there was family worship, each evening the lad said his prayers. Sunday was the New England sabbath when the world seemed to stand still, and cold meals added to the religious observance an additional touch of austerity. Bennie went to the South Congregational Church in the morning with his father and with both his parents in the afternoon. His mother read him Bible stories and those tract-like story books in which our grandparents so delighted. Learning hymns, too, was his portion. Such training had its effect. He early had religious experiences and enjoyed a vivid and childlike faith in his Heavenly Father and his Savior. He

171

was a sensitive child with a delicate organization closely bound
to that of his mother.

Life with her, as her husband had learned, was not the easi-
est. Her ill health and her "nerves" made her exacting, and
she seemed unable to express her affection. It was much easier
for her to chide than to praise; and she bitterly reproached
herself in later years because she had never found the way to
open her heart. Bennie and his father were patient, even
tempered and affectionate, and life went on with the boy as
the center of the home. In spite of it all, he was a good deal
of a boy and ran as wild with his playmates as his mother's
watchfulness would allow; besides, when he was at Lowell, there
were his cousins. He was always eager for his father to come
home from his office, and when the latter tarried his son would
start down town to hurry him up, a custom which was a brake
upon Pierce's social inclinations.

During these years the general's practice and success steadily
increased. His income grew and his fame grew faster. He was
not a great lawyer nor a deep student of the law, but he possessed talents which made him powerful. His greatest asset
was his facility with a jury. He had a native kindliness and
sympathy and a deep interest in individuals which he used to
great effect. He knew numbers of people and he never forgot
their names. When he faced a jury he studied it, he knew its
individual members and he directed his case to them.

He was master of clear oral exposition, and did not complicate
the legal aspects of a case, but simplified them, endeavoring to
bring the question at issue to fundamental, clearly explained
principles. Most valuable of all his talents was his oratorical
ability. He was master of his voice and could concentrate his
personality to the point of hypnotic power. Observers recalled
in later years how his intense efforts in concentration caused a
glow to suffuse his countenance, which some even described as
giving the effect of a halo. He didn't convince juries, he converted them; and after his fervent pleas tears often would well
up in the eyes of Main Street jurymen unaccustomed to such
emotional treats. He bore himself courteously to court and
clients, and to opponents as well. When he thought he de-
tected fraud he would excoriate a witness in a manner quite
imposing. He spent much time in preparing his cases, analyzed

MRS. PIERCE AND BENNIE

them thoroughly and had an excellent memory, so that he was never at a loss. He was careful to advise against litigation wherever possible and did much to bring about peaceful settlements. Added to all these talents, he was fortunate in having as a partner the shrewd and able Josiah Minot; and a number of young law students who passed through their offices and worshipped him—Carroll, Dana, George, Sidney Webster and others—were his eager coworkers. To them he imparted that feeling of equality and self-confidence so pleasing to youth.

His practice was varied. Cases of all sorts came to his office, civil cases, criminal cases, libel, forgery, murder, trespass, slander, damage suits for injuries to persons or animals, prosecution of unlicensed rum selling. Increasingly important was a new class of cases—corporation law was developing. Corporations had been increasing in numbers and in wealth. They had many problems requiring legal advice, not only matters of their own organization, but in addition questions involving their relations with the public. Agricultural New Hampshire distrusted banks and railroads and watched the advance of these corporations jealously. The new class of mill owners along the Merrimack also paid well for legal advice.* In court, before legislative committees, in lobbies and at conventions, not to mention inter-corporation negotiations, good political lawyers were needed. Retainers of no small size came to Pierce from corporation officials who appreciated the value of his political influence and his skill with a jury. His most famous cases were the Wentworth murder case and the Farnsworth forgery. The latter cause seems to have been the only one which he

* Bill to J. M. Harper and Benj. Sanborn (illustrating Pierce's fees)

1849	March	6.	To services in trial of case Baxter	
			Bowman vs. them	$ 50.00
	Sept.	2.	To term fee in suit	5.00
1850	Jan.	14.	" paid for copies	4.50
	March 11.		" service in preparing for trial	30.00
	Sept.	19.	" term fee and preparation of suit	15.00
1851	March	8.	" services and arguing case	150.00
				$254.50
	Sept.	29.	" term fee	5.00
1852	March		" " "	5.00
				$264.50

pleaded outside of his immediate radius, going to Boston to lose it. His reputation as a lawyer, though not as a politician, was decidedly local.

During these years he was by no means out of politics. The Mexican War having been in many respects political, the Whigs were doing their best to discredit it. While Pierce was away Burke had thought it wise to defend him from Whig slanders, particularly the charge that he had refused to accept his commission without three months' pay in advance. When he returned he found himself immediately involved because Whig spokesmen declared he had come home disgusted with the war, and later they charged his report had caused Polk to recall Scott. Vigorous defense of the war was his first problem, and he made speeches and wrote letters, denying the charges as well as glorifying our arms; incidentally, he retracted his former slighting opinions of West Point. While he was laboring in defense some few people thought of him as a possible Presidential candidate for the year 1848, and one or two New Hampshire politicians like Harry Hibbard began to suggest the possibility. The general himself and his brother officers of the Aztec Club hoped to nominate their comrade Persifor F. Smith, but New England was for Woodbury, and Pierce soon climbed on the bandwagon.

The free soil issue once more presented itself. After the defeat of 1846 the Democrats had succeeded in recuperating sufficiently to win in 1847 and 1848, and they had learned something. They caused the legislature and state convention to pass resolutions endorsing the Wilmot restriction on slavery extension, and attracted some attention thereby. Burke and the more strait-laced at Washington regretted these resolutions, and the *Union* expressed its disapproval when New Hampshire congressmen voted for the proviso. Pierce, on the other hand, was more of an opportunist in this matter, and he realized that after the disaster of 1846 the party must make some concessions to the anti-southern feeling or lose power permanently. His vision was clearer in 1848 than it proved to be in 1854.

When Woodbury was defeated at the national convention in 1848, and the followers of Van Buren bolted and held a separate convention at Utica, the latter considered the Woodbury partisans as possible allies. Before the meeting at Utica Benjamin

F. Butler of New York wrote to Pierce asking him if he would permit his name to be used as a possible presidential candidate by the Van Burenites; presumably he refused, and when Van Buren was finally nominated remained loyal to New Hampshire's son, Cass. That fall he was offered the nomination for governor. The Whig-Free-Soil coalition was going to make a vigorous fight and the Democrats wanted his strength, but he refused. He preferred to retain his sway over the rank and file without the responsibility of office. Numerous other leaders resented his popularity and his power; a popular hero with no ambitions was apt to be arbitrary and hard to handle. Regardless of these conditions success crowned the Democratic efforts. Cass carried the state with more votes than Polk had received, and the next March, when the opposition coalition fell apart, the Democrats won the governorship with ease.

The restoration of harmony in the Democratic ranks and the return of the party to power had once more demonstrated the strength of the state organization. In the party councils Pierce held a position of great influence. He was one of a small fraternity of lawyer-politicians who were prominent before the Merrimack bar, and were known as the " Concord Clique " or " Regency," so dominant were they in state politics. The most active Democrat in Concord was Pierce's close friend, General Charles H. Peaslee, a man of Pierce's own age, who had been busily occupied at the capital since 1824. Peaslee had led the campaign to establish a state insane asylum, and for many years had been adjutant general of the state militia, an office he had resigned in 1847 to go to Congress. For six years thereafter he represented the district at Washington. He was a genial man and a successful jury lawyer, but there was much of the " shrewd Yankee " about him. He was fully aware of Pierce's value as a political asset for the New Hampshire Democrats, and his friendship for the general was to have a very important influence upon future events.

Another Democrat of mark in Concord was Judge Nathaniel G. Upham. After ten years on the bench Upham had been chosen to manage the new railroad enterprise, and since 1843 he had been successfully organizing the transportation interest which was steadily developing. He was an enterprising manager with a keen interest in politics. Third in this group was

Nathaniel B. Baker, younger than the others, who had gained his Concord experience as a law student first with Pierce and Fowler and later with Peaslee. He had edited the *Patriot* with Carroll until 1845, and in 1850 and 1851 was speaker of the house. He had developed greatly the arts of companionship, becoming one of the most popular men in Concord.

The press was represented among these associates by William Butterfield, editor of the *Patriot*; he had been imported from Nashua to take charge of the paper shortly after Henry Carroll died in 1846, and his tall, cadaverous figure with its mannerisms, and his peculiarities of temperament, were colorful features of Concord politics. Then there was Joseph Robinson, a small man, sprightly and capable, who had started in Concord as a school teacher; later he had developed a fondness for politics and business which made him postmaster during Polk's administration. A rising power in the party was the youthful John H. George. To him Pierce was much attached; their fathers had been cronies, and young George upon leaving Dartmouth had come to Pierce's law office. He was a headlong, heedless, downright chap with boundless force and little tact. He was breaking into the political game, and his energetic activity was to bring him early to the top.

Among the many other young men whom Pierce helped to advance was Sidney Webster, Peaslee's nephew, who had graduated from Yale in 1848, and was now beginning the study of law in the office of Pierce and Minot. Very close to the general, but behind the scenes, was his partner, Josiah Minot. Minot was fifteen years younger than Pierce and had come to Concord only recently—in 1844. He was an able lawyer and a shrewd financier who contributed to the firm, as Fowler had done, the talents which Pierce lacked. Pierce and Minot were more compatible than Pierce and Fowler had been, for Minot was in full sympathy with his partner. Their association was to be lasting, and Minot became entrusted with the management of Pierce's business affairs. Among his marked peculiarities was a " passion " for self-effacement; he hated contact with his fellow-men and avoided pleading in court wherever possible. His timidity, however, seemed only to contribute to his shrewdness, and he was a powerful behind-the-scenes manager. With this group was Moses Norris of Pittsfield, in Merrimack County,

Hale's colleague in the Senate, not a very close friend of Pierce
nor in the inner circle.

No town group, however powerful, can exert much control
without allies; therefore the " Regency " kept closely associated
with it certain chieftains from other portions of the state.
Closest to Pierce were leaders in his old county, Hillsborough.
At Nashua dwelt Charles G. Atherton, a man always peculiarly
connected with him. Atherton had succeeded him as speaker,
as congressman and as senator, and though early rivals they
had become friends and allies. Atherton, next to Woodbury,
was the New Hampshire politician best known in Washington;
he had been author of one of the " gag " resolutions in Congress
and was trusted by southern leaders. Northern opponents considered him, like Pierce, a " dough-face." He was a shrewd
Yankee, a man of no striking characteristics, but a power in the
state. At Manchester, Richard H. Ayer, a railroad promoter,
and George W. Morrison were the principal bulwarks against
the rising free soil sentiment. Morrison strikingly resembled
Pierce in cast of countenance and sought to imitate Pierce's
mannerisms quite successfully, too successfully for Pierce's liking, because he began to be accused of imitating Morrison.
Back in Hillsboroughtown, his brother, Henry D. Pierce, and
his former law student, Samuel H. Ayer, were managing things
political, or at least trying to.

To the eastward in Rockingham, Levi Woodbury was titular
chieftain, but his elevated position on the supreme bench kept
him aloof from practical politics. Richard Jenness and George's
cousin, Albert R. Hatch, were active there, the latter especially
allied with Pierce and the Concord group; but in this county as
in Strafford, the free soil heresy was too strong. John P. Hale
and Amos Tuck were powerful in this region and could too
often carry elections. Local politics was further complicated
by Pierce's rival, so-called, John Sullivan Wells. Wells was a
close connection of the powerful Sullivans and he and Pierce
should have acted in harmony for family and traditional reasons, because Benjamin Pierce and John Sullivan had been
close associates. However, they were covertly antagonistic.
Their principles and their dislike of the free soil heresy coin-
cided, but their experiences in party councils and before the
bar produced a certain amount of distrust. Wells had travelled

down from the north country to settle in Exeter and become attorney general. He was a striking figure, nearly six feet tall, with prematurely white hair and a florid complexion. He had a high-pitched, musical voice, well-developed oratorical skill, and the impressive, commanding authority of the Sullivans. He was eminently a man of the forum and the hustings. Pierce was always willing to trust him, but his close friends felt that Wells's loyalty could not always be counted upon.

Over the mountains, in the valley of the great river, Pierce for years had been closely associated with Edmund Burke, who, like Atherton, was well known in Washington. He had been connected with Sullivan County politics for more than ten years, and the *Argus and Spectator* was his organ. He had been congressman when Pierce was in Washington, and commissioner of patents during Polk's régime, after which he became one of the editors of the Washington *Union*. He had done much for Pierce during the Mexican War, but their relations after the general's return had been growing apart. Burke was a " hedgehog," and his irascible temper and unwillingness to accept any sort of domination made him an independent politician. He had lost ground while away in Washington for five years, and resented the control which the " Regency " had gained over the party. While he always professed continued friendship for Pierce, he hated some of his associates, especially Butterfield. The result of this hatred was a newspaper war between the *Patriot* and the *Argus and Spectator* which increased the ill feeling between the river towns and the capital.

Last but not least were the north country chieftains in close alliance with the " Regency." In the far-away hill towns dwelt a group of barons who ruled the yeomen in feudal fashion. Their titular chieftain was old Major John W. Weeks, and his younger associates were Colonel Edward E. Cross, Judge Richard Eastman and Governor Jared W. Williams; with them was John H. White, who had fallen away under Hill's banner in the days of the " conservative " revolt and was now seeking a means, of restoring his fortunes. Their spokesman was James Madison Rix, who had been editing the *Coos Democrat* since 1838. He was of spare frame with a large head, black hair, and keen black eyes; he, too, possessed nervous energy that stopped at no obstacle.

Closest to Pierce in the North country was Harry Hibbard of Bath, Grafton County's leading Democrat. Hibbard was not a man one would expect to find in politics; he was a quiet, dignified, and self-contained gentleman with charming manners and a frail constitution. He had a deep interest in literature, had written some poetry, and contributed to the pages of the *Democratic Review*. Since 1843 he had been in the legislature where he became speaker of the house and president of the senate. In 1849 he went to Congress where he was to remain six years. He had senatorial ambitions, but Hale had prevented their fulfillment in 1847 and Norris had defeated him in the caucus of 1849.

Such was the state of the party control; these were the leaders the laymen followed. Among his associates, Pierce occupied an enviable eminence; his military services, his wide acquaintance outside of the state, and his large following among the voters gave him an independent position which some of the leaders were growing to resent. However, he and his friends had conquered Hill, and once at least he had beaten Hale. A third trial of strength and leadership was to be even more spectacular.

XXIV

" DICTATOR "

IN these years of prosperity and complacency, Pierce had withdrawn somewhat from active politics and his friends of the Concord Regency and their allies had been more in the arena. They had continued their warfare with the Whigs on the basis of the Wilmot Proviso. This principle they had endorsed in platform and legislative resolutions in 1849 demanding freedom in the Mexican cession and condemning the Southern proposal to provide federal enforcement of the fugitive slave law. News of these resolutions of course brought objection and reproof from the South. Southern commentators could not or would not see how the Democrats were pursued in the North by Whig and free soil " allies " and their strictures caused bitter comment among the Northern leaders. Pierce himself is quoted as saying: " The fact of the matter is, the South is so exhorbitant in its exactions of us that it will end by breaking us down." Furthermore, many held that the South had not been loyal to Cass and by supporting Taylor had caused the former's defeat. Now the energies of Northern Democratic leaders were earnestly directed toward finding a formula that would bring back the Van Buren supporters of 1848 or at least give none others the excuse to leave the party on that issue.

When the congressional struggle over the government of the Mexican cession began again with the assembling of Congress in December, 1849, the New Hampshire *Patriot* advocated the Wilmot Proviso and when the committee of thirteen finally evolved the compromise scheme, the organ was not enthusiastic. " We need not repeat that we do not approve of this mode of settling the matter; although we admit that even this is better than no adjustment of the question. We would rather pass this bill, than, by defeating it, . . . leave the territories without government." The *Patriot* counselled New Hampshire's congressmen to battle for the Wilmot Proviso as long as there was a " reasonable prospect of securing it."

Pierce himself became very apprehensive of disunion and

when the compromise was first rejected by Congress he told an audience that he wanted to die with the Union. Also it may be hazarded that the death of General Taylor affected the New Hampshire point of view. With the President dead, the possibilities of electing a Democrat in 1852 brightened and the New Hampshire leaders thought of Woodbury's chances and some may have thought of Pierce again. Perhaps it would be better not to antagonize the South further. At any rate, they decided to support actively these measures and when they were finally passed began a vigorous campaign for popular endorsement even of the unpopular fugitive slave law. In October the state convention approved the measure and Pierce went to a meeting at Webster's old home in Franklin where he and the great Whig fraternized and joined in commending the recently enacted laws. In November a giant Union meeting was held at Manchester and Pierce's fervid speech supporting all the measures including the fugitive slave law was long remembered.

While he was rejoicing in the renewed life of his beloved Union, he was called upon to serve as one of Concord's delegates in a convention to revise the archaic state constitution. When this body assembled in November at the state house, he was chosen to preside over its deliberations. For two months the delegates exhaustively overhauled the fundamental law. Most important as far as results were concerned, was the action on the qualifications for office-holding. Catholics had been barred from holding office and this restriction had become an object of political controversy as the Catholic population increased. Since 1844, Pierce had been advocating the removal of this bar and now he actively promoted the change. Judge Woodbury spoke to the delegates in favor of the reform, and Pierce left the chair to argue in the same cause. Their pleas were successful. His further efforts were spent, so the press charged, in altering the system of representation so as to fasten the control of the Democratic party on the legislature; but his position as presiding officer generally kept him from debate and the record is barren. Just before the assemblage broke up, he had the satisfaction of transmitting to President Fillmore resolutions endorsing the compromise measures. The convention had resolved to "firmly stand by and maintain the compromise measures of the last session of Congress," after an attempt to condemn the fugitive slave law and the Texas debt settlement had been overwhelmingly voted down. The work of revision was presented to the people for their approval in the form of fifteen amendments to the constitution.

During the protracted weeks of amending Pierce had been drawn back into the midst of state politics. The Democrats in their October convention had enjoyed a spirited contest for the gubernatorial nomination. Governor Dinsmoor had sought re-nomination, the "Regency" had put forward another candidate, and the Hillsborough delegation supported Reverend John Atwood. The latter at length had been accepted as a compromise candidate. Although this convention adopted a platform which denounced slavery as a "curse" which the party would use its best efforts to prevent from spreading, it condemned secessionists and abolitionists alike, and concluded by endorsing the compromise of 1850: "Our hostility to the introduction of slavery into free territory, however great it may be, shall not prevent us from congratulating the country and the friends of freedom throughout the world" upon the compromise measures omitting any specific reference to the fugitive slave law.

Reverend John Atwood was neither a happy politician nor a discerning leader. He was known to have free soil sympathies, and the free soil politicians thought they saw a chance to capture the leadership of the Democratic party, or at least to discredit its spokesmen who, like Pierce, were intent on keeping peace with the South. So John H. White, ancient "conservative" and passé Democrat, acted as the mouthpiece of the Manchester free soilers. They formed an alliance with the leaders of the mill towns who were not so regular as they once had been, and talked "free soil" more than Pierce and his fellows relished. Rural ideas could not forever dominate; the mill workers of Manchester hated slave labor which they felt helped to keep them in wage slavery under oligarchic control, something which the independent farmers on their broad acres were slow to realize. The Manchester-Concord free soil group, therefore, through White undertook to commit Atwood to their views in order to break the influence of the Regency. They enquired of Atwood whether he was opposed to the "oppressive" fugitive slave law and whether as governor he would favor "all peaceful and constitutional measures to effect its

early repeal." Atwood had free soil leanings and he wanted
to be honest, so he wrote a reply repudiating the fugitive slave
law because it denied a trial by jury and required a service of
the people of the free states which he felt " neither the constitution nor conscience " could require. He showed this letter to
Goodale, the editor of the Manchester *Democrat*, free soil organ,
and left it with him, but did not make up his mind to publish it.

As was to be expected, rumors of his letter began to spread,
and early in December Pierce and the other members of the
constitutional convention heard them. Pierce and his close
friends suspected at once that a plot was on foot to spread free
soil heresy among the Democratic party and to challenge their
leadership. Such a scheme was too dangerous to be ignored.
Pierce and a few others decided to warn Atwood. They invited
him to meet them in Manchester and in the conference which
followed Atwood admitted to Pierce, not only that he had written the letter, but that it was in the hands of Goodale. Pierce
and his associates convinced Atwood of the unwisdom of his
course and he agreed to recall his letter. The group went to
Goodale and he surrendered it with a copy, swearing that no
other copy existed. When the letter and the copy had been
destroyed Pierce returned to Concord, liking Atwood no better, but feeling that the candidate had been saved from an
indiscretion.

A week passed, and then late one evening Pierce was surprised
to receive a call from Perkins Gale, a prominent Baptist layman,
who wanted him to accompany him immediately to his home.
There he found Atwood and his own brother Henry. Only that
day, the clergyman told them, he had learned that Goodale had
lied, that the Manchester editor had another copy of Atwood's
letter and had published it. Atwood had been hard at work all
day at his home, but as soon as he had heard this news, he had
harnessed up and driven the long distance from New Boston to
seek advice. Henry Pierce, who represented Atwood's district,
and the general then had been called in. After going over the
situation they agreed that Atwood should write another letter to
counteract the first one. Then and there they composed it, and
Atwood agreed to sign a statement that although he was opposed
to the fugitive slave law he realized that it had not been passed
as a single measure, but as " a link in a series of measures of

compromise and concession," and he would stand by these measures "as a whole" with the firm conviction that such was his "duty as a patriot and a Christian." Pierce went to bed with the feeling that Atwood had been saved again. The second letter was published in the *Patriot* next day.

In spite of his second letter some editors began attacks upon Atwood for the sentiments contained in his first epistle. Many were suspicious of his good faith, and the *Argus* came out in a bitter editorial. Such abuse stung Atwood, and on Christmas Day he wrote to Pierce complaining that he was being sacrificed after he had retracted; in this letter he stated specifically that he had written the retraction for publication. Sentiment toward Atwood did not improve, and after some preliminary hints the Manchester *Democrat* published a statement signed by several men in that town. They alleged that the day after his trip to Concord, Atwood had told them he had been coerced into signing the retraction, after obeying a summons to appear before the party leaders, and that the letter had been published without his permission.

Pierce now was made to appear in the columns of the free soil journals as the leader of those who had coerced Atwood, and then surreptitiously published his forced retraction. The general demanded in writing that Atwood deny these statements. Atwood did not reply, whereupon the *Patriot* gathered together all the documents in the case and published them, withholding only the dominie's Christmas letter which had been marked "confidential." The collection Butterfield headed by an editorial to the effect that Atwood was fast losing public confidence and unless he restored his reputation for veracity, which Pierce's letter questioned, he would be no fit candidate for governor.

Atwood resented Butterfield's threat and shortly replied; he did not remember, he said, what had passed before his fireside in his conversation with the free soil junta at Manchester. He had been tired and distraught after an almost sleepless night, and had taken little note of the conversation. He had been upset also by the immediate publication of his letter of retraction which he declared he had not expected to have published so soon. He further reiterated that the fugitive slave law was

law, and although he didn't like it as a good citizen he was
bound to obey it. He ignored Pierce entirely.

To Pierce this " whining about fireside conversations " was
evidence of his " miserable double dealing." Atwood was be-
traying his party by trafficking with the enemies of the national
Democrats. Pierce felt that he had " uttered a tissue of falsehoods which are made the foundations for the basest and most
virulent assaults upon individuals [Pierce and his brother] and
the party." Worse, Atwood had denied to those slandered " a
simple act of justice, an act demanded by the most ordinary
sense of honor." Pierce in this frame of mind called upon Atwood in no uncertain terms for permission to use his Christmas
letter with its admission of his intention to publish the retraction. He sent his demand to Atwood by special messenger, but
the clergyman after reading it gave it back to the messenger
and refused to reply. He felt Pierce was pushing him too far
and he was defiant.

As with Hale, so with Atwood; Pierce was ready. Atwood
must be removed as the party candidate, and a new and true
press must be established in Manchester. Goodale's *Democrat*
must be destroyed. Pierce's influence was potent. After some
hesitation the state committee recalled the October convention,
Atwood's name was withdrawn, and Gov. Dinsmoor almost
unanimously renominated. Rare in the annals of American
state politics is such an occurrence, and it demonstrated the
strength of the feeling against political free soilers among New
Hampshire Democratic leaders.

Atwood refused to accept the verdict of his party and the
contest waxed warm. His friends singled out Pierce and the
" Concord Clique " and charged them with the most flagrant
kind of " dictation " and despotic rule. Pierce fired back with
charges of treachery to the platform, disloyalty to the party,
disruption of the party, and personal unreliability. Prompt
action had been necessary to maintain party orthodoxy. *Sub
rosa*, if they wished to make Woodbury President they could
not afford to tolerate Atwood's heresy. On election day no
candidate received a majority, but the choice of a Democratic
legislature insured the re-election of Dinsmoor.

Pierce and the national Democrats reigned supreme. He had
won his greatest triumph, a triumph by no means unnoticed in

the South. Never before or afterwards was there to be such a moment of power. The Atwood affair was the climax of Pierce's career.

But even climaxes are seldom perfect. On that election day the voters had rejected the work of the constitutional convention. The frugal farmers resented the long, expensive session and the wholesale changes, which the Whigs considered political moves to fasten Democratic power upon the state. In the hope of salvaging some of the wreckage the convention reconvened in April, 1851, and after considerable urging by Pierce they resubmitted three propositions—to abolish the property and religious qualifications for holding office, and to permit the legislature to submit constitutional amendments to the people. The new proposals could not be voted upon until March of 1852.

Spring and summer moved along, and 1852 must be prepared for. The death of Taylor had given the Democrats renewed hope for regaining the presidency, and the convention in June of 1851 enthusiastically presented Judge Woodbury's name and elected Pierce's close friend, Charles G. Atherton, as delegate-at-large to Baltimore. Pierce followed his legal routine. Like the other townspeople he was much excited by the holocaust which laid most of business Concord in ashes that August; and he was somewhat disturbed also by the suicide of the Democratic nominee for the governorship. But most important of all was an event of the waning summer, an event the consequences of which gradually sapped Pierce's peace of mind and changed the course of his life. On September 4 Levi Woodbury died.

A CROWD OF STRANGE EXPERIENCES
1851-1853

XXV

A PAWN IN THE GAME

DURING the years of Pierce's political career New England's situation in national politics had never been happy. Since the defeat of the younger Adams, as Pierce came into the arena, no New England man had been nominated for the presidency. In the Democratic party, especially, New England cut a small figure. Woodbury and Bancroft had achieved a certain influence, but the accepted leaders and standard bearers came from other sections. Woodbury's name had been occasionally mentioned for the presidency and had received votes in national conventions, but it was not until the bolt of 1848 that New England Democrats entertained much hope. After that disaster some one was wanted to heal the breach; obviously a southern man could not do it, a safe northern man was needed. Cass, the candidate of the west, had failed; Van Buren had eliminated himself; might not New England Democrats pit Woodbury against Pennsylvania's favorite, Buchanan? A good deal of pipe had been laid, but Woodbury's death put an end to that plan.

New England Democrats felt themselves in too strong a position to warrant a cessation of effort, just because their candidate had died. A new man must be found. Sentiment among the leaders was not unanimous and the lack of unanimity was going to cause trouble. In the first place, a Boston group led by Benjamin F. Hallett and Charles G. Greene, editor of the *Post*, were in favor of renominating Cass; they had as associates a number who had been active for that candidate in 1848 and who now thought victory for him in 1852 was the surest way to advance their political fortunes. The chief supporters of Woodbury in New Hampshire and Maine were naturally disinclined to accept this scheme and sought to find the new man nearer home. Senator Hamlin of Maine, Isaac O. Barnes of New Hampshire and Massachusetts who was Woodbury's brother-in-law, Charles H. Peaslee, and John H. George, now chairman of the state central committee, were active in this second group.

189

We may suspect that the latter two and their New Hampshire friends had never been any too faithful to Woodbury, entertaining hope that one of their own number might prove more available. Ever since the Mexican War General Pierce, in their minds at least, had been a potential candidate.

Among Woodbury's friends, especially outside of New England, there seemed to be more or less agreement at first that General William O. Butler of Kentucky was the man and that New England must be satisfied with the vice-presidency. The bulk of the Woodbury strength, including those who had been closest to him, accepted the Butler candidacy, and a number spoke of Pierce as a possible vice-presidential nominee; to Peaslee and George, at least, came the thought, why not run him for the presidency? Confusion reigned in the party, the principal candidates had too many enemies; was not this the opportunity for a new man, a New Englander, General Pierce? Thus it happened that Peaslee and Hibbard, New Hampshire congressmen, and Senator Hamlin, went to Congress in December of 1851 with Pierce plans, and with their minds set on making opportunities.

Congress was not long in session before the complexity of the situation became apparent. Cass, Buchanan, Douglas, Marcy, Butler had so divided the field that the possibility of any one of them obtaining a two-thirds vote seemed an absurdity. The Cass forces were sufficiently alarmed by the growth of Butler sentiment to attack it, and Francis J. Grund charged in the Baltimore *Sun* that it was a free soil move originated by the Van Buren forces. Grund predicted that if Butler were nominated Pierce would be made Vice President, Benton secretary of state, and Blair would become the official editor; northern and southern Union Democrats would be discarded. In this confusion, Pierce's close associates in New Hampshire saw their opportunity. While Pierce was being advertised for Vice President by the Woodbury forces, their ambition grew.

Peaslee took charge of plans in Washington, George managed affairs in New Hampshire. The mass convention set for January 8, 1852, to nominate a candidate for governor, vice Luke Woodbury, suicide, would be an outstanding occasion, well-advertised; and there Pierce's name should be proclaimed as New Hampshire's contribution to the Baltimore Convention, without specifying which office they wished him to have.   Peaslee should prepare an article, to be published in the Washington *Union* early in January, showing Pierce's activity and leadership in the Hale and Atwood matters; and in answer to the Grund attack he was to publish a Pierce letter written in 1850 fully endorsing the Compromise.   George made the local convention arrangements.   At first he hoped to import some national figure such as Benton or Dix, but finally home talent was selected and William L. Foster, another ardent young Democrat, a relative of George's, was chosen to make the nominating speech.   The resolution was carefully phrased, avoiding a definite statement; it merely presented Pierce as " worthy . . . of high place among the names of the eminent citizens who will be conspicuously before the national convention."   In Washington, Peaslee found it necessary to bring pressure upon the editors of the *Union* to publish his article, as they were not anxious to do anything which might antagonize senatorial candidates; but the pressure was brought, and Donelson prepared an editorial to explain carefully that the *Union* had no favorites. Three days after the New Hampshire convention met, the *Union* published the article.   The chess players had moved a pawn.

*   *   *

Pierce was spending the winter in his usual routine and had survived a very dreary season.   The snow had been unusually heavy with a fall totaling thirteen feet.   Late in October the first storm had ushered in winter and the last came in April. Sleighing was good from November until March.   The thermometer had borne mute record of the ruthlessness of the cold, twice drawing its mercury down to 20° below zero.   Those interested in the weather recorded that the sun shone but rarely.

No winter, however frigid, could congeal New Hampshire's political enthusiasms, and the January convention put the heating ingenuity of the householders through that acid test of warming the " spare room."   The Democratic " organization " needed enthusiasm, because Atwood again was leading the free soil forces, attacking Pierce, the " Regency," and the " Concord Clique."   " Dictator " Pierce felt called to the stump, and while preparing for the January convention he invaded Atwood's territory to make a speech at New Boston on the day after New Year's, 1852, a speech he was long to remember.

Through two hours and a half he harangued the crowd in defense of himself, refuting the charges that he was a " boss " and a slave sympathizer. Slavery as " involuntary servitude " was recognized in the Constitution where it had its place as part of one of the great compromises which had made possible the adoption of that instrument of government. The difficulties attendant upon the drawing up and ratifying of that document he described graphically and at length, dilating upon the great benefits which the Constitution and the Union had bestowed upon the country. The main part of his speech, however, he devoted to explaining his treatment of Atwood. He declared he had ever been his friend and had sought earnestly to avoid a break, but when Atwood persisted in his dangerous and un-Democratic free soilism, there was no alternative but the course adopted.

During the progress of this speech he was heckled, especially about the fugitive slave law. In answer to questions he admitted that he disliked the law and thought it inhumane; but he quickly veered off this dangerous topic to ask if there were any Revolutionary soldiers present. There happened to be one in the vicinity, but as he turned out to be an Atwood man the speaker again had to turn to something else. The official account of the speech in the *Patriot* said nothing about any heckling; but in unfriendly papers the fugitive slave law item appeared and it was not to be forgotten. A few days later came the special state convention. Noah Martin was nominated for governor and the Granite State Democracy endorsed its favorite son for an office not yet specified.

Just how much of a surprise the action of the state convention was to Pierce, is a matter of uncertainty. He had consistently declined any opportunity to return to Washington, ever since he had left the city ten years before. He was prosperous and comfortable in Concord, and it is hardly probable that four of eight years of the dull routine of presiding over the United States Senate could seem attractive. However, in spite of his well-known preferences, his friends had seen fit to make capital by using his name. As the possibility of success seemed remote, perhaps he was not particularly put out; at least he was going to correct any impressions of seeking office on his part, so he wrote to his old friend Atherton, delegate-at-large to the Baltimore convention, that the use of his name, " in any event, before the Democratic National Convention at Baltimore, would be utterly repugnant to [his] tastes and wishes." This letter he wrote as he "thought and felt." To Pierce the possibility seemed fantastic in its unreality. The *Patriot* published his letter with the editorial comment " but we do not understand from [it] that he forbids the use of his name entirely, in the Democratic National Convention, or that he would decline a nomination tendered him by the great party to which he belongs." So the flame died down as quickly as it had flared up. One or two comments of a complimentary nature from the New Orleans *Courier* and the Chicago *Democrat,* and the matter attracted no further attention, although the New York *Herald* predicted more would be heard of it.

Having thus dismissed the matter, Pierce refused even to talk about nomination possibilities when the subject was broached, and went to work in preparation for the court terms and the spring election. The latter contest would determine whether with three parties in the field the Democrats could regain a majority of the vote, and also whether the voters would agree to admit Catholics to the privilege of holding office. Democratic success would also mean the retirement of John P. Hale from the Senate. Election Day brought a great party victory; Atwood and Hale were both decisively beaten, and great was the rejoicing. A grand jubilee was held at Manchester and Pierce sent a toast: " The Compromise Measures of 1850 and the New Hampshire Democracy: Upon the former, the latter have fixed the seal of their emphatic approbation. No North, no South, no East, no West, under the constitution; but a sacred maintenance of the common bond and true devotion to the common brotherhood."

Again there was one drawback to complete satisfaction for Pierce. The voters had refused to accept the amendment giving Catholics office-holding privileges—the necessary two-thirds vote had not been obtained. Pierce was disappointed because he felt that his state stood branded with intolerance. Peaslee was urging him to come south for a visit and he was seriously considering going. Now he replied to the letter of Charles

O'Conor, a prominent Catholic layman of New York, who the previous December had requested information in regard to the Catholic "test," and told him he would be in New York in May; he had postponed answering his letter until after the election, hoping he might report that the test had been abolished. Meanwhile, spring court business was piling up, and in Washington the players were deep in their game.

* * *

Pierce's Washington friends had found many obstacles to contend with. The closest friends of Woodbury regretted the fact that the New Hampshire convention had not specifically nominated Butler and Pierce. The general's letter to Atherton proved a wet blanket which made the task harder. How could their insinuations of availability be effective if their friend publicly refused to be considered? Most unpleasant, however, was the opposition close at home. Edmund Burke, who had been Pierce's friend in the Polk days, had no use for his Concord associates. The *Argus and Spectator*, the Newport, N. H., paper in which Burke was interested, still was carrying on its bitter feud with Butterfield's *Patriot*, and the rivalry was breaking out continually. Senator Norris, who had defeated Pierce's friend Hibbard for the honor, was also unsympathetic with the plans of Pierce's intimates. Consequently Burke and Norris had not been consulted about the Pierce candidacy by Peaslee and his associates, and when news of the use of Pierce's name came to their ears and they were questioned by outsiders, they discounted Pierce's availability and damned his qualifications with faint praise. Pierce would do nothing to improve their feeling by taking any conciliatory measures, as his personal relations with Burke had lost their confidential character.

By March, however, the tide turned. Butler's boom, which had been carefully nursed, collapsed, his letter which acknowledged responsibility for the recent Kentucky resolutions, and endorsed slaveholding in the territories, received too much publicity. It destroyed him in the North. Where would the Woodbury group turn? Some thought of Sam Houston. Others again sought for a new man. The great success of the New

Hampshire Democrats in their spring election was most opportune.

Peaslee and his friends sought to make the most of this opportunity and capture the Butler strength.   John H. George
corresponded with a Washington retainer, Albert G. Allen, who
had a government position, and with Sidney Webster, Peaslee's
nephew, who was spending the winter in Washington.   They
plotted anew, with occasional prompting from Peaslee.   The
latter in the meantime had enlisted aid from Benjamin B.
French, a former clerk of the House, who had made his home
in Washington.   Thus a friendly article praising Butler appeared in the *Patriot,* while Pierce's Manchester toast was published in the *Union.*   Plans were discussed for more publicity,
and the little scheme gained valuable support.

Burke, who had dismissed the idea of Pierce's nomination
as of no consequence early in the winter, returned to Washington late in March on pension business; he too had seen how
hopeless the fight was becoming and had become impressed with
the feasibility of nominating his old friend Pierce.   He set
himself at work among a large circle of prominent friends to
sound out the prospects.   A few days later Caleb Cushing, accompanied by his former aide, Paul R. George, half-brother of
John H., came to Washington to try a case before the Supreme
Court.   He was a most ambitious man and a born schemer.
With General Gideon J. Pillow and a few other Mexican War
officers, he had cherished the idea, since their service in Mexico,
that they might control the destiny of the Democratic party.
Pillow always claimed the credit for Polk's nomination, and
he and Cushing had some such scheme in hand for 1852.

Pillow had been in leisurely correspondence with Cushing and
the latter had been thinking of a trip through the South in the
interest of President-making.   After Woodbury's death he had
some thoughts of Butler.   Pillow, for his part, had one great
objective and that was to defeat Scott, and he was undoubtedly
thinking of a ticket with Pillow's name on it.   At length, he
wrote Cushing that he would be in Washington in April.   He
suggested that they meet there and that he then accompany
Cushing back to New England, presumably to organize the Mexican War officers in support of a ticket of Pillow and Pierce or
vice versa.   When they met in Washington they found the quiet

boom for Pierce in process, a boom that fitted into their plans.
The original Peaslee-George nucleus was now reinforced by
Burke and the Mexican War generals. But Pierce had declined to permit the use of his name; would he consent to a
nomination? His friends must be entirely assured before they
could continue. His views must be definitely known. He must
be told just how things stood, how Cass, Buchanan, Douglas,
and Butler were in process of defeating each other, and that
with proper discretion he might very well be the successful
nominee. He must commit himself. On April 8 French wrote
him a letter, and next day Burke sent him a similar inquiry.
The latter had labored with Grund and the same day the *Sun's*
representative had published another Washington letter; this
time he declared that all the prominent candidates were unavailable, a new man must be found. Who was this new man
to be? Nobody could say, surely, but an active few were
wondering whether they might not predict. Evidently some
pieces were going to be removed from the board.

XXVI
A STAGGERING POSSIBILITY

CONCORD was all agog this April. The spring term of the court of common pleas was about to be holden. That in itself was an event of no more than passing interest, but this spring an unusually savory case was on the docket. In the little town of Loudon not far to the north of Concord, malicious tongues had been wagging for many years. Back in 1840, said the gossips, Almira Dame had made a sad misstep. Now for one reason or another this scandalous morsel had been rolled about on gossipy tongues for many years and had become the center of a bitter neighborhood war of words, many in Loudon taking Almira's part and many attempting to cast continual infamy upon her head. Finally she would stand it no longer and went to Lawyer Butters; the result was a suit for damages for slander to be pressed against two of her tormentors, Mr. and Mrs. Kenney. So Butters went to Concord and retained the prominent General Pierce, noted far and wide for his skill with a jury. The case was docketed for April 6.

Loudon was so near, the touch of scandal so seductive, and the fame of the legal talent so attractive that a large audience was assured. To Pierce it was an opportunity to aid a lady in distress, so he eagerly lent himself to the cause and became the leading figure in an unusual trial. Most of Loudon were there as witnesses on one side or the other, and gleefully they mounted the witness stand for their little hour of glory. It was a hard trial for Judge Sawyer, presiding; these "ladies and gentlemen" had little idea of the rules of evidence; and tattle, tattle, tattle, went their tongues, with frequent interjections, objections, and corrections by counsel and justice. All that week Pierce sat beside his client, a "slight figure, dark hair, sharp features, . . . [wearing] a fitch tippet and cuffs to match." Disputes over testimony, hour after hour of slanderous gossip rehearsed by the witnesses, oratorical appeals for justice to an unprotected woman, so the week passed until a very much interested jury went into retirement and decided that for such

197

slander the aggrieved party should receive damages to the amount of $808.54. Each juryman had suggested a sum, they were added up and divided by twelve and the result obtained. It had been an exciting but satisfying week.

Fresh from this forensic triumph, an $800 slander suit, Pierce was confronted with letters from French and Burke, practically inviting him to be President of the United States. French's letter arrived first. In January, when New Hampshire nominated him, Pierce had been very sceptical about any hope for success; but the course of events since then, as reported from Washington, was changing the situation. Perhaps a deadlock was imminent, which would be very dangerous to a party so lately rent by schism. Possibly he was needed, possibly New Hampshire could bring glory to herself and her partisans through him. He suffered from a mixture of emotions; all the disadvantages of Washington were still disadvantages, all the influences drawing him away were still as strong as ever, except that he had accumulated some property—but the thought of the Presidency! French's letter must be answered one way or the other. He must commit himself somehow.

By Monday, April 12, he had his answer ready, and he wrote it hurriedly. In substance, he must leave the matter in the hands of his friends at Washington to determine "what is my duty and what may be the best interest of the party." That night Burke's letter came, and it may possibly have been a surprise as his Washington friends had been reporting Burke as hostile. Pierce was again immersed in a trial, but Tuesday night after midnight he wrote Burke a letter similar to that written French. He definitely committed his cause to Burke, Norris, Hibbard, Peaslee, and French and urged Burke to get into immediate touch with French. "I wrote in a hurry and hope he will not speak of anything I have said except to you and the other New Hampshire men without consultation with you and them." His record must be kept clear. So in the small hours of the morning the die was cast. He was definitely committed but he still doubted the possibility of his nomination.

Court continued with Pierce in most of the cases, and more letters came from Washington including one from Peaslee which detailed the situation and reported that there was less need for a trip south than had been earlier supposed. Whether for this reason or others, Pierce decided not to leave New Hampshire, and made preparations for court at Amherst. A severe storm added to the interest of the season. Hard rain and melting snow brought a freshet and the whole intervale was flooded. The train service was disrupted: one day no mail came through at all, and the trains were much delayed on the days following. But with the retiring of the waters came two visitors who bore tidings.

During their April sojourn in Washington, Pillow and Cushing had joined forces behind Pierce in some form of Pierce-Pillow combination. Pillow undoubtedly hoped to head the ticket and spoke to Cushing about assuming the cabinet post of Secretary of State if he were elected. Pillow and Cushing then went on a trip north together to round up their old comrades in arms. They stopped off in New York and then went on up to Hartford where their fellow officer Colonel Thomas H. Seymour was soon to be inaugurated governor. They conferred with him, went on to Boston, and thence to Concord where they arrived on April 30. Here they spent the night and were given a reception, but between whiles they had an opportunity for a frank talk with Pierce. Cushing and Pillow told him how excellent were his chances. Back to Boston they went, and off to Amherst went Pierce, to attend court with a letter from Burke in his pocket containing more favorable news. Burke had spent an active month in Washington; Norris, too, was interested. His other Washington friends all were working quietly, and as the bitterness among the supporters of the prominent rivals became deeper, the chances for a dark horse were ever improving and a friend of Pierce was generally at hand to mention his name—casually.

Amherst court came and went and then Pierce had to go to Plymouth session. He wanted to see Burke, who had returned from Washington for a few weeks before going back for the convention, so he decided to go to Goshen to look after a plumbago mine in which he was interested, stopping to see Burke at Newport on the way. Bad weather intervened and he invited Burke to come to Concord with Reding and Tilton, two of the delegates, to confer with him. Atherton and Ayer, two more of the delegation, were also to be present. Burke could not or would not find this meeting convenient; therefore

Pierce went over the situation with Atherton and Ayer and
perhaps others of the delegation, without Burke, on May 17.
A day or two later, Pierce went to his plumbago mine and met
Burke at the hotel in Newport. At these conferences and in
a letter or two Pierce with much caution and some misgivings
carefully emphasized his position. " My name must in no
event be used until all efforts to harmonize upon one of the
candidates already prominently before the public shall have
failed. Perhaps when the convention comes together there will
not be found that want of harmony now anticipated. If, however, there shall arrive a time in the convention ' when ' (as
Dougald Stuart says) ' the highways are broken up and the
waters are out '—then you will of course seek harmony at all
events and take such measures as the interests of the party and
the country may demand." The New Hampshire delegation
had agreed to scatter their strength and see how the balloting
went. If a deadlock ensued and some other state started his
name, then they were to vote for Pierce. Only as a last re-
source was his name to be used. The delegation went off to
visit Washington before the convention and Burke returned
there as well. They left Pierce the harder part; he had to
wait.

Tantalizing fragments of news came up from Washington.
Peaslee wrote George that everything

> appears well for Gen. Pierce. . . . His name is familiarly
> talked of by the members as the man upon whom all
> would unite . . . he has not been thrust forward in a man-
> ner to obtain the enmity of the friends of other candidates
> or any clique of the party. Two months ago I was fearful
> he would not be enough thought of to be instantly brought
> up at the convention as a compromise candidate but I am
> now satisfied he must be in the minds of all . . . the ultra
> men of the south say they can cheerfully go for him and
> none, none say they cannot. The battle is now waging so
> hot among the friends of the different candidates that I
> do not mention his name to their violent friends except
> incidentally or when they allude to it and then not in a
> way to excite alarm. . . . One thing I feel confident of, no
> mistake has yet been committed.

After the New Hampshire delegation departed and he had
seen Burke, Pierce prepared for a trip to Boston, which may

have had as one of its purposes similar conferences with Massachusetts and Maine delegates. The last week in May he and his family left Concord. Bennie was left with the Aikens at Andover and Mr. and Mrs. Pierce went on to Boston, where they visited the Lawrences and the Masons. While Mrs. Pierce visited during the day, Pierce made the Tremont House his headquarters. They all knew what was in the wind. Packard came down from Brunswick, and meeting Mrs. Pierce at the Lawrences', bowed low and elaborately saluted her as the future " Presidentess."

Meanwhile a last-minute problem had arisen. Just as Pierce was about to leave Concord he had received a letter from Robert G. Scott, a Richmond editor, requesting his views upon the Compromise of 1850, in the form of replies to three questions which he was asking each of the Presidential candidates. This it later turned out was a scheme fathered by the Ritchies of the Richmond *Enquirer* to make the Compromise of 1850 the platform of the party. These questions were: " Would you do everything in your power to sustain the compromise and the fugitive slave law? Would you do all you could to prevent change in the fugitive slave law to make it less effective? Would you veto a law impairing the fugitive slave law? " Pierce was not keen to answer, because he would have to make a public statement as to whether he was a candidate or not, something which he was not willing to do. He took the letter to Boston and talked it over with delegates whom he met, especially his old army associate, Major Lally, one of the Maine contingent. There evidently was a feeling that his views on the Compromise should be down in black and white, but how should it be done? Finally, after Lally had left, Pierce wrote a letter to him on the subject and dispatched it by John Glockin of the old Ninth Regiment who delivered it to the major at Baltimore. It proved to be the most important letter of his life.

I intended to speak to you more fully upon the subject of the compromise measures than I had an opportunity to do. The importance of the action of the convention upon this question cannot be over-estimated. I believe there will be no disposition on the part of the South to press resolutions unnecessarily offensive to the sentiments of the North. But can we say as much on our side? Will the North come

cheerfully up to the mark of constitutional right?   If not,
a breach in our party is inevitable.   The matter should be
met at the threshold, because it rises above party and looks
at the very existence of the confederacy.

The sentiment of no one state is to be regarded upon this
subject; but having fought the battle in New Hampshire
upon the fugitive slave law and upon what we believed to
be the ground of constitutional right, we should of course
desire the approval of the democracy of the country.   What
I wish to say to you is this: If the compromise measures are
not to be substantially and firmly maintained, the plain
rights secured by the constitution will be trampled in the
dust.   What difference can it make to you or me, whether
the outrage shall seem to fall on South Carolina, or Maine
or New Hampshire?   Are not the rights of each equally
dear to us all?   I will never yield to a craven spirit, that,
from consideration of policy would endanger the Union.
Entertaining these views, the action of the convention must
in my judgment be vital.   If we of the North, who had
stood by the constitutional rights of the South, are to be
abandoned to any time-serving policy, the hopes of democracy and of the Union must sink together.   As I told you,
my name will not be before the convention but I cannot
help feeling that what there is to be done will be important
beyond men and parties—transcendently important to the
hopes of democratic progress and civil liberty.

Now came the period of final suspense, and again nothing to
do but wait.   Last minute reports from the south were hopeful.
June 1, and Tuesday; down in Baltimore the convention was
meeting.   Letters and telegrams came urging an answer to the
Scott letter; Peaslee, Hibbard, and Upham so advised.   He received an anonymous letter from a " well-disposed man " in
Hillsborough county predicting his nomination as a result of
his friends' active planning during the last two years.   It was
not his first letter from this source, but he did not burn it, as
he had the last, with the characterization that it was a " damned
silly letter."   Late telegrams and Wednesday's morning paper
bore the facts as to organization of the convention and the adoption of the two-thirds rule.   Wednesday Pierce went back to
Concord and waited with his friends at Gass's.   No more news
that day, except that the platform would be postponed until
after the nomination, and the credentials committee had recommended that the Massachusetts free soiler Rantoul be ousted

THE PRESIDENTIAL NOMINEE

in favor of a conservative contesting his seat. The atmosphere at the American House became more intense. Thursday—Rantoul was unseated by the convention—served the abolitionists right. Then toward night word came in of balloting: Cass was leading, he had 119 scattering all over the Union; Buchanan was next with ninety-five, Douglas and Marcy were way down in the twenties; there were 288 all told and 192 were needed. Cass had nowhere near enough. Late in the evening it was known that Cass had lost some to Douglas and was about down to Buchanan; seventeen ballots had resulted in no choice. Would there be a deadlock?

Friday—another day of waiting. Sixteen more ballots. Strange things were happening. Cass dropped out of sight almost, Douglas climbed, then Buchanan forged ahead; Kentucky tried out Butler; all this in the morning session. In the afternoon Douglas seemed to be attaining the goal; but there was a stampede to Cass: he reached 123 and the convention adjourned for the day without an evening session. Thirty-three ballots and it looked as though Cass would go over in the morning. Pierce went back to Boston.

Saturday was a pleasant day, just the day for a drive, a drive away from this tense excitement of waiting for the telegraph, and the uncertainty of ballot after ballot. So Mr. and Mrs. Pierce drove out away from Boston to Cambridge, and to Mt. Auburn where the thousands who had found their last dwelling place in that beautiful spot lay untroubled by the uncertainties of half-desired, half-feared success. About noon the horses' heads were turned toward Boston, and presently those in the carriage noticed a rider coming at breakneck speed. It was Colonel Barnes, and as he checked his horse beside the carriage he shouted the news; the convention had nominated Pierce. The general could hardly believe it. Mrs. Pierce fainted away.

Back to Boston they rode and Barnes explained how Virginia had nominated the general on the thirty-fifth ballot, how his name had received only a few votes from Virginia, Maine, New Hampshire, and Massachusetts for ten ballots, while Marcy climbed. How Kentucky had started over on the forty-sixth and on the forty-ninth James C. Dobbin of North Carolina in an outburst of oratory had led a stampede which accomplished the result. The Tremont House and the Lawrence home were

busy places. Further news came that William R. King of Alabama was to be the vice-presidential candidate and that acquiescence in the Compromise of 1850 was to be the platform.
Congratulations by personal calls, wire and mail began to pour
in; it was all so overwhelming. Mrs. Pierce could not stand it;
this result was too dreadful. So the general must take her away.
They spent the weekend at the Brattle House over in Cambridge
in a vain effort to quiet her nerves, and perhaps his too. Monday he sat for his daguerreotype and then they left for the sea
breezes of Newport.

The game was over. The New Englanders had won. The
Mexican War generals had made a significant advance in their
campaign to defeat Scott.

XXVII
RUNNING FOR PRESIDENT

PIERCE'S hope that a short trip would provide a respite for him and his wife before the active duties of the campaign began, was vain. Hardly had they arrived at Newport and renewed old acquaintance with the officers at Fort Adams before the campaign intruded upon their holiday. The Boston *Evening Journal* started out that first Monday with a charge that Pierce's military services had been stained with cowardice, basing the accusation on information received from Concord. To be confronted by this accusation as he was renewing his army associations was humiliating, and the general sat down in the Bellevue House and wrote a furious letter to George denouncing the item. His army friends sympathized and began a rather general testimonial writing. From Newport, Mr. and Mrs. Pierce went to Providence, and in the midst of the bustle of the City Hotel they were overwhelmed by felicitations, but Pierce had a few minutes' quiet when he called on ex-Governor Dorr in his peaceful retirement on Benefit Street. In this city, the candidate was greeted by charges of drunkenness and hostility to Catholics. But the summer had only begun. Returning to Boston they spent the week-end at Andover.

Pierce was having difficulty in grasping the strange turn of fate; and the ensuing weeks of new experience and unusual life served only to deepen his confusion. To emerge suddenly from the obscure round of a local dignitary and to enter the glare of nation-wide publicity was a violent and unsettling transition. In this hour of uncertainty and shock Pierce was to get scant sympathy from his family. Little Bennie wrote his mother, " Edward brought the news from Boston that Father is a candidate for the Presidency. I hope he won't be elected for I should not like to be at Washington and I know you would not either." Pierce had never been able to share any ambitions he might have with his wife, and now his son was just as little interested. Nevertheless, they must all go back to Concord and

appear squarely in the public eye.   Monday brought them home
on the morning train.

New Hampshire's capital had enjoyed a most unusual state
of excitement ever since the Saturday noon when the news came.
Concord for the space of the next eight months was to be the
heart of the political world, and the life of the quiet town was
to be metamorphosed; for the nonce it was a national center,
an experience quite unusual.   During the last few days, Main
Street had been one continuous political meeting; the local
orators were hoarse from their florid efforts.   Now that the
general had returned, the whole town thronged to extend their
congratulations.   Wednesday evening the Concord brass band
serenaded him, and in answer he came to the door and made
his first public utterance in a " happy and complimentary manner."

The campaign was formally inaugurated by an unusual occurrence.   Contrary to custom, the committee on notification
from the national convention was coming in person to inform
Pierce of his recent honor; but unfortunately, its membership
had not been happily chosen.   Dickinson of New York felt
that he should have been chairman because he had made the
motion for the committee, but by accident or design a friend of
Marcy's, Corning of New York, had been appointed.   He had
been unable to serve, yet the misunderstanding remained to
fester in the troubled days that lay ahead.   John S. Barbour,
Pierre Soulé, Jacob Thompson, and Alpheus Felch finally made
up the committee, and they appointed Bunker Hill Day, June
17, as the time of their arrival in Concord.   At noon they appeared at Pierce's home and handed him the letter of notification.   There were no ceremonies or formal speeches, and following an hour of general conversation Pierce invited them to
enter carriages and inspect the town.   After a dinner at the
American House and speeches from the balcony to the assembled townspeople, the visitors were further regaled by a
trip to Lake Winnepesaukee and an excursion on its waters.
During the course of the entertainment Pierce presented the
committee with his letter of acceptance; rejoicing that his
nomination pointed to the " overthrow of sectional jealousies,"
he accepted the nomination and the platform, which had the
full " approbation " of his judgment.   The letters of notification and acceptance were straightway published.

During these crowded days immediately after his return to Concord, the candidate had been learning the details of the proceedings from the returning delegates, his many visitors, and the numerous correspondents who now were favoring him with their letters. He was told that on Friday, when the thirty-third ballot seemed to indicate that Cass might be chosen or the convention disrupted, the supporters of Buchanan whose chief members were the southern *bloc* (Virginia, Alabama, Georgia, Mississippi and North Carolina) met with Pennsylvania in an all-night caucus to seek a solution. Finally they achieved a plan. A nucleus was to remain loyal to Buchanan, but various other candidates were to be brought forward for defeat in order to demonstrate that Buchanan was the only available candidate; at least they would prevent the nomination of Cass or Douglas. Pennsylvania, Georgia, and Alabama were to continue voting for Buchanan while North Carolina, Virginia, and Mississippi voted for others, to see if any considerable number of delegates would follow. The question was what names to suggest. Such an event was the opportunity upon which the Pierce supporters had been figuring. Peaslee, Atherton, Cushing, French, Burke, and Hibbard had been carrying on a campaign of constant suggestion. They had obtained the ear of some prominent Virginians, especially John S. Barbour, and had supplied the Lally letter at the psychological moment. Consequently the caucus included Pierce's name with those of Marcy, Dickinson, and Butler as the candidates to be tried. Marcy had failed, Dickinson was unable to allow his name to be used, Pierce had been nominated. The result, Hallett wrote, " came from Virginia and the magnanimous South as a peace offering of union and brotherly concord to the North." King had been nominated as a solace to the Buchanan strength, and after many weary hours Hallett had hit upon phraseology for a platform agreeable to all except Virginia, Alabama, Louisiana, Arkansas, and New Jersey. Fortunately these latter states had withdrawn their objections, and all pledged themselves to " abide by, and adhere to " the Compromise of 1850.

Besides learning the particulars of his nomination Pierce received many felicitations and much advice. The leaders all fell in line. Cass, Marcy and Dickinson sent congratulatory letters; Douglas offered his pledge of support through a friend;

Buchanan's supporters felt themselves responsible for the nomination, but their chief kept silent. The vice-presidential nominee, King, was quoted as saying that though he would have refused to run with some men he was proud to be on this ticket. All Pierce's close friends and many others advised him to say and write nothing. As Gideon Welles wrote: " There are honest differences among good democrats. . . . Be the candidate of all . . . [Jackson] wisely refrained from giving his opinions on conflicting views among his supporters. It was the great error of Van Buren, of Cass that they wrote letters."

The nomination of General Winfield Scott by the Whigs gave the campaign further impetus and the battle was on. It was before the day of active campaigning by the candidates themselves, consequently Pierce found his activities confined by custom within a very narrow range. He might write letters, he might journey to one or two important centers and mingle with those interested; but he early concluded to follow the advice given him by the elder statesmen, to do as little as possible and to say almost nothing. The party leaders throughout the country could do the work, the party press could blazon his record. Pierce's part in the campaign was chiefly a dignified retirement in Concord, where he made it a point to be polite, pleasant, and non-committal to the hundreds who came north to satisfy their curiosity or to seek advantage. At this sort of campaigning he was adept, and his gracious reception of his many visitors made him hosts of friends. Throughout the country Granite Clubs were organized, hickory poles were set up and Pierce was hilariously hailed as Jackson's successor, " Young Hickory of the Granite Hills."

Certain problems which Pierce felt called upon to handle personally interrupted his attention to visitors from time to time. In the first place, there was his biography. Many were asking " Who is Frank Pierce? " and a good account was more than usually important. C. Edwards Lester had published immediately a biography under the pseudonym " Hermitage," presumably from information given by close friends of Pierce. Greene of the Boston *Post* was writing one, and B. B. French was preparing another for a New York agency. Pierce had his own ideas on the subject and immediately thought of his friend Hawthorne, now famous as a writer. He requested an intimate,

NATHANIEL HAWTHORNE

Thomas J. Whipple, to get in touch with him, but Hawthorne anticipated him. In congratulating Pierce he wrote " It has occurred to me that you might have some thoughts of getting me to write the necessary biography. Whatever service I can do you, I need not say, would be at your command; but I do not believe that I should succeed in this matter so well as many other men. It needs long thought with me, in order to produce anything good." However, Pierce overbore him and he set to work somewhat hesitantly.

Pictures were also necessary. As soon as he was nominated he was daguerreotyped many times. Engravings and woodcuts were promptly made and scattered broadcast. At least two artists came to Concord to make oil portraits, and the work of Tenney was thought of sufficient merit to be copied in steel engraving. As the campaign progressed Hawthorne wrote a friend that " his portrait is everywhere and in all the shop-windows and in all sorts of styles—on wood, steel and copper, on horseback, on foot, in uniform, in citizen's dress, in iron medallions, in little brass medals and on handkerchiefs."

Any candidate must submit his past to hostile scrutiny, and scarcely was Pierce nominated before opponents began to find flaws. There was no issue at stake, since both sides had endorsed the Compromise, and the campaign early confined itself to comparing the personalities of the two candidates in order to disprove the qualifications of one or the other. Abuse was the order of the day. Pierce was branded as a coward, a drunkard, and an anti-Catholic. The first of these charges angered him and his friends rushed to his rescue by publishing testimonials. The second charge was carried on largely by whispering and was met by certificates of character from medical and clerical friends. Neither of these two was calculated to do much harm, but the third was perilous. Religious antagonism was reviving, and the recent influx of a large Irish population made it politically dangerous. If the Catholics should support Scott, their influence might be deciding. The weak point in Pierce's position on this question was the fact that New Hampshire had refused to abandon the Catholic exclusion provision in her constitution. As the Granite State was predominantly Democratic, foes of Pierce immediately charged that the Democrats of New Hampshire must be anti-Catholic or they would have voted out this constitutional provision. Much was made of this charge in New York and Philadelphia, and Pierce's friends were somewhat at a loss how to meet it. Among New York Catholics his correspondent, the prominent Charles O'Conor, defended him, producing the letter Pierce had written in March; and in Philadelphia, George M. Dallas explained the situation in a public speech. The Democrats prepared to prove that the clause was defeated because a two-thirds vote was required for approval and the party could not control so large a proportion of the vote of the state. To this end campaign documents relating the facts were distributed by the national committee.

Pierce devoted considerable attention to this issue himself. He began correspondence with Dr. William J. Barry in Baltimore, who had the ear of Archbishop Purcell, and with George F. Emory of Boston, who had influence with the Catholic press and the editors of the *American Celt* and the Boston *Pilot*. Besides communicating with these two men, he wrote to several others, such as James May of Pittsburgh and John E. Warren of Plattsburgh. Soulé undertook to interest Kossuth in using his influence with the foreign vote, and Democrats generally worked vigorously to counteract prejudice. The only public notice the candidate gave the troubled question was the publication of a letter he wrote June 30, declining to attend a Fourth of July celebration in Philadelphia. In it he referred gracefully to the services of the foreign-born in the American Revolution.

The other troublesome issue with which Pierce had to cope was slavery. In spite of the fact that both parties had accepted the Compromise of 1850 as the final word, the dreaded question could not be avoided. His New Boston speech, made the previous winter, appeared in the *Republic*. In it he had characterized the fugitive slave law as inhumane and opposed to moral right but had given his opinion that it ought to be enforced and accepted as a part of the Compromise. Immediately the New Hampshire men in Washington were called upon to explain, and a lively correspondence ensued. Pierce presumably was puzzled. He did not remember exactly what he had said. He had been " unwell " at the time and his rapid fire method of speaking extemporaneously made it difficult for him to recall

his remarks with any definiteness. He convinced himself, however, that his meaning had been distorted, and wrote his friends
that he had been misrepresented. A statement to this effect
which he made to De Leon, editor of the *Southern Press*, was
published; and some affidavits from auditors of the speech were
produced to prove that the words had not been uttered. The
opposition obtained counter affidavits and a pamphlet war ensued. A. G. Brown of Mississippi wrote Pierce at Peaslee's
request that the " South was satisfied." Southern Democrats
cared little what he had said, but they did not want the Whigs
to have any advantage. Pierce himself never made a specific
denial, but contented himself with general remarks about misrepresentation and distortion of the truth.

In such wise the campaign drifted somewhat listlessly through
July. Concord was terribly hot that summer; day after day of
drought had parched and scorched the grass, had thickly over-
laden the streets with dust, and had added nothing to the comfort of the candidate who was besieged by indefatigable visitors
and deluged by mail. His thoughts turned to a vacation, and
after considering a trip to Fortress Monroe he finally chose Rye
Beach.

Most of New Hampshire is either pleasant plains or granite
hills, but in one corner lies a stretch of beach which seems like
an outlet for that self-contained and pent up state. The shore
presents a rocky surface for the waves to beat or to caress as
befits their mood. Off on the horizon are the Isles of Shoals,
rocks scornful of the sea, where travelers may find their haven
seemingly in the very bosom of the temperamental ocean. Like
many another of his fellow citizens Pierce and his family sought
the sea. They made their way thither encouraged by the news
of party victories in Iowa, Missouri, and even North Carolina,
home of William A. Graham, the Whig nominee for Vice President.

Rye Beach, especially the Ocean House, became a Mecca
during August, and the hotel proprietors rejoiced. Mississippi-
ans, Louisianians, Wisconsinites, travelers from every corner
came, and the general was constantly occupied. His secretary,
Sidney Webster, was with him. Minot sent packages of letters.
Caleb Cushing sailed up occasionally from Newburyport in his
fishing boat. Politics and the campaign were the all-pervasive

topics and the interest was general. Mrs. Pierce alone remained aloof. She alternated between sickness and health, but gradually improved and began to look forward " with less despondency to her brilliant fate that is, when she feels comfortably well, at other times the expectation seems too heavy to be borne." She was somewhat comforted by the presence of friends and relatives. Her sister, Mary Aiken, and her aunt, Abby Means, both waxed enthusiastic over the prospect. They found the general in high fettle behaving " just like a good noble soul," and Mrs. Means was " never more sensible of his charming manners."

Pierce moved about more during this period of the campaign. Occasionally he went over to Portsmouth. When Hillsborough was made the scene of a great barbecue to which all prominent Democrats in the land were invited, he went back as far as Concord and on August 18 greeted many of the enormous throng who were passing on to the rally. The next day the officers of the famous Ninth held their reunion at Concord and Pierce made them one of his few speeches of the summer, avoiding politics. Later on, he went to see Hawthorne and about the first of September visited Portland and Brunswick where he and Hawthorne attended the fiftieth anniversary of the admission of the first students to Bowdoin. Here he met a few of his old friends and naturally shone forth as one of the most distinguished sons.

Pierce and Hawthorne came back to New Hampshire together and the latter went to the Isles of Shoals where Pierce joined him for a few hours. The biography was printed about this time and presumably Pierce never knew what this little volume cost its author. To the general's unreflecting mind it was all very simple. Hawthorne was an author, authors wrote biographies, he needed a biography, what was easier? But to the more sensitive artist it had been difficult. Writing was a matter of brooding and inspiration, of fancy and creation, and the necessary hurry was foreign to his mode of production. He had done it, however, but never deemed this effort worthy of inclusion with his other works.

As fall approached, efforts redoubled and the uncertainty increased. Pierce continued to be plagued by slanders. In September the *Old Defender*, a Baltimore paper, published the

statement that while in Mexico Pierce had had his face slapped
by a brother officer, Magruder.   The general was sensitive about
his courage and military prowess and he immediately wired a
denial; but how could he disprove the charge?   Magruder was
in California.   Besides, there had been a dispute while Magruder was in a " peculiar state of mind," but no blows.   While
Pierce was worrying over this, he received a very friendly letter from Magruder himself which showed the best possible
feeling.   Thus armed, Pierce rejoiced that Providence had
interposed to " vindicate the truth."   The press now easily disposed of the charge.   Accusations of intemperance also continued to be whispered, and when some one wrote asking him
to make up his mind " not to allow another glass of intoxicating
liquor of any description to enter his lips as a beverage," he
replied that there was no occasion to make such a resolution.
" It was formed long since . . . and will never be shaken."

The time for the important fall elections which served as
barometers was at hand, and attention was focused on Pennsylvania.   New Hampshire speakers were sent thither, and
Foster, Whipple, and Morrison stumped the state to show the
Keystone voters what New Hampshire was like.   They zealously
combated attempts to alienate the Catholic vote, and when October 12 came the voters turned out to give the state to the
Democrats.   Such a victory, coupled with similar triumphs in
Ohio and Indiana, called for a celebration in Concord, and two
hundred marched to Pierce's home to demand a speech.   He
had not expected them and was not very graceful in expressing
his surprise.   He told his neighbors that he refused to permit
himself any elation at the result; he would calmly trust in the
wisdom of his fellow citizens.

He tried to divert himself with fall court duties and made an
occasional trip to Boston, but the last few weeks were not con-
ducive to calm.   Fortunately visitors continued to seek him
and they were not all men.   Charming and vivacious Mrs. Senator Clay of Alabama, who was ailing sufficiently to make it
necessary for her to visit most of the health resorts that summer, came to visit the general, accompanied by her brother.
Arriving unannounced, they went immediately to a hotel which
had assumed the name of the Pierce House.   When the Democratic candidate heard of her arrival he hastened to inform her

that she was in a Whig hostelry and she immediately and indignantly left for an abode of the true faith. Pierce gallantly attended her and took her for a drive at five o'clock the next morning, pointing out the show places of Concord—the capitol, his house, Count Rumford's former home and the insane asylum, talking volubly all the while. Mrs. Clay shortly departed for another cure, an enthusiastic campaigner. Meanwhile most of his local friends were away on the stump. Those who knew the candidate were much in demand, especially in New York, to give a personal touch to the campaigning for their comparatively unknown friend. So Pierce had sent them on with letters of introduction and Atherton, Low, George and others were leading an exciting and a glorious life. They spoke often, mingled with the politicians and wrote home apprehensive reports. They worried Pierce about finances. The national committee had hoped to collect more than $20,000 by levying an assessment of $100 on each congressional district. They had looked for $60,000 from the financial districts: $25,-000 from Wall street, $15,000 from Chestnut street (Philadelphia), $10,000 from State street (Boston) and $10,000 from Baltimore. But it had been slow in coming in. At the last minute they were rescued by August Belmont, who assumed the burden. The Whigs, too, worried Pierce, with their plots for fusion with the Free Soil party which had nominated his arch enemy, John P. Hale, for President. Some of the reports of this fusion were very discouraging. Moreover, his friends feared that the New York vote would be lost because of the Marcy-Dickinson feud. Thus the last weeks passed—broken, as the campaign drew to a close, by a long foreseen sorrow. On October 24 Daniel Webster died, and the nation turned to brief mourning. Concord went to the capitol to do him honor, and Pierce added his eulogy to those delivered by Judge Perley and Colonel Kent. His tribute to Webster, like his remarks on the death of Clay in June, gave him an opportunity to stress his praise of the Compromise measures.

The general attended the funeral at Marshfield in company with the city officials of Boston, but the night previous he had spent at the home of J. E. Thayer in Boston. He had ascertained from John V. L. Pruyn, who had been to see him at Concord, that Marcy was in the city, and he sent for him. The two had quite a talk and Pierce learned much of the New York situation and the difficulties he would have to face if elected. The next day the open-air funeral proved very impressive, and it served to relieve the tension of waiting.

The end was at hand, the suspense could not last much longer. Election Day came, and as the returns straggled in the result was soon apparent. The Mexican War generals could now rest content. Scott's political ambitions were permanently frustrated. By eleven that evening, Pierce realized that he was to be the next President of the United States. He allowed no demonstration and next morning he went back into the land of hills where at his sacred places, his birthplace, his old familiar haunts, his father's grave, he sought to take courage for his overwhelming task. He could hardly sense it; but he, Franklin Pierce, was to reign in the chair of Andrew Jackson.

XXVIII

PREPARING TO BE A STATESMAN

WHEN Pierce returned from Hillsborough Friday, November 5,
to prepare for his new task he was deeply conscious of heavy
responsibility. This responsibility was twofold, for he was both
President-elect and titular chief of a powerful and victorious
party. His position was likely to be difficult because of the
bitterness of sectional rivalry. The disunion crisis of 1850
barely had been averted by the compromise of that year, and
while the country was at the moment calm, Pierce was too fully
alive to the dangers just escaped not to realize that skillful administration would be necessary to maintain equilibrium.
Politically, his situation was difficult because of the factional
organization of his party and the size of his victory; he had
carried all states except four, Vermont, Massachusetts, Kentucky, and Tennessee.* In 1848 the party had been badly split,
in 1852 it had been wondrously united. Could this harmony
be maintained? Too many would want rewards and there
were not nearly enough positions to go around; the ideals and
interests of the factions were so divergent that quarrels were
bound to arise.

These problems called for no small skill and there was much
speculation as to how this comparatively unknown and inexperienced man would handle the situation. Opinions varied.
Hawthorne, fresh from writing Pierce's life, summed it up to
their mutual friend Bridge.

* The electoral vote was 254 to 42. The popular vote stood

Pierce	1,601,274
Scott	1,386,580
Hale	155,825
Webster	7,425
Troup	3,300
Broome	4,485

Pierce's majority was under 50,000 in a vote of over 3,100,000. In the
free states he was a minority candidate; 14,000 more votes were cast
against him than for him.

I have come seriously to the conclusion that he has in him many of the chief elements of a great ruler. His talents are administrative, he has a subtle faculty of making affairs roll onward according to his will, and of influencing their course without showing any trace of his action. There are scores of men in the country that seem brighter than he is, but [he] has the directing mind, and will move them about like pawns on a chess-board, and turn all their abilities to better purpose than they themselves could do. . . . He is deep, deep, deep. But what luck withal! Nothing can ruin him.

So spoke his friend. In Boston, R. H. Dana, Jr., wrote in his diary the day after election, " The country ' gone with a rush ' [for Pierce]. A New Hampshire Democratic, doughface, militia colonel, a kind of third-rate county, or at most, state politician, President of the United States! " So spake State Street. Would he measure up to the expectations of Hawthorne or was he cast in the mould described by Dana? [1] *

His two immediate problems were the selection of a cabinet and the preparation of an inaugural; the one would provide the organization, the other the principles which would harmonize section and faction, and advance the interests of nation and party. During the summer he had had much time to think over the possibilities, but the uncertainties of the campaign had prevented crystallization of his thoughts. With the result finally determined, plans could be definitely decided upon and ideas formulated.

Before he could come to any conclusions, a purely local question assumed disproportionate importance in Pierce's mind. John P. Hale's term in the Senate was about to expire, the Democrats possessed a comfortable majority in the legislature, and his successor was to be chosen at the winter session just assembling. Pierce was fully alive to the importance of his relations with the Senate and was very anxious to have ex-Senator Charles G. Atherton for his personal representative in that body. He and Atherton had long been on the stage together and Atherton was well versed in senatorial ways. In fact Pierce considered this senatorship no less important than a cabinet position and set himself to press Atherton upon his party caucus. All candidates acquiesced except John S. Wells

* The numbered notes are found at the end of the volume.

and Edmund Burke, who had always been independent of the
"Concord regency." At the moment, their truculence accomplished nothing. Atherton was elected to be the President's experienced spokesman. But Burke believed he had been defeated by false charges and he was to cherish a grievance.[2]

Meanwhile, in the major problems before him, Pierce was
progressing toward solution. He very largely kept his own
counsel and his circle of intimates was limited: in Concord,
Senator-elect Atherton and Congressman Peaslee, his partner
Josiah Minot and perhaps one or two others; at Boston, a
small coterie. Concord was not suitable for private conferences
as it was off the beaten track of travel and besides was so
small that the arrival of distinguished strangers was sure to
be noted. To avoid publicity, Pierce went often to Boston and
met the important politicians like Marcy at the Tremont House,
where arrivals were not such an event. Here Caleb Cushing
and Charles G. Greene received his confidences. Cushing particularly struck Pierce as a man of many ideas and active mentality. Pierce requested men like Jefferson Davis, whose names
might cause comment, to address to Greene telegrams intended
for himself; and he had them enclose their letters in two
envelopes, the outer bearing Greene's name, thus insuring to
his plans that secrecy he was determined to maintain. In such
an environment the general outlines of policy were worked out
during November.

Accident dictated the first step. In his immense congratulatory mail he found a letter from his former war chief, William
L. Marcy, who not only congratulated him but invited him to
accompany him on a southern trip, which he was making for
the benefit of his invalid son. As Marcy stated his intention of
sailing soon for Savannah, Pierce realized he must act quickly
if he wished more of his advice. He had been impressed at
their recent meeting. Marcy was certainly of cabinet stature,
besides he was well versed in the complexities of New York
politics. The situation in the Empire State had been thrust
upon Pierce by various delegations during the summer, and he
knew that he had three factions to deal with, whereas Polk had
been troubled by but two. The old barnburner-Van Buren-
free soil group, after bolting in 1848, had come back to the party
fold. Their return had split the hunker or anti-free soil faction

into two parts; one group, the " soft-shells " or " softs," had co-operated in the reunion and sought to forget the past; to this Marcy belonged. The other section, the " hard-shells " or " hards," opposed the reunion and demanded that the " barn-burners " be punished; Daniel S. Dickinson was their prophet. All three groups had supported Pierce and the Baltimore plat-form in 1852; therefore the President-elect knew that all would expect recognition and patronage. With this in mind, he telegraphed Marcy November 11, asking him to come to Boston for an interview.

On the day set for their conference, the complexities of the New York affair were further demonstrated. Just before Pierce took the train for Boston, a delegation of " hards " headed by Augustus Schell, representing the " General Committee of the Democratic party of New York City," arrived in Concord to offer him the hospitality of their city and to enlighten the President-elect upon the desirability of appointing Dickinson to a cabinet position. As Pierce was on the point of departure, they decided to accompany him and discuss the situation in Boston that evening. There was some talk on the train going in, from which the " hards " gathered that their stock was not very high; and when they came to Pierce's room that evening and found Marcy there, they were much concerned for the fu-ture. As Pierce kept Marcy with him during the entire inter-view the delegation obtained little satisfaction from their trip. When alone, Pierce and Marcy went carefully over the situation. Pierce told Marcy that he wanted to harmonize the New York factions and wished a cabinet member from that state to direct the work; he had thought of Marcy or John A. Dix, prominent " barnburner "; Marcy as occupying a middle ground might be best, but he had bitter enemies; so had Dix. Dickinson who was opposed to harmony would not do at all. Another diffi-culty was the fact that Marcy had been a member of the Polk cabinet. How could he take him and not Buchanan? All told, it was a vexing problem. Marcy went away with the impres-sion that whatever happened, Dickinson would not be favored and that Pierce was considering him or Dix. The matter was left open and Marcy sailed for the south.[3] Buchanan also was considered as a possible secretary of state, a natural choice as he had held the office before and had been a leading contender at Baltimore; but Cushing has the credit or blame for persuading Pierce not to follow this plan.

By December, Pierce had reached some tentative conclusions. The fundamental proposition which he decided to adopt was harmony; by cabinet and inaugural he aimed to conciliate as many of the factions as possible. He determined to forget past heresies, especially the bolt of 1848, to question the loyalty of none who had accepted the Baltimore platform and voted for him. For this reason he would head his cabinet with a prominent " barnburner " and a leading " southern rights " advocate. Such a policy would allow him to cover with a broad principle a political debt. He owed the southern group who had nominated him particular recognition. If he did not take Buchanan, their original candidate, he must choose a prominent member of their clique. Such favor to the militant South would make desirable a similar recognition of the radical North. He would also need to invite one of the Cass faction, and to select a particular friend of Buchanan from Pennsylvania, as well. Dobbin, whose oratory had led the stampede which nominated him, should have a place. A representative of the Blair-Benton-Butler alignment was to be included; strong Union men from the various sections would fill the remaining posts.

His inaugural would stress a vigorous foreign policy of territorial and commercial expansion backed by an adequate army and navy; this would please " Young America " and the so-called progressive wing of the party, besides being generally popular. His would be a reform administration: economy and integrity would mark the public service and the Whigs must go. Strict construction would be his constitutional doctrine. The rights of the South must be respected, including slavery, for he sympathized with the southern fear of loss of property. His most cherished policy was the maintenance of that greatest of blessings, the Union, a task which could be accomplished only by faithful adherence to the Compromise of 1850, a policy which would appeal to conservatives and lovers of the Union. In a word, his inaugural was to provide expansion for the radicals and the preservation of the Union at all costs for the conservatives; unwittingly he had planned to carry out what proved to be a most dangerous and difficult combination of policies.

Having decided upon these general plans he sought the

men to aid him in carrying them out. He was determined to
have his own administration and though he was favored with
floods of advice from those who thought his inexperience war-
ranted it, he gave little comfort to the importunate. He began
by making tentative advances in four directions. As he had
determined to invite a " barnburner " into his cabinet Marcy
was automatically ruled out in favor of Dix. The latter's name
was put on the slate, a course which Senator Atherton may
have strongly influenced, but one which was also affected by
the fact that Blair, who had the ear of Benton, had written
Peaslee a hearty recommendation of the New York leader;
hence his appointment would serve two purposes. Dix the
" barnburner " it must be, and Pierce invited him to conference.
For the southern rights leader, Jefferson Davis was his choice
or perhaps R. M. T. Hunter; at any rate he wrote to Davis [4]
inquiring whether he could come north to discuss the situation.
Pierce's former colleague in the Senate, Alfred O. P. Nicholson,
came to consult with him about Cass's wishes; and he sent a
letter to Buchanan.

The responses to these approaches soon began to be received.
His interview with Dix, which presumably took place in Boston
about November 29, was satisfactory. He showed the " barnburner " his inaugural as tentatively written, and explained his
policy. He was gratified at Dix's warm approval and gave Dix
to understand that he was being seriously considered for a
cabinet position.[5] Davis responded that he could not come
north, so Pierce decided to send for Hunter. Just then Nicholson arrived and Pierce went over with him the question of
Cass's choice. Pierce seems to have considered the Tennessee
senator the appropriate man for postmaster general, but he declined, intimating, however, that he would accept the post of
secretary of the treasury. Pierce did not fall in with this suggestion and then Governor McClelland of Michigan was fixed
upon as the best choice for the post office. Nicholson journeyed
back to Washington to consult Cass and the northwestern leaders, carrying with him a letter inviting Hunter to come to Boston
for consultation. In a few days Nicholson reported back that
Cass was much pleased with McClelland for postmaster general
and that Hunter would come north very shortly. Cass in the

meantime wrote McClelland that he expected he would receive the office in question.[6]   Finally, the response from Buchanan came, and Pierce considered it all that could be desired.

Pierce realized there was much expectation abroad that Buchanan would be placed in the cabinet.   However, he had persuaded himself (presumably aided by Cushing) that he did not want any active Presidential aspirants in his official family; he wished to mould his own administration.   Still, he could not afford to offend Buchanan: hence the careful wording of his letter to the former premier.   In it he had spoken of his earnest wish for Buchanan's advice, of his great regret at the distance which separated them.   "I do not mean to trouble you with the many matters of difficulty that evidently lie in my path. So far as I have been able to form an opinion as to public sentiment and reasonable public expectation I think I am expected to call around me gentlemen who have not hitherto occupied cabinet position, and in view of the jealousies and embarrassments which environ any other course, this expectation is in accordance with my own judgment, a judgment strengthened by the impression that it is sanctioned by views expressed by you . . . you will confer a great favor by writing me, as fully as you may deem proper, as to the launching (if I may so express myself) of the incoming administration, and more especially in regard to men and things in Pennsylvania."

Buchanan was not to be outdone.   He replied to the effect that he was glad Pierce had not offered him a place in the cabinet, because declining it would have placed him in a very embarrassing position; so great was the pressure of his friends and the public to accept.   He did not agree with Pierce that the Polk cabinet should be proscribed; and, after a long dissertation on Pennsylvania politics, he recommended James Campbell for the cabinet or, if he was not acceptable, then ex-Governor Porter.   He also advised Pierce to come to Washington and consult all groups.   Pierce concluded the elaborate ritual with another expression in like spirit.   "Language fails me to express the sincere gratitude I feel for your kind and noble letter." [7]   Christmas Day he held a conference at the Tremont House with Hunter, at which Nicholson, Cushing, and Atherton were present.   Hunter was offered a position in the cabinet and went back to Washington to talk it over and think it out; he seemed rather doubtful about leaving his important position in the Senate and entering a hybrid cabinet with a "barnburner" like Dix, but Pierce was optimistic about his acceptance.[8]

With these responses, mostly favorable, in hand Pierce felt that it was time to give the public at least an inkling of his plans, for press and private speculation were teeming with guesses and claims to knowledge and inside information. Therefore appeared in the *Patriot*, December 22, what was generally considered an "inspired" editorial. The President-elect, declared the writer, had been called to office by the unsolicited suffrages of the American people. He was the representative of the whole country and as such would appoint a truly national cabinet composed of men of broad national views, men who would not use their places for their own emolument, or as a stepping-stone to future promotion. No section of the party was to be proscribed, members of Polk's cabinet would be equally eligible, there would be no distinction between "old fogy" or "young America." Those who were shrewd interpreters of events may have been a little dubious as to the wisdom of this plausible scheme; certainly it awakened hope in the minds of many of doubtful orthodoxy. Perhaps none took more pleasure in this doctrine than Caleb Cushing, whose Whig days were not long past and who presumably had urged this policy. Having progressed thus far, Pierce felt the need of more detailed knowledge as to the Washington reaction to his combination plan of "barnburner" and southern rights representatives—Dix and Hunter—so Atherton went to Washington at New Year's to consult. Then the unforeseen precipitated chaos.

XXIX

TRAGEDY

PIERCE's time during December had been by no means entirely engrossed in politics. He and his family had enjoyed the hospitality of the Lawrences in Boston. Very shortly after election Amos A. Lawrence had written him a cordial note tactfully offering any financial aid necessary to prepare for his assumption of the Presidency; Pierce replied appreciatively but indefinitely. About Thanksgiving time he and his family went to Boston to visit. The elder Lawrence and his sons were staunch Whigs and had voted for Scott; but they liked Pierce, and enjoyed their close connection with the prospective chief magistrate. So they placed every facility at his disposal, and it was no longer necessary for him to go back and forth to Concord so often. He stayed almost continuously at the Lawrences until the approach of Christmas, when a eulogy of Webster which he was to deliver called him back to Concord and Mrs. Pierce and Bennie went to Andover for the holidays. They had planned to come back to Concord immediately after New Year's but on January 1 learned that the elder Amos Lawrence had died. In order to attend the funeral with them, Pierce returned to Boston. Mrs. Pierce and Bennie prolonged their stay in Massachusetts until January 6 when they were to return to Concord with Pierce for the final necessary preparations before leaving. On the day set, all three boarded the morning train; but they had proceeded scarcely a mile when there was a sudden snap and jar, then a violent shock as the car in which they were seated toppled off the embankment and rolled into the field below. Mr. and Mrs. Pierce were practically uninjured; but Bennie had been caught in the wreckage and horribly killed before their eyes, the only immediate fatality.

The next few days were filled with slow-passing hours of stupefying grief, paralysis of thought and dazed half-living. Arrangements were made for the funeral from the Aiken's and for the burial at home. Their pastor conducted the service and twelve of Bennie's school fellows were his pallbearers. As the body was carried down Main Street, Concord stopped briefly to pay its respect, until the procession passed into Minot's enclosure. Next morning Pierce went back to Andover to do what he could to comfort his prostrated wife.

It had been a terrible and shattering experience to these worshipping parents, to see their only boy horribly mangled before their eyes, an experience from which neither of them ever recovered. They had been wont to forget whatever present misfortune they encountered in thoughts of their boy's future: his growth and development had been their chief interest. Pierce's great justification for assuming the burdens of the Presidency had been the thought of building a heritage which might aid Bennie's advance in life. Now this great station was no longer a half-compensated responsibility, but an impending horror. Mrs. Pierce was completely distraught. She sought consolation in her religion, and her husband was much influenced by her ideas. Together for many a day they submitted themselves to a rigorous Calvinistic self-questioning, and sought to solve the riddle of their sorrow by discovering the purpose in this stern decree of a just God. Pierce had never experienced signs of grace and was now more than ever conscious of faults and weaknesses which bore the marks of sin. Might not this bereavement be punishment for his transgressions? Mrs. Pierce may have felt the force of his suggestion, but she did not adopt it. She found her solace in a most destructive solution of the problem. God, said she, had taken their boy so that Pierce might have no distraction, caused by his preoccupation in the child's welfare, to interfere with his attention to the great responsibilities which were to be his. His high honor had been purchased at the price of his son's sacrifice.

It is difficult to express adequately the effect which this interpretation of the tragedy worked upon the President-elect. It became the fact of greatest importance in his life, troubling his conscience, unsettling him almost completely, and weakening his self-confidence for many months to come. At a time when he required peace and self-control for summoning all his powers to the big tasks awaiting him, he was distracted and worn by heart-searchings. Burdened with a dead weight of hopeless sorrow, he entered his office fearfully. He could not undertake its duties with that buoyant and confident assurance which so often in itself invites success. Unless some happy turn of chance produced a more inspiriting psychology, he was to work under a permanent handicap. His was not a frame of mind to command success or to invite inspiration. Much of the difficulty which he experienced in administration during the next four years may be attributed to this terrible tragedy and its long-continued after effects.

XXX

ASSUMING A BURDEN

LIFE had to be faced again; public responsibilities crowded upon the President-elect. Hardly had he returned to Andover after the funeral, than accumulating mail forced his attention to public affairs. As he wrote Davis, it was very difficult to give any concentrated attention to his political problems, " How I shall be able to summon my manhood and gather up my energies for the duties before me, it is hard for me to see." [1] His task was made all the harder by the news which came to him. First, he received a letter from Hunter declining the cabinet post. His family was very much averse to it, his position in the Senate was important and satisfying; some suspected he was not keen about entering a cabinet with the heretic Dix. [2] On January 17, Pierce went back to Concord to receive Atherton's report on Washington reactions to his cherished scheme. Atherton, too, had been affected by death; in the short space of a fortnight his father and only sister had died and he had been compelled to cut short his visit at the capital. When Pierce met him in the South Main Street house it was anything but a cheerful conference; not only did their mutual sorrows obtrude, but also Atherton's report was gloomy. Criticism of the appointment of Dix was universal; regular Cass Democrats and southern rights men would not hear of this honor to a renegade of 1848; he would have to be given up. Atherton's report of Dix's unavailability was further confirmed by Sidney Webster, who had gone to Washington to obtain admission to practise before the Supreme Court, by John H. George who had carried New Hampshire's electoral vote to Washington, and by the reports of other friends. Coupled with Hunter's refusal these objections served to cast down Pierce's entire structure and destroyed his scheme. Furthermore, his desire to appoint Dobbin to the cabinet was made difficult of fulfillment by the fact that the North Carolina electors had recommended Robert Strange. It was almost too much. As he wrote his wife, " If I had my energies all invigorated by the circumstances most

favorable to me personally, they would be taxed to their utmost in pursuing a path hedged in and blocked as mine is." [3]

His first step toward reorganization was to secure a release
from Dix, whose hopes he had raised too soon. He communicated with the ex-senator, spoke rather indefinitely of a foreign
mission, perhaps to France, and received a letter from him expressing a willingness to abide by any judgment Pierce might
make. [4] Thus freed, Pierce was about where he had started.
He had an embarrassment of riches from which to choose, for
since the election pressure of all sorts had been brought to
bear upon him. From New York, the three factions still
pressed Marcy, Dickinson, and Dix. Scarcely two days after
his return to Concord two delegations were upon him once
more, but he met them both together. A friend of Marcy
who saw him at that time was encouraged because Pierce
asked him for Marcy's address. [5] Buchanan's faction in Pennsylvania continued to press Campbell, whose services in mar-
shaling the Catholic vote had been instrumental in carrying
Pennsylvania, while Buchanan's opponents were just as intent
on Dallas. Various electoral colleges had offered favorite
sons: North Carolina had endorsed Robert Strange, Virginia
had recommended J. S. Barbour, Ohio had set the seal of her
approval on Samuel Medary, Illinois had done the same for
McClernand. [6] In addition, there were a number of others
whose prominence demanded Pierce's consideration. Howell
Cobb of Georgia, who had sturdily fought for the Compromise
of 1850, was the chief hope of the southern Unionists. Jesse
D. Bright of Indiana had many backers in the Northwest and
in the South; many Cass men urged him. Robert J. Walker
was always prominent. Louis McLane, who had been in Jackson's cabinet, seemed so desirable an adviser that Pierce nearly
approached him about becoming secretary of state; and his
son Robert also had strong recommendations. [7] The Douglas
men wished a representative but seemed not to concentrate on
any one. In fact there were few Democrats of any importance
who were not pressed in one way or another upon the unde-
cided President-elect.

About February 1, after many slates had been made and
broken, the final decisions were reached. Instead of his original plan of Dix and Hunter Pierce decided to substitute Marcy

and Davis as the symbols of the Baltimore reunion. Marcy
while never a " barnburner " was friendly to them; this course
Cushing urged. Davis would make a southern rights representative about whom there could be no doubt, as he had been much
more active than Hunter. If the Dix-Hunter combination had
seemed to favor free soil, the Marcy-Davis arrangement would
be more sympathetic to southern rights. Furthermore Pierce
accepted McClelland and Campbell as the choices of Cass and
Buchanan. However, he had disappointed Blair and Benton by
the rejection of Dix and he had not yet found a secretary of the
treasury. Marcy and Nicholson had brought to his attention
James Guthrie of Louisville, a very active financier and railroad
builder, who was perhaps the leading operator in the Kentucky-
Tennessee area. He had also been recommended by Blair as a
Union Democrat. He would choose him and Dobbin, another
Union man, to offset the Calhounite, Jefferson Davis. He had
received North Carolina assurances that Dobbin would be as
acceptable as Strange, but he did not learn until later that his
choice had really been a Nashville Convention man in 1850.
The last place was to go to Cushing, who had worked for him
with their Mexican War associates and with Wise and the Virginians. Wise, certain newspaper editors, and even Edward
Everett favored him for secretary of state, for his ideas were
those of Young America. Pierce had come to depend upon him
since June, but seems never to have thought of him for the foreign office, nor to have actually decided in what berth to place
him until about the last minute. There was one notable omis-
sion in this slate: all interests were represented save that of
Douglas, no real friend of his was included.

Though the men were selected, Pierce was not yet sure of the
position to be assigned to each. Time was growing short and he
must confer with them. He had gotten his inaugural together
with the help of Chief Justice Gilchrist of New Hampshire.
Now each of his choices must read it and agree to its principles
before receiving an invitation. So a series of conferences was
imperative. He saw Cushing first. The latter had been suffering from scarletina and was not released from quarantine until
January 31. Pierce saw him in Boston next day. The others
were not so conveniently located and must be written to. Sidney Webster wrote Marcy asking him to come to Washington by

the eighteenth or the twentieth of February, stating no reason, not even mentioning Pierce's name. Pierce telegraphed Davis the same request. These three Pierce knew personally, but the other four were strangers, and, consequently, he had to be a little more explicit. On February 5, he wrote identical notes to McClelland and Guthrie and presumably to Dobbin stating that he expected to reach Washington about February 20, and as he wished to have "a free consultation in relation to the formation of my cabinet and the acceptance of a seat in it" by each of them, he requested that they arrive there a day or two in advance of him. He mentioned no specific post in any case and enjoined the strictest secrecy. To Campbell, one of his friends, presumably Webster, sent an invitation to a conference on cabinet matters when Pierce was shortly to pass through Philadelphia. Not a breath of this got to the press.

As a matter of fact, he had come to tentative decisions as to the allocation of the posts. Marcy was to be premier; Guthrie, Davis and Dobbin were to manage the treasury, the army and the navy. Cushing was to be attorney-general. McClelland and Campbell were to have the interior and the post office, but he wanted to talk to them before final assignment. His inaugural, too, was in shape and he was committing it to memory. At the same time, he was putting his private concerns in order.

His law practice and business affairs in general were to be left in the care of his partner, Josiah Minot, assisted by John H. George, who was to enter the firm. Mr. and Mrs. Williams would continue to keep the South Main Street house. Pierce had a special wardrobe made for his new duties, including a broadcloth dress coat and trousers and resplendent vests. Sidney Webster was going to be the President's private secretary, despite his youth and inexperience, and his old orderly sergeant, Thomas O'Neil, who had served him so well during the Mexican War, was to be his bodyguard. Mrs. Pierce was to have a companion in the person of her girlhood friend, who had been her uncle's second wife, Mrs. Abby A. Means, a lady of independent income and social experience, who was also, as her diary shows, delightfully human. Her role was to be a vital one, particularly since Bennie's death, for as Lawrence wrote, "[Mrs. Pierce's] misfortune has paralyzed her energy entirely; and from present appearance she has not bodily vigor enough to rally." She had not returned to Concord but had spent most of the interval in Boston at Robert Mason's.   On the eve of the inauguration, Atherton and Mrs. Means would escort her to Baltimore where she would stay until the festivity was over and the capital city less confused.   Thus the last arrangements were completed.

The President-elect finally left Concord on Monday, February 14, and stayed in Boston with Mrs. Pierce until Wednesday. Then he bade her a sad farewell, ordered a bouquet and a bracelet to be delivered to her later in the day and set forth to his great responsibility with Webster and O'Neil.   He had proudly planned to have Bennie with him on the great day so that he could witness his father's triumph and remember it ever afterward.   Now he must go through the ordeal alone—and with a sense of guilt.

XXXI

THE INAUGURATION

His journey to Washington was anything but a triumphal procession. Even before his misfortune he had determined to travel quietly, and his progress now was almost furtive. His old friend, Governor Thomas H. Seymour of Connecticut, escorted him through New England, even venturing to have a national salute fired in his honor at New Haven; elsewhere there was no demonstration. At midnight he arrived at New York, but before entering the station his car was detached, he alighted, and was driven directly to the Astor House, thus avoiding the throng at the depot. Next morning he was up at early dawn and with O'Neil promenaded Broadway unrecognized. In the forenoon he was visited by a number of his old friends and some new ones, including the aged mother of John Mitchell, the Irish exile; at eleven he and Governor Horatio Seymour of New York sought to escape the crowd by having themselves rowed over to Bedloe's Island to pay their respects to the widow of General Worth. Here the sentry at first refused to let him land because he had no pass, and even threatened the visitors with his bayonet, a queer experience for one about to become commander-in-chief of the army. Also the surf was so high, that the President-elect was quite drenched and upon returning to the hotel had a chill. Thus incapacitated, he refused to receive any ceremonial visits, and limited his guests to four or five at a time. That afternoon he left for Philadelphia, where in the quiet and seclusion of McKibben's Merchants Hotel he spent the week-end. Friday morning he received several hundred visitors, and became very much fatigued. He walked and rode, visited Mrs. Twiggs, the wife of a Mexican War associate, had two interviews with Campbell, and on Sunday attended church services twice. Monday afternoon, quite unexpectedly, he left accompanied by Pierce Butler as well as Webster and O'Neil, and by 8.30 that evening was in Washington. He had ridden in the rear car from Baltimore, and almost before the train stopped he jumped off and was hastily driven to the Willard, leaving the Mayor of Washington and his welcoming committee to seek him in vain.

He found Marcy, Guthrie, McClelland, and Dobbin already in town, but Davis had not arrived though summoned by telegraph a second time. On Washington's birthday Pierce saw Guthrie, Douglas, and Everett in the morning and had a long conference with Marcy in the afternoon; in fact so busy was he that he did not show himself to the celebration parade. Sometime during the day the usual congressional committee informed him of his choice by the electoral college. After interviews with McClelland and Dobbin his cabinet plans were finally settled upon as far as possible without word from Davis; the latter would not be able to arrive until after the inauguration, so the matter must remain open. However, the slate reached the press with the names correct, although the places were not always accurately assigned.

A few last-minute changes were incorporated in the inaugural; the most notable referred to territorial expansion. Pierce had written that new possessions " will be sought not with a grasping spirit," but Washington advice caused him to change it to " should they be obtained it will be through no grasping spirit," an expression which showed conservative influence. He could not forbear intruding his overwhelming sorrow, and therefore inserted the following introduction. " It is a relief to feel that no heart but my own can know the personal regret and bitter sorrow over which I have been borne to a position so suitable for others rather than desirable for myself." His grief, nervousness over the new responsibilities, and the recent shock given his system by the accident, had combined to put him in an unfortunate frame of mind. People, too, were importunate, throngs invaded the city, and all seemed under the imperative necessity of seeing the President-elect. Sidney Webster was kept busy answering letters and warding off importunities. Already the drive for office had begun; hundreds were in the city armed with letters of introduction of varying strength, and with their hearts set upon serving their country. The President-elect was more than ever tired.

A number of social diversions added to the burden. Fillmore gave him a dinner at the White House. He attended Crittenden's wedding. Thackeray and Irving were both in Washing-

ton, and he attended a lecture by the former. The Secretary of
the Navy invited him to inspect Ericsson's new ship.

On March 2 he went to Baltimore to spend the night with
Mrs. Pierce. He found her in a pitiable state of mind. That
morning she had learned from her cousin, Senator-elect Atherton, that Pierce had desired and worked for the Presidential
nomination while allowing her to believe he did not want it.

What she said to him that night we do not know, but unexpectedly early the next morning, he returned to Washington,
leaving her "confounded." She had had much more she wanted
to say to him and she had particularly wished to give him a
locket containing Bennie's hair to wear next to his heart. Now
she had less faith in her husband than before and greater woe;
he probably suffered from a greater sense of guilt. There
seemed no end to the tragedy.

The fourth of March was early ushered in by the roll of
drums and the sound of music. Pierce arose and arrayed himself nervously in his fine clothes, with that blind fear which
always preceded his set speeches; it certainly would be a relief
to have it over. What if he should forget his speech? Outside
the skies were gray, a raw northeasterly wind made the thousands of spectators shiver, and snow fell continuously, melting
almost as quickly as it struck the ground. About noon Fillmore
called for the President-elect, and in an open barouche escorted
by numerous military organizations and fraternal orders Fillmore and Pierce with Senators Bright and Hamlin made their
progress down Pennsylvania Avenue. The throngs cheered and
their plaudits were like strong stimulant to the incoming magistrate. He rose in the carriage and lifted his hat again and again
as the way to the capitol was traversed. Hail to the Chief!

Having arrived at the north gate of the capitol grounds, the
presidential party passed through a covered way to the north
door. Here in the Senate chamber the Congress, the Supreme
Court, and the diplomatic corps were assembled. As Vice-
President-elect King was far away in Cuba, engaged in a vain
struggle with death, there was no preliminary inauguration.
Shortly after Pierce entered the chamber on the arm of Senator
Bright, the throng proceeded to the east front. Here Chief
Justice Taney administered the oath, and Pierce raised his right
hand and broke the nation-old precedent by affirming, rather

than swearing. So 'midst the falling snow and in the presence of a vast concourse of his fellow citizens, Young Hickory became fourteenth President of the United States.[1]

His first presidential acts were to take off his overcoat, and break another precedent: he declaimed his inaugural without sign of a note or manuscript. As he proceeded he warmed to the task, he turned several times to Fillmore and those behind him, and his speech was punctuated by the cheers of his hearers. Certain phrases attracted much attention and caused an individual behind Senator Everett several times to exclaim, " By G—, he's up to the mark! "

> . . . My administration will not be controlled by any timid forebodings of evil from expansion. . . . The great objects of our pursuit as a people are best to be attained by peace, and are entirely consistent with the tranquillity and interests of the rest of mankind . . . open new channels of trade . . . upon every sea and on every soil where our enterprise may rightfully seek the protection of our flag American citizenship is an inviolable panoply for the security of American rights . . . reject the idea of interference or colonization on this side of the ocean by any foreign power beyond present jurisdiction as utterly inadmissible.
>
> In the administration of domestic affairs . . . devoted integrity in the public service . . . rigid economy. . . . No reasonable man . . . will expect the Administration . . . to retain persons known to be under the influence of political hostility and partisan prejudice. Having no implied engagements to ratify, no rewards to bestow, no resentments to remember, and no personal wishes to consult in selections for official station, I shall fulfill this difficult and delicate trust, admitting no motive as worthy of my character or position which does not contemplate an efficient discharge of duty and the best interests of my country . . . to regard strictly the limits imposed by the Constitution. . . . With the Union my best and dearest earthly hopes are entwined. . . . I believe that involuntary servitude as it exists in different states of this Confederacy, is recognized by the constitution. I believe that it stands like any other admitted right, and that the states where it exists are entitled to efficient remedies to enforce the constitutional provisions. I hold that the laws of 1850, commonly called the " compromise measures," are strictly constitutional and to be unhesitatingly carried into effect . . . I fervently hope

that the question [of slavery] is at rest, and that no sectional or ambitious or fanatical excitement may again threaten the durability of our institutions or obscure the light of our prosperity. . . .

We have been carried in safety through a perilous crisis. Wise counsels, like those which gave us the Constitution, prevailed to uphold it. Let the period be remembered as an admonition, and not as an encouragement, in any section of the Union, to make experiments where experiments are fraught with such fearful hazard.

Fillmore escorted him back to the White House and then took his leave. All that afternoon the muddy-footed throng pressed in to greet their new chief magistrate. Because of his mourning there was to be no inaugural ball, so the crowd was more eager than ever. After seemingly endless hours of hand-shaking, the last of the public had departed and Pierce had time for a brief word with Marcy, who had remained until the end. Mud, empty refreshment dishes, and silence now reigned in the Executive mansion.

The President and his private secretary were not long in deciding to retire, but where were they to sleep? The servants were not within call and Pierce had not yet had a moment to look at his new quarters. After a little search, they found a candle and ascended the stairs. In the private apartments all was confusion and nothing was ready. After a ghostly inspection of these deserted, disorderly rooms so dreary in the feeble light of the flickering candle, Pierce pointed to one and said to Sidney, " You had better turn in here and I will find a bed across the hall."

Pierce was alone at last and in the White House. Finally he was possessed of that will-of-the-wisp of his ambition, so often happily lost from sight. Yes, he was President of the United States, but how little satisfaction that honor seemed to bring. If only Mrs. Pierce did not dread it so, if Bennie were here to join in his father's honor. But no, only Sidney was with him, he was really alone, alone with himself and that weakening sense of his own woes and insufficiencies.

XXXII

A NEW WAY OF LIFE

===

To awaken in the White House the morning after inauguration as the master of the executive mansion, is an experience vouchsafed to but few Americans and one sufficiently unique to merit record; but neither Pierce nor any of his fellow executives have favored the annals of history or science with reminiscences of that event. For Pierce to open his eyes and find himself, not in the cottage on South Main Street but in Millard Fillmore's bed, should have inspired the new executive with some unusual thoughts and reflections; but such is the mind of man that we may presume rather that his thoughts were mostly disconnected trivialities threaded in and out with a normal distaste for getting up. He and Sidney Webster had a great deal ahead of them for that day and innumerable days to follow. They had to learn the ways of a new house, sample new cooking, open a new office, and assume new responsibilities of unusual magnitude and uncertainty. So many things were unsettled and not even the cabinet was complete; Jefferson Davis had not yet arrived, and persuading him to accept a ministerial post might be difficult. Fortunately the Senate had adjourned until Monday, leaving the week-end in which to settle that doubt.

After breakfast he and Webster began familiarizing themselves with the executive's offices. They found them not very commodious. For business purposes three rooms were set aside in the southeast portion of the second floor of the White House; there were an anteroom at the head of the stairs, the President's own private office, and a smaller office at the southeast corner for his private secretary and the executive files, all with connecting doors and also opening on the corridor, where visitors might overflow if the anteroom became too crowded. The President's private office served also as cabinet room and contained Old Hickory's high desk and the long mahogany table around which that body sat in deliberation while Andrew Jackson's portrait over the fire-place kept watch over Young Hickory and his advisers. Here the President was to see his many callers, confer with his cabinet in a group and as individuals, discuss matters of policy with the various senators and members of Congress, attend to his large correspondence, and transact the various matters of departmental business which must be decided by him. Sidney Webster, his private secretary, was at first his only assistant; but shortly the Senate appointed an assistant secretary of that body in the person of Benjamin B. French and detailed him to serve at the White House, signing the President's name to the multitudinous land patents, all of which must be validated by that process. Other force the President had none, not even a messenger to send on departmental business. The government did supply a doorkeeper and his assistant but they were constantly on duty, so that Pierce had to depend on Sergt. O'Neil, his bodyguard, or upon the house servants, for any service which he might need. Thus equipped, the President sat down at his desk by the south windows and became literally enchained through long hours each day by the miscellany which then even more than now fell to the lot of the American chief executive.

All that first day many thronged his new office to present good wishes, to satisfy curiosity, and to talk business. The office seekers were there in full force, and carefully or openly, according to their temperament, expressed an entire willingness to hold office under the new administration. Sidney Webster was almost bewildered by a host of new and miscellaneous duties which he was expected to perform in the midst of constant interruption. The big event of the day was Davis's arrival, and it took all Pierce's persuasive powers to prevail upon him to enter the cabinet. Davis was reluctant because of his own health and that of his family. He was comfortably situated on his Mississippi plantation, and a change to Washington and its official cares was not attractive. Also we may hazard that Davis was not sure how this new association with men of all shades of opinion might affect his standing in Mississippi, where the Compromise of 1850 was not very popular. In the end the President had his way and his cabinet slate was completed.

The first Sabbath gave Pierce the opportunity to revisit old haunts. He went down to the 4½ Street Presbyterian Church and heard Dr. Byron Sunderland preach, as he had listened to other divines that long score of years before. Sunday also gave the President an opportunity to become better acquainted with his new home. The White House, or the Executive Mansion as it was officially designated, was an uncomfortable and inconvenient dwelling which presented a somewhat worn and dilapidated appearance both outside and in. Its thirty-one rooms were distributed over two stories and a basement, the latter quarters extending out from the house, east and west in two long colonnades. The first floor was largely public; the great east room filled that end of the building completely, while along the south front were the three parlors finished in green, blue, and red; from the blue room it was but a step out upon the portico overlooking the gardens. At the southwest corner the state dining room with its accommodations for the gastronomical delight of the dignitaries was an object of interest to all visitors. From the hall in the west end the private stairway led to the family apartments, and in the northwest corner was the butler's pantry with communication to the kitchens below and the family dining room adjacent on the north front. On this front also was the main entrance under its columned portico, opening into a wide reception hall decorated with busts of Columbus, Vespucius, Lamartine, and other notables; to the left the crowds found the public stairway which they ascended to the executive offices above. These public rooms were all much in need of redecorating and refurnishing; fortunately Congress had just provided the money.

The second floor, as has been seen, was devoted in part to Presidential duties. Adjoining the offices on the east end were two chambers, one for his private secretary and one used as a state bedroom. These rooms were shut off from the rest of the second floor, where the President's family enjoyed most of the little privacy they could command. In their apartment were seven chambers, the library, and the recently installed bathroom which boasted one of the few bathtubs in Washington. The library had once been the famous oval salon which Mrs. Fillmore had fitted up for a sitting-room, and which Congress had just voted to supply with books for the President's use. In this rather restricted space, the President and his family were " at home." In the basement and colonnades were the storerooms, the servants' quarters and the kitchen; and in the east colonnade a carriage house was going to be installed for the

President's new equipage. The house was lighted by gas, but was so damp and so badly heated that Congress had been moved to make an appropriation for a heating and ventilating system.

The mansion stood in the midst of extensive grounds. Directly in front of it in an oval grass plot stood David's Thomas Jefferson in bronze, gazing calmly at Jackson's dangerous balance across the street in Lafayette Square. To the rear were sloping gardens and to the eastward, close by the greenhouse and kitchen garden, were the stables which were to house the President's carriage horses and his black saddle-horse. Just beyond the stone wall which marked the southern boundary of the President's garden, lay the unkempt maze of stagnant pools and pestilential sogginess which merged into the vile Potomac flats; here flourished the mosquitoes which carried malaria or intermittent fever. An occasional breeze wafted an unpleasant stench when temperature and tide were right. In early March no place ever looked more forlorn or presented a more melancholy environment to a sad and lonely man.

Sunday proved but a brief interlude and on Monday the crowds again invaded the mansion. Not only had the inauguration attracted people, but the Mechanics Institute fair and a telegraphic convention had brought their share of the populace, and all sightseers knew that the President was their fair game, to say nothing of the office seekers; deserving Democrats were very much in evidence, and the Whig clerks calmly or nervously lived in the shadow of the axe. Most welcome perhaps of the callers that day were twenty-two of Pierce's former brigade officers who came at the invitation of their chief to share his glory. Shortly after noon Senators Walker and Phelps were announced and informed him that the Senate was awaiting any communications which he might be pleased to send, whereupon Sidney Webster went down the avenue with eight messages. The first recalled all previous nominations not acted upon by the Senate and the other seven nominated to the Senate for its advice and consent:

William L. Marcy of New York—Secretary of State
James Guthrie of Kentucky—Secretary of the Treasury
Jefferson Davis of Mississippi—Secretary of War
Caleb Cushing of Massachusetts—Attorney-General
James Campbell of Pennsylvania—Postmaster-General

James C. Dobbin of North Carolina—Secretary of the Navy
Robert McClelland of Michigan—Secretary of the Interior,
vice the members of Fillmore's cabinet resigned. They were
straightway confirmed.

That afternoon these new officials received their commissions
and next morning were sworn in at their various offices, where
they were introduced to the principal assistants. Most of these
latter gentlemen greeted their new superiors with all the warmth
which would naturally accompany the sure knowledge that they
were about to lose their positions. Davis, accompanied by the
officers of the army, then went to the White House where he
introduced his staff to the President, and Dobbin likewise presented the officers of the navy. Next evening Pierce gave his
first official dinner, the guests being the members of the retiring
Fillmore administration, and Thursday he went over to Baltimore to spend the next day, her birthday, with Mrs. Pierce.
She was fairly comfortable but they decided that she should
remain where she was a few days longer until the rush was over.

When Mrs. Pierce arrived at the White House within the
next fortnight she found that she was to have little to occupy
her. A New Hampshire hotel proprietor, William H. Snow,
and his wife had been brought to the White House to act as
steward and purveyor to the kitchens, to manage the servants
and to have general oversight over the comfort of the official
family—to hire the caterer when state dinners or receptions
were given and to take charge of the accounts. The gardens
were the province of Watt, one of the regular staff of public
gardeners which the government maintained, and the stable
was presided over by Henry, the coachman, who wished it well
known that while he sometimes wore a blue coat with plain
brass buttons together with whatever pantaloons he might have
on, he was not a liveried servant. As Mrs. Pierce was so
stricken, the duties of hostess were to fall largely upon the
shoulders of Mrs. Means.

With these household arrangements completed, Mr. and Mrs.
Pierce, Mrs. Means, and Sidney Webster developed a routine of
semi-public, semi-private life. In many ways it was not a cheerful environment or one which would contribute to the success
of the administration the invaluable elements of social leadership and influence. The President naturally had much to di-

vert him, but Mrs. Pierce remained socially alone and among
strangers; she was without any outlet and simply surrendered
to an all-enveloping melancholy from which she attempted to
find no relief.   To nurse her grief she very successfully secluded
herself from all forms of public notice, sitting upstairs writing
little pitiful pencil notes to her lost boy, reproaching herself
for not having tried harder to express to him her great love.
Needless to say the White House was anything but a social
center and the hospitality of the mansion was administered
rather artificially.   That spring social functions were kept down
to the very minimum.   The President had to hold public receptions, but with the exception of one or two evening affairs held
before Mrs. Pierce arrived, these were confined to the hours
between twelve and two.   The only state dinner was that
tendered to Fillmore and the retiring cabinet; and while Pierce
entertained a number of politicians at meals, Mrs. Pierce did
not appear at table when there was company present.   Nevertheless people thronged to the White House and delegations of
Indians, mail contractors, local militia, visiting conventions, all
sought to be introduced to the President.   Occasionally when
old friends came in, such as Hawthorne who was in Washington
in April, the atmosphere was a little brighter, and Mrs. Pierce
even consented to go to Mt. Vernon escorted by the noted author.   Such visits of New England relatives and intimates were
Mrs. Pierce's chief recreation, since she made few new friends
in Washington.   Visits to the White House were to be treasured
recollections stored up by the Boston and Andover nieces,
nephews, and cousins.

During these new experiences Pierce was as usual a man of
mercurial mood and quickly changing emotion.   His life since
the preceding summer had been a continuous series of shocks
and strains.   He had arrived at Washington tired and depressed,
and the burdens of these first weeks had added a new
seriousness to his personality.   Observers noted a change in his
appearance and a somber quality in his bearing that was new,
quite different from his generally spontaneous affability.   On
the other hand one close to him could say that he was the same
free and easy Frank Pierce who " talks and laughs as in olden
times."   But there was a change; his sorrow, his new responsibilities, and the Washington climate were combining to under-

mine his health. As early as April press reports began to appear containing news of illness, and although the *Union* denied these rumors Washington correspondents reiterated them. On June 21 he was ill enough to cancel all engagements and the increasing heat oppressed him. The hordes of mosquitoes made it impossible for him to escape the malaria, which was to trouble him a good deal, just as it had made miserable many of his predecessors.

If anything were needed to deepen the melancholy tone of these early weeks in his new life, it was provided by the death of Mrs. Fillmore at the Willard Hotel and by the passing of Vice President King. By special act of Congress King had been permitted to take the oath of office in Cuba, but with the approach of spring he had returned to Alabama, consuming his remaining strength in the journey. Eight days after his arrival, on April 19, he died. King's demise, coming with news of the President's illness, caused many to speculate on the chances of David R. Atchison, president pro tem of the Senate, for succession to the chief magistracy.

All these difficulties combined to turn Pierce's thoughts more toward religion, where Mrs. Pierce had ever found her solace. Those few visitors who entered the private apartments could see upon the center table in the oval library a small and dingy black book, and if by chance the caller looked more closely he saw it was Thornton's *Family Prayers*; inscribed on the fly leaf was " Franklin Pierce with the sincere regard of Amos Lawrence, April 27, 1842." From this book each morning he read prayers to his family and the servants, and if one thumbs through it today he will find the pencil marks bracketing out the prayers for the President. Grace was said at meals, and on Sunday the family regularly went to church, Mrs. Pierce urging all the servants to attend service " for her sake " at least. Generally Mr. and Mrs. Pierce worshipped at the old 4½ Street church where the Rev. Byron Sunderland preached; at other times they visited the Presbyterian church on 9th Street. When Mrs. Pierce was able to go, they drove in the new carriage; but when Pierce went alone or with Webster, he walked. In the White House itself there was a strict sabbatarian rule, as there had been in Polk's day. No business was transacted and no mail was opened. Indeed the Executive Mansion assumed

an austere air of New England piety, which was quite out of
harmony with the prevailing tone of light-hearted gayety that
marked the colorful social life of the capital.

In this depressing environment and under these melancholy
circumstances, Franklin Pierce was initiated into his new responsibilities and set at work upon the task of determining the
policies of his administration. Fully realizing the difficulty of
his position, he nevertheless felt confidence in the earnestness
and efficiency of his associates and in his own " correct principles." He was resolved, as he told Senator Everett, to do what
was best for the country, " irrespective of factions or the opposition or wishes of individuals."

WORKING OUT AN EXECUTIVE PROGRAM
1853-1854

XXXIII

DISTRIBUTING THE PATRONAGE

Not the least of the new President's tasks was that of establishing harmonious working relations with the seven men who were to share with him the duty of advancing the interests of nation and party. The seven presented a diverse group of varying experience, representing widely different sections and exhibiting contrasts of personality which foretold friction. Of the number, four were strangers to Pierce, and among the three whom he knew, Cushing was the only one he had seen often of late. Fusing these disparate elements into a unified and smooth-working cabinet, which was to last four years unbroken, was not the least of Pierce's achievements and demonstrated a tact and leadership which would have been more useful if they could have been exercised over a larger group.

First in rank was William Learned Marcy, sixty-six years old, a veteran in the public service who had been governor, judge, senator, and secretary of war. He was tall, heavy and square shouldered. His face was wrinkled and his deep-set eyes, shaggy brows, and close lips could assume a ferocious aspect or a quizzical look, the despair of those who braved his gruff and often forbidding manner to seek information which he did not wish to divulge. The new secretary of state had spent his life in politics, going from position to position, as he phrased it. "in learning trades." His shrewdness was combined with a sense of humor and a philosophical calm which made him an unsatisfactory enemy. He had command of a literary style which made him no mean antagonist with a pen and fitted him peculiarly for writing state papers. As far as his new duties were concerned, he was not hampered by any training in, or knowledge of, foreign affairs. His experience in diplomacy had been confined largely to the intricacies of New York politics, a limited but instructive preparatory school.[1]

Next in order was another substantial figure, James Guthrie, sixty years of age, over six feet tall and of very sturdy build, a veritable picture of strength and endurance. He was plain,

247

rather unattractive, and presented a sleepy-looking appearance which his soft drawl accentuated. His movements were slow, as he had been lamed in a fight in his youth, but he was really energetic and determined, peremptory, rapid in execution and decision, and sometimes obstinate. His life had until then been spent in business, where he had made a fortune in a number of enterprises including railroads, but he had had little experience in politics outside of the Kentucky legislature. His tall figure crowned with a broad-brimmed "Quaker" hat was to become a familiar sight in the vicinity of the treasury. Sound business sense was to reign in that office while he occupied it.[2]

The third member of the cabinet was Jefferson Davis, forty-four years old, army officer, planter, and senator. Much of his life had been spent in positions of command, and he possessed many of the qualities of a martinet. He was not gifted with a sense of humor and his mind ran in straight channels of order and precision. His ideals of administration were more fitted for the war department than for practical politics. His natural reserve, which passed for haughty indifference, was accentuated by ill health, for will power alone enabled him to overcome the neuralgia which so frequently tortured him. His thin, stiff figure and serious manner gave him more the appearance of a New England deacon than a "fire-eater"; yet underneath this awesome exterior there was a human being whom few ever knew. Of all the members of the cabinet, he seems to have had the largest political following, but his influence upon the policies of the administration seems not to have been as great as generally stated.[3]

Fourth in the group was its most extraordinary member. He was fifty-three and had started out as a Whig legislator and member of Congress from Massachusetts. During Tyler's regime he had weakened his Whig ties, becoming a Democrat under Polk. He had been first envoy to China and a brigadier-general in the Mexican War. As an anti-coalition Democrat he had been made a member of the Massachusetts Supreme Court, and it was from that bench, while he was an active candidate for the distinction of becoming Massachusetts' most unpopular citizen, that Pierce called him to his council. Only New England could have produced Caleb Cushing and only

New England would refuse to tolerate him. A man of boundless energy, vast learning on all subjects, he fairly dripped with erudition. His fame as a lawyer was widespread, and no better attorney-general could have been found as far as his legal duties were concerned.

As a politician Cushing was Pierce's gravest cabinet error, unless possibly Marcy has that uncoveted distinction. He had absolutely no sense of politics or sense of humor. A politician all his life, he had not the most elemental knowledge of its art. He thought and acted along lines of rational, legalistic procedure, and then wondered what was wrong with irrational and emotional humanity when it would not follow him. He was to be the brains of the administration, but unfortunately that group needed a knowledge of politics and human nature more than it did legal lore and the principles of logical thought. He had acquired the reputation of being unstable and was looked upon as a turncoat. Hawthorne recorded Pierce's comment that the unreliability, the fickleness, usually attributed to Cushing, was an actual characteristic but " intellectual, not moral." He had " such comprehensiveness, such mental variety and activity, that, if left to himself, he could not keep fast hold of one view of things and so could not, without external help, be a consistent man. He needed the influence of a more single and stable judgment to keep him from divergency." Thus equipped he was not to prove the ablest of political councilors. Confident in the knowledge of his accomplishments, he had never found it necessary to acquire a fund of political common sense. Had he possessed such common sense he might have been a great man rather than a millstone around Pierce's neck. Unfortunately he was more intimate with Pierce than any of the rest and his influence seems to have been greatest.[4]

James Campbell can be described as quiet, methodical, efficient, stubborn, and strait-laced. He was only forty, inclined to stoutness and could be jolly. He had been trained as a Philadelphia lawyer and city politician and had served as judge and attorney-general of Pennsylvania. As he was a member of the Catholic church his choice by Pierce was a monument of enlightened tolerance but not of political foresight, as events were to demonstrate.[5]

James Cochrane Dobbin like Campbell was a young man.

thirty-nine years of age, of limited local experience. He had been a lawyer, had served one term in Congress and more recently had been an active member of the North Carolina legislature. He was a small duodecimo edition of a man, with a high forehead, delicate features, and elegant manners. He worked prodigiously and seemed to be the most retiring and self-effacing member of the administration. His health was not very robust and tuberculosis crept on him as his term advanced. Politically, he seems to have been effective in keeping North Carolina in line, but there is so little on record about him that he remains but an indistinct personality.[6]

Robert McClelland was another comparatively young man, having reached the age of but forty-five. He had migrated from Pennsylvania to Michigan in territorial days and had combined law and politics; he had served in the state legislature and when a member of Congress had voted for the Wilmot proviso. This heresy he had abandoned when the Compromise of 1850 was passed, and as its supporter he had been elected and re-elected to the governorship of Michigan, an office which he held when Pierce made up his cabinet. He was soon characterized as the " pugnacious " member of the council and devoted himself to an able administration of his department, to the general dissatisfaction of the politicians. He was not prepossessing in appearance and was forbidding in his official manner. Meticulously exact in his conduct of affairs, he, too, had few of the arts of the politician.[7]

Such a group was the cabinet of a politician inexperienced in national administration. The majority were young and comparatively without executive training; in fact only Marcy and McClelland had ever held any political administrative post. However, they had all given a pledge to their chief to support his policies, and were a unit in their determination to carry on their duties according to the principles of strict construction and common honesty. There was to be no taint of Galphinism or corruption if they could help it; honest Democracy had succeeded corrupt Whiggery.

Handicapped as they all were by their lack of experience, they would have profited by an uninterrupted opportunity to master their new duties. Such a privilege, however, was not to be vouchsafed them, as Pierce had to call them to his office in immediate and daily session on that insistent political problem—the patronage. Over seven hundred appointments had to be made in the near future and thousands were applicants for these positions. The problem of selection was made more difficult by the factionalism so apparent in the party. Southern rights advocates and free soilers as well as national compromise men were in active opposition each to the others. The last named felt that they alone were orthodox and resented favors shown the radicals, while the two extreme groups, having returned to full loyalty in 1852 and having made victory possible, demanded the rewards of repentance. Unfortunately for the contentions of the orthodox compromise men they alone could not carry a national election. Pierce by his cabinet appointments had made it clear that he was not sensitive about past factionalism, and his hybrid ministry could not very well afford to be so. Schism was to be banished and Pierce was determined to proceed according to the policy he had been developing since his election; the party must be made a unit on the basis of the Baltimore platform, and the distribution of the patronage must not only provide an efficient and honest public service; it must also build up a loyal united Democracy.

The cabinet assembled to this task daily at ten and sat for at least two hours reading recommendations, discussing qualifications, balancing possibilities, trying to evolve logical plans. of appointment which would convince by their very fairness. Pierce himself put much faith in the workability of his scheme, and was quoted in the *Union* as saying " if a man who has attained [this] high office cannot free himself from cliques and act independently, our constitution is valueless." He told one of his friends who sought a place which Pierce wanted to give to some one else, " political services and personal friendship furnish no claim to office "; a doctrine more ideal than practical. The difficulties were immense and the President soon complained that the pressure for office was so great that he had no leisure to examine credentials or mature decisions. He was glad to leave all minor appointments to departmental heads, for upon him came the continuous pressure for the important offices. War with England might threaten, our flag might be insulted in Cuban waters, our business interests might suffer in Central America and Mexico, but these serious questions must be pushed aside to give place to deserving Democrats.

Some sort of method was devised. All important positions seem to have been discussed in full cabinet. According to one account, the council considered the patronage by states, the large numbers of letters of recommendation sent to the President and his advisers were arranged under the head of each position in each state, and these files were considered in cabinet sessions. With the opinions of the writers of these letters, were weighed their importance and standing. When these results had been harmonized with the various wishes of the cabinet, selections were made. Each officer had general charge of his departmental appointments, and when Jefferson Davis objected to some of Campbell's post-office appointments in Mississippi, the President sustained Campbell and made it a point to persuade Davis to agree. In many cases the recommendations of senators, representatives, or local leaders were accepted without much question. Pierce is quoted as having invited the senators from Iowa, Jones and Dodge, and her lone Democratic representative to tell him whom they "wished removed and whom appointed in Iowa."

The philosophy of apportionment is well illustrated by Guthrie in a letter he wrote rather incoherently to a Kentucky constituent.

> You will understand that there are some twelve full missions and with the seven cabinet offices, nineteen places considered equal to full missions and that Kentucky in getting a cabinet officer was not considered entitled to a full mission unless she presented a gentleman of national reputation and character justifying the selection over a state not having a cabinet officer. . . .
>
> Kentucky might have claimed and been entitled to a second rate place but I was placed with my obligations to my old friend Judge Brown, his son being an applicant, and with my obligations to my friend Ward and my promise to his wife, his son-in-law, Hunt, being an applicant, to say nothing of Andrew McKinley all of Louisville in an awkward position to press the claims of either or of any one from any other place in Ky. and finding inherent difficulties in the appointment of the two remained, no such appointment has been made from Kentucky.

These perplexing problems Pierce started out to solve in such manner as should demonstrate his capacity for leadership.[8] Not in vain had Cushing whispered in his ear, " General, be King."

By the end of the first week in office a number of patronage decisions were ready, and on March 15 Sidney Webster carried to the Senate a batch of forty-seven appointments from fifteen states and territories. Most interesting to Pierce were the rewards to his friends. Peaslee received the most important New England gift, the collectorship of the port of Boston, and Greene of the Boston *Post* became naval officer at the same port; Concord, also, had been in his mind and Jacob Carter had been appointed postmaster. From that date names were sent to the Senate almost daily and the cabinet continued to meet each morning. Of particular importance were the appointments to the bureaus of the interior department and the filling of the vacancy in the Supreme Court. Loren P. Waldo of Connecticut, George W. Manypenny of Ohio and Charles Mason of Iowa were chosen to preside over the pension, Indian, and patent offices, and John Wilson, Whig though he was, was retained in the land office, because of his knowledge and efficiency, endorsed by such men as Cass and Gwin. For filling the vacancy in the Supreme Court Pierce adopted the unusual means of appointing a judge upon the recommendation of the court itself: Judges Catron and Curtis brought him letters from all the justices (whether Whig or Democrat) recommending John A. Campbell of Alabama, and Pierce gave him the honor.[6]

While these general appointments were being made, particularly perplexing problems had been demanding time and thought, namely, the disposition of the patronage in the great commercial centers of New York, Philadelphia, and New Orleans. These positions were not only of great importance and from a political and financial standpoint much sought after, but in each locality there were bitter factional fights. In New York, there were " hardshells," " softshells," and " barnburners," in Philadelphia, Buchanan and anti-Buchanan men, in New Orleans the Slidell faction against that of Soulé; these rivalries presented difficulties, especially as Pierce was determined to harmonize them. Many slates were made and broken, and differences of opinion appeared in the cabinet.

The New York situation proved the most difficult. Pierce was determined to apply his rule of ignoring past schism even to the bolting "barnburners" and planned to recognize the three factions equally. Before doing so he called in Hunter and the southern group and persuaded them to swallow this bitter pill. They finally consented after entering upon " an honorable understanding that the Barnburners who were appointed should abstain from agitation." They were led to this arrangement, so Hunter told Everett, because the conservative New York Democrats were certain that any other course would produce an instant revival of agitation.[10] Fortified by this agreement Pierce called upon Dix to assume the office of assistant treasurer so that he, as a prominent " barnburner," might take his place with collector Dickinson, " hard," and naval officer Redfield, " soft," in the first rank of New York appointments. He assured Dix that he wished him to accept this position but temporarily as a personal accommodation to him; within a few months they might talk of the French mission. John L. O'Sullivan, one of the President's friends and a " barnburner," was requested to write to the editor of the *Evening Post* saying that the patronage of the New York offices was to be divided evenly among the factions.[11] Without waiting to hear from Dix, the President sent this slate together with one similarly made up for Philadelphia to the Senate next day, and the nature of his ideals of patronage distribution for the first time became authentically public. Two days later the Baltimore appointments were disposed of, and on April 6 those for New Orleans were sent in, arranged on the basis of an equal division between the Slidell and Soulé factions.

Of course such an equal distribution which favored no group was satisfactory to none except those who had received more than they expected. To those groups like the " hards " in New York, the " Buchaneers " in Philadelphia and Slidell and his friends in New Orleans, who had expected to dominate, the division was gall and wormwood. The bitterest objection was made to the appointment of Dix, the bolter of 1848, and many looked to the Senate, still in special session, to reject the nomination. In the secret debates on the appointments bitter attacks were launched against the President's non-exclusive policy. Pierce was much gratified with their failure, for on April

6 Dix was confirmed: in fact only eight Senators voted against
the nomination.   Their identity was significant.   Six were Democrats; their leader was a follower of Cass, Bright of Indiana,
whose opposition to Pierce was to become notorious; he was
joined by James M. Mason of Virginia, Atchison of Missouri,
Butler and Evans of South Carolina, and Rusk of Texas.   The
bolters were among the most powerful Democrats in the Senate,
and the press discovered the identity of all of them, save Evans,
and made it worse by adding the names of Thomson of New
Jersey and Brodhead of Pennsylvania, neither of whom had
voted against Dix.

The confirmation of Dix did not settle the New York matter,
however, for Dickinson refused to be a party to this harmony
arrangement.   O'Conor, who was now the newly appointed district attorney, was called to Washington by McClelland, and
shortly thereafter it was decided to offer the collectorship to
Greene C. Bronson, another " hard."   He reluctantly agreed to
accept after much importunity on the part of O'Conor and a
personal letter from Marcy.[12]

Having apportioned the domestic plums Pierce and his advisers now turned to the diplomatic appointments.   As appropriations for the salaries of the new diplomats were not available until July 1 their nominations had been postponed until
local matters had been cleared away.   The three key positions
were the missions to England, France, and Spain.   Pierce was
partially committed to give Dix one of these and Virginia another.   When Dix had released Pierce from appointing him to
the cabinet, a foreign mission had been mentioned and the " Old
Dominion," with no place in the cabinet, was certainly entitled
to an important diplomatic post.   Pierce discussed the Virginia
situation with Wise soon after the inauguration, perhaps with
the idea of offering him a position, and he also told John Y.
Mason to hold himself in readiness for a summons to Washington.   Wise declared he would not accept a foreign post as he
was too poor, but strongly recommended Buchanan for the
British mission.[13]   What passed between Pierce and Mason,
history does not relate.

Pierce, under no necessity to hurry, and busy with local patronage, was deliberate in making up his mind.   He made a few
appointments, most noticed being the nomination of Hawthorne

to the very lucrative consulship at Liverpool, which the author accepted in order to become familiar with England and in the hope of accumulating sufficient fees to make him independent the rest of his life. The President filled the newly created mission to Central America by nominating John Slidell, whose previous assignment to Mexico had given him some experience of a rather unsatisfactory nature in the ways of Latin American diplomacy. Shortly thereafter he wrote to Buchanan, offering him the British mission. Buchanan and Slidell were intimate friends, and had they both undertaken the task, might have been a potent pair in straightening out the Central American tangle in which England so largely figured. But Slidell was not willing to be exiled to Latin America, his ambition demanded a major post, so he declined. Slidell's refusal left Pierce free to reward the former's Louisiana rival, Pierre Soulé, by whom he was much impressed, and after a breakfast conference, the President sent the Louisiana Senator's name to his colleagues for confirmation as minister to Spain. Had Slidell been given that post instead of Soulé, Pierce would have had an expert and shrewd diplomat at Madrid and a warm friend in the Senate; by sending Soulé to Spain, Pierce paved the way for one of our diplomatic fiascoes, and Slidell succeeded to his rival's place in the upper chamber in no friendly mood to the President. The appointment of Soulé now left only one major place vacant, and presumably that was to go to Dix, although Virginia's claims had not been satisfied.[14]

Soulé, as might have been expected, accepted the post at Madrid enthusiastically; for a republican exile from monarchical Europe to return to one of the most aristocratic courts as our minister created a situation full of dramatic value, which Soulé could well appreciate. Neither he nor any of the Pierce administration seemed to sense the incongruous and undiplomatic character of the appointment. Buchanan was not so eager. He had doubts, and after consulting a number of his friends he decided to see the President before making up his mind. He arrived at the capital the same day that Soulé was appointed. The next afternoon he had dinner with the President in company with John Slidell and Charles O'Conor and afterwards went into conference with Pierce. Buchanan wanted to make sure that his appointment would not deprive his followers in Pennsylvania of the patronage they were expecting; he did not want to remain away more than two years; and, most important, he wanted full control of the negotiations with Great Britain at London; in the latter regard he was afraid Marcy might not wish to relinquish the honor of settling these questions, especially as Polk had set the precedent of conducting British negotiations in Washington. Pierce hastened to set Buchanan's mind at rest on all these questions. The Pennsylvania statesman was being drawn from the country at large as a diplomatic expert and his appointment would in no wise affect the Pennsylvania dole. If the negotiations were concluded Buchanan might return within eighteen months. As for Marcy's objections to the control of the negotiations in London, he grew quite excited and declared that the President, not the secretary, had the controlling voice. With his fears thus quieted Buchanan consented to go. His nomination was confirmed forthwith and it was agreed that he should sail for Europe June 20.[15]

With the most difficult of the foreign appointments made (except that to France) and the Senate adjourned, Pierce turned to local patronage once more and then tackled the remainder of the diplomatic posts. A long list of these appointments was announced on May 23, Virginia having the lion's share. A few days later the District of Columbia appointments were disposed of, and by July 1 practically all of the patronage had been given out. No announcement of the French mission had been made, as it was understood that public avowal of the Dix appointment had better wait until after the summer elections in the southern states.[16]

Since his inauguration the President had made more than seven hundred appointments, feeling keenly all the while the discomforts of the patronage distribution. Literally hundreds of applicants had sought interviews with him, and all sorts of pressure and importunity had been brought to bear upon him and his ministers. The various factions in the party, entirely unsympathetic to equal distribution, demanded each the lion's share of the plums. The problem had been made more difficult by Pierce's temperament. He lacked a sustained feeling of self-confidence and was desirous of approbation. Consequently, he endeavored to be gracious and accommodating to all who sought. His graciousness was interpreted by many to mean approval of their requests. Since his reactions were generally affirmative, he often was convinced by a plea and made a snap judgment to grant it, which later consideration and the advice of others showed unwise or inexpedient. Consequently, he had to withdraw the hastily given or implied acquiescence. A temperament and mode of action like this inevitably brought forth charges of bad faith and instability, the former unjustified, but the latter unfortunately founded on fact. A man as suggestible as Pierce was hampered by having seven advisers of varied opinions; had he possessed but one, or a close coterie of like-minded friends such as he enjoyed at Concord, he would have more nearly approximated the decisive politician that he had been in New Hampshire.

Yet in spite of his difficulties, he had finished the job, and the completion of it was a relief, especially as the weather was becoming torrid. Pierce was badly prostrated by the heat, for by July 4 the thermometer had reached 99¼. On that day, when some experimental soul grasped the bulb of the Smithsonian thermometer, he reported that the mercury went down three degrees. But whether pleasant or scorching in Washington, there Pierce must remain. Many administrative matters, particularly foreign relations, were clamoring for his attention.

XXXIV

SHAPING ADMINISTRATIVE POLICIES

WHILE politics and the patronage had been the necessary evils of the first months of the Pierce regime, they could not entirely monopolize the attention of the new administrators. No President ever took his administrative duties more seriously than Pierce, and he sought to master the complicated details of the executive departments. Almost incidentally in these first months, but more extensively as the patronage began to be disposed of, Pierce's ministers brought to the council table the concerns of their several offices that needed general discussion.

By far the most extensive and interesting were the problems which Marcy brought over from his department. The new secretary of state was quartered in the ancient two-story brick building adjoining the White House on the 15th Street, or northeast, corner, officially designated as the Northeast Executive Building. Here he not only presided over all foreign affairs but also affixed the great seal, acted as keeper of the rolls, directed the government of the territories, and had oversight of judicial and legal appointments. He soon determined that there were too many of these domestic matters burdening his attention; so he called in Cushing and made an arrangement whereby the attorney-general took charge of the judicial and legal appointments connected with the federal courts. With desk somewhat cleared he could turn a less divided attention to foreign affairs.[1]

Of our foreign relations Marcy knew little and had to depend upon his assistants, spending what time he could spare from the patronage distribution in study of his new duties. Unfortunately his chief clerk, William Hunter, a man of long experience in the state department, became dangerously ill, and there were difficulties in procuring the assistant secretary of state for whom Congress had just provided. Marcy was disappointed in not obtaining the services of George Sumner, brother of Senator Sumner, in this capacity, and A. Dudley Mann whom he did appoint was abroad and unavailable until after May 1.

259

The new secretary found his office in general confusion. Webster had been ill and absent for a considerable period during his last term of office, and Everett's brief incumbency had not provided sufficient opportunity for catching up. Worse hindrances were the patronage distractions. As Marcy wrote Buchanan after two months in office, " [he] had not been able, since his appointment, to devote one single hour together to his proper official duties. [His] time had been constantly taken up with office-seekers and cabinet councils." In the midst of these interruptions and distractions Marcy had to study the correspondence with the various countries in order to prepare himself to instruct the numerous diplomats, who after July 1 would be going forth to carry out the policies of the Pierce administration.

The President had spoken in his inaugural about territorial expansion and trade extension, but Marcy soon discovered that the United States must pursue a defensive as well as an aggressive foreign policy. Relations with Great Britain, Mexico, and Spain were not harmonious, and our interests in various parts of the Western Hemisphere seemed in danger. So to defense Marcy, with the active interest of his chief, first turned his attention.

There was friction with Great Britain in Central America and in Canada, friction of such a character that occasionally the hot-headed talked of war. The question of trans-isthmian communication had brought the United States into dispute with Great Britain several years before, and the Whigs had endeavored to resolve these difficulties by the Clayton-Bulwer treaty in which both sides agreed to extend their interests no further in Central America and to refrain from exercising exclusive control over any canal which might be built in that region. In spite of this treaty, reports came to Washington that British interests were being extended, and the Democrats in Congress had been quick to blame Whig diplomacy during the preceding session. No sooner had the Senate come together in special session after the inauguration, than the debate was resumed and became all the more interesting because Clayton himself was once more a member of that body. Marcy must consider the problem of British aggression, and, if any were discovered, find means to check it.[3]

The exact status of our fishing rights in Canadian territorial waters was a second troubled question, especially as Great Britain maintained there a fleet which might at any time be provoked to fire upon the American flag. As many Canadians were anxious to further their interests by establishing reciprocity with the United States, there was the possibility of gaining fishing rights in return for trade concessions. Everett had made some progress in negotiations with John F. Crampton, British minister at Washington, and when Marcy entered the department he found the *projet* of a treaty already prepared.[4]

An unexpected incident connected with the Central American difficulty brought British relations forcefully before the administration. American interests were established at the mouth of the San Juan river on the eastern coast of Nicaragua in the vicinity of a " free city," called Greytown, maintained by the British under grant from their protectorate, the Mosquito Indians. The Accessory Transit Company, in which Cornelius Vanderbilt was largely interested, had established the headquarters of its trans-isthmian route at a little settlement across the bay, called Punta Arenas. The officials of this company had continual difficulty with the citizens of the " free city " who were British in sympathy, and as a result the Fillmore administration had sent Captain Hollins down there with a war vessel to protect American rights. April 1 and 2 brought news dispatches to the effect that the naval force had captured Greytown. In reality Captain Hollins had merely landed marines at Punta Arenas to protect the property of the Accessory Transit Company when the officials of Greytown threatened to destroy it. The news caused a flurry and Pierce faced his first real diplomatic problem. He was immediately urged to sustain Hollins's action and he had a long conference with Joseph L. White, counsel of the company, who came to Washington for that purpose.

As soon as Hollins's report arrived, April 4, Dobbin replied very briefly to him, sustaining his course and ordering him to stay on the ground. Within the next ten days the matter was discussed more fully and Dobbin prepared the first definite statement of the Central American policy of the Pierce administration. Hollins was informed that he was not performing his action, as his Whig instructions had led him to think, under the clause of the Clayton-Bulwer treaty which provided that Great Britain and the United States should exercise joint protection over interoceanic communication interests, but " because American citizens are largely and chiefly interested in said company [Accessory Transit Company], the charter of which was granted and guaranteed by the State of Nicaragua . . . long before any attempt was made to convert Greytown into what is now alleged to be an independent city " under a charter from the King of the Mosquitoes. He was resisting " an unauthorized attempt to disturb the rights of American citizens and the United States desire that the American citizens ' shall realize that upon every sea and on every soil where our enterprise may rightfully seek the protection of our flag, American citizenship is an inviolable panoply for the security of American rights,' " —this last was a quotation from the inaugural.

The episode was without further consequences for the time being, but it emphasized the need of a diplomatic representative in the vicinity. Since Slidell had declined the post, Pierce planned to send down immediately Solon E. Borland, lately Senator from Arkansas, and recently appointed governor of New Mexico. His mission became all the more urgent when a dispatch was received by Crampton and read to Marcy, in which the British interpretation of the Clayton-Bulwer treaty was set forth in such manner as to " claim the same right to intermeddle in the affairs of Central America that they had before it was concluded." As Marcy said, if the United States yielded " to the construction given to [the treaty] by the British Government, very few of the objects which constituted our inducement to enter into that compact have been obtained." Therefore, before the official attitude of his administration was fully formulated, Pierce sought to hurry off Borland in advance of the other diplomats. Orders for his transportation were issued June 1. His instructions, bearing date of June 17, informed him that Great Britain was willing to abandon its protectorate over the Mosquito Indians if the Nicaraguan government would treat them fairly and allow them compensation for territory which they would be expected to relinquish. Borland's first duty, therefore, was to urge Nicaragua to make an arrangement with these Indians similar to that made between the United States and Indian tribes, and to assure Nicaragua that the United

States had ever stood by her in resisting the pretensions of Great Britain.

Next he was to urge Nicaragua to adjust her boundary with Costa Rica so that no areas of doubtful ownership might be left for nations like Great Britain to encroach upon as the latter country had done at Greytown.   Further, to obviate this difficulty, Borland was to do all he could to encourage the re-establishment of the Central American confederation in place of the five weak and quarreling states which had lately risen out of it; a strong unified state could much more easily oppose British advance.   In the meantime, the United States wanted to be as friendly as possible in order to establish closer commercial relations, and Borland was to demonstrate the value of an understanding like the Monroe Doctrine.   The treaty made with Nicaragua during the last administration was deemed unsatisfactory, because it contained an article concerning an interoceanic canal supposedly at variance with the Clayton-Bulwer treaty; consequently Borland was to endeavor to conclude another treaty without that article and in the meantime do all he could to aid the work of the Accessory Transit Company.[5]   Borland delayed starting because of ill health, but in spite of administration apprehensions no new difficulties arose.

Having thus instructed Borland to resist British pretensions, Pierce and Marcy next had to devise instructions for Buchanan, and define therein their official attitude toward the Clayton-Bulwer treaty.   Marcy had been in correspondence with Clayton and Buchanan as to its meaning, and he had been studying it himself, only to find it more enigmatical, the longer he pored over it.   The preparation of these instructions brought up Pierce's earlier agreement with Buchanan that he should have full charge of all British negotiations in London to further his scheme for trading off Canadian reciprocity for British retirement from Central America.   Since the date of this agreement, Marcy had become more and more convinced that Canadian matters should be taken up immediately and concluded with Crampton, especially as Great Britain had just renewed her naval force in those waters and war might break out at any time.   As the weeks passed and Buchanan heard no more, he became uneasy, and a visit he paid to Washington in May did not reassure him; the President was too vague in his replies.

Finally in June Buchanan pressed the matter to a definite decision, and learned what he had suspected. Pierce had changed his mind. Fear of an armed clash in Canadian waters and his own New England interests had persuaded the President that Marcy was right. The Canadian matters should be settled immediately in Washington. In two rather indirect and clumsy letters Pierce had to withdraw his early promise to Buchanan, and practically dared the new minister to resign. Buchanan saw the weakness of his position because refusal at this point would certainly be attributed to peevishness at his inability to have his own way, and after a conference with Pierce when the latter passed through Philadelphia, he yielded with as much grace as possible.[6]

Meanwhile Marcy had drawn up Buchanan's instructions and forwarded them to him. He was ordered to protest the extension of British Honduras, the control of the Mosquito coast of Nicaragua, and the exercise of covert jurisdiction over the Bay Islands, rightful possessions of Honduras. He was to endeavor to persuade Great Britain " to withdraw from all control over the Territories and Islands of Central America, and if possible, over the Belize [British Honduras] also, and to abstain from intermeddling with the political affairs of the governments and people in that region of the world."

While considering the Central American problem Marcy had pushed his conversations with Crampton in regard to Canadian matters. There seemed need for haste because American fishermen were arming to withstand the British fleet. Crampton went north to caution the British admiral; but nevertheless Pierce decided to send an American fleet to these troubled waters in July, under instructions: " If on any occasion you discover attempts maturing to deprive any of our citizens of their just rights, you will respectfully but firmly remonstrate, and if persisted in, you will take such steps as in your judgment will be best calculated to check and prevent such interference, never resorting to violence except as a matter of self defence and necessity." About August 1, Marcy and Cushing went to Berkeley Springs with Crampton, where they worked over the British *projet*; and after consulting Everett, Marcy submitted a *projet* of his own, which Crampton sent back to England for consideration. Meanwhile Israel D. Andrews, our consul at St. John,

New Brunswick, was instructed to do what he could to mobilize Canadian opinion in favor of the treaty and was given funds for that purpose.[7] Thus Pierce demonstrated his determination to maintain American rights and interests at all costs against the traditional enemy, but negotiation after all was to be the better part of valor.

The next foreign controversy concerned the Mexican situation. Here relations were most unsatisfactory. Boundary disputes and Indian depredations continued despite the treaty of 1848. Rival American capitalists were pressing the State Department for support, and complicated negotiations and Congressional action. The Garay-Hargous interest represented by Senator Benjamin of Louisiana and A. G. Sloo's associates served by Senator Slidell claimed right of way over Tehuantepec Isthmus and they wanted government support of their contentions. The Fillmore Administration had gone so far as to press the Sloo claim, and a treaty was in process of negotiation when Pierce was inaugurated. Also, many people felt that we had not acquired enough of Mexico, and if a southern Pacific railroad were to be built, a certain amount of additional Mexican territory was essential.

Pierce had been in office scarcely three weeks when first rumor, and then confirmed news despatches, brought word that Santa Anna, widely suspected of unfriendliness toward the United States, had been elected President of Mexico once more. Shortly thereafter news arrived that the treaty ratifying the Sloo grant had been signed March 21. When this treaty, known as the Conkling convention, arrived in Washington, it was found to bind the United States and Mexico to joint protection of the Sloo concession. Simultaneously, came news that Governor Lane of the territory of New Mexico had brought the boundary question to a point of crisis by issuing a proclamation declaring that the Mesilla valley, an area in dispute, belonged to New Mexico and by this act taking possession of the region. To complicate matters further, a Frenchman, Count Raousset-Boulbon, in connivance with the French consul, Patrice Dillon, was using San Francisco as a base for plans looking toward the acquisition of Sonora, and an adventurer, William Walker, was becoming interested in a similar scheme.

To straighten out this confused situation, especially as Lane's proclamation brought protests from Santa Anna, Pierce and his

advisers took up Mexican relations early in May. They decided
to uphold Lane's contention that the Mesilla valley belonged to
the United States, but to permit no steps toward taking forceful
possession. Lane was recalled and David Meriwether of Kentucky was sent out as governor with instructions to refrain from
seizing the valley and to avoid collision with Mexico, pending
negotiations. James Gadsden, a South Carolina railroad promoter suggested by Davis, was then selected as minister to Mexico, and his instructions were pondered. The Conkling treaty
was held to be unsatisfactory, because it abandoned the Garay-
Hargous interest; but what attitude the Pierce administration
was going to adopt toward that interest, they were not ready
to decide. They concluded, however, to negotiate for sufficient
territory south of New Mexico to provide a route for a possible
southern Pacific railroad, and Gadsden accordingly was instructed to treat for the purchase of an additional area. He
also was delegated to secure our release from the obligation to
protect Mexicans from Indian incursions, and to provide for the
settlement of claims and the improvement of commercial relations. Later in October when Gadsden reported that Santa
Anna was in sore straits for money and probably ready to cede
land, Pierce and Marcy sent down C. L. Ward of Pennsylvania,
the active partner pushing the Hargous grant. They despatched
him secretly with verbal instructions to offer $50,000,000 for a
large area to include much of northern Mexico and all of lower
California.[8] Pierce, like Jefferson, was not averse to adding
large areas to the national domain. Expansion southward was
about to begin, so Pierce hoped.

The third set of diplomatic problems which Marcy brought
to the cabinet table were those connected with Spain and
Cuba. The hint in Pierce's inaugural, that he was interested
in acquiring further territory, was interpreted by many to mean
Cuba. New York Steamship interests were eager. Polk offered
$100,000,000 for the island, but without success, and the Taylor-
Fillmore administration had witnessed foolhardy attempts on
the part of American citizens to aid in freeing Cuba by filibustering. These private ventures had made negotiations very
difficult, and the flag of the United States upon merchant vessels
plying between Cuban and seaboard ports had been insulted.
Controversies of this description were aggravated by the fact

that our diplomatic officials could not treat, or make adjustments, with the Cuban authorities, but must take up all questions with the Spanish government at Madrid by way of Washington, a mode of procedure extremely slow and tantalizing. By no means the least of the complications was the evident willingness of Great Britain and France to interfere in order to prevent the increase of American influence in Cuba. These powers were suspected of blocking our attempts at purchase. In the last months of the Fillmore administration after Pierce's triumphant election Secretary Everett had rebuffed a proposal made by Great Britain and France, at Spain's instigation, that the powers and the United States disclaim intention of acquiring Cuba and discountenance such attempts by others, in a letter that borrowed Democratic fire.* Pierce hoped that Cubans aided by Americans would revolt and, like Texas, seek admission to the Union as a state. With the President's knowledge, a Cuban junto was negotiating with his Mexican War associate, General Quitman, to lead such an expedition, and Pierce appointed the latter's intimate, Alexander M. Clayton, Consul at Havana. Marcy in his first instructions to Soulé marked time, endorsed Everett and told Soulé to persuade Spain to make more flexible commercial and diplomatic arrangements to insure the security and development of American commerce in the West Indies. Our "security" was his principal interest.⁹

Having mapped out a policy for protecting American interests, the Pierce administration sought to promote trade. Marcy wrote a series of instructions to our minister in Brazil and our chargés in Ecuador, Bolivia, Peru, New Granada and Venezuela, seeking to bring about a concert of action which would convince Brazil of the advisability of opening up the Amazon to our traders. Another subject of diplomatic instruction, especially to our chargé in Peru, was concessions in guano, a commodity much in demand for the manufacture of fertilizers; and the administration sought to follow up the commercial advantages recently obtained in the La Plata region by their predecessors.¹⁰ Even greater possibilities were visioned in the far east. There lay a tempting source of wealth,

* The French minister reported to his government that this letter had been written to forestall Pierce and to strengthen the Whig position for 1856.

as none knew better than Cushing, who had negotiated the
first treaty with China. Now there was rebellion in that ancient empire, and American interests might profit thereby.[10]
As Marcy wrote:

> Immediately after the extension of our laws over Oregon
> and the acquisition of California, not only [Hawaii] but
> also the whole of Polynesia, assumed an increased impor-
> tance [to the United States]. More recently this impor-
> tance has been vastly augmented by the wonderful events
> in China, events which threaten the overthrow of the
> Tartar rule, and the establishment in its stead of a gov-
> ernment more in accordance with the tenets of Christianity
> and by the probable abandonment, at a day not distant, of
> the non-intercourse system of Japan.[11]

Pierce and Marcy soon learned that China was of the more immediate concern, as Great Britain was endeavoring to use the
rebellion as a means of gaining more trade facilities and was
asking the coöperation of the United States. Pierce favored
such a policy and Marcy so instructed Humphrey Marshall, then
commissioner to China, but these instructions left the form of
coöperation to Marshall's judgment, as the President did " not
enjoin upon him coöperation [with the British] but only cordial
relations and free conference with them."

Pierce thereupon sought an enterprising Democrat to send to
China in Marshall's place. He considered himself fortunate
when he prevailed upon no less an individual than Robert J.
Walker to accept the commissionership. Walker, however, was
not destined to go to China. His wife, who was ill, became so
much worse as the time for parting neared that it was feared his
leaving might kill her, so he declined the appointment late in
August after having drawn his expense allowance. It is interesting to note that this decision was made not long after the
administration began to speak favorably of a Pacific railroad,
a project in which Walker was deeply interested. Pierce finally
appointed Robert McLane, who was instructed to seek reciprocal free trade from the celestial empire, and was empowered to
call in Perry's fleet if necessary.

Hawaii, too, offered opportunities, so thought American interests who were working for annexation; the strength of the
English and particularly the French, in this region, meant that

the islands must be watched.   Marcy sought to warn the other
nations against too close a connection with Hawaii, and arrived
at the conclusion that these islands must inevitably come under
the control of the United States.   As a preparatory measure he
began to feel out English and French official attitude toward
American annexation.   News of Perry's trade negotiations with
Japan also was awaited with interest.[12]   But for both Japan and
Hawaii more information must be received before any action
could be taken.

Pierce's foreign policy was broader than defense and expansion; it sought to preach democracy and defy monarchy.   Two
opportunities the administration utilized to spread the propaganda for democracy and to proclaim America's mission to the
world.   Marcy prepared a circular to our foreign representatives in which he promulgated a series of new regulations.   Administration of fees was to be more exact, only Americans were
to be employed as clerks in the legations abroad, and finally, he
added the striking regulation which was to cause so much comment.   For a democracy to permit its representatives to participate in the monarchical ceremonies of European courts decked
out in gold lace and ostrich feathers seemed highly inappropri-
ate; Marcy therefore suggested the advisability of using only
American evening dress, a recommendation which caused admiration, amusement, and some consternation among its recipi-
ents.[13]

A second occasion to defy monarchy soon presented itself.
Late in July news was received that Martin Koszta, by birth an
Austrian subject but lately a resident of the United States who
had declared his intention of becoming a citizen, had been arrested in Smyrna for activities in the Austro-Hungarian revolu-
tions of 1848-9.   Thereupon Captain Ingraham of the United
States navy, whose vessel, the *St. Louis*, was then in Smyrna
harbor, threatened to fire on the Austrian war vessel in which
Koszta was held unless he were surrendered.   His threat caused
Koszta to be turned over to the French consul until diplomacy
could intervene.   Pierce and Marcy were forced to take official
cognizance of this matter when the Austrian charge, Hülsemann,
presented demands from his government for the custody of
Koszta, a disavowal of the acts of Ingraham, and satisfaction to
Austria for the " outrage."   Marcy studied the matter carefully,

and then in a very able document imitated Webster's exploit of a "Hülsemann letter," upholding American rights and refusing Austria's demands. When the correspondence was released for publication September 30 it was received with general acclaim; Pierce could cherish with satisfaction one of the few hits of his administration.[14] The new President had great hopes of a successful foreign policy, and he and his advisers had embraced a wide field of interest.

Extensive though they were, foreign affairs by no means monopolized the administrative energies of the cabinet. Guthrie entered upon his duties more readily than Marcy, as he had been long in business and was used to promoting enterprises. He found himself established in the long, colonnaded, unfinished treasury building on 15th Street, which had been started in Jackson's day. It was situated just south of the state department, and its north and south façades, as well as the west colonnade, were still unbuilt and would be as long as the state department and the President's stable and kitchen garden remained where they were. The magnificent eastern pillars effectually darkened many of the rooms, and the building was so crowded, especially by the land office, now a bureau of the interior department, that space had to be hired across the street in order to accommodate the first, third, and fifth auditors. The treasury was a complicated department which included customs service, revenue-cutter service, coast survey, lighthouse system, bureau of weights and measures, and a bureau of construction, as well as the accounting system established by Hamilton.

Guthrie, like Marcy, was to have an assistant secretary, and for this office he chose Peter G. Washington, who had been Polk's sixth auditor and was familiar with treasury procedure. In general he made a clean sweep of his bureau chiefs but he retained two Whigs, Elisha Whittlesey, first comptroller, and Philip Clayton, second auditor. He had found three problems of more than usual importance awaiting his action; in the first place a surplus was piling up in the treasury, assuming awkward proportions; secondly, the late Whig administration had not been over zealous about enforcing the independent treasury act, and government money was not all in the treasury, by any means; thirdly, charges and suspicions of fraud floated around too lightly for the peace of mind of the secretary. Guthrie had started immediately on the problem of the surplus, with plans for paying off portions of the public debt. He issued a notice that the indebtedness due July, 1853, would be paid any time after March 10, and he began to buy United States stocks at market prices through brokers. Furthermore he set about erecting barricades around the treasury. He had found that the late secretary made contracts with New York financiers such as Simeon Draper, whereby they kept public money to buy up United States stock for the treasury, to pay interest, and to facilitate the transfer of public funds by draft. These practises Guthrie deemed violations of the independent treasury act. He canceled these contracts as soon as he could, called all government money into the treasury and subtreasuries, and even went so far as to ship $500,000 in gold from New York to St. Louis, rather than resort to bank drafts. Simultaneously, his attention was called to abuses in the contract system, for at that moment a select committee of the Senate was investigating the subletting of contracts, a system whereby people with influence were wont to obtain contracts which they sublet to their personal profit. Such abuses, the administration decided, would be punished hereafter with forfeiture. Guthrie also terminated a practice among treasury officials at New York whereby they had profited to the extent of one-half the customs fines levied upon all those detected in undervaluations. His order resulted in a considerable monetary loss to the customs officials and did not help to smooth out New York's political situation. Guthrie's strict construction measures, at variance with the easy-going methods of Secretary Corwin, served to show the world that the Pierce administration was determined to prevent corruption such as Galphinism. The ruthless secretary earned the title of " the prairie plow." [15]

When Davis entered the war department, northwest of the White House, he like Guthrie found his office space very much crowded and his records in danger of fire. The war department, like the treasury, housed a bureau belonging to the interior department. It was the Indian office, and the secretary of war was renting the Winder building across 17th Street which he shared with the pension office, another bureau of the interior department. Davis did not have as many patronage worries as some of his colleagues, but his administration was hampered by the fact that the commander of the army, Major General Scott, maintained his headquarters in New York rather than be in Washington near Davis. They enlivened the next four years with an almost continuous quarrel. Davis brought to the war department his West Point training and his military experience; he intended to standardize the army and bring it up to date in equipment and organization. To this end he began a thorough study of the American war machine in comparison with those of Europe. Problems of immediate concern were the occasional Indian uprisings which confronted the secretary with the puzzle of how to stretch a small army along a far-flung frontier. Moreover, at its last session Congress had voted the war department an appropriation for equipping and dispatching engineering detachments to survey the possible routes for a railroad to the Pacific coast. Davis, who had been much interested in this project while in Congress, immediately organized four such expeditions; the first under Isaac I. Stevens, newly appointed governor of Washington territory, set out under instructions early in April, and the other three under army officers departed in May. Their surveys were to mark the routes which were to be used by four of the future great transcontinental railroads.[16]

Dobbin, situated just south of Davis, was perhaps more comfortable as to quarters; but he had a run-down navy and an age-ridden personnel to worry over. Besides the routine of supervising the various squadrons scattered over the seven seas Dobbin had the oversight of several special expeditions. Hollins was looking after American interests in Central America; a fleet had to be assembled and sent to Canadian waters; Page's expedition, which was exploring the La Plata region, was continued by Dobbin; and he organized a surveying party to locate a route for a Panama canal. Perry's expedition to open Japan to our commerce had left not long before the Pierce administration opened, and the new secretary as well as his colleagues hoped for its successful termination. Dobbin was an enterprising man and he and Davis planned to ask Congress to appropriate the necessary funds to make the United States armament second to none in strength and efficiency.[17]

Cushing found himself in a most anomalous situation. He was technically a cabinet officer without a department. How-

ever, as he entered his office on 15th Street in the building which
he shared with the first auditor of the treasury, he was determined to change things.   Congress had recently raised the salaries of the cabinet to $8,000, although the money for the in-
crease had not been appropriated, and for the first time the
attorney-general found himself upon an equal footing financially
with the rest.   Cushing therefore set about creating a department for himself.   While working out this scheme he added
new functions to his office by transfer from the state department,
and engaged busily in writing numerous, voluminous opinions
upon the variety of questions referred to him.   With prodigious
industry he tackled the confused tangle which his predecessor
had left for him to straighten out; straightening out tangles was
one of Cushing's diversions.[18]

Campbell settled himself in the general post office at Seventh
and E Streets and found that he, like Marcy, had problems
world-wide in their extent.   There were the appointment and
superintendence of twenty-three thousand postmasters scattered
all over the land; their appointment he could turn over to the
veteran first assistant postmaster-general, Selah R. Hobbie, who
named men commended by the members of Congress or local
political leaders and troubled Campbell only where there was
serious contest.   The difficulties which concerned the new chief
most were the deficit, the mail contracts, the unsatisfactory
status of mail arrangements with England, France, and Mexico,
and the usual charges of fraud and laxity in the accounts.

The annual deficit ran in the neighborhood of $2,000,000 and
had come to be a habit.   Campbell hoped to cure it, partly
through economies in payments for carrying the mail.   The
problem met him immediately, for nearly a thousand mail
contracts had to be let in April.   They were looked upon by
steamship and railroad companies as legitimate subsidies.   Demands for high rates of compensation Campbell felt called upon
to resist; this thankless task was not to contribute to the administration's popularity.   Campbell disposed of the contract-let-
ting in three weeks, an unusual feat; and then began a study
of other possible economies which might be effected in his
department, meanwhile preparing material for Buchanan to
present to the British government in seeking a new postal convention.   His final ambition was to eliminate fraud.[19]

McClelland found his physical situation the most difficult. His department in most part consisted of four bureaus which in 1849 had been detached from other departments, namely, the land, Indian, pension, and patent offices. As yet this department had no building, and while the secretary shared the unfinished Greek temple which housed the patent office on the old national church reservation, F Street between Seventh and Ninth, his other bureau chiefs were still unwilling guests of their former cabinet heads, which they were likely to remain until the west wing of the patent office should be completed. He was further hampered by lack of a seal, because all his official papers had to be sent to other departments to be validated. Moreover, McClelland suffered from an insufficient number of clerks, and a large mass of unfinished work left over from the previous administration. He set himself to improve routine methods. The clerks were required to work regularly from eight to three, and strict rules were established against stepping out to get a drink, engaging in conversation, and participating in other diversions.

The secretary was called upon almost immediately to administer a reclassification of the civil service. At the last session Congress had provided that on July 1, 1853, all clerks in the departments should be classified into four groups upon the basis of examinations given to all, so that the inefficient might be weeded out and the competent divided into groups with different salaries according to ability and experience. Examinations were held during June everywhere except in the state department, which did not come within the provisions of the act, and on July 1 the changes were made. Of this work two-thirds fell upon McClelland's department, because of the large number of his clerks. Congress also had placed upon McClelland's shoulders the responsibility for treaties of land cession with the Indians in Kansas, preparatory to opening it to settlement. He went over the problem with Manypenny, the Indian commissioner, and sent him out to make the necessary arrangements. As he became better versed in the far-flung ramifications of his department he, like his colleagues, studied carefully its many opportunities for fraud and sought to find means of preventing chicanery. The public lands, the Indians, and the pension system provided immense opportunities for graft and corruption, and the new secretary found the cleansing of his Augean stables a truly Herculean task. His temperament was fitted for this kind of work and it was not long before a number of individuals realized that the interior department was no longer quite the place of easy opportunity it once had been.[20]

Pierce himself took a very active interest in the work of all his ministers; and while he left them a very free hand in administering their various duties, he tried to master the details of the entire complicated organization. He shirked no labor and encouraged consideration of manifold problems in cabinet meeting. In fact, the council chamber became a general clearing house for departmental business, and the President's office was the real center of government. Pierce, however, did not confine his executive functions to this room. He early acquired the habit of visiting the various departments and bureaus at least once a week, inquiring about details, chatting with the chiefs and the clerks, and keeping in personal touch with his organization.[21] In fact, such peripatetic administration was a diversion to him and a relief from the routine of his office, which had been especially trying. Pierce had lived the roving life of a circuit lawyer for so long that settling down to the binding monotony of heavy office work was hugely onerous. He applied himself diligently, however, and as the months went by administrative policies began to take shape in spite of the many distractions of politics.

XXXV

ON THE DEFENSIVE

ONE of the first tests which a President of the United States has to meet is the popular reaction to his initial appointments. Press, politicians and, to a certain extent, the public are bound to comment, and much is gained or lost in reputation as these reports are predominantly favorable or otherwise. While Pierce had been busy with patronage and administrative problems, the press had been actively scrutinizing his work. From the moment of his inaugural utterance, Whig editors had searched his every word and act for material to be used for partisan purposes, especially in several congressional campaigns that were being fought in the South that spring and summer; seventy-seven congressmen were yet to be chosen, most of whom were from that region. Two important lines of attack developed. In the first place, the tone of the inaugural and the appointment of men like Davis, Cushing, John A. Campbell, Pierre Soulé, Borland, and Gadsden indicated a tendency to radicalism; territorial acquisition and protection of American rights abroad smacked too much of " Young America." Secondly, after having been elected upon a platform featuring the Compromise of 1850, both fire-eaters from the South and Wilmot proviso men of the North, men of doubtful party regularity, had been given generous shares in the patronage to the exclusion of Compromise Union men. Had these charges emanated only from Whigs, they would have been of little moment, but they were echoed in other quarters.

Abroad the administration evoked a certain amount of unfavorable comment. The London *Times* spoke of the inaugural as a " mixture of looseness and pretension . . . which awakens suspicions as to the sobriety and good sense of its author," and lamented the passing of Clay and Webster. In less than three months the *Times*' New York correspondent, C. Edwards Lester, a disappointed office seeker, began his series of very unfriendly letters which were published in this important English journal.[1]

At home protests began to be heard even in the Democratic

ranks. In the first place the cabinet was obnoxious to some.
Caleb Cushing's appointment was perhaps the most objection-
able. Only a few years before he had been a Whig tainted with
abolitionism; now he was in the cabinet; hosts of Democrats,
especially in New England, were bitter against the recognition
of this " turncoat," to the exclusion of so many who had been in
the party for years. Unpopular in other quarters were the appointments of Davis and Marcy; the former because of his alleged secession sympathies and the latter by reason of the bitter
opposition of the " hardshell hunkers " of New York. No
southern unionist, or Compromise of 1850 Democrat, had been
appointed, much to the chagrin of this element; Guthrie and
Dobbin who had been chosen to satisfy that group failed to
do so, especially as Dobbin turned out to have been a southern
rights sympathizer. But criticisms of a President's newly selected cabinet are not generally very open, there are too many
other places still in jeopardy; so the disappointed bided their
time.

With the successive announcements of the appointments next
in importance to the cabinet, during the spring, louder mutter-
ings of discontent began to be heard. The recognition accorded
states' rights men, such as Soulé and others, not only furnished
ammunition to the southern Union Whigs, but also caused many
Democrats in both sections to complain. Union men who had
supported compromise in 1850 and since, men such as Howell
Cobb, Jeremiah Clemens, and Henry S. Foote had expected the
loyalty of their faction to receive a higher reward than the appointment of their most bitter enemies to office.

Northern selections as well called for criticism. Many in
both sections resented the favor shown to the bolters of 1843.
As was to be expected, the Cass regulars, whose hopes had
been destroyed by the defeat of that unfortunate year, were
most bitter. The New York " hards," Senator Bright, and some
" hardshell " New England Democrats were very outspoken in
their contempt for the new scheme. Important too was Francis
J. Grund, Washington correspondent of the Baltimore *Sun* and
the Philadelphia *Public Ledger*. As early as April 12 his column in the *Public Ledger* attacked the administration for neg-
lecting Union men all over the country; Davis, Soulé, and John
A. Campbell were his special targets. In private correspond-

ence to Marcy and others he vowed vengeance; incidentally he
had failed to obtain a consulship he desired.[2] These criticisms
the *Union* answered again and again, explaining that it was not
what a man had been but what he now was that counted.   Loyal
adherence to the Baltimore platform was the only test.

The climax of fault finding came in June, and from a source
which proved most humiliating to the President personally.
Open warfare developed in his own state. The trouble had
really started immediately after the fall election when Pierce
had openly smoothed the path of Atherton to the Senate. Men
like Burke resented the influence of the Concord group, the
President's failure to consult more widely, and his appointment
of southern rights men and " barnburners " to high office. Here
Pierce was not served very well by his friends, for the Concord
group most publicly through the columns of the *Patriot* carried on an aggravating feud with Burke and blatantly arrogated
to themselves full control of state matters; besides, Pierce made
little effort as far as is known to show Burke any appreciation
of his valuable services at the Baltimore Convention. Burke
felt aggrieved and decided to assert himself. He marshaled the
opponents of the Concord regency with such effect at the June
convention that he was able to write its platform. He brought
in a series of resolutions which condemned the administration
policy of appointments. Upon this insubordination the Baltimore *Sun* commented, " we shall, in due time, see more of like
demonstrations," [3] a prediction which was immediately borne
out by similar activities staged by " hards " and " barnburners "
at the expense of the administration in a special session of the
New York legislature.[4]

These reactions were but the natural result of a large-scale
distribution of patronage. Multitudes had to be disappointed,
and many of the attacks from within the party came from men
who had not received what they wanted. If the organization
effected by this distribution proved efficient, the discontented
would have to fall in line eventually. Meanwhile the party was
successful in the spring Congressional elections in New Hampshire, Connecticut, South Carolina, Rhode Island, Louisiana,
and Virginia. Thirty-one Democratic Congressmen were chosen
as compared with one Whig, a net gain of eight. Pierce could
count these results as gratifying, but he had made bitter ene-

mies, and their tactics during the next few months were to cause him much worry.

In order to protect himself, Pierce began to realize the necessity of paying more attention to his own publicity agents. In this respect he was then, and continued to be, badly served. In the first place, he and his cabinet were close-mouthed and would not talk for publication. Secondly, the so-called administration organ was ineffective. Since Thomas Ritchie had been forced out in 1851, the Washington *Union* had been owned by Robert Armstrong of Tennessee, and its editors had been men of little influence. When Pierce came to Washington he had hoped that Nicholson would take editorial charge, but the latter had not been able to make satisfactory arrangements with Armstrong. In the meantime the organ was conducted to nobody's satisfaction by Charles Eames and Roger A. Pryor, a Massachusetts-Virginia combination, aided by John W. Forney, clerk of the House of Representatives, and Caleb Cushing who wrote many editorials. The President felt more and more embarrassed by having no confidential friend in the editorial office of the *Union*; and when it became known that opponents of the administration in the party were going to establish a " hard " national organ in Washington under Beverly Tucker, Pierce bestirred himself. Armstrong precipitated the matter by discharging Pryor because of a disagreement, whereupon Pierce interfered and insisted upon Nicholson's retention under a satisfactory arrangement; he forced out the unpopular Eames, despite the objections of Marcy and Davis. Thereupon Nicholson with the assistance of Harvey Watterson, an old crony of Pierce's congressional days, undertook about July 1 the conduct of the *Union* with continued help from Forney and Cushing. Plans were also projected for establishing Forney in New York in charge of an administration paper to be launched during the summer.[5]

As the organ was being tuned, Pierce planned another appeal to popular interest. In New York City the United States was to hold its first world's fair at the newly erected Crystal Palace, to which Queen Victoria was sending as her personal representatives, the Earl of Ellesmere and Sir Charles Lyell, the geologist. When the committee in charge had come to Washington to invite the President to attend the opening ceremonies of the fair he had been doubtful of the propriety of such a journey but finally he had decided to go. It was stated in the press that a desire to be especially courteous to the Queen's representative was his chief motive; such an action would be timely, as the President was about to send a fleet to Canadian waters to protect our rights. Moreover, the President's personal appearance might aid the New York situation, which was becoming increasingly more difficult. In the course of this journey from the capital to New York, Pierce and the three members of his cabinet who were going with him, Guthrie, Davis, and Cushing would be expected to make a number of addresses. Such public utterances would provide him with an opportunity, seldom afforded the President in those days, of speaking directly to the public. He was little known personally, relatively few had seen him; would not this royal progress through Baltimore, Philadelphia, and New York provide an opportunity for his magnetic personality to win those whom he met and make him a popular figure? It was to be quite a different journey from that which he had made in February.

The several speeches were planned carefully beforehand and subjects deemed important were selected for emphasis. The first was the compatibility of the idea of union with the principle of states' rights, the glory of the union and the rights of the states—truly national ground; this was the principal theme and it was iterated and reiterated with many illustrations drawn from the Revolutionary War appropriate to the historic localities which they were to visit. Free trade was also to receive its endorsement and much was to be made of American idealism; however, this last was what might be expected as it was standard Democratic doctrine.

But that was not all: Pierce and his cabinet decided to treat another subject which could not help arousing much public interest. Pierce was ruling in a railroad era, and many projects were seeking endorsement and aid from the government; one of the most important and widely advertised was a railroad to the Pacific. Robert J. Walker was interested, Colonel Benton was agitating for a road, the California Senators, especially Gwin, were ever pushing the idea, and many promoters less well known were active. These interests early had sought to engage the attention of Pierce, and only a few days after the inauguration he was quoted as having told one promoter that he had been elected President of the United States and not of a railroad company.   At the outset some of his cabinet were more sympathetic than he; Davis had organized transcontinental surveys, and Guthrie's attitude was the one natural to a promoter fresh from a railroad boom in Kentucky.   The *Union* ventured occasional articles on the subject.   Then came the big Memphis convention, where a thousand southern delegates stated in unmistakable terms that they favored railroad transportation to the Pacific.   It might be a political error to oppose these importunities, especially as the *Tribune* was advocating a scheme for rejuvenating the Whig party upon a Pacific railroad platform.   Pierce and his advisers may also have had some idea of interesting capitalists, especially in New York and Philadelphia, who up to date tended to be somewhat resentful of the administration's strict construction policy.   For any or all of these reasons it was decided that Davis and Guthrie should give administration endorsement to the railroad idea; they were to make the practical speeches, and leave the President the Union and American ideals; Cushing could fill in wherever necessary. With the speeches prepared, and departure arranged for July 11, the President allowed himself the relaxation of a drive on Saturday evening with his friend French.   He talked over his addresses with his erstwhile assistant secretary, who was duly impressed: " the speeches Pierce will make on this tour, will add unfading laurels to his brow . . . and will be most enthusiastically received by the whole nation."   He furthermore confided to his brother, " Frank Pierce *is* a great man, he is at least a head and shoulders greater than I took him to be before he became President.   He is the best President we have had since Jackson, and for the times, the very man we ought to have! " [6]

The President with his party left Washington for the north Monday.   His first stop was Baltimore, where he mounted a horse, received the local militia, and made a glowing speech, mostly about the Star-Spangled Banner.   It would have been an auspicious beginning save for the fact that he caught cold, and a night's sleep in Barnum's Hotel did not throw off the discomfort.   Next morning he went on to Philadelphia with a stop for dinner at Wilmington; in both places he had to curtail his own speaking, but at Philadelphia the important work of the trip was accomplished. After the parade in which Pierce again appeared there was a dinner. The President's cold debarred him from anything but a few remarks, for every word "was like a knife in his lungs." But in the course of the speech-making Davis gave a flaring address, punctuated by "enthusiastic applause," in which he showed the need for a Pacific railroad for national defense. To provide one, "the application of the war power of the government in this case would be within the strict limits of the constitution." Then "the smoke of Pennsylvania coal might be seen on the desert waste, . . . and Pennsylvania iron, with the very stamp of her own foundries upon it, might be seen creeping in a long, serpentine track to the slope of the Pacific." In these views the secretary of war said the President concurred and Buchanan thereupon complimented them. Guthrie, when his turn came to speak, added that if there was sufficient money in the treasury after the debt was paid "why, for purposes of self-defense, shall we not extend a railroad to the Pacific?" The press now heralded the pronouncement of the administration in favor of steam transportation to the coast.

In this brief stop at Philadelphia Pierce was scheduled to interview Buchanan. Although the latter had received his instructions and his commission he was still fussing about his control of British negotiations and had made an appointment to talk it over with the President once more. He met Pierce at the dinner where the President was on one side of the mayor and Buchanan on the other. Pierce leaned over behind the mayor's back and "strongly expressed the hope" that Buchanan would accept the mission; they found this mode of consultation rather unsatisfactory and agreed to discuss it after dinner. That function, however, so Buchanan recorded, "was kept up until nearly midnight, the President cordially participating in the hilarity of the scene." As a result they decided to postpone the interview until the following day. Next morning they had a rather disconnected interview, partly at McKibben's and partly on the ferry going over to Camden, and Buchanan was finally persuaded.

The Presidential party after stops at Trenton, Princeton, New Brunswick, Rahway, and Elizabeth, and another parade and overnight stay at Newark, finally arrived at New York. There at his reception in Castle Garden the President made his longest speech. His effort was marked by rhetorical idealism and reflected, a little turgidly perhaps, his "sincere and anxious purpose" to aid in the onward march of the Republic. The parade that followed was marred by a shower which caused the President to ride his horse under an umbrella, unaware of a rather damaged hat which had been crushed when his horse collided with General Sandford's. Between the horse and the shower Pierce looked rather bedraggled when he approached the Crystal Palace. He stopped first in a saloon for a glass of water, with just enough brandy to prevent further taking of cold, and then in the anteroom of the Palace, where a clean shirt and a clothes brush did their best. When he appeared upon the platform, he looked tired and old. His voice failed him and he had to curtail his speech; the affair was further marred by the absence of Lord Ellesmere, who was ill. After this ceremony, the President hurried to the Astor House, exceedingly fatigued and laboring under severe "physical debility." By nine o'clock, however, he was sufficiently recovered to dance in the ladies' parlor.

The final day of festivity was a full one. Presumably there were conferences on the New York political situation, seemingly with little fruit. That night there was a big dinner and the last speeches. Pierce, in his, alluded to the illness of Lord Ellesmere upon whom he had called that day and expressed the hope that their only international rivalry might be the "rivalry of earnest, determined, steady effort to promote the elevation of the race and peace and good neighborhood among nations and men." Then after Davis had described the glories of free trade, the President went to Castle Garden to hear Madame Sontag sing Meyerbeer's "Robert Le Diable." He appeared much preoccupied, except when Sontag sang "Roberto tu che adoro," whereat he turned with compliments to Lady Ellesmere. For the rest he seemed scarcely conscious he was at the opera. He left soon after, and with difficulty fought his way through the crowd. Next day he hurried back to Washington, the only recorded incident of the trip being the receipt at Princeton of a bottle of pale ale from Mrs. Senator Thomson. He reached home late at night and had to take to his bed, sick with fatigue and cold. It was at this time that Forney, who had

been with the President on most of the trip, wrote Buchanan
" Pierce has had a fine reception but I deeply, deeply, deplore
his habits. He drinks deep. My heart bleeds for him for he
is a gallant and a generous spirit. The place overshadows him.
He is crushed by its great duties and he seeks refuge in . . . .
His experience convinces me that a great mistake was made in
putting him in at all." So the President had shown himself to
the people. His efforts to keep up under his cold and under
the awful burden of hospitality had brought forth unkind comment like the above. However, he had persuaded Buchanan to
go abroad, and capital ought to be pleased with the railway pro-
nouncements. The press speculated at length as to the meaning
of these Pacific railroad allusions.[7]

XXXVI
ATTEMPTING PARTY DISCIPLINE

WASHINGTON summer was at its height when Pierce returned to the White House. He found his dwelling anything but a restful place because it was largely in the hands of workmen who were painting, papering, and installing a new heating plant. As usual there was plenty to engage his attention. Columbian College held its commencement exercises, and he went, attended by most of his cabinet. The bricklayers at work on the new capitol extension called to present a wage difficulty which the President courteously promised to consider; he went over the matter with Captain Meigs with the result that the men received more pay for more work. He received a delegation of Pottawatomie Indians who came to protest against the dishonesty of their agent. That summer there was a frightful scourge of yellow fever in New Orleans which attracted nation-wide sympathy; Pierce contributed fifty dollars to the relief of the city. He gave a like amount to help finish the Washington monument which had attained a height of but 128 feet. In spite of the heat, and the dread of disease, the administration maintained its good humor. As several were going away shortly, they attempted to finish up a number of patronage matters on July 22. "Guthrie came clumsily along with a heap of commissions to be filled up preparatory to signing. 'You'd better not trouble yourself about 'em,' said Marcy, 'you'll get a spiteful paragraph for every commission you sign.' 'Yes, but I'll only get my share with Campbell, and the sec. of state. Dobbin gets but very little yet.' 'Oh, yes, Dobbin scuds along very smoothly under bare poles, being of the navy; I seem to get it on all hands.' 'Oh yes,' said Guthrie, 'and how can you expect anything else, being the chief of sinners!' Marcy bowed in comic acknowledgment of the one-sided compliment and retired." Marcy and Guthrie were becoming whist cronies.

August was a dull month, and the pressure of work relaxed. Marcy and Cushing went to Berkeley Springs with Crampton to try to finish up the fisheries treaty; Davis went off on a tour of inspection through New England; Campbell, who had been quite sick with "cholera," went home to Pennsylvania; Dobbin became ill; late in the month Pierce let Sidney Webster have a month's vacation, to recuperate from too much work and the Washington climate. Pierce, with Guthrie who seemed to take no vacation, and McClelland who had just returned from a sojourn in Michigan, kept watch over affairs of state. The President allowed himself some recreation and relief from the discomfort of the workmen-ridden and paint-smelling White House. There were concerts on the lawns, during which he mingled with the people, and occasional excursions. One in particular must have been a pleasant relief when Pierce and Dobbin, who was recuperating, went down the Potomac on the U. S. S. *Engineer* which was the *Mayflower* of that day. Entertained by music from the marine band, they sailed down as far as Indian Head, enjoying the placid beauties of the river and the inspiration of Mount Vernon. On the anniversary of Contreras and Churubusco the officers of the President's old brigade came to wait upon him; and so midsummer drifted away with only occasional unpleasant incidents, such as the importunate pleas of the friends of a local wife murderer who sought a stay to ward off the death penalty; they sought in vain.

Politically, the summer had not been as successful as Pierce had hoped. The August elections had demonstrated unexpected Whig strength, and while three congressmen had been gained in Alabama and North Carolina, the Democrats had just managed to hold their own in Kentucky and had lost a representative in Tennessee. Furthermore, a hot contest was pending in Georgia which would not be settled until October. With this party situation confronting him, Pierce was pressed for a decision as to the French mission. Dix was still in the subtreasury at New York awaiting the President's pleasure; the Unionist faction in Georgia were hoping that Pierce would at last recognize Cobb by giving him the post; and leverage was being exerted from Virginia for the same place. The Old Dominion had received no substantial recognition, and in view of the leading part which her delegates had taken in nominating Pierce, her political leaders were anxious for the plum. Pierce sent for Dix to acquaint him with the pressure from Georgia, but the assistant treasurer did not come; he sent a friend instead who got nowhere with the President.   To meet Georgia attacks, Dix wrote a letter for publication explaining clearly his position on slavery, and sent several of his speeches to Pierce to demonstrate his respect for southern rights.   Finally, by September 3, Pierce made up his mind that he could not appoint Dix and wrote him frankly that it would be more advantageous for his administration to name some one else to the French mission; in the course of the next few weeks the place was offered to John Y. Mason of Virginia.   Dix and the " barnburners " now had just reason to feel ill used, and New York matters rapidly approached a crisis.[2]

Bronson had proved an unfortunate choice for collector, for he had shown no willingness to coöperate with his " barnburner " associates in dividing the appointments equally among the various factions.   A contributing cause may have been Guthrie's decision denying customs collectors their fees, restricting them to their salaries.   Bronson's expectation of $25,000 annually was reduced to $6,000.   If he was seeking martyrdom, he was approaching it.   At the primary meetings held in late summer to choose delegates for the state convention, the true nature of the so-called coöperation to be expected from the " hards " was disclosed.   Because of his refusal to coöperate, Bronson was slated for removal about the time that Dix was dropped, but nothing was done immediately; and then the September convention staged a new schism.   As Marcy had feared, the " hards " refused to participate, and nominated a ticket of their own.   Their recalcitrancy produced two tickets, both claiming strict orthodoxy.   Delegations from each convention immediately came to Washington, where the " hards " discovered that Pierce considered them the " bolters "; both Bronson and O'Conor dared to endorse the " bolting " ticket, refusing to affiliate longer with the free soilers, as they called their " soft-barnburner " opponents.   Supporters of Bronson openly declared that Pierce would not dare punish the collector because, said they, Bronson and the " hards " had the whole South behind them as well as the Cass party in general.   The President would think twice before he removed an important official protesting against the favor shown free-soilers.   Governor Marcy made a trip to Albany and wrote back to Cushing that Bronson should be removed.   Within two weeks, Bronson was ordered to recognize all factions in his appointments and stop favoring the " hardshells."

While the effect of this order was being awaited, official announcement of the appointment of John Y. Mason as French minister was released to the press and brought a serious complication. James Gordon Bennett of the New York *Herald* had set his heart upon the French mission; he had made known his wishes to Pierce soon after the election and he had lived in hopes. Now his columns, always unfriendly to Marcy, turned against Pierce; and the oft-repeated burden of his editorials was that Pierce was a free soiler who fellowshipped with John Van Buren. In Washington Beverly Tucker began the *Sentinel*, which was to play the same tune. Finally, to make Pierce's journalistic woes even more pronounced, C. Edwards Lester, who had been the recipient of Cushing's confidence, now used his position as American correspondent of the London *Times* to demonstrate the " moral prostration " of the new President because of his " false, feeble, and fatal policy " of selling his friends " for the sake of buying his enemies and thus losing both." Lester had failed to obtain a consulship.

The New York situation proceeded to grow intolerable. Bennett kept baiting the administration, especially Davis, calling the latter's position most ridiculous—a " fire-eater " endorsing John Van Buren and the " barnburners." To this Davis replied that he did not like the policies of Van Buren et al., any more than he approved of Dickinson's anti-slavery speeches of 1847–9 or Bronson's letter of July 15, 1848, to a Van Buren meeting, but the past was the past. " Holding, as I do, that party organization is a necessary means to insure success to principles on which parties are formed, I cannot but lament the division which has, without recent cause, opened the old wounds in our party." The *Union* prolonged the dispute by digging up the records of the " hards " a few years back and engaging in an active use of personalities. Finally the insurrection came. On October 17 Bronson wrote a letter to Guthrie refusing to be dictated to, as to appointments, and O'Conor wrote a letter to the *Union* declaring that the administration was " free soil." It was open rebellion.

Bronson's letter was received at a time when the administration was rejoicing over an endorsement. There had been considerable doubt as to the strength of the party in Georgia because of the divided condition of the organization. In the October election, after a campaign in which the opposition pointed to the New York distractions and charged that Pierce was forgetting the rights of the South, a sweeping victory had been achieved. The confusion of his opponents was a source of great satisfaction to Pierce, August doubts were forgotten, and he was ready to deal with Bronson. Young Hickory tore a leaf from Andrew Jackson's book, and Guthrie removed the collector. Dix resigned as assistant treasurer, the naval officer, Redfield, "soft," was put into the collector's office, John J. Cisco, "hard," received Dix's post, and two "barnburners," John R. Brodhead and John L. O'Sullivan, received Redfield's office and the mission to Portugal, respectively.

Pierce had carried out his original policy of treating all factions equally with the result that all were now equally disgruntled. "Barnburners" resented the disappointment of Dix, "hards" were vengeful because of Bronson's removal, and the "softs" were dissatisfied because the administration policy had caused the "hards" to bolt and to invite defeat in the coming state election. The whole affair had been badly handled; instead of removing Bronson for using his office to meddle in politics the administration had removed him for failing to use his position to build up the party. Cave Johnson back in Tennessee remembered the days when he had been in Polk's cabinet, and wrote his former colleague, Buchanan:

> I suppose Mr. Polk and yourself would have quietly invited Mr. Bronson to Washington, had a private talk with him, by way of *consultation*, rather than *dictation* and the whole difficulty would have ended by acquiescence in your views or resignation and without an appeal to the public. It does not look well for cabinet officers to write letters or make speeches justifying appointments or removals or exercising influence in state elections.

But Pierce and Guthrie were not Polk and Buchanan. New York seemed hopeless; so Pierce and Forney gave up the idea of establishing an administration press there. The field was left to the blasts of the *Herald*, the *Evening Post*, and the *Tribune*, a formidable trilogy of enemies.[3] The discipline had failed.

The situation was by no means improved by an attempt at vindication. If the removal of Bronson seemed to be an undue favoring of free soil, that impression must be eradicated. So Caleb Cushing tried his hand at epistolary practice and wrote a letter denouncing the coalition which Massachusetts Democrats of late had been arranging with free soilers. Such a custom he declared to be unorthodox, and furthermore penned his most famous literary achievement, " the dangerous elements of abolitionism . . . shall be crushed out." His letter was straightway telegraphed to Mississippi for use in the fall campaign to counteract the Bronson removal. In fact the knowing ones declared that this was the reason for writing the letter. The " ukase " as it was called, with its phrase " crushed out " traveled from lip to lip and succeeding events were to make unfortunate use of it. The letters of Guthrie and Cushing demonstrate the political unwisdom of October, 1853, in spite of the fact that they were based on the seemingly solid rock of party harmony, unity, and purity. Though Cushing might philosophize that all administrations had bolters and that these renegades harmed only themselves, others felt differently. As one wrote:

When the powers that be, avow that any party, especially if it be a reform party in a great moral question, shall be suppressed, and crushed by proscription—all history shows that the attempt must fail. I think the course taken will hasten another anti-slavery movement, more violent than any we have yet witnessed.

This man, Pierce would have told you, was a disappointed office seeker. So he was, but his disappointment had somewhat clarified his vision.[4]

Discipline had been administered but insubordination was by no means quelled. The lid blew off in New Hampshire and the battle of the factions grew warmer in New York as the November election approached. The New Hampshire developments were peculiarly unpleasant to the President because of Burke's insistence upon drawing Pierce into the quarrel. Butterfield, George, and the others of the Concord clique, had been resisting Burke's senatorial ambitions by charging that he was the President's enemy, and had opposed his nomination. Finally, to prove that he was not unfriendly, but had done much to elevate

Pierce, he wrote a long article which was published in the *State Capitol Reporter* on October 22, in which he described how *he* had really procured the nomination of Pierce. He described the letters he and the President had exchanged in April and May, 1852, the conference they had held at Newport, New Hampshire, and showed how a plan of procedure had been worked out and followed, so as not to bring Pierce's name out until at just the psychological moment. Those unfriendly to the President, like the editor of the New Hampshire *Statesman*, could talk of how Pierce intrigued and plotted to capture the nomination. A week later Burke published a large number of letters which he had solicited from delegates to the Baltimore convention from all parts of the country, describing his efforts to secure the nomination of Pierce. These papers arrived in Washington in due time, and anger and chagrin were the portion of the President. Only those who care as much for appearances as did he can understand how he felt. Prior to these revelations it had been supposed by most people that he had been the spontaneous choice of the convention and that the honor had come to him all unexpectedly. Now it was spread abroad that he had intrigued to obtain the office and that the whole proceeding had been arranged beforehand. This revelation was a great blow to his pride, in spite of the fact that it was not strictly true.

Other offensive personalities were indulged in. A New York "hard," Cooley, by name, in a public speech accused the President of drunkenness. As a result of these attacks, Nicholson wrote a long defensive article entitled "Assaults upon the President's Personal Character," in the course of which he denied one or two of Burke's minor statements and called upon the New Hampshire delegation to come forward with the facts, an invitation which they did not accept. The President's private life, Nicholson went on to state, was in every way exemplary, as he knew from daily association. A few days later the *Union* published a letter from one who had become acquainted with Pierce's intimate friends, who assured his readers that Pierce was strictly abstemious; the assurance seems to have been borne out except perhaps on the New York journey. Then came the final round of hostilities before the meeting of Congress, the November elections, in which the Democrats won in New Jer-

sey, Louisiana, Maryland, and Mississippi; Massachusetts as
usual went Whig and the split in New York had made Democratic defeat there inevitable, besides demonstrating a very
unwelcome truth. The " hards " had received more votes than
the President's friends, proving that the former were no mere
faction but on paper at least a majority of the party; this the
" softs " denied, claiming that many Whigs had voted the
" hard " ticket.[5]

The sum total of this nine months of politics and patronage
demonstrated how far the President's plan of impartial reward
of all factions was lacking in success, if not an absolute failure.
The one great state, New York, which Pierce had hoped to
salvage permanently for his party, had been divided hopelessly
once more, and in all probability permanently lost. An important section of the party press was hostile and a number of
Democratic senators and congressmen were coming to Washington to make war upon a President of their own party. The
presumptuousness of this accidental President and his small-
potato cabinet in their inflated pride and inexperience, attempting to impose a reorganization of their own invention upon the
old and tried leaders of the party! Such was the state of mind
of certain of the party chieftains as they arrived at the capital.
Cass had openly accepted the new order [6] but it was among his
followers that the objections were the loudest. Douglas, or
perhaps more accurately, many of his supporters had been disappointed. Sectional jealousy, instead of being allayed as
Pierce had hoped, was strengthened; many in the South thought
that free soil doctrines were approved; in the North a number
suspected that Pierce was bending the knee to secessionists.
The question remains, would Pierce have succeeded better if
he had built his administration of " Compromise " men, and
had abandoned the extremes in each section? Could he have
attracted enough conservative Whigs to have established a
strong conservative party as Buchanan did temporarily in 1856?

Pierce realized that the conservative element in the Democratic party alone could not carry elections. 1848 had proved
that, and besides he fondly considered himself the harmonizing
agent of the Democracy and dreamed of a united party such as
he had known in Jackson's day. With such hopes and dreams
the course which he followed was inevitable. It had proved to

date a doubtful venture, and his effort to administer discipline in New York had failed utterly. In spite of this failure, would Congress sustain him? If his administrative program and his organization could persuade or compel a congressional majority, all would be well. Much would depend upon the strength of the program Pierce was preparing to present to Congress in his annual message.

XXXVII
PREPARING THE ADMINISTRATION
PROGRAM FOR CONGRESS

WHILE the President had found in his appointments an ample opportunity to demonstrate his political policy, there had been no means of indicating his administrative program. His inaugural had contained only the broadest outline, and the speeches on the New York trip had been suggestive, rather than definite. The coming of Congress in December called for a detailed accounting, and these reports to the legislative body from the President and his subordinates would give him the first real chance to set forth the policy which the past months' experiences had matured in the minds of the executive heads.[1]

The annual review was quite a task and started early in the fall. The various bureau chiefs first prepared summaries of their activities and recommendations, for their cabinet superiors, who in turn made formal reports to the President. There were three exceptions to this rule as Guthrie under the law reported directly to Congress, Cushing having no department made no report at all, and Marcy, as was the custom, informally supplied data for the President's summary of foreign affairs. With this material before him, Pierce set out to write his message, which he did mostly in his own hand. The process of inventory and report occupied the better part of October and November and was the cause of unwonted activity in the departments, protracted cabinet meetings, and much thought and labor.

Guthrie presented quite a list of achievements. He had reduced the debt by $12,703,329 or about seventeen per cent. He had enforced the independent treasury act and instituted a number of reforms in the service including the collection of many old accounts. The treasury was still troubled by a large balance which at the moment amounted to over $14,000,000. He had been collecting statistics and opinions and had worked out a revision of the tariff on the basis of a general tax of 25 per cent on imports with a large free list and a 100 per cent duty on brandy and liquors. This tariff he recommended in order to reduce the revenue to its proper amount.

Davis reported an army on paper of 13,821 officers and men, of whom 10,417 were in actual service; 8,378 of these were on the frontier. The frontier problem bulked large in Davis's mind. Indian uprisings had been reported, the bogey of foreign attack was still alive, and he was painfully aware of the inadequacy of his force and equipment. He therefore asked for more men, more posts, an armory for the west, and above all for adequate transportation by rail to the Pacific coast, so necessary for insuring prompt moving of men and equipment in time of need. He detailed at length the railroad surveys and the geographical difficulties which had been encountered in the process of making them. However, he went on to add:

> If I seem to have pressed the magnitude of the obstacles to a successful execution of the contemplated work, it has not been to suggest the abandonment of the undertaking, but only to enforce the propriety of much caution in the preliminary steps, and the necessity for concentrating all the means which can be made available to the completion of so gigantic a project.
>
> Preconceived opinion or prejudice, personal interest, and sectional rivalry, must be held subject to the developments of instrumental survey, and subservient to the purpose of final success, or the result to be anticipated is failure. And when from the consideration of the magnitude of the difficulties to be overcome we pass to the importance of the effects to be produced, there is enough to sustain patriotism in the sacrifice of any personal or local interest which may be involved.[2]

He also stated that there were other " duties and interests of vital importance " calling for a railroad, but as they were not within his province he would not consider them. In the meantime he recommended experiments with camels.

To increase the efficiency of the army he suggested a plan for improving the personnel by providing higher pay for officers and men, by promoting non-commissioned officers to the commissioned ranks, and by establishing a retired list. Finally, as most internal improvements which the government undertook were constructed under the supervision of army engineers, Davis included some remarks about the unsatisfactory nature of these enterprises, which he considered of doubtful constitutionality. He suggested the advisability of trying the scheme which Polk had advocated of granting to the states the right to levy tonnage duties, and with the proceeds manage their own improvements. It was evident Davis had made a thorough study of his department.

Dobbin pointed out the need for reorganizing and enlarging the navy. The staff of officers was especially in need of pruning to remove the inefficient and the superannuated; promotion should be based upon merit and achievement, not seniority. To improve the morale of the enlisted men a better system of rewards and punishments should be introduced, and to increase efficiency a bureau of personnel similar to the adjutant general's office in the army should be provided. His most important recommendation arose out of the fact that our navy was " much less than one fifth of that of several of the greater powers of Europe . . . not larger than that of certain other powers of Europe which are not of the first rank." [3] It consisted of about seventy ships, few of which were propelled by steam, and the personnel was limited by law to 7500 men. He requested the building of six additional steam frigates and an increase of his force to 10,000 men. He believed in preparedness.

Campbell's report was largely filled with his difficulties with railroad contractors, the deficit in departmental revenue, and the unsatisfactory nature of our postal relations with England. He also dilated upon the state of the ocean mail service, the steamship company contracts, and the inefficiencies of the accounting system as applied to the returns of the postmasters. He made few recommendations. The most important of these asked for an assistant postmaster-general to handle the Pacific coast mail, more agents to superintend mail-carrying and detect fraud, and more pay for postmasters.

McClelland's report contained a summary of the returns of his four bureau chiefs. Attempts had been made to check pension frauds, but new laws and a revision and codification of the old were needed. The patent office had been brought back to order but the force of patent clerks was too small and the system of appeals to the courts needed revision. As to the Indians, they had been more peaceful than expected but their condition was deplorable. McClelland reported his reforms for

preventing frauds upon the aborigines and protecting them better from their own improvidence. He recommended that more
reservations be set aside for them in which they might be
colonized, and that cash annuity payments be abandoned as
soon as possible in favor of payment in goods. Both he and
Commissioner Manypenny dwelt at length upon the latter's trip
to the unorganized territory west of Missouri and Iowa, to arrange for treaties of cession with the Indians there preparatory
to opening the region to settlement. Manypenny regretted
that the act providing for these treaties had been interpreted by
a number of people as a declaration that the territory was about
to be opened to settlement, for though none from Missouri and
Iowa had actually located in the Kansas region, many had gone
in and explored land. Whether designedly or not, McClelland
failed to allude in any manner to Manypenny's statement to the
effect that " the interests of the Indians require that a civil government be immediately organized in the territory." [4]

The most interesting part of McClelland's report was found
in his own statements and those of John Wilson, the land commissioner, in regard to the public lands. McClelland set forth
the general belief that our land system " is founded in correct
principles and needs but little modification or change. The
pre-emption feature might possibly be advantageously enlarged
and made more liberal. Sound policy requires that every
encouragement should be held out for actual settlement and
cultivation." [5] It was his opinion that liberal grants should be
given for railroad purposes. The lands already had been very
profitable to the government; it had cleared $53,289,465 from
their sale and stood to gain $300,000,000 more. By granting
lands to be used for railroads, the remaining areas would be
made much more valuable, lands now unsalable would become
desirable, new regions would be peopled, and, as Wilson added,
" hundreds of thousands of laborers can find constant employment on them, and each, by a very small amount of labor, can
secure the blessings of a ' homestead,' without feeling degraded
by having it conferred on him as a gratuity, even if it were
constitutional thus to benefit a few at the expense of the many.
To grants of this character for railroads, canals, &c., not one
tangible or substantial objection can be presented." [6] Although
McClelland omitted any comment upon possible homestead

legislation he endorsed Wilson's railroad grant idea with two important statements. " The strongest political and economic considerations, therefore, dictate this course." " The right to donate a part for the enhancement of the value of the residue can no longer be justly questioned," if provided with proper safeguards.[7]

With these ideas as a basis, Pierce labored upon his message and gradually during November it took shape. The predominant thought with which Pierce was filled as he sat down to outline his policies was similar to that which he had enunciated in his inaugural; here he had an opportunity to enlarge upon it and make it more specific. He expressed the prevailing feeling of unlimited confidence in the resourcefulness of the American people and in the exceptional excellence of their institutions as established by the mighty men now dead. But his confidence was qualified: the glorious potentialities of the Republic would be realized only if the institutions and ideas of the past and the simple virtues of the pastoral age were rigorously maintained. In other words Pierce's great weakness as a publicist was here displayed in his fundamental attitude toward his duties. He would administer government by strict adherence to precedent rather than by creative statesmanship. Creative statesmanship was unknown to him except as a dangerous violation of tried doctrines advocated by men both unstable and unprincipled or by dangerous fanatics.

He was not able to enlarge very much on foreign affairs because only a few of the diplomats had left the country and there had not been time for many developments. However, he made plain the three lines of his foreign policy: he was going to maintain and protect American rights against all aggression, he would endeavor to extend our interests, especially those of trade, he would show to the world the example of our democracy. As a great achievement, he stressed the Koszta incident, and sent the correspondence to Congress. We were " at peace with all foreign countries."

At home the country was " exempt from any cause of serious disquietude " because there was a general recognition of the great American solution to the problem of sectionalism, namely, the Union composed of states with their " institutions," " welfare " and " domestic peace " " alike secure under the sacred

ægis of the Constitution." To maintain this domestic peace he
outlined a laissez-faire policy to be maintained by the central
government. Reduction of the revenue by revising the tariff
according to Guthrie's plan, was his first proposition. Increases
in the army and navy as recommended by Davis and Dobbin
received his endorsement, and he cautiously approved the recommendations of McClelland and Wilson for land grants to
railroads. He concluded his summary of the departments' reports by suggesting a reorganization of the federal judicial
system, and offered to submit a plan if Congress so desired;
Cushing evidently had not been idle. In disposing of these
departmental matters Pierce had reserved three topics for special treatment, and he devoted a generous portion of his message to their consideration.

These three issues were all a part of the great problem of
expansion, which always raised constitutional doubts as to the
powers of the federal government. The first was the question
which had been a matter of dispute for forty years, namely,
should the federal government aid commerce and community
development by making public improvements within the various states? On this subject the President summoned the Democratic precedents from Jackson's day, and stated various practical objections such as waste and lack of jurisdiction; he failed
to recommend the appropriations needed for continuing those
works then in progress, and after suggesting the possibility of
abandoning the so-called system he asked Congress for " a deliberate reconsideration of the question." His statements, while
indicating disapproval, were in no sense direct and straight-
forward, and showed an unwillingness to demand any set policy.

The question of a railroad to the Pacific he dealt with in like
manner. Most tentatively and guardedly did he endorse this
project, within the limits of strict construction of the Constitution as far as embraced under the war power, but he felt that
the connection of the government with such a project should be
" incidental rather than primary," that is, the government
should grant subsidy to some private corporation rather than
undertake the project itself.

The third matter of moment was the question of the relation
of the sections, especially as regards slavery. Here he again
expressed his firm belief in the efficacy of the Compromise of

1850, which had brought peace after the dangerous crisis of that year. " This repose is to suffer no shock during my official term, if I have power to avert it. . . . While men inhabiting different parts of this vast continent can [not] be expected to hold the same opinions . . . they can unite in a common object and sustain common principles essential to the maintenance of that object."

This extended discussion he concluded with a statement of his views on the fundamental problem of the republic, namely, its rapid expansion. By 1900 the republic would have a population of 100,000,000 not only because of natural increase and immigration but because of " the probable accession of the populations already existing in other parts of our hemisphere, which within the period in question will feel with yearly increasing force the natural attraction of so vast, powerful, and prosperous a confederation of self-governing republics and will seek the privilege of being admitted within its safe and happy bosom, transferring with themselves, by a peaceful and healthy process of incorporation, spacious regions of virgin and exuberant soil, which are destined to swarm with the fast-growing and fast-spreading millions of our race." There was a dream of Empire, and what an accurate prophecy! Such expansion was certain to produce further problems of conflicting sectional influence. The United States therefore " could only be kept in national cohesion by the strictest fidelity to the principles of the constitution . . . the minimum of federal government . . . strict deference to the sovereign rights and dignity of every state." The states must not be reduced to a provincial relation to central authority. Between the sections a spirit of " mutual forbearance, respect, and non-interference " was necessary, and throughout the land there must flourish a spirit of integrity in the public service accompanied by an economical fiscal administration.

This message, like its author, was optimistic and indecisive, and drew largely upon precedent and the wisdom of the fathers. It carried a sustained note of deference to the judgment of Congress and made explicit recognition of the coördinate nature of the legislative and executive branches of the government. Pierce was not going to attempt to lead Congress, but to supply it with a statement of an orthodox Democratic President's creed, which they might find useful as a standard of party and Congressional action. The message demonstrated very clearly the President's great weakness as a statesman. He did not understand that the feeling for the Union, the nationalism which he so cherished, was not the spiritual possession of the republic. He did not realize that before the nation could be truly unified it must have more social unity; and he did not understand how deep-seated was the incompatibility between the sections, or how intense was the rivalry which he sought to reconcile and satisfy by " mutual forbearance, respect, and non-interference."

* * *

But Congress was not to meet without another misfortune. As Pierce was working on his message word came that Atherton was dead. The assembling of Congress was but two weeks away when Pierce found himself suddenly and without warning deprived of his spokesman in the Senate. With politics in such an uncertain state, the President more than ever needed his friend to represent him. But neither illness, nor Atherton's death, nor political turmoil, seemed for the moment able to shake the confidence which Pierce had gradually been acquiring as his administration advanced. He felt ready for Congress:

> *Faction* is powerless here, you would be surprised to see how perfectly so. The message . . . I think you will pronounce . . . sound. There are parts of it which will strike you as *broad* as well as sound. . . . Labor and confinement have shaken my health a little, but my constitutional elasticity will bring me out. The interest with which friends and foes have been looking for the message has naturally enough made me anxious.
> So far as that is concerned it is over now—my best powers have been given to duty, consequences may take care of themselves.[8]

XXXVIII
CONGRESS ASSEMBLES

PIERCE did not suffer from any illusions as to his power over Congress, he did not have to learn that the executive and legislative branches of the government are coördinate and equal. His message stressed that idea and invited coöperation between Congress and the Executive in carrying out a joint program. But many freely predicted that the political troubles of the last few months would make coöperation difficult. While the President had been guilty of no statement or action based upon incorrect principles, his handling of the patronage had caused noisy factions and important newspapers to demand that Congress rebuke the President's presumption. Would Congress heed this demand or would they accept his policy? If Congress refused to coöperate how would the President handle the situation? Gideon Welles, for one, feared that he was no Jackson.[1]

The thirty-third Congress, which was foregathering to consider Pierce's program, contained generous Democratic majorities in both houses. The Senate assembled in full consciousness of its responsible position. Few legislative bodies in the world had more power, and their prerogatives had been increasing, especially under Fillmore.[2] Under Webster, Clay, and Calhoun this chamber had become a temple of wisdom, and though the giants had gone to their reward their successors were fully conscious of reflected glory. The Senate with its power of confirmation and its share in the control of relations was a body with which the President must establish satisfactory relations if he were to succeed. Sixty-one solons finally came together in the upper house to participate in the winter's legislation.

Most prominent of them all perhaps, though no longer in his prime, was Lewis Cass, defeated Presidential candidate in 1848 and author of the Nicholson letter, who had been in Washington much of the time since Jackson's regime. He was ancient and obese now, disinclined to labor but willing to make long, rather tedious speeches of no particular merit on the great questions of the day. When gas fixtures were being installed in one of the committee rooms of the Senate his colleague Hamlin of Maine remarked that it would be better to hang " Old Cass " there, he would answer the same purpose.[3] Next in prominence was Judge Douglas, chief spokesman of the exploiting West, a man small in stature, inclining now to *embonpoint*. He had striven vainly for the nomination in 1852 and was held by all hands to be actively looking into the future. He was a " shrewd Yankee," politically opportunistic, ruthless, facile and daring. Western development, land speculation, railroad promotion, all these were dear to his heart and necessary to his fortune. He was a dangerous man in the eyes of many, especially in the South, but to " Young America " he was an idol.[4] A third figure from the West was Jesse D. Bright, whom one Washington " bud " characterized as " not a refined-looking man. He has a large stomach and little legs, too much ' animality ' about him." He too was a speculator, close friend of the banker Corcoran and politically allied to Cass, largely, it may be suspected, because he wanted to use Cass's prestige in his fight with his colleague Pettit and Governor Wright for the control of Indiana. Pierce had not heeded his pretensions, and he was the President's bitter enemy from the start.[5] These three men were the outstanding Democratic Senators from the free states.

Among their associates from the West were the patriarchal Henry Dodge of Wisconsin and his lank and impassive son, Augustus Caesar, representing Iowa with the irrepressible raven-haired George W. Jones.[6] Almost by themselves were Gwin and Weller from California. The former was a tall and striking Tennessean, crafty and calculating, who with his colleague and their House associates, was there to promote railroad, mail, and telegraph service to their far-away Golconda, ready to threaten secession if these services were not extended. They knew neither North nor South but only California.[7] The East sent no outstanding Democrats; Hamlin of Maine was a coming man and perhaps the most influential.[8]

The chief exponents of the southern interest in the Senate were a group of four men. On the south side of F Street, three doors west of Ninth, almost within the shadow of the patent office, stood one of Washington's usual brick houses. Here apart from the ordinary congressional boarding-house life lived five men during the sessions of Congress, four of them senators; David Rice Atchison, of Missouri, acting Vice President, next in line for the succession should accident or illness remove Pierce; James Murray Mason of Virginia, chairman of the foreign relations committee; Andrew Pickens Butler of South Carolina, chairman of the judiciary committee; and Robert Mercer Taliaferro Hunter, also of Virginia, chairman of the finance committee. These four, heirs and assigns of the political estate of John C. Calhoun, formed the mess which sought to lead the South. While they could not be said to dominate, they often could block legislation effectively and had always to be reckoned with. Atchison was florid, forthright, impetuous, hot-tempered and convivial. Mason was pompous and self-important, a Dombey, thick-skulled and ruffle-shirted, as one characterized him, "feebly forcible and forcibly feeble." About Butler we know little; in appearance his white head made a contrast to his red face, and he was generally respected except by the more bitter anti-slavery senators like Sumner. Fourth and last was Hunter, quiet and unobtrusive, a strange contrast to the others, and known as the financial brains of the Senate.[9]

Another personage from the South who acted with his southern colleagues, though rather independently, was John Slidell, a newcomer in the Senate, originally of New York, now of Louisiana, a cosmopolitan who played a lone hand. He had a hobby and that was the establishment of James Buchanan in the White House; and he had a mission and that was the destruction of Pierre Soulé's faction in Louisiana. He was a cold, reserved man whom few could penetrate. He had hoped for a European embassy where he might promote manifest destiny and his own manifold financial interests. Failing this, his attitude toward Pierce was cold and critical, more especially since Pierce and Davis were very friendly to his rival, Soulé.[10] Besides Slidell, there were other southern Democrats of prominence, such as Evans of South Carolina, who had been a judge and who struck one observer, who had expected swashbuckling southern chivalry, as being as "plain and simple-minded as a Methodist clergyman of the old stamp."[11] Picturesque Sam Houston sat in his seat in the Senate [12] and whittled, occasionally sending a wooden heart of his own make to some fair observer in the gallery. James A. Bayard of the famous Delaware family, like Bright and Slidell, was disaffected over patronage matters.[13] Freshly arrived was Clement C. Clay of Alabama, destined to be one of the President's few friends in the Senate.[14]

On the Whig side there was a smaller group of more able or at least, as the future was to demonstrate, more fortunate men. Seward, in many respects the ablest man in the Senate, with Fish, Sumner, and Everett combined ability, learning and respectability such as no other group could. The pompous and self-loving Chase and his less polished and more ruthless colleague, Ben Wade, represented a rising power in the West. From the South came the impetuous, turgid and alcoholic Toombs, whose tongue outran his discretion, and the suave, smooth Benjamin with the perpetually smiling mask that covered a soul devoid of humor or apparent feeling. The border states were represented in part by two veterans, John Bell and John M. Clayton, who contributed long experience and wide acquaintance with public affairs to the Senate proceedings.[15]

Grouped as to parties, there were thirty-seven Democrats, twenty-two Whigs and two Free Soil men. Of the Democratic majority twenty-one were from the free states. The committees in the Senate were chosen by the party caucus and then elected by ballot. Their composition was governed by seniority, and of the five or six members of each, the Democrats usually had four. While the South held three of the most important chairmanships, foreign affairs, finance, and judiciary, and two others nearly as valuable, they had an actual majority on but three committees. Western senators had eight of the eighteen major chairmanships, the East five. Few members of the Senate had served very long; Atchison with a record of ten years was the dean of the Democrats, and Clayton who had returned for his third term since 1829 was the senior Whig, with eleven years to his credit. Only six Democrats and three Whigs had served more than six years. The old order had just passed and the new generation had not known power long. If the Democrats could agree among themselves, they were in comfortable control; but the tendency to vote according to personal preference and sectional interest had become increasingly pronounced.

In the House there was a distinct absence of well-known men of any party. Only eighty of the 234 had been re-elected, which

made the proportion of new faces unusually large.* One studies the rolls of that House almost in vain for familiar names;
most of them have departed without leaving a trace of their
identity. The Democrats were in the great majority, having
more than twice as many as the Whigs (159–71). Virginia had
perhaps the strongest delegation. Bayly, Millson, Bocock, " Extra Billy " Smith, Faulkner, Letcher, and McMullen, seven out
of the thirteen were active and often in debate. Bayly with
his golden spectacles and curly blond hair, soft negro dialect
and unfortunate propensity for alcohol, was to be chairman of
the foreign affairs committee, while Bocock was to be head of
naval affairs. George S. Houston of Alabama, a Union Democrat, sagacious, ponderous, and convincing, known as the noisi-
est member, was to preside over the ways and means committee.
Orr of South Carolina, Clingman of North Carolina, and especially Jones of Tennessee were to be indefatigable in their participation in the proceedings; the last-named was known as the
most acrid member of that House, seemingly never off the floor
and silent on no legislation, the Cerberus of the treasury.

Influential were the two Stantons of Kentucky and Tennessee
and a newcomer from Alabama, Philip Phillips, who soon
gained reputation for himself as one of the ablest lawyers on
the floor. By no means can we omit Cobb of Alabama, irrepressible advocate of land legislation, or the talented and handsome John C. Breckinridge, in contemporary eyes one of the
most valuable congressmen, if we are to judge by the outside
effort and money contributed to his election the previous August. The East did not furnish many Democratic members of
note. Pennsylvania and New York sent down the most, but the
names of none of them strike any responsive chord of recognition. From the West it was different. Ohio, Indiana, and Illinois had important delegations. Disney of Ohio, Cass's special
representative; Richardson of Illinois, Douglas's henchman;
Hendricks, Dunham, and English of Indiana; all these were
men of mark, while ex-Senator Benton of Missouri, now in the
House, was perhaps the most outstanding of all.

The Whigs likewise were men of relatively little prominence,

* The Washington *Star* of January 12, 1854, reported upon investigation
that there was neither a confirmed drunkard nor an otherwise dissipated
man among all those coming for their first term.

other than Haven of New York, Chandler of Pennsylvania, Campbell of Ohio, the Washburn-Washburne brothers from Maine and Illinois, with Preston and Ewing from Kentucky, and most noteworthy of all, Alexander H. Stephens of Georgia. The free soilers were few in number but conspicuous; their principal representatives were Gerrit Smith and the patriarch Joshua Giddings.

Linn Boyd, a ponderous compromiser from Kentucky, was to be re-elected speaker.[16] He was harmless and served as a compromise between Orr and Disney, representing southern and Cass factions; Guthrie considered him as opposed to the administration. The compromise speaker took pains to see that the committees were made up nicely, to give each section its fair distribution: of the twenty-four major chairmanships, the slave states had twelve, the East six and the West six. All important committees had nine members each, six or seven Democrats and two or three Whigs. Of sixteen major committees, the slave states had a majority on six (counting both Democrats and Whigs): ways and means, claims, foreign affairs, territories, military affairs, and naval affairs; the East dominated but two, manufactures and invalid pensions, although there were 92 eastern members as compared with 90 slave-state members. The West with only 52 members of course could not expect much, and received little; true, on agriculture and public lands there were four westerners each, but on ways and means they had none, and on roads and canals, and on commerce, to which internal improvements would go, they were well hidden with but two. The reason for this was not so much attempted domination by the slave-state leaders as the fact that southern congressmen stayed in so much longer. Considering *Democrats* only, no eastern congressman was further along than in his third term, one from the West was entering his fourth, but in the South there was one eight-term man, the speaker, three six-term men, three five-term men, four who were beginning their fourth; the slave states had twenty-nine Democrats who were serving at least their second consecutive term, while East and West together could only muster thirty such Democrats. Had those who made up the important committees apportioned them by mathematics, a fairer distribution could not have been made; the South with 41 per cent of the Democrats got 43 per cent of the assignments,

the West with 23 per cent of the Democrats got 25 per cent of
the assignments.   The southern Democrats had advantage in
strategic location, but that was due them because of their
marked seniority of service.   Such was the Congress with which
Pierce had to deal.

In his relations with Congress the President suffered severe
handicaps, in spite of his previous congressional experience.
Few who had known him in his former Washington sojourn
were still in active service; not one of his senatorial colleagues
remained in that body.   He lacked personal friends, and, worse,
he lacked the devoted service of any faction whose position and
power depended upon his success.   He had been chosen by the
party leaders to tide over a dangerous emergency.   Just as soon
as the party had been successful in the 1852 election the emergency for which he had been created, in a sense, was passed, and
party leaders had no further need of him.   This position he did
not understand, in fact he was under an illusion.   He considered
himself his party's leader, which he was not, and had endeavored to impose upon it a program of party policy for which he
had neither the authority nor the backing.   He had demanded
recognition for all who had accepted him, and he had ignored
party history, especially the dark pages of 1848.   Instead of
calling the party chiefs, especially the senators, around him
and giving over the various principalities to their jurisdiction,
thus tying their fortunes to his own, he had ignored them, treating their party rivals as well as he treated them.   Consequently
no one had a vested interest in his welfare, for if he triumphed,
their enemies triumphed as well.

Another aspect of this situation Slidell well summarized:

> [In the Senate] while there is a general disposition
> [among the Democrats] to give [Pierce] a fair and frank
> support I do not believe that there is one man upon whose
> personal devotion he can count.   Every measure proposed
> by him will be received with the respect due to the official
> chief of the party but there is probably not a member of
> the Senate who does not consider his own individual opin-
> ion in every other respect entitled to quite as much con-
> sideration as that of the President, in other words he is the
> " de jure " not the " de facto " head of the party.[17]

To aid in overcoming this handicap Pierce had counted much
on Atherton, but Atherton was dead.

His cabinet could help but little in relieving this situation. Marcy's influence was nullified because of his inability to straighten out the New York situation. Cushing was like an old man of the sea upon Pierce's back. Dobbin, Campbell, Guthrie, and McClelland were men of only local influence. In fact Davis was the only member of the cabinet with real standing, and that was purely southern. This was not a group of advisers who would make any impression upon Congress, especially upon the Senate, who under Fillmore had become accustomed to dominate and resented Pierce's independence of them in patronage matters.

Another set of factors complicated the situation. The treasury was burdened with a heavy surplus and as times were flush, speculation was the order of the economic world. Knowledge of this surplus and the great size of the nation's estate attracted the scheming and the ambitious to Washington to persuade Congress to vote subsidies. The platform of the party featured laissez faire and economy; but hope sprang eternal, especially in the breasts of the railroad promoters, for had not Davis and Guthrie given cause on the New York excursion? Prominent Democrats were interested; no less a man than R. J. Walker was promoting a $10,000,000 Atlantic and Pacific railroad scheme and looking to the government for aid. Steamship lines also hoped for subsidy in the form of mail contracts, to aid them in their competition with the merchant marine of rival nations. Croswell, Law, and other such enterprisers had headquarters in New York city and were rumored to be connected with the " hards " and to be opposed to the strict policies of the Pierce administration. The public lands were a great attraction and many were the schemes pressed upon the government for their distribution to railroad promoters, to individuals, and to needy groups. River and harbor improvements, marine hospitals, drydocks, new federal buildings in many parts of the United States, all attracted those who wished to profit by contracts for the construction of public works.

Many private claims for every conceivable object were pressed annually upon Congress, and the situation in this regard was becoming worse because of the multiplication of professional claim agents or " undertakers." Their " lobby " had in fact become so numerous and importunate that a Senate committee had been appointed to investigate; and during the recent special session of the Senate they had reported upon the danger and had urged measures of reform to prevent the abuse of private bills for individual relief, chief of which projects was the establishment of a court of claims. The belief that the pressure upon this session of Congress would be great was widespread, and Pierce was determined to resist it. Many senators and congressmen who had plans of their own and whose political fortunes hinged upon the favors which they could obtain for their constituents, were bound to resent his strait-laced attitude.[18]

Finally, a condition which was to make Pierce's position still more difficult was inherent in the change which had come over congressional politics since the days of his service. When he had been in Congress he was a member of a strong, well organized party in which discipline was maintained, to whom the Whigs were a real menace, an enemy to be feared. Of late years, the old partisanship had died; there had been an era of good feeling. Senators and congressmen had been voting regardless of party labels, according to their sectional or personal predilections. Spiritually, the Jacksonian religion of Democracy was as dead as Jackson, but Pierce by past experience was not equipped to realize it. As Congress convened, the *Union* made an evangelist's plea for a quickened partisanship.[19]

XXXIX
" SOCIETY " RECEIVES ITS DUE

WASHINGTON, as Pierce had long ago discovered, was a social as well as a political capital, and each President was obliged to organize a social administration. The facilities for entertainment at the Executive Mansion had been improved recently, thanks to the generous appropriation made by Congress. The redecorating and refurnishing of the previous summer had been done under the watchful eye of Captain Lee, whom Davis had detailed from the army for that purpose. An entire new heating plant, installed by Walworth and Nason of Boston, furnished the latest type of hot-water and hot-air furnace, and a glass and bronze screen, erected in the main hall of the house, shut off the drafts produced by the constant ingress of people on public business. The house was now much warmer and the pervading dampness somewhat dissipated.

The public rooms on the main floor had been entirely redecorated. A. T. Stewart furnished the heavy window draperies and the new floor coverings; the most marvelous of the carpets was laid in the east room; it was bright red and weighed a ton. The walls had been refrescoed and much additional furniture provided, including some of the late Vice President King's Parisian furniture which had been purchased and " done over." The dining room had received a new suite of black walnut furniture, the chairs cushioned with green brocatelle and the table supplied with a new china service of white porcelain with a deep red border, numbering 450 pieces, and fifty-five dozen " handsomely engraved and richly cut " glasses; the silver service, too, had been renewed and completed by Bailey and Company of Philadelphia.[1]

Until Congress assembled the President and his family had lived very quietly. Mrs. Pierce had the companionship of Mrs. Means; and occasionally her relatives, the Masons, the Aikens, and the Lawrences came to visit at the White House. These visits increased with the coming of Congress, because William Appleton, a Boston congressman, was also a relative and the

Boston kinsmen now came to visit both families. After Congress assembled there were occasional dinner parties, though a full series of formal dinners was not inaugurated that winter. At these parties, the guests arrived at six and were ushered into one of the parlors. Shortly the President and Mrs. Pierce joined them. The President introduced the guests to his wife, and Sidney Webster assigned an escort to each lady. Upon entering the dining room everything was found in the latest mode; place cards were new then and attracted attention. There were table decorations of fruit and flowers, and stiff formal bouquets for the ladies. The President said grace, and then the meal was served under the direction of Peter, formerly a retainer of one of the family, Mrs. Copley Green. The servants passed all of the dishes to each guest and then removed them; though wine was served the President took none. His evident enjoyment in presiding at his well-appointed table was noted by those favored with his hospitality. At the close of the dinner the guests returned to the parlors, and about eight-thirty the party broke up.[2]

The President was the servant of the people; as Pierce once said to a group visiting him, " You need no introduction to this house, it is your house and I am but the tenant for a time." As their tenant the President must ever be ready to display the dwelling to his landlords; in February, 1854, 5,000 people called, though not all saw the President. A certain social etiquette had developed which dictated a set public routine each winter. The season opened with the New Year's reception. On that day all Washington held open house and the President received the public in his mansion. At eleven in the morning the diplomatic corps arrived in state uniforms and waited upon him; at noon the White House doors were thrown open, and the people thronged the public rooms until they became so crowded that thousands, so the papers said, were prevented from shaking the President's hand. After this event, public receptions were held each week on certain days from twelve until two, and evening receptions each Friday from eight until ten, when the President received with Mrs. Means and Marshal Hoover. Washington society on these occasions glittered under the gas light and chattered to the strains of the marine band. With the coming of April, these evening functions were discontinued, but in May

their place was partially taken by the Saturday afternoon concerts of the marine band on the south lawn of the White House.
At these affairs the President generally mingled with the throng
or appeared upon the portico.[3]

In organizing his social routine the President was severely
handicapped. The tragedy of the previous winter combined
with Mrs. Pierce's customary ill health and melancholy to
prevent her from giving any attention to society, much less
playing the leading part befitting her as mistress of the White
House. Also three of Pierce's cabinet, Guthrie, Cushing and
Dobbin, were widowers; consequently the social prestige of the
administration rested chiefly upon Mrs. Marcy, Mrs. Davis, and
the widowed daughter of Secretary Guthrie. None of the administration could be classed as brilliant and effective at entertaining. As Charles Mason confided to his Diary after a call at
the Executive Mansion, " Everything in that mansion seems
cold and cheerless. I have seen hundreds of log cabins which
seemed to contain more happiness."

Pierce had to depend largely upon his own social resources
and here he was at his best. He was very fond of society and
went about Washington extensively, very shortly becoming a
well-known figure along the avenue where he enjoyed the hom-
age and the friendly greetings of those whom he met. He obtained his exercise chiefly by horseback riding, and black
" Union," with the President astride, might be seen almost any
time. Tradition has it that he was fond of riding out late at
night to enjoy the solitude after a busy day. He paid many
calls on his friends. Mrs. Davis, after her little boy was born,
was a great source of interest to Mr. and Mrs. Pierce; and Mrs.
Pierce used to invite her to ride quite frequently. The President had other intimates, among whom were Senator Clay of
Alabama and his vivacious wife. To one of his temperament,
in his situation, the warmth and cordiality of southern hospitality, so in contrast to the stiffness of staid New England, were
an immense relief and pleasure. The political effect of this
social sympathy will always be a source of speculation.[4]

Public functions of all kinds drew Pierce. If a church were
dedicated, a commencement held, or a prominent person buried,
he and various members of his official family generally were
present. The President lost no opportunity to break the con-

fining demands of his labors and his melancholy home atmosphere by mingling in crowds and appearing at public entertainments. Music and the theatre especially attracted him. Usually accompanied by Webster and other friends, but never by Mrs. Pierce, he regularly attended the various concerts given in Washington. Many artists stopped to entertain the capital, and Pierce not only enjoyed their art but often welcomed them to the White House. It must have been very pleasant to receive the ovations which were his when he entered the crowded concert hall, especially on the brilliant occasion when Ole Bull, Strakosch, and the "wonderful little Patti" gave a joint program. But to the musicians, Pierce's attendance must sometimes have been disconcerting, as when the Germania Musical Society was forced by Pierce's untimely entrance to swing from the midst of Beethoven's *Fourth Symphony* into *Hail Columbia.*[5]

As the winter's social regime was assuming its usual gay air, Congress was getting back into harness and politics was starting to simmer. Committee work in the morning, sessions in the afternoon, and receptions in the evening, were the usual order; and not the least part of the nation's business was influenced and guided at the evening functions. Society and politics in Washington have always been in entangling alliance.

XL

OPENING SKIRMISHES

WHEN news came to the White House that Linn Boyd had been elected speaker and that the houses were ready for business, Sidney Webster started down the avenue with the message, and the papers throughout the country, provided with advance copies, published it broadcast. Pierce eagerly awaited political and popular reactions. He knew from his own congressional experience that little legislation could be expected from Congress in December; but his relations with the houses might be clarified by votes on incidental questions. Each house must elect a printer, and the usual choice would be the publisher of the party organ who would thus be rewarded with a very lucrative plum. Armstrong, as owner of the *Union*, had enjoyed the contract during the last Congress and naturally looked for continued subsidy. However, his paper, under Nicholson's editing, had been very active in defending the President's appointment policy. So it was foreseen some time in advance that the opponents of the administration would attempt to defeat him, as an early test of strength. "Every man who secretly wishes ill to the administration will vote against Armstrong if they can make a respectable show."[1]

The first episode in the printing test occurred in the House two days after Congress assembled. Armstrong was easily elected printer, but twenty-three Democrats bolted, twenty of them voting for Beverly Tucker. Nine New York "hards" were among those bolting in company with two of the same brand from Wisconsin and some Virginia and South Carolina personal friends of Tucker. Little political significance would have attached to this minor bolt, had it not been for the outcome in the Senate. Five days later the Senate balloted secretly and Armstrong was defeated by Tucker, 26–17. Somehow the details got out and the press reported that Bright and Fish had arranged a combination whereby nine Democrats—Atchison, Bright, Brodhead, Evans, Hunter, Mason, Weller, Wright, and one unknown—had joined with the Whigs in electing Tucker.

Armstrong's unexpected defeat was hailed by the " hards " as a rebuke to the administration. Pierce and his friends explained it on personal grounds; a number did not like Armstrong, and the Virginians who were very clannish wanted to help their friend. Armstrong had displaced another Virginian, " Father " Ritchie, under unpleasant circumstances. Here was an opportunity to repay a grudge in no way connected with Pierce. The significant fact remained, nevertheless, that the Senatorial managers, Atchison, Hunter and Mason (Butler had not yet arrived) had done something which was viewed by others, if not by themselves, as showing a disregard for the administration; and they had joined with Whigs and free soilers to do it. The combination did not augur well for party solidarity. As Joseph Lane put it:

> The election of Bev. Tucker . . . will I am inclined to think have the effect to waken up the [Administration]. A new chapter has been opened, and they that can see had better read before it be too late, the democratic senators who brought about this result are true men, sound national democrats who have on all occasions supported democratic principle, and always will, but who are unwilling to see the democratic party, *abolitionized,* and they will support the administration in all sound democratic national measures, but will not go for the confirmation of unsound men.[2]

Another opportunity was presently given the suspicious to be confirmed in their belief that dangerous opposition to the President's policy lurked in the Senate. Jesse D. Bright, ever mindful of Pierce's failure to bolster his Indiana pretensions, brought in a bill to make it necessary for the President hereafter to submit his nomination for assistant secretary of the treasury to the Senate for confirmation. Had this bill passed it would have deprived the secretary of the treasury of the right to name his own chief officer without Senate approval. Democratic leaders in the Senate realized that the bill presented an " awkward issue " but as they did not think it important enough to imperil other projects by a fight, they ignored the " issue " and let the bill pass without discussion or recorded vote. Not so in the House, where the measure caused debate and some members claimed that the move was a rebuke to Guthrie for his interference in New York politics. Since it was Bright, the most

" disaffected " Senator, who introduced the bill, some malice may be suspected; but as the House failed to pass it, the administration forces were seen to have retained control.[3]

Before the House concluded its debate on the assistant secretary bill, Gerrit Smith and Joshua Giddings on behalf of the free soil group tried unsuccessfully to raise the slavery issue. Smith attacked Marcy as having defended Koszta and liberty abroad while remaining indifferent to slavery at home; and Giddings scolded the President for recommending that the long-standing *Amistad* slave claims be paid to Spain. Neither onslaught was effective and slavery seemed dead.[4] There was further House rally to the President's support, according to some newspaper editors, in the laying on the table of motions intended to provoke premature discussion of the Pacific railroad and internal improvements.[5]

So far, lines had held in the House; but the disgruntled " hards " from New York were determined to bring forward their grievances. The picturesque " Hell's Kitchen " congressman, Mike Walsh, had started in before Christmas, but the real assault came when the House assembled after New Year's. Then Francis B. Cutting rose. Taking as his excuse the " inflammatory article " which had appeared in the *Union* during the holidays charging Bronson with insubordination, he moved that the House call for the correspondence connected with the collector's removal. Next day his motion was promptly voted down 105–66, with only eleven Democrats in the minority. This vote, compared with that against Armstrong for printer, showed that only seven Democrats, five of whom were from New York, had voted twice against the administration. Not content with this defeat, the " hards " determined on another move. On January 16 a resolution was introduced declaring that the letters of Guthrie and Cushing were violations of states' rights, and directing the judiciary committee to prepare a bill to prevent outside interference in state elections. The resolution produced no record vote but it did provide opportunity for an extended debate. For the next three days a number of speeches were made which aired the whole " hard-soft-barnburner " controversy, and the policy of the President was attacked and defended. During this debate the " hards " harped on the free soil sympathies of the administration, and Cutting charged a coalition with free soilers for the re-election of Pierce.[6]

The various roll calls in these six weeks showed that the administration was safe as far as the House was concerned but that danger lay in the Senate. The election of Tucker and the passage of the assistant secretary bill had been ominous; yet Pierce and his advisers felt that these defeats could be discounted if the President were upheld on the real test question. From the opening of the session they had been anxious about the Senate's action in the case of Bronson's successor. If Redfield were confirmed the President's patronage policy would be endorsed and his prestige strengthened. It was to safeguard Redfield's confirmation that the administration Senators had made no objection to the assistant secretary bill; and Redfield under Marcy's tutelage was carrying on a campaign to convince Douglas that he ought to be confirmed.[7]

As the vote on Redfield approached, the " hards " and the New York *Herald* accused Pierce and his administration of free soil sympathies, and Bennett offered a reward for Pierce's " Scarlet Letter " in which, so it was claimed, he had endorsed Van Buren in 1848. To scotch this charge Pierce wrote up to New Hampshire to obtain a copy of the letter which, far from endorsing Van Buren, had been so unfriendly that the " barn-burners " had thrown it away without publishing it.[8] These free soil charges and Bennett's slanders were disturbing to Pierce because he prided himself on his " national " point of view and he was becoming increasingly sensitive upon the subject. If Congress would only drop politics and buckle down to legislation!

XLI

REACHING AN ACCORD WITH THE SENATE

PIERCE found his hopes for arranging an accord with the Senate strangely entangled in an unforeseen legislative problem. While the question of Redfield's confirmation was still unsettled, though Congress had been almost two months in session, and while the President was chafing under charges of free soil sympathy and prejudice, he was unexpectedly confronted with a question which he rather short-sightedly had expected to avoid. He had lost no opportunity to express his confident belief that the Compromise of 1850 had driven the slavery question permanently out of politics, and he had expected to spend his energy in pursuing a vigorous foreign policy and in fighting graft, waste, and whiggery. No vainer hope did man ever entertain.

Western urge had pushed the frontier up to the border of the unorganized territory, powerful rival railroad interests were involved, and the opening to settlement of the remainder of the Louisiana purchase had been agitated from time to time in the preceding years. During the previous Congress a bill for this purpose had failed for want of southern votes.[1] However, laws had been passed providing for railroad surveys in this territory and for extinguishing Indian titles to the land in question. The surveys were in process and Commissioner Manypenny had gone into Kansas to make the necessary arrangements with the Indians. Although the Pierce administration had warned those interested that no land was open to settlement, numbers of people took the laws and Manypenny's visit as sure evidence that the territory would be opened in short order. Much activity had taken place on the border; claims had been staked out, unofficial delegates had been sent to Congress, and legislation could not be postponed much longer. Bills to organize Nebraska territory were introduced into both houses the moment Congress met and were referred to the territorial committees. Senator Douglas, chairman of that committee in the upper house, had been interested in pushing a measure for this purpose during several sessions. He was intrigued by the land

319

speculating possibilities of the West, and was especially desirous of promoting a Pacific railroad through the area. However, he realized, from the vote in the last session, that he could not succeed without a few more southern votes.

Atchison, by reason of Missouri's interests and local politics, was vitally interested in the removal of the Missouri Compromise restriction against slavery in the territory in question; and he was insistent that such a repeal be incorporated in Douglas's bill. Douglas knew that the Missourian's influence with his southern messmates was such that they would vote for the bill only if he acceded to Atchison's demands. The Illinois Senator realized the political difficulties involved in attempting a repeal and therefore he sought to satisfy the southern group indirectly. He used the phraseology of the acts organizing Utah and New Mexico. Under these statutes the territorial legislatures were authorized to exercise all rightful powers of legislation consistent with the Constitution and a provision to except slavery had been stricken out in the Senate in 1850 by motion of Moses Norris. The question of the actual legal presence of slaves in the territories was to be decided by the courts, and special machinery was provided to permit reference of such cases to the Supreme Court. Furthermore, the Utah and New Mexico acts had provided that these territories should be received into the Union, " with or without slavery," as their constitutions " may prescribe at the time of their admission." In copying these provisions, Douglas completely ignored the Missouri Compromise which forbade slavery in this area. In his accompanying report he declared it was not his purpose either to affirm or repeal the ancient compromise but merely to carry into practical operation the propositions and principles of the Compromise of 1850, one of which he declared to be that " all questions pertaining to slavery in the territories and in the new states to be formed therefrom, are to be left to the decision of the people residing therein, through their appropriate representatives."

Douglas was not close to Pierce. In spite of his ardent campaign for him in 1852, Douglas and his friends had been largely ignored in the patronage and he naturally did not consider himself in Pierce's confidence. It seems that he did not consult the White House at all about his Nebraska bill report. Nevertheless, the *Union* endorsed it; and Pierce evidently anticipated no

particular difficulty about it, accepting it because it was almost
identical with the Compromise of 1850 and therefore in accord
with the Baltimore platform. As far as is known, Pierce gave
it no particular thought or attention. He held the Missouri
Compromise unconstitutional; Cushing agreed in, if he did not
suggest, the belief, and later gave an opinion to that effect.
But it was not to be so easy.

Henry Clay's successor, old Archibald Dixon, a Kentucky
Whig, ruined Douglas's scheme. He moved as an amendment
to the bill a direct repeal of the slavery restriction in the Missouri Compromise. His proposal placed the southern Democrats in a predicament; they could not permit the southern
Whigs to be more southern than they were. Besides, they saw
the weakness of Douglas's proposal and had doubts among themselves whether under his scheme any slaves could be taken
legally into the territories until after statehood. Therefore,
although there was no particular popular demand in their section for the repeal, they felt called upon to exact from Douglas
the acceptance of some such amendment as the price of their
support; politically they could not do otherwise. If Douglas
wanted his bill to pass he must consent, a fact of which he was
only too well aware.[2]

Pierce and the administration presumably considered Dixon's
move as a Whig trick to stir up trouble for the Democrats. But
past experience made it apparent immediately that the Dixon
amendment might command stronger backing than the Whigs
could give it. Northern Democrats took fright. Cass came to
the White House to urge the President to oppose this scheme,
so dangerous to party harmony, especially in the North, and
Marcy held a like opinion. The President assured Cass that he
would not sanction the move. On Friday, January 20, the
Union contained an editorial condemning both the Dixon
amendment and another, introduced by Charles Sumner, to
reënact the Missouri Compromise restriction, as partisan and
uncalled-for attempts to stir up strife. Next day the cabinet
completed an amendment to be proposed, to the effect that
" the rights of persons and property shall be subject only to
the restrictions and limitations imposed by the Constitution of
the United States and the acts giving governments, to be adjusted by a decision of the Supreme Court of the United

States." [3]   The administration did not wish to raise a storm by
a direct repeal of the Missouri Compromise and Pierce and
Cushing were so sure the old law was unconstitutional that they
felt a reference to the Supreme Court should be satisfactory to
the South.   They hoped a majority would unite in this method
of carrying out the Compromise of 1850.

Breckinridge brought this amendment to Douglas and the
southern managers.   The latter refused to accept it in the place
of the repeal clause.   Douglas was in a tight place, and he had to
work quickly, for the bill was on the calendar for Monday and
the chairman wanted no debate until his plans were perfected
and his final draft fortified with the assurance of united party
support.   If he did not accept the repeal, he could not expect
his bill to be passed.   On the other hand, if he did accept the
repeal it seemed certain that Pierce would rally the northern
senators to the administration amendment and would definitely
push Douglas into the position of violating the Baltimore platform by promoting the reopening of the slavery question.
Somehow, within the next twenty-four hours, he must persuade
Pierce to abandon his amendment and accept the repeal.   The
next day would be Sunday and the President transacted no business on that day.   Douglas was in desperate plight and he was
not going to let Pierce's scruples stop him.   Davis, he knew,
favored railroad development and the repeal of the Missouri
Compromise, so he went to him and prevailed upon him to persuade Pierce to see Douglas on the Sabbath.

Davis succeeded and Douglas marshaled Atchison, Mason, and
Hunter of the Senate and Breckinridge and Phillips of the
House to accompany him to the White House.   Douglas and
Atchison went up first and no one has ever revealed what they
said to Pierce, but when the others arrived in the President's
library an air of very chilly formality pervaded the room.   The
President was not sympathetic and uttered a caution, " Gentlemen, you are entering on a serious undertaking, and the ground
should be well surveyed before the first step is taken."   Then
began the discussion.   For Pierce here was a true dilemma.
He was pledged not to reopen the slavery controversy but he
was also pledged to the Compromise of 1850.   Several very
practical problems confused the issue.   His recognition of the
" barnburners " had led to frequent accusations of free soil sym-

pathy; he chafed under that charge. Here was a way to disprove it and do so in terms of the Baltimore platform; Nebraska would be treated like Utah and New Mexico. Moreover, there was the Pacific railroad scheme; it might turn out that the most practical route lay through this territory; if so organization was necessary. Most important, however, and perhaps the real makeweight, was the nature of the relations between Executive and Senate. The Senate must confirm his appointments; there was already disaffection, and Redfield, the key appointee, was still unconfirmed. Also the Senate must ratify treaties; just that last week the Gadsden treaty had been received and the fisheries-reciprocity treaty was pending with Great Britain. To a great degree the success of his foreign policy depended on Senate approval. In face of these facts, here were the most powerful of the Senators standing before him in his library demanding his assent to the repeal of a law he believed unconstitutional, and the substitution therefor of a principle upon which he had been triumphantly elected. He might, of course, refuse and stand by his amendment, threaten to use the patronage and call upon the conservatives to support him. Such a course would be extremely hazardous and in all probability would bring on a war with the Senate which would prove disastrous to party harmony and the administration program.

The force of all these circumstances was overpowering. With some hesitation, for he remembered the warnings and doubts of Cass and Marcy, Pierce gave his assent. Douglas, however, wanted it in writing. The President had a way of changing his mind when later advice was given; so the Illinois Senator, in the course of the ensuing discussion of the phraseology of the amendment, got Pierce to draft it and took with him, after the close of the conference, the President's manuscript. Pierce's draft stated that the Missouri Compromise " was superseded by the principles of the legislation of 1850, commonly called the compromise measures, and is hereby declared inoperative and void; [and] . . . the people [of a territory or state are left] perfectly free to form and regulate their domestic institutions in their own way." The visitors departed after receiving the President's final admonition to be sure and consult Marcy; when they arrived at Marcy's home he was dining out. They made no further effort to see him.

Next day, while Douglas was presenting the amended bill to
Congress, the President informed his advisers of his commit-
ment and Cushing undertook to prepare an article for Tuesday's
Union announcing that the " policy of the administration . . .
[was] directly involved " in the repeal. Pierce had essayed to
sponsor his first important measure and the problem of marshal-
ing all his forces was uppermost. He was not sure how Marcy
would stand. The secretary of state had been extremely doubtful the previous week about repealing the Missouri Compromise,
but on the other hand he was very directly concerned in Redfield's confirmation, and senatorial coöperation in foreign affairs was essential for his success. As soon as Douglas brought
in the amended bill, Fenton and some of the " soft " Congressmen from New York went to the White House perplexed at the
new move. There Pierce told them decidedly that they were
expected to support this bill as a return for the patronage recognition which they had received. To Marcy they next proceeded. They found him in no pleasant frame of mind. He
told his intimates that while he believed in the correctness of
the position he knew that the measure might have unfortunate
consequences and he would not command his followers in the
New York delegation. In fact he asked their advice as to his
resignation. This, however, the " softs " felt would never do,
because whoever filled his place would hardly favor their views
and in all probability would be chosen from the opposite camp.
Marcy was persuaded, and when next he came to cabinet announced his approval of the repeal. Pierce was much relieved;
his advisers were still a unit.[4]

On Thursday Redfield was confirmed by the unanimous vote
of the Democratic senators present. Pierce's policy of patronage distribution had received the endorsement of the highest
authority.[5] The much desired accord with the Senate had been
achieved. What price victory!

XLII

INAUGURATING A FOREIGN POLICY

PIERCE cherished dreams of a vigorous, expansive foreign policy. His scruples would not permit a very broad domestic program, but the Constitution wrote no " laissez-faire " across the pages of the state department instructions. Diplomacy offered an un-hampered field for constructive achievement and now that his relations with the Senate were clarified, the way was clear. Sufficient time had elapsed to reap results from the work of the lately appointed diplomats, and European conditions were shaping in such a way as to compel American attention.

The first concrete results of Pierce's diplomacy arrived in Washington but a few days before the Sunday conference on Nebraska. Gadsden had sent home his completed treaty with Mexico, and what a disappointment it was! The amount of land which Gadsden had been able to purchase was woefully small and the United States was committed to the satis-faction of the Garay claimants while Mexico was freed from all responsibility arising from this grant, which she had annulled. Pierce and Marcy by this time had decided to ignore both the Garay and Sloo pretensions and they were by no means willing to assume the controversy. Whether the treaty did not deserve the same fate as the Conkling convention, which favored the Sloo promoters, was a question which the cabinet proceeded to debate at length. The President and his advisers labored with the problem intermittently for nearly a month. They finally sent the treaty to the Senate February 10 with several amend-ments, among which was one striking out reference to the Garay concession and substituting the general assertion that the United States would assume all just claims of its citizens against Mexico arising since 1848. In the Senate this treaty vied with the Kansas-Nebraska bill for the center of the stage. The Gadsden purchase was the first step in expansion.[1]

Further expansion and indeed the major field of American diplomacy was about to be complicated by a European war. From time to time during 1853 rumors of conflict between Tur-

325

key and Russia had been prevalent, and at Thanksgiving time
news arrived of an actual outbreak.   It was suspected that Great
Britain and France would become involved, to prevent Russian
aggrandizement in the Near East, and such an event was sure to
have important effects upon Pierce's program and upon American commercial interests.   One of the principal foundations of
the Pierce-Marcy foreign policy was the conviction that Great
Britain and France were in league to thwart American expansion
and harm American interests.   Marcy suspected such an understanding in regard to Cuba and the Hawaiian Islands.²   In fact
ever since the joint proposals of Great Britain and France, during the Fillmore administration, that the United States unite
with them in guaranteeing Cuba to Spain such suspicions had
been growing in strength at the state department and were quite
in accord with the popular anti-British prejudices of the day,
so ably represented in the cabinet by Cushing and Campbell.
The *Union* had been harping on the theme, making special use
of the rumor that through British instigation Spain was preparing to free the Negroes in Cuba, Africanize the island and
thus make it an undesirable place to Southern annexationists.³
The very thought of such a possibility made southern slaveowners apprehensive; they had never forgotten the stories of
the French refugees from Haiti in the 1790's.   Suspicion of
British opposition to American acquisition of Cuba was shortly
changed to certainty when the papers of February 20 featured
a speech made by the British foreign secretary at the opening
of Parliament.   When Lord Clarendon was explaining the nature of the Anglo-French alliance for the purpose of making
war upon Russia, he touched on affairs in America.   There was
" no portion of the two continents with regard to which the
policy of [England and France], however heretofore antagonistic, [was not then] in entire harmony."   Furthermore, about
two weeks previously Crampton had presented Marcy with a
despatch from Clarendon which seemed to make the fisheries
treaty very remote.⁴

Spain further focused the attention of the administration
upon Cuba by offering another one of her periodic insults to
the flag.   March 7 brought word that during the preceding week
Spanish authorities in Cuba had seized the cargo of the *Black*

Warrior flying the American flag, upon a trumped-up charge of violation of port rules. Public opinion immediately flared. General Quitman and the Cuban junto were perfecting their plans for the filibustering expedition. Spain had gone too long unpunished; there was an urge for decisive action. Pierce was having the first taste of international crisis.[5]

Congress called upon the President for information, and cabinet consultations were frequent that first fortnight in March. Marcy had received intelligence to the effect that Mexico had granted permission to a Havana company to supply themselves with Indians from the Yucatan for use as apprentices. This report, untrustworthy though it might be, seemed to bear out other rumors that Spain was getting ready to free the Negroes.[6] Just how was the United States placed? Was there an Anglo-French understanding with Spain in regard to Cuba? That question which had troubled the Fillmore administration was still unanswered. Were England and France encouraging Spanish insults? Was Spain preparing to free the Negroes and Africanize Cuba? Would war be necessary? Feeling in the cabinet was pronounced. Campbell wrote Buchanan a heated denunciation of British activity.

> I believe fully, notwithstanding all the assertions and protestations of Mr. Crampton that England is very busy in Cuba at this time and that Spain is acting entirely under her direction. This is believed too everywhere in the southern states and recent facts only show it more conclusively. If [matters with Great Britain] cannot all be arranged now and be put on a satisfactory basis when she is about to engage with Russia, they must soon be settled with us at the cannon's mouth.[7]

What policy should the United States pursue towards the allies? The Russian minister was endeavoring to learn from Marcy how the United States would stand in the inevitable war. He even went to the President, who told him, " We desire most sincerely to remain neutral but God alone knows whether it is possible." Great Britain's policy might completely " Russify " the United States, so Marcy thought.[8] What measures should the administration take against Spain, and could the occasion be utilized to gain Cuba? Such questions gave the cabinet

much material to debate. The President was not well and was
much cumbered by a seemingly endless amount of work, but
in those confused days of illness, of Kansas-Nebraska and of
foreign affairs, preliminary steps were taken. Pierce described
to Buchanan his state of mind in this troubled period; " Nothing can be more apparent than that an overruling Power is
and has been controlling in the form and destinies of men and
of nations, nor can anything be more idle than to foresee or
grasp the consequences. All we can do is to act with a wise
and comprehensive view of what may be seen and ought with
exercise of judgment and vigilance to be anticipated." Fortified by this philosophy, Pierce' sanctioned instructions to Buchanan to find out Clarendon's meaning; [9] an agent, Charles W.
Davis, was sent to Cuba very secretly [10] to investigate the reports
of Cuban Africanization; and a message was prepared in reply
to the call from Congress.

The document which Sidney Webster carried down the avenue on March 15, was a resounding composition in Pierce's
most exhilarating vein. Spain's action, he declared, was " so
clear a case of wrong that it would be reasonable to expect full
indemnity therefor as soon as this unjustifiable and offensive
conduct shall be made known to Her Catholic Majesty's Government; but similar expectations in other cases have not been
realized." He briefly indicated the difficulty of negotiating
because of the fact that while the " outrages " were perpetrated
by Cuban officials all matters of redress had to be taken up with
the foreign office in Spain—a tedious and unsatisfactory process.
He reported that he had taken measures to set this machinery
in motion and uttered a scarcely veiled threat, " In view of the
position of the island of Cuba [and] the relations it must ever
bear to our commercial and other interests, it is vain to expect
that a series of unfriendly acts infringing our commercial rights
and the adoption of a policy threatening the honor and security
of these states can long consist with peaceful relations." If all
possible peaceful negotiations failed, he would use any power
Congress might grant to " obtain redress for injuries received,
and to vindicate the honor of our flag." He concluded by suggesting to Congress the propriety of adopting such provisional
measures as the exigency might seem to demand. The message,

as was readily seen, was not exactly a manifesto but indicated a sufficient sense of national pride; also it shifted some of the responsibility to the shoulders of Congress. In the meantime, Marcy instructed Soulé to demand an apology and damages from Spain, and on April 5 Pierce transmitted to Congress a document prepared by Marcy detailing sixteen cases of Spanish disregard for our rights in Cuban waters. The secretary of state was even more worried about our security in the Caribbean.[11]

While waiting for Congress to act and Spain to reply, Pierce saw opportunity beckoning. Almost at once Marcy received a despatch from Soulé dated before the *Black Warrior* affair. This despatch indicated that politics in Spain was confused almost to the point of the revolution which Pierce may have expected him to encourage, and Cuban negotiations were therefore now appropriate. Buchanan almost simultaneously reported that Clarendon had assured him his remarks referred only to joint operations in the La Plata region, and that England and France had no understanding about Cuba. Finally Mason reported that the entrance of England and France into the Russo-Turkish war on the side of Turkey was inevitable; * their whole energies would now be concentrated in Europe.[12] The opportunity was too good to miss; seldom did destiny present such a chance.

Marcy instructed Soulé to negotiate for the acquisition of Cuba, April 3. He was still convinced that continued Spanish possession of that island was a menace to our security, but he preferred negotiating to filibustering. Next day he wrote to Gregg in far away Honolulu authorizing him to make an annexation treaty with the Hawaiian king. Sometime during these weeks, Marcy went to the Russian minister and told him that if the rumored desire of Russia to sell Alaska were real the United States would buy.[13] A few weeks later after Mason had reported that the French foreign office " disclaimed all desire to

* The entrance of England and France into the war was announced as early as March 8 in the press (Philadelphia *Public Ledger*) and Mason's despatch of February 20 speaking of the fact as beyond a doubt was received March 11. Official declaration did not take place until March 27 and word of it was not received by Marcy until April 18.

interfere in the internal affairs of [the Dominican Republic]
much less acquire any rights or control there," and had recalled
their indiscreet representative, W. L. Cazneau and Captain
George B. McClellan were sent to the Dominican Republic to
seek a commercial treaty and the cession of a coaling station on
Samana Bay.[14] Destiny was manifesting itself once more and
Pierce and his foreign minister were its willing servants.

In this year in which Pierce and Marcy had been working on
foreign policy, they had learned something of its intricacy.
Pierce had entered office in a state of confusion about foreign
policy. Despite the prevailing antipathy to Britain which was
an important item in the Democrats' political stock in trade, he
wished to make friends with England. But he was one of the
junto of Mexican War generals and close friends among them,
like Cushing, felt quite the contrary. He was volatile and somewhat given to flamboyant utterance which must later be repudiated in quieter moments. He soon was in a predicament for he
quickly learned that Marcy was cautious and diplomatic where
he was inclined to be favorable to heedless action. The result of
this difference in temperament had been a compromise, Pierce
had appointed a series of undiplomatic, or worse, representatives abroad, including such men as Soulé, Borland, Sanders,
DeLeon, Sickles, and O'Sullivan, who were sent out with conservative instructions. Pierce had started out under the influence of Young America, but Marcy and experience had been
gradually toning him down.

Pierce and Marcy had also discovered what pressure meant.
Young America was always demanding. Territory must be acquired. Those with the daring to acquire it should be encouraged. The example of Texas and the Mexican War was always
before them. Filibusters should solve the problems in Central
America and Cuba by aiding the inhabitants to free themselves
and join the Union. Then, too, there were the promoters,
steamship and trans-isthmian transit operators. Cornelius Vanderbilt, George Law, William H. Aspinwall, John L. Stephens,
Prosper M. Wetmore, Marshall O. Roberts, Edward K. Collins,
P. A. Hargous, represented by Senator Benjamin, and A. G.
Sloo, represented by Senator Slidell, were insistent that the State
Department be the instrument to advance their interests. Pierce
and Marcy may have wondered sometimes whether they were
managers of foreign policy or errand boys of business.

DISAPPOINTMENTS AND DEFEATS
1854-1855

XLIII

THE FIRST ADMINISTRATION MEASURE

In the first year of his administration Pierce had become committed quite characteristically to a program which had been dictated largely by chance. European conditions and events in Cuban waters had provided the opportunity for launching an ambitious policy of expansion; and unforeseen circumstances had forced the President to commit himself to the promotion of territorial organization on the basis of popular sovereignty. Almost in spite of himself, therefore, the main policies of his administration had been determined upon and he was to be judged by their success or failure.

Instead of using his influence with Congress to promote tariff reduction and a Pacific railroad and to prevent internal improvements at federal expense, he had employed it to obtain support for the Nebraska bill, and the opposition groups had cleverly focused public attention upon this measure. If his administration and his party were to retain prestige they must pass the bill which had now become the object of bitter attack. All the anti-slavery agitation which Pierce had hoped to avoid had broken forth again. Almost before Pierce had time to think, his action stirred free soil senators and representatives to organize anti-administration opinion along the old lines of opposition to southern pretensions and encroachments. A flood of protest began to pour in from northern sources. Editorial guns, led off by the *Tribune* battery, began to thunder at Pierce who so lately had promised to do all he could to prevent the recurrence of sectional strife and was now fathering a bill certain to precipitate a new crisis of regional rivalry. They little knew, or at least would not admit, that he had been forced into it.

The center of debate was Congress, and while Pierce and his cabinet were deep in foreign problems the Senate became the daily forum for the oratorical efforts of the pros and cons. There seemed little doubt but that the Senate would pass the bill after it finished talking, but Pierce was not taking any

333

chances. Now that the project had been forced upon him, he could not afford the loss of prestige which the defeat of his first administration measure would bring. He was especially anxious to have the northern Democratic senators in line, those from New England in particular. The leading New England Democrat was Hamlin of Maine, who felt slighted in the patronage distribution, and with him the President labored. Cushing tried his hand first, and went down the avenue to the St. Charles to suggest important patronage concessions which Hamlin had not hitherto enjoyed. Hamlin received these overtures coldly, so the President summoned him to the White House. By the usual indirect methods the subject was broached, and when Hamlin expressed his disapproval of the bill the President began to exert pressure. He pointed out that it was a party measure and that party loyalty demanded his support. He even harked back to the days of Jackson and recalled the fate of Calhoun and Hugh L. White who had broken over party traces. Hamlin might have replied, as Douglas is credited with having retorted to Buchanan later, that Andrew Jackson was dead. Hamlin was obdurate.[1] Senators, so Young Hickory discovered, could not be disciplined like Atwood or removed like Bronson.

However, Hamlin's vote was not needed. As it turned out, Douglas succeeded in stopping the flow of oratory on March 3, and at five o'clock the next morning the booming of cannon from the navy yard told those who heard and understood that the President's first administration measure had passed the Senate. Later in the morning, he learned that the victory had been generous, 37–14; Hamlin of Maine, James of Rhode Island (his colleague Allen was absent but voted " nay " later), Houston of Texas, and Dodge and Walker of Wisconsin, alone of the Democrats, had voted against the administration; fourteen northern Democrats had voted " aye." As Mason of Virginia later said, and as Pierce believed, the Democrats by " mutually laying down prejudices " had proposed " a system of legislation which would quiet once and for all the distracting question of slavery "[2] by removing it from Congress and transferring it to the territories. If the House accepted the law, the subject could not arise, they thought, anywhere except thousands of miles away at territorial elections; besides, as numerous senators north and south hastened to proclaim, slavery could not exist in

Nebraska anyway.[3] Such was the statesmanship of the Pierce administration, somewhat under senatorial pressure.

The passage of this measure through the House was to present a much more difficult problem than its adoption by the Senate. While the smaller body had been debating the bill, House orators had been discussing it in committee of the whole on other measures. The members were more than usually hesitant and confused.

A tangled web of sectional and economic interests was clogging the wheels of legislation. Almost simultaneously with the passage of the Nebraska bill through the Senate, the House put through a homestead measure. Newspaper correspondents declared the fate of the two was intertwined.[4] Also, a few days later, select committees in both houses presented a bill for two Pacific railroads, one through the southern area and the other through Nebraska, a significant compromise scheme.[5] The Senate, meanwhile, had sent over a flock of bills designed to grant lands for railroads to five southern and three northern states. Propositions for patent renewals and extensions were being pressed by resourceful lobbies. All these measures represented conflicting interests; many of them could expect success only in alliance with others; they offered a splendid opportunity for log-rolling. To make these bargaining possibilities more complicated, there were pending both a deficiency appropriation bill, which originally provided for a number of uncompleted public buildings in various sections of the country and a rivers and harbors bill. In grappling with these problems, the Democratic and Whig parties in the House had disappeared. In their place was a group of *blocs* struggling for some interest, railroad, land, internal improvement, or claim. Only by coalition and mutual agreement could a majority be procured. It was the European *bloc* system without any responsible ministry to guide arrangements.

Pierce found the passage of the Nebraska bill further complicated by the unexpected death of Armstrong, the House printer. A successor must be chosen and naturally Pierce was anxious to advance his friend Nicholson. In order to thus favor him, Pierce engineered an arrangement whereby Armstrong's interest in the *Union* passed to John W. Forney, clerk of the House, in spite, so it was said, of the opposition of Marcy and Davis.

Nicholson was duly elected March 1 and in a few days the *Union* announced that its views on the Nebraska question had modified. Originally it had proclaimed that support of the Nebraska measure was a test of party orthodoxy. The *Union* now announced that the President would not regard as party enemies those opposing the details of this bill but on the other hand, he would not permit any party patronage to be used against those who supported it. This change of policy, said the New York *Herald*, was the price of the printing,[6] though according to Marcy the new pronouncement represented a real change of view on the President's part; presumably Young Hickory had found it unprofitable to play Jackson.[7] House members would not stand presidential dictation of tests.

Meanwhile, Pierce calculated that the bill would pass the House by a majority of at least twenty and possibly forty in spite of the excitement upon the subject in the northern and western states. His composure, however, was destined to receive a rude shock, for the "hards" started to make trouble once more. On March 21 Congressman Cutting moved that the Nebraska bill be referred to the committee of the whole instead of the committee on territories, an action which would destroy its chances of passing because there were already so many bills upon that committee's calendar. Against Richardson's protest, the House so voted, 110–95, and to many it seemed that the measure was practically defeated.[8]

Pierce and his cabinet began to bestir themselves. As Guthrie wrote:[9]

> The condition of the Nebraska Kansas bill is not what we expected or hoped and we have been disappointed in some on whom we relied but I still think we shall pass the bill and in all the month.
> We loose (*sic*) a member in Maryland, one in Virginia, one in Louisiana, three in Mississippi and Benton of Missouri that ought to vote [for] the bill and we may loose (*sic*) some others on mere quibbles, yet the question must be settled and not allowed to disturb and divide the Democratic party in the coming election and in my opinion and in that of the best judges in the house the bill [will] yet pass.
> These territorial bills passed, the abolition whigs and fishy democrats will have to fight against the principle of self government and for repeal of that principle and must fail.

As Campbell put the matter:

> The question is a barren one in some respects for it seems to be admitted on all sides that no part of the territory is fitted for slave laborers but still our Southern brethern (*sic*) say and with great force and truth: we offered to run the line of 36° 30′ to the Pacific but you refused, don't disregard us now by shutting us out of any part of the common territory.   They ask us further to take this whole subject from Congress and leave it to the people alone to say what institutions they will have amongst them.[10]

Pierce did everything he could for the bill.   He wrote editors like Rix up in New Hampshire urging them to defend this eminently just, wise, and patriotic policy.[11]   He had an interview with ex-Senator Clemens and Senator James, in which he argued that the Kansas-Nebraska bill was a proposition in favor of freedom.   If it passed, although we might absorb the whole of Mexico not another slave state would ever come into the Union. He expressed surprise that the North opposed the bill if the South were willing to take it.   The interview was given wide publicity.[12]   In addition, Pierce used the patronage to exert influence upon congressmen.   He had not become acquainted with many of them, and had consulted with few beyond his small circle of intimates, but now necessity produced a change. Representatives in future debates were to tell of Executive pressure, but whether it came from him directly or from the House managers, it is difficult to say.[13]   Pierce was never very adept at persuading dissenters.

Let the means have been what they may, the administration and congressional leaders succeeded in their efforts.   The adverse majority which had been victorious on March 21 was overcome by May 8, when Richardson, the manager of the bill in the House, was ready to force the issue.   He opened his maneuvers by moving to go into committee of the whole, which carried 109–88; and then he moved to postpone consideration of all bills prior to the Kansas-Nebraska bill.   Eighteen roll calls postponed the eighteen bills that stood in the way of number 236, which was the House edition of the Nebraska bill. Within two weeks the rest was accomplished; and after stormy scenes and a final thirty-six hour session, marked by proceedings that nearly brought bloodshed, the disputed measure passed,

113–100 (twenty-one absent). To this figure the original party majority of 159–75 had fallen. Forty-three northern and two southern Democrats had revolted, thirteen were absent and one had died. Of the 159 Democrats only 100 had voted for the bill and they could not have carried it. Had it not been for the aid of thirteen southern Whigs and the brilliant floor leadership of the Whig, Alexander H. Stephens, the bill would have been lost. Pierce, his cabinet and Senator Douglas had failed to rally their party in the House behind the Administration's most significant piece of legislation.

On May 30, the President signed what he considered his first great measure, expressing the hope that the slavery agitation was forever allayed. There was short life for his satisfaction, however, for he had failed to reckon with the strength of popular opinion. Sidney Webster almost immediately recorded, "The President is and will be more than heretofore embarrassed by inducements held out during the pendency of Nebraska." [14]

ENTERING WORLD POLITICS

PIERCE and Marcy found foreign affairs becoming more complex with each week during the spring of 1854 and the President shifted his attention continually from domestic to foreign concerns and back again. The Gadsden treaty was before the Senate. The Cuban problem was increasingly difficult, British negotiations were troublesome, and the Crimean War developed a series of questions in international law which caused the President and Marcy many a puzzled hour and produced many a debate in the cabinet.

Pierce was to have further reason for rueing the Gadsden treaty. The debate over its ratification, which was the Senate's chief business after the Kansas-Nebraska bill, degenerated into a contest between the backers of the Garay and Sloo grants. In the course of the frequent secret sessions the President's name was drawn into the matter. The Garay people claimed that Pierce had verbally instructed Ward to press the insertion of the Garay claim in the treaty and then, after his instructions had been followed, had stricken out the reference. To settle the dispute regarding Ward's real instructions the Senate asked the President for information. On April 1, he replied with a denial that Ward had been so instructed, and added that although Ward had failed to convey to Gadsden " the correct import of remarks made by me anterior to his appointment as special agent, I impute to him no design of misrepresentation." After more debate the treaty, with the Garay section restored, was rejected by the Senate on April 17. Pierce did not relish the rejection of his first treaty, and declared in private that the Senate's action would be the cause for a new war with Mexico. A week of busy influences followed, a new arrangement was made and the treaty reconsidered. The Garay claims were abandoned, it was the Sloo grant which was to be protected; and in this shape the treaty was ratified on April 25. Such a victory could give the President little satisfaction. His wishes had been disregarded, his diplomacy had been subordinated to the purposes of private interests. During the struggle he more than once had been on the verge of tearing the whole thing up and starting over, but Rusk and other senators importuned him and he reluctantly accepted the mutilated treaty, to avoid another war with Mexico.[1]

With the Mexican treaty ratified, Cuba was left to vie with Kansas-Nebraska for Pierce's attention. The reactions of the public followed two contradictory lines. When the President's *Black Warrior* message [2] was received in the House, Joshua Giddings attacked it with particular bitterness, and his words represented the feelings of many in the North. Cuba was identified immediately as a southern interest, so that discussion of Spanish relations was bound to bring up the slavery issue. On the other hand, men like Clingman of North Carolina and Perkins of Louisiana wanted to introduce measures to aid the President in defending America's honor, a move which would precipitate a congressional struggle. As long as the fate of Kansas-Nebraska remained in doubt, more debate on slavery was the last thing Pierce wanted, and he therefore exerted his influence to keep the hot heads down.[3] Nevertheless, the question did arise occasionally, and was used successfully as an argument for passing a bill to provide for six new frigates.

Of greater danger to Cuban diplomacy than congressional debate was the possibility of some rash act by overzealous citizens. Interest in Cuba was most pronounced in New Orleans, where General Quitman was organizing another filibustering expedition " to free Cuba." In order to help this undertaking, Slidell moved in the Senate on May 1 to suspend the neutrality laws for a year, an action which would serve as a blanket permit for filibustering. Also, there was a renewal of agitation over the dreaded Africanization of Cuba, a proclamation by the Cuban authorities for the registration of Negroes being interpreted by southerners as the first step toward emancipation. Senator Mallory of Florida introduced a resolution to the effect that the recent Cuban proclamation was " calculated to excite the just apprehensions of the Government of the United States of a settled design to throw Cuba ultimately into the hands of its negro population." A few days later a similar declaration, sent up by the Louisiana legislature, was presented to the Senate. All these resolutions went to the foreign relations committee, which on May 23, through Mason, induced the Senate to call upon the President for information in regard to the slave situation in Cuba. By this time Davis, the secret agent, had returned and confirmed the reports from the American consuls in Cuba, which Marcy had been receiving for six months, that Spain was proceeding with plans for slave liberation but no reply to the Senate request was then made.[4]

During these same May days, Pierce and his advisers had been considering Spanish relations as complicated by a report from Soulé. He had visited the foreign minister at Madrid with a dramatic demand for satisfaction for the *Black Warrior* outrage, threatening to break off diplomatic relations if his insistence were not met immediately. Now nothing was ever done "immediately" in Spanish diplomacy and the foreign minister rebuked his haste. Soulé sent an account of his rebuff to the administration, expecting to be sustained in his precipitancy. If we are to believe press comment, some of the cabinet wanted to plunge headlong. However, there were never enough votes in Congress for that, so Pierce decided to negotiate further; a new Spanish minister was en route to Washington and it was hoped more could be done with him than through the temperamental Soulé. That gentleman had made himself ludicrous by his social and diplomatic antics; therefore, in order to lend force and dignity to the negotiations at Madrid, the administration determined to send two commissioners to Spain to aid him. Rumor had it that these two citizens were Howell Cobb and George M. Dallas.[5]

This plan for renewed negotiation made it imperative to curb the filibusterers. Pierce and Marcy realized that nothing could be more disastrous to effective negotiation with Spain than a rash outbreak: the administration already had had to deal with California filibusterers planning a raid on Mexico. Consequently, Pierce prepared to issue a proclamation against Quitman's Cuban expedition, similar to the one he had launched against Walker's Mexican foray in January. His plan for a commission and a proclamation was bound to bring trouble in Congress if not carefully handled. On the one hand, an appropriation to pay the commissioners must be obtained, against northern opposition in all probability; and on the other, the southerners interested in the filibuster must be held in line, after they learned that Pierce was not going to wink at Quitman's expedition but invoke the law against it. Nothing could be done until Kansas-Nebraska was out of the way; but no sooner was that bill passed than a new difficulty presented itself. The Senate foreign relations committee decided to report Slidell's motion to suspend the neutrality laws. Before doing so, they informed the President. He summoned the Democratic members of the Senate foreign relations committee and Bayly of the House committee to confer with Davis and himself. Mason, Douglas, and Slidell, accompanied by Bayly, went up to the White House May 30, the same day that the President signed the Kansas-Nebraska Bill. Pierce there informed them of his plan to send commissioners and his determination to issue a proclamation against the filibusterers. In other words, he would pin his faith upon negotiation and frown upon violence. Slidell immediately protested.

Quitman's expedition was popular in New Orleans. Many had been disappointed when no action followed the President's message of March 15. A proclamation would look too much like backing water, to please an ardent " Democracy." The President explained that negotiations would be ruined by any filibustering activities and persisted in his idea of a proclamation. Perhaps he suspected that Slidell's objections were colored by his enmity toward Soulé. Defeated in his first proposal, Slidell then asked that the proclamation be delayed until the President send in his message requesting a commission; the latter would take away some of the bad taste of the former. The President was unwilling to accede to this, for the Quitman expedition might break out any time and the Senate was in a recess for a few days; it would be dangerous to delay the proclamation until they resumed deliberation. So it went, back and forth, until finally Marcy was delegated to telegraph the district attorney at New Orleans that decisive measures to obtain Cuba were about to be undertaken. This wire would calm New Orleans' disappointment in the proclamation; Pierce further promised to send in the message concerning the commission when the Senate reassembled June 5. Presumably nothing more would be done to press Slidell's resolution to abrogate the neutrality laws. During the interview, Pierce waxed eloquent in expressing his determination to uphold the honor of the flag, and announced to his hearers that toward the close of the session he would ask Congress for an appropriation of millions to be used in case the commission failed to achieve its purpose.[6]

Next day the proclamation was issued, but when Congress reassembled June 5, no message came before it. The President kept assuring questioners that it would soon be ready, and as late as June 24 Marcy sent a confidential instruction to Soulé, informing him that when Congress made provision the President was going to send over a commission to help Soulé accomplish the objects in view without the hazard of those protracted delays which usually attended the ordinary course of Spanish diplomacy.[7] But the message was never sent in. The simple truth was that the Nebraska bill had spent the strength of the administration; it could not count on the Democratic majority to uphold another proposition that was tied to southern interests. As Marcy put it, " the Nebraska question has sadly shattered our party in all the free states and deprived it of that strength which was needed and would have been much more profitably used for the acquisition of Cuba." [8] Yet southerners like Stephens were declaring that the administration was " vacillating about Cuba " and " not worth shucks." [9] It was truly a hard position; many in the North in arms about the violation of the Missouri Compromise, the vociferous southern interests complaining because no decisive action was taken in regard to Cuba.

In the last days of the Nebraska struggle and while Pierce was maturing the latest phase of his Cuban policy, Lord Elgin arrived in Washington with power to conclude the fishery-reciprocity negotiations which had been at a standstill since the previous autumn. Within a few days, Marcy and Elgin signed a treaty giving fishery concessions to the United States and arranging for tariff reciprocity with Canada on certain classes of raw material. Marcy feared that opposition might arise from Pennsylvania, Maryland, and Virginia because of " free coal." He wrote letters to various men whom he thought might be in a position to offset the coal interest; Pierce persuaded the doubtful southern senators; his endorsement of the Nebraska bill proved a valuable ally. In fact when the vote was taken only two of the Democratic senators voted " nay."

His second treaty gave the President much satisfaction. As
Sidney Webster wrote many years later, "Pierce believed that
if the treaty could be ratified . . . and be permitted to work
its sweet will during the years to come, a peaceful merger of
[Canada and United States] . . . was, sooner or later, inevitable." [10]

No such disposition to settle did Great Britain display in
regard to Central America. In fact that tangle had been complicated by Minister Borland. He had been talking freely in a
tone hostile to Great Britain, and had negotiated a treaty with
Nicaragua which apparently guaranteed to that republic territory which Great Britain occupied. The administration was
not satisfied with Borland, he resented their dissatisfaction, and
after pigeon-holing his treaty they were glad to grant his request for a recall. He already had endangered negotiations
with Great Britain, but before he left Nicaragua he was to
make one more contribution. At Greytown he endeavored to
protect an American ship captain accused of murder; in the
resulting melée a broken bottle considerably marred his countenance, and the property of Vanderbilt's steamship company was
endangered. When Borland arrived in the United States,
Pierce was not long in sending Hollins back with a warship to
protect American life and to exact satisfaction from Greytown
for damages suffered by the Accessory Transit Company and
for the insult to the American representative. Such a warlike
demonstration was undertaken with all the more enthusiasm
because a week or so before Buchanan had reported that the
British government rejected the Pierce-Marcy interpretation of
the Clayton-Bulwer treaty and seemingly were going to do
nothing to adjust matters. England's pretensions must be with-
stood. [11]

While considering these varied diplomatic problems of the
spring of 1854, Pierce and Marcy dreamed of playing a larger
part on the stage of world politics, of developing policies toward the belligerents in Europe which would best further
American interests. In this respect relations with Great Britain
assumed primary importance. That nation was much interested in preventing American merchants from giving commercial aid and comfort to the Russians. Our shippers had been
quick to seize the advantages of the neutral carrying trade, and

Great Britain had not failed to note their activity. American diplomats had been wont to contend for the principle that free ships make free goods, but heretofore the British Government had refused to accept it. Now they saw that an opportunity might be gained from concession. Pierce was probably much surprised to learn from Buchanan early in April that Great Britain had adopted the principle for the duration of the war and furthermore would be willing to accept it permanently, but with a proviso. In return for this concession the United States was to agree to the abolition of privateering. Great Britain feared American ships might take service under Russia and prey upon British commerce. Pierce readily understood this was an impossible arrangement; privateering was our principal weapon in wartime and we could not surrender it. By April 13, Pierce authorized such a reply to be transmitted through Buchanan, but instructed him nevertheless to seek privileges for American shipping affected by the proposed blockade. A call was arranged from the House and on May 11 Pierce sent in a message and documents to inform the people that he would not surrender American privateering.[12]

After refusing the British overtures, Pierce and Marcy decided to press, on their own initiative, the idea that free ships make free goods, without making compensating concessions. Pierce awaited developments. Marcy approached Russia and found that country eager for the sympathy of the United States, and although not ready to sell Alaska, willing to make a treaty. Consequently the preliminaries were undertaken, and on July 22 an agreement was signed " recognizing as the Law of Nations, the rule that free ships make free goods except contraband and that neutral property on board belligerent vessels (except contraband) is not confiscable." After this initial success, the corps of American diplomats were generally instructed to propose similar treaties to the governments to which they were accredited. No other important nation proved to be particularly interested.[13]

Besides presenting the possibility of commercial advantage, the Crimean War suggested to the Pierce administration the idea of assuming a new rôle in world politics and promoting peace. Even before the war was officially begun, Pierce had been importuned to take steps to insure the speedy conclusion of hostilities. Elihu Burritt, indefatigable worker for peace, had waited upon the President to urge this policy. The President with his usual courtesy invited him to dinner, March 24, and he had the rare opportunity of dining not only with Pierce but with Mrs. Pierce as well. Burritt was surprised to hear the Executive condemn the horrors and follies of war which had been impressed upon him during his service in the Mexican War. He was encouraged to hear Pierce speak in favor of arbitration although the President felt that it was difficult to find impartial arbitrators for American disputes in the face of European prejudice against the United States. He went on to say that he would enforce the Monroe Doctrine, and that he condemned the efforts of England and France to curtail our commercial enterprise by thwarting our Cuban plans. Mrs. Pierce and Mrs. Means were interested listeners and asked many questions.[14]

Pierce did not take the steps to further the cause of arbitration which Burritt had hoped, but he and his cabinet had ambitions to act as peacemakers. Such a rôle could be assumed naturally because Russia had offered her services in the War of 1812. Before moving in this direction, on July 1, Pierce sounded out Crampton and a plan was matured in cabinet which Pierce hoped to submit to the belligerents in August whereby the United States would offer to mediate.[15]

The plan never was perfected; when these July days with their unbearable heat had passed, the British attitude was so unfavorable as to make it impracticable. Captain Hollins, failing to obtain redress, at the instance of the Accessory Transit Company, it was reported, blew Greytown off the map. Such a feat of arms was quite a shock to Pierce and Marcy; they had not contemplated so spectacular a demonstration and they could but wonder how England would take this explosion and what its effect would be upon the structure of their diplomatic house of cards.[16] For at the same time, Marcy was receiving protests from the French government against what they claimed was " a gross breach of respect to France "; the French consul at San Francisco, Patrice Dillon, had been brought into a United States court for aiding the Mexican filibustering expedition of January, and had hauled down the French flag from his consulate in protest.[17] With Great Britain and France furnished with grievances, and with Prussia and Austria reported as about to offer mediation, Pierce and his advisers laid aside the lines they had prepared for their appearance upon the stage of world politics, and turned to the feverish work necessary in dealing with Congress in its last stifling days. Besides, word came that revolution was brewing in Spain, perhaps aided by Soulé as expected, and now that Quitman and his aides were under indictment and out on bail, negotiations for Cuba might again intrigue the Administration.

When Pierce had commenced implementing his foreign policy, there had been two instruments available, filibustering and diplomacy. Chance, the Crimean War and Marcy had turned the scales in favor of diplomacy. But there was little chance of success. Neither Pierce nor his associates comprehended the reputation which the United States had acquired in the European chancellories, nor what strong containing forces these antagonists could bring to bear upon the so-called "Manifest Destiny" of the republic. Typical perhaps of the opinion of which Pierce was so blissfully ignorant are the words of Palmerston. "These Yankees are most disagreeable fellows to have to do with about any American Question; they are on the Spot, strong, deeply interested in the matter, totally unscrupulous and dishonest and determined somehow or other to carry their Point. . . . [They] are such Rogues and such ingenious Rogues that it is hardly possible to hope that even if the present Questions were settled to their liking . . . [through filibusters] some independent North American State would not be established in Central America, in alliance with the United States if not in Union with them, *in short Texas over again*." [18] Pierce, on his part, had confided to Crampton that he wanted very much to make friends with Great Britain. But his efforts were already giving warning of dismal failure.

IN describing the city of Washington as the home of the President and the meeting place of Congress, no one can dilate at too great length upon the heat of its summers. The many ways in which the history of this republic might have been altered, if Congress had held its summer sessions in some cool spot, can never be adequately conjectured. The summer of 1854 was no better than usual and to many seemed worse. Marcy wrote feelingly: "The thermometer is at 99°, the nights afford no relief. The state of the weather produces a lassitude which incapacitates for mental labor, and the pressure of incidental business attending the close of the session of Congress was never in my experience so great as at present."[1] Cholera, too, infested the seaboard cities and added fear of disease to the discomfort of the heat. In such an atmosphere Pierce had to wrestle with foreign problems and with Congress in its final crowded weeks.

The last battles were being fought by the various *blocs* demanding railroad grants, homesteads, river and harbor improvements, and claims; and these conflicts were complicated by all sorts of echoes of the Kansas-Nebraska struggle. After some sparring among these groups in the Senate, the railroad unit decided not to press the Pacific railway bill, presumably until after the surveys should be completed; and in the House, after once having been defeated, the bill granting land to Minnesota for railroad purposes was finally passed. Other states had strong prospects of similar rewards, until irregularities connected with the Minnesota bill were discovered, whereupon that act was promptly repealed under the spur of indignation. The greater struggles took place over other questions related to the disposition of the public lands, and it was in this realm that Pierce made his second attempt to lead Congress, this time not by advocating an administration measure but by vetoing a bill.

In the midst of the Kansas-Nebraska fight Congress had passed a bill which was submitted to Pierce on April 27. Miss

Dorothea Dix, representing the philanthropic tendencies of the day, for six years had been urging the sale of public lands for the benefit of the indigent insane. Her bill provided for the distribution of ten million acres among the states in proportion to their population for this charitable purpose. Many speculators looked upon the scheme with complacency, as a mutual opportunity for them and for charity. Ten million acres would be placed upon the market and a large proportion would be under the control of the politicians in the eastern states. Dodge of Iowa prophesied that this bill would cause the whole of the public lands to be swallowed up and would establish a system of trading and peddling at all the state capitals. Such a type of legislation Pierce had feared from the beginning, and he courageously set himself to oppose it by his veto, a custom not at all usual among American Presidents. He expended a great deal of thought upon his veto message and studied numerous authorities, for he realized that this sort of bill would be most difficult to oppose: all philanthropy and charity would unite to condemn him.

On May 3, after a week's thought and effort, he sent in an elaborate message interposing constitutional and legal objections. Under the Constitution the Federal government had no right to dispense charity, he maintained. If it started to aid the indigent insane the next step would be care of the indigent not insane and thus the whole problem of poverty would become federal, a situation obviously not provided for in the Constitution. Also the public lands had been pledged as security for the Mexican War debt, and little land could be disposed of legally before this obligation had been discharged. Incidentally he reiterated by indirection his willingness to sign bills granting lands to states for railroad purposes. He took the ground that " profitable management sometimes requires that portions of [the public domain] be appropriated to local objects in the States wherein it may happen to lie, as would be done by any prudent proprietor to enhance the sale value of his private domain." [2]

The veto brought down a storm of philanthropic protest upon the Executive's head and precipitated two legislative questions. First, would the Senate sustain the President, and second, what light if any did the veto shed upon his probable attitude toward the homestead bill, passed by the House and now before the smaller body? The first question was decided in the affirmative when the Senate voted to sustain the President, only Brown, Gwin, Hamlin, and Stuart of the Democrats voting to override. Regarding the second question Cass argued that as a " prudent proprietor " Pierce would sign a homestead bill; others including Hunter insisted he would veto it, because these were lands which the President had said were pledged to secure the public debt.[3] The details of what followed are still obscure, but Hunter engineered a substitute for the homestead measure in the form of a graduation bill, which provided that poorer lands might be purchased more cheaply. The proposition was said to represent Pierce's wishes, and the western senators reluctantly agreed to accept it because they found that there were not enough votes for the homestead plan.[4] If this be true, Pierce's relations with the Senate were still on a very satisfactory basis. But not so in the House.

The last weeks of the deliberations of that body were marred with charges of fraud and the manipulation of legislation. Investigating committees sat hearing testimony as to the integrity of Congressman Bayly, the activities of lobbyists, and the culpability of officers of the House who had changed the wording of a land grant bill to suit some Minnesota railroad interests. Meanwhile the House itself was debating departmental and river and harbor appropriations. In these last weeks they considered most of the recommendations of the cabinet which had appeared in the President's message. Throughout the session they had shown themselves somewhat less willing than the senators to fall in line behind the administration. After the first unfortunate measures like the election of Tucker as printer and the passage of the assistant secretary bill, in fact after the famous Sunday conference on the Nebraska bill, the Senate had generally coöperated with the executive. But in the House it had been different; a number of Democrats had seen fit to attack various members of the cabinet.

Letcher and Bayly of Virginia had criticized McClelland and Davis for advocating railroads at government expense. Others censured Guthrie, especially, because he had contracted an expensive lease for the site of the new assay office on Wall Street; his arrangement to rent the plot for fifteen years at

$53,000 a year seemed to a number of southern Democrats most extravagant! It could not get through as part of the deficiency measure, but finally slid into law as an amendment to the civil and diplomatic bill.[5] Orr criticized Guthrie's tariff suggestions, as being such as every Whig would sustain; these recommendations for tariff and Pacific railroad made the South Carolinian conclude that Guthrie's Democracy was about as orthodox as John Tyler's Whiggery. Besides, early in the session, Guthrie and Senator Gwin had had words at the Treasury so violent that the altercation appeared in the papers. Davis's managerial activities, too, came within the limelight, when Stanton of Kentucky declared that the secretary of war " had gradually and insidiously " brought many civil positions under his jurisdiction and filled them with his underlings. The attack so stirred Davis that he enlisted Barry of Mississippi to move an investigation, whereupon Stanton explained he had not meant the present secretary of war but secretaries of war in general.

Campbell fared the worst, perhaps; the committee on post offices and post roads reported out bills against his recommendation; and when at his suggestion they raised the salaries of postmasters, they ignored the careful and economical plan he had made and adopted one that ruined his hope of decreasing the departmental deficit. His enforcement of the law providing for mails on the Mississippi was so strict that no company would carry the mail, and it threw him open to biting attacks from the congressmen in that region, which resulted in the passage of an act reversing his rulings. In defending him, Olds, the chairman of the House committee, admitted that he was too close and economical in the administration of his department.[5] The Senate voted down his request for a new building.

The recommendations of the President and his cabinet were generally disregarded. Nothing was done about the reduction of the revenue except to vote money for the Gadsden purchase and for the final payment of the Texan debt. A majority of the ways and means committee composed of the Whigs and a few Democrats prepared a tariff bill of their own, disregarding Guthrie's proposals; the orthodox Democratic minority presented the secretary's bill to the House; but neither of these measures received any consideration. McClelland had made many suggestions but few of them obtained action. Although

Dobbin's plea for more war vessels had been quickly heeded,
under stimulus of a possible war with Spain, his recommendations for reorganizing the navy failed; the Senate had provided
for the creation of a retired list but the House refused its assent.
Davis's recommendations concerning reorganization and increase in pay for officers and men were only partially accepted.
The Senate wished to provide for the retirement of officers, and
increases in pay for both officers and men; but the House refused the retirement provision and the officers' new salary scale.
The popular branch would provide only for the privates' increase.   In addition, Congress removed the armories from military control and placed them under civilian management,
against vigorous protest by Davis.   Cushing's scheme for reorganizing the courts, which he had prepared for Congress, and
his plan for a law department, were ignored.[6]

The President himself had suffered, not so much in actual
criticism as in certain disconcerting votes which were taken in
the last days of the session.   Badger, a Whig, and others in the
Senate, had endeavored to lighten the burden upon the President's person and pocket by appropriating more money for
his White House entourage.   It was proposed to provide another secretary, a clerk, a messenger, and an assistant messenger,
also a steward to be responsible for the furniture and other
equipment, and a furnace man; stationery, too, was to be supplied.   These items were approved by the Senate but the House
non-concurred, after Giddings facetiously had moved an appropriation of $500 to provide for " one lady of the bed
chamber "; the House was of the opinion that these expenses
should come out of the President's salary of $25,000.   Hibbard
made it a point to say that neither the President nor any of
the department heads had asked for these extras, but the implication remained that the President's own party was not particularly interested in their leader's comfort.[7]

Most unpleasant of all the affronts which the President received was administered by the more friendly Senate.   At the
same time that news came of the bombardment of Greytown
there arrived reports of a revolution in Spain.   National feeling was stirred by the prowess of our navy; a change in government in Spain might make negotiation easier.   Pierce had told
senators he would bring up the subject again before adjourn-

ment and ask for an appropriation. Here was his chance. On July 26 a long editorial appeared in the *Union*, presumably by Caleb Cushing, putting forth the doctrine that Cuba should be purchased but " if a purchase cannot successfully be negotiated," then upon the principle of self-preservation, and in accordance with the admitted doctrine promulgated by Burke, and acquiesced in by British statesmen, our government should abate the nuisance and remove the danger by an open and national enforcement of the principle. Papers which had been asked for in regard to the Cuban slave trade in May, were sent to Congress this same day, and opportunely the *Africa* arrived on the day following, bearing much news of Spanish disturbances.

In order to insure favorable action in the Senate, Pierce sought to conciliate the interest which his May proclamation had rather chilled. Cushing breakfasted with Slidell, and after some other business had been discussed, proposed to the senator that he introduce a resolution asking for information upon the state of negotiations with Spain, so that the President might reply and ask for resources to be placed at his disposal. Slidell was not interested, but spent some of his time in lecturing Cushing because Buchanan and John Y. Mason were not kept informed as to the state of Cuban negotiations. Disappointed in Slidell, Pierce persuaded James M. Mason to make the call, the resolution was drawn up at the White House and on August 1 introduced and passed. Immediately Pierce's message, prepared beforehand, was dispatched to the Senate. In this document Pierce defended his action in issuing his proclamation against the Louisiana filibusterers, and intimated his desire for resources to be placed at his disposal during the absence of Congress. The foreign relations committee, Mason, Douglas, and Weller, wanted to propose a grant of ten millions to be tacked on to the army bill, and this was mentioned in the press as the plan to be followed, but when Mason polled the Senate he found it had no chance of passing. The committee was forced to fall back upon a proposition of Slidell's, to endorse the President's policy but make no recommendations, on the ground that the time between sessions was so short. Mason softened the blow as much as possible in presenting the report, August 3, but for Slidell and others who were much disappointed at the President's lack of earlier success it was an expression of want of confidence.[8]

The President's last contest with Congress during this troubled session was over the " pork barrel." Pierce had anticipated trouble in this matter and he was not disappointed. Congress had failed to heed the warning of his annual message, or the suggestion of Davis, that tonnage duties be permitted the localities to provide them with funds to manage their own enterprises. Instead, they had put together a large rivers and harbors bill which must inevitably come to the President. The situation was complicated by the fact that in July a bill had been sent him providing for the improvement of the Cape Fear River in North Carolina. This measure was desirable because some work of the federal government to protect the foundations of a fort had caused the current of the river to deposit mud in such a way as to obstruct the passage. Pierce felt that the federal government should undo the damage it had wrought; but how would it look for him, after his utterances, to sign an internal improvement bill? To forestall any misunderstanding, he took the unusual course of sending a brief message with his approval of the bill explaining that " the obstructions which the proposed appropriation is intended to remove are the results of the acts of the General Government."

A great deal of politics had entered the history of the general river and harbor bill. Some of its provisions were inserted by its opponents to aid in its ultimate defeat, in particular one $50,000 item to improve the Appomattox and another to continue connecting the waters of Indian river and Mosquito lagoon at the Haulover in Florida. These appropriations were so patently a waste of money that the President had declared his intention to veto them and friends of the bill feared that unless some arrangement were made with him the measure was as good as dead. While proof is not conclusive, there is some reason to believe that Senator Stuart and perhaps others conferred with Pierce or Davis and as a result brought in a series of amendments designed to remove the scruples of the administration. First, it was proposed to give the secretary of war power to suspend the application of any appropriation contained in the bill and to report his action to the next session of Congress; thus such items as the Appomattox appropriation would not be taken seriously. Stuart then had the amendment amended to substitute the President for the secretary of war; but Toombs further amended the amendment, to forbid the President to make any of his decisions on constitutional grounds. Thus amended, the amendment failed 35–14. Next, the managers of the bill tried to strike out the objectionable items, but the opponents of such legislation joined the Whigs in voting to *retain* them. In such objectionable shape the bill passed 31–17, with the Democratic party split almost evenly in two, thirteen votes for and fourteen against.

As the measure did not pass the Senate until August first, the President had little time to think about or prepare his veto message. Whether he had expected the bill to fail, or to come to him in such shape that he could sign it, or whether he had put off the message because engrossed in last-minute foreign problems, does not appear. At any rate he had no veto ready. So he contented himself with sending in a brief veto and promising an extended paper at the next session. When his message of disapproval arrived in the Congress on August 5 western Congressmen rose up and protested. As Senator Dodge of Iowa remarked, nothing the West had urged had passed; homestead, railroads, and now rivers and harbors, each had been pressed in vain; all they had received was the Kansas-Nebraska and graduation acts which were not unmixed blessings. Westerners openly threatened that hereafter regardless of party they would band together to enforce their will. Hibbard, the President's closest friend in the House, in the last hours rose to defend him. Said he, the President has only been doing his duty in following the principles laid down by the fathers of the Democratic church, and this appeal to sectional interest is regrettable but on the whole harmless. For, he continued, "we have had political coalitions heretofore. Attempts at combinations of sectional elements for factious purposes are now being made in various quarters. With what success remains to be seen. They have never been ultimately profitable in the past. My own opinion is, that they will be equally futile and disastrous for their originators in the future." Within a few hours many of his hearers were on their way home to contribute to the organization of the Republican party.[9] Hibbard was not gifted in reading handwriting upon the wall nor was Pierce for that matter.

Having thus enforced his will upon Congress once more, the President went to the Capitol accompanied by his cabinet on Saturday, the last day of the session. In the Vice-President's room he placed his signature upon the army, navy, and post office appropriation bills, upon an act putting his cherished Canadian reciprocity into effect, upon twenty-three other bills and a joint resolution. Having finished about two o'clock, he with Campbell and Webster passed into the rotunda to wait for his carriage. Here an intoxicated young fellow greeted the President, shook hands with him, and then invited him to have a drink. This invitation the President freezingly and quickly declined, whereupon the youth began to enumerate the various great men with whom he had imbibed. At that moment the President's carriage arrived and as Pierce was entering it, the enraged and befuddled young South Carolinian hit him with an egg, providentially hard-boiled. Pierce turned around and had him arrested, but later Cushing went himself to the police station and withdrew the complaint; meantime, the youth upon sobering up a little had attempted suicide with a pen-knife: a little incident in itself, but trying to the poise of anyone who was never quite sure of his own dignity.[10]

Did Pierce's thoughts wander next morning, as he sat listening to the Reverend Byron Sunderland preach the gospel " in the purity of Trinitarian understanding "? Did he by any chance, that rainy August Sunday, cast up the accounts of the Congress about to go into history? The session had been so jammed by Nebraska that little legislation had been passed. Of his principal recommendations only two—the six-frigate bill, enacted under the excitement of the *Black Warrior* affair, and an increase in army pay, had become law. Most of his suggestions had been ignored or defeated. But on the other hand, he had had the satisfaction of signing the Nebraska bill, and of being sustained in his veto of the grant of land for the insane. In foreign affairs, the Gadsden, Reciprocity, and Russian treaties stood to his credit. Besides, there were negative achievements as well. " Economy " had been practised, although to the point of depriving the President of an adequate staff; no flagrant speculators' bills had been passed, no land had been thrown away, no " pork barrel " had been corned. He could still find hope for the future.

XLVI

ANOTHER CUBAN HOPE

THE failure of Congress to provide Pierce with the desired millions for Cuba left him rather at a loss as to the next move. Without funds, the means at his disposal were limited to the routine appropriations. He must use regular diplomatic channels or none at all. Disguise the matter as he might, Pierce had realized for some time that Soulé could do nothing alone. As no extraordinary commission could be sent to aid him without money, he must find some other means. Buchanan supplied them.

August Belmont had once suggested to Buchanan that the way to acquire Cuba was to use backstairs influence on the Spanish royal family and to call in the aid of the great European banking houses. Being an agent of the Rothschilds, Belmont thought that if he were appointed American chargé at the Court of Naples where relatives of the Spanish royal house ruled, he might aid. Also, the Barings, the Rothschilds, and other large holders of Spanish bonds would be interested in having Spain sell Cuba, because the large sum thus received would insure the payment of the debt, which of late was not a very good risk.

When Buchanan wrote his long letter of advice to Pierce in December, 1852, he outlined the plan to the President-elect and later successfully urged the appointment of Belmont to a diplomatic post; the financier was sent not to Naples but to the Hague. From this center he went occasionally to Paris and became more convinced after further investigation that his scheme was practical. After the *Black Warrior* affair, Buchanan adverted to the matter once more in a letter to Slidell, and the latter pressed it upon Pierce.

Just before Congress had adjourned, Marcy received a letter from Buchanan in which the latter again put forward his scheme. " It would be manifestly to the interest of the holders of the Spanish debt as well as of Spain herself " for Cuba to be sold and Buchanan did not believe that Great Britain would

interpose any serious obstacles. The refusal of Congress to provide any money had left Pierce without a plan. This scheme
of Buchanan's might have something in it. Into the midst of
the puzzle came Mr. Sickles.

When the *Atlantic* entered New York harbor at the time the
President was having his little brush with the Carolinian inebri-
ate, it brought Daniel E. Sickles, secretary of Buchanan's legation, fresh from London. He spent Sunday in New York and
next day went to Washington with despatches. He called upon
Pierce and the President invited him to stay at the White House,
where he was entertaining General Joseph Lane of Oregon, then
a convalescent. The White House was reputed to be the coolest
abode in Washington.

Pierce and Sickles were kindred spirits. Sickles talked much
in his usual free vein. He had a great deal to say about the
revolution in Spain and related at length his conversations with
a prominent Spanish republican in England. The Spanish
revolutionaries were going to free the slaves in Cuba once they
got in power, and to this end the British Anti-slavery Society
had offered them funds to aid in the revolt; these funds
they had refused. Uprising in Spain might also mean revolution in Cuba. Sickles further discussed Buchanan's scheme for
bringing influence to bear upon the Spanish government through
financial and family pressure and presumably told of his own
conferences with Belmont and the latter's quiet investigations.
The effervescent diplomat also talked to Marcy though not as
freely as to the President. Sickles's warmth easily kindled
Pierce's tinder-like emotions and he in return talked freely to
Sickles, much more freely than Marcy relished. Just at this
moment, Pierce received from Mason a long report upon the
French attitude toward Cuba. Buchanan and Mason were the
ones to guide Soulé to take advantage of this unexpected opportunity; perhaps they could put Buchanan's scheme to work.

In these few days of ardor the decision was made to authorize
Soulé to call Buchanan and Mason to conference, presumably
in Paris. Pierce asked Sickles to return to Europe immediately
and deliver advices to all three of the diplomats concerned.
Sickles had expected to remain in the United States, but he
agreed to the mission. Marcy sat down and instructed the
diplomats in the following terms:

I am directed by the President to suggest to you a particular step from which he anticipates much advantage to the negotiations with which you are charged on the subject of Cuba.

It is not believed that Great Britain would interpose in any hostile sense to prevent the cession of Cuba to the United States. Yet she might be disposed to obstruct this as she did the annexation of Texas.

But the present government of France is less responsible to public opinion than that of Great Britain, it is not checked by any effective parliamentary influence and it has already indicated a tendency to intermeddle in the affairs of the American Continent.

These and other considerations which will readily occur to you, suggest that much may be done at London and Paris either to promote directly the great object in view, or at least to clear away impediments to its successful consummation. . . .

Toward this end, Soulé was to invite his colleagues to Paris " to consult together, to compare opinions as to what may be advisable, and to adopt measures for perfect concert of action in aid of your negotiations at Madrid . . . you are desired to communicate to the government here the results of opinion or means of action to which you may in common arrive, through a . . . confidential messenger, who may be able to supply any details not contained in a formal despatch." The instructions were dated August 16 and their bearer departed for Europe three days later, charged in addition with the President's verbal assurance that he would be watchful on this side of the water and take efficient measures to turn to account any insurrection which might occur in Cuba.

Pierce was enthusiastic again. Sickles's visit had acted like a tonic. As the President wrote Buchanan, " Mr. Sickles' visit at this time is, on several grounds, very opportune and if he has participated in the pleasure he has conferred, he will have no occasion to regret it. He will have much to communicate verbally with regard to home and other affairs." The President had been so attracted to this convivial and congenial spirit that presumably it never occurred to him to suspect he might be making a blunder in choosing Sickles for a confidential mission. He never learned to be suspicious of other people, and near the end of his life remarked that he always trusted a man until he found him wanting. Pierce's instincts were not sure enough to make such a course safe.[1]

XLVII

POPULAR REACTIONS

THE President, thus revivified by Sickles's visit, and by Bedford Springs water, soon recovered from the fatigue of the last days of Congress. With rest came optimism and in spite of his problems, foreign and domestic, he confided to his brother-in-law, " I am neither annoyed nor painfully anxious. To the extent of my responsibility I shall be willing to be judged by results." [1] Results, too, would soon be coming in.

Through all the heat Pierce had remained at his post with Congress. Hardly an hour's relief had he allowed himself from his routine. Early in the summer he and Mrs. Pierce had sailed down the Potomac on the U. S. S. *Engineer* with a party, including Cass and Dobbin, and after spending the night at Piney Point had gone on to Old Point Comfort for a week-end by the sea. These few days had to suffice until the adjournment; it was not until the last of August that he left Washington again. Then, with Mrs. Pierce, Secretary Davis, Webster, and Marshal Hoover, he spent a week at Capon Springs in Virginia.

When he returned to his task on September 9, he found nothing of pressing importance and could give some attention to the fall elections. 1854 was a year of congressional campaigns and the first real chance to sense public opinion. The months since the introduction of the repeal of the Missouri Compromise had witnessed stirring political activity of two sorts. An appeal to independent Democrats, which Chase, Sumner, and their friends issued in January, had been followed in a number of the states, generally in the West, by coalitions based upon opposition of the repeal. Such groups, regardless of party, began to hold meetings to plan for political action to defeat the Democratic supporters of the bill. In Wisconsin and in Michigan, closely followed in Ohio and Iowa, the idea began to take form that opponents of the repeal should organize a coalition party, and on July 4 the famous Michigan convention was held which nominated such a fusion ticket. The West was bitter over the repeal and much disturbed because

Congress was deaf to most of their pleas for aid in the form of land grants or internal improvements. Almost simultaneously with this political development came another and very curious one. The visit which the Pope's *nuncio*, Cardinal Bedini, had made to the country in the early part of the year, had been the signal for active demonstrations of anti-Catholic sentiment and the revival of nativism, especially in the East. This phenomenon had appeared in spring elections in Louisiana, in New York state, even in Washington itself, where a nativist mayor had been chosen.[2] These two disquieting signs were undeniable omens of future political confusion.

The spring election in New Hampshire, though nominally a Democratic victory, had been inconclusive, but less than a month later the Connecticut Democrats had been defeated by a coalition of Whigs and anti-Nebraska Democrats. Dissatisfaction in New England was growing and an unfortunate incident had kindled further resentment. Amos A. Lawrence had written Congressman Appleton that the success of the Nebraska bill would mean the nullification of the fugitive slave law, and he had predicted that thereafter no slave would be captured in a northern state. As early as March three runaways arrived in Boston in three days. Such a condition was bound to cause trouble, and late in May a fugitive, Anthony Burns, was pursued and captured in the Massachusetts capital. Bostonian indignation reawakened so threateningly that the alarmed marshal called upon the United States troops for aid. When the report came to Pierce, he wired, " Your conduct is approved. The law must be enforced." Four days later, on May 31, he telegraphed the district attorney: " Incur any expense deemed necessary . . . to insure the execution of the law," and he sent the adjutant general of the United States to Boston to supervise federal protection. When Commissioner Loring had delivered Burns to his master, the President provided a revenue cutter to transport the slave safely back to Virginia.

Pierce's execution of the fugitive slave act, coming hard upon the heels of the repeal of the Missouri Compromise, stirred up popular resentment against the administration in New England. It brought in the President's mail items such as the following: " To the chief slave catcher of the United States. You damned, infernal scoundrel, if I only had you here in Boston I would

murder you." This amused Pierce at the time but there was
to come a day when such strictures were to be bitterly resented.[3]
The issue of slavery was not so easily banished.

At no time during his administration could Pierce count on
his own state. The previous June had witnessed Burke's insubordination and this year brought a fresh disappointment. Opposition to Nebraska invaded his own party. Pierce was anxious to have Hibbard, who had voted for the bill, elected to
the Senate; but Morrison and Kittredge, the other two congressmen, had voted against the measure and they sought endorsement. This Nebraska rivalry produced a feud. At the June
convention the administration forces won a resolution endorsing
the Nebraska bill, but they got no farther. The legislature balloted for senator off and on through the session, and then adjourned without a choice.[4]

In New York, the " softs " had not adopted such a course as
pleased the President in regard to endorsement of the Nebraska
bill and he was determined that they should have no more favors. When O'Conor resigned, he saw his chance to administer
chastisement. Both " hardshells " and " softshells " besieged
him early in July to appoint a new district attorney to their
liking. Marcy plead the " softs' " cause and presented Lorenzo
B. Shepard for the place. But Pierce would not; the New York
City Democracy had fluked on Nebraska; instead of passing
strong resolutions in its favor they had temporized; Governor
Seymour had appointed an anti-Nebraska Democrat to the state
bench. Still Marcy insisted, for he was in receipt of angry letters from New York. Governor Seymour was furious at Pierce's
stand; he declared the President was a " fool who [aspired] to
be a knave." Unmoved, Pierce turned to his old congressional
associate, John McKeon. He had been on more than one side
of the fence, and though he once had pursued a course which
caused him to be accused of abolition sympathies he now was
a " hard," and Tammany was violently opposed to him. Nevertheless Pierce sent in his name, July 10. At this result Marcy
felt as " deeply mortified as a man can be. . . . I have pressed
my advocacy of Mr. Shepard—and more particularly—my opposition to McKeon very far.—I fear too far, and probably have
given some cause of dissatisfaction." [5]

After this rift in his official family came the elections in North

Carolina which were somewhat encouraging, but the real test would be made at the fall polls, starting with the vote of Maine in September. That New England commonwealth always had been a center of Pierce's interest. He had attended college there. Many of his friends lived there. It had been, next to New Hampshire, the banner state of Democracy in New England, and Maine leaders had been very potent in aiding his nomination. Support from this state could surely be counted on. Then the news came: Maine had repudiated him. His old friend Parris was defeated for governor and the Democracy, suffering a thirty per cent defection, had lost two congressmen. The new party calling themselves Republicans had spread to the East, and under the leadership of such erstwhile Democrats as Hannibal Hamlin were organizing and winning victories based upon opposition to Pierce's administration and its measures. The pretensions of this group Pierce and his friends would not recognize. These pseudo-Republicans, sailing under false colors, were none other than Know-Nothings or abolitionists in disguise, often united with Whigs and temperance groups. Forney opened the guns of the *Union* upon them as foes of civil and religious liberty, anti-democratic, foreign to American institutions. The *Union* also attacked the new doctrine of " no more slave states " as anti-national and opposed to the rights of the South; on the other hand southern sectionalism was rebuked as well. " Nationalism and Democracy " was written boldly on the broad pennon of the Pierce administration, and that flag was nailed to the masthead.[6]

With the issues laid down, the practical problems of politics continually confronted him. New York was much in the foreground, for the disastrous quarrel there remained in evidence. Bronson had been nominated by the " hards " for governor, and during September Seymour was renominated by the regular Democratic party. Seymour again demanded support from the administration, although he felt he could not rely on the good faith of Pierce; the McKeon incident still rankled. But now Pierce was willing to help; he could not afford the entire destruction of the party in New York. The post office entered the contest; two department agents were appointed whose real function was to go to New York and line up the office holders for Seymour. In addition, Skinner, a trusted clerk in the depart-

ment, went to New York with a letter from Marcy containing
assurance of administration support; he attended a meeting
called at Albany to make decisive plans.[7]   Later great efforts
had to be made in New Hampshire; much of the President's
prestige depended on a victory there the next spring.   The
President himself was taking a personal interest in the disposition of New Hampshire post offices.   And it was well he was,
for at this time Burke was sending out little notes to Pierce's
enemies as follows: " The result of the late elections [Maine]
must, I think, convince every intelligent democrat of the utter
impossibility of the re-election of General Pierce to the Presidency."   Burke called a meeting for October 11 at the Eagle
Hotel.[8]

So September drifted into October, and the second Tuesday
was at hand.   It would reveal much, for on that day the voters
of Ohio, Indiana, and Pennsylvania would go to the polls.   As
long as the Democratic party held those states it would be safe.
The returns began to come in, and gradually the enormity of
the result became apparent.   The opposition in various guises
had elected their tickets in all three states, and the Democrats
suffered a net loss of thirty-one congressmen.   On that one day
half the party majority in the House was lost, and in view of
the divided condition of New York only further losses could be
looked for in the few states voting in November.   The very next
day, October 11, the disaffected met in the Eagle Hotel at Concord, and the press of the country carried the news that some
New Hampshire Democrats had repudiated the President and
were advocating the nomination of Sam Houston in 1856 to save
the party.   Visitors reported the President very uneasy about
the whole situation.   Marcy philosophically expressed the
thought of the administration, " The prevailing humor of the
people is to find fault and be dissatisfied.   While this humor
prevails, doing well does not much avail."   Forney dramatically
recorded:[9]

> Our columns are broken, but thank God, we have not
> lost our colours.   Now our giant has touched Mother Earth,
> I expect him to recover strength again.   Non-Intervention,
> self government, Independence, Liberty, Religious, Moral,
> Social, Political it is the true cross itself we carry on our
> banners.   We shall have a smaller party than usual for a
> few brief months, but our devotion to principles will soon
> fill our ranks with bold and energetic Democrats.

Final political disaster came in the November elections. New Jersey and Delaware fell away before a combination generally Whig and Know-Nothing; Douglas failed to hold the Illinois legislature, where an anti-administration senator was forecast; Cass and McClelland lost Michigan; Wisconsin went over to the opposition. In New York, with four tickets in the field, most of the successful officers were fusionists; the vote for governor was so close that the *Union* did not need to admit Seymour's defeat until January. Massachusetts, Cushing's state, went completely and hopelessly Know-Nothing. One fact was written down: the Democratic majority in the House was destroyed. In 1852 Pierce had carried every northern state except Vermont and Massachusetts; in 1854 his party lost every northern state except New Hampshire and California.

XLVIII
THE END OF CUBAN ANNEXATION

WHILE the October and November elections spelled Democratic defeat and popular repudiation of the Nebraska policy, Pierce's last Cuban card was thrown away by his agents. The loquacious Sickles had gone, with great éclat, from London to Paris, and thence to the Pyrenees, to find Soulé. Quite by chance, as Sickles appeared in Paris, he found in that capital a congregation of Americans: A. Dudley Mann, assistant secretary of state; John L. O'Sullivan, American minister to Portugal; John A. Dix; and John Van Buren. Such a gathering, European journalists were convinced, could not be fortuitous, and the overflowings of the exuberant Sickles about the proposed Cuban measures added to the story. Pierce was much disturbed to read in the papers about the congress of American diplomats at Paris meeting to perfect schemes the nature of which was variously estimated. The bright light of publicity and falsehood could bode no good for his plans. Rumor after rumor appeared in the press, but more disquieting were letters conveying Buchanan's reaction. He wrote at length to Pierce expressing his disapproval of the whole proceeding, especially as it had been so blazoned abroad by Sickles. The best way to have worked out his plan of mobilizing the bondholders would have been through Belmont, but why call in Mason and himself, and more especially, one reads between the lines, the indiscreet Soulé:

> Should you deem it proper to cause me to be specifically instructed to that effect, and furnish me with the necessary means from the Treasury, to be strictly accounted for, I think I could, with the assistance of Mr. Belmont, ascertain the names and places of residence of the principal Spanish Bond holders and probably induce them to unite in an effort to prevail on the Spanish Government to sell Cuba to the United States. Capital and Capitalists are proverbially timid, and nothing of this kind ought to be attempted until after the éclat by the public journals to Colonel Sickles' journey to Paris and Madrid shall have passed away.

To this letter Pierce made no reply; he would hope against hope.

Nothing more of an official nature came to Washington, except notification that after some correspondence Soulé had arranged to hold the conference at Ostend in the second week of October. The meeting, like all other details of this *secret* conference, was duly recorded in the press and elicited much comment. On Friday, November 3, the *Arabia* docked and McRae, the consul at Paris, came ashore with despatches bearing the official results of the conference; Sickles was not entrusted with them, he already had talked too much. On Saturday McRae arrived in Washington, and then Pierce heard the results. The important papers were two in number: one, dated October 18 at Aix-la-Chapelle where the ministers had adjourned from Ostend, was the result of nine days of conference signed by Buchanan, Mason, and Soulé; the other was a covering letter from Soulé.

The report of the three ministers recommended that the United States submit to the Supreme Constituent Cortes of Spain, which was about to assemble, an offer of $120,000,000 for Cuba. The diplomats sketched a series of arguments demonstrating that the sale of the island would be best for Cuba, Spain, and the United States. Finally they gave their opinion that *if the Spanish government really freed the slaves and Africanized the island,* then the United States government would need to consider whether the law of self preservation did not require the seizure of Cuba by force. Soulé's letter was more explicit and daring. He hoped for peaceful acquisition of the island, but if that were not possible, what a glorious time it would be for conquest! Great Britain and France were at war elsewhere and could scarcely object. These ideas Soulé described as " sentiments according strikingly with the intimations repeatedly thrown out in your despatches to me."

Thus did the chosen diplomats of the administration permit themselves the luxury of dubious phraseology, at the same time that they declined the responsibilities which Pierce and Marcy had allotted to them. Their instructions specifically bade them " compare opinions " and " adopt measures for perfect concert of action " to converge from Madrid, London, and Paris, upon the desired project. But instead of sending Pierce a constructive plan for European diplomacy, they merely expressed their joint opinion as to the attitude which the administration should assume in Washington, to which Soulé could not forbear to add his private enthusiasms.

Scarcely had the President and his advisers begun consideration of the report and Soulé's effusion, than the New York *Herald* capped the climax of futility. This paper was the one most read in Europe. In it, of all places, appeared a strained version of the Ostend report, a version which all diplomats would see. The *Herald* announced that the three conferees had advised their government to declare, in effect, "that our safety demanded and our interests required we purchase or take Cuba at once." A more unfortunate set of circumstances cannot be imagined.

At home the elections had shown how little hope there was of any Cuban legislation in Congress. What remained for Pierce and his advisors to do? Nothing, but fix on some reply, eventually to be published, for Marcy to send to Soulé and his colleagues. Their plan for making an appeal to the Cortes was not practical; as Marcy wrote, "How that could have been done without insult to the Executive government of Spain is past my comprehension." Likewise, after Buchanan's letter of protest against the conference, and all the publicity, any work with the bondholders seemed in Washington at least to be out of the question. So, following a week of consultation, Marcy was empowered to instruct Soulé to try negotiation once more, to mingle with the prominent politicians at the approaching Cortes and determine whether the sale of Cuba had any chance of being consummated. If not, Soulé must drop the matter and confine himself to pushing demands for damages and claims.

Marcy also inserted a paragraph for safety's sake, to refute the New York *Herald* and to reply to Soulé's covering letter. He pointed out to Soulé that some parts of the report could be interpreted to mean that the proposition to buy Cuba should be made, accompanied by a threat that if Spain would not sell, the United States would seize the island. Such an interpretation might be made, "but other parts of the report repel this inference." Marcy went on to assure Soulé that the President entertained no such inference, for the very idea that the self-preservation of the United States depended on the acquisition of Cuba was absurd.   In such wise the Pierce administration rebuked Soulé.

Copies of this instruction were sent to Buchanan and Mason and these gentlemen read them with mixed feelings.   Buchanan wrote Marcy, " In your Dispatch to Mr. Soulé on our report I am glad to perceive that you exonerate us from the charge so extensively circulated that we had recommended to offer to Spain the alternative of cession or seizure.   How preposterous and suicidal would have been such an idea!   How surely would it have defeated the great object we had in view—the peaceful acquisition of Cuba."   Mason was much astonished and puzzled by Marcy's despatch to Soulé, and wrote Buchanan: " It suggested propositions which are not in the Report.   It disputes about a proposal of cession or seizure which I had not supposed was suggested or hinted at.   I am very glad you wrote the private letter * of which I return the copy which you sent me.   I have reason to fear that Mr. Soulé accompanied the Report with a despatch which he never submitted to me.   Did you see it?   In that despatch there may be found the explanation of Governor Marcy's remarks."

Soulé had committed the worst possible blunder and, furious at Marcy's reply, he resigned; Mason had a stroke of apoplexy.

What Really Had Happened

Pierce's choice of the trumpeting Sickles had been the initial blunder.   The latter's vociferous return to Paris had aroused Buchanan's misgivings; he distrusted any such conference. Therefore, when Soulé chose Bâsle in place of Paris (which Marcy had suggested) because the ex-Frenchman was *persona non grata* at his native capital, Buchanan demurred, and advised that they come to London where the continental spy system was not so effective.   After some little correspondence, Ostend finally was agreed upon.   Soulé invited Sickles to attend the conference as its secretary, although Buchanan thought he ought to be at London in charge of the legation while the minister was absent; Marcy, too, was not pleased at Sickles' presence; Mason had little confidence in the meeting and did not take it seriously, referring to it as an opportunity to " loaf."

The indifference and disapproval of Mason and Buchanan,

* The quotation just preceding is from that letter.

therefore, were to act as dampers on the ardent hopes of Soulé and Sickles. The latter was present at Ostend, though he was not permitted to act as secretary, and he was by no means a silent observer. He was fresh from invigorating conference with Pierce, Forney and Cushing and brought with him the spirit of the July editorials in the *Union*, a spirit which had its origin in the filibustering attempts of the preceding years, and such sentiments fitted in with Soulé's own exuberance. In such wise, the diplomats conferred nine days, three at Ostend and the remainder in Aix-la-Chapelle. Soulé prepared notes of the tenor of the sessions, but it was Buchanan who wrote the report which Mason and Soulé joined him in signing.* According to a later comment of his, Buchanan phrased the document as he did in the hope of utilizing Spain's financial difficulties as best he might, now that his original plan of secretly mobilizing the bondholders had been rendered impossible. He felt that if a definite offer of a large sum of money were made to the Cortes, the influence of the Spanish bondholders, the Spanish clergy, and the commercial classes in England might possibly be enlisted to urge the consummation of the bargain. Spain was " hopelessly bankrupt and her creditors " could have " no hope of payment but in the sale of the island." As Spain was proposing to raise money by selling church property the clergy would, he hoped, see the sale of Cuba as a more desirable alternative. At that time Buchanan did not explain this situation and it would seem that Pierce and Marcy did not understand what he was driving at; Soulé's covering letter was the focus of their attention.

It is doubtful whether Soulé had much confidence or interest in Buchanan's scheme, he was more enamored of the possibility of obtaining Cuba by force. He had talked with Sickles and had studied long and closely Marcy's instructions which had stressed concern over our commercial security in the Caribbean and anxiety about the possible Africanization of Cuba. One phase of the instructions of April 3 had impressed him, " Should you, however, become convinced that Spain will not . . . entertain a proposition for a transfer . . . you will then direct your efforts to the next most desirable object, which is to detach that island from the Spanish dominion." But Marcy had carefully defined that proposal to " detach." Spain " might be induced

* See Appendix.

to consent to [Cuban] independence." Marcy wished to make available any " assistance this country might give to the people of Cuba, to enable them to induce Spain to consent to their independence " in case Spain should relax her strict rule and allow political organizations advocating independence to exist in Cuba. Such was Marcy's scheme of " detachment "; seizure by force lurks nowhere in the meaning of those instructions. Soulé, however, thought otherwise and wrote the explanatory letter which accompanied the Ostend report.*

* * *

Thus the last hope of acquiring Cuba faded. If cleverly handled, the scheme of Belmont and Buchanan might have been worth trying; but what was diplomacy worth, when entrusted to such gasconading " Young Americans " as Sickles and Soulé with the prying New York *Herald* alert for news sensations? The administration blamed Congress; if that body had voted the means asked for in the *Black Warrior* message, they were confident they could have succeeded.[1]

* The last previous word on the subject had been written by Everett, a Whig, in his note of December, 1852, to Great Britain and France. These Democratic ministers may have had some partisan desire to offset that despatch with one of their own equally or even more positive.

XLIX

SALVAGING THE PROGRAM

THE Autumn defeats and a return of the chills and fever did not provide much inspiration for the annual message, nor did the financial panic and the cholera epidemic so lately menacing. But another attempt must be made to salvage the administration program, and the department chiefs busied themselves restating their recommendations. There was more than ever an air of efficiency around the bureaus, and the press commented on the improved system and order in departmental work, which increasing business transactions and growing population had enlarged in bulk between twenty and thirty per cent in the course of the year. Guthrie reported the need of new revenue laws, especially recommending a revision of the tariff; the surplus was still large. Davis recounted the horrors of the Indian wars and asked for four new regiments; he presented to Congress an elaborate scheme for reorganizing the army. Dobbin recounted the exploits of the navy, among which was an exploring expedition across the isthmus of Panama; he endorsed their report that a trans-isthmian canal was " totally impracticable " with the statement, " This, I apprehend, settles the question forever." In spite of his six new frigates, he demanded more ships. Campbell was worried by the deficit in his department and urged a system of registering valuable mail matter. He still had difficulty with the steamship companies and asked Congress to stop the subsidy to Collins. Had he wished to make the administration more unpopular, he could not have succeeded better than by his urgency for increases in the postage on newspapers. The proposal influenced editorial writers adversely in forming their opinions about one member at least of the Pierce regime. McClelland reported a new policy upon the part of the administration in regard to railroads. Hitherto, in anticipation of probable congressional grants of land to states for railroad purposes, the secretary had withdrawn much public domain from sale. The unfortunate circumstances which had killed railroad legislation in the last session had so impressed

372

the administration that it had restored all such land to public sale, and McClelland now announced that no more withdrawals in advance of legislation would be made.

Pierce contented himself for the most part with summarizing the reports of his ministers. Only one did he elaborate, McClelland's remarks on railroad land grants. Since his last message, twenty-eight proposed roads in eleven states and one territory had sought to obtain nearly 20,000,000 acres from the government to aid in building 5,000 miles of railroad, which were to cost over $150,000,000; and in addition the bill granting land to Minnesota for railroad purposes had produced a situation in Congress which provoked a scandal. To the cautious President, the matter was getting out of hand. When could the government stop if it once started? He complimented Congress upon the ability which it had demonstrated at the last session to move slowly.

The chief purpose of the President's message was to restate his foreign policy and publicly reply to Great Britain on the Greytown incident. His desire, he told Congress, was first of all "to maintain peace and friendly intercourse with all nations." "Amicable relations between [states] and reciprocal good will are essential for the promotion of whatever is desirable in their moral, social and political condition." Secondly, he had steadfastly refrained from any entangling alliances or interference in the affairs of other nations. Thirdly, he had sought to aid in "giving widest range to our foreign commerce." In spite of our "systematic abstinence from intimate political connections with distant foreign nations," certain European nations had not reciprocated. "Increasing disposition [had] been manifested by some of its Governments to supervise and in certain respects to direct our foreign policy." Some European powers had regarded with disquieting concern the territorial expansion of the United States and seemed to resent the growth of our foreign commerce which was now "nearly equal to that of the first maritime power of the earth, and exceeding that of any other." Such was the present state of our foreign relations.

In summarizing at length both his efforts to secure the adoption of the principle that "free ships make free goods," and his other diplomatic activities, he ignored Cuba. He concluded the foreign section of his message with a justification of Hollins for his bombardment of Greytown. " It certainly would have been most satisfactory to me if the objects of the *Cyane's* mission could have been consummated without any act of public force, but the arrogant contumacy of the offenders rendered it impossible to avoid the alternative either to break up their establishment or to leave them impressed with the idea that they might persevere with impunity in a career of insolence and plunder." He had utilized the most open and emphatic medium for replying to Great Britain's protests; for the presidential message is a document which all political Europe reads.[1]

On the day Congress met, Alexander H. Stephens recorded: " Everything is flat. Nobody cared a cent for the message or anything else. I don't believe that the tide of popular feeling or popular interest in public affairs ever ran so low as at present in this or any other free country." [2] Stephens was no optimist, but the situation truly was a disheartening one. Congress was in a chastened mood. The Whigs naturally saw little ahead, and the Democrats had been badly defeated. A new and unknown force made even the most experienced politician wander and grope in uncertainty. Besides, disaster had been frequent in the past year. The European war, the crop shortage, epidemic, financial panic, shipwreck, and political disintegration had left deep scars upon 1854.

Congress quickly settled down. In the Senate, the president pro tem, Atchison, was not even interested enough to come back for the opening weeks; so Pierce had the very doubtful pleasure of knowing that his worst senatorial enemy, Jesse D. Bright, as the new presiding officer, would succeed him if anything befell him.

Pierce spent a good deal of December in preparing the official party statement on the rivers and harbors question, as he had promised in August. This document was a lengthy effort which appeared December 30. It laboriously argued that the federal government undoubtedly had powers which could be applied to rivers and harbors for military and naval purposes, also powers which had been used to aid navigation by building lighthouses and beacons; yet the question which " of the infinite variety of possible river and harbor improvements, are within the scope of the power delegated by the constitution " still remained unsettled. The Constitution, he held, " had of necessity left to Congress much of discretion in this matter." Feeling strongly that any concessions by the Executive would let loose a flood of appropriation items similar to those vetoed by him in the last session, he laid down as a policy that two conditions should govern any legislation. One, that for all such works both soil and jurisdiction should be transferred to the United States, and the other, that each item should be passed as a separate bill. As the best policy, he recommended that appropriations of the central government be confined strictly to " works necessary to the execution of its undoubted powers," and the rest be left to individual enterprise or to the states " to be provided for out of their own resources or by recurrence to the provision of the Constitution which authorizes the States to lay duties of tonnage with the consent of Congress." His line of argument pleased the promoters and western developers not at all. This appropriations message was rather an anti-climax, as the House had sustained his veto three weeks before by a narrow margin, but it might come in handy for campaign purposes.

New Year's as usual marked the inauguration of the social season; and on this occasion Mrs. Pierce finally made her Washington début, receiving with her husband. The White House was so jammed that guests had to make their exit by a window; and in the city the loveliness of the beautiful winter day was almost too stimulating. A crowd of rowdies made the rounds of the open houses in true gang spirit. At Davis's and at Dobbin's they broke glasses and carried off food in their hats, while at Mr. McGuire's they took a turkey from the table and tore it apart in the hall.

Mrs. Pierce continued her social duties at the Friday receptions where dazzling costumes were the order of the evening. But here, too, all were not of the *beau monde* or the *bon ton*. One night two Kentuckians, one blanket-clad, stamped in, and in tones in no wise subdued wanted to know " whar Frank Pierce was." Their amazement may be imagined when Marshal Hoover asked for their cards. Shortly thereafter a new experience was vouchsafed the occupants of the White House when a consignment of presents arrived from Japan, sent by that government in recognition of the recently established official relations. Silks, swords, writing tables, vases, umbrellas, mats, jars, cabinets, agricultural implements, plants, sugar cane, two birds and seven dogs, the latter so small that they were a constant menace under foot, represented the flower of Japanese art and civilization, and became the marvel of many a wondering visitor. The President did not know what to do with it all. Congress eventually supplied a special greenhouse for the plants, and the art objects were variously distributed. Mrs. Davis received one of the dogs, to the great annoyance of the many who stepped on him.

Congress in the meantime had shown itself more inclined to business than usual. The Democrats in their speechmaking sought to explain their recent discomfiture. The Know-Nothings with their anti-American, intolerant, and undemocratic views and principles, came in for many hard knocks, while the opposition consumed time in attacking the Kansas-Nebraska policy. Unpleasant rumors and press reports of difficulties in Kansas, between Missourians and eastern immigrants at the recent delegate election, were cited occasionally; but as yet these clouds upon the political horizon were no larger than an opposition congressman's hand.

The administration forces tried to make capital out of the foreign situation. Marcy opened his files to Senator Mason, who appeared at his seat armed with data to prove, as Pierce had hinted in his message, that Great Britain and France had united all over the world to block the advance of the United States. The former had violated the Clayton-Bulwer treaty and brought on the bombardment of Greytown. Both powers had violated the Monroe Doctrine constantly. They had attempted to force Guatemala to recognize a disputed Belgian claim; they had meddled in our attempt to annex Hawaii; they had interfered when we tried to make a treaty with Ecuador looking to commerce in guano; they had thwarted plans to obtain a coaling station in San Domingo. He concluded with the announcement that " measures if not now in progress, will be speedily taken to bring this matter of European interference in questions purely of American and domestic interest to an issue." [3] Pierce still hoped that a vigorous foreign policy might retrieve the fortunes of the Democratic party, in spite of the Cuban failure.

Near the close of the session the legislative mill began its

output. The product was not all to Pierce's liking and, as in
the last season, he prepared to use his veto. When the French
spoliation bill came to him in February, he decided not to sign
it. The bill had been before Congress ever since Jackson's
French treaty failed to provide for this class of claims, owned
principally by insurance companies. The Whigs generally had
sponsored the bill and Pierce considered it a raid on the treasury. He had voted against it when in Congress, Polk had
vetoed it, and so Pierce naturally did likewise in spite of the
earnest persuasion of so close a friend as Nicholson.[4] He took
the occasion of his message to defend his use of the veto: he
was not going to permit himself to be classed with Tyler. The
veto was received by Congress, February 17, with scant enthusiasm. Some Democrats took occasion to condemn executive
usurpation bitterly, and the Washington *Union* expressed disappointment, but the President's judgment was sustained.[5] He
again had protected the treasury.

A second bill roused Pierce's ire, and he prepared a second
veto. The mail steamer appropriation measure came up to the
White House with a number of unsavory provisions. Collins's
subsidy was continued instead of being cut off, as the administration had recommended. Collins was also freed from the
obligation to maintain five ships in service; and, worst of all,
Congress was no longer permitted to terminate the contract by
six months' notice. Pierce resented this proposition to make
the government subservient to Collins. Government and business were becoming too intimate. It was the evening of March
3 in the final hours of the session, so his veto was sent in immediately. A riotous scene ensued. Hunt made a fiery denunciation of executive usurpation and Campbell called for a revolution; but in spite of the noise the President was sustained,
98–79, and the measure without its obnoxious features was
tacked on to the naval appropriation bill.[6] Pierce's strict view
again had triumphed. Yet for the second time, business men
had been given opportunity to sneer at the " stingy " and unsympathetic attitude of the government toward business enterprise.

In the last hours of Congress, the President felt called
upon to kill a third congressional product. As he sat in the
Vice-President's room on the final night, considering the flood

of last-minute legislation, he was confronted unexpectedly with an internal improvement bill making provision for deepening the channel over the St. Clair flats and in St. Mary's river in Michigan. As he wrote later, " I had no previous knowledge of the pendency of the bill and was thus called upon to examine it without any opportunity either of investigation or of deliberate reflection so as to satisfy myself whether its provisions were or were not compatible with my convictions of constitutional obligation." The measure was sponsored by powerful northwestern interests in a region where the Democrats needed friends; still Pierce refused to sign it, and favored it with a " pocket veto." Senator Stuart of Michigan was furious, all the more so because Pierce had recently signed a bill improving the Savannah river in Georgia. In Pierce's mind there was a clear distinction. The Georgia bill was to remove an obstruction placed in the river during the Revolutionary War, a valid exercise of federal power. To many, this so-called discrimination seemed but another evidence of what was known as " southern domination " of the administration. Pierce attempted an explanation to Stuart, but presumably without much success.[7]

The army bill provided for the four new regiments Davis had requested, and their officers had to be appointed immediately, although there was hardly time for the Senate to act on them. Pierce hastened to send in a list of sixteen officers for the new commands. When one scans the list and reads the names of Lee, the two Johnstons, Bragg, and Hardee, it seems almost like the roster of the Confederate Army. Twenty-five civil appointments also, were sent in at the last moment; Pierce's old friend Judge Gilchrist was going to be brought from Concord to be chief justice of the new court of claims, and best of all, Josiah Minot was to be fifth auditor of the treasury and near at hand. Here at least was one friend that he could count on.

The Democrats had been able to salvage some of the party program in this short session, possibly in spite of, or perhaps because of, the fact that many were preparing to leave, not to return; mayhap because, as one observer noted, " no man seemed responsible for [the session's] success or hardly to care for it." [8] At any rate, several administration bills were passed. Following Guthrie's recommendation, acts to regulate steamship travel, to provide for the safety of passengers, and to safeguard the coasts to prevent loss from shipwreck secured enactment; the sum of $300,000 was voted for an extension to the treasury building. For Davis, four new regiments were provided, and an appropriation of $30,000 to experiment with camels and dromedaries for army transportation. Dobbin received four new revenue cutters, besides two acts, which he had requested, for reorganizing the navy and establishing a retired list, and for providing better discipline. The difficulties McClelland had reported in the graduation act were remedied, and certain other of his recommendations, including increased salaries for federal judges, were heeded. Campbell was authorized to establish a registered mail system and to require postage stamps to be affixed to all mail matter; and he was given an appropriation of $300,000 to enlarge his building. Congress on its own initiative had established a court of claims, authorized the construction of a telegraph line to the Pacific by providing a right of way and promising protection, and had reorganized the diplomatic service in a manner quite unsatisfactory to Marcy.[9] It had voted 160 acres of land to all veterans, their widows or minor children, a blanket grant which Pierce signed in spite of its size; he had a tender spot for old soldiers.

On the other hand, a number of bills of executive interest had failed. In spite of a caucus agreement that the tariff should be revised, all efforts proved futile; and after some desperate parliamentary moves in the last hours, its friends had to let it die rather than submit to a legislation-destroying filibuster; protectionism was raising its head once more.[10] The Pacific railroad bill had failed by one vote in the House, and when Davis reported, February 27, the results of the surveys and recommended a southern Pacific railroad [11] nobody paid any attention to him. Cushing's plans for a reorganization of the judicial system and a law department also fell by the wayside, and Dobbin received little increase in his naval force. The thirty-third Congress had passed into history. Pierce in his relations with it had experienced all the difficulty inherent in dealing with an " equal and coördinate " branch of government.

L

THE ROUTINE OF ADMINISTRATION

WHETHER there is much satisfaction in tenure of the Presidential office is a matter of debate, but if the occupant of that high station is to obtain any personal satisfaction, the opportunity for the maximum lies in the mid-period of his term. Between the final adjournment of his first Congress and the first regular meeting of his last are nine months during which the President may enjoy comparative freedom. He has inaugurated his policies and distributed most of his patronage, it is not yet time to prepare very actively for the next election, and he has no Congress on his hands. The routine of administration is the order of the day.

The months from March to December, 1855, were Pierce's heyday. During this time he was by no means free from problems but they did not compare with those which he faced in 1854 and in 1856. Physically he was more comfortable than usual. During his term of office he was much troubled with malaria, but this spring was unusually cool and pleasant for Washington. There was no hot weather until July, and progress had been made in draining and cleaning up some of the malarial areas. The artist, Carpenter, stayed at the White House painting portraits of the President and some of his cabinet, and the bright and robust picture that he made of Pierce shows evidence of more abundant health than the rather wan Healys and the Brady photographs of the last days of his term.

During the months that followed the adjournment of Congress, Pierce devoted himself wholeheartedly to administration. As President of the United States, he had before him a constantly changing miscellany of interests and duties, and he took this miscellany very seriously. He was fond of detail and went about from department to department giving personal attention to matters. He encouraged his cabinet to bring him a variety of items, large and small, and he took pains to investigate many difficulties, real or imagined, carried to him by individuals from outside. Access to him was easy and many disgruntled people

came with their grievances. His manner was sympathetic and
he seemed to like people to come; possibly it increased his feeling of importance. Undoubtedly he spent long hours and
wasted a great deal of time in pleasant puttering around. This
absorption in detail was a concomitant of his inability to handle
major issues more successfully, and in settling many little problems he found a sort of compensation for his failure to handle
the large ones.

The miscellany before him had no bounds. The items which
came to his desk from the departments dealt with matters from
all parts of the world, and every section of the large area under
his supervision. The signing of commissions alone called for
many hours of tedious routine. His mail was large, but Sidney
Webster and his assistant, Henry Baldwin, handled and distributed most of it to the various departments for reply. The
output of letters from the White House does not seem to have
been great. Pierce himself sent very few letters and when he
did, they went out in his own hand.

Following press comment was another chore which was largely
managed by Sidney Webster. He read to the President such
items as he thought he ought to hear. Constant association with
Webster who idolized him, and with his cabinet who by now
were his fast friends, isolated him too much in a sheathing of
friendly coöperation and encouragement which blinded him to
and protected him from the ruthlessness of the criticism that
was so prevalent. It was not an environment to force upon him
the reality which his nature so carefully avoided.

A troublesome administrative problem which cursed him continually was the patronage. He never seemed to find the ability
or the ruthlessness necessary to deal with it firmly and satisfactorily. He had such difficulty in making up his mind that
often when he had made it up he sought to unmake it. The
Oregon situation was a case in point. A few days after his
inauguration, he and Joe Lane had agreed on the Oregon appointments, and Pratt and Deady were named judges. In the
months that followed, Douglas and Shields called upon Pierce
and " made charges of a character that made it absolutely necessary and proper to withdraw " Pratt's appointment. The Pennsylvania delegation meanwhile made a vigorous demand for a
territorial position for a local man named McFadden, but there

was none vacant. Their importunities persisted until Cushing made a discovery. Deady had been nominated and confirmed as Mordecai Deady when his name was Matthew. The error made it necessary to revoke his commission; but instead of giving him a new one, Pierce or Cushing gave the place to McFadden. When Lane returned to Washington, he immediately began to investigate, and when he finally arrived at the truth he convinced Pierce that Deady should be reinstated. Then McFadden went elsewhere.[1]

In another instance, Pierce wrote his friend George, " I deem it my duty to remove Mr. Rosser the present Secretary of the Territory of Minnesota and will nominate you for the office if you have decided to remove to the West." [2] But in spite of his duty, the President never removed Rosser. At another time, Pierce wrote Marcy, " I am extremely sorry to disappoint our friends in Maryland in relation to the consulate at Galway but Mr. Holmes was removed through mistake and I feel under obligations to confer upon him this appointment." [3] Characteristic was a letter he wrote for Campbell, to be sent to Douglas, " The number of robberies which have occurred at the P. O. at Chicago, the loose and irregular manner in which the office is conducted, the fact that two clerks, both relatives of the Post Master have been found guilty and the want of faith in some of the employees still in the office renders it absolutely indispensible that a change should be made without delay." He appreciated Cook's integrity, he said, and wanted to remove him in the manner " least disagreeable." [4] Douglas presumably objected, for Cook was not removed, not even agreeably. His lack of firmness and decision in the patronage Pierce combined with an exceedingly strait-laced exactness in administering rules and laws. He was always confident when he did not have to use discretion. If he had a rule or a statute to follow, he would stick to it through thick and thin. It was only in connection with matters that were without rules, like the patronage, or beyond the usual, like Cuba and Kansas, that he floundered.

Even in these instances he sought for " principles " for guidance, as when he attempted to develop a formula for patronage distribution. In administering the departments he and his cabinet sought honesty, efficiency, and promptness in business dealings and in performance of duty. They attempted to enforce this standard among the government officials. No groups of political appointees who consider their offices rewards for services rendered are apt to take very kindly to discipline, especially when it requires strict accounting in money matters. The numerous rules and circulars issued from time to time by the various ministers left many disappointed or discharged officeholders who bore no good will to the administration. The Massachusetts district attorney, Hallett, became furious at Comptroller Whittlesey's strictness in regard to accounting. In the New York row, one of the grievances was Guthrie's severe application of laws which cut off profitable income. The secretary of the treasury even went so far as to construe a measure granting increases in salary so as to exclude the employees of Nicholson, proprietor of the *Union*.[5] Another famous case concerned a law granting a certain Richard Thompson a sum of money. The original bill had contained a proviso to the effect that the approval of certain Indians must first be secured, but when the question of payment arose, it was found that the final copy of the act signed by the President contained no such proviso, and no one seemed to know when or how it had disappeared. Pierce thereupon went *behind* the law and refused the payment.[6] Administration of this character did not enhance the popularity of the President or his advisers with those who should have been their chief supporters, namely, the officeholders.

The early months of 1855 witnessed the development of three administrative problems which Pierce and his cabinet found particularly perplexing. In the first place, Congress had passed a bill reorganizing the diplomatic service. The service needed it badly enough but Marcy never had had time to give much attention to it. During the recent session, however, his assistant, Dudley Mann, and Perkins of the House foreign relations committee got at it and wrote a new measure which Marcy declared he had not seen while it was in the making. This law stipulated that after July 1 there should be only one grade of foreign envoy, and it provided a salary scale ranging from $7,500 to $17,500 per annum, doing away with outfit and infit sums heretofore paid each diplomat. The act was intended to abolish the grade of minister resident, which had superseded that of chargé d'affaires since July 1, 1854, and to put all in the minister plenipotentiary class thus raising the salaries and giving automatic promotion to many of the diplomats. It also placed most of the consuls on fixed salaries and provided that the fees which had previously gone to the consul should now go to the government.

The law thus enacted caused Pierce and Marcy much perplexity. Did it mean that the President had to promote the appointees involved, re-commission them and send them to the Senate once more or make new appointments? Pierce and the cabinet resented this intrusion by Congress upon Executive prerogatives in spite of the fact that it would increase the salaries of a number of their own appointees, and finally Cushing in an elaborate written opinion advised that the portions making promotions mandatory be ignored. The administration feared embarrassment if some of the names had to be submitted a second time to the Senate. As a result the numerous ministers resident were not promoted and did not receive the salary increases which the law provided; only the ministers plenipotentiary received the new salaries. In the meantime, the consuls were placed upon salary, a change especially hard upon Hawthorne, whose Liverpool consulship up to that time had been raining gold into his strong-box. The attorney-general's decision may have been good law but it was poor politics and did not increase the good will of a number of the diplomats.[7]

In the second place, Congress had passed a bill pruning the naval service of its dead wood. The inefficiency of the commissioned personnel and the clannish family organization of the officers of the navy had attracted Dobbin's attention as soon as he became head of the navy department. In his annual reports of 1853 and 1854, he had urged the legislation which previous secretaries had been recommending, and his appeals finally resulted in the appointment of a board to study the efficiency of the naval officers and recommend for retirement or dismissal those who were not up to standard. During the spring Dobbin organized the board, and late in the summer of 1855 it reported to the secretary. The final decision was the responsibility of the President. He conferred with Dobbin and then called the board before him. He questioned them carefully as to their mode of procedure and the principles of their action and finally concluded that although he did not agree with the board's decision in every case, still it was better not to tamper with their judgment. Whereupon, September 12, the President approved their findings. Of the 712 officers, forty-nine were dropped and 152 were retired on diminished pay. Naval officers generally have influential relatives. The result was a storm of protest that beat unceasingly but to no avail upon Pierce and Dobbin; it did not add to the popularity of the administration in naval circles.[8]

The third administrative problem was raised by the passage of an act conferring upon General Scott the rank of lieutenant-general by brevet. General Winfield Scott and his officers of Whiggish tendencies had been thorns in the flesh of Polk during the Mexican War, and Pierce in turn was afflicted with these barbs. The situation was complicated because Scott had been overwhelmingly defeated for the Presidency in 1852 and he and the secretary of war were temperamentally incompatible. To Davis's mind Scott was lax in discipline, and he did not agree with Scott's financial claims. As regards these, there were two subjects at issue: first, the question of settling Scott's accounts arising out of his collections of tribute in Mexico; and second, by the recent act of Congress raising his rank, Scott now claimed a tidy amount of back pay and an increase in salary.

Relations between Scott and Davis had been growing more and more difficult ever since the beginning of the administration. Scott had moved the headquarters of the army to New York City so that all communication had to be carried on by letter. Davis had sought to tighten discipline by curtailing Scott's power to grant furloughs. The President had refused to allow his claim for a five per cent collection commission upon the Mexican tribute. The storm began actually to break, however, when Scott received his long-desired promotion. Scott interpreted the act to provide him with a sizable sum in back pay, because his new commission was antedated to the Mexican War, and also an appreciable increase in his regular salary. But there was no provision for all this financial outlay in the act. Davis held that such being the case, no increases should be allowed. Scott maintained that the salary and allowances of the law which had created the lieutenant-generalship for George Washington were still in effect; and he also made several other favorable constructions of laws providing allowances whereby he was to be substantially the gainer. In this tangle Pierce was to lean heavily upon his attorney-general.

From July until October, 1855, these questions were intermittently before the cabinet. Davis and Scott engaged in an unseemly exchange of vituperative letters ill befitting the position of either. Finally, in October, the President had the matter placed squarely before him. Davis was opposed to granting Scott any increase of pay, but Cushing submitted an opinion to the effect that the general was entitled to more salary. Pierce considered the question for two weeks, studying Davis's and Cushing's views. Cushing was the weightier servitor to Pierce's mind and he overruled Davis. However, he curtailed some of Scott's demands for forage, rations, servants, fuel, and quarters so that the newly promoted general won $592 per month rather than the $858 he claimed. Davis was so incensed that he threatened to resign, but Cushing at length convinced him.

While Pierce was considering this salary matter, the question of Scott's Mexican accounts came up for final settlement. Then it was discovered that Pierce's refusal of the claim for five per cent had not been sent to the war department, but by accident or design had been kept upon the executive files. Pierce now transmitted his decision that Scott might keep the balance of the funds in his possession, which, while falling short of the five per cent demanded, amounted to a fair-sized commission. As was usual with Pierce, he had settled all these questions by a series of varied and quasi-expedient decisions, most of which were in the nature of compromises.

Presumably they were not to Davis's satisfaction. At any rate, he went on accusing Scott of " grasping avarice," " lawlessness," and " disobedience," whereas Scott characterized his superior's correspondence as showing " no improvement in courtesy, candor or justice." " Such continued recklessness of character could only proceed from one whose low ambition is flattered with the title of ' The Favourite.' " Thereupon Davis rejoined with " Your petulence, characteristic egotism and recklessness of accusation have imposed on me the task of unveiling some of your deformities." And so on until Davis terminated the correspondence, May 27, 1856, feeling that having stamped Scott with falsehood at every turn, he was now gratified " to be relieved from the necessity of further exposing your malignity and depravity." It is conceivable that Pierce, who had some sense of humor, although Davis and Scott had none, as he read this correspondence, threw back his head and laughed; but perhaps his sympathy for his secretary of war prevented that.[9]

From the above miscellany, chosen almost at random, it is easy to see some of the reasons for the intense unpopularity of the Pierce regime. As an administrator, Pierce was unable to rehabilitate his political fortunes. He carried out matters of routine according to excellent standards and in each case had a satisfactory sense of honest purpose, all of which was to his credit. But he and his advisers lacked that saving sense of pragmatic judgment which would have permitted them, without violating their sense of honor, to have made their justice more convincing. Instead of building up a loyal *esprit de corps,* his policies had served to antagonize too many important factions among officeholders, diplomats, army and navy officers. Whether these factions could have been potent in a more fortunate period is problematical, but in the growing sentiment of dissatisfaction toward the administration their opposition bulked large.

LI

PUTTING DOWN THE KNOW NOTHINGS

"Public sentiment in this country is in a transition state, so far as the principle of party organization is concerned. Old parties, old names, old issues and old organizations are passing away. A day of new things is at hand."[1] So Alexander H. Stephens had spoken during the late session of Congress. Pierce would not have made so broad a statement; he would have applied it only to the Whigs. The Democracy was sound except for a few misguided defectionists, but the opposition was being transformed.

The elections of 1854 had demonstrated that Congress was lost and that a strange and mysterious force had entered American politics which upset all calculations. How far was Know-Nothingism going to spread? The spring elections of 1855 would demonstrate to some degree at least how formidable might be this new alignment in 1856. Early in the year, Pierce had turned his attention to stemming the tide of Democratic defeat. The task of retrieving was particularly difficult to a President who lacked administrative genius—one who refused to relax his strictness to conciliate the disaffected. New Hampshire, his native state, had offered him of late little comfort. The failure of the legislature to elect Atherton's successor the previous June had been a sore trial, not only because it showed the weakness of his home support but also because, so the Senate decided, this failure to elect automatically brought old Governor Williams's term to an end. Hope thereafter fixed upon the March election of 1855 to restore the Democracy.

Had the President a party in New Hampshire? Could the Democracy rally once more, crush Know-Nothingism and elect two senators and a congressional delegation? Preparations had been going on for some time. Federal office holders had been raising money in New York, and Webster was in correspondence with George. Webster was worried about Butterfield and the *Patriot*. The editor seemed to trim on slavery and although he asked Webster's advice often enough, his pen

didn't seem quite sure.   Wrote Webster, " If [Butterfield] trims
on the slavery question all is up.   The humiliation then will be
complete.   What a sad mistake is being committed if any fear
is to be evinced of encountering the slavery question and defy-
ing all.   The President feels of course most solicitous that his
party friends shall not merit the reproach of avoiding and
shirking the great living issues upon which the democracy are,
everywhere else but in New Hampshire, a united, brave and
determined body."

But how could an election be carried in New England on
such doctrine?   Webster and his chief were certainly out of
touch with New Hampshire opinion.   Following Senator Norris's death in January, Governor Baker had appointed John S.
Wells as his successor.   After an interview with the newly arrived senator, Pierce realized a little of the difficulty of the
situation.   He harked back to former days in writing George,
" It is quite evident that reasonable hope can only be predicated
upon the supposition that our efficient and able men are everywhere to enter the lists in earnest.   If the battle is fought as was
that of 1840, I have not a doubt that you will be victorious." [2]
But this was not 1840.   The President bestirred himself to send
speakers; he even attempted to conciliate the New York " soft "
leader, Governor Seymour, by appointing John B. Miller secretary of the Peruvian legation, and Seymour promised to speak
in New Hampshire.   A few days later, Pierce withdrew Miller's
name because he found he was anti-Nebraska and feared a fight
in the Senate over his confirmation.[3]

Pierce wrote George rather mysteriously but characteristically, " I have attended to the matter to which you particularly
refer, not of course by making any direct reference to it.   I am
confident that our friends need apprehend nothing from that
quarter.   Write me again on the receipt of this and say what
you want which we can supply."   Webster sent up $2,000 con-
tributed by the friends of New Hampshire in Washington, and
Cochrane collected $1,000 from the New York office holders to
be sent to the Granite State.   As the election approached, Pierce
received rather discouraging reports and attempted to fortify
himself for a shock.   The shock came.   New Hampshire was
completely lost, senators, congressmen, state ticket, all were

captured by the coalition.[4] Not that the Democratic vote had fallen off so much; it was within 2,000 of normal, but from somewhere 32,000 Know-Nothings appeared and 6,000 new voters cast their ballots against the old regime. In less than a month Connecticut and Rhode Island each elected Know-Nothing tickets, and news of serious rioting at an election in Cincinnati between " Americans " and " Germans " had shocked the country. Certainly the northern masses were being stirred by something, but what it was Pierce could not understand. As Marcy commented:

> The party condition of the United States is anomalous. The sudden rise and wonderful progress of the Know Nothing organization cannot be externally accounted for. It is hardly fair to ascribe it to the unpopularity of the administration or in any considerable degree to the Nebraska measure. In no place has it appeared in such overwhelming strength as in Massachusetts. That state was more decided against the Administration than any other before the action upon the Nebraska Bill and every member of Congress opposed it yet those who were signalized by their opposition to the bill found no favor from the Know Nothings when up for re-election. The new sect has triumphed as completely over the Whigs where they were strong as over the Democrats. In many places where their success was most complete, they have already met with reverses. It would be strange indeed if it should assume the character of a permanent party.[5]

How far would the new party sweep? What part would it play in 1856? The answer to these questions depended upon its ability to break into the South. If the order proved as popular there as it had in the North, no one knew of what heights of power it might attain. With such a situation confronting them, Pierce and the leaders of the Democratic party looked eagerly for tokens which would predict the future. The spring election in Virginia seemed to be the most valuable indicator. The powerful southern Whig party were not unaware of the advantages which this strange enthusiasm offered in their section. If their rather indifferent ranks could be stirred up and further recruited on the issues of Americanism they would enjoy a revival. In the South where the population was homogeneous and predominantly of English descent, the foreign menace aroused strong prejudice, especially as the new comers were supposed to be opposed to slavery and were concentrated in the North. The Know-Nothings were showing strength in the South and if they could carry one or two of the important states there might be hope of establishing a permanent and successful national party. Virginia was to provide a test vote this spring. As Marcy wrote, " The result of the Virginia election will have some effect upon the party's future. If the Know-Nothings are defeated in that state, as the Democrats think they will be, their career will be arrested and their decline may be as rapid as was their rise." [6]

With such issues at stake, the Virginia contest became the center of political attraction during April and May. Henry A. Wise was leading the Democratic ticket in opposition to a cleverly devised group of all opposing elements headed by Flournoy, nominee of the Know-Nothing party, for the governorship. Anything that Wise did was apt to be startling and his campaign was spectacular. Election day, May 24, found him triumphant and brought a feeling of relief to Pierce. When the national council of the Know-Nothings, held in Philadelphia that June, suffered a split over the slavery question, Marcy's prediction was fulfilled. The danger of Know-Nothingism was passing. Still the administration was apprehensive, so uncertain was politics, and continued its efforts to exterminate the menace.

Office holders with Know-Nothing sympathies were removed; even the President's old friend Benjamin B. French lost his position because of Know-Nothing sympathy in the Washington city election, and John Wilson, for many years commissioner of the land office, was deposed for similar cause.[7] Pierce was particularly sensitive on the subject because his cabinet officer, Campbell, was a Catholic, and many insinuations were made that Pierce was under the thumb of the church. It was charged that the hierarchy had arranged with Pierce for the appointment of Campbell and that the papal *nuncio* had boasted of the fact in Madrid before the inauguration. A lady from Baltimore, Miss Carroll, was publishing articles about the Catholic sympathies of Pierce which later came out in book form.[8] The axe fell many times in the departments and among the office holders in the states. Pierce was determined to do what he could to root out this intolerant and unpatriotic order that put their secret, clandestine oaths above their obligations to support the Constitution. Fighting the Know-Nothings, however, was like Don Quixote's tilting at windmills. A new party was coming out of the West far more potent than the Know-Nothings. Pierce spoke of them slightingly as " coalitionists " and " abolitionists," but they called themselves Republicans.

LII

DIPLOMATIC FENCING

THE routine of administration and the political conflict with the Know-Nothings were liberally seasoned with increasingly difficult problems of diplomacy. Pierce's interest in such matters was ever very lively; in fact, it was the center of his thought. He and Marcy worked together, and most of the important despatches and instructions were considered in full cabinet. Marcy submitted his finished products to the President for his approval, and while Marcy had the stronger mind and the shrewder intellect, the President was very persuasive and could be determined. Therefore, it is hard to separate the contribution of the two and definitely allocate responsibility for the various policies. Pierce several times overruled Marcy, and his influence in foreign matters should not be underestimated.

Just before the adjournment of Congress, Cuba had resumed its front-page position, a place which it was destined to maintain much of the time during the spring. Congress had called for the Cuban correspondence toward the end of the session, and on March 2, after Soulé had visited the state department, it was sent in, just in time to be made public before Congress adjourned. Monday, March 5, the press had it and the veil over the Ostend conference finally was officially rent; the Ostend report was printed in full. The Baltimore *Sun* carried headlines: "The Ostend conference, Bold and Important Recommendation, Cuba at any cost." [1] This interpretation was what had been feared by the administration, and the opposition papers pounced upon this document which they spread abroad as the Ostend "Manifesto."

A few days later, a report was printed that the Spanish Cortes had declared, "The sale of Cuba would be the sale of Spanish honor." The *Union* felt that this declaration showed the futility of negotiation and sought to rouse feeling. Here was Spain with a secret police in our country watching every vessel that went out and invoking the neutrality law if a keg of powder, old musket, or rusty cutlass went on board. Great Britain and

France were protecting and upholding Spain in this course because the former wanted the slaves freed and the island turned into a second Santo Domingo. The time was evidently at hand, the paper declared, to determine whether the acquisition of the island was not necessary for American self-preservation.[2] Four days later, Spain came to the aid of the *Union*.

When the *Crescent City* arrived at her New York slip on March 14, she brought with her the news that the *El Dorado*, flying the American flag, had been fired upon by a Spanish frigate. For the next two weeks, the press was carrying numerous items about Cuba; one described how the American vice-consul at Sagua la Grande had been arrested and our national emblem torn down. There were conflicting reports from Spain, one to the effect that the Spanish were willing to make amends for the *Black Warrior* and another that the ministry had announced that the slaves in Cuba were to be freed. The first report proved to be true but the second false. Such was the situation which confronted the Executive and his advisers.

Pierce found his position difficult, for he was embarrassed by several unfortunate circumstances. In the first place, there was natural resentment at the Spanish insult, all the more galling because these affronts seemed to be becoming habitual. The President as well as some private citizens, generally southern, shared in the common indignation. A second complication intervened when Spain, by apologizing for the *Black Warrior* outrage and making amends, showed a disposition to right these wrongs, although without hurry. Finally, Pierce faced the disillusioning fact that there was little or no hope of congressional support. The last assemblage of solons had been unwilling to give any aid, although it had been Democratic; the next Congress, which was nobody knew what, would be much less likely to help. National pride called for some action, and the expansionists again demanded Cuba, stirred by the *Union*.[3] Pierce knew that Quitman was once again preparing to invade Cuba. Despite popular clamor this must not be. Quitman was called to Washington and showed the plans of the Cuban fortifications. The general then realized that he could not hope to succeed and quit.

Because of the end of filibuster hopes, Pierce tried to placate Young America by a show of force—a resolution doubtlessly influenced by the fact that Pierce was conferring frequently with Soulé. When Dobbin was able to return to his duties after a month's illness, the home squadron of six vessels was sent to Cuban waters with orders, dated April 10, to prevent Spanish ships from searching and seizing our merchant marine. Those desiring Cuba now began to be hopeful; here was positive action at last, war perhaps, and Cuba might be captured. This might be the view of the *Union*, but it was not that of the administration. As Marcy wrote:

> Cuba would be a very desirable possession if it came to us in the right way but we cannot afford to get it by robbery or theft. The conduct of Spain and the Cuban authorities has been exaggerated, even misrepresented in some of our leading journals, particularly in the *Union*. I cannot speak of the views of the conductors of the latter paper for I have little or no intercourse with them. From what I have seen in it, I am not much surprised at the opinion it is for war right or wrong but I venture to assure you that such is not the policy of the administration. It does not want war, would avoid it but would not shrink from it if it becomes necessary in the defense of our just rights.[4]

The *Union* was becoming a positive nuisance, and within four days of this letter the editors became aware that they had seriously embarrassed the administration before the country by their too ardent demands for war. Whether, as Sidney Webster recollected forty years later, "this step was not suggested or inspired by the administration or by any member of it," or whether pressure in fact was exerted, on April 19 the *Union* published a statement: "The administration, we believe, has never inclined to have an organ. The only relation of this press to the administration is that the latter does not find fault with our sentiments, and that we have found no occasion to disapprove of its acts."[5] This affirmation in the *Union*, coupled with the fact that the naval expedition was soon found to be coöperative and peaceful rather than warlike, seemed tame after the bold display of force. The expansionists were bitterly disappointed, and complained openly about the ineffectiveness of the administration. Soulé wrote Buchanan, "General Pierce I am sure with some two or three other members of his cabinet was ever right both in his head and in his heart; but he has been wanting in firmness and that has destroyed him." From Soulé this is curious, for if ever a man destroyed the Cuban prospect it was Soulé.

The truth was that Pierce had turned to negotiation once more. When Soulé had resigned early in the year, Pierce sought to reward John C. Breckinridge, who had done yeoman service in the Kansas-Nebraska struggle, by offering him the Spanish mission. After some hesitation, Breckinridge declined; he could not afford it; Soulé had so effectively ruined any chance of acquiring Cuba that there was no reputation to be gained there, and besides he had other ambitions. At length, Pierce had selected an Iowa lame duck, Augustus Caesar Dodge, whom he appointed in February. The ensuing difficulties had postponed his mission, and for a while after the *El Dorado* incident Dodge did not expect to go, so sure was he of war. After hostilities had become unlikely, the new minister was sent forth with instructions dated May 1, to the effect that the United States wanted Cuba peaceably and in no other way.[6] The war party had been defeated and " Finis " had been written upon the acquisition of Cuba. Pierce could take no warlike steps to obtain the island with public opinion so unfriendly, for he would have to call Congress in extra session and the House was now hostile. If he did precipitate war, Congress could not be counted on to sustain him.

Cuba was not the only diplomatic disappointment, as Pierce was called upon to witness an almost total collapse of his expansion program. In November 1854, the state department had received a draft of a treaty for the annexation of the kingdom of Hawaii, which Gregg had made in consultation with the king, and Marcy placed it before the cabinet. This treaty stipulated annexation of the kingdom in return for immediate admission into the Union as a state and liberal financial provision for the royal family. Such a proposition the cabinet finally decided could not be accepted. Hawaii must remain a territory for a time and the financial contributions must be appreciably reduced, because annexing Hawaii would be difficult at best. Marcy had instructed Buchanan to ascertain the attitude of Great Britain; he replied that Clarendon was opposed. Crampton and the French minister as well had interrogated the secretary in such a way as to convince him of the hostility of their governments. Hence the covert reference to the attitude of

Great Britain and France made by Pierce in his late message. Congressional approval also was uncertain, especially as Clayton, a leading Whig Senator, held that Upshur, a Whig secretary of state, had renounced the idea of acquisition in a promise to Great Britain a decade before. For any or all of these reasons, the projected treaty was sent back to Commissioner Gregg for revision, January 31. However, the Hawaiian king had died in the meantime. As his heir was anti-American, he put an end to all negotiations for annexation, and Pierce and Marcy had to be content with a reciprocity treaty arranged in Washington during the summer. Forty years were to elapse before Hawaiian annexation became a fact.[7]

The acquisition of Samana Bay from the Dominican Republic likewise had received a setback. Cazneau had negotiated a commercial treaty containing the cession of Samana Bay, but the British and French representatives had made such a protest that the Samana item was stricken out before the treaty was finally signed in October, 1854. To make the negotiation more complicated, the Dominican Senate had mutilated the treaty (under the same influence, it was charged) in such fashion that it could never be ratified by the United States. One of the worst changes provided that Dominican Negro citizens should be on an equal footing with American citizens in the United States. Cazneau withdrew the treaty rather than transmit it to Marcy, and as negotiations were hopeless Marcy recalled him in December. Hope in this instance did not die, for after some further consideration, our consul Elliot was instructed in October, 1855, to try again.[8]

In such manner were piled up evidences of British and French interference in American expansion. But what had become of the measures which, Mason had promised the Senate, would bring an end to this interference with American interests? A fleet had been sent to the West Indies and Marcy had been contemplating a protest to the British through Buchanan, but the spring passed without action. New factors had entered the already sufficiently complicated relations with Great Britain.

In the first place, Central American negotiations were becoming even more impossible. Clarendon had made the bombardment of Greytown an excuse for further delay, and the tone of the President's message had been very distasteful to him. Once again private citizens were interfering with diplomacy and renewing the danger of trouble. Colonel Henry L. Kinney had acquired near Greytown a grant of land once given to the Shepherd brothers of Georgia, and he planned to develop an " agricultural settlement " of Americans in that region. For this purpose he formed a company in which such administration associates as Sidney Webster, Nicholson, and Forney were interested financially. Moreover, Pierce may have given this Mexican War comrade the nod in December, 1854. His proposal would serve to neutralize British influence in Nicaragua and would also aid in building up the Accessory Transit Company. Great Britain, meanwhile, warned the Central American republics; and the representatives of Nicaragua and Costa Rica expostulated with Marcy.

Pierce and his advisers at first held Kinney's venture to be in the nature of a peaceful business operation with which the government could not interfere. But so persistent became the Latin diplomats in protesting against this " invasion " of Nicaragua, that Marcy at length was impelled to publish some correspondence with Kinney in the *Union* of February 7, 1855. These letters contained Kinney's avowal that his expedition was peaceful and legal, and Marcy's reply that if they were going peacefully to Nicaragua and would submit themselves to its jurisdiction, then the United States would not interfere; but Marcy expressed a determination to enforce our neutrality laws. In spite of this warning, Kinney made preparations for an expedition that did not promise to be peaceful.[9]

While the administration was sifting this possible breach of neutrality, the tables turned. March 21, the public prints bore the news that Great Britain was building up her armies in our principal cities. Immediately, Crampton came to inform Marcy that the recruiting was unauthorized; but the district attorneys of New York and Philadelphia declared that the enlistment continued. Cushing investigated and reported to the cabinet, with the result that on March 26 the administration ordered arrests of the violators of our neutrality acts and instituted legal proceedings.[10] An administration protesting British violations must watch its own regard for law. Kinney had quarrelled with Cushing and the Transit Company; "Joe" White said he was through with him so Pierce's district attorney had him indicted together with Fabens, our agent in Nicaragua.   Although they were acquitted for lack of evidence, a strict guard was placed around Kinney's ship and Fabens was dismissed from the service, steps which did not deter Kinney from going to Greytown, albeit minus his ship.[11]

British recruiting was not without its effect upon our relations with that country.   Aberdeen had fallen, to be succeeded by the bellicose Palmerston, and although Clarendon remained as foreign secretary, his diplomacy became less urbane.   Clarendon and Buchanan had a heated interview on April 5, which left the American minister hopeless of procuring any Central American adjustment as long as Palmerston remained in power.   He planned to return home in October.[12]   Pierce and Marcy long had suffered a disadvantage because of the Greytown incident, but now they saw a little light.   Perhaps the proper use of the recruiting incident would be a stronger weapon than a protest against British interference in our expansive plans.   So Marcy postponed a projected note on that subject, and turned to the new line of attack.   On June 9, he instructed Buchanan to call Clarendon to account for British recruiting, and he planned to follow this move by an ultimatum on Central America.   Palmerston must be handled in Palmerstonian fashion.

In the meantime, the idea of filibusters which Pierce seems once to have entertained must be given up.   Alas, it was impossible once again "to do a Texas."

LIII

THE TERRITORIAL PROBLEM

FOR several weeks after the adjournment of Congress, Pierce was able to enjoy comparative quiet. With the exception of the Cuban flurry there was not much out of the ordinary to deal with. Unluckily, the calm was short lived. April was not very far along before disquieting news came persistently from the West.

From the days of the ancient empires, the government of provinces has been a problem to tax the ingenuity of the ablest rulers. The United States, sprawling out over the continent, had adopted a system of territorial management which compromised between executive control and self-government and placed upon the President the responsibility for the administration of these outlying districts. Many factors combined to make Pierce's territorial rule particularly difficult. In the first place, the provinces were far away. Oregon, Washington, New Mexico, and Utah were beyond satisfactory communication, and correspondence had to be carried on with the full knowledge that no answer could be received in less than two, and in some cases three, months. Minnesota was more favorably situated but in Kansas this element of distance played a large part in the approaching difficulties. Even when he used the telegraph as far as St. Louis, Pierce could not get a message through to Kansas in less than a week, and a letter generally took two. He could not get replies in less than two weeks and often an exchange of letters took a month. Consequently, the President was handicapped in dealing with this troubled area. The slow communication of that day almost parallels that between the American colonies and Great Britain, and is not readily understandable now when telegraph, telephone, cable, and radio bring Alaska and the Philippines within an hour or two of the President.

The Indian problem further embarrassed provincial administration, and the restless, unsettled, lawless nature of the frontier made stable government a matter of chance. At the same time sectional rivalry was contributing uneasiness; men of northern and southern sympathies often met for the first time within the area of the territories and called sectionalism to aid them in their struggle to advance their personal fortunes.

Finally, the type of official whom Pierce could obtain to go forth to the boundaries of civilization was a hindrance to good government. He had to depend chiefly upon politicians who were either a failure at home or who saw possibilities in a new community. Neither of these types made the most honest or the most careful governors. Fortunately, Pierce found some men with the public service at heart who wished to obtain honor and preferment in western administration, and in at least one emergency he drafted a territorial expert, Geary, to straighten out a dangerous situation.

During this spring of 1855, the full difficulty of the far-off situation really became apparent. Pierce had had a number of premonitory warnings. He had experienced difficulty in Oregon, almost immediately upon his inauguration, by reason of his patronage distribution; and the Rogue River Indians had since been in insurrection. In the first months of his regime, the actions of federal officials in New Mexico had caused apprehension of hostilities with Mexico. The previous summer had been marred by Indian hostilities in Washington Territory over which Davis and Governor Stevens displayed some temper in their relations. In the unorganized areas Indian disturbances had broken out in 1854 with the massacre of a military detachment by the Sioux; so that late in the year the administration decided on a punitive expedition against these savages. One of the best Indian fighters, Harney, who was on leave in Europe, was summoned home. When he arrived in Washington, Pierce characteristically addressed him, "General Harney, you have done so much that I will not order you but I do wish you would consent to assume the command and whip the Indians for us." During 1855, not only the Sioux but also the Snakes and the Cheyennes were on the warpath, and a serious outbreak in Washington Territory was made by the Yakimas. The campaigns against these tribes had been aided somewhat by organizing the four additional regiments but the army had its hands full before Kansas burst into flame. The three territories which worried the President most were Utah, Minnesota, and Kansas.

Pierce's predecessor had appointed Brigham Young, head of the Mormon church, governor of Utah, and in that distant and isolated region he had been holding undisputed sway. The difficulties which many of the California immigrants experienced as they passed through the territory, brought numerous complaints to Washington. The climax came when Captain Gunnison and a detachment connected with the Pacific railway survey were killed in Utah. The Latter Day Saints blamed the tragedy upon the Indians, but there were many who laid it at the door of the leaders of the sect. Captain Steptoe was due to arrive in Salt Lake City in August, 1854, commanding a military detachment to undertake the surveying and building of military roads. Pierce gave him the additional task of ferreting out the murderers and himself undertook to solve the problem of government. He had already appointed territorial judges for Utah but he had not disturbed Young; in fact Young had informed his people that he expected to be retained in his present post. Pierce, however, made up his mind to the contrary and when the Senate convened in December, 1854, he sent Steptoe's name to that body for confirmation as governor. The President told Bernhisel, the Utah delegate, who urged the reappointment of Young that he thought the choice of a non-Mormon would be better for the Latter Day Saints as it would aid in removing the common prejudice against them. Young and his followers could scarcely credit the news that he had been superseded, and in meeting, the people acclaimed Young governor and expressed hostility to anyone whom the faraway Washington authority might send.

At all events, the office was going to be no sinecure and Steptoe hesitated. After four months in the territory, he joined at Christmas with the territorial officials, the army officers and merchants in petitioning Pierce to re-appoint Young. Pierce approached John W. Geary of Pennsylvania about the position, and wrote out to Salt Lake City inquiring whether Judge J. F. Kinney would accept if the Captain declined it. Kinney wrote to Cushing that he would take the office, but no move was made. In the meantime, Steptoe wintered in Salt Lake City and succeeded in capturing the reputed Indian murderers of Gunnison. Much to his chagrin, these individuals were punished very lightly by a local jury, whereupon Steptoe left for California.

Young, in the meantime, reigned supreme.   The official register
of September 30, 1855, bore his name as governor, and presumably after Steptoe came back east and visited at the White House
in October, the President decided that wisdom and the public
peace demanded that Brigham Young be left undisturbed.   This
decision many felt to be a characteristic shirking of responsibility in order to avoid trouble, but one, at least, who was well acquainted with the situation, was sure that the President had done
wisely.   It is doubtful whether his successor shared that view.[1]

Minnesota was in a more settled area and the problems which
she had been presenting to Pierce were not so much those of
frontier instability as the more sophisticated questions of the
relations of railroads to the public lands and party politics.
The Minnesotans were anxious for development and so were
numerous speculators.   One group interested New York capital
in rail construction, and had proceeded along the usual lines.
Congress had granted public lands to a number of the newer
states to aid them in building railroads.   In anticipation of
such grants the Minnesota group were chartered by the territorial legislature as the Minnesota and North Western Railroad
Company and were given lands to be theirs when Congress made
their grant.   As soon as the charter was voted, in 1854, the Minnesota delegate, Henry M. Rice, a man endowed with political
cleverness, pushed the railroad land grant bill in Congress.
The Democratic party in Minnesota, however, was divided into
two factions, and Governor Willis A. Gorman was friendly with
Henry H. Sibley rather than with Rice.   The promoters of the
new railroad being of the Rice group, Gorman came to Washington to oppose their scheme.   With Sibley he succeeded in
framing the railroad bill so that the Minnesota and North Western would be barred from receiving any of the land granted to
the territory.   To prevent this exclusion required some sleight
of hand; somehow two or three little words were changed after
the bill had passed, and the law which Pierce signed permitted
the Minnesota and North Western to receive their grant.   The
plan almost succeeded, but it had been discovered in time to
arouse a storm of indignation which caused the repeal of the
law and turned Pierce and McClelland against land grants for
railroad purposes, as the 1854 message well demonstrated.

No sooner was the repeal signed than the railroad wanted to

press a suit to test its validity.   Officials approached McClelland
without success, but during the winter they planned to arrange
a case in Minnesota.   The administration learned in December,
1854, that the district attorney had acquiesced in a move to test
the repeal in the courts.   Pierce and Cushing did not relish this
connection of the government with the railroad; Cushing was
especially incensed because Warren, the district attorney, had
violated the attorney-general's rules and had failed even to mention the case.   Warren was removed but Pierce found that his
Minnesota troubles had only begun.

The President had been aware of Minnesota's party difficulties
ever since he had appointed his old army associate, Gorman, to
avoid making a choice between the Sibley and Rice factions.
Gorman was not an adept at political management and had not
improved matters.   He had favored the Sibley group, enemies
of the powerful and enterprising delegate to Congress.   Thereupon Rice tried to persuade Pierce to remove Gorman, during
the first session of the 33d Congress, but dropped his importunity in the course of the railroad bill contest.   After Gorman's
efforts had largely defeated the Minnesota and North Western
plan and widened the schism in the party, Rice came back to
the second session determined this time to have Gorman's head.
Rice was close to powerful influences; he had become associated
with Douglas, Bright, Hunter, Forney, Breckinridge, and the
banker Corcoran in a real estate project at the western end of
Lake Superior in Wisconsin.   It was just across the St. Louis
river from Minnesota, and was known as Superior City.   This
town was planned as a great depot for lake traffic, and from it
the Minnesota and North Western would go up into Minnesota,
providing rail connections to a growing region.   Gorman had
endangered this speculation by his opposition to the railroad,
and Rice could count on the sympathy of his fellow promoters,
more especially as he planned to push John C. Breckinridge for
the governorship, a move which gained Guthrie's aid.   Rice
thereupon made charges against Gorman to the President and
to the secretary of the interior, to the effect that the governor
(by supporting the Sibley faction presumably) was ruining the
party.   Worse than that, he was incompetent and perhaps corrupt, especially in his dealings with the Indians.

Pierce really wanted to do something for Breckinridge and

besides did not think Gorman suited for the place; on the other hand, he could not dismiss Gorman without some unprejudiced investigation of his purported misconduct. To get the facts he sent J. Ross Browne, a confidential agent of Guthrie who was well versed in frontier ways, ostensibly to examine into land sales for McClelland. When Browne returned towards the end of March he reported that there was nothing to Gorman's discredit. Such a report surprised Pierce and disturbed him, for he already had told Guthrie and Breckinridge that he intended to remove Gorman and appoint Breckinridge. Since no charges had been substantiated the President now felt obliged to retain his appointee, and so informed Rice and Guthrie. The Minnesota delegate, who had been haunting the White House, was furious at this decision, but he could do nothing until Douglas came back to Washington. Rice felt he could count on Douglas's aid, for their political and financial fortunes recently had become closely knit; each needed Minnesota politically and each was heavily interested in the Superior City development. On April 11, they went up to the White House to have it out. The four-hour interview was largely about Douglas's political affairs, but before they left the Minnesota matter was brought up. When Douglas and Rice charged Browne with an attempt to whitewash Gorman, and the President called the attention of his callers to Browne's charges that Rice was mixed up in a land fraud, the interview became heated. Douglas insisted that Gorman's removal was necessary to save Minnesota to the party and stressed Breckinridge's services, his deserts and his needs. Afterwards Rice claimed that they had convinced the President and that he had given them strong assurances that Breckinridge would be appointed at once. Whether Pierce made this pledge or not, is very doubtful; but at all events, his resolution was weakened to the extent that in May he sent Sidney Webster out to investigate further. Webster was gone six weeks and when he returned, Gorman was not removed. As a result the powerful " Superior " group were no friendlier: Rice wrote, " Pierce is a miserable weak squirt. The administration is sunk so low that it is death to any man that attempts to sustain it." [2] Meanwhile Pierce went out of his way to be friendly with the senator. Douglas went back to Illinois that summer and left his boys in charge of their uncle. In an accident Douglas's brother-in-law saved one of his nephews at the cost of painful injuries to himself. Pierce went immediately to the Douglas home when he heard of the mishap and wrote the senator a reassuring account of what had occurred. He continued to call frequently and to supply Douglas with news of the sick-room. Territorial troubles, however, were just beginning in earnest.

The President's experiences in connection with Utah and Minnesota had brought him a clear perception of the fact that territorial troubles were no rarity, that insubordination and lawlessness were not uncommon, that provincial governors often had malignant enemies who made charges which a President must discount. Consequently, when the cloud of Kansas trouble drifted into the territorial sky the horizon was so spotted with other provincial storm signals that Pierce was not much impressed by its density or its storm-carrying possibilities.

LIV

SQUATTER SOVEREIGNTY IN PRACTICE

THE President had taken a great deal of satisfaction in convincing himself that by the enactment of the Kansas-Nebraska bill he and his party had laid the slavery question away permanently, and he had determined to exercise the greatest pains in a correct administration of its provisions. The working of this law would be a great triumph of the basic principles of local self-government, which were the foundation of American democracy. To allay all suspicion of sectional favoritism, he had determined to appoint a northern man governor of Kansas and a southerner governor of Nebraska. Upon the recommendation of Forney and Asa Packer, congressman from the Easton district in Pennsylvania, he offered the Kansas governorship to Andrew H. Reeder of that city, a respectable lawyer without much political experience. He was now forty-seven, impressive and deliberate, somewhat inclined to corpulency and, as events proved, quite lacking in tact. He was firm in his support of the bill and had full sympathy with the southern position. After some deliberation, he decided to accept the proffer and make his home in Kansas, where he would hold an honorable position and also would be enabled to make paying investments for himself and his friends. Although he was commissioned June 29, 1854, he delayed setting out for Kansas until early fall on the plea of winding up his business. Pierce had appointed an estimable man, one who was much abler than the average political aspirant for office; but Reeder lacked even the remotest concept of the frontier, had never known administrative experience, and was without that " sturdy combativeness " requisite for dealing with the situation. Moreover, the fact that he was a northern man awakened suspicion in the South that the President was trying to make Kansas a free state. His appointment of Reeder to that pivotal position was Pierce's initial mistake.

The next phase of the difficulties in this territory to come to Pierce's attention, was the question of fraud in connection with Indian lands. In considering the Kansas question it is very easy to focus on slavery and forget real estate. After the passage of seventy years, however, it has become apparent that Pierce had clearer vision than some of the critical historians of his day. He realized that the land speculator often lurked behind the impressive figure of the agitator for freedom or slavery. Hardly had the ink of his signature dried on the Kansas-Nebraska bill when the wires flashed westward the welcome news that Kansas land could be acquired; and the summer of 1854 saw a stream of population going into the new territory. Naturally those on the ground were not blind to opportunity, and officers and men at Fort Leavenworth, citizens of western Missouri, and wandering speculators began to pick out promising lots and plan to acquire them under the preemption act of 1841. The way was not plain, however; for much desirable land, though acquired by the United States in the recent treaty with the Delaware Indians, was held in trust for them to be sold at auction so that the Indians might reap the benefit of the speculators' ardor. Another very desirable area was occupied by half-breed Kansas Indians as a perpetual reservation under the Kansas treaty of 1825. Many of the hopeful land hunters were ignorant or careless of these restrictions and began speculations which the authorities of the Indian office held to be unlawful. Backed by an opinion of Cushing, the Indian agents were ordered to drive the squatters from the Delaware lands, and then the trouble began. The Indian agents, especially B. F. Robinson for the Delawares, began to protest the activities of the army in engaging in speculation and encouraging squatters who were planning an association to prevent any competitive bidding at auction. Worse still, Robinson and others began to complain of Governor Reeder.

The governor had not arrived until October 7. He established himself at Fort Leavenworth and immediately gave encouragement to the pre-emptioners by a public speech in which he disparaged Cushing's opinion. He had been in the territory but a few days when he and several of the territorial officials made an inspection trip, one object of which was to look for desirable lands. Much of the good land had already been staked out, so late was he, but he was not without a scheme. Under the Kansas Indian treaty of 1825 certain half-breeds had been granted the occupancy and use of lands on the Kansas

River; Reeder and his associates now sought to contract with some white men who had married descendants of these half-breeds for the sale of their lands, planning to send the contracts to the President for his approval. Congress had sometimes given half-breeds permission to alienate their lands and therefore the governor seemed to expect the President would allow the sale. Reeder moved rather secretly in the matter and did not avail himself of the services of the Indian agents, dealing directly with the occupants of the reserves. The lands in question were about one hundred miles from the Missouri border and here Reeder expected to establish the capital of the new territory, a procedure which could not fail to enhance real estate values. Meanwhile certain speculating interests who had been looking with longing eyes on these lands determined to do what they could to prevent the governor from completing his scheme. By November 6 protests from the Indian agents against Reeder's deals were on their way to Washington, charging him and his associates, including two judges, with unlawful conduct and also with cheating the Indians. Similar charges were made against the military authorities at Fort Leavenworth.

The administration took no action until January 10, when Reeder's contracts came to Manypenny for opinion. The commissioner was in no mood for favorable consideration. Such a scheme as Reeder wished to promote had been declared illegal in 1833 by the then attorney-general, Taney, and the Indian office had generally followed his opinion. A similar application recently had been refused and the disappointed contractor had publicly charged Manypenny with favoring government officials such as Reeder by giving information about the good Indian lands. The Indian commissioner smarted under the charge and it did not take him long to denounce Reeder to the President and disapprove his contracts; the new governor was robbing the Indians by offering such a low price, and besides the papers were carelessly drawn and incomplete. Pierce contented himself with sending back Reeder's papers without approval. An Ohio congressman, presumably a friend of Manypenny, moved that the documents be called for, and on February 3 the President sent them in. The mass of papers aimed to show that the President and the Interior department were attempting to protect the Indians, and contained in full the story of Reeder's deals accompanied by the charges against him and Manypenny's denunciation of his conduct. Reeder had to do something to justify himself, so he forwarded counter-charges against Agent Clarke and pondered a withering reply to Manypenny. Then came March 30, election day in the territory; up to that time the trouble had been, in Pierce's eyes at least, almost exclusively an unsavory real estate scramble in which his own appointees, governor and judges, had openly participated to a degree approaching corruption.

After March 30, however, rumors and reports of disorder and fraud began to appear in the press. Missourians, angered by the organized activities of the Emigrant Aid Company, had invaded a number of the polling places on election day and cast sufficient votes to elect a pro-slavery legislature, so the free-state people charged. Whether the invasion changed the general result is a matter shrouded in doubt; presumably it did not. At any rate Governor Reeder, under threats of personal violence, accepted the situation, certified to the election of most of the members, and issued a call for the legislature to meet in July at the new town of Pawnee near Fort Riley. This location was over one hundred miles distant from the Missouri border and was partly under his ownership. Since his arrival, he had invested impartially in southern and northern deals. But he had been learning that southern large estate operations meant slow settlements and slow appreciation, while northern dealings in small lots meant quick turnover. He would get rich quicker in a free Kansas. But Governor Reeder realized that his position was precarious. Now in his danger his southern sympathies were fast evaporating. To protect himself he challenged Manypenny in bitter and inflammatory language to prove his charges or resign. With the group among whom his natural sympathies lay, the southern element, he was also at odds; numerous enemies among them were accusing him of undue partiality for the New England faction and unlawful assumption of authority. All of his personal relations were strained by his lack of tact and his nervous apprehension of violence. He determined to go east for sympathy and reinforcement, not unmindful of his land purchase contracts still unapproved. His authority in Kansas had been so flouted and his own person so endangered that he wanted to find out from Washington whether the government would permit such disregard of federal power. On his way to the capital, he stopped at his home in Easton, and there on April 30 he made a speech recounting the violation of Kansas by the Missouri invaders.

His Missourian opponents were not slumbering. Atchison, too, had come east, and his influence among senators and his personal position were giving much weight to his words. He came to demand a new governor. He believed that Reeder was in full sympathy with the group who had attempted to make a mockery out of " squatter sovereignty." Even before the Kansas-Nebraska bill had been passed, New England promoters had organized a company which hoped to collect $5,000,000 for the purpose of making Kansas a free state. Missourians believed unhesitatingly that people were to be recruited by the Emigrant Aid Company and paid to go from New England to prevent slavery from extending. Such a procedure was in violation of the spirit of fair play, for the southern propagandists had felt that Kansas should be left to southern emigrants while the North could have all of Nebraska to roam in. The Missourians thought that in organizing the Kansas invasion they had merely sought to protect themselves. Reeder, said Atchison, had stealthily played into the hands of the New Englanders. He had not arrived in the territory until late in the fall. He immediately had devoted more attention to land speculation than to government, and when he did call for a poll, instead of providing for the election of territorial officials, he had ordered only the choice of a delegate to Congress. He had delayed taking the census and holding the territorial ballot until spring, in order that New Englanders might have time to arrive; and when he finally took the census he had failed to advertise the fact or to include in the count a number of the pro-slavery people. When Missourians had gone into Kansas to vote, as they contended they might well do, since the law of 1854 in regard to suffrage qualification was so indefinite, Reeder had attempted to nullify some of the returns. He had capped the climax by calling the legislature to meet off in the interior, where there was no adequate housing, on a town site which he was financially interested in developing contrary to law. So Atchison argued and the strident and impetuous, influential and important senator, now thoroughly aroused, was insistent in his demands that the President remove Reeder. He would not listen to reason. Pierce could not fail to be impressed.

When Reeder arrived in Washington on May 4, therefore, Pierce was facing a dilemma. Reeder undoubtedly had been speculating and his operations had received undesirable publicity. Also, he had become quite naturally identified with the northern group in Kansas; he hardly would appreciate the attempted dictation of his course by Missouri politicians, nor was it pleasant to have one's life threatened. But the President, in common with a multitude of New Englanders, had long despised abolitionists. There were reasons enough, public and private, for this zealous dislike. Following the natural course of his prejudice, he resented the activities of the New England Emigrant Aid Company; and by this time he had come to believe that the trouble in Kansas had followed from their efforts to anticipate the normal course of migration; they were not "playing the game." By their unwise and fanatical course they had stirred up the resentment of the Missourians and caused the trouble. Pierce from the beginning had been able to convince himself that under normal circumstances slavery had no future in Kansas; he and most northern Democrats wanted Kansas to be free. The Aid Company by insane conduct had destroyed what they desired most and had let this avalanche loose upon him.

Then there were private complications. Amos A. Lawrence was deeply interested in the Aid Company, and he kept the President informed of their doings and sent news from Kansas, though Pierce could not see how so solid a business man could have permitted himself to become involved in so treasonable an occupation. At this very time, there were visitors at the White House. About April 19, Lawrence's step-mother, Mrs. Pierce's aunt, came down from Boston with her niece Jane Mason and her nephew, Lawrence's business partner, Robert M. Mason. Mrs. Lawrence, an active lady of seventy-two, did not approve of Pierce's administration and was a staunch Whig. It was she who had whispered a year before, "He's too small for the job." To Robert Mason, Pierce expressed his regret that Lawrence had mixed in this business (Kansas). Mason did not remain long, but Mrs. Lawrence and her niece visited until May 9, when William R. Lawrence, Amos's brother, came down to escort them home. During this visit, the Reeder matter was pressing. Reeder was coming to the Executive office while the guests were with Mrs. Pierce a few doors down the corridor. Amos A. Lawrence promised to write his mother to see if she could aid Reeder, and he himself came to Washington a day or two before they left. So Pierce, in those April and May days, was beset by two powerful propulsions. There were potent politicians like Atchison and on the other hand opposite influences such as the Lawrences with all their financial, social, and family prestige. These counter-forces we know of definitely; undoubtedly there were many others. Reeder did not depend entirely upon anti-slavery sympathizers for support. Many good Democrats, especially in his own state of Pennsylvania, felt that southerners like Atchison were unreasonable. Excitable Forney declared the South was overreaching by making this demand.

To extricate himself from this dilemma, Pierce adopted a politician's device. Reeder was not a success; his speculations, his disrepute with the southern faction, but more especially disorder and lawlessness wholly beyond his control had destroyed his effectiveness as a governor. If he returned to Kansas, his authority would be flouted and his position would be as dangerous as it would be ineffective. Clearly, as a matter of administrative policy, a new man was necessary, a fresh start must be made. But Reeder had friends and had done his best to steer a middle course; to remove him would seem to be an abject surrender to southern demands. Either course was fraught with unpleasant political and personal consequences. Therefore, Pierce hit upon the device of endorsing Reeder's course and getting rid of him. Reeder had come back with a grievance, he wanted to be vindicated, he wanted to go back to Kansas and show the southern party that he had the authority of the federal government behind him. From May 5 for a fortnight Pierce and Reeder thrashed the matter out.

Pierce took the governor to task for his land speculations and for certain illegal acts reported by Manypenny whereby he had fixed election districts, appointed voting places and established the executive offices within Indian reserves in violation of the organic act. Furthermore, he objected to his Easton speech; it did not censure the Emigrant Aid Company, it bore too heavily upon the Missourians. If the election were so irregular and fraudulent why had he accepted it? " Which shall we believe, your official certificates under seal or your subsequent declaration to us in private conversations? " In spite of these shortcomings, Pierce told the governor he stood ready to endorse his official course. He said the same thing to others, including Lawrence, and approved an article supporting Reeder which the latter's friend Forney had prepared for the *Union*. Such was the first part of Pierce's scheme and it caused southern pressure for removal to be much increased.

His next step was to express to Reeder deep solicitude as to the probable consequences of his return to the territory. In the excited state of the community he feared that the governor might suffer personal violence, in which event the whole North would be inflamed, and civil war would probably ensue with results such as no man could predict. Similar sentiments, Reeder later testified, he reiterated a number of times; but the governor refused to take this obvious hint to resign. His obtuseness made it necessary for Pierce to come out in the open. He proposed to remove the incumbent painlessly. Reeder was to write a report explaining his policy as governor and justifying it, closing his letter with an offer, in view of the disturbed condition of the territory, to step aside for a new appointee if the President thought wise. Pierce in return would write endorsing his policies but agreeing that perhaps a new man might be more effective. Reeder was to close the correspondence by a response that he " was not prepared to say " that the President had acted unwisely. With this correspondence duly exchanged, Pierce would appoint a strong northern man as Reeder's successor and give the ex-governor another position as a public mark of favor. Reeder testified that the Chinese mission was involved, but this the *Union* later denied.

Reeder considered the proposition and finally consented, providing the correspondence could be agreed upon in advance. Then began a series of drafts. Reeder wrote some to which Pierce objected; then the President tried his hand at it. But it all came to nothing, as they could not agree. Upon what specific points they disagreed, the record does not show; but it may have been that the President insisted upon holding the Emigrant Aid Company primarily responsible, and refused to issue a proclamation pledging the administration to a fair execution of the Kansas-Nebraska bill and the use of troops to secure it. When, according to his own story, Reeder finally refused to step aside, the President told him that if he did remove him it would be because of his land speculations. Reeder denied these purchases were speculations, and just before leaving he said that he had procured additional documents which proved these were not unlawful and that they were then before the President. The latter replied that he had had no time to consider these papers " but that if the vacating of [Reeder's] office could be satisfactorily adjusted, he thought all these matters could be arranged in such a shape as to promote [his] private interests." Reeder according to his own report was so insulted that he withdrew in silent contempt.*

Reeder's refusal of the President's plan brought the whole matter back to the beginning. His disposal was considered at length in cabinet and Reeder's congressman was called in. In the meantime the case became more involved because Reeder had ignored Manypenny's request that he publish the Commissioner's reply to the diatribe of March 30 which the Kansas governor had given to the press; and furthermore Manypenny's investigation of Reeder's charges against Clarke, the Indian agent, had brought a warm defense from that gentleman and counter-charges against Reeder which did not simplify the situation. Clarke's letter was sent to Reeder June 5 for answer and the cabinet continued their review of the affair. Finally the views of Marcy and McClelland prevailed. Reeder was to have another chance or at least be permitted to return to Kansas, and in the meantime Marcy and Cushing were to ask official explanations from Reeder and from the members of the territorial judiciary who had joined him in purchasing lands. Letters to this effect were written June 11 and 14, and Reeder went back to Kansas before replying in full. As Secretary Davis had just lost a much-loved child and was absent in Mississippi during most of late May and June, he was not present to join in these conferences. What effect that fact had upon the cabinet decision is a matter of speculation.[1]

* This is distinctly a Reeder story with no corroboration except that one of the drafts in Pierce's handwriting still exists, and that when the Reeder testimony was made public, it was not denied.

LV

SUMMER MISCELLANY

PIERCE was going to take more rest this summer. His first summer had been marred by patronage troubles, the peace of his second had been destroyed by Congress, but now there was more prospect of repose. The Know-Nothings had divided at Philadelphia; Reeder had gone back to Kansas; Webster had reported from Minnesota that matters there need not be disturbed. The President felt the need of a change for the absence of his secretary and three members of his cabinet at one time during May and June had piled extra responsibility on his shoulders. Now that Webster had returned and matters were not pressing, he could go with Mrs. Pierce to Cape May. There they stayed at Congress Hall and enjoyed the sea for ten days while Washington sizzled in its first hot spell.

When the President returned to Washington, Marcy left for Old Point Comfort with the British correspondence, to prepare an ultimatum to Palmerston on the Central American question. Pierce busied himself with the reorganization of the interior department before he had to return to the Kansas problem. In June, three of the four bureau chiefs in the interior department left the service. Wilson of the land office was removed for Know-Nothing sympathies. Waldo of the pension office was made a judge in Connecticut and Mason of patents went back to Iowa, permanently, so the press said. Pierce now had an opportunity to reward further his best friend Minot, so he advanced him from fifth auditor to head of pensions, and Thomas A. Hendricks of Indiana was placed in charge of the land office. Later on, Mason came back as his own successor.[1]

Kansas was not to be disposed of as easily as the cabinet had thought. Governor Reeder had returned only to enter into a bitter quarrel with the legislature, arising from the fact that he had called them to meet in the capital of his own establishing, Pawnee City. A valid reason for haling them there, in his mind, was the distance of the settlement from Missouri influence, then, too, real estate values in his town-site would be increased. But Pawnee City was a very uncomfortable place with inadequate facilities, and the legislature almost immediately moved back to Shawnee Mission against the will of the governor. Reeder thereupon refused to recognize them and the situation became impossible. In the meantime, Marcy and Cushing addressed letters, the one to Reeder and the other to the judges and district attorney who were involved in the land speculations, asking for explanations. Reeder wrote a long justification of his course, which arrived while Marcy was away. Meanwhile, reports of the deadlock between governor and legislature were coming to Washington in greater volume and Pierce concluded that he had to find a new governor. Reeder by his speculation and quarrels had proven that his usefulness was at an end. His insistence on establishing the capital at his own town-site was the last straw. Marcy was still away and Pierce did not wait to consult him, although the territorial management was under the state department; Davis in the meantime had returned.

Pierce decided to end the Reeder transaction. While negotiating about his resignation Reeder had resubmitted his contracts with extensive briefs and documents to demonstrate their propriety. Pierce had pigeon-holed them waiting for developments; now he sent them over to the Indian office, July 11, we may judge as a matter of form. Mix, the acting commissioner, replied in a long and elaborate opinion of July 23 to the effect that the revised papers made the transaction no more creditable. Upon the basis of this opinion, Pierce ordered the acting secretary, William Hunter, to dismiss Reeder July 28, because his letter explaining his land sales was unsatisfactory, just as he had told Reeder he might do in their May interviews. This course Pierce wrote Marcy was " inavoidable."

But the President wished to be non-partisan and impartial about Kansas; so a few days later Cushing dismissed Judge Elmore,* a southerner, to offset Reeder's removal, and Judge

* Elmore claimed that this move was not unexpected and wrote Cushing August 23: " I felt confident that the President's course being dictated altogether by political policy which would not be successful without the removal of an equal number of Territorial officers from the North and South, was fully determined upon—on the date of your letter of the 14th of June." Atty. Gen. MSS.

Johnston was dropped for the same reason. Colonel William R. Montgomery, commandant at Fort Riley, who had permitted the Pawnee Association in which Reeder and his fellow speculators were interested to occupy and take possession of 400 acres more or less within the military reservation, was courtmartialed and dismissed from the army. Pawnee City itself was destroyed and its site reincorporated within the reservation by Pierce's orders. In this manner did Pierce place the seal of his disapproval upon land-speculating territorial officials; just how much he was actuated by the importunities of Senator Atchison and the pro-slavery faction can only be measured by the depth of his resentment against the Emigrant Aid Company, and his disgust at Reeder's seeming espousal of their cause. As far as Pierce personally was concerned, his decision was the result of a complex jumble of emotions rather than any calculated desire to please the South. He still thought himself impartial and discounted the popular clamor following his act; it would only be " temporary." Whether he would have carried out this wholesale removal if Marcy had been in Washington must also remain a matter of speculation.

The removal of Reeder brought forward the problem of his successor. The southern party had resented the appointment of a northern man when Reeder was chosen, and they now pressed the name of Woodson, a Virginian who was secretary of the territory and reliably pro-southern. The President saw no reason to abandon his original scheme, so he selected a second Pennsylvanian, Congressman John L. Dawson, only to have him decline. For next choice he called upon Wilson Shannon of Ohio. On paper this selection was eminently fitting; Shannon was Manypenny's brother-in-law, he had been governor of Ohio, had executive experience, was much more tactful, and like Reeder had no anti-slavery prejudices. His appointment was announced in August and a month later, I. M. Burrell of Pennsylvania and S. G. Cato of Alabama were given the places of Johnston and Elmore.[2]

While engaged in the Kansas removals, Pierce had been planning for another respite. Mrs. Pierce continued unwell, the President was none too vigorous, and the last half of July was terribly hot. He expected to leave early in August for Old Point Comfort where he and Marcy might enjoy a sojourn together; unfortunately Mrs. Pierce became very ill and vacation plans had to be postponed. It was a part of the torture which the officials had to endure—those stifling, insufferable nights in the pocket of the Potomac Valley. But as long as Mrs. Pierce was too sick to leave, her husband turned his attention to settling the far eastern question during the interim.

Pierce and his advisers were under the necessity of reconsidering their far eastern policy this summer. Treaty relations with Japan and Siam were in an unsatisfactory state; Perry's agreement had not provided adequately for commercial relations. McLane had resigned and left China in the midst of the Taiping rebellion, sending home a recommendation that the United States navy join with the British and French in obtaining treaty provisions by means of gunboats, since our commercial privileges in the celestial empire were not to our liking. Pierce already had declined to participate in a naval demonstration, and now he needed a new deputy to collaborate with other nations in obtaining more concessions peacefully. China seemed to be one ground where Great Britain, France, and the United States could meet on a coöperative basis. The problem of finding a new commissioner to China as well as a representative to negotiate with Japan and Siam had been difficult, and Marcy had been looking four months or more.

By August first, the secretary had found the man he wanted for the Japanese mission in the person of Townsend Harris, a successful New York merchant who knew the East. Pierce invited Harris to the White House for conference and next day had him to dinner, after which the President wrote Marcy that he had been very favorably impressed and would appoint Harris consul-general to Japan, commissioned to visit Siam. Within two weeks, Pierce also chose his new Chinese commissioner. Dr. Peter Parker had been second in rank in China under McLane and had lived in that empire for twenty years. He knew its language and customs thoroughly, a rare thing for an American, so Pierce decided to adopt the unusual course of promoting him.[3] Before he reached this decision, his attention was recalled to British matters.

As the President had been delayed by Mrs. Pierce's health longer than he had expected, Marcy had finished his Central American instructions without him and sent them to him for his approval. Marcy directed Buchanan to secure " a definite and final statement " from the British government. Would they retire from the Bay Islands? He reminded his minister once again that the American interpretation of the Clayton-Bulwer treaty demanded the withdrawal of Great Britain from these islands, from the Mosquito coast and from that part of the Belize lying between the Sibun and the Sarstoon rivers. August 6, Pierce wrote Marcy, " I am much pleased with the dispatch—no substantial alterations have been made and it will be sent with your signature by today's mail." That same day startling intelligence reached the President.

Suspicions which the administration had entertained for some time were confirmed. A chance phrase which Marcy had noticed in a British instruction read to him in May had caused the secretary to suspect that Great Britain had originally authorized recruiting activity. Judicial proceedings had since been taking their course and the district attorneys especially in New York and Philadelphia had been actively investigating. As late as July 15, Marcy had sent a second instruction to Buchanan giving more evidence of British recruiting. Now came definite proof that Crampton had been engaged in enlisting men and arranging with agents for recruits at the same time that he had assured Marcy that such was not the case. This knowledge was disconcerting, especially as it was received simultaneously with a note from Clarendon assuring the American minister that orders had been issued that all such activity cease. Was Crampton disobeying the orders of his home government or had these orders never been issued? Pierce sent for Marcy to come home although he wrote Campbell that he was aware of no urgent necessity to hasten his (Campbell's) return. When Marcy arrived, Cushing had prepared an opinion as to the legal aspects of British violation of our neutrality laws. Now the United States had a definite advantage in the diplomatic duel. The discomfiture of the Greytown episode could be forgotten and Marcy sat down to sharpen his sword, or perhaps more accurately to mend his pen, for the new encounter. Pierce and his advisers decided that the first step would be a note to Crampton containing definite charges and confronting him with Clarendon's note.[4]

When these decisions at length were made, the President was

free to take his deferred vacation. Old Point Comfort was abandoned, as Marcy had returned to Washington, and the Virginia Springs were chosen instead. A change was imperative because Pierce was suffering from certain symptoms which warned him that the chills and fever so unpleasant the previous autumn were returning. With Mrs. Pierce, Webster, and Marshal Hoover, he left Washington August 16 and sought the comfort of Virginia hospitality. That noon they arrived by train at Staunton where a public dinner awaited them at the Virginia Hotel.

The President, in spite of the warnings preceding chills and fever, had to make a speech and visit the Insane Asylum and the Deaf and Dumb Institute, with Senator Mason. From Staunton, accompanied by Mason and J. S. Barbour, Jr., the party went to Warm Springs by special train where they arrived in the evening. Next morning he was prostrated by the ague and had to stay where he was over Sunday. The malady took its course, but by Tuesday they were able to arrive at their destination, White Sulphur Springs. Here they were met by a delegation, ex-President Tyler made an address of welcome, and Pierce once more must speak.

The viewpoint on public affairs which he wished to impress upon the nation is well illustrated by a paragraph. " The President said he apprehended that the great danger to be guarded against, at the present time, was the prevalence of heresies which were in direct antagonism with the basis, doctrines and principles of the constitution and perhaps he might say, a general want of deference to the authority of law. Let it be remembered that whenever in a state or territory, from the Atlantic to the Pacific coast, a single citizen of the Republic is deprived of the right guaranteed to him by law, then is a blow aimed at the constitution itself."

Rest and pleasant surroundings did their work very well and both the President and his wife improved. They enjoyed the Springs for a week and then came back by easy stages. At Charlottesville, they had another royal reception at the Tavish House, and the President spent the evening listening to the sprightly Mrs. Pryor execute the " lilting puerilities of the innocuous Henselt " as she played " L'Elixir d'Amour " and " La Gondola " on the pianoforte. All too soon he returned to Washington to assume the burdens of his station.[5]

DECISIVE ACTION
1855-1856

LVI

CHOOSING TO RUN

THE fall of 1855 marked the beginning of the third and most effective period of Pierce's presidential experience. Since the spring of 1854, when he had made himself responsible for the program of territorial expansion and popular sovereignty, his administration had been troubled by a disconcerting number of disappointments, the most far reaching being the popular repudiation of his party at the polls. His foreign policy too had been subjected to trying reverses, and his relations with the leaders of his party were on occasion difficult. As autumn advanced in 1855, however, Pierce seemed to gain new strength. The British situation was lightened by the enlistment disclosures, and at home the approach of a presidential year was to aid Pierce in assuming a more forceful position as executive.

Whether Pierce would follow Jackson's precedent of seeking two terms, or that of Polk in being content with one, was a matter which it was hard for him to decide. He had hoped that he would not have to decide it, that his services would make his party spontaneously desire his renomination. Such was not the case and it became apparent that he and his friends must take the initiative if a renomination was to be forthcoming. The summer of 1855 was the natural time for the first appearance of moves preparatory to the conventions of 1856. In New England, where delegates were chosen early, advances began to be made in Pierce's behalf, although Webster told Forney at the beginning of July that they were not authorized. Still Forney wrote Breckinridge, August 8, that it was " well understood now that Pierce is a candidate and if he goes on carrying delegates in New England and can unite the south he will be most formidable in the National Convention "; this although in the meantime Pierce himself had assured Forney that these activities did not " meet his sanction." Perhaps Webster was correct in his view that the President was resolved to be respected in the convention and if not nominated himself at least to have a hand in the final choice. By August 26, Forney was writing Nicholson that "the Presidency is beginning to move upon the waters." [1]

The political situation was altogether more auspicious since Know-Nothing strength was on the wane. The August elections in North Carolina, Tennessee, and Alabama had been generally favorable. The returns showed the net gain of a congressman in each of the first two states, and Andrew Johnson had been re-elected governor of Tennessee. Kentucky had been a disastrous failure; election day had witnessed riots at Louisville and the "Americans" had won, but as Pierce had been unable to carry the state in 1852 it was not considered a setback. In Maine, the "Republican" candidate failed of election by the people although the legislature presumably would choose him. The latter result to Pierce was glorious. "A great Administration triumph on the Kansas issue," he told French. To the President's Maine-stimulated imagination, New Hampshire, Connecticut, New Jersey, Illinois, Indiana, Iowa, and several other free states would follow; in one year the Democratic party would be stronger than it had been before and the Union stand firmer and more permanent than ever. Said one observer, " he was very much excited, and very sanguine." [2] Guthrie wrote Breckinridge, September 14, that "things now taking place" demonstrated that the present incumbent would have to be nominated for the succession in 1856. The "fifteen slave states can hardly withhold their sanction to his administration. His recard is all right and five of the Northern States will send delegates. Twenty states will be a strong capital in the convention."

The campaign against the Know-Nothings was carried on ruthlessly. Postmasters were changed, Guthrie made a clean sweep in the treasury, custom houses, and lighthouses, of all connected with that heresy.[3] As the Pennsylvania election was approaching, Glancy Jones invited Pierce to attend the State Agricultural Fair at Harrisburg, which he did on September 26, presumably to aid the state ticket; he met a number of people, some politicians no doubt, and nobody knows what he did or did not accomplish.[4]

By October the situation had cleared somewhat and the weeks ensuing showed that Pennsylvania, Indiana, Illinois, Wisconsin, and New Jersey had come back to the Democratic fold. Buchanan repeatedly had written from England that he was not a candidate. Cass had written Nicholson in the same tenor and Douglas had told Forney that he was not in the running and had authorized Beverly Tucker to make such announcement in the *Sentinel*. Forney had gone to the President to tell him he would stand by him, though he thought his case hopeless with Marcy, Guthrie, and Davis almost open candidates.[5] This last surmise on Forney's part seems not to be substantiated, though friends of the secretaries were using their names and creating a situation which may have influenced Pierce to place the subject before his cabinet. Presumably about the first of November when the encouraging returns from the October elections had been digested, he discussed the matter with them and received their advice to plan for a renomination.

Thereupon Nicholson began "laying pipe" and wrote letters to various influential politicians enlisting their aid. Pierce's line of approach was the one most natural to him, being based on his innate shrinking from personal antagonisms. It showed again his inability to evaluate political enmities. To J. Glancy Jones, that chief lieutenant of Buchanan whom Pierce had helped in September by going to Harrisburg, Nicholson suggested a line of *rapprochement* with the Buchanan forces. Let there be no issue between Pierce and Buchanan. The Pennsylvania voters preferred Buchanan and it was right that they should. Pierce would have no objection to Pennsylvania declaring for Buchanan so long as no issue was made between that politician and the President which would prevent the Buchanan men from turning to Pierce if their first choice proved unavailing. To this plan Jones agreed. In somewhat similar terms Pierce explained to Forney his sentiments toward Buchanan's candidacy. Forney in an emotional interview had offered to resign from the *Union* if his friendship for Buchanan embarrassed the President, but Pierce assured Forney he would not go into Pennsylvania as others had done to win Buchanan's friends. Said the President, "All I ask at your hands is that you give me, as I know you will, the benefit of fair treatment. I am irrevocably in the field. You may rely on it I never will take a nomination if it is to be had by conflict with others." He would as soon expect Sidney Webster not to be his devoted friend as to expect Forney to desert Buchanan. All this was

said in Pierce's "frank and generous way," for, as Forney reported, "he can be so beyond most men." However, all Buchanan's supporters were not agreed. Many knowing politicians perceived Pierce's weaknesses and realized Buchanan's
strength. Buchanan's declination was not always heeded and
sentiment for his renomination was quietly at work.[6]

The formal launching of Pierce's candidacy was to take place
in New Hampshire. Peaslee was watching and laboring from
the Boston custom house and in Concord preparations were
being made to lead off in the fall convention. Proper resolutions endorsing the President on truly national ground were
prepared, circulated in Washington, approved and sent to
George; on November 14 they were adopted by the convention,
and the delegates to the national gathering were instructed to
vote for Pierce's renomination.

The President's hat was in the ring and he planned to conduct
his campaign along lines described by Sidney Webster:

> General Pierce while he is a candidate for renomination
> is not the antagonist of any other candidate. He desires a
> nomination only when the convention at Cincinnati con-
> sider that he is the best and most available candidate. His
> purpose is to treat every candidate, who sustains his ad-
> ministration and its measures, with that kindness and con-
> sideration which by his position he owes to every man in
> the democratic family. In Pennsylvania he is the friend
> of Mr. Buchanan and Mr. Dallas. In Virginia, he treats
> Mr. Hunter and Mr. Wise as alike entitled to his confidence
> and esteem, and he does so because he supposes them all
> devoted to the measures of his administration. In a word,
> he has no quarrel with anybody who is a democrat; his
> friends can conduct and will conduct the canvass as they
> see fit but probably will not do anything which his judg-
> ment disapproves.[7]

Presidential nominations are not generally obtained that way.

LVII

ASSUMING LEADERSHIP

PIERCE's message of 1855 marks the high point of his statesman-ship. In preparing this document, he designed to demonstrate his leadership and place himself at the head of his party to cope with the hostile majority in the House and to prepare for the campaign of 1856. The Democratic party needed a leader and must be rallied on a platform of compelling issues if it were to regain what it had lost in 1854. Pierce and his group had ignored as long as they could the new political alignment. No longer could they dismiss with sneers the " fusionists," " coalitionists," " abolitionists," or " Know-Nothings," as they were wont to designate the new Republican party. In 1854 it had been largely a western movement but the elections of 1855, though more encouraging to the Democrats, had shown that this new Republican party was organized in Maine, Vermont, Massachusetts, and worst of all, New York. The administration had been as unsuccessful in uniting the " hards " and " softs " in 1855 as before, and the election of that year proved the Democratic party to be, numerically, no longer a force in New York state. Pierce determined his message should expose this new combination and rally all true national men against its menace. He set himself to provide his party with a platform; no doubt he had also his own fortunes in mind.

In view of the circumstances, the reports of the secretaries were of minor importance that fall. If they had been unable to persuade a Democratic Congress to grant their requests, they could expect little from the hybrid opposition now about to assume control. There was little that was new in their recommendations. Guthrie foreshadowed federal supervision of banks by suggesting that if their unsupported issues of paper money became much more numerous the government must consider the advisability of taxing their circulation. Davis modified his recommendation of the southern path for a Pacific railroad to the extent of mentioning that the expense of the route along the 35th parallel (the central route) had been esti-

mated at a figure much too high. Dobbin, besides reporting
the dispatch of Commodore Paulding to Nicaragua and the exploits and rescue of Dr. Elisha Kent Kane and his party in the
arctic, made a stirring plea for a larger navy; small boats were
necessary, sloops of war that could enter southern as well as
northern harbors; as the navy now stood, in spite of the six
frigates, it was too feeble to command our coast. To these departmental recommendations the President paid but little heed
in his message, giving them little space. Two ideas dominated
his writing as he drew up this document.

The first of these was the British situation. The Central
American matter was still unsettled; Clarendon had submitted
an unsatisfactory reply to Marcy's ultimatum. The enlistment
dispute was in an unpleasant stage. Buchanan had reported that
Clarendon considered Cushing's statements in the published
correspondence of the enlistment trial harsh and unjust, especially those regarding Clarendon's note to Buchanan on the subject—" most insulting " in fact; Crampton had denied complicity in the matter. The situation had become further involved because Great Britain was sending to American waters
what purported to be a heavy squadron. Buchanan was told
by Clarendon that the fleet was not large and was planned
originally for three reasons: because it was thought that a Russian privateer was being equipped at New York; that Celtic
sympathizers were planning an expedition from the United
States to invade Ireland; and that the American steamer *Fulton*
had been observing the fortification of the West Indies. Buchanan was able to convince Clarendon that the suspected boat
was not a Russian privateer, but a barque built for the China
trade, and that the Irish invasion was fanciful. Thereupon the
fleet was reduced to four vessels rather than the seven originally
planned and Clarendon expressed friendly feelings and desire
to keep the peace; but he made no satisfactory conciliatory
moves to settle the questions at issue. Such was Buchanan's
last dispatch before the meeting of Congress.

With these data arriving piecemeal, Pierce prepared his report on British relations, and when John Appleton, Buchanan's
new secretary of legation, arrived from London a day or two
before Congress was to meet, the President invited him to stay

at the White House, and read his message to him. Appleton's comment to Buchanan was informing.

> I am amazed at the coolness with which the whole war blast has been received here. The tone of the message is not bellicose at all. On the contrary, I have found it necessary to strengthen it to prevent us from appearing ridiculous abroad. The President read me that portion of it relating to enlistments and to Central America. The former question is stated to be still the subject of discussion. The latter subject is stated pretty fully and then after mentioning our demands for the ultimate views of the British government and the character of those views, the President hopes that "renewed negotiations" will lead to favorable results. Was there ever anything like that? To exhaust discussions (after five years) to demand an ultimatum and then to talk about "renewed negotiations"—But the President has promised to reform this conclusion and is talking about the danger of delay.[1]

Pierce did make some changes in his statement of the Central America case. While he removed mention of "renewed negotiations" he said that because the "British Government, in its last communication still declares that it sees no reason why a conciliatory spirit may not enable the two Governments to overcome all obstacles to a satisfactory adjustment of the subject," it appeared to him "proper not to consider an amicable solution of the controversy hopeless." But he added this paragraph:

"There is, however, reason to apprehend that with Great Britain in the actual occupation of the disputed territories and the treaty therefore practically null so far as regards our rights, this international difficulty cannot long remain undetermined without involving in serious danger the friendly relations which it is the interest as well as the duty of both countries to cherish and preserve. It will afford me sincere gratification if future efforts shall result in the success anticipated heretofore with more confidence than the aspect of the case permits me now to entertain." Not a very bellicose statement but at least it indicated some strength to the British ministry, for whose eye it largely was cast. He further strengthened his position in the enlistment controversy by giving public warning that our laws forbade any American citizen from participating, a statement aimed at Americans who might wish to aid Russia in that way.[2]

The second phase of Pierce's message was domestic politics. Here he called in Cushing. The Republicans must be put in their true light. As a preliminary he reviewed with extreme brevity the reports and recommendations of his cabinet. He dismissed the Kansas difficulties with a paragraph in which he asserted that while there had been " acts prejudicial to good order," none had occurred " under circumstances to justify the interposition of the Federal Executive." He could only intervene " in case of obstruction to Federal law or of organized resistance to Territorial law, assuming the character of insurrection." If such disturbances occurred he promised " promptly to overcome and suppress " them. Kansas had not yet begun to bleed and " unwarranted organized interference," he maintained in private conversations, had come to his attention only after Reeder's acts had put it beyond the power of the President to do anything (a thought quite in line with his convenient concept of the limited powers of the executive). In fine these United States were at peace, wasting their strength " neither in foreign war nor domestic strife. Whatever of discontent or public dissatisfaction exists is attributable to the imperfections of human nature or is incident to all governments, however perfect, which human wisdom can devise. Such subjects of political agitation as occupy the public mind consist to a great extent of exaggeration of inevitable evils, or overzeal in social improvement, or mere imaginations of grievance, having but remote connection with any of the constitutional functions or duties of the Federal Government."

He could not deny, however, that there were elements of danger in the situation which, so far as they exhibited a tendency " menacing to the stability of the constitution or the integrity of the Union and no further," he presented to Congress. The government had been founded on the principle of mutual concession and recognition of the reserved rights of the states. Now this principle was in danger of being overthrown under the guise of social reform by the North upon the plea that the South for years had been an aggressor. This charge of aggression the President refuted by an appeal to history; the South had always minded its own affairs, in fact had made concessions in the form of the Missouri Compromise, a measure of doubtful constitutionallty. Not content with this, the North sought to exclude slavery from all territories, and the ensuing struggle had resulted in the Compromise of 1850 which organized the new territories " without restrictions " on slave-holding and left their citizens to judge " in that particular for themselves." He contended further that the North had abandoned the idea of the Missouri Compromise by refusing to extend the line to the coast. As Pierce put it, the Missouri Compromise " had been stripped of all moral authority." The substitution of the Compromise of 1850 for the Missouri Compromise principle justified the repeal of the Missouri Compromise and the extension of the rule of territorial sovereignty to the Kansas-Nebraska area, thus providing a " complete recognition of the principle that no portion of the United States shall undertake through assumption of the powers of the General Government to dictate the social institutions of any other portion."

Those who attacked this fulfillment of the spirit of American Constitutional government, he rebuked severely. " If the friends of the Constitution are to have another struggle, its enemies could not present a more acceptable issue than that of a State whose constitution clearly embraces ' a republican form of government ' being excluded from the Union because its domestic institutions may not in all respects comport with the ideas of what is wise and expedient entertained in some other State." Such exclusion would be a violation of the fundamental compact and Pierce queried, " Would not a sectional decision producing such result by a majority of votes, either Northern or Southern, of necessity drive out the oppressed and aggrieved minority and place in presence of each other irreconciliably hostile confederations? " Conditions at present represented either " disunion and civil war " or " mere angry, idle, aimless disturbances of public peace and tranquillity." If they represented disunion, " Disunion for what? If the passionate rage of fanaticism and partisan spirit did not force the fact upon our attention, it would be difficult to believe that any considerable portion of the people of this enlightened country could have so surrendered themselves to a fanatical devotion to the supposed interests of the relatively few Africans in the United States as totally to abandon and disregard the interests of 25,000,000 Americans. . . . Are patriotic men in any part of the Union

prepared on such an issue thus madly to invite all the consequences of the forfeiture of their constitutional engagements?
It is impossible."

In these words the President wrote the platform. As leader
of his party, he promulgated a doctrine calculated to restore the
country to its senses; briefly, the " friends of the Constitution "
of whatever political faith could look to him and to his supporters as the saviors of the Union by the protection of constitutional rights. He placed the onus upon his opponents; these
sons of darkness were attempting to destroy the children of
light. A crisis was approaching. Pierce felt the call to leadership, and a new strength of will was growing within him.
Would the Pierce who had purged the party of Hale and Atwood return once more?

LVIII

THE FIRST STEP

WITH his message practically finished, Pierce and several of his cabinet went down to the Navy Yard the Saturday before the meeting of Congress to watch the launching of the great frigate *Minnesota*. Here was a tangible achievement; this imposing ship, an added sinew to the arm of American power which would contribute much to our ability to resist the encroachments of England. With these great vessels coming rapidly into commission, Britain's gestures were not to be feared. Time was to show how idle was the British menace; the impending danger was from foes much nearer. That same day the disturbed and shaken governor of Kansas was telegraphing from his Missouri retreat to the President for troops. Kansas had begun to bleed. The telegrams had to be relayed, however, so the calm of the President's Sabbath was not broken by this startling news. He and his guest, Appleton, conversed presumably on the topics of the moment and of these not the least troublesome was the question of what would happen next day when Congress assembled. No party was in control; the Democrats had caucused the night before and Richardson, the henchman of Douglas, and a Virginian, A. D. Banks, had been nominated for speaker and clerk although Pierce as in 1853 would have preferred Orr. Forney was to be printer to the Senate.[1] The President and his party knew that there was little likelihood of an immediate organization.

On Monday, December 3, befell what to Pierce must have been three calamities; though two of them were foreseen, they were none the less bitter. The House failed to organize; the balloting showed that the Democratic caucus nominee could count on only seventy-four votes, which were between forty and fifty less than needed; consequently the message could not go in nor become public. Then John P. Hale was sworn in as senator for a term of six years; Pierce felt his native state might have spared him that humiliation. But worse than these, came the telegram from Governor Shannon asking for soldiers to sup-

435

port the law in Kansas. His reply was immediate. "All the power vested in the executive will be exerted to preserve order and enforce the laws." He promised troops to be detailed " on the receipt of your letter " reporting particulars. However, the crisis quickly passed, for in a few days Shannon advised that he had made a truce between the contending factions; the day for troops was not yet.[2]

In the meantime day by day went by, ballot after ballot was taken, and no nearer seemed the organization of the House. The situation was growing serious. One of Pierce's chief hopes from his message was to impress the British Ministry and public with the need of changing their policy toward us. Parliament was to meet about February 1 and it was important that American policy be well in the public eye before the debate in this body began. But if our own government was broken up by failure to elect a speaker, and the message undelivered, the United States could expect little but ridicule and contempt from the British. Pierce urged this argument upon House leaders as he besought them to secure organization in time for his message to be sent to England. He was going to submit to Congress some of Palmerston's correspondence dug up from the state department files in the hope it would cause the premier's downfall—correspondence dated prior to the Clayton-Bulwer treaty which seemed to bear out American contentions in regard to Central America.

The President's wishes had little weight with Congress and the last days of the year approached with nothing accomplished. Alexander H. Stephens grew impatient and suggested to Howell Cobb that the President send in the message without waiting; the Senate was organized. Cobb and Stephens then went to the White House to urge this procedure. " At first he did not seem to take to it at all; he was timid and shy; but after a while said he would think of it and consult his cabinet. The thing was so unprecedented, he was afraid of it." December 29 Pierce went to see Toombs about the plan and Toombs endorsed it. Stephens further helped by finding a precedent in British parliamentary history. Without more urging Pierce conferred with Cobb, Stephens, and Quitman whom he had summoned that Saturday morning, reached his decision the same day and sent in his message on Monday. Cobb commented:

If he had had bold counsellors from the beginning, he would not be in the position he is and I expect he begins to think so himself. The credit is given to the President for the boldness of the move and that is right. I don't know which was most astonished when the message was delivered, his friends or his enemies—all were taken by surprise. This is the advantage of the head of a party doing a thing first and consulting about it afterwards. Had he consulted too many, there never would have been unanimity.[3]

Pierce at last had done something original. The same steamer that bore the message to England carried Marcy's letter instructing Buchanan to demand Crampton's recall for his recruiting activities. Pierce was going to strike out. Would Congress and the people be impressed by their leader's program?

LIX

AN UNPLEASANT TURN

<hr>

SOME eleven years before in another January, Pierce had felt himself called upon to set out at dusk one bitter New Hampshire day and drive far into the night to arrange for the punishment of a party traitor. He had been successful, the traitor had been withdrawn temporarily from public life, and for several years the renegade's political fortunes had been precarious, with Pierce alert to block any permanent success. But the outcast had not been discouraged. Several times the wheel of fortune had turned, and on the first Monday in December, 1855, John P. Hale as a Republican was sworn into the United States Senate once more after an absence of two years. The failure of the House to organize prevented much debate, but as soon as Pierce sent his message to the Senate discussion began, with Hale participating.

John P. Hale started the new year and his second senatorial term with a bitter personal attack upon Pierce. January 3, he spoke at length excoriating the President for both his foreign and domestic policies, tearing his message apart and denouncing it as a public bid for support for renomination. What right had the President to send this message before the House was organized? It was a breach of the privileges of the Senate and could "only be excused by an illusion that the President must have got into his head from an unfortunate remark which fell some days since from [Clayton] that the country was waiting with great anxiety to hear it."

What right had the President to classify all his opponents as enemies of the constitution? He quoted a conversation he said he had overheard.

A Southerner: "It is one of the best messages that ever was written and Pierce is the best President we have ever had since Washington."

His companion: "Well—you will renominate him, will you not?"

438

Southerner: " No, that is another thing; his message is a little strong to get northern votes with; we shall not use him anymore."

The President, so Hale declared, had no more chance of being renominated than a Senate page.

Such an attempt to throw cold water upon Pierce's hopes met a response from the weather. January, 1856, was a terrifically cold period. A great snow fell a few days after the advent of the year and for a month the ground was covered and sleighing was popular. The thermometer seemed to have become congealed around twenty degrees and the inhabitants thought back a quarter of a century without being able to recall a parallel. Such arctic weather had caught Washington unprepared; the barnlike public buildings had refrigerative qualities undreamed of and the Senate chamber, which depended largely for its heat upon four fireplaces, presented a strange appearance. It was the day of shawls and long tippets, and grave senators now appeared in their seats and addressed themselves to the questions of the day stuffed far beyond their normal size, which made some of them at least quite enormous. One observer who noted the frequency with which they gathered around the fireplaces declared that they cared more for the state of the fire than for the state of the nation.[1]

New Year's day, 1856, inaugurated Pierce's most brilliant social season. Mrs. Pierce received with him, and in the months that followed the White House was more of a center of attraction than it had been previously. The usual Friday evening receptions were resumed and a round of official dinners was inaugurated. The diplomatic corps, the Supreme Court, senators and congressmen, came upon invitation to the President's table.

The first evening levee, held on January eleventh, was a notable affair. Receptions were much better managed now than when Pierce first gave them. Sidney Webster, Marshal Hoover, and Commissioner Blake had worked out a smoother order of procedure. Men were relieved of their wraps in the entrance hall, the private dining room to the right was used as a ladies dressing room. The guests passed through the " Crimson Parlor " to the oval blue room where the President received the gentlemen, introduced by Hoover, and Mrs. Pierce welcomed

the ladies, presented to her by Blake. Mrs. Pierce was there
doing her duty; "traces of bereavement" were "legibly written
on a countenance too ingenuous for concealment though a winning smile ever" accompanied her welcoming words. Thence
the crowds passed through the green drawing room to the
"East Room." It was a motley throng. Representatives from
certain dressmaking establishments came there dressed in the
latest fashions to advertise their "emporiums," "one or two
specimens of the antique who by the free use of rouge and
pearl-white excited the mirth of the lovers of landscape painting" also mingled in the throngs. Then this was Dr. Lydia
Sayer's winter; she was in Washington advocating the wearing
of bloomer costumes by the ladies. Occasionally an advocate
of this style would appear at the White House in costume and
the expectation of such appearance increased the male attendance. Such was the crowd that ebbed and flowed through the
gas-lit rooms as the marine band played under the staircase;
Il Trovatore provided the favorite airs that winter.

On the evening of the second reception Washington was there
in usual throng. A group entered with the rest, Senator Hale
escorting a party through the crowd. In due time they approached the President. He greeted the ladies and passed them
on to Mrs. Pierce; but to John P. Hale he turned his back. His
resentment at Hale's bitter personal attack, the first one made
against him on the floor of the Senate, would not permit any
social amenities.[2] Hale's lack of anything like sensitivity
robbed this snub of its sting and furnished the New Hampshire
senator with more reason for continuing the war which he pursued zealously until Pierce faded out of public life. Hale had
chosen a winning cause. As Washington left the White House
that night, to the strains of *Yankee Doodle*, it had much to talk
about.

LX

COPING WITH TREASON IN KANSAS

WHEN Pierce had drafted his message, Kansas was calm. Although Shannon's telegrams of December had been temporarily disquieting the governor had reported a return of peace almost immediately. Under these circumstances he had not revised his message and his reference to Kansas was brief. Shortly after the end of the year news from the territory again became alarming. The free state sympathizers were about to set up an organization of their own and disregard the lawful territorial government. Such action to Pierce was treason. Meantime, Congress was still unorganized, and while Pierce felt that the situation was so dangerous as to make immediate legislation necessary, there could be no laws passed without congressional organization. In the hope of quickening the consciences of the House combatants, the President decided to send in a message on Kansas, setting forth the gravity of the state of affairs. As Pierce had no sympathy for the treasonable free state organizers, it was hoped by many and perhaps by the President himself that his message would persuade the southern Know-Nothings, generally known as South Americans, to unite with the Democrats, most of whom were southerners, and organize the House. Thus measures might be taken to suppress the anti-southern move in Kansas. To aid this plan, Richardson withdrew from the contest for speaker, and Orr, the South Carolinian, was substituted.

January 24 came the President's message and Orr was presented by the Democrats. The message was direct and to the point in its analysis of Kansas troubles. In the first place as to causes: Reeder had not gone out till late, he had paid more attention to land speculation than to taking the necessary census, he had failed to have delegates and members of the legislature chosen at the same time (had he done so, Congress would have had jurisdiction over the election). But this was not all; misguided individuals in other parts of the country had attempted to force the trend of immigration into an anti-slavery channel;

441

their efforts had caused resentment on the part of neighboring
citizens (Missourians) and acts had resulted which though provoked were unjustifiable. Notwithstanding these unwarranted
acts, the proper authority, the governor, had duly canvassed the
votes and declared a legislature elected; his word was final and
no authority existed which could overrule it. Then had occurred an unseemly quarrel between governor and legislature
over the place of meeting, in which the former quite unlaw-
fully had attempted to discredit the latter. Their quarrel gave
an opportunity to the free state element to claim that the legislature was no longer lawful. They began to act independently
of it, elected a delegate to Congress although there was one
already, called a convention, drew up the so-called " Topeka "
constitution which they submitted to their followers, adopted
it by a popular vote of anti-slavery men and finally chose state
officers and a legislature—all in defiance of a lawfully constituted and functioning territorial government. This was revolution.

As executive, Pierce could do nothing but uphold the territorial government against this rebellious free state organization
and place at the marshal's command such federal forces as were
available in the territory. " But it is not the duty of the President of the United States to volunteer interposition by force to
preserve the purity of elections, either in state or territory."
All this trouble had been caused by propaganda and unfounded
or grossly exaggerated reports. Such foolishness had hindered
the working of nature which through climate and topography
would have made the territory free soil. Pierce pledged himself to use force in supporting the law and upholding the
territorial government, but he saw danger ahead and consequently made two recommendations to Congress. First, that
they provide for a constitutional convention and the speedy
admission of Kansas as a state, and second, that an appropriation be made for expenses necessary to maintain order.[1]

The " South Americans," however much they might agree
with the philosophy of the message, refused to throw away their
party identity by organizing under a Democratic caucus nominee; so nothing was accomplished except to deepen the conviction among observers that Pierce was wholly with the South.
Pierce would have denied that he was anything except a true

nationalist trying to uphold law and order and suppress treason. Balloting for a speaker continued and the long delay became a matter of deeper concern to the President. Europeans were jibing at the downfall of democratic government in the United States. The end of the controversy, however, was near at hand.

On February 1, three resolutions were offered, declaring respectively that Nathaniel P. Banks, the Republican candidate, Mordecai Oliver of Missouri, a Whig, and William Aiken, a South Carolinian, Democratic in sympathy but not a participant in Democratic caucuses, was each elected speaker. They were defeated 115–102, 116–101 and 110–103. The tallies showed the Democrats that Aiken could command more votes than Banks, as the "South Americans" generally voted for him; consequently some of them, thinking thereby to elect Aiken, decided to join the Republicans, who were advocating that a plurality elect, as it had done in 1849–1850. These hopes were shared by the President. He was greatly relieved and when greeting Aiken at the White House reception that evening he congratulated him wholeheartedly on his probable election. But this was a delusion and a snare; just as soon as twelve Democrats had hopefully voted for a plurality resolution and permitted the Republicans to gain their point, Banks was elected 103–100.* The strategy of Pierce and the Democratic leaders had failed to save the House committees.[2]

While waiting for Congress to act in the Kansas matter, Pierce was called upon to do more than report to that body. The disorder which had accompanied the free state election January 15 continued into the days following, and resulted in death and retaliation; the so-called treaty that Shannon had negotiated in December proved of no lasting strength and the bitter winter became the real truce-maker. Shortly after the "state" election its leaders, Lane and Robinson, realized that the pro-slavery men were bound to renew attempts, in the name of law and order, to destroy the irregular and "treasonable" organization of the free state men. So they in turn sent a demand to the

* Forney wrote to Buchanan that they had enough votes to elect Aiken after Richardson was dropped, but Hickman and Barclay refused to vote for Aiken, the first because he was anti-Nebraska, the second a good-hearted but light-headed young fellow. Five others, "South Americans," did the same and Aiken failed.

President, on January 21, for protection by the United States troops stationed at Forts Leavenworth and Riley; and two days later they requested the President to issue immediately a proclamation ordering the invading Missourians to disperse. The so-called Topeka constitution had provided that the first " state " legislature, that which had just been elected, should meet March 4. It is hard to tell which prospect, the meeting of the so-called state legislature or the invasion of the Missourians, was for Pierce most unpleasant to contemplate. Evidently the situation required some action; so Pierce and his advisers decided to issue a proclamation condemning the irregularities of both parties and commanding all flouting of law and duly constituted authority to cease; Cushing set to work to draw it up. In the second place, Shannon, now visiting in Ohio, was summoned to Washington for consultation concerning the use of troops; and finally, two commissioners, one from the North and one from the South, were to be sent to Kansas " to use their influence to adjust the differences there." Horatio Seymour was the northern man selected for this task, and Marcy undertook to persuade him to accept.

On February 11 the proclamation drawn up by Cushing was issued. It recited that one group was attempting to take over the government of Kansas by force, that another on the borders was preparing militant intervention, that people in remote states were sending armed men and money to aid revolt, and that parties in the territory were inviting states to intervene. The proclamation commanded these irregular combinations to disperse or be dealt with by local militia and federal troops; " all good citizens " were called upon to aid in suppressing such encouragement of violence. Three days later Governor Shannon arrived in Washington for a protracted interview with the President and Marcy who ordered him back to Kansas and bade him be there before the Topeka legislature came together; they provided him instructions to Colonel Sumner which placed the federal troops at his disposal. Shannon departed the 16th and two days later the President sent the Kansas documents to Congress. Meanwhile, the Senate committee on territories, under Douglas, already was busy preparing a statehood bill. While these plans were being concluded Seymour had declined to serve as a Kansas commissioner, giving his opinion that such a commission would only embarrass regular officers, lessen their authority, and impair their usefulness. The administration gave up the idea of pacification, revolution was to be " crushed out." [3]

The transmission of the Kansas documents to Congress was immediately followed by a speech from Toucey who acted as the President's spokesman in the Senate. He reiterated the particulars of the President's recent message and pointed out that although protection had been granted Lane and Robinson as soon as they called for it, free state supporters refused to be satisfied. He also started an offensive campaign by declaring that if the Kansas outrages were to end the Republicans would have no excuse for existence—that they were not really anxious for peace. Wilson and Hale rejoined with scathing denunciations, the latter referring to Toucey slightingly as the President's senator. Thus the dispute went on, and it redoubled when the Senate was presented with the administration's solution of the Kansas difficulty.[4]

Senator Douglas from the committee on territories brought in, March 12, a Kansas bill and a report in which he embodied the President's Kansas theory. That report Glancy Jones described as an attempt to give Douglas the credit of Kansas-Nebraska and picture the President as a late supporter. The bill authorized Kansas to form a constitution and state government when her inhabitants numbered 93,420 (the number required to entitle her to one congressman under the existing ratio). As Calhoun, the surveyor of the territory, had reported to Marcy recently that there probably were not more than 30,000 then living in Kansas, this would postpone statehood indefinitely and leave the region under the control of the territorial legislature. A few days later, Douglas made an extended speech upholding the administration's contentions and declaring that Pierce was entitled to the thanks of the whole country for the promptness and energy with which he had met the crisis. Naturally, the Senate was not unanimous in agreement. Pierce had played directly into the hands of the Republicans and they were quick to take advantage.[5]

LXI

A RISING POWER

PIERCE'S Kansas program of neutrality and law enforcement placed in the hands of his enemies the most dangerous weapon which he could possibly have forged, at the moment when these same enemies had reached a position from which they could most effectively use it. For exactly two years a new enthusiasm had been spreading among the people, an enthusiasm which was an emotional outbreak much deeper and wider than a political reorganization. The latent antagonism toward the South which lurked in the North had burst forth again, and to the Democrats the renewed bitterness was assuming alarming proportions. As Pierce had demonstrated repeatedly in his acts and utterances, he refused to consider the tide of feeling anything but a misguided and mistaken prejudice fostered by disappointed and designing demagogues. To his mind the Whigs were bankrupt and their leaders were hoping to profit by a new agitation. Pierce was wrong, or rather only partly right, in his diagnosis. Not only were northern politicians seeking new power; there was an even greater source of strength to the movement. The enthusiasts of the North were arming for a new expedition in the anti-slavery crusade, in a manner well calculated to appeal to a generation of youth alive to the excitement of a political revival.

The resentment which the repeal of the Missouri Compromise aroused had not crystallized immediately because of a competing interest, the Know-Nothing enthusiasm. The returns of the elections of 1852 and 1854 had shown that there were about 1,200,000 voters willing to vote against the Democrats in the northern states. In 1852, 1,022,757 called themselves Whigs and 157,745 Free Soilers. In 1854 it may be estimated none too accurately that of this approximate 1,200,000, about 520,000 had become Free Soilers and the remainder were still Whigs or had become Know-Nothings; it was impossible to tell which.

It was apparent that these elements thus divided could make

446

but ineffective opposition to the Democrats and fusion seemed
the natural path to victory. But upon what basis was fusion
possible? Two methods appeared available, one to organize a
Know-Nothing or American Party, in reality a revamped Whig
party still representing both sections, the other to mobilize a
northern party upon a free soil basis. Whether either or neither of these methods could be utilized had been a matter of
uncertainty, and meanwhile in 1855 the Democrats had regained ground. Evidently fusion must be accomplished in
time for the elections of 1856 if there were to be any hopes of
success.

The possibility of a Presidential victory in 1856 was a powerful stimulus to organizers and a number became active, for
without such a victory the political fortunes of men like Seward
and Chase would be in eclipse. After the schism in the Know-
Nothing party at the June Council of 1855, the free state group,
known as " North Americans," tried to arrange a fusion with
the Republicans on the basis of their anti-foreign, anti-Catholic
principles. On the other hand, two groups of Republicans, the
Ohioans with middle-western allies who looked to Chase as their
leader, and an eastern group, which contained the followers of
Seward and a remnant of the Jacksonians such as Francis P.
Blair and his family, were attempting to arrange a fusion on the
basis of opposition to the extension of slave territory. The two
Republican factions finally agreed to an organizing convention
to be held February 22, 1856, at Pittsburgh, the same date upon
which the Know-Nothings were holding a national nominating
convention at Philadelphia. On Washington's Birthday, 1856,
therefore, the decision as to the future was taken. The Republicans definitely organized on a free soil basis and the southern
branch of the Know-Nothings refused to make any peace with
the " North Americans." If the Republicans and " North
Americans " could unite there would be possible a real northern
party with a chance for success.

The Republicans in Congress and out began an intensive campaign to stir up resentment against the South and indefatigably
to promote the free soil crusade. Kansas made admirable
propaganda. The difficulties in that troubled territory were
advertised and magnified so that all the world might see. Congress was in session and there was no easier source of publicity.

With untiring energy and shrewd knowledge of American political psychology the hopeful leaders of the new cause scrutinized
every act of the Pierce administration and found them all wanting, and newspapers like the *Tribune* reported every occurrence
in Kansas and found them all drenched in blood. Hale had led
off in January in the Senate and with the President's Kansas
message, his proclamation, the documents he sent to Congress,
and Douglas's report came new opportunities which the Republicans were not going to miss. Wilson, Wade, Lewis D. Campbell, Grow, Sherman, and many others made innumerable
speeches and devised well advertised parliamentary tactics to
keep the issue going strong. They pilloried the President as a
weakling who had sold out to the South in hope of renomination,
the creature of a dangerous and callous oligarchy which demanded the spread of a cruel and barbarous institution. Seward even went so far as to arraign him as a tyrant, and likened
his policies toward the oppressed Kansans to the despotism of
George III. So heavy was the flood of criticism that history,
swept along by its very mass, has generally accepted it as truth.[1]

Pierce was in an unhappy position, for the "South Americans" were attacking him viciously on the other flank. As
Senator Clay of Alabama put it:

> The Abolitionists charge that the President approved the
> Nebraska Kansas bill to open new fields for slavery; the
> South Americans, that he did so to enlarge the area of free
> soil. The Abolitionists say his Administration has been
> exerted to make Kansas a slave state, the South Americans,
> to make it a free state. The Abolitionists abuse the Presi-
> dent for removing Reeder; the South Americans for ap-
> pointing him. The Abolitionists say he was removed too
> soon; the South Americans, too late. The Abolitionists
> say he was removed for no official delinquency; the South
> Americans that he was retained after repeated delinquen-
> cies. The Abolitionists complain that squatter sovereignty
> is frowned upon and threatened with suppression; the
> South Americans that it is countenanced and encouraged.
> The Abolitionists complain that the proclamation is leveled
> at Free-Soilers; the South Americans, at pro-slavery men.

Clay even went so far in his speech as to express the hope
that if ever the Republicans got into control, the South would
take up the sword in self-defense.[2] Clay in private also under-

took to remonstrate with Hale for his agitation of the slavery question. No good, he felt, could come from it. To this Hale characteristically replied, " Mr. Clay, it sent me to the Senate and *I* think there is something in that." [3]

In the meantime the Republicans were looking for a candidate who would command the support of the " North Americans " and conduct a campaign which would make out of the fusion movement a permanent party.

LXII

THE APPROACH OF THE CONVENTION

THE rapid rise of the new political power further stimulated Pierce to decisive action. His renewed ambition and the unfriendly composition of the lower house pointed his behavior and made more decided his purposes in so far as administrative acts were concerned. On the other hand, he could not bring himself to work directly for his own nomination. Frankly, he did not know how. He had been the convenience of others generally, and his offices had come to him because he was useful as a compromise choice to settle differences between contending parties. The only place he had really striven to obtain was his brigadier generalship. So in 1856 he rather fatalistically was inclined to let events take their course. He laid down a platform for his party, he proceeded to enact a vigorous policy, and to demonstrate his loyalty to sound doctrine. Such acts he considered the best bid for renomination. His office holders must do the practical work, must lay the pipe. He was quoted as saying he would not use the patronage to further his renomination, but it is doubtful whether his cabinet were as scrupulous, and officials like Charles Mason found him keenly concerned in the bearing of appointments upon his candidacy.[1] His fortunes as spring advanced fluctuated, and with them his hopes.

The January conventions were disappointing. Alabama alone declared for him. Even the states of Davis and Guthrie were non-committal. Tennessee, Georgia, Ohio, and Iowa gave no instructions, Indiana went for Bright and the New York factions were going to plague the Democratic assemblage by sending contesting delegations. Much attention was focused on the Virginia convention, February 28 and March 1; but that state, so largely instrumental in his nomination in 1852, followed her usual custom of giving no instructions. North Carolina, however, wheeled in line behind New Hampshire and Alabama.

Worse than the conventions were the elections. Once again

New Hampshire smote her famous son.   As in the other spring
campaigns Pierce had exerted himself.   Sidney Webster collected funds.   Cochrane levied assessments on the New York
office holders at pay day amounting to $1,468.   Fowler, New
York postmaster, sent up $500.   A check for $2,500 was dispatched from Washington with the authorization to use $500
more if necessary.   Pierce prevailed upon Orr and Cobb to go
up and address the voters.   Their speeches produced a curious
effect, as the Democrats had been waging their campaign on
Pierce's issue, namely, that the Kansas-Nebraska act was a measure for freedom, and here came the southerners with their
doctrines of states' rights and slave protection.   Pierce franked
2,000 speeches to New Hampshire voters and just before the
election wrote George in strict confidence: " I am fully aware
of the expenses necessarily incident to a contest like that thro
which you are now passing.   The enclosed is for your *ward*
only and to be known to no one but yourself."

But again New Hampshire was unappreciative.   The ticket
was defeated and in spite of the fact that friendly papers made
much of the greatly increased Democratic vote, it was still a
defeat.[2]   Pierce felt it deeply and temporarily gave up hope.
In a few days, he wrote his brother Henry inviting him to visit
the White House.   He said, " You ought to come on every account but I desire to see you especially to converse about plans
for life when my labors here shall come to a close."   He began
to plan for his retirement and decided to visit Concord as soon
as Congress adjourned.   He wanted to buy some property and
make preparations for a home.[3]   A few days later the Connecticut election proved equally disastrous.

Pierce was going to be a very hard candidate to renominate.
In the first place, in the North the shame of the repeal of the
Missouri Compromise was bitterly felt, and Pierce was held
responsible for the subsequent difficulties in Kansas.   Nor did
he add to his popularity by his public messages attributing
these disturbances primarily to the activities of the Emigrant
Aid Company.   On the other hand, southern support had reservations; Alexander H. Stephens wrote, " It is only within the last
six months that the position of Mr. Pierce has been such as to
receive my commendation."   He blamed him for sending
Reeder to Kansas and for his desire, as Stephens saw it, to

make Kansas a free state; then too he had not stood by northern
supporters of the Nebraska bill as he should, but conferred
patronage upon their opponents.   His policy toward the whole
matter had showed " Fickleness, weakness, folly and vacilla-
tions." [4]   Atchison wrote, " If the General Government would
only leave Kansas to the nurture of the Border Ruffians we
would soon have peace in that quarter, but as General Pierce
has taken the matter out of our hands God knows what shall
come of it.   I do not complain of him for I believe his motives
are good but I doubt his policy." [5]   Many considered his Kansas
procedure indecisive and hesitant, and pointed to his failure in
regard to Cuba and his long patience in the matter of England's aggressions, as evidence that he was not a strong or forceful executive.   His patronage blunders and his changeableness
in appointments combined with the strictness of his administrative rulings to make him enemies.   Worse than all this, his
regime had been marked by personal feuds.

His administration had been inaugurated to the accompaniment of the feud between Dickinson and Marcy.   Guthrie and
Bronson had waged their famous war.   Cushing publicly had
expressed a desire to " crush out " abolitionists.   Davis had
quarreled with Henry S. Foote, with General Wool, and with
General Scott.   Many of the naval officers were in high dudgeon.
Reeder hated the President.   Borland and Soulé nursed grievances and lately old Sam Houston had charged Pierce with
having trifled with the best interests of the country.   McClelland and Campbell were very unpopular with many monied
interests, especially speculators.

All this mountain of personal unpopularity contributed to
his difficulties; but the chief trouble was the realization by
many practical party leaders that Pierce was a weak candidate
and if nominated hardly could be elected—the larger interests
of party success consequently dictated the choice of another
man.   Many were looking around for some one who could
cement the broken ranks of the party shattered by Know-Nothingism and Black Republicanism.   To a great many James
Buchanan loomed as the figure of unity.   He was well known
and his availability had been widely considered for years; indeed it may be said that the dominant element in the party
had preferred him in 1852.   Furthermore, he was not an un-

tried man as Pierce had been; he had had a great deal of experience; he knew the governmental machine and its handling
thoroughly.

During nearly three years he had been abroad and had participated in none of the domestic predicaments of the administration.   Although he had repeatedly declined becoming a candidate, and the strong desire which he had once felt for the office
did not seem to have maintained itself, to many politicians he
seemed the only hope.   More especially was this true because
of the action of the Pennsylvania machine.   His henchmen
there found that as the choice of delegates approached in the
fall of 1855 their enemies were attempting to make capital out
of Buchanan's refusal to run and were putting forward Dallas
as Pennsylvania's choice.   Also another faction, under the lead
of Campbell and the federal office holders, was pushing Pierce
and at the same time endeavoring to gain control of the state
machinery.   Thereupon Buchanan's old phalanx felt that to
maintain their domination they must bring him forward as if
he were actually a candidate.   This they succeeded in doing
and their activities gave the impression that Buchanan was
openly in the field.

About the intentions of Cass and Douglas there seems to have
been similar doubt.   Early in the year 1856 it was understood
that neither would be candidates; and the former seems hardly
to have been considered but to have been abandoned for the
latter.   Douglas on February 8 arrived in Washington for his
first appearance that session, having been detained by a " protracted illness." [6]   He returned with the realization that Illinois
had temporarily deserted Democracy.   It may be that he was
doubtful about going for the nomination, but he had supporters,
and as one of them put it:

> The position his friends have forced him into is this.   He
> must permit them to use his name or be driven to ignore
> the great act of his life—yet while he will do this, he will
> not deny to others the same rights his friends claim for him,
> maintaining all the time such a position as will enable him
> to do the most effective service for the nominee. . . . He is
> here going all the time and if he does not work a change in
> a few weeks, I shall be surprised.[7]

Pierce's unpopularity, as well, especially in the North and West, may have contributed to a belief on Douglas's part that his leadership was necessary to save the election of 1856. At any rate, on March 3 his relative, Senator Reid of North Carolina, wrote that he had called on Douglas and found that his position in regard to the Presidency had "somewhat changed. He is now in the hands of his friends, or in other words before the people." His supporters began to circulate around the country reporting to him on his prospects, carefully refraining from doing anything to antagonize Pierce workers. Douglas was reported as declaring his intention to run with Pierce as his second choice.

Evidently Pierce was to have two opponents of first importance as well as such less influential men as Senator Hunter of Virginia, Senator Bright of Indiana (whom rumor reported as aiming at a combination ticket of Hunter and Bright), and Governor Wise of Virginia, foe of Hunter, who hoped to inherit the Buchanan strength and climb to glory in that manner. "Sam" Houston also wanted to be President and had the active support of Burke and the anti-Pierce faction in New Hampshire. Loudest of all was the New York *Herald* which kept up a continual devastating barrage of attacks and slighting statements such as the following: "He is a made man altogether exceedingly anxious to please everybody and allowing the last man who sees him to take him captive. He is wholly without moral courage." [8] As a friend of Breckinridge put it:

> Pierce has to encounter so many objections and prejudices that I think every consideration demands that he should not be nominated. He has no real strength but there is so much weakness in him *personally*, for instance you may hear it often said "anybody but Pierce." There is undoubtedly an *active* opposition to Pierce in our ranks which we are bound to respect.[9]

More than ever did Pierce need a firm, steady, and respected organ; but the *Union*'s influence was so vitiated by the equivocal position of Forney, known friend of Buchanan, as to be almost useless. Forney's enemies went after him the instant the new Congress opened. He wanted to be printer of the Senate, and therefore Forney and Nicholson had been nominated; but Bright, Hunter, Mason, Butler, Bayard, Brodhead, and Brown of Mississippi prevented his election. The Virginia Senators, always his enemies, went to the President about it and demanded that Pierce cast him loose. Pierce persuaded Forney to withdraw from the race and arranged a compromise whereby Nicholson was to get the printing but Forney was to have charge of the paper. Then came personal difficulties. Forney struck out an " inspired " article written for the *Union* rebuking attacks upon the President in the *Pennsylvanian*. Pierce ordered the article printed. " We had some words," reported Forney, and the article did not go in; Forney ceased going to the White House. After Nicholson was elected printer, pressure was again brought to bear to separate Forney from the *Union*, in spite of the fact that Pierce had once declared that " all hell should not make him break with Forney." Such pressure was especially strong from friends of Buchanan, who did not want Forney's connection with the administration continually brought up as an earnest that Buchanan was not really a candidate. So March 28 Forney withdrew, and Nicholson in complete control began to line up the administration batteries and repel the charges. The *Herald* said that Pierce dismissed Forney; the *Union* said that Nicholson bought him out.[10] This paper was a continual source of weakness to Pierce throughout the whole course of his administration.

When Buchanan arrived April 23 from England and heard of Forney's difficulty with the President he wondered just how much of Pierce's displeasure with Forney would reflect upon him. To find out where he stood, he sent Glancy Jones to the White House. Pierce told Jones he did not blame Forney but he was much displeased at the course of Van Dyke, the Philadelphia district attorney, and the *Pennsylvanian* (nevertheless Pierce would not or dared not remove Van Dyke). Jones assured the President that Buchanan was friendly and reprobated all personal attacks on him. After the long interview Jones could assure Buchanan that he would be cordially received.[11]

Buchanan's strength was manifest from the enthusiasm with which his home-coming was greeted. His candidacy seemed formidable. Such conditions led the supporters of Pierce and Douglas to seek an understanding. The details of this *entente*, spoken of by the press and private correspondence of the day, are not available; the delegate from Minnesota, Douglas's intimate, wrote:

> Douglas and his friends are prudent here and I believe that there is a good understanding between him and Pierce. The war waged by some of Buchanan's friends has had the effect to unite the others. I also believe that Pierce sees his own condition and that his friends will not urge him if they see that the effect will be to nominate Buchanan. I know you are right in regard to Douglas and Pierce.[12]

Pierce was approaching the convention with a support coming mainly from the South and from certain federal office holders elsewhere. Consequently, if he could command most of the South and New England, this force with Douglas's western followers might control the choice of the convention. However, it was an uncertain coalition. Virginia could not be counted on, no one knew how Cass's supporters in Ohio, Indiana, and Michigan would line up, and besides there was schism in New England. Many of Pierce's erstwhile friends and supporters had forsaken their allegiance. N. G. Upham, who in 1852 had been eager for Pierce, now was writing Benjamin F. Butler to organize what support they could to coöperate with Forney in behalf of Buchanan. Upham himself was not a delegate but he was doing what he could to establish a Buchanan nucleus in the President's own state. Butler was also canny, not disclosing his hand, and certain other New England politicians such as Charles L. Woodbury were out for the main chance; many had a confirmed distrust of Cushing. The result was to be apparent in the convention.[13]

LXIII

DEFIANCE OF GREAT BRITAIN AT LAST

BRITISH relations had vied with Kansas and partisanship in creating problems for the President this spring of 1856, and certain steps were taken which Pierce's friends attempted to utilize to his advantage in the struggle for the nomination. At no period, thus far in Pierce's administration, had British relations been satisfactory. Rumors of the embarkation of a large British fleet to be stationed near American shores rekindled the embers of animosity which the senators further stirred in debate and the New York *Herald* fanned by bellicose editorials. On the other hand, Marcy commented to Buchanan that the " strengthening of the British fleet in this quarter [was] regarded as a harmless menace. Our people rather admired the folly of the measure than indulge any angry feelings on account of it "; Marcy was philosophical and deliberate about everything except filibustering. Buchanan was more than ever anxious to come home and impatiently urged the choice of his successor until at length Pierce selected George M. Dallas to replace him and awaited Clarendon's reply to the demand for Crampton's dismissal.[1] The opening of Parliament gave Clarendon an opportunity to make public comment upon American relations, and when reports of his remarks arrived February 19 Pierce was much surprised. According to the news despatches, Clarendon asserted than an offer to arbitrate the Central American difficulties had been ignored by the United States and that Great Britain had explained Crampton's acts to our satisfaction. Such a speech was startling, but it was just a newspaper statement; official information would soon be at hand.

On Sunday, February 24, the official mails reached New York and the next day Marcy came over to the White House with the papers. Buchanan's despatches told the President what he wanted to know. Clarendon had never made any direct offer to arbitrate, although he had suggested it, and he had given no reply to Marcy's demand for Crampton's removal; Clarendon's reference to our satisfaction was based on correspondence which passed before Crampton's complicity was proven. Pierce held a long cabinet. There was going to be action this time.

Pierce wrote a brief message calling for $3,000,000 for fortifications and improved arms. The *Union* declared Clarendon's statements untrue. The President transmitted to Congress the full details of the enlistment matter. The war dogs were barking again; Crampton must be dismissed.

Not so fast. Wednesday, Pierce and Marcy spent most of the day at the state department going over the despatches. What was the status of this arbitration offer anyway? That night at eleven o'clock a messenger from the British legation arrived at Marcy's office with a note from Mr. Crampton. The careless British Minister apologized for having neglected to apprise Marcy of Lord Clarendon's offer of arbitration, which he had been ordered to present last November. He had not read the despatch carefully and had neglected to note the instructions! After this, Pierce could only arrange to send Crampton's note to Congress and let the war spirit collapse. Clarendon's offer must be refused but the correspondence involved would take a long time; and in the meanwhile, Clarendon had not replied to the request for Crampton's dismissal, he was too busy with the Paris peace conference. They were tantalizing, these British negotiations, and explanations to the public who craved spectacular action were difficult. The fortification message and the *Union*'s denial of Clarendon's assertions had whetted the popular appetite and the tame climax did not add to the President's reputation for firmness and decision.[2]

The Senate during the interim took up the question, both as presented by the President's fortification message and by his reports on the enlistment and Central American arbitration issues, which reports had been submitted in response to calls introduced by Mason. The Senate voted ten new sloops of war, of a type which Dobbin had recommended, and considered a bill appropriating $3,000,000 to increase the efficiency of the army; this latter, however, it did not finally pass until July. Of course the anti-administration House paid no attention to the Presidential proposals. In spite of a rather hasty speech by Mason on these questions, the Senate foreign relations committee decided to make no recommendations until they could see how the peace conference in Paris was progressing.[3] The speeches made in the Senate told the British that the upper house was behind the President, but otherwise the affair drifted off into obscurity.

March of 1856 was a very uneventful month in Washington. After the stirrings of February it was tame, so the newspaper men felt; but afar off action was brewing which would eventually shake Washington not a little. The grey-eyed man of destiny, William Walker, who had first given Pierce trouble in '53, when he sought to filibuster from California into northern Mexico, was once more aiding the stars. He had gone into Nicaragua, war-torn and revolution-drugged as usual, and after many adventures had emerged so triumphant that John H. Wheeler, Pierce's minister, had recognized Walker's tool, Rivas, as president. Such recognition Pierce and his cabinet, in the grip of a strong anti-filibustering complex, felt to be premature, so they rebuked Wheeler and withdrew recognition. But Walker, like any soldier of fortune, had stirred the American imagination, an imagination so easily awakened in the 'fifties by adventurers. His success, and cut rates offered by the Accessory Transit Company, had lured many an imaginative citizen toward the southern cross. Nevertheless, as with Kinney, so with Walker, Pierce could not afford to have these violations of neutrality going on constantly while he was belaboring Great Britain for the same thing. The President had sent Commodore Paulding, with a warship to keep watch, and had issued a proclamation on December 8 forbidding American citizens to participate in these ventures; Cushing had ordered the district attorneys to be vigilant. When the rather shady Parker H. French came to the United States with credentials from Walker's president as minister, Marcy would have none of him. Attempts to prosecute French for recruiting only served to advertise him, and the outward flow of " peaceful emigrants " was so continuous that Marcy grew " touchy " about the inability of law officers to prevent filibustering and Cushing drew heavily upon his extraordinary vocabulary of expletives whenever the subject was mentioned.

Walker's power began to inflate him. He banished Colonel Kinney, whose forlorn fortunes had finally petered out at Greytown, although Cushing, Webster, Forney, and others in Wash-

ington (some whispered the President himself) had been interested in the promoter. Then the adventurer moved forward
and engaged with some of Vanderbilt's agents to double-cross
that wily financier by revoking the charter of Vanderbilt's
steamship company without warning and giving it to the new
company formed by his agents. Vanderbilt made use of some
of his picturesque language and girded himself, by writing
Marcy. Senator Clayton called the attention of Congress to
the revocation. Vanderbilt seconded his letter by himself and
Pierce received a call from the commodore and General Webb,
a favor he shared with Cushing. The President was not sympathetic; Vanderbilt's steamboats had been the main instrument
for conveying filibusterers to Nicaragua and discrediting his
efforts to enforce the neutrality law. If the filibusterers now
turned on the commodore, it was but poetic justice and in this
frame of mind the President calmly disregarded a senatorial
call for papers introduced by Seward.

While Pierce was declining Vanderbilt's requests to punish
Walker, he was also resisting pressure to acknowledge him.
Influential men headed by Douglas sought to persuade the President to recognize the adventurer who was really successful. His
sympathy might come in handy if the British must finally be
punished in Central America for Walker was at war with Costa
Rica; no one knew where his power might end. The New York
Herald kept up a more or less continuous demand for recognition while the cabinet deliberated; but Marcy was stoutly opposed. Nevertheless, Pierce felt he must know more about conditions down there, so John P. Heiss was sent to Nicaragua to
observe and report. In the meantime nothing more was heard
from England. Clarendon and the diplomatic world were at
the peace conference and Mason was sending home gossipy
letters from Paris and incidently worrying lest the British suddenly attack the American fleet in the Mediterranean.[4]

Pierce's attention of course was diverted often by domestic
details, administrative and social. Indian atrocities had become so continuous in Washington and Oregon that early in
March the President had appealed to Congress for $300,000 to
quell the uprising; strange to say, Congress had responded
favorably and in April Pierce and Davis had the details of
these distant operations to manage. Spring also brought social

diversions.   The final reception of the season was held, at which
a visiting delegation of Seminoles approached as close as possible to the marine band and refused to pay attention to anything else.   For twelve weeks the White House had been a social
center; and a series of dinners had marked this most brilliant
winter of Pierce's dull social reign.   On the evening of the 17th
of April, Pierce and Webster went to the National Theatre to
hear Donizetti's *Daughter of the Regiment* given by Pyne and
Harrison's English Opera Company, gracefully concluded by
the singing of " Hail Columbia."   Two days later, Pierce, Dobbin, and Webster went to Annapolis to inspect the new frigate,
Merrimac.   There was elaborate ceremony: the President was
received at the state capitol where he was formally welcomed
by the commissioner of the Maryland land office and Captain
Goldsborough, commandant of the Naval Academy, gave a ball
in his honor that evening.   Accompanied by Governor Ligon,
he inspected the cadets and embarked on the *Merrimac* while
the new vessel steamed out and was put through maneuvers.
After a " hasty collation " on board, Pierce went back to Washington.   Spring was there with all its charm, and the outdoor
concerts began to be the center of gossip and good fellowship.
Then came events fast and furious.

A flood of tidings began to pour into the executive buildings
and Washington was agog with rumors.   There had been a riot
on the isthmus of Panama and Joe Lane had brought a telegram to Pierce April 30 from the president of the Pacific
Steamship Company asking for a war vessel to restore order
and safe trans-isthmian transportation.   The same day, John
P. Heiss returned from Nicaragua and letters were received
from Walker, describing how he had intercepted the British
mail for Costa Rica and found official intelligence that England
was willing to sell arms to Costa Rica for use in their war with
Nicaragua, to drive out the " north Americans."   On May 2,
Pierce received the treaty with the Dominican Republic which
Consul Elliot had negotiated, and which failed to include cession of Samana Bay.   In less than a week, further tidings came
that a British naval officer had stopped an American steamer,
the *Orizaba,* in Nicaraguan waters and had demanded her papers.   On May 10 a private letter from Dallas reported that
Clarendon would not recall Crampton.

Emerging from the drenching flood of these varied tidings, Pierce no longer resisted the British phobia. Great Britain had become intolerable, indignity after indignity had been heaped upon the United States and Young Hickory would brook this sort of thing no longer. There must be retaliation; Marcy had counselled deliberation too long, the time had come for action. A new minister from Walker's government, a priest, Vigil or Vijil, had arrived May 5. The padre was quite a different type from the notorious French, he was educated and respectable, a man of standing in his community. Pierce was struck with the idea of receiving him, thus recognizing Walker and bidding defiance to Great Britain. After that, Crampton must be summarily dismissed.

Marcy objected to the first part of the program; Walker was a disreputable adventurer supported by filibusterers who had broken the laws of the United States. How would it look to recognize him as we dismissed Crampton? Great Britain had gone too far once too often, countered the President; before we knew it she would have armed forces in Nicaragua. Pierce was determined; he decided to recognize Vijil and report the whole affair to Congress. Marcy was unconvinced.

The President went vigorously to work and on May 12 had concluded his labors. He wrote Marcy: " I was up till a very late hour last night or rather a very early hour this morning and am experiencing too seriously the effects of an unusual amount of labor to go out to-night. Hence I send by Mr. Webster a rought draft of the message of which we spoke on Friday. Altho' I cannot have what would have afforded me great relief, the approbation of your judgment in relation to the reception of the minister from Nicaragua it is pleasant to beleive (*sic*) that I can have your advice, as my friend in all matters connected with myself or our country, and to know that I can never fail to appreciate a friendship so generous and true, as that which has been exemplified by you in all our intercourse." Marcy could but acquiesce, and wrote Dallas that Crampton was to receive his passports. The secretary apprehended grave difficulties from the recognition of Walker.

On the thirteenth Paulding was sent to San Juan with a war vessel to protect traffic and the day following Vijil was received. Pierce with an accompaniment of voluminous documents explained to Congress that recognition was accorded so that satisfactory arrangements might be made to keep trans-isthmian communication open. Four days later there arrived Clarendon's polite and indirect refusal to recall Crampton; consequently it was just as the Democratic convention was assembling that the British Minister was handed his passports. Senator Mason immediately telegraphed the news to Cincinnati. He did not include the fact that Marcy simultaneously had authorized Dallas to treat again in regard to Central America, but with no arbitration unless direct negotiations were hopeless.[5] How would Palmerston receive our defiance? Would Mr. Dallas be sent home? Pierce again had acted decisively. The convention was ever nearer at hand.

LXIV

THE CALAMITIES OF A MONTH

THE advance of May brought the delegates to Washington on their way to the Cincinnati convention. Seemingly they were at sea; Douglas was tied to Pierce by the Kansas-Nebraska bill, Cass was out of it, the Buchanan men were not active. Many called at the White House, proffering friendship and support; Pierce was still President. On May 21 his principal managers arrived in the persons of Hibbard and Peaslee who were still faithful and Greene of the Boston *Post*. John H. George, who had reached political maturity, was with them as a member of the national committee wearing the fallen mantle of Atherton, but the latter was dead and Burke was in another fold: the phalanx of 1852 was badly shattered. They had their head-quarters at Willard's, but a curtain is drawn over their last-minute negotiations; no record seems to have survived.[1] Just before Buchanan's return, Peaslee had written confidently to George. Undoubtedly the Nicaraguan stand had aided Pierce somewhat and the rumors of Crampton's dismissal, if substantiated, would prove advantageous. In the midst of these more favorable signs a conflagration broke out.

Few months have been more murderous, in peace times, than May, 1856. Just as the cycle began, news came that some Kansans of Lawrence had shot Sheriff Jones, perhaps fatally. May 8 Herbert, member of Congress from California, killed one of the waiters at the Willard. That same day, John P. Heiss, recently back from Nicaragua, assailed Wallach, the editor of the *Star*, for an article on Nicaragua. The 15th there was a murder at the Navy Yard. The 22d Preston Brooks entered the senate chamber and thrashed Senator Sumner, a proceeding which caused northern senators to arm openly and organize for protection. Throughout these days pneumonia was taking a heavy toll of death from the nation. But worst of all was the disquieting news from Kansas. As early as the 14th dispatches had arrived describing a new outbreak in that unhappy territory. On hearing of these, Pierce naturally blamed the free state men. He is quoted as having said, " If there is to be armed resistance to the laws of the country and the constitutional rights of the south, it might as well occur at this time and in Kansas as elsewhere." But the news was getting worse. Sheriff Jones was on the road to Lawrence. A grand jury under Lecompte's instruction had indicted some of the free state leaders for treason and shortly thereafter the marshal also set out with a large posse of pro-slavery men to arrest the accused at Lawrence. That town was reported in a state of siege, a veritable reign of terror. Finally on May 24 came a wire that Lawrence had been sacked, a report Pierce doubted at first, but one which proved true. Just before the convention met, as an anti-climax, came incomplete news of the Pottawatomie Creek massacre.

Such fruit of the Kansas-Nebraska policy aroused a general resentment sufficient to show how dangerous the support of that doctrine was to prove. Popular indignation was great, and it became increasingly clear to a number of wavering delegates that only the strongest kind of candidate would prevent a party disaster. It is claimed that these last-minute calamities cost Pierce a number of votes. The conservatives were taking fright.[2]

Of Pierce's thoughts and plans during this fateful month of May, we know very little, but it would seem that the major part of his time was devoted to considering the complicated problems presented by Nicaraguan and British relations. His decisions in these questions meant a considerable amount of message writing to which he added the preparation of two more vetoes, vetoes which Mason believed would " tend to exasperate feeling and render his nomination under the 2/3 rule more doubtful." Two internal improvement items, one for bettering the mouth of the Mississippi, and the other similar to the measure he had pocket-vetoed the previous session concerning the St. Clair flats and St. Mary's river in Michigan, came to him (by pre-arrangement, so it was said). He showed his orthodoxy and his sectional impartiality by vetoing them both.[3] The record of his administration was now complete. He had kept faith with Jacksonian principles and he had defied Great Britain. The rest was up to the convention. The crowds left Washington to cross the Alleghenies to the first Democratic convention in the West. Congress was deserted and the President awaited news in the uncertainty of abnormal quiet.

LXV

DISILLUSIONMENT

ROUTINE duties occupied the President somewhat; he and his cabinet visited the Smithsonian Institution. Douglas was superintending improvements on his grounds. Congress had adjourned, ostensibly to prepare the halls for the summer sessions, and workmen were occupied with taking up carpet and laying down matting. The telegraph operators seemed to be the only busy people in the capital city.

Though the convention was not scheduled to meet until Monday, June 2, crowds of delegates spent the previous weekend in Cincinnati, and news of their doings was interesting reading to the President. Nothing had been certain in the last days of conference in Washington. The Buchanan supporters, including Slidell, had talked much with Douglas in the weeks preceding, and had thought they had him where they wanted him, namely, in the position of making a perfunctory showing and then withdrawing in favor of Buchanan. At the last minute, however, Slidell received bad news. S. L. M. Barlow of New York was living in Cincinnati, stationed there on railroad business, and his contact with the assembling delegates brought him some surprise. Buchanan had no organization, no headquarters, and he was convinced that the Pierce and Douglas forces were in agreement. He communicated hastily with Slidell and offered his house as headquarters. Slidell was disturbed and hurriedly made up a party of some of Pierce's worst enemies, Senators Bright, Bayard, and Benjamin.[1]

At Cincinnati, they settled in Barlow's house and began work to offset the Pierce-Douglas coalition. The success of such an arrangement would depend upon the ability of Douglas to marshal the West to unite with Pierce's southern support. If Douglas could command Indiana, it might be feasible. The President and his advisers calculated that he would have 145 on the first ballot and Douglas forty; then if the "softs" from New York were admitted, or even half of them, a union of these forces would control the nomination, giving the necessary two-thirds

majority, 198. Calculations like these worked out very nicely
on paper and were backed up to a certain extent by written and
oral pledges from the delegates.[2] Paper reckonings and pre-
convention pledges, however, have a way of being unreliable.
The first blow came on the Friday night before the convention
when the various state delegates caucused in Cincinnati.
Bright, exasperated because Douglas would not use him as
second choice, committed Indiana to Buchanan, and sufficient
progress was made by the Buchanan strength to make Pierce's
chances rather dim. Friday night was referred to as his Water-
loo.[3] But until the ballots were cast there was yet hope.

Pierce's interests were in the hands of Hibbard and Peaslee,
George and Greene, and various other federal office holders and
friends of the cabinet. They established headquarters on
Fourth Street just opposite the new custom house in the upper
rooms of a restaurant called the "Custom House Retreat."
They were in consultation with many southern delegates and
had "wires" through to the Douglas leaders. Their first task
was to get the "softs" recognized as the New York delegation.

The convention was slow in beginning to ballot. Monday,
Tuesday, and Wednesday went by and, contrary to the procedure at the last Baltimore convention, the platform was
adopted first; it incorporated the Kansas-Nebraska principle
and the idea of our necessary prepondcrauce in the Gulf region.
Although not a word was said about the Pierce administration,
its principles were thus endorsed. Thursday morning came the
first open defeat. Though the report of the majority of the credentials committee favored the administration delegates from
New York, the minority report was adopted. This admitted the
"softs" only on an equal basis with the "hards" and no endorsement was given to the claims of either; it was done by a
vote of 137 to 123, Virginia's fifteen suffrages being cast against
the "softs" and with the Buchanan forces. At last the wires
brought news of balloting. Thursday afternoon at two the
candidates were presented and the first poll taken. It stood
Buchanan 135½, Pierce 122½, Douglas 33 and Cass 5. Pierce
had counted on 145, but Kentucky instead of yielding twelve
gave him only five, Massachusetts instead of thirteen only nine,
Ohio four and one-half instead of ten. The great disappointment was Virginia; she had nominated him in 1852 and now

dropped him. Wise had swung the delegation for Buchanan
on the unit rule, and Hunter and Mason could but acquiesce.
The rest of his support was about what he had expected—most
of the southern states except Louisiana, Delaware, Missouri, and
the greater part of Kentucky and Maryland; the " softs " from
New York; Rhode Island, Vermont, and New Hampshire, together with nine out of Massachusetts' thirteen. Connecticut
and five out of Maine's eight he had lost; New England, therefore, was divided; and from the West he had but a feeble minority in the Ohio delegation.

Ballot after ballot followed, his forces held for five votes,
then on the sixth Tennessee dropped away, and on the seventh
Arkansas, Georgia, and his Kentucky adherents. Through the
following seven ballots of that day he held his remaining
strength except for the loss of Vermont and Rhode Island.
North Carolina, South Carolina, Mississippi, Alabama, Florida,
and Texas, with the New York " softs," his own New Hampshire,
and that part of Massachusetts that Peaslee could hold, were
practically all he had. Finally after the fourteenth ballot the
convention adjourned till Friday. That Thursday night, like
the momentous Friday four years previous, witnessed much
planning. Friday morning, when the convention met, an arrangement had been made between some of the Pierce delegates
and some of the Douglasites. Hibbard arose and withdrew
Pierce's name, the larger part of his votes went to Douglas,
whether with Pierce's approval or not is unknown. The scheme
was to block Buchanan and thus force a compromise candidate,
anybody but Buchanan. On the second ballot that morning,
Douglas reached Pierce's greatest strength, 122; then, in spite
of the bargain and in spite of the fact that some claimed Douglas
could yet be nominated, Richardson arose and withdrew his
name, reading a letter from Douglas dated two days earlier.

Buchanan was an old man and in all probability would not
seek a second term; the good will of his supporters would be
very valuable to Douglas in 1860; Slidell presumably had not
conversed at length with Douglas in vain. Thus was Pierce defeated for renomination, and the telegraphic news reached him
just before noon, almost on the fourth anniversary of the fateful
day in Boston. The conservatives had triumphed for their demand for a safe and experienced man, who could command con-

servative Whig and American support, had been met. The veteran Buchanan was to save the party from the terror of the times. It was cold comfort that the convention, *after* Buchanan's nomination unanimously adopted the following resolution:

> *Resolved:* That the administration of Franklin Pierce has been true to the great interests of the country. In the face of the most determined opposition it has maintained the laws, enforced economy, fostered progress, and infused integrity and vigor into every department of the government at home. It has signally improved our treaty relations, extending the field of commercial enterprise and vindicated the rights of American Citizens abroad. It has asserted with eminent impartiality the just claims of every section and has at all times been faithful to the constitution. We therefore proclaim our unqualified approbation of its measures and policy.[4]

The victors could afford to be generous.

This result, though perhaps all too plainly foreseen by most of the President's entourage, was painful. As Marcy commented, " The President bears his disappointment manfully. He has now I believe less confidence in the faith of men than he had [before the convention]. If delegates had redeemed their voluntary pledges to him and his friends, the result would have been different. The President was less hopeful as the day for the meeting of the convention approached." But there was no outward show of disappointment; Saturday night when five thousand rejoicing Washingtonians gathered in front of the White House, the President came to an upper window and spoke to them. He wholeheartedly endorsed the nomination, he told them, men were dwarfs, principles alone were abiding, the Union was the great ark of safety against general wreck and universal ruin.[5]

Perhaps there could be peace now. At any rate the illusion of glory had departed.

FINISHING HIS WORK
1856-1857

LXVI

KANSAS AS CAMPAIGN MATERIAL

THE convention had spoken and Pierce realized that his days as Chief Executive were numbered, whereupon he set himself to so use these last months as to leave the least possible unfinished business for his successor. To accomplish this he must give his chief attention to Kansas. Since the middle of May affairs in the territory had become more and more involved. The first tidings of the difficulties at Lawrence which he received were fragmentary and disconnected. He immediately feared that troops had been used needlessly, and telegraphed Shannon May 23: " Has the United States Marshal proceeded to Lawrence to execute civil process? Has military force been found necessary to maintain Civil government in Kansas? If so, have you relied solely upon the troops under the command of Colonels Sumner and Cooke? If otherwise, state the reasons. The laws must be executed; but military force should not be employed until after the Marshal has met with actual resistance in the fulfilment of his duty."

Later that day, Davis had brought over Sumner's report, which had just arrived. Sumner explained that he had not been called upon to supply a posse, although he had offered one, as the governor did not wish to decide what kind the civil officers should use. Sumner reported that the use of civilian forces made bloodshed imminent. The President instantly sent Shannon another telegram, cautioning him, " My knowledge of the facts is imperfect; but with the force of Col. Sumner at hand, I perceive no occasion for the posse, armed or unarmed, which the Marshal is said to have assembled at Lecompton. . . . You must repress lawless violence in whatever form it may manifest itself." These telegrams took eight days to reach Shannon, during which the sender waited for news. When fourteen days had elapsed without reply Pierce on June 6, Buchanan's nomination day, had sent Shannon another wire to inquire why his previous dispatches had not been acknowledged. If his forces were not strong enough he ought to have notified the President, so read the telegram, and the concluding admonition was " Maintain the laws firmly and impartially and take care that no good citizen has just ground to complain of the want of protection." To make certain that these orders reached Shannon a special messenger was sent with duplicates. The press continued to carry conflicting accounts of friction and within a few days came Shannon's report, previously mentioned, of the events around Lawrence and the Pottawatomie murders.[1]

These renewed outbreaks raised up two schools of Kansas advisers. One held that there should be better military supervision and protection, to which end on June 10 Crittenden moved in the Senate that General Scott be sent out to take charge of the troops. To this school the principal Buchanan leaders in Washington belonged, and while they did not endorse the Scott project they were anxious to maintain an adequate military force in the territory. Their apprehensions were much increased by the importunities of a second school which demanded that the soldiers be withdrawn altogether as the cause of the difficulties. Needless to state, this group was ultrasouthern; its chief protagonist was Stringfellow, who had come on from Kansas to make these demands. He had a strong supporter in Davis, who was partially motivated by the fact that the troops were needed farther west to quell Indian uprisings which were straining the capacities of the small army to the utmost. In fact, before any word had come from Shannon, orders had been issued for taking detachments from Kansas to serve under Harney in his active compaigning against the redskins. Should these orders be carried out?

The matter came up in cabinet on June 16 when Davis advocated withdrawal and was opposed only by McClelland. The Buchanan men took alarm, and even Cass ventured to go to the President to remonstrate against the removal. Shortly Whitfield, the regularly elected Kansas delegate, came to Washington to urge withdrawal and not long after came a letter from Shannon protesting against it. Pierce, in face of such conflicting advice, finally evolved his own policy and this time overruled Davis. Sending Scott to Kansas was out of the question; his relations with Davis and his politics made that impossible. But the commander-in-chief realized the need of a more responsible authority than Colonel Sumner, against whom Harney had filed charges of insubordination, so on June 27 General Persifor F. Smith, Pierce's old Mexican War friend, was ordered to proceed to Kansas. The President took him into conference to impress upon him his desire to establish order. The Nebraska bill must be fairly administered so as to deprive the Republican party of their chief issue; Pierce and Smith were both good Democrats. Also the orders permitting Harney to detach troops were countermanded in spite of the Indians. Kansas was to have an adequate military force to suppress Buford and Jim Lane alike.[2]

Pierce's determination to bring order in Kansas was further strengthened by the outcome of the Republican nominating convention at Philadelphia. On June 19 that body had named John C. Frémont and at the same time had received most of the " North Americans " as allies. Frémont and the Republicans, thus strengthened, were in a position to wage an intensive and exciting campaign for not only were they a new party with no past record to hamper them but in addition they had an idealistic program, an emotional appeal, an attractive and romantic candidate, and, without any southern branch, they could cater directly and openly to northern interests and prejudices. They were making an enthusiastic drive for northern electoral votes on a platform of Pierce's mistakes with " Bleeding Kansas " as one of their most valuable issues. Against them the Democrats could counter only with popular rule, " squatter sovereignty," and this weapon would be ineffective if Kansas continued to suffer civil war, and to afford a horrible example of the impracticability of the Democratic dogma.

The Democrats in Congress sought to settle the question by an attempt at legislation known as the Toombs bill which provided machinery to take a census in Kansas, to hold an election (participated in only by those with three months' residence in the territory) for members of a constitutional convention who were to prepare a constitution for the consideration of Congress. Such steps were to be taken under the immediate supervision of five commissioners, appointed by the President, who were to be charged with full responsibility and equipped with due authority to insure a fair working out of the cherished doctrine of popular sovereignty. The Toombs bill appealed to Democrats as a vindication of their doctrine and to southern sympathizers who saw in it their last chance for a slave state, for String-fellow, fresh from Kansas, reported that there was still a faint hope that in an election Kansas might vote slave. The scheme also appealed to Douglas and the President and although Douglas gave out that they were not on good terms, possibly because the President resented Douglas's inopportune withdrawal at Cincinnati, the two conferred in some manner, perhaps through intermediaries. Thereafter, Pierce gave strong assurances he would appoint a group of commissioners of the most reliable reputation and temperament, and Douglas for his part reported the Toombs bill back from the committee on territories June 30.

On the next two days it was debated. Republicans immediately raised the objection that the success of the bill depended upon the character of the commissioners. They openly declared their distrust of the President, professing to doubt that he would appoint impartial representatives. To this Cass replied that he had assurances that the President would appoint a group above cavil: " I feel myself at liberty to say that if the commissioners are selected under the bill by the Executive, they will be selected impartially from the different shades of party in the country and the best men that can be got." Toombs likewise came to the President's defense: " I think [the President] has not been justly dealt with by his friends. He has maintained his faith when others have yielded to temptation and I give the honest judgment . . . that no truer, juster, more patriotic, more impartial or more national man has ever succeeded to the chair of Washington than Franklin Pierce."

Hale, however, could not forbear to administer his little dig by declaring that in spite of his patriotism and that of his honored father, Pierce could not be trusted to make good appointments; and he brought up the broken promise not to permit slavery to come up during his term. Without much difficulty the bill passed the Senate July 2; and after the House almost simultaneously had passed a bill admitting Kansas under the Topeka constitution, the Senate substituted the Toombs bill therefor. The great problem now was to get the hostile House to accept the Senate measure. The President did what he could toward this end and worked quietly to dispel the idea that he was under southern domination, a notion widely held. He even went so far as to confide the probable personnel of the commission to Lawrence, who approved of his choices and wrote to Haven, the leading Whig-American congressman, disclosing the fact of his approval although he did not feel at liberty to reveal the names. These efforts were in vain, for instead of even considering the Toombs bill the House was stirring up more trouble and providing more campaign documents for Frémont.[3]

The fact was that no one understood the Kansas struggle. Pierce interpreted it as a free-soil, pro-slavery political contest, an interpretation all too simple. It can be seen now as a power struggle to control the machinery of territorial development. The first legislatures would have great resources to assign and, in this day of rapid railroad projection, the profits might be high for those in on the ground floor.

This power struggle was being carried out under unusual circumstances. The settlers were not just the usual territorial pioneers from other sections of the transmontane region. Organized groups had been recruited from New England and the lower South which knew nothing of prairies and would buy land only in familiar wood and meadow regions along rivers. Thus, there was an intensity not found elsewhere about the contest for these restricted locations on the fringe of the plains.

A further element of confusion was one for which the Pierce Administration was responsible without seeming ever to realize it. They had opened the territory before the surveys. Therefore, for months it was not possible to locate and record land titles. Not until 1856 were the plats ready. Therefore, for two years, no one was sure of his property. There was no defense against claim jumping except force, and there was plenty of both. No wonder there was confusion and strife. No wonder Kansas "bled." And then Republican journalists so skillfully advertised the blood-letting as the work of pro-slavery border ruffians whom Pierce, they said, encouraged, or at least refused to restrain.

LXVII

KANSAS IN CONGRESS

THIS month of July, during which the fate of the administration plan remained hopeless, was another of Washington's most unpleasant displays of meteorological temperament; hardly a breeze broke the torrid spell. In the midst of the heat, the President was ill again, and many remarked how broken and wretched he looked. But from heat, malaria, and Kansas there seemed no relief. By July 10 news came that Colonel Sumner six days earlier had dispersed the Topeka legislature by armed force. The disruption of this peaceful meeting caused a great deal of indignation, and shortly Pierce and Davis disavowed it. Davis wrote what practically amounted to a censure of Sumner and the friendly Senate made a call upon the President July 21 for papers, which enabled Pierce to make public a report of Davis to the effect that no orders for this act had been given from Washington.[1] Pressure for Shannon's removal, which had begun immediately after the Lawrence disaster, continued and demands persisted for the release of those participants in the free state movement who, upon Lecompte's charge to the grand jury in May, had been indicted and arrested for treason. S. C. Pomeroy had arrived from Kansas and Amos A. Lawrence sent him to Pierce with a letter which he presented July 24 in an interview as interesting as it was spicy.

Upon Pomeroy's request that Shannon be deposed, Pierce renewed the promise of removal he had formerly made. He well knew by this time that Shannon was not fitted for the post, but he wanted an official report from General Smith before acting. A new appointment would be made before the President left town at the close of the session. Furthermore, he promised to dismiss the marshal, Donalson, if the charges made against him should be substantiated. So far, so good. Then Pomeroy brought up the cases of treason. The free state agent urged the release of the culprits, among them notably Dr. Charles Robinson. But Pierce did not agree, for Robinson and his associates, according to the President's view, had violated the law and should be punished for their revolt against constituted authority. Pomeroy denied that any of his friends had committed treason, whereupon Pierce contradicted him. As Pomeroy reported:

> He was very severe upon the " unauthorized " free state movement. Both of us got hot and showed some passion. I content myself by feeling that I did not show more than he did. He would be willing to have Congress pass a Resolution to instruct him to direct the prosecuting Attorney in Lecompton to enter a " Nole prosequi " or have a change of venue.

Whether Pomeroy invoked the spirit of Bunker Hill which Pierce inherited from his father, as Lawrence advised him to do, we do not know.[2] At any rate, after word of increased hostilities appeared in the press the President, on July 28, removed the incompetent Shannon and appointed John W. Geary of Pennsylvania, at this time working Virginia mines with hired slave labor. Now for the first time Kansas was going to have a governor who really knew something of the frontier. As to the treason cases, during a debate upon them precipitated in both houses August 4 and 5, it was stated by Republicans and Democrats, notably by Representative Orr of South Carolina, " that if the executive promises are to be relied on, these prosecutions are to be dismissed." [3] But before it could be accomplished, a congressional impasse intervened.

The House still persisted in its determination to refuse to permit further use of regiments in Kansas. As the second week in August passed, and the agreed-upon date of adjournment approached, it became apparent that there was a deadlock. The Senate would not accept the House amendment to the army bill which forbade the President to use troops to enforce the laws of the territorial legislature. After a stormy session, Pierce in the Vice President's room at the capitol was notified, at noon on August 18, that Congress had adjourned without passing the army bill. This failure to provide produced a particularly unfortunate situation because it was a very bad time to leave the country unprotected. Not only were there troubles in Kansas which required troops, there was still possibility of war with Great Britain. The Indians, too, were restive; Governor Stevens lately had declared martial law in Washington [4] and General Harney had been encountering trouble with the Cheyennes. Civil government also seemed to have broken down in California, as the press that summer was full of the activities of the Vigilance Committee in San Francisco. To an administration charged with the maintenance of peace and order, these were serious calamities. So Pierce boldly issued a call for a special session to meet within three days in spite of the fact that many of his party wanted to leave the issue as it was, with the blame upon the " black Republicans " for " disarming " the country in its hour of need, because it would make good election material. Also many southerners were much disappointed for Kansas without troops might have become pro-slavery. But the Executive would not let the Kansas issue destroy the army.

The President detailed to the recalled Congress the dangers of disbanding the federal forces, and the pressure of events had even more effect. Pierce had closed the armories and dismissed the workers; there was no money to pay them, must they starve? Like magic, Jim Lane descended upon Kansas with an army. Report had it that these abolitionists had freed the treason prisoners and bloodshed was going to be the order of the day. Then a delegation of free soil sympathizers came to the capital to implore protection; the Missourians, in their turn, they said, were now about to enter the territory to drive out Jim Lane. Douglas rose in the Senate and charged that Lane had been encamped on the Iowa frontier watching for news of the failure of the army bill as a signal for his Kansas invasion. Geary was anxiously awaiting the action of Congress before setting out, and Kansas was left to acting governor Woodson, ardent pro-slavery man. Finally after a hopeless week of voting, a few " Americans " gave up playing politics and Pierce had the opportunity to write his name upon the army bill.[5]

LXVIII

ESTABLISHING PEACE IN KANSAS

PIERCE was well rid of Congress and its members were hurrying away to participate in the Presidential campaign. They had been but a source of disappointment to the President, for not only had they completely disregarded his legislative recommendations but they had passed five internal improvement bills over his veto; Tyler, alone of the Presidents, had been so disregarded. Nevertheless, the army bill was law and Geary could go to Kansas carefully instructed to preserve order but to remain neutral; for this last Pierce gave him every assurance of support and sent more troops to Smith. His policy in regard to Kansas he made public in an interview which he gave on the day Congress finally adjourned. In spite of the fact that he was just recovering from another attack of chills and fever and necessarily had been at the capitol for the last hours of Congress, he received a delegation from Kansas come to beg protection for the free state element, and spoke his mind to them at length.

Although he admitted both sides to be guilty, he as usual placed the major blame upon the Emigrant Aid Company, especially for sending to Kansas men who were openly war-like. He said that he was doing all he could with his limited constitutional powers; that they must look for redress to the civil courts which were functioning. In fact, he had never heard of any authentic case of an individual applying to the Kansas courts in vain; moreover, if he ever did, he would remove the official involved. Finally, their reports did not coincide with those which he was getting from General Smith, and in affairs so far away he had to rely upon official sources. The true solution of the matter lay with the Kansans themselves, he told them, for if they frowned upon bloodshed and lawlessness it could not continue; if both sides could get rid of about one hundred trouble-makers all would be peace. The Lawrence invasion was without authority and many other mistakes had been made, as he had admitted when he removed Governor Shannon, but now he had sent out an impartial man. If the new governor should catch either party in acts of violence, summary justice would be administered. The civil power of the territory must be maintained; but he would not change his policy of non-interference between the factions unless, in cases of violence, civil law ceased to function.

It was such a sensible, reasonable speech, so convincing, but not a sentence of it showed the slightest grasp of frontier psychology and society.[1] Talking of Lecompte's court as a remedy to citizens of Lawrence!

To complete that eventful day and to fill the days following, wild dispatches describing war in Kansas appeared in the press, and a report came from the generally confident Smith calling for more troops; the free state men were in arms and were expected to destroy the capital. Cabinet meetings were almost continuous and as a result of these prolonged deliberations Marcy sent a special messenger to instruct Geary to organize the militia and Davis peremptorily ordered Smith to suppress insurrection against the civil authority. Davis furthermore ordered the governors of Illinois and Kentucky each to have two militia regiments ready to send into the territory upon General Smith's requisition. Rebellion was to be put down; Jim Lane and the Emigrant Aid trouble-makers must be taught to respect law. Having dispatched a messenger with all these orders, the administration gave them to the press, September 6, and the *Union* stated that the President's desire was to carry out the Kansas-Nebraska bill and to make safe the " unembarrassed judgment and uncontrolled will of the actual bona fide settlers." Insurrection within or aggression from without would be subdued.[2]

Meanwhile, having published to the world his determination to bring peace in Kansas, Pierce went off for a few days of rest. He had expected to go north for a vacation when Congress adjourned in mid-August, and in fact Mrs. Pierce and her sister had gone up to New York August 12 and thence to Long Branch, New Jersey, where Pierce expected to join them when the army bill was passed. Affairs in Kansas, however, made that impossible. Yet rest was necessary. Dobbin had gone home September 2 and the next day Campbell followed. Finally on Saturday Pierce and Webster went down to Warrenton Springs, Virginia, for the week-end. Monday morning found them back, and awaiting the President was General

Smith's report of the 29th. In this dispatch he recounted free
state outrages. He also stated he had just learned that Shannon
had retired and Woodson was calling out militia, into which
would be incorporated all the parties coming over from Missouri. This force moving under orders from civil authority,
Smith, acting as aid to the same authority, saw no way to oppose.
He further recited that the treason prisoners were not secure,
because there was no fund to feed them and they might at any
time be turned over to the territorial militia.

Neither Pierce nor Davis, seemingly, cared to have the militia
moving about under Acting-governor Woodson, especially with
a Missouri contingent. Consequently, that very day, Davis
wired Smith that all military operations were to be carried on
in Kansas by Smith alone and that he was not to use any
militia or permit its employment unless regularly mustered into
the service of the United States by Geary; and Marcy wired similar orders to Geary who was expected to arrive about that
time. Needless to say, Smith's report did not diminish the
unfavorable opinion which the President held of the free state
leaders. He was under great apprehension lest Fremont be
elected by reason of all this trouble.

Pressure for the release of the treason prisoners continued.
Lawrence wrote a letter which Mrs. Robinson copied and signed
and her communication begging for her husband's release was
sent to Mrs. Pierce, accompanied by one from the elder Mrs.
Lawrence, which she gave to her husband just about this
time. Whether because of this or not, we do not know, but
Pierce wrote to Lawrence's brother that he had telegraphed
orders satisfactory to their wishes and especially to those of
Mrs. Lawrence, whose good opinion he declared he valued
" more than that of all the politicians." Cushing wrote the
district attorney to send the treason indictments to Washington.
Then when the treason cases came before Lecompte, the district attorney and all witnesses were absent (we may suspect
as the result of the President's telegram), and Lecompte admitted them to bail; next spring a *nol. pros.* was entered.
Pierce would have released them unconditionally had not Lane's
invasion reawakened his ire. The Massachusetts crowd, thought
the President, had certainly made enough trouble, but Geary
and Smith would straighten it out now. If they could not,
nobody could.[3]

LXIX

PREPARING FOR RETIREMENT

As September drew to a close, Kansas seemed quieter, and the President convalesced from the malaria. He could now afford to devote a little time to plans for his approaching retirement. His brother Henry had been to Washington for a visit in July, and they had hoped that the President could go back to Concord for a little while after Congress adjourned in order to buy some property and prepare to build a home. He proposed at first to leave about September 20 and Webster and George began to make arrangements. As Webster wrote, " A large, a tremendous reception is vital." So his New Hampshire friends raised money and laid plans. On September 6 the New Hampshire State Agricultural Society invited Pierce to attend their fair during the second week in October, but he replied that he could not tell just when he would be able to come. In fact, Kansas was so threatening he did not care to leave his post. Nevertheless, the New Hampshire preparations went on.

On September 22 a meeting was scheduled to be held at Depot Hall in Concord to make plans for the reception. The meeting turned out to be more like a riot; the Republicans appeared in full force and quite overwhelmed the administration men led by George, who had called the meeting. The next day Pierce to his chagrin read how his fellow townsmen had voted that it was " inexpedient for [them] as citizens of Concord to give President Pierce a public reception at this time." He learned that in their judgment he had used his office to betray the rights and liberties of the people of the northern states into the hands of an usurping southern oligarchy: by his Cuban attempt, by the wicked repeal of the Missouri restriction, by his manifest endeavors to aid the South in establishing slavery in Kansas, and by his slanders against many including a large majority of Concord's citizens (*i.e.*, supporters of the Emigrant Aid cause). Consequently the most fitting reception, this gathering resolved, would be " solemn, mournful silence." Prior to this insult, Pierce had been rather doubtful about his time of departure;

but, as he characteristically wrote editor Butterfield, September 24, " the action on the part of the disunionists leaves me no ground of choice. I shall reach Concord on the forenoon train on Thursday, October 2nd." His bitterness was lightened by knowledge that black Republicans and disunionists had been responsible, and that there were friends like Abbott, Gilmore, Stearns and Smart, who though opponents remained " personal friends in relation to whom political differences have never been strong enough to create personal alienation." [1]

One of the most painful aspects of this disappointing four years was thus illustrated once more for so many of his friends and supporters had fallen away. Burke had led in 1853 and ever since there had been a series of defections. Atherton had died, Baker had migrated to Iowa, the Kansas measure had sent Hibbard, Kittredge, and Morrison, the three congressmen into enforced retirement, and Hibbard had been defeated for the Senate. Upham, whose ambitions for a consulship had been denied by the President, had aided the old Woodbury forces (C. L. Woodbury, Barnes, and B. F. Butler) in organizing pre-convention support for Buchanan in New England. Benjamin B. French, who had longed to become marshal of the District of Columbia and whom Pierce had practically beheaded during the Know-Nothing extermination, and his brother Henry F. French were numbered among the alienated. The little group, who so suddenly had been thrust into prominence, had expected great things and fat plums from their chief, favors which pressure from other sections forced him to deny. He fatuously had hoped that the strength of friendship would only be proven by these disappointments; but he had been mistaken.[2]

Erstwhile friends became his enemies. Upham spoke of him as an experiment which had proved a failure. Bancroft, smarting under Cushing's elevation, remarked, " He has got round him so many Whigs, that democrats are crowded out of an organization pretending to the democratic name." He was blamed by northern Democrats for their misfortunes because of his espousal of the Kansas bill. " He has deserted his native state, his native New England—to immolate himself on the altar of slavery." " He is a poor critter, weak and faltering and false to his best friends, . . . a weak and miserable poltroon "—so spake the French brothers. Kittredge declared that Pierce had

" the G— d——edest black heart that ever was placed in mortal
bosom." John S. Wells was the only convert Pierce had made,
and his futile efforts for the governorship had caused him to
remark that he had been " crucified again." George and Butterfield were trying to hold the fort in Concord but they had just
been humiliated. Peaslee in Boston and Minot, Cushing, and
Webster in Washington had remained loyal, it is true, but the
enthusiastic coterie who had planned so shrewdly in 1852 had
been scattered. Pierce in less than four years was returning
home uncertain whether scant courtesy, even, would be vouchsafed him by his fellow townsmen.

Preparations went on in spite of a return of chills and fever
while cabinet meetings continued to consider the dispatches
from Kansas. These tidings were hopeful and on September
27 word was received from Geary and Smith to the effect that
an invasion of some thousand Missourians had been turned back
peacefully by their efforts, the only fly in Geary's ointment was
the fact that he was not sufficiently aided by civil authority; as
a remedy he contemplated martial law. Marcy telegraphed
back approval of his course, but ordered him not to proclaim
martial law as that did not lie within his power. That Saturday
night the *Union* came out with the news that law and order were
prevailing in Kansas.[3]

The journey to New Hampshire was hurried with no stops
for ceremony. Accompanied only by Webster, Hoover, and
General Anderson of Tennessee, he spent the first night in New
York and the second night with J. H. Cutter at Hollis, Massachusetts. Thursday noon he arrived in Concord escorted by
the Manchester Veterans. He was not received in silence; the
countryside had sent throngs to greet the President. He
mounted a horse, and rode down Main Street to the cheers of
the multitude. He had a reception in the state house yard
with the usual speeches, John H. George doing the principal
honors. That evening there was a levee at Depot Hall and
next day he and Henry journeyed alone to Hillsborough where
he passed the night in his old home. Saturday he went back
to Concord and on to Andover to spend Sunday with the Aikens.
Monday and Tuesday were spent in Concord, where he looked
at property, and when he left for Portsmouth Wednesday it
was rumored he had bought the Hoyt farm in East Concord.

ON THE EVE OF RETIREMENT

At Portsmouth he boarded the *Wabash*, which was about to make a trial trip to Annapolis, and enjoyed the hospitality of the navy. He arrived at Annapolis October 16, but weather prevented his landing and he did not reach Washington until next day, when his train was greeted by a salvo of artillery and the District military escorted him to the White House. Here he learned that Geary had reported "Peace now reigns in Kansas," [4] and under the inspiration of that welcome news he set himself to the preparation of the final account of his steward-ship, and to watch the concluding weeks of the election campaign.

He was sincerely interested in Buchanan's success and that of his party. As he wrote Breckinridge, "No election so important as that before us has occured (*sic*) since the foundation of the Government. I consider the continuance of the Union as directly involved in the result. . . . The question between sectionalism and nationality has never been so distinctly presented before." His cabinet, especially McClelland, were like-wise anxious for success. Campbell, in spite of the distrust of the Buchananites, was faithful and active. Pierce himself may have thought that his trip to New Hampshire would be of some value. He had great pride in his native state and did not want to have it said that his own home had permanently deserted the party of its usual choice; never yet had New Hampshire failed to vote for the Democratic presidential candidate. Also, he had sought earnestly to bring peace in Kansas and thus deprive the black Republicans of their chief issue. Meanwhile these op-ponents had been making an effective campaign, so effective that many of the southern leaders were apprehensive. Wise had called a conference of governors to meet at Raleigh to consider a course of action if Frémont should be successful, and Senator Mason had written to Davis inquiring about arms which might be issued to Virginia, because he felt Frémont's election would demand secession. But the October voting, the results of which arrived just as Pierce returned, showed that the Democrats could carry Pennsylvania, and much anxiety was thereby re-lieved.

Cabinet meetings, held twice a week as usual, were reported dull and without interest. Everyone was awaiting the final re-sult. On November 4 Pierce assured Slidell, upon meeting him at the *Union* office, that Buchanan would carry New Hampshire.[5] But he was mistaken. New Hampshire voted for Frémont. A few days after the election the President wrote Buchanan, for the first time since his nomination:

> No patriotic citizen of the Republic can have failed to breathe more deeply and freely since all doubt was removed from the result of the election. I congratulate my country and congratulate you.
>
> Good men everywhere may now retire at night with renewed confidence in the power of constitutional obligation over the minds of our people.
>
> [If people support the Cincinnati platform and you] I think we may safely count upon a triumph over sectional fanaticism for many years. I need not speak to you of my mortification at the result in New Hampshire. There is a measure of relief in the fact that in this most exciting crisis the largest democratic vote ever polled in the state was given to you. . . . It is certainly no alleviation to know that the mastering power which overthrew our party there was a perverted and desecrated pulpit.

His bitterness against abolitionists and their clerical leaders amounted to hate. He concluded by inviting Buchanan to stay at the White House when he came to Washington in February.[6] The President could console himself with the knowledge that the Democrats had regained Congress and were still in control of the federal government.

LXX

THE FINAL ACCOUNTING

WITH Buchanan safely elected attention could be given to the final reports. President and cabinet worked together in this last joint enterprise, and some of them perhaps speculated about the next cabinet. Whether any hoped to hold over, they do not seem to have revealed.

McClelland as usual was the first [1] to complete his task and he displayed in orderly fashion the achievements of his four years' work. 93,976,772 acres of public land had been disposed of, over 63,000,000 acres in the form of military bounties, railroad grants to the states, or swampland grants. The land system had been extended over the whole of the Mexican cessions, as well as Oregon, Washington, Kansas, and Nebraska. Six new surveying districts had been established and in all regions nearly 60,000,000 acres had been surveyed. In the pension bureau he had 13,932 persons upon the rolls who drew slightly over $1,360,000 annually; and of these pensioners 9,585 had been added during the outgoing administration. He felt that the pension system was too loose; doles should be stopped when need for them had ceased; and he made his parting recommendation that indigence should be the only ground on which revenue should be granted veterans. As it now stood, the really needy obtained too little and the rest too much. As to patents, he reported that the average number of annual applications for the years 1849–1853 had been 2,522; now the average was well over 4,000. The patent office had outgrown the system under which it was operating and Congress might well devise another. Besides issuing patents, the commissioner of that bureau was entrusted with aid to agriculture; in 1853, $5,000 had been allotted for this purpose; the last appropriation had been $105,000.

The work of the Indian bureau had doubled under his tenure; its jurisdiction had been extended to cover 500,000 additional square miles of territory; fifty-two Indian treaties had been negotiated, extinguishing title to 174,000,000 acres at a cost of

$11,000,000. There were 300,000 aborigines and they cost the government annually more than $2,600,000. He had been checking up the accounts of all Indian agents and requiring statements of them. Most Indian annuities were still paid in cash, which he considered unfortunate as it paralyzed efforts for permanent improvement. The best way to care for the redskins was to colonize them or place them on reservations, isolating the various tribes within set limits, taking care of them under agents, teaching them to work, and giving them Christian instruction; he made no mention of Manypenny's report that the Indians were on the verge of a general war in the territory of Washington. The activities of all these bureaus McClelland had found scattered over the capital city, and unorganized. Now, the west wing of the patent office was practically completed, the north front was begun, and both the land office and the Indian bureau were housed with the patent bureau and the secretary in their Doric temple.

Equally elaborate though less in the nature of a review was Guthrie's financial statement. When he entered office, he had found the debt standing at $69,129,937.27; to date this had been reduced to $30,963,909.64. For the fourth time he urged the reduction of the tariff; and in response to a call from the last House he incorporated in his report a most lengthy and meticulous survey of all phases of our economic life, as a foundation for tariff revision. He reported on his methods for safeguarding the collection of the public funds and urged Congress to enact additional safeguards, making more useful the independent treasury system. He, too, had introduced order and regimen; he had attempted to build a stout wall around the national treasure.

Davis was still fertile in suggestions as to army improvements. He now recommended the abandonment of the array of scattered small posts, isolated in the wilderness, and proposed instead that large garrisons be maintained in civilized centers with flying columns, that could be swiftly dispatched where needed. He again reported on railroad surveys and emphasized the increased practicality of the southern route as the result of more recent reckonings. He rejoiced that troops had checked civil strife in Kansas and restored order and tranquility there, " without shedding one drop of blood."

Dobbin reported that the six frigates were nearly completed, and detailed the widespread activities of the navy in exploring and opening roads to commerce; its latest exploit was the sending of a ship southward for cuttings of sugar cane which would enable the planters of Louisiana to renew their stock. The marine corps should be enlarged and more sloops of war built.

Campbell had the least satisfactory record to disclose. His deficit was larger than ever, no adequate postal arrangements had yet been made with Mexico, and neither Great Britain nor France would agree to the improvements in service which he desired. During the first year of his incumbency he had been able to reduce the arrears, but since then Congress had increased the salaries of the postmasters and had imposed the expensive Mississippi River mail service upon his department. Great extension of the mail service had been made, especially by railroad, the mileage of that branch being now 20,000, or just twice what it had been in 1853. Once more he recommended elimination of the franking privilege.

As the substance of these last reports was being considered, Pierce was pondering his own closing words to Congress and the nation. Plainly the thought dominant in his mind was the satisfaction which he felt at the outcome of the recent election. His party, his views, his administration, had been endorsed by the people, and the menace of black Republican triumph averted. In this mood he utilized his message, not to review the achievements of his administration—and there were a number—nor to suggest new plans, but to lecture the Republicans at great length upon the incorrectness of their views and the blindness of their folly. The people, he declared, " asserted the constitutional equality of each and all of the States of the Union as states; they have affirmed the constitutional equality of each and all of the citizens of the United States as citizens, whatever their religion, wherever their birth or their residence; they have maintained the inviolability of the constitutional rights of the different sections of the Union, and they have proclaimed their devoted and unalterable attachment to the Union and to the constitution, as objects of interest superior to all subjects of local or sectional controversy, as the safeguard of the rights of all, as the spirit and the essence of the liberty, peace, and greatness of the Republic." In doing this they had " at the same time emphatically condemned the idea of organizing in these United States mere geographical parties, of marshalling in hostile array toward each other the different parts of the country." He proceeded with a scathing indictment of this "attempt of a portion of the states by a sectional organization and movement to usurp the control of the government of the United States."

However, he was not quite so bitter as last year, when he had classified his opponents as enemies of the Constitution; in fact, he expressed his confident belief that the great body of them were "sincerely attached to the constitution and the Union." Nevertheless, their course unconsciously and indirectly, step by step, had been leading to ultimate disunion and civil war. This he endeavored to demonstrate, rehearsing once more the syllabus of errors attributable to the North. He detailed anew the nature of the Kansas-Nebraska bill, defending his policy toward the territory. "We perceive," he wrote, "that controversy concerning its future domestic institutions was inevitable; that no human prudence, no form of legislation, no wisdom on the part of congress could have prevented it." With this consoling thought, he justified his non-interference in territorial elections by want of power. "If he had such power the government might be republican in form but it would be a monarchy in fact; and if he had undertaken to exercise it in the case of Kansas, he would have been justly subject to the charge of usurpation and of violation of the dearest rights of the people of the United States." However, that was all past, peace reigned in that area. With the hope that neither the territory nor Congress would permit any obstruction or abridgment of the constitutional rights of the citizens of the United States in Kansas, he left the subject. The work of the departments he passed over perfunctorily and devoted most of the remainder of his message to foreign affairs.

At length, he could report that all difficulties with Great Britain were settled. During the summer and fall the snarl had unraveled itself with at least a semblance of satisfaction. About July 4, he had received word that Dallas was not going to be handed his passports. Great Britain showed no resentment at Crampton's dismissal, except to send no successor while Pierce was in office. Furthermore, Clarendon and Dallas made a draft of a treaty which they submitted to Pierce in September. In it, Great Britain and the United States agreed jointly to propose to Nicaragua and Costa Rica an arrangement whereby the Mosquito Indians, with a definite, established boundary, should be either an independent state under Nicaraguan protection or a part of the Nicaraguan Republic. Costa Rica should have certain rights of navigation on the San Juan River, and Greytown was to be a free city under the sovereign authority of Nicaragua. Furthermore, Great Britain and the United States agreed to fix the boundaries of Belize and to recognize the arrangements made by Great Britain and Honduras whereby the Bay Islands were constituted a free territory under the sovereignty of Honduras. This treaty was considered in cabinet in September, and was finally accepted with certain modifications which made its boundary terms more definite, reduced the Mosquito reservation in size, and made sure that isthmian transit trade would not be subject to the discretion of the inhabitants of Greytown as to tonnage duties. Dallas was instructed not to sign any treaty unless the latter stipulation was inserted. With such reservations, Pierce's approval was dispatched on September 26. October 17 the treaty, with the " Marcy " exceptions largely incorporated, was signed and it now was ready for Congress. In rather indirect manner and with no apologies, Great Britain was withdrawing from Nicaragua and Honduras in accordance with the demands of the Pierce administration.

A second diplomatic item which Pierce dwelt upon was his effort to influence the work of the peace conference which had closed the Crimean war. This conference had proposed to abolish privateering, to agree that a neutral flag protected enemy goods with the exception of contraband of war, that neutral goods with the exception of contraband of war would not be liable to capture under an enemy's flag and finally, that blockades to be binding must be effective. These propositions had been presented to the United States by the French Minister late in May, and Marcy had spent much of the hot July in drawing up our reply. As to the last three points, Pierce and his advisers were agreed; but the first in regard to privateers they were not willing to accept; the United States could not surrender so important a protective device. Consequently they decided to suggest an amendment: " And that the private property of the subjects or citizens of a belligerent on the high seas shall be exempted from seizure by public armed vessels of the other belligerent, except it be contraband." This counter proposal Marcy signed on July 28 and submitted to the Washington representatives of France, Russia, Austria, Prussia, and Sardinia.[2] As yet Pierce could report no positive results from his proposals. A third section contained a detailed account of the violation of American property on the isthmus of Panama and informed Congress that the President had taken measures to secure damages and provide for greater security for American interests.[3]

He concluded by congratulating the Republic on " peace, greatness and felicity." The Revolutionary forefathers had created the nation, the next generation had consolidated it, and the duty of this third generation was to " maintain and extend the national power." To do this " in foreign relations we have to attemper our power to the less happy condition of the Republics in America and to place ourselves in the calmness and conscious dignity of right by the side of the greatest and wealthiest of the Empires of Europe. In domestic relations we have to guard against the shock of the discontents, the ambitions, the interests and the exuberant and therefore sometimes irregular impulses of opinion or of action which are the natural product of the present political elevation, the self-reliance and the restless spirit of enterprise of the people of the United States." Thus platitudinously he ended as he had begun his preachments to the nation at large.

Many people read this message with approval, some with amusement. Far away in Springfield, Illinois, one of the local political leaders, Abraham Lincoln by name, recorded his opinion:

> Like a rejected lover making merry at the wedding of his rival, the President felicitated himself hugely over the late Presidential election. He considers the result a signal triumph of good principles and good men, and a very pointed rebuke of bad ones. He says the people did it. He forgets that the " people," as he complacently calls only those who voted for Buchanan, are in a minority of the whole people by about four hundred thousand votes—one full tenth of all the votes.[4]

* * *

While this final inventory was being made late in November, the Executive was stricken again; neuralgia was his master and its sharp pains necessitated cessation of labor. Then came a letter from Geary charging Chief Justice Lecompte with gross partisanship and improper conduct in admitting a pro-slavery murderer to bail when bail was refused to free state culprits. His letter carried conviction, and besides it was not the first charge against Lecompte; the free state men had been after his scalp since the treason cases. So the President determined to dismiss him and give the position to a Kentuckian. He wanted very much to accomplish this before Congress assembled, for in that case he could give the new justice a recess commission and the Senate could take its time in acting, whereas if it was not done until Congress convened he could not commission until the Senate confirmed. However, bad fortune and his own habit of procrastination defeated his plan. With Guthrie he talked over the judgeship and decided on James O. Harrison; but would he accept? On November 27 they telegraphed to Breckinridge asking him to find out. Breckinridge's reply of " yes " did not arrive, however, until after Congress had met. Geary also had requested the removal both of the marshal, Donalson, who had aided Lecompte and disobeyed Geary's orders, and Indian Agent Clarke who had committed murder. Pierce tried to do as requested; he got rid of Clarke just before Congress met and commissioned Isaac Winston to succeed him. Donalson already had resigned, but his successor, William Spencer, was not named in time and had to await confirmation. Pierce wrote Geary on December 12, warmly commending the governor and urging him to continue to " be so just and true to the right that no man might challenge [his] impartiality," and to " cultivate kind relations with Judge Cato " (the pro-slavery associate justice).

Three days later Pierce sent Harrison's appointment to the Senate, accompanied by Geary's minutes and correspondence. But at the same time he failed to send Lecompte a letter of dismissal; therefore since the Senate refused to confirm Harrison, the Kansas justice remained in office as did Donalson, whose successor was not named until February 11. In the meantime General Smith was promoted and Pierce hoped that Kansas was disposed of finally.[5]

LXXI

A PRESIDENT DEPARTS

Passing administrations like dying years run their courses quickly, almost imperceptibly. No longer was the White House a center of attraction where hopes and fears were dispelled or confirmed. " The King is dead. Long live the King." Elsewhere a new " sovereign " was preparing to assume the office conferred upon him by his " peers." At Wheatland, near Lancaster, not in Washington, was the stage set and the political drama unfolding. Nevertheless Pierce had to live out his last three months, and a variety of political, social, and administrative interests and functions gradually spread themselves out on the calendar.

Politically the President became once more a center of some notice because of the contents of his message. The Republicans naturally were going to do their best to demolish his strictures upon their principles and tactics. Congress met on December 1 and the very next day Hale rose in his place and launched an attack upon Pierce; Hale's pursuit was relentless and on December 11 he returned to it, when in a most aggravating manner he referred to his speech of the previous January in which he had predicted Pierce's discomfiture. He exulted in his complete success as a prophet. Seward, Fessenden, Wade, and Wilson in the Senate, with Campbell and Sherman in the House, carried on the attack, even going so far as to allege that the President did not write his own message but had delegated it to Cushing. Also, because he had injected politics into his farewell, they charged he had lowered the dignity of the Presidential office. Mason and Pugh came to the President's defense, but their speeches did not equal those of their opponents in effectiveness or in number. With the passing of December Congress turned to legislation and other interests developed. The Pierce wing of the party was particularly concerned over the prospective cabinet. Pierce's immediate friends were anxious about the New England member; the choice seemed to have narrowed down to Toucey of Connecticut

and Clifford of Maine.   The latter was *persona non grata,* hence
their efforts concentrated on Toucey.[1]

Society, as usual during the winter months, had its round of
festivity.   The event of December was the coming of Thalberg,
the celebrated pianist, who gave a gala concert at Carusi's
saloon.   Washington's élite were there in their splendor and
the Chief Executive was an appreciative listener.   The next
day the virtuoso called at the White House where Pierce received him cordially and presented him with a finely bound
copy of the account of Perry's Japanese expedition.   A few
days later the President gave a dinner to a number of his Mexican War associates including Shields, Quitman, Weller, and
Cushing.   Then came the first of January—for the last time the
President descended the stairway, faultlessly dressed, to usher in
a new year.   1857 was to bring disaster to many; but another,
not Pierce, would have to bear the brunt of administration.   At
eleven the diplomatic corps, the cabinet, the officers of the military and naval establishments, came to pay their respects; and
at noon the doors of the White House opened to " The people
of the United States."   The President, flanked by the mayor and
the commissioner of public buildings, received them all in his
usual pleasant manner.   The arrangements had been perfected;
the throng was admitted without the usual crush, and then it
was guided around, so that instead of the customary general condition of frustrated locomotion, you went, you greeted the
President, and presently almost before you realized it you
were out.

1857, like 1856, was ushered in to the accompaniment of two
months of severe cold, unusual not only for Washington but
also for all sections to the north and west.   The harsh winter
had been anticipated by severe fall rains and December had
been bitter, but January brought storm after storm and an
arctic temperature.   The climax came on that memorable Sunday, January 18, when there enveloped the capital a blizzard
which was termed by old residents the most awful in the city's
history.   Everything was at a standstill, train communication
was practically cut off and for a weak the seat of government
was blockaded.   Mrs. Davis lay dangerously ill and Pierce almost collapsed plunging through the drifts to inquire for her.

In spite of the weather society would have its day and the city was agog with the last festivities of the old regime and preparations for the inauguration of the new order. On Jackson Day the veterans of the War of 1812 held their annual convention and many of the old soldiers came to the White House to pay their respects to the President. On the fifteenth the United States Agricultural Society was received in the East room and to them Pierce announced his future plans. He was going back to New Hampshire, there to spend the coming years in the quiet and peace of agricultural pursuits. Cincinnatus was returning to the plow, which, as Marshall P. Wilder told him in responding, was leaving a high position and ascending to a higher.

The last social season opened with a levee on January 17, described as having the largest attendance of any in the administration. Two weeks later Buchanan arrived unexpectedly, after Washington had burst from its snow grave, and his coming made cabinet gossip the fashion. He appeared at the Friday night reception and was officially received by Pierce. Whether Buchanan consulted his predecessor at all as to the future does not appear, although the retiring President offered him the usual courtesies and Buchanan in return invited him to remain in the White House until he could leave conveniently. Pierce must have realized early that none of his cabinet would be retained in the new administration and his interest seems to have centered on who would be the New England representative, at least so Sidney Webster said. He naturally hoped for Toucey, a true and faithful supporter.

This closing month of power went even more quickly than the others. In its early days Colonel Henry D. Pierce came to pay a final visit to his brother's splendid tenement. A fortnight later the President had his last public triumph. A grand concert for the relief of the poor was held at Carusi's. A varied musicale was arranged with selections from Rossini, Mendelssohn, Weber, and Meyerbeer, not to mention an inevitable polka. A place had been reserved for the Chief Executive but he slipped into a seat in the rear. He did not escape notice, however; there was a roll of drums, the simulated thunder of cannon and the orchestra burst forth with the strains of " Hail Columbia " " with great effect."

February 24 was held the last Tuesday afternoon reception and preparations were made for the final Friday evening levee.

All Washington was there to bid farewell to the retiring executive; fully two thousand ladies in full dress graced the occasion. But even this farewell could not pass unmarred. One of the departmental clerks in the exit rush charged a citizen with picking his pocket. Next morning the accused visited the clerk at his office to seek redress and in the fracas that ensued the former was killed. The Pierce administration closed as it had opened, under the shadow of death.

As the social amenities were being concluded an administrative miscellany presented itself to Pierce and his cabinet. They put the finishing touches on their foreign policy by suggesting to the European powers a series of treaties embodying the proposals of the Paris Conference with the Pierce-Marcy privateering amendment incorporated, a project not destined to meet with any success. As a second constructive effort, Marcy instructed the commission which had been sent to Colombia to negotiate along novel lines for damages suffered in the Panama riot of the previous spring. They were to present the project of a treaty by which Aspinwall and Panama should be made free cities under American protection and the railroad line across the isthmus should be placed under American authority. This arrangement Marcy declared was "not designed for exclusive advantage of the United States but to secure common use of the Panama route to all foreign nations." If the plan succeeded the United States would then propose to Europe to neutralize the route. The scheme anticipated the "Canal Zone" idea but Colombia refused to entertain it then.

Pierce was somewhat disturbed by disquieting news from China to the effect that the British had bombarded and entered Canton and that the United States flag had been carried into the captured city with the British. This was not in conformity with administration wishes, and the cabinet decided to refuse the French suggestion of armed coöperation in bringing China to more liberal commercial views. Finally, just as the administration was closing, a messenger arrived from Mexico with five treaties which Forsythe had negotiated, including a commercial treaty, a postal and a claims convention. The commercial arrangements were unexpected, as they provided for a loan of $15,000,000 in return for tariff reductions favorable to the United States and the adjustment of claims; this "dollar"

diplomacy was too new and arrived too late in the administration to receive its sanction. In what was practically his last
instruction, Marcy refrained from giving his approval to Forsythe and left the covenants for the next administration. Thus
were foreign relations disposed of; Cuba had not been obtained,
the *El Dorado* incident was unredressed, and the Dallas-Claren-
don compact remained before the Senate.[2]

Cushing was troubled by last-minute filibustering expeditions
to Nicaragua and Venezuela; these illegal forays had been the
bane of his existence. Dobbin was issuing final commands to
Captain Mervine who had gone on a hunt for a guano island in
the south seas and had returned reporting himself unable to
land. He was now ordered to go back and try again. Davis
was arranging for that expedition to punish the Cheyennes
which had been delayed by the use of the troops in Kansas.
Since Geary's glowing reports of peace and quiet he had felt
free to detach troops, and disposed of a number which Geary
suddenly found need of in February. Smith could not return
them, which gave Geary and others ground for charging that
Pierce was heeding the southern desire that Kansas be left to
the mercy of the Missourians.[3] Simultaneously, the President
and all the cabinet were occupied with the plans for laying the
Atlantic cable. Its promoters had conference at the White
House, and Pierce upon call from Congress submitted correspondence showing that the cable company were petitioners for
an assurance of government messages and for the use of a
naval vessel to aid in laying the wires. The country at large
entered into the project.

In spite of Geary's constant expressions of confidence, the
administration was not to have the satisfaction of a peaceful
leave of Kansas. Reports had been generally optimistic, though
early in January there had been some anxiety about the scheduled meeting of the " free state legislature "; and Pierce and
Marcy had worked over a despatch cautioning Geary about
taking at their face value certain promises made by the free
state men that they would make no trouble. However, fears
had been groundless, only a few so-called legislators came together and then broke up. There remained, however, the question of the Senate's attitude toward the removal of Lecompte.
The judge immediately had written back home to his Maryland

Senator, Pearce, and had furnished him with a defense against Geary's charges which read very plausibly; this he later elaborated and sent to Cushing. His letter Pearce submitted to the President, who again was impressed by plausibility. He had Marcy send it to the long-suffering Geary for his reply. Also the Senate called for Lecompte's letter to Cushing, and these two letters were sufficiently pleasing to southern senators to cause them to refrain from confirming Harrison. Lecompte continued to preside over justice in Kansas.

Out in the province difficulties were increasing. When the territorial legislature met they immediately entered into a quarrel with the governor. In the last days of the administration Geary, whose life had been threatened, answered Marcy's letter by refusing to make further statement in his controversy with Lecompte and demanding that the full records of his governorship be published that the world might judge. The press bore reports of the renewed trouble. " Terrible outbreak in Kansas. Governor Geary assaulted. Several persons shot," so read the headlines. Where was the peace that had been reigning in Kansas? Well, another administration would have to seek that phantom.[4]

Amidst these duties and last-minute problems the third of March finally arrived. Mrs. Pierce took her leave of the White House and went to Secretary Marcy's, where she and the President planned to remain awhile until it should become warmer in the north. Many called to bid Pierce good bye, as did the mayor and other officials of the city of Washington and the justices of the Supreme Court. The final cabinet meeting was held and then came the closing hours of Congress. By ten the President and his advisers, except Marcy and Dobbin, were in the Vice-President's room at the capitol awaiting the final flow of enactment. Prior to this day, little legislation of note had been passed; the only bills of particular interest to Pierce were that granting an increase in pay to army officers and one providing for courts of inquiry to review the naval retirement cases. But now the parliamentary wheels began to turn; the measure granting government aid to the Atlantic cable, a bill for overland mail service to the Pacific, a number of private items and some appropriations, and the navy proposition for five of the sloops of war which Dobbin had been recommending, all came to

Pierce for signing. After several hours the President retired for his last night in the White House. Next day he endorsed the rest of the appropriation enactments, and his last signature was affixed to a tariff bill, which after four years of urging finally had been passed to provide for a reduction of the revenue.

March 4 itself was a balmy day, quite in contrast to the stormy occasion four years before. Washington was crowded with the usual inauguration throng and all were awaiting the noontime pageant. That morning the President took official leave of his cabinet; Davis came in at nine a little before the rest and they talked for a while. Pierce was much affected. "I can scarcely bear the parting from you," he told Davis, "who have been strength and solace to me for four anxious years and never failed me." [5] The others came in and the farewells were said. As noon approached it was time to be leaving for the capitol, but no carriage appeared to take him to meet Buchanan. Finally he had to order his own carriage and proceed to the Willard. Together he and Buchanan, with Senators Bigler and Foot, entered a barouche and the parade moved slowly down the avenue midst the lines of the applauding crowd. It was soon over, the oath and the inaugural, the ride back; Pierce escorted Buchanan to the White House door and then retired to the home of Secretary Marcy. His "crowded hour of glorious life," not all glorious by any means, had passed into history.

Some time during that day he received a parting letter from his cabinet and sent each of them a grateful acknowledgment. He utilized this opportunity to place before them his evaluation of his own administration. His words are significant because they so accurately reflect his personality, showing his mental reaction to the total experience of the presidency. He wrote:

Your uninterrupted manifestation of personal friendship for me, during the past four years leaves no occasion for reassurance of your cordial regard, now that we are about to separate.

I participate fully in the gratification which you express in reference to our daily intercourse, happily undisturbed by any element of discord. And I shall ever hold in grateful appreciation the extent to which my most severe and perplexing official labors have been lightened by your unfailing and cheerful cooperation.

It will I am sure be an agreeable recollection to us all, that whatever else the Administration may have done or omitted to do, it has not sought applause by the adoption of temporizing expedients, nor immunity from censure by the negative character of its policy and measures. The violent assaults which it has encountered on the one hand and the zeal with which it has been defended on the other are conclusive upon the point that it has been one of positive good or positive evil.

The exercise of the veto power on sundry occasions involving in some instances large individual pecuniary interests and in others questions of public policy of an exciting character:—the discussion in annual and special messages of controverted constitutional principles and of the rights of the states under our system, have undeniably been a fruitful source of complaint and vituperation. These were matters which could alone be determined by my own judgment and conscience and in the responsibility of which no one could participate.

You may, I think, recur with just pride to the condition of the Country during the four years now about to close. It has concededly been a period of general prosperity: defalcations on the part of federal officers have been almost entirely unknown:—the public treasury with more than twenty millions of dollars constantly on hand has been free from the touch of fraud or speculation:— long pending foreign questions, have been amicably and advantageously adjusted:—valuable addition has been made to our already vast domain and peace has been maintained with all the nations of the earth without compromise of right or a stain upon the national honor.

Whatever of credit pertains to the Federal executive in the accomplishment of these results is attributable in great measure to the fidelity, laborious habits and ability of the heads of the different departments.

In my final retirement from active participation in public affairs I shall observe the career which awaits you individually with the interest of constant and unabated friendship.[7]

Your friend
Franklin Pierce

WATCHING EVENTS
1857-1869

LXXII

WANDERING

MAKING up his mind had never been one of Pierce's easy accomplishments, and when he left Buchanan at the door of the White House he was free to avoid this necessity with the greatest of impunity. He was comfortably off, for during his Presidency he had saved half his salary, and his inventory showed a capital of $78,000 carefully invested by Minot. He had no responsibility except a solicitude for Mrs. Pierce's comfort and seemingly no intention of going back to his profession. In fact the American tradition for ex-Presidents was dignified and idle retirement. Van Buren, Tyler, and Fillmore were all submerged, and when Van Buren and Fillmore had re-entered political life the results had not been particularly pleasing. So under these conditions the next three years were largely spent in a vain attempt to restore Mrs. Pierce's health, or at least to make her more comfortable and less melancholy, by a change of climate and by wandering amid new scenes.

Before leaving the White House they had decided that an immediate return to the March climate of New England would not be wise, so they accepted the Marcys' invitation to stay with them in Washington during the remainder of the month. These few weeks were marked by many incidents of peculiar satisfaction to the ex-President. Washington was thronged with the inauguration crowds, and many friends and acquaintances came to pay their respects. Marcy ventured the opinion that no occupants of the White House ever left it with such deep feelings of affection from the people of the city. The one cause for concern was political; Buchanan, in spite of protestations to the contrary, was reorganizing the government service for the benefit of his particular supporters. Many a Pierce man was officially decapitated. The new king was reigning in his own right.

With the approach of summer New England was a safe climate for Mrs. Pierce; so presently after a visit in Philadelphia they went to Andover and Pierce made his first public appearance since the inauguration. On June 1 at an anniversary banquet given in Faneuil Hall by the Ancient and Honorable Artillery Company he was among the speakers and he lost no time in preaching to New England. We must learn to respect our own rights and the equally sacred rights of others. The Constitution and the Union must be preserved, that latter word had more power for good to the human race than any other known in the English language. The Union could be preserved only by a faithful and sacred maintenance of the Constitution —not in one but in all its provisions. When he read this speech Jefferson Davis immediately sat down and wrote an appreciative letter.

The summer was spent at several places in New England, and at varying intervals news of death came to sadden the leisure of retirement. First Marcy, then Dobbin, and finally Mrs. Campbell; all died before August was over and the cabinet circle was sadly depleted. Hardest for Mrs. Pierce to bear was the death of her intimate companion, Abby Means. Finally, while at Portsmouth in the late summer it became necessary to plan for a winter in a milder climate. After considering a number of possibilities it was decided to go to the island of Madeira where their friend, Marsh, was consul. To this place Buchanan offered passage on the *Powhatan*.

They set sail late in November for their first extensive trip. Prior to this time their orbit had been a narrow one, but now with leisure and a competence they could discover the world. After a pleasant winter on the luxuriant isle of Madiera, Mr. and Mrs. Pierce went to Europe and began a leisurely tour through Portugal, Spain, France, Switzerland, Italy, Austria, Germany, Belgium, and England. Most of the summer of 1858 they idled away on the shores of Lake Geneva and the winter was spent in Italy. Here they met Hawthorne in Rome and renewed the old friendship. The author was struck by the change in his friend, by his whitening hair and furrowed face, and by a " something that seemed to have passed away out of him, without leaving any trace."

During his foreign sojourn Pierce eagerly read what political news he could gather. Campbell, McClelland, Cushing, and Davis wrote him occasionally; Guthrie alone was unheard from, but seemingly through no lack of friendship. Pondering on

frauds uncovered and Buchanan's other troubles, Pierce rejoiced
at the consciousness of the " integrity, Patriotism and devotion
to the best interests of the country to the exclusion of selfish
purposes and interests which characterized every member of
my cabinet." His successor's increasing difficulties afforded
Pierce a degree of self-satisfaction of which he was quite unconscious. He could not help it. The much-touted, experienced Buchanan was succeeding no better than he had succeeded.

At length in the summer of 1859 they set foot once more on
their native land. They had traveled far and seen much, but
Mrs. Pierce had received little permanent benefit. All the way
she had carried Bennie's Bible and a little box which Abby
Means, her " dear true friend," had given her, in which she
carefully treasured locks of hair of her " precious dead," her
boys, her mother, her sister. Perhaps the keepsake she valued
most of the European purchases was an Etruscan bracelet containing a strand of her husband's hair, which he had given her
at Rome. Sorrow so assiduously nursed could not be dispelled.
Existence for her continued as aimless as ever, but there were
the many souvenirs, the Florentine pictures, sixteen rather obscure " old masters " which they had bought, and the various
experiences to be talked about and described.

The return to Boston brought many welcoming letters, and
one or two significantly raised the question of the Presidency.
Mississippi and Alabama friends, notably Jefferson Davis, and
also Caleb Cushing, were not willing to accept a letter he had
written from Europe as a final decision. He must realize that
if the times needed him he must still serve his country. But
Pierce was not to be thus tempted. He wrote an ardent Alabama partisan that he had reason to believe his friends would
regard his wishes. While he dabbled a little in New Hampshire
politics he spent most of the fall at Andover, planning for a new
home, and for the coming winter. He and Mrs. Pierce bought
some sixty acres, on Pleasant Street on the fringe of Concord,
but decided to avoid the cold weather by visiting the West
Indies. Meanwhile some few friends like John H. George were
quietly maturing a plan to support Douglas, with the hope of
bringing Pierce forward after the Illinoisan failed.

In the midst of his home-making and winter-spending plans,

Pierce like thousands of others was startled by John Brown's attempt to operate after the Kansas fashion in the vicinity of Harper's Ferry.   When the fanatic had been duly hanged, popular sentiment demanded expression and meetings were held in glorification or protest.   The conservatives of Boston and New York organized anti-Republican and Union-saving meetings to denounce the Harper's Ferry episode.   To two of these December gatherings Pierce was invited to speak, and in declining sent letters deploring the ruthless invasion of Virginia " in violation of all law, human and divine."   However, he saw some good in it, for he believed that it would awaken the multitudes of " conscientious and patriotic " citizens in the South who would not " willfully and deliberately shake a single column which sustains the fabric of our existing institutions; multitudes who have been misled upon the question of duty and personal obligations, and who now, when they have practical illustration, drawn in blood, of the teachings to which they have listened, and to which they may have given their assent, will pause long enough, at least to take counsel of intelligent reason."   He denied that there was an irrepressible conflict; the first fifty years of our history had proved that there was none.

In this frame of mind he went on with his preparations for the southern tour.   Just after Christmas, he with Mrs. Pierce arrived at New York where the Clarendon Hotel was their home until they sailed January 7.   Pierce talked politics incessantly and found conditions which dismayed him.   Serious dangers threatened the Union.   " Orders for merchandize and for various articles of manufacture are being constantly countermanded by the Southern people," he wrote his brother, " social intercourse between the North and South and business arrangements also are being seriously disturbed and if the interruption becomes much more complete, political relations cannot long be maintained."   He did what he could at long distance to aid George in organizing a Union-saving meeting of a non-partisan character at Concord, and on the night before he sailed he wrote Jefferson Davis a fateful letter.

In it he recounted a conversation in which a Mr. Shipley had expressed his belief that Davis would be the best candidate for 1860.   This judgment Pierce affirmed and said that it was growing in New England.   " Our people are looking for the ' coming man.'" He regretted that he was going to leave the country; were it not for the illness of Mrs. Pierce he would not think of going. More of that letter later on. Next day they sailed for Nassau.

At this pleasant spot they spent five months in the society of Miss Vandervort, whom they had met in Europe, and the circle that clustered around British and American officialdom. In the meantime a few old supporters were nursing the hope that the Democratic convention might create a situation which again would call forth their chief. To his friends assembled at Charleston under Minot's leadership, Pierce sent a letter saying the use of his name was utterly out of the question.

The approach of summer and Sidney Webster's wedding brought them to New York early in June. Things political were in turmoil. The Democratic party had actually done in 1860 what some feared it would do in 1852; its convention had broken up without a nomination. Now the adjourned convention was about to reassemble at Baltimore. Two weeks of scheming had produced much fruit, and Pierce hardly had landed when Cushing and others approached him as a possible harmonizing candidate. This, however, he would not approve and wrote a strong letter to Cushing to that effect. He was not a leader of forlorn hopes and he had suffered enough in the Presidency. Mrs. Pierce was more unwell than ever; Dr. Peaslee was resorting to heroic cures. Meanwhile some still hoped, but in vain; the northern Democrats would not yield, it was Douglas or nobody. Baltimore proved just as disastrous as Charleston, and two Democratic tickets were presented, Douglas and Johnson leading one and Pierce's old friends, Breckinridge and Joe Lane, the other. A crisis was at hand; unknown fates were impending. Pierce's wanderings were over.

LXXIII

STRIVING TO SAVE THE UNION

PIERCE had delayed establishing a home for three years. He had bought property and had been considering building without actually beginning operations, principally, it seems, because Mrs. Pierce preferred visiting at Andover with her relatives, to remaining very long in Concord with its memories of Bennie. Now, however, they were going to live in Concord occasionally. The Williamses had purchased a larger house on South Main Street not far from their old one; and Mr. and Mrs. Pierce would be very comfortable there, at least till their new dwelling was built. Concord, of course, had altered. A few days after he had left in 1853, it had voted to become a city, a change which Pierce had opposed; and during his administration the government had been reorganized. A mayor and council had replaced the selectmen; no longer was there a town meeting. A new court house and city hall had been built and the old building where he had been so active was gone. Gas lights, too, illuminated the streets and the young city even boasted a sprinkler. Old faces had passed. Atherton and Ayer no longer frequented their former haunts. Most lamentable of all, a strange, mongrel party possessed the state house and offices, and the New Hampshire Democracy for six years had not known the taste of victory. At intervals, Pierce became a familiar figure once more along Concord Street and he resumed a place in the public life of the state; in that year Dartmouth honored him with an LL.D.

He continued to observe the political struggle. As to the Presidential contest he wrote Hallett that neither ticket in his opinion could be held binding, but he hoped Democrats could unite on Breckinridge and Lane. In any event, it would be best to nominate a representative electoral list, with an understanding that it was a compromise ticket which would vote for either Douglas or Breckinridge according to circumstances and previous agreement. The Breckinridge and Lane campaign committee seized upon this letter and made a document out of it. In application of his doctrine Pierce tried to help arrange such a fusion movement in New Hampshire. Minot and George, the leading organizers of the state Democracy, either did not favor his scheme or were unable to achieve it; for the state convention, while nominating an electoral ticket of excellent men, endorsed Douglas. Although Pierce would have preferred Breckinridge, his belief in party regularity made him follow the state convention. It may be surmised that the action of some of the papers in announcing that Honorable Edmund Burke, with the aid of General Pierce, was getting up a Breckinridge ticket, somewhat strengthened his regularity; for he still wrote of Burke as " this very bad and unprincipled man." In this wise he finally refused countenance to the Breckinridge ticket, as having been nominated irregularly. He did not participate actively in the campaign except in an advisory capacity, and his advice was little heeded. While there is no proof so far discovered that he voted in 1860, if he did we can rest assured that he voted for the regularly nominated electors, in spite of the Douglas resolution attached to them.

As the election approached and the preliminary rounds in September and October indicated Republican victory as sure, Davis and a few others thought that, as a last expedient, Douglas and Breckinridge might be persuaded to withdraw in favor of Pierce, and James Campbell so wrote the latter. Pierce immediately vetoed this scheme, but expressed confidence that Guthrie and Horatio Seymour might provide a ticket in favor of which not only Douglas and Breckinridge, but also Bell, might withdraw. Davis and Campbell circulated this idea somewhat late in October, but without any result. Nothing, evidently, could be done to stem this Republican tide.

Election day in 1860 produced a result which all had foreseen, but it proved none the less painful to Pierce and his fellow " National Democrats." It was a " distinct and unequivocal denial of the coequal rights " of the states, and such a sequel was " fearful." However, this fear was not shared by most of the New Hampshire politicians, and Pierce presumably felt like Cassandra as he left Concord for Andover a few days after the election. A very bad cold, too, contributed to his low spirits.

Not long after the election it became apparent that, unless something could be done, the unity of the Republic was to be destroyed. South Carolina's steps were ominous and Pierce soon began to receive appeals for action. Jacob Thompson, secretary of the interior, wrote him, and the first assistant post-master-general, Horatio King, likewise, the latter pleading, " Give us a letter which may serve to strengthen the arm of the conservative men of the south in this fearful crisis. *You are emphatically the man for the work.*" But Pierce hesitated: he felt somehow as though he had said all he could say. Besides he was paralyzed by the suspicion that if he were in the places of his southern friends he would be doing what they were doing, driven at length to extremes by years of unrelenting aggression. It was not the fact of Mr. Lincoln's election—that in itself was constitutional—it was the meaning of Lincoln's election, that the South resented. They considered it an endorsement of resistance to the fugitive slave law and of Lincoln's prophecy that in the end the United States must be either all free or all slave, because of the irrepressible conflict. If our fathers had been mistaken when they formed the Constitution, " the sooner we are apart the better," though he himself felt these fears were all unfounded, if each side would look at the matter rationally.

His indecision was overcome by the gravity of the situation; and as the dangers multiplied Pierce matured three successive plans of action. To Thompson he wrote the first: " No wise man can under existing circumstances dream of coercion. The first blow struck in that direction will be a blow fatal even to hope." He expressed some faith that there might be " indica-tions of a disposition to repeal laws directed against the consti-tutional rights of the southern states, such as ' personal liberty ' bills, etc. and if we could gain a little time, there would seem to be ground of hope that these just causes of distrust and dis-satisfaction might be removed." Much would depend upon the tone and temper of the early sessions of Congress. But if recog-nition of coequal rights could not be obtained and expectations were disappointed, " life itself, my friend, will lose its value for you and me." His first desire, then, was that the North might repeal the " personal liberty " acts. Pierce did not realize the strength of anti-southern feeling in the North.

His unhappiness was made all the more intense because he had little else to occupy him than thoughts upon this subject. Having once been chief magistrate, the cares of the nation seemed personal and the responsibilities still his. Also the sorrow was deeper than that, because he had come to cherish sorrow, and here was a new cause for pain. Something he loved which he called the Union, which in essence was a fellow-ship, a friendship, a great emotion or a sentimentality if you will—this ideal was being destroyed, destroyed by those whom he had been despising and fearing and fighting as a source of evil for the last twenty-five years, the political abolitionists. The return of the cough which had plagued him so in his con-gressional days did nothing to encourage optimism.

In this gloomy period came news of the secession of South Carolina and the conventions to be held in the other southern states. They brought a new appeal for aid from Washington. Judge John A. Campbell of Alabama, whom he had appointed to the Supreme Court, wrote that he had been urging Buchanan to send commissioners to each of the states about to hold con-ventions. Would the general consider acting as a commissioner to Alabama? This letter reached Pierce at Andover on Christ-mas Eve while he was confined to the house with his cold. He immediately made a trial answer and when Minot came down from Concord, Christmas Day, they went over it carefully to-gether. In it he set forth his second plan. He spoke of his ill-ness as probably making it impossible for him to travel, and then penned an urgent plea for the South to remember the hun-dreds of thousands who had always steadfastly defended their rights in the North. The southern states must not act precipi-tately but give their northern friends an opportunity to right the South's wrongs peacefully. If after six months or so this had proven impossible, then there must be a sad farewell which would in no sense justify a war. His letter was widely pub-lished in the South, especially in Alabama, but without effect. Pierce did not realize the strength of anti-northern feeling in the South.

When news came of the dispatch of the *Star of the West* to provision Sumter he wrote his wife: " I cannot conceive of a more idle, foolish, ill-advised, if not criminal thing . . . will not the first act of war, the useless sending of this steamer, and the first hostile gun reverberate and blaze along the whole southern line, calling men to arms? " Shortly after, Lawrence went to Washington, and while there engaged in that prevalent occupation of trying to find a way out. The peace conference was about to meet and ex-President Tyler was in the capital. The idea gained some limited currency that if all the ex-Presidents attended this conference their prestige might be a valuable factor. Lawrence therefore wrote Pierce to sound him out.

The latter at the moment did not think it much of a suggestion. His cough still troubled him, he could see no point for " effective interposition." The extremists in both sections were alike earnest for civil war, and the conservatives were either supine or too thoroughly controlled by party affiliation. Besides, as he believed, " the North have been the first wrong doers and [he had] never been able to see how a successful appeal could be made to the south without first placing [the North] right."

In April the dreaded crisis broke. Lincoln decided to maintain the garrison at Sumter and the flag of the United States was fired upon by its erstwhile defenders. The week-end of April 12–14 clearly defined the issue. Sunday brought to Concord the news of the surrender, and though many attended the evening lecture of the President of Antioch College on the theme " The first chapter of Genesis not in conflict with the researches of Modern Science," it may be suspected that the thoughts of the audience wandered away from the fall of man to the fall of Sumter, which was to prove another terrible calamity. Monday morning's mail brought the President's proclamation and call for volunteers. The situation looked almost hopeless but Pierce determined on his third and final expedient. He reconsidered Lawrence's suggestion and wrote Van Buren, proposing that he call the ex-Presidents to Philadelphia to see if they could not issue some appeal which might arrest popular clamor.

Meanwhile, in Concord, public spirit surged and a Union meeting was held to rally patriotic fervor. Pierce was out of town, but on his return next day a committee waited upon him and requested that he give a public declaration. He agreed and that evening from the *Eagle* balcony he addressed the crowd. Opposed as he was to secession and coercion, he had recently read alleged declarations of the vice-president and secretary of war of the Confederacy that Washington was to be attacked. This aggression was just as bad as coercion. So he endorsed the patriotic resolutions passed the previous night, and then delivered a brief panegyric upon the flag and its glorious history. It was an occasion for patriotism and stern duty. He would never cease to hope " so long as the fratricidal strife is not more fully developed than at present, that some event, some power " might yet intervene. " I do not believe aggression by arms is a suitable or possible remedy for existing evils." But should " a war of aggression be waged against the National Capital and the North, then there is no way for us as citizens of one of the old thirteen States, but to stand together and uphold the flag to the last, with all the rights which pertain to it; and with the fidelity and endurance of brave men, I would advise you to stand together with one head and one mind. . . . Born in the State of New Hampshire, I intend that here shall repose my bones. I would not live in a state, the rights and honor of which I was not prepared to defend at all hazards—and to the last extremity."

This speech he somewhat qualified in a private letter. " It was very unfortunate that Mr. Walker . . . and Vice President Stevens should have spoken of an assault upon Washington and armed aggression upon the North. I do not believe that the Confederate Government ever entertained such a purpose except in retaliation for invasion of the seceded states. Still, the official position of the two gentlemen named gave weight to their words and I was ready to meet and resist such threats at all hazards."

Within a day or two he received a polite and typical letter from Van Buren in which the latter declined to take any responsibility for issuing a call to the ex-Presidents but suggested Pierce do it. Pierce had not moved any further in that direction but had been concentrating his efforts upon persuading his friends in Virginia to stand firm against disruption and to secure a compromise. Just before her secession he had telegraphed Governor Letcher: " Virginia can yet save her children." Now with the Union seemingly quite destroyed he gave himself over to bitter reflection. " To this war . . . which seems to me to contemplate subjugation I give no countenance— no support to any possible extent in any possible way—except thro' inevitable taxation, which seems likely to bankrupt us all. Come what may the foul schemes of Northern Abolitionism, which we have resisted for so many years, are not to be consummated by arms on bloody fields, through any aid of mine." To the end of his days he always believed that war could have been avoided if there had been the same self-sacrificing devotion to the public good that carried the nation through the Revolution and made possible the adoption of the Constitution.

LXXIV

OPPOSITION TO THE WAR

EVENTS of the first months of the war were to drive Pierce into open opposition. During that strange summer of 1861 he had postponed his home building once more, and financial difficulties had suggested the possibility of his return to law practise. But instead, after arranging for spending the late summer at Rye beach, he suddenly changed his plans for some unknown reason and departed on a brief trip of less than three weeks " in fulfillment of a long cherished purpose to visit the Great West and obtain a better idea of its boundless resources." He went as far as Detroit and Saginaw City, Michigan, where he called on McClelland, Cass and his niece, Fanny McNeil Potter; and then he journeyed to Louisville where he visited Guthrie.

On this excursion he was not at all reticent in private conversation. He criticised the war-making and was especially bitter when at Detroit he learned that his old friend James G. Berret, ex-mayor of Washington, had been imprisoned in Fort Lafayette. He was overheard to say such acts would precipitate fighting in the North. He also declared that he would rather see Joseph Holt as President than anyone else. He made a few speeches in which he glorified the Union and the Constitution and said nothing of the war. So brief a journey would hardly merit record had it not been for its consequences.

Christmas Eve Pierce was at Andover where he was surprised by the receipt of an official letter from Seward, the secretary of state, enclosing a copy of an anonymous communication which contained a reference to General P—— having taken a trip for the purpose of aiding an anti-war organization known as the Knights of the Golden Circle, " a secret league, the object of which [was] to overthrow the Government." This allusion Seward called upon him most curtly to explain. Although he had some inkling that he was suspected, the receipt of this letter made Pierce furious. The affront, and the insult of having his patriotism questioned on so slight evidence by highest authority, were a bitter stroke. He answered the secretary's

letter indignantly. Seward straightway apologized, saying that
he had received this charge and wanted to give Pierce an
opportunity to meet it; the actual note had been written by a
clerk who had done the job tactlessly.*

The correspondence in this matter Pierce showed to various
Democratic friends and they urged him to give the letters to the
press. He took no steps, however, until March when the Detroit
Tribune circulated the charge. Their item, containing the
anonymous letter, was spread broadcast by Republican papers
including the Boston *Journal* and the New York *Evening Post*.
The unpleasant notoriety roused Pierce once more and at his
request Senator Latham introduced a resolution in Congress
calling for the submission of the correspondence to that body.
Seward's apology was thus made public and the fact was brought
to light that a Dr. Hopkins, who had been arrested on suspicion,
had fabricated the accusation as a hoax. Unfortunately, these
revelations did not aid Pierce very much in the war-inflamed
public mind, and the impression became deeper that he was
disloyal.

He in his turn became increasingly bitter. In his most intimate correspondence he was unrestrained, as one after another
the various policies of the Lincoln administration were promulgated, such as the arrest of the members of the Maryland
legislature and the arbitrary imprisonments in Fort Warren.
When martial law was proclaimed, he felt that despotism had
succeeded representative government. Sovereign states, constitutional rights, trial by jury, legal protection for person and
property were destroyed.

Nothing in the course of hostilities did he condemn more
bitterly than the emancipation proclamation. This act showed
that the true purpose of the war was to wipe out the states and
destroy property; objects which made the war flagrant treason
to the constitution. He could not understand how the people
of the United States would tolerate this attempt to " butcher "
their own race for the sake of " inflicting " emancipation upon

* The maneuver of the secretary was not based entirely on this anonymous letter. There were a few other items besides, on the state department
files, which in those suspicious times were sufficient to move Seward to give
Pierce an opportunity to explain. Today the flimsy character of the evidence seems most apparent.

the four million Negroes who were in no sense capable of profiting by freedom.

Again, he had hopes of raising an issue that would bring the Democratic party back to power. Encouraged by the numerous victories in the fall of 1862, he urged that the spring campaign be waged on the " great issue of Executive usurpation against the constitution, against freedom of speech and of the press, against personal liberty." He declared that the Emancipation Proclamation as issued in its final form demonstrated that Mr. Sumner and the whole band of abolitionists had triumphed through Mr. Lincoln, who was " to the extent of his limited ability and narrow intelligence their willing instrument for all the woe which [had] thus far been brought upon the Country and for all the degradation, all the atrocity, all the desolation and ruin " which to date had been accomplished. For this proclamation invited the black race " in six entire States and in parts of several others to rise and with all the barbaric features which must be inseparable from a successful servile insurrection to slay and devastate without regard to age or sex," white men, women and children. His bitterness was extravagant; not one act of Lincoln's administration could he commend. On the other hand, he never carried his opposition to the war to the point of justifying the South in its struggle for independence. In destroying the Union they had committed a useless sin. For as Hawthorne said at the time, Pierce retained his faith in the Union " in all the simplicity with which he inherited it from his father. It has been the principle and is the explanation [of his career] . . . it would ruin a noble character (though one of limited scope) for him to admit any ideas that were not entertained by the fathers of the Constitution and the Republic. . . . There is a certain steadfastness and integrity with regard to a man's own nature (when it is such a peculiar nature as that of Pierce) which seems to me more sacred and valuable than the faculty of adapting one's self to new ideas, however true they may turn out to be."

Popular reaction to his course was unpleasant. Old friends fell away to join forces with the war party. Caleb Cushing followed the crowd, became a Republican and sought a commission, demonstrating once more his facility at changing his policies. Pierce heard of the course of these former associates with regret. In regard to one of them he wrote his wife: "I know him, and know that he can do what I can not do—bow to the storm" and he added a comment which suggests that Mrs. Pierce did not agree with him: "My purpose, dearest, is immovably taken. I will never justify, sustain, or in any way or to any extent uphold this cruel, heartless, aimless unnecessary war. Madness and imbecility are in the ascendant. I shall not succumb to them, come what may. I have no opinions to retract, no line of action to change."

Of course this determination did nothing to temper the slights or to lighten the load of political abuse which came his way. Concord was too small a place to lose one's self in, and the bitterness of neighbors is most difficult to endure. Consequently they were much at Andover; occasionally he went to Hillsborough. The press was unkind enough to state that he had been driven from Concord as no one would speak to him.

Not since his speech in April, 1861, had Pierce been heard publicly, but his emotions were too deep-seated to be denied utterance; and when, after a large Republican rally at Concord on Bunker Hill Day, 1863, the Democrats planned a counter-gathering on July 4, he consented to be the principal orator. So at noon in Capitol Square he was introduced as the president and principal speaker and launched forth. He deplored the state of the country, dwelt much on its past history and the Revolutionary fathers. He attacked the President for his arbitrary acts, his dictation "when we must or when we may speak." "True it is, that any of you, that I, may be the next victim of unconstitutional, arbitrary, irresponsible power." The conflict he spoke of as this "fearful, fruitless, fatal civil war . . . prosecuted upon the basis of the proclamations of September 22 and September 24, 1862 . . . upon the theory of emancipation, devastation, subjugation, it cannot fail to be fruitless in everything except the harvest of woe which it is ripening for what was once the peerless Republic. . . . How futile are all our efforts to maintain the Union by force of arms. . . . Through peaceful agencies, and through such agencies alone, can we hope [to achieve] . . . the great objects for which, and for which alone the Constitution was formed." Having thus expressed his views at length he concluded with the greatest literary effort in his career of platitudinous oratory. He conceived an amazing metaphor well reflecting the perfervid obsessions of a war-tainted imagination.

> If you turn round and ask me, what if these agencies fail, what if the passionate anger of both sections forbids; what if the ballot box is sealed? Then, all efforts, whether of war or peace having failed, my reply is, you will take care of yourselves; with or without arms, with or without leaders, we will, at least, in the effort to defend our rights as a free people, build up a great mausoleum of hearts to which men who yearn for liberty will in after years with bowed heads and reverently, resort, as Christian Pilgrims to the sacred shrines of the Holy Land.

There were other speeches, and the meeting lasted five hours; but in the meantime telegrams had been received by the *Statesman* telling that at Gettysburg what seemed to be a great military victory was being won, and while Pierce was preaching his counsel of despair this word threaded in and out through the crowd. In vain might John H. George declare it to be a " damn Abolition lie "; it was true and made the reading of the ex-President's great effort peculiarly anticlimactic. He concluded his day by calling upon the crowd to contribute to a fund to aid the sick and wounded. He subscribed $50 himself and $350 was raised. John H. George quite jubilantly waved a handful of money. " The Republicans say we help the rebels; but this is the way we help our soldiers." Pierce passed the rest of the day quietly with Hawthorne who was visiting him, its end somewhat saddened by the word that his old friend Colonel Cross of the 5th New Hampshire Regiment had been killed.

The day's work had been done, the last shred of public reputation which Pierce had, save with his old political friends, was destroyed. From this speech he never recovered. When Hawthorne against the advice of his publishers dedicated his book, *Our Old Home*, to Pierce shortly thereafter, inscribing in an open letter printed therein his great faith in his friend's devotion to the " grand idea of an irrevocable Union "; many, like Emerson, bought the book but cut out the letter and the dedication.

LXXV

THE DISSOLUTION OF A PERSONALITY

To write of the decline of a personality is not a gracious task, for when an individual begins to loosen his hold upon life, generous impulse bids a quick passing over the painful process. The remaining six years of the life of Franklin Pierce are marked by many signs of failing spirit and power. Death continued to afflict him, weaknesses overcame him more completely, his constitution, so robust yet so badly used, began to fail in its functions.

On December 2, 1863, Mrs. Pierce died. Hawthorne came to him immediately and together they looked at the shrunken figure in the coffin, which strangely affected the author. To him it seemed like a carven image laid in its richly embossed enclosure and there was a remote expression about it as if it had nothing to do with things present. The two friends remained together during the ceremonies and on a bitter December day stood by the graveside in the Minot enclosure. The wind was penetrating and Pierce leaned over to wrap Hawthorne's collar more securely around his neck.

Death had brought to an end the union solemnized in Colonel Means's mansion nearly thirty years before. Franklin Pierce and Jane Appleton had shared some joy and more sorrow, had received much honor and had learned to endure much bitter condemnation, in those thirty years. She had never been happy for long; disease or death or her husband's interests and failings had been constant sources of anxiety and melancholy from which she never had learned to free herself. Deeply religious, hers had been the religion of acceptance, not of conquering power. He, realizing the fundamental incompatibility of their backgrounds, temperaments, and interests, had sought to recompense for that fact by all the tenderness, consideration, and affection which his sentimental nature could shower upon her. How well or ill he succeeded we cannot judge, for she had slight powers of self-revelation and gave little expression to her inward thoughts.

In the spring of 1864, death came again; this time to his oldest friend, Hawthorne, who had not been well for a year or more. The two friends were journeying together in the White Mountains, in a vain effort to revive the author's failing spirits, when the end came. While Pierce was packing up Hawthorne's few belongings, he noticed in the bottom of the valise an old pocketbook, seemingly empty. He found therein his own picture which his friend had been wont to carry on his journeyings. The funeral was imposing because of those who attended: Emerson, Whittier, Lowell, Longfellow, Agassiz, and Alcott, that charming fellowship of the New England literati. Pierce was there too, but the bitterness of the times excluded him from a place among the pallbearers.

Through these bereavements there was a continuous manifestation of public slight, even as shown at Hawthorne's funeral. Not very long after his Fourth of July speech, the fateful letter to Jefferson Davis, which he had written in 1860 just before sailing to Nassau, was unearthed by northern soldiers in their marching through the South. It was lithographed and spread broadcast, even used as a political document, especially in New Hampshire. An anonymous writer signing himself a " Democrat " delved into the past and prepared a pamphlet in which he told the story once more of Pierce's broken pledge to keep the slavery question out of politics, of how he had used soldiers in an attempt to make Kansas a slave state. The pamphleteer included this Davis letter, which he declared demonstrated that the subject of secession was seriously considered at that date " in the secret deliberations of the South," that Pierce, far from discouraging the idea, had actually encouraged it by suggesting that if the South did secede the fighting would not be along Mason and Dixon's line, but in the streets of northern cities and towns. He concluded by quoting from the Fourth of July speech, and likening Pierce to Benedict Arnold. So bitter did public feeling become, especially in his own state, that Minot attempted to combat it by taking three Union-saving letters Pierce had written in December, 1859, and publishing them, together with the Davis letter in a pamphlet entitled *The Record of a Month.*

In spite of it all, a very few of his friends felt that he would be the best candidate for the Presidential nomination in 1864.

He knew the fallacy of this idea and refused to consider it; he urged that the Democrats unite on General McClellan, Seymour, or Guthrie, standing on a platform of the restoration of the Union by a cessation of arms and an appeal to reason. If the issue of pacification were not presented there might as well be no contest.

The end of the war was at hand but peace was not to come without another dark hour. Good Friday night, 1865, brought dispatches that Lincoln had been shot and that murder was abroad in the capital city. Early next morning Pierce went to the post office to get the latest news and waited there with the anxious crowd till the final word came that the President was dead. The great calamity stirred Concord and in this " holiday of sorrow " Pierce shared deeply. A mass meeting to give public expression of grief was held late that dismal day, and as the early shadows of the stormy evening began to fall, a crowd gathered, determined on they knew not quite what. Every house must show a draped flag and they began to seek out those where no sign of mourning or patriotism was visible. George Williams, a lad in Pierce's household, was with the crowd when he heard the proposal that they go to Pierce's. He scampered away and found the general lying down in his library rather indisposed by the excitement of the night and day. When Pierce heard that the mob was on its way he lost no time in getting up, and when the shouts were heard before his door he took a small flag in his hand and went out to face the crowd.

They demanded a speech and while he was denouncing the crime of the previous night and expressing his condemnation of the assassin, someone yelled " Where is your flag? " To this he replied " It is not necessary for me to show my devotion for the Stars and Stripes by any special exhibition upon the demand of any man or body of men. . . . If the period which I have served our state and country in various situations, commencing more than thirty-five years ago, has left the question of my devotion to the flag, the constitution and the Union in doubt, it is too late now to resume it by any such exhibition as the enquiry suggests." The oldtime fire burned once more within him, the power of his speech was still potent, and when he finished the crowd dispersed, leaving the rain as the only remaining visitor on that doorstep.

So the war ended; but the Union soldiers then, and as they formed later into the Grand Army of the Republic, remembered his opposition to the struggle and forgot his support of its charities and his solicitude for the welfare of the men on the field. For fifty years no sign of recognition did the state give to the public career of its only President.

The renewed association with death, the political bitterness of the war period, the slights of townspeople and former associates—all these troubles, coupled with the demands of age and his way of life, told upon his spirits and his health. After Mrs. Pierce's death there seemed little reason to resist the appetites which so long had plagued him. So on the Main Street, more occasionally at his cottage, which he purchased in 1865, at Little Boar's Head by the sea, but never at Andover, his propensity for alcohol overcame him. It was not that he indulged freely but that any indulgence had so marked an effect; his will bowed before the stormy craving and the defeat was made easy because he felt that he had inherited the weakness. Some of his friends tried to help him, others merely served as boon companions. Sickness was frequent. In December, 1864, February and June, 1865, his illnesses were such as to cause his relatives anxiety and he complained much of a heavy cough. A climax came in the fall of 1865 when his life was despaired of. Yet his constitution was strong and his vitality so sustaining that he pulled through; but the experience had made a deep impression.

All his life, since the days of his close association with Zenas Caldwell, he had never satisfactorily worked out the problem of religious faith. He had been in two worlds, the world of politics which was generally not at all interested, or, if so, after the manner of the agnostics; his married life on the other hand had been almost excessively religious. His own relatives seem not to have done more than pay formal acknowledgment to religion, but his wife's family were all most earnest adherents to orthodox faith. For forty years he had never met the question more than half way; he professed to be an orthodox believer, but moving experience, which would lead to public profession, he seems never to have felt; nor did he have the willingness or the confidence to accept the discipline. He did his best to invite the experience, was regular in his church attendance, and

especially after the death of his boy he became even more observant as his White House customs show.　However, when the
war difficulties approached, orthodox Congregationalism, especially under the political preachers, such as Henry E. Parker
of the South Congregational Church, who stormed against the
sin of slavery, became so distasteful that he went less and less
within its churches.

Meanwhile he had become intimate with Dr. Eames, rector
of St. Paul's Episcopal Church, and he and a number of other
Democrats found that from his pulpit came no politics, but
sermons dealing with the problems of religious life.　So he had
become accustomed to going into the peaceful quiet of St.
Paul's, especially after Mrs. Pierce's death, and he found the
society of Dr. Eames comforting and congenial.　When, therefore, he recovered from his illness that fall, the world at large
was astonished to read that on Sunday, December 3, 1865,
Franklin Pierce had presented himself at St. Paul's font, and
had there promised to " renounce the devil and all his works,
the vain pomp and glory of the world, with all covetous desires
of the same and the sinful desires of the flesh, to no longer follow nor be led by them, and to obediently keep God's holy will
and commandments and to walk in the same all the days of his
life."　Whereupon Dr. Eames baptized him, and in the spring
his old friend Bishop Chase confirmed him.

> While Thee I seek, protecting power,
> Be my vain wishes stilled
> And may this consecrated hour
> With better hopes be filled.

Thus did " Brattle Street," his favorite hymn, express the long-
ings which at last had been satisfied.　It had taken many long
years; only when his life had been lived, did the seed planted
by Zenas Caldwell come to fruition.

With renewed health and greater peace of mind his autumn
softened into a brief Indian summer.　Once more he moved up
and down Main Street, an example of stately courtesy, with high
hat and cape, and with a greeting and stately bow for many acquaintances; a red-faced man with a propensity for shaking
hands, who did not look his age.　Especially was he the children's idol.　Those then in their early youth have told me of

his irresistible attraction and the great prize set upon little favors with which he was wont to delight the heart of a child. Julian Hawthorne, then a boy in his teens, gives his impression of him thus:

> There was a winning, irresistible magnetism in the presence of this man. Except my father, there was no man in whose company I liked to be so much as in his. I had little to say to him, and demanded nothing more than a silent recognition from him, but his voice, his look, his gestures, his gait, the spiritual sphere of him, were delightful to me; and I suspect that his rise to the highest office in our nation was due quite as much to this power or quality in him as to any intellectual or even executive ability that he may have possessed. He was a good conscientious, patriotic strong man, and gentle and tender as a woman. He had the old-fashioned ways, the courtesy, and the personal dignity which are not often seen nowadays. His physical frame was immensely powerful and athletic, but life used him hard and he was far from considerate of himself, and he died at sixty-five, when he might under more favorable conditions, have rounded out his century.*

Miss Lena Minot, Miss Almira Fletcher, William J. Ahern and others echoed this, as I sought out those who remembered him. A less sympathetic description was phrased thus:

> Pierce was amiable and kindly, and possessed the rare gift of personal magnetism. Nature sometimes endows men and women with this quality in lieu of all other advantages. Not much above the average in intellect, and, as Hawthorne afterward confessed, not particularly attractive in appearance, with a stiff military neck, features strong but small, and opaque gray eyes,—a rather unimpressive face, and one hardly capable of decided expression.†

Older friends he had, too, John H. George, Colonel Thomas J. Whipple, Richard S. Spofford, and best of all his old partner and business adviser, Josiah Minot. Part of the picture would be omitted if his horses were not brought in, Union and Grey Eagle of earlier years, and his last companion, Ethan, who knew his moods and even understood his words. Ethan it was who always brought him safely home, even if he went to sleep and let drop the reins.

---

* Hawthorne, *Hawthorne and his Circle*, 359.
† Stearns, *Life and Genius of Nathaniel Hawthorne*, 62–63.

In these last days, Concord knew him less, especially in the summer. He had purchased some eighty-four acres at Little Boar's Head on the New Hampshire coast and here he built a cottage, marked out the ground for building lots, and sought to develop the area as a summer colony. A few farms were located in the vicinity and not very distant were the hotels on Rye Beach. His cottage was a small, two-storied building on high land. From his door the " head " dropped abruptly, about fifty feet, to a rugged beach where the ocean moved restlessly a stone's throw from the house. The beach itself was covered with many boulders and ledges with no sand within half a mile. From his windows he could enjoy a far-reaching prospect off to the Isles of Shoals, Cape Ann, and Eastern Point. Here Pierce spent many a day alone or with his cronies, living over the past, dozing, and occasionally stirring himself to new plans.

In this period he bethought himself of his possessions, for he had been prosperous of late, and he made a long and elaborate will to distribute his competence of nearly $90,000. His brother Henry and his nephew Kirk were to have substantial legacies; old friends were to be remembered; he planned some small public benefactions. The residue of his estate was to go to his nephew Frank, whom he had sent to Andover and to Princeton, and who was following his footsteps in the law. His two swords were left to the two nephews " with the hope that should occasion arise for their use, in repelling foreign agression, in vindicating the rights of American citizens the world over, or in the faithful upholding of the sacred Constitution framed and adopted by the fathers of the Revolution, the weapons may not be dishonored in their hands." Distribution of his bounty, however, was not to wait until his death. He was interested in his numerous nieces and nephews, especially in his namesake, Frank H. Pierce, and in Julian Hawthorne. These boys he helped to educate, and watched their careers with interest. Mrs. Hawthorne constantly besought his aid and advice, which he gladly gave. When President Lord of Dartmouth fell into a predicament because of his disapproval of the war, Pierce was active in raising an annuity for him. One of the last things he did was to unite in a subscription to be presented to his brother-in-law, Alpheus S. Packard, who was still serving their Alma Mater.

This revival of interest was but a flicker.   His strong constitution had been too badly used to last out its appointed three score years and ten.   Late summer of 1868 found him ill again and his mind seemed to grasp the approach of death.   He wrote Bridge:

> Does it ever occur to you, Bridge, that we are rightly classed among the old men now?   It is quite certain that those who were not old, but prominent, during my day, and those who were in the early struggle with me among the first class Mr. Sullivan, Mr. Bartlett, Mr. Jos. Bell, Mr. Atherton, Sr., and Mr. Farley and among the second Judge Gilchrist, Mr. Choate, Atherton, Jun., and at last Mr. Norris, Mr. Wells, and most of their more humble compeers, have gone before.
>
> I do not, my dear friend, look upon it gloomily, but sometimes when I seem to be gathering up vigor so slowly I doubt if I take into account, fully enough, my protracted and severe illness, or the fact that nearly sixty-four years of pretty strenuous life have passed over my head.   I am driving out more or less, daily, and can repeat, with more or less comfort, " Thou art my God, my time is in Thy hand."   Give my love to dear Mrs. Bridge.
>
> Always, early and late, y'r Friend,
>
> Franklin Pierce.*

In the spring he summoned his strength for his last journey. He had always treasured the inheritance of his father's membership in the Order of the Cincinnati, and as their triennial convention was to be held in Baltimore that May of 1869, he " could not resist the impulse to manifest by his presence, the profound respect he entertained for the noble men who founded that society, and for their descendants, who were endeavoring to maintain it over an *undivided* Union."

Before these associates he delivered his last public speech. Referring to the Howards of Baltimore who had been imprisoned in Fort Lafayette during the war, he said, " If the Howards were disloyal, I was disloyal too, tho' I do not believe that I ever saw a day when I would not have made any possible, personal sacrifice to maintain the Constitution of my country and the Union based upon it.   The opinions or perhaps it would be

* Bridge, *Personal Reminiscences of Nathaniel Hawthorne*, 180.

better to say the convictions which have controlled me may have been matters neither of merit or demerit. Some men are so constituted that they do not incline to bow before a storm. At all events, I was not educated in the school where it has been taught that the great work of the fathers was ' a covenant ' or a ' league ' with anything evil. Other lessons were taught at my father's fireside."

That summer he was still able to go to Little Boar's Head, but illness, the dropsy, overtook him there, his system had broken down and he was barely able to return to Concord. Early in September he took to his room and it was only a matter of time. There in the quiet of the southeast chamber he lay as the sands ran out of the glass. Concord passed beneath his window and the townspeople were mildly interested in his struggle. In moments of consciousness he could gaze half-comprehendingly out of the window over Concord Street, across the familiar Merrimack, that river of broken waters which then, as in so many autumns past, was flowing unevenly through its intervale decked with patches of evergreen and flaming splashes of turning leaves. Beyond the river lay the dark plains, and in moments of imagining perhaps he thought of his beloved white hills. Unconsciousness drifted over him slowly and as the days of autumn advanced, more frequently. Finally just before the dawn of October 8, 1869, he died.

They laid his body in state in the capitol where he had won his early triumphs. There the townspeople came to pay their final tribute and satisfy their curiosity, the little children from the schools passed by hushed and uneasy. U. S. Grant, another unfortunate inhabitant of the White House, declared a period of national mourning.

On the appointed day, friends bore the casket into St. Paul's for the final office, and thence to the Minot enclosure where was to be the grave of the fourteenth President of the United States.

Once long ago Seneca, in quoting his daily wisdom text to Lucilius, copied an item from Hecato: "What progress you ask, have I made? I have begun to be a friend to myself." Franklin Pierce had never been a friend to himself.

LXXVI
RECASTING A STEREOTYPE

MOST men can avoid a biographer and pass into oblivion leaving hardly a trace. Not so a public man, particularly in the American democracy. The intensity of political contest, the disputes over policy and legislation mean that the biographies of politicians of any prominence will be compiled many times by many tongues and many pens. In their day, the deeds of these public figures will be observed by the multitude, their words will be heard and read by a lesser number. From the flood of utterance regarding their behavior and from their own words and deeds a stereotype is almost inevitably constructed which is accepted by contemporary opinion and usually shapes the judgment of posterity.

This stereotype may frequently bear little resemblance to the real personality which it presumes to represent. Sometimes the image presents the figure at an advantage; sometimes it is less than just. But whether better or worse than reality, the picture is generally a simple one in black or white, of evil or of virtue. The popular comprehension has no mechanism to grasp or to weigh complexity. He who runs can read only so much, and he who shouts in a political campaign must lose the zest for shouting, if he permits himself to be confused as to whether the man of the hour may be neither hero nor villain.

In the gallery of American political leaders there are many stereotyped figures, few more easily recognized than certain of the Presidents of the United States, notably Franklin Pierce. The stereotype of him created during his unfortunate life has received almost universal acceptance. Before his death he was described by Gideon Welles as "a vain, showy, and pliant man . . . [who] by his errors and weakness broke down his Administration, and his party throughout the country." * Eighty years later, Allan Nevins described him as "one of the quickest, most gracefully attractive, and withal weakest, of the men who have held his high office . . . on the whole a man of shallow nature." †

* Gideon Welles Diary, March 11, 1868.
† Nevins, *Ordeal of the Union*, II, 41–42.

The picture is consistently uncomplicated, a picture of more or less unrelieved weakness. But does this stereotype represent an adequate understanding of the fourteenth President of the United States?

Long pondering over the facts of Pierce's life lead to the conclusion that the accepted stereotype should be replaced by a much more complex representation. Pierce was not this simple example of weakness, but rather a personality of such varying strengths and conflicting inadequacies that his resulting confusion takes on the aspect of high tragedy indicated by a desperate struggle of heroic proportions. Much of his life was spent in the turmoil of an inner conflict, of sporadic episode and varying intensity.

The impulse basic to this conflict was physical. He was the child of a rugged father and a neurotic, volatile mother who gave him a body and a nervous system both strong and weak. He was sturdily built and seemingly robust, capable of great exertion and elastic recovery from fatigue, but he appeared susceptible to respiratory ailments; he was, in the modern phrase, "allergic" to alcohol, and during Washington summers suffered from malaria.

This inner conflict was further aggravated by certain environmental influence. He spent most of his life in New England, a region where religion was a prominent element in shaping behavior. But neither his parents nor their particular social group in his native Hillsboro were notably pious. Not until he went to Bowdoin College did he observe the obvious piety of the cultured New Englander and awake to the fact that he was lacking in a religious experience. So many others professed a sense of regenerating grace, but to him it came not. As he climbed up the ladder and when he married into the dignified ranks of the Puritan hierarchy, he appears to have had an increasing sense of not belonging. He was different, not of the elect.

His marriage further complicated and confused his existence. Pierce, a young frontier Democrat, married a daughter of a well-established New England family, closely connected with ecclesiastical and educational leadership, with the lords of the loom and the merchants of State Street. Her family were of the New England aristocracy of mind, mart and pulpit. She had a select group of impressive relatives to whom she was attached by deep ties of affection. It was all so obvious that these people moved in a different orbit than that of the Pierces. Their very lives emphasized the difference of background of the two young people. The emotional effect of adjusting to his wife's relatives added to the intricacies of his problem of existence.

His preoccupation with politics likewise contributed to his domestic infelicity. He had been born to politics. He had entered it early and his rise had been quick and easy. His ambition grew with his success and he naturally acquired faith in his capacity to advance. He gloried in the sociability of politics and in the sense of status gained by almost continuous office holding. But political activities were convivial and consuming of time and substance without much material recompense. His wife and children must be thought of. She was an invalid and they must live expensively. She resented the alcoholic temptations to which politics subjected him. She took no satisfaction in his success and it is probable that with her Whig background she was ashamed of his Democratic associations. So at the age of thirty-eight, he decided that he must lay aside his ambitions, a devastating experience.

The summary disposition of his political prospects led him for a time to secure some relief from tension. He and Jeanie sought to live for their children, a desire which became more intense after the loss of two boys. Their absorption in the life of little Bennie, their sole remaining child, became excessive. Mrs. Pierce lived for the boy rather than for her husband. As she was too frail to keep house, she had plenty of time to brood, to indulge in self-pity, to make long visits with her relatives away from her husband. Then when they were together, she was often melancholy and querulous. They loved each other deeply, but they were constantly and mutually irritating. He developed an unusual self-control and capacity for expressive tenderness which she seems not to have been able to return. In the meantime, they could forget much in their consuming affection for their boy, even presumably accepting a sort of fiction that Pierce was going to serve in the Mexican War and yield to the draft for the Presidency solely because it would make Bennie proud of his father and give the boy such a wonderful advantage in life.

For many years this inner conflict was not too devastating.

Pierce was able, in large things, almost uniformly to command success. His political career was a phenomenal, almost Horatio Alger story of from log cabin to White House. He was never defeated for office. In New Hampshire politics his leadership was decisive and effective. President Polk sought to include him in his cabinet. At length he completed the long rise from state legislator to President of the United States. At the age of forty-eight, he was elected the youngest chief magistrate of the Republic.

Then came the demoralizing tragedy of that dark winter of 1853. Not only was there Bennie's horrible death, but Mrs. Pierce was led to believe that her husband had sought the Presidency while maintaining to her that he was doing everything he could to avoid it. In two short months, she had lost her boy and her faith in her husband's integrity. Hereafter, she could look accusingly at him; his presidential ambitions were the cause of the boy's death.

Whatever else the White House was to be for the new President, it could never be a home. Mrs. Pierce chose her own apartments and retired to them. She never recovered from these shocks, complicated as they were probably by phases of her menopause. Her relations with her husband were thereafter painfully altered. In these two months he can be said to have lost his son, his wife, and his capacity to command success. He entered the Presidency with all his latent sense of insecurity exposed, sin-conscious, nervously shocked and conditioned to a hitherto unexperienced sense of inadequacy.

There is no method of demonstrating a "might have been," but it should be noted that prior to 1853 he had succeeded reasonably well in meeting, at least adequately, the demands made upon him by public life. Had he entered the White House with the confidence which his great victory should have supplied, and been able to live a happy, normal family life, with his nervous system unshaken and, as hitherto, resilient, it may at least be wondered whether he might not have risen to the challenge of the Presidency. He was only forty-eight, in the prime of life, enjoying a zenith which should have still afforded much capacity for further development and maturing of power.

As it was, Pierce entered upon his duties deprived of the capacity for leadership which upon occasion he had hitherto exercised. So he set about to carry out his duties not as a leader but as a group associate. He must share and delegate, in reality abdicate, his executive function to a group. His native friendliness and his new sense of sorrow and inadequacy demanded a circle of sympathetic intimates who would uphold him and relieve his sense of loneliness. Fumblingly, and in confusion, he chose such a group as his cabinet with the aid of his New England cronies, Mexican War associates and certain other political acquaintances of earlier days. His old Mexican War chief, ex-Secretary of War Marcy, became his premier. He included two of his military associates, Davis and Cushing, and Dobbin, the man who had turned the tide in his favor at Baltimore. The three others represented Buchanan and Cass, his principal rivals, and, by one construction at least, the old Jackson-Van Buren-Benton-Blair interest, in the persons of Campbell, McClelland and Guthrie. He depended upon them and his very young and inexperienced friend, Sidney Webster, who was to be his private secretary. He bound them to him by his charm and his obvious need for sympathy.

Unfortunately, they were poor choices for strength, wisdom, and political advice. Campbell, Dobbin, Guthrie and McClelland were men of purely local political experience. And the other three, despite their greater experience, had serious handicaps as advisers. Marcy was old, and plagued by a badly demoralized local constituency, the shattered New York Democracy. Davis was a peculiarly imperceptive military martinet who loved his chief, but was too engrossed in his West Point ideas, the demands of his young wife and his growing family and his nervous illnesses. He was already indicating that capacity for political failure which was to be so amply demonstrated by him when he became President of the Confederacy. Caleb Cushing was a maverick of no stable principles, with a perverted instinct for seeking the winning side, who could change horses at will. He was a learned genius with a minimum of judgment and stabilizing sense who was capable of frightful labor and who was possessed of a terrifying knowledge of law and other learning. He was a poor business man and constantly in debt while in the cabinet. But he was so impressive to Pierce that the latter never seems to have suspected how bad his judgment was. Finally, his secretary, Sidney Webster, did not have the experience or the wisdom necessary to fill his most exacting post and failed to develop the qualities most necessary to enable a private secretary to protect a harassed executive. Neither in meeting the public nor in comporting himself with the importunate and the influence-peddlers does he seem to have developed the most helpful skill.

None of these men was really in a position to give sound or perceptive advice. None of them had much political know-how, except perhaps Marcy, and his constituency was in such revolt as to deprive him of any real confidence in his capacity to control political forces. Besides, Pierce did little to make their administrative task easier. He was so eager for appreciation and comforting good will in the midst of his tragedy that he developed little capacity to defend himself from importunity. And importunity was everywhere. As a Democrat succeeding a Whig he had a vast mass of patronage to dispose of, and then there were projects of all sorts for contracts and administrative favors. The White House was the scene of constant importunate visitation.

In normal times Pierce found it easier to say "yes" than "no," but now in his new bewilderment, his confusion was much greater. He felt so much the need for human sympathy that he seemingly could not bear to make people hostile by refusal. So he took refuge in a cordial indefiniteness that was frequently interpreted as an affirmative. When his decision finally was made in the negative, he was accused of lying and hated as a deceiver. Nor did his cabinet appreciate his easy willingness to agree to review their administrative decisions when those refused complained to him. Nevertheless, despite, or perhaps because of, this trying and tragic volatility, these cabinet ministers were drawn instinctively to their charming and distraught chief. He on his part abdicated his responsibility, even his individuality to them, his new creation, "his" administration. To this group he surrendered any capacity for leadership he once had and functioned merely as a member of an executive committee, not as a chief executive.

As this group had no leader, it could exercise no more leadership than a political cabal can. Whether or not they recognized their situation, they did the only thing which a leaderless group can, they adopted a set of rules based upon such a group of prin-

ciples as they could agree upon. As they were men of different
minds, representing different sections, and, in some cases, opposing concepts, they could agree only on something of a negative
compromise rather than a positive plan for aggressive action.
They looked to that which had been tried in the past and denied
innovation.

Pierce and his counsellors thought in terms of Jackson and
Polk. They were honest, consistent, *laissez-faire* Democrats who
made no concessions to the importunate. At the same time, they
rewarded all factions in the distribution of patronage, treated all
alike, forgot past factionalism, even the schism of '48, and accepted all as regulars, worthy of patronage who acknowledged
and supported them. Such a program to their minds was so
rational and so Democratic that they stuck to it with ever increasing consistency. This consistency was their faith and their
refuge, their refuge against their insecurity and their consciousness of their lack of status. For none of the real leaders of the
party were among them and they seemed instinctively to recognize their individual lack of prestige. The real leadership, such
as it was, was in Congress, as was clearly demonstrated when the
Administration was, in effect, forced to sponsor the Kansas-
Nebraska bill by the pressure of the Senate leaders.

The efforts of these men to establish their reputation and to
secure Pierce's re-election by affirmative policy were concentrated in the field of foreign policy. Here they sought to protect the rights of United States citizens, extend national interests and defy Great Britain. Polk's success in this field, the
manner of the acquisition of Texas and the Mexican War experience were all deeply engraved on their mental tablets. But here
again their leaderless structure was so apparent. Pierce had at
his table the conservative Marcy, the somewhat heedless Cushing,
and the radical Davis. Marcy wrote the instructions which were
generally sound and within the structure of effective diplomatic
argument, but Pierce, Cushing and Davis had a hankering for
dashing and bizarre diplomats. Never was such a crew recruited in any one administration as Borland, DeLeon, O'Sullivan, Sanders, Sickles and Soulé. They were all attractive and
even charming, especially Soulé, who was several times a guest
at the White House, and the perceptive Mrs. Means recorded a
prediction that Pierce would regret his appointment. This

need so strongly felt to satisfy all shades of opinion together
with the confused world situation meant that in foreign as in
domestic policy their efforts were vain. Never once did their
policies, pay off. Some of the quixotic episodes like the Ostend
Manifesto made their enemies even more virulent and added to
the growing belief, even among their friends, of their incapacity.

In sum, these eight men formed a most unusual group made
congenial, in part at least, by their corporate misfortunes and
by the growing realization that no one of them, save Davis, had
any identity or future, once he left the circle. Consequently,
they became one of the most compact and smoothly operating
small groups which American politics has ever known and the
only presidential cabinet to remain intact for four years. They
achieved this distinction despite the fact that never once during
their service, when there was a possibility of making capital out
of political perceptiveness, were they able to do it, never once
did they develop the capacity to placate a formidable enemy or
to make a significant friend.

The difficulties of their situation should not be measured
merely by their individual or corporate handicaps. Their difficulties were also due to general situations then conditioning the
American scene. Several unusual and disturbing developments
were confusing politics and the public attitudes which influenced
them. During their term of office the nation experienced outbreaks of two violent emotions. Two of the strongest prejudices
which have been operative during the nation's history have been
the antipathies which so many have held against foreigners and
slaveowners. The influx of foreign immigration, growing industrialization, and the western pressure of settlement caused a revival of anti-foreign, anti-Catholic, and anti-Southern prejudices
in the 1850's. The Kansas-Nebraska Act and the organization of
Bleeding Kansas added fuel to these always smouldering embers.
Under such circumstances, the Administration position was
made doubly difficult by the presence in the Cabinet of James
Campbell, a Catholic, and Jefferson Davis, Southern Rights defender and Calhoun's heir.

Less obvious as a confusing element was an intense power
struggle going on behind the political scenes, a struggle for control of the law-making, money appropriating and administrative
functions of the federal government. Hundreds of schemes were

pushed forward for some sort of federal aid by steamship, railroad, real estate, manufacturing, internal improvement, banking, and other speculative interests. Generously financed lobbies were hard at work for tariffs, subsidies, contracts, patent extension projects in myriad forms. Washington was a community of importunity. Pressure was everywhere, often subtle and insidious, frequently dominated by men of large capacity for affairs. In the midst of this stood the President, a small-town country lawyer who did not even manage his own small capital but turned it over to his law partner.

He and his advisers had seemingly done everything to alienate the "business interests." Cushing, himself improvident and in debt, often construed the law strictly and against their promotion schemes. Campbell was strict with the postal contractors, refusing service where it did not pay. McClelland did his best to thwart speculators. Guthrie, himself a man of affairs and a vigorous speculator, was determined to have things managed his way and to use his power. He enforced regulations to the dismay of fellow operators. He applied the Independent Treasury Act literally and kept government money out of the hands of bankers. He antagonized the expansive banker and speculator, Corcoran. He deprived the collectors of the customs of their lucrative fees, allowing them only their salaries, and thus deprived his party of potential "sinews of war." Marcy eventually refused Vanderbilt the aid he required and joined with Cushing in quenching filibustering backed by speculative interests. This administration in sum would know no fear nor favor. They maintained the most granite-like opposition to grants, subsidies and higher tariffs. They reached a low point in political imperceptiveness when they combined to write a veto message killing a philanthropic project promoted tirelessly by Miss Dorothea L. Dix to provide for the care of the indigent insane, and thereby brought the wrath of thousands of women down upon their heads. These attitudes raised up for Pierce and his colleagues an implacable series of enemies, many of whom would not express themselves openly but would stimulate and subsidize others to do so in ways not always to be identified.

This opposition was in part responsible for the fact that Pierce had such a bad press. Not the least of the President's many misfortunes was the fact that so many skilled journalistic pens were leveled at him, some of them subsidized by bitterly hostile interests roused by his refusal to advance their projects and by his thwarting of their schemes. Most disastrous was the fact that he had offended James Gordon Bennett of the powerful *New York Herald* and thereafter he was written down as "poor pierce" for multitudes to see. The great Horace Greeley of New York's *Tribune* was likewise on the constant offensive against these "tools of the slave power" and his words were read by thousands daily and tens of thousands weekly.

Against these journalists and the many others who echoed them, the Administration had no distinguished press upon which to call. Their so-called organ, the *Washington Union*, met no greater success than much else that they did, despite the political experience of Senator Nicholson, the immense erudition of the ever-writing Cushing, and the dynamic enterprise of Forney, who by amazing imperceptiveness, was kept on even while supporting Buchanan's rising fortunes. It was these opposition journalists, the disgruntled Democratic editors and the rising Republican scribblers, on occasion backed by certain inconspicuous men of wealth and schemes, who made inevitable the stereotype which was to be cast of Pierce.

And he and his associates had so little skill themselves, nor could they command more to break the mould into which the President was being cast. His state papers, in which they all had a hand in the main, read well now, even though somewhat turgid, but there was little interest in them then. They were not in the spirit of the times. Close study of these efforts to be strictly constitutional, impartial and patriotic can arouse much sympathy today, but, at that time of romantic impulse, logic and impartiality were not appreciated; rather, they were disdained. The public of that day could only understand irrational and emotional appeals.

Basic to all Pierce's political difficulties was a great social and political transformation which few, if any, of his contemporaries understood in all its ramifications. The American estate was so vast and the population so sparse that people were very mobile and institutions highly flexible. One great movement of population was reaching out into the unoccupied West, another was directing an influx into the growing cities and factory towns of the East. Westward expansion, industrialization and urbanization were all working toward the creation of new communities, states and political constituencies. This activity was not taking place with uniform momentum. There was much less of it in the slave labor region. There was, consequently, a very decided difference in activity and enterprise in the slave and free labor sections. In the one, there tended to be stability and lack of interest in things new, in the other, feverish enterprise and restless imagination.

Those managing the federal government were increasingly conscious of the fact that this expanding society contained two elements operating at different speeds and with increasingly conflicting objectives. As new communities were formed and new states sought admission, questions of political power and control became more divisive and more difficult to deal with. When Pierce came into office, Southern and Northern interests were in temporary, uneasy equilibrium but the map and the census predicted that it would be short-lived. New states were in the making, and the physiography of the regions in which the new communities were springing up seemed to dictate that most, perhaps even all of them, would be free labor in their character. Each new state would diminish the influence of the South in Congress and in party conventions. Southern politicos were used to dominance in Washington and now there seemed handwriting on the wall.

All sorts and kinds of individuals and interests which had been thwarted by Southern defensive *laissez-faire* negativism were eager to take advantage of any opportunity to cooperate in forming a political combination strong enough to overthrow the Southern control. The Democratic party was accepted as the Southern instrument and Pierce and his associates were more and more written down as dough faces, abject servants of the lords of the lash. That they were men of high principle, upholding a time-honored constitutional interpretation created by the Founding Fathers to promote the stability of the Republic, mattered not a wit. They were pilloried as tools and lickspittles.

Finally, the calendar was contributing to Pierce's difficulties, for it was dictating a change in the course of American politics. The well-known parties, Democratic and Whig, had been fighting each other for twenty years, the life of a generation. Time was inexorably prescribing a change in leadership. The older generation of statesmen, Calhoun, Clay, and Webster, had passed from the scene. Benton was in eclipse. Democracy is periodically chary about using its best men and, particularly in these periods of transition, uses them sparingly. As yet, a younger group had not reached sufficient stature to take over, certainly not Pierce and his cabinet. It was Pierce's misfortune to be elected to the chief-magistracy at a moment when probably no one was prepared for it or when no one could have occupied it successfully.

Today, it is difficult to discover any formula of success which Pierce and his associates might have created and applied. We can only attempt to understand better what they did. In the field of domestic policy, their most spectacular act which brought upon their heads such great condemnation was the endorsement of the Kansas-Nebraska bill. Their motives for this can now be much better comprehended. This endorsement was the price they had to pay for the legislative cooperation which they believed indispensable. Without this support, they could not have carried on politically and for it they had to pay. But when we come to the almost unbelievable stupidity of permitting Young America to play such a role in their foreign policy, it is more difficult to find even an explanation. The nation's experience in Texas and in the Mexican War and the current bitter hatred of Great Britain must share the responsibility. Yet the consistent failure of their efforts, the diplomatic chaos resulting from negotiations with Spain and action in Central America, the fatuous negotiation with and repudiation of filibusters, and the prostitution of diplomatic relations with Mexico in the interest of steamboat and railroad men, all this never opened the eyes of this administration to the incongruity of Marcy and Young America both trying to direct foreign policy. Never for a moment did even the more sophisticated Marcy seem to realize what fools and knaves he and his diplomats appeared to Europeans to be. Basically it was all part of the crazy romanticism of the decade, the naiveté which conditioned the folly and absence of any approximation of realism which did so much to bring on the strife of 1861–1865.

One course perhaps might have been open to Pierce. He might have tried to make a fight against the southern Congressional leadership, by dismissing Davis and attempting to rally the northern cohorts of his party. But we can believe now that his capacity for leadership had been so impaired that he was too emotionally dependent to take such independent action. Furthermore, had he tried it he probably would have found himself, like Tyler, without a party. It is difficult to believe that the newly organizing northern politicos would have accepted him as leader in their first campaign. What he could do in New Hampshire, before the tragedy, backed by a strongly unified Concord Regency, he could not do in Washington, himself so unstrung and with an Administration representing such diverse interests.

Pierce, in fact, was caught in a great political reorganization which he did not understand. He and his associates saw wicked men undermining the virtues of the forefathers; they must protect their values. They did not perceive the necessity for new concepts nor for a more complex series of values. Rather he and his associates resented the contempt of those who charged them with weakness and failure, and this resentment strengthened them in their stubborn course. But they were really trying to hold back the tide. Had Pierce not been demoralized by the disasters of the winter of 1853, it is just possible that his political instincts, already well developed, might have matured under challenge sufficiently to carry him through. Certainly he was young enough to be capable of further development. But his misfortunes prevented any achievement of greater political perceptiveness and skill. He was left inflexible and incapable of growth. As Hawthorne diagnosed the situation, "It would ruin [this] noble character (though one of limited scope) for him to admit any ideas that were not entertained by the fathers of the Constitution and the Republic." * This steadfastness and integrity in behaving within his limitations Hawthorne thought wholly admirable, even sacred, but it was little aid in assisting Pierce to become a statesman.

The 1850's unfortunately did not demand steadfastness and integrity; they encouraged daring and ruthlessness. The obvious rewards of enterprise were so tempting politically that the standards of truth and consistent intellectual and moral integrity fell before the surge of ambition and power mania. The structure of the nation collapsed with it and the building could only

* *New York Times*, April 28, 1887, p. 10.

be re-erected after a blood purge had drawn the fever from political emotions.

Pierce's greatest misfortune was that, disorganized and numbed by personal tragedy, he seemed to understand little of the forces outside himself which were combining with his inward insecurity to make him one of democracy's most unfortunate victims. It is only his due that the stereotype created in his lifetime be replaced by a more realistic portrait. Reconsideration of his complex life experience reveals not mere weakness, but a difficult combination of inner conflict, tragedy and national confusion which prevented him from meeting the challenge of his great responsibility.

NOTES

Chapter I, pp. 3–6

1. This characteristic autobiography of the somewhat illiterate old gentleman is among the papers of Albert Baker in the possession of Mrs. Mary Beecher Longyear, who through the kindness of Miss Louise Guyol graciously permitted me to use them.

2. Franklin Pierce's grandfather, Benjamin Pierce (d. 1764), was of the fourth generation descended from Thomas Pierce who had migrated to Charlestown, Mass., in 1634–1635. Thomas Pierce's grandson Stephen had moved to Chelmsford (now Lowell), Mass., about the end of the 17th century. Of English stock, the Pierces had married into families of similar origin such as Cole, Parker, Fletcher, and Merrill. Pierce, *Pierce Genealogy (Descendants of Thomas Pierce); Farmers' Monthly Visitor*, I, 49, XII, 194.

3. He was promoted to the rank of ensign as a result of bravery in rescuing the regimental standard at the Battle of Bemis Heights, Oct. 17, 1777. *Ibid.*, 194–195; pension application of B. Pierce, dated Sept. 8, 1819, N. H. Hist. Soc.

4. He was taken prisoner by the British and held at New York during this period. Before his exchange he was insulted by a British officer, whom he later met after the surrender of New York, fought and grievously wounded. *Farmers' Monthly Visitor*, XII, 195.

5. Col. Samson Stoddard of Chelmsford had extensive lands in New Hampshire and Vermont. One of his tracts was situated between the Contoocook and Connecticut Rivers in Cheshire Co., N. H. *Ibid.*, 196.

6. On May 24, 1787, Pierce married Elizabeth Andrews (1768–1788, Aug. 13), daughter of one of the leaders in the frontier community. By her he had one child, Elizabeth, at whose birth she died. Feb. 1, 1790, he married Anna Kendrick (1768–1838, Dec. 10), daughter of Benj. Kendrick, a local magnate in Amherst, N. H., the county seat. They had eight children: Benjamin Kendrick, Aug. 29, 1790; Nancy, Nov. 2, 1792; John Sullivan, Nov. 5, 1796; Harriet B., 1800; Charles Grandison, 1803; Franklin, Nov. 23, 1804; Charlotte, died in infancy; Henry Dearborn, Sept. 19, 1812; *Pierce Genealogy*.

7. Appointed Brigadier General, June 14, 1805, as soon as the first Republican governor assumed office. *Visitor*, 196.

8. Benjamin Pierce to Col. Hunt, undated, N. H. Hist. Soc.

9. Autobiography.

547

Chapter II, pp. 9–13

The sources for Pierce's childhood are not very numerous. In the eighties John M. Irelan, who was writing a series of Presidential "lives," went to Hillsborough and collected a number of reminiscences and local traditions which he embodied in his *The Republic: Life and Times of Franklin Pierce*. Much later Mary H. Northend did the same thing and incorporated her results in two books—*Historic Homes of New England* and *We Visit Old Inns*. Hawthorne and other campaign biographers supplied a few details. The letter of Fanny Currier to Pierce alluded to in this chapter was written September 23, 1852, and is in the N. H. Hist. Soc. In 1841 Charles James Smith, one of Pierce's law students, published the *Annals of the Town of Hillsborough*. Later works are Hamilton Hurd, *History of Hillsborough County*, and George W. Browne, *History of Hillsborough, N. H., 1735–1921*. His schooldays in Francestown are described in Cochrane and Wood, *History of Francestown, N. H.*, and reference to his schooling in Hancock is found in Hayward, *History of Hancock, N. H.* Thirty years later, Pierce in a public speech alluded appreciatively to his life at Mrs. Woodbury's in Francestown. *Patriot*, May 15, 1851.

Pierce described his mother in a letter to McNeil, Dec. 14, 1838, which, together with a number of interesting letters written home by his brothers in the War of 1812, are in the N. H. Hist. Soc. The Baltimore *Sun*, Jan. 9, 1855, contains a speech he made while President, referring to his boyhood experiences in the War of 1812. A few details are found in Secomb's *History of Amherst, N. H.*

Chapter III, pp. 14–27

The fact that both Longfellow and Hawthorne were students at Bowdoin during most of Pierce's collegiate experience has made the material in regard to the general college environment plentiful. All the biographies of these two men give descriptions, the most notable for the purpose of this biography being Horatio Bridge, *Reminiscences of Hawthorne*. and Samuel Longfellow, *Life of Henry W. Longfellow*. The detailed *History of Bowdoin College* begun by Nehemiah Cleaveland and completed by Alpheus S. Packard, Pierce's brother-in-law, has considerable valuable material. Other items of interest are the historical sketch by George P. Little in the *Bowdoin General Catalogue of 1894*; Hatch, *History of Bowdoin College*; John Clair Minot, *Under the Bowdoin Pines*; Hawthorne's *Fanshawe* and his preface to the *Snow Image*. A book that should have contributed more than it did is Hawthorne's *Life of Franklin Pierce*. Stephen M. Vail's *Life in Earnest; or, Memoirs and Remains of Rev. Zenas A. Caldwell, A.B.*, contains an account of the friendship of Caldwell and Pierce which has a very valuable supplement in a frank account which Pierce himself wrote in response to a request from Sprague, editor of the *Annals of the American Pulpit*; this, however, was not used for that purpose and still remains in manuscript in the hands of the Pierce family. The N. H. Hist. Soc. has a few letters written during his college life, two from his father, Oct. 19, 1820,

June 5, 1823, a draft of a letter in answer to the latter, one written to Col. McNeil, Jan. 10, 1823, and another to his father, July 22, 1824, and an interesting letter of reminiscences written by his classmate, Wm. H. Codman, after his nomination to the Presidency, June 14, 1852.

The Bowdoin sources have been well preserved. The broadside catalogues published annually 1820–1824 and the commencement programs are preserved in complete files. The *Laws of Bowdoin* were published in a number of editions, that of 1824 being used for this purpose. President Allen published his addresses to the students in *A Decade of Addresses*. References to the fire in Maine Hall and Pierce's commencement are found in the New Hampshire *Patriot* of March 18, 1822, and September 6 and 13, 1824, and the Hallowell (Me.) *Advocate*, Sept. 4, 1824. The manuscript records of the Faculty of Bowdoin have been preserved, and I am very much indebted to Dr. Gerald G. Wilder, Librarian of Bowdoin, for searching them for Pierce items as well as for his criticism of the foregoing chapter.

CHAPTERS IV–VI, PP. 28–59

These chapters are based on a large file of letters which Pierce wrote at short intervals during these years to his sister Elizabeth and her husband John McNeil. This file, deposited in the N. H. Hist. Soc., begins in 1824 and continues with satisfying regularity for more than twenty years. Pierce was very fond of his sister and her husband, and his correspondence with them was spontaneous; few correspondence files more valuable for biographical purposes could be found.

The details of political activity are filled out from the newspaper files of the period, collected very completely by the N. H. Hist. Soc. Of most value are the *N. H. Patriot,* which Isaac Hill edited, and the *Amherst Cabinet.* See also Robinson, *Jeffersonian Democracy in New England,* and Edwin D. Sanborn, *History of New Hampshire,* Frank B. Sanborn, *New Hampshire* (American Commonwealth Series), and Everett S. Stackpole, *History of New Hampshire,* for background.

For legislative history the press is the most important source, supplemented by the *Journal of the House of Representatives of the State of New Hampshire* for the June sessions, 1829–1832, and the December session of the latter year and the *Laws of the State of New Hampshire* passed during these sessions. *The History of Concord,* edited by James O. Lyford, Bradley, *Biography of Isaac Hill,* Robinson, *Jeffersonian Democracy in New England,* Darling, *Political Changes in Massachusetts, 1824–1848,* and *From the Diary and Correspondence of Benjamin Brown French,* edited by Amos Tuck French, have some interesting items, and the Plumer MSS. in the N. H. Hist. Soc. contain scattered references. The Pierce family have a few valuable papers for this period including even the bills for his legislative expenses.

CHAPTERS VII–XIV, PP. 63–111

Biographically the most valuable sources for the period of Pierce's congressional experiences are his letters written to the McNeils previously referred to and two series written to his partner, Asa Fowler, and to Albert Baker. I am indebted to the American Council of Learned Societies for a grant in aid which enabled me to have photostats made of the Fowler MSS. Three other groups of manuscripts from this period are also valuable. The Lawrence papers deposited at the Mass. Hist. Soc. consist of a large and complete collection of the letters to and from, and the diaries of, Amos Lawrence and his sons; there are numerous letters to and from the Pierces in these papers. The second group consists of typewritten copies of letters written by Benjamin B. French from Washington to his relatives in New Hampshire and their replies; these are deposited in the Library of Congress. The third group are the letters which John Fairfield of Maine wrote to his wife from Washington; as Fairfield was part of the time a messmate of Pierce's he made a number of interesting allusions to him although they do not seem to have been very friendly; these letters are in the Library of Congress, and extracts from them have been published in book form, Staples, *Letters of John Fairfield*.

An interesting contemporary collection is the manuscript diary and letters of Benjamin Tappan, Senator from Ohio. This collection, while having practically nothing directly bearing on Pierce, supplies interesting atmosphere. I am greatly indebted to Dr. John K. Wright for the use of these papers.

The official sources for Pierce's congressional career are the files of the *Congressional Globe*, 23d–27th Congresses and the congressional documents. Pierce made twenty-three speeches reported at any length. The most important of these are on the subject of slavery and were delivered on Dec. 18, 1835 (*Globe*, 24: 1, 33), Feb. 15, 1836 (*Globe*, 24: 1, 165–167), Dec. 18, 1837 (*Globe*, 25: 2, 37), Jan. 9, 1838 (*Globe*, 24: 1, App. 54–55), Feb. 21, 1839 (*Globe*, 25: 3, 208); the Pinckney report is in *Repts. of Coms. No. 691*, 24: 1 (Ser. 295). His speeches on military affairs were delivered June 30, 1836 (*Globe*, 24: 1, 600–602), on West Point, July 4, 1838 (*Globe*, 25: 2, App. 488–491), Jan. 9, 1840 (*Globe*, 26: 1, 109), July 14, 1840 (*Globe*, 26: 1, 524–525). Incidental remarks of interest are found on July 28, 1841 (*Globe*, 27: 1, 258), Dec. 21, 1841 (*Globe*, 27: 2, 40). His pension speeches were delivered Feb. 27, 1834 (*Globe*, 23: 1, 206–208), Dec. 18, 1838 (*Globe*, 25: 3, 45), March 4, 1840 (*Globe*, 26: 1, 233–235), May 1, 1840 (*Globe*, 26: 1, App. 465), July 29, 1841 (*Globe*, 27: 1, 263). He made but three speeches on financial matters, April 28, 1836, June 5, 1840, and July 26, 1841. After the Whigs obtained control he made three attacks upon them, June 25, June 30, 1841, and Feb. 14, 1842. His one speech for home consumption was given Jan. 28, 1841 (*Globe*, 26: 2, App. 192–193). The two reports with which he had most to do besides the Pinckney report were the West Point Report, *Repts. of Coms. No. 303*, 24: 2 (Ser. 306), and the Reuben M. Whitney Report, *Repts. of Coms. No. 193*, 24: 2 (Ser. 307).

CHAPTERS XV–XIX, PP. 115–144

The manuscript sources for this period, 1842–1847, are more limited than for previous chapters. The letters to the McNeils are much fewer as a good part of the time they lived in New Hampshire. Pierce's correspondence with Edmund Burke found in his MSS. is important, and it is at this point that the Pierce papers in the Library of Congress begin. Scattering items are found in the Jackson and Polk papers in the same repository. In the N. H. Hist. Soc. besides the McNeil correspondence there are the papers of John P. Hale. Even more important than manuscripts is the local press of the period, especially the two *Patriots,* the *Statesman* (Whig) and the *Herald of Freedom,* all published in Concord.˙ For Concord days and ways see Bouton, *History of Concord;* Rolfe, *Reminiscences of Concord;* Cook, *Wayside Jottings; Saunterings about Concord;* McFarland, *Personal Recollections.* Most valuable of all for the Concord background is that most excellent of local histories edited by James O. Lyford, *History of Concord, N. H.*

The interesting railroad history of the state has never been written. Items of particular concern on this subject are found in the *Patriot,* April 29, May 20, June 3, July 8, 15, 22, 1839, Jan. 13, 27, Mar. 30, June 8, 22, 29, 1840, Jan. 1, 8, July 2, 9, Aug. 26, Dec. 9, 23, 1841. Acts of incorporation of New Hampshire railroads (Concord R. R., Keene R. R., Boston and Maine R. R., Nashua and Lowell R. R.) are found in the *Laws of the State of New Hampshire* passed June Session 1835 (ch. 1, 7, 14, 37 of the private acts). General railroad laws are found in *ibid.* passed June Session 1836, ch. 237 of the public acts (act of June 16, 1836); *ibid.,* passed November Session 1836, ch. 280 of the public acts (act of Jan. 13, 1837). The famous act of June 20, 1840 (ch. 498 public acts passed June, 1840), repealed the two last-mentioned acts as well as the act of Jan. 14, 1837 (ch. 100 private acts passed Nov. Session 1836), and was supplemented by the act of Dec. 23, 1840 (ch. 563 public acts of Nov. Session 1840). The railroad question was finally settled by the act of Dec. 25, 1844 (ch. 128 public acts passed Nov. Session 1844), which gave the railroads the right to take land under the " sanction and the assessments " of a board of railroad commissioners which was created by the act. See also Lyford, *History of Concord,* II, 866–904.

The temperance situation and the free-soil agitation are best described in Lyford. The latter movement is discussed from the point of view of the free soilers in John L. Hayes, *Reminiscence of the Free-Soil Movement in New Hampshire in 1845.* For Hale's career see Chandler, *Statue of John P. Hale,* and the John P. Hale MSS.

Chapters XX–XXII, pp. 147–168

Pierce's war experiences are set forth at length in his diary and in his letters to his family and friends. His diary, now at the Huntington Library, was published in part by Hawthorne in his *Life;* however he omitted important parts and also sought to improve upon his friend's English; a photostat of the diary is in the Library of Congress. His letters are found in the three collections of his papers, in the George MSS. in the N. H. Hist. Soc., and in the Burke and Polk MSS. in the L. of C. Several of them are printed by Irelan and some found their way into the press. Polk's *Diary* and the Washington *Union, National Intelligencer* and Boston *Post,* as well as the local press, furnish items, as does his testimony before the Pillow court martial, *Sen. Doc. No. 65*, 30: 1 (ser. 510). The setting of his service is best found in Smith's *War with Mexico*. Through the kindness of Col. John W. Geary, I had access to his father's unpublished journal kept during the war; and Prof. Milledge L. Bonham graciously permitted me to read that portion of his biography of his grandfather, one of Pierce's associates, which deals with the period.

CHAPTERS XXIII–XXIV, PP. 171–186

The sources for this period of Pierce's life are the most unsatisfactory. The McNeil correspondence is closed, the general died in 1850 and his wife no longer kept her brother's letters. Burke was back in New Hampshire and his relations with Pierce were no longer so cordial. Of increasing importance are the papers of John H. George.

Pierce's career as a lawyer is best characterized by David Cross in a speech which he delivered before the New Hampshire Bar Association, March 15, 1900, "Franklin Pierce the Lawyer." This speech was printed separately and as an appendix to the proceedings of the *Dedication of a Statue of General Franklin Pierce*, etc., edited by Henry H. Metcalf. Other speeches in the latter volume and some items in Lyford's *Concord* are interesting in this regard, as are the *Reminiscences of Hon. William L. Foster*.

Through the courtesy of Hon. Gist Blair I was permitted access to the Levi Woodbury papers in his possession.

CHAPTERS XXV–XXVII, PP. 189–215

When John P. George of Concord, N. H., died in 1925, Maj. Otis G. Hammond, Director of the New Hampshire Historical Society, discovered in his attic, boxed up and forgotten, not only the political correspondence of his father, John H. George, containing numerous letters from Pierce, but also the bulk of the letters received by Pierce during the campaign of 1852. This large body of manuscript, over 2,000 letters, was transferred to the New Hampshire Historical Society and forms the main source for these chapters. An account written previous to this discovery, which goes into the details of the pre-convention campaign and discusses the action of the convention much more fully, is Nichols, *The Democratic Machine, 1850–1854*; it contains an extended bibliography. The George letters and the campaign correspondence have been photostated and the photostats are in the Library of Congress.

A number of biographies appeared during the campaign. Hawthorne's work was not ready until mid-September and in the meantime others had been busy. C. Edwards Lester, a newspaper correspondent, published the one referred to in this chapter. Charles G. Greene published another which he had written for his paper, the Boston *Post*, and his work, somewhat revised by George and Webster, was sent on to Peaslee, who had it printed as the official pamphlet life to be distributed by the National Committee. Benjamin B. French prepared a biography for which Sidney Webster drew a portrait, and the biography was published as the second number of *Papers for the People*. Pierce's friend, Col. Seymour, then governor of

Connecticut, sent to Concord a newspaper man, D. W. Bartlett, and Pierce had quite a conversation with him in which he related a number of anecdotes of his past life. Bartlett thereupon wrote a " life " running into three hundred printed pages. This pretentious work, bound in cloth and in paper, was published about Aug. 25, some weeks before Hawthorne's book appeared. Pierce resented the publication of Bartlett's work, especially as it was advertised as " authorized," and he had some warm correspondence with Bartlett as a result. Thousands of copies of it were purchased and we may presume it hurt the sale of Hawthorne's delayed volume.

Besides biographies, the campaign produced much printed matter. The central propaganda agency was the National Democratic Executive Committee located in Washington and largely operated by Peaslee and John W. Forney. The committee began their distribution in July and circulated at least sixteen varieties of pamphlets. Charles G. Greene of the Boston *Post* was active in preparing them and the New York *Evening Post* published at least ten documents. Prior to the convention a group of " Young America " Democrats in New York City formed a " Jeffersonian Union," presumably to aid Marcy's chances; and they began to publish. After the convention they continued throughout the campaign and printed at least eighteen numbers of " Papers for the People." The pamphlets from these various sources specialized in vindicating Pierce's character and pointing out Scott's weaknesses; they were almost entirely personal in their character, and the Whig pamphlets, seemingly much fewer in number, were written in a similar vein.

GENERAL NOTE ON THE SOURCES FOR 1853–1857

The sources for the Pierce administration are disappointing from a biographical standpoint. Pierce seemingly destroyed his papers for those four years, carefully saving a few odd pieces such as some letters from Geary in the matter of Kansas, some vouchers for the expenditures of I. D. Andrews in promoting Canadian enthusiasm for the reciprocity treaty, and a few miscellaneous items noted in the calendar of the Pierce MSS. in the Library of Congress; these papers include most of his rough message drafts. The New Hampshire Historical Society has his letters to George and those from Sidney Webster to the same person, items provokingly few, together with some miscellaneous papers. The family have another miscellany including his accounts, some canceled checks and even his bankbook. The great mass of White House correspondence, official and personal, except as it is found in the files of the departments, has disappeared.

A second difficulty has been the fact that the Pierce administration was early discredited and his party with him; consequently there are relatively few biographies of his associates or those in sympathy with his point of view and of those an even smaller number are of much value. Davis and Cushing alone of the cabinet have volume biographies; Dr. H. Barrett Learned has an extended account of Marcy in *American Secretaries of State*, v. VI. Of the Democratic leaders, in Congress and out, there is surprisingly little data. Of the four leading Senators, Mason, Hunter, Butler, and Atchison, we know tantalizingly little. The first two are represented by family

memoirs and small collections of MSS. of too little importance, and Butler
and Atchison have well nigh disappeared from view. Perhaps best represented are the Georgian group, Cobb, Toombs, and Stephens, and their
correspondence is very enlightening. The chief manuscript sources are the
voluminous papers of Marcy and Buchanan, as I am informed that the
Cushing MSS., not now available, contain little for the period of his at-
torney-generalship.

For the general policies of the administration the Presidential messages
and reports of the Cabinet, regular and special, found in profusion in the
Congressional documents and the archives of the departments, are the primary sources. The archives of the State Department are the most easily accessible and the most satisfactory to use. The papers of the attorney-general
down to 1870 are in the Manuscript Division of the Library of Congress and
are also readily available. I found the War Department very willing to
permit access to its voluminous files for specified information. Through
the kindness of Dr. Newton D. Mereness I obtained photostats of the Reeder
material in the archives of the Interior department.

Little work has been done to provide us with secondary material in regard to administrative history. The work of Marcy in the State Department has been carefully studied from the State Department archives by Dr.
H. Barrett Learned in his penetrating account in *American Secretaries of
State*, v. VI. The work of the other cabinet officers has never been studied
except incidentally. Dr. Chas. O. Paullin in his studies of the history of
the navy department found in *Proceedings of the U. S. Naval Institute* makes
us wish that similar research might be done in the history of other departments.

Wallach's Washington *Star* is the best source for the social and personal
side of Pierce's administration. The paper was a daily which displayed
sympathy for Pierce and also had a sense of news, incorporating notes about
the lighter side of life which the more political presses omitted. Next in
importance is the daily column of Washington correspondence appearing in
the Baltimore *Sun* signed " Mercury." Mercury's column eschewed politics,
leaving that to " X " and " Ion," and devoted itself wholeheartedly to local
Washington news. The Lawrence MSS. in the Mass. Hist. Soc. contain
valuable accounts of visits to the White House and observations on the
mode of life which its occupants adopted.

For politics the most valuable newspaper commentaries on the Pierce
Administration I have found to be the Washington *Star*, the Baltimore *Sun*,
the Philadelphia *Public Ledger*, the New York *Herald*, and the Washington
Union. The *Star* was the most observant newspaper of the day and contains more real news about the activities of Pierce and his cabinet than any
of the others. The *Sun* had two correspondents, " X " and " Ion," the first
of whom was Francis J. Grund; their daily letters, especially during Congressional sessions, are valuable, although their speculations and assertions
as to probable happenings and motives are often more interesting and ingenious than accurate. Grund also was " Observer " for the Philadelphia
Ledger. The New York *Herald's* correspondent had excellent avenues of
information but the hostility of the *Herald* to Pierce and his administra-

tion, especially Marcy, makes its statements occasionally too harsh to be accurate. The *Union* is a queer puzzle. It contained the official news, and Cushing wrote much for its columns; in that sense it was an administration paper. Nicholson and Forney, its principal editorial writers, however, were not always on good terms with various members of the administration. Marcy had no use for Nicholson. Guthrie refused a claim which the editor made for increased compensation for printing. Forney was very friendly to Buchanan, and all told the relationship in many ways was most unsatisfactory. The columns of this paper bore little real news and it is valuable largely for its editorials, whenever one can be sure they represent administration feeling. The accurate use of this journal is a difficult historical problem.

CHAPTER XXVIII, PP. 216–223

1. Bridge, *Reminiscences of Hawthorne,* 131; Adams, *Richard Henry Dana,* I, 226.

2. *N. H. Statesman,* Nov. 27, 1852; Henry F. French to B. B. French, Nov. 26, 1852, French MSS.

3. Pierce to Marcy, Nov. 9, 1852, Thomas to Marcy, Nov. 20, 24, 1852, Marcy to Berret, Jan. 15, 1853, Marcy to Wetmore, Jan. 19, 20, 1853, Marcy MSS.; Slidell to Buchanan, Dec. 19, 1852, F. Byrdsall to Buchanan, Nov. 24, 1852, Buchanan MSS.; Marcy to Bancroft, Nov. 10, 1852, Bancroft MSS.; *Magazine of History,* XVI, 24–25.

4. Pierce to Davis, Dec. 7, 1852, Pierce MSS. (L. of C.).

5. Dix, *Memoirs,* I, 271; Dix to Pierce, Jan. 29, 1853, Dix MSS.; Dix to McClelland, Sept. 23, 1853, McClelland MSS.; Marcus Morton to Azariah Flagg, Dec. 6, 1853, Morton Letter Book; N. Y. *Herald,* Dec. 9, 1852; Stanton, *Random Recollections* (2d edition), 90.

6. Caldwell, *Bench and Bar of Tennessee,* 230; Andrew Johnson to Milligan, Dec. 28, 1852, Dreer Coll., Hist. Soc. Pa.; Nicholson article in Appleton's *Biographical Encyclopedia;* Nashville *Union,* Mar. 8, 1853; Washington *Star,* Nov. 29, 1853; Blair to Van Buren, Dec. 27, 1852, Van Buren MSS.; Nicholson to Pierce, Dec. 16, 1852, N. Y. Hist. Soc.; Cass to McClelland, Dec. 17, 1852, Jan. 10, 14, 20, Feb. 14, 1853, Burton Collection; Wentworth to Douglas, Dec. 12, 1852, Douglas MSS.

7. Buchanan, *Works,* VIII, 492–500.

8. Thomas to Marcy, Dec. 20, 27, 1852, Wetmore to Marcy, Dec. 28, 1852, Campbell to Marcy, Dec. 31, 1852, Marcy MSS.; Blair to Van Buren, Dec. 27, 1852, Van Buren MSS.; N. Y. *Herald,* Dec. 24, 26, 28, 30, 1852, Jan. 3, 1853; Boston *Atlas,* Dec. 28, 1852; Hunter, *Memoir of Robert M. T. Hunter,* 106–107; Journal of Amos A. Lawrence, June 8, 1853, Lawrence to Mrs. Pierce, June 22, 1853, Mass. Hist. Soc.

CHAPTER XXX, PP. 227–231

1. Pierce to Davis, Jan. 12, 1853, Pierce MSS. (L. of C.).

2. Hunter, *Memoir,* 107–108; Paul R. George to John H. George, Jan., 1853, N. H. Hist. Soc.

3. N. Y. *Herald,* Jan. 5, 1853; Boston *Atlas,* Jan. 10, 13, 1853; Hunter, *Memoir,* 109; Thomas to Marcy, Jan. 11, 16, 1853; Berret to Marcy, Jan. 14, 1853, Marcy MSS.; Blair to Van Buren, Jan. 11, 1853, Van Buren MSS.; Pierce to Mrs. Pierce, Tuesday [Jan. 18, 1853], Pierce MSS. (Hillsborough); Albert G. Allen to George, Feb. 7, 1853, N. H. Hist Soc.; Robert K. Bryan to D. S. Reid, Jan. 20, 1853, Reid MSS.

4. Dix to Pierce, Jan. 29, 1853, Dix MSS.

5. *Magazine of History,* XVI, 25; Thomas to Marcy, Jan. 13, 15, 16, 18, 1853, Pruyn to Marcy, Jan. 18, 21, 1853, Marcy MSS.; N. Y. *Herald,* Jan. 22, 23, 1853.

6. *Ga. Hist. Quart.,* VI, 36; Boston *Atlas,* Jan. 17, 1853; N. Y. *Express,* Jan. 7, 1853; Chase to Hamlin, Feb. 15, 1853, Chase MSS.; Day to Chase, Dec. 9, 1852, Blair to Van Buren, Dec. 27, 1852, Jan. 3, 11, 1853, Van Buren MSS.

7. Cushing to P. R. George, Jan. 27, Feb. 2, 1853, N. H. Hist. Soc.; Isaac R. Diller to Douglas, Dec. 6, 1852, Douglas MSS.

8. Webster to Marcy, Feb. 6, 1853, Marcy MSS.; Greene to Davis, Feb. 2, 1853, Pierce MSS. (L. of C.); Pierce to McClelland, Feb. 5, 1853, in private hands; Campbell to Buchanan, Feb. 13, 1853, Buchanan MSS.; Robert K. Bryan to D. S. Reid, Jan. 20, 1853, Reid MSS.; Norton *Democratic Party in Ante-Bellum North Carolina,* 162, 250–251; Pierce to Guthrie, Feb. 5, 15, Filson Club.

CHAPTER XXXI, PP. 232–236

1. Baltimore *Sun,* Feb. 14–Mar. 4, 1853; Campbell to Buchanan, Feb. 25, 1853, Buchanan MSS.; Greene to Davis, Feb. 18, 1853, Pierce MSS. (L. of C.); Richmond *Enquirer,* Mar. 4, 1853; Parker to Breckinridge, June, 1853, Breckinridge MSS.; Parker to Buchanan, Feb. 26, 1853, Buchanan MSS.; Allen to George, Feb. 7, 1853, N. H. Hist. Soc.; Butt, *Taft and Roosevelt,* I, 363; Everett Diary, Feb. 23, Mar. 4, 1853.

CHAPTER XXXII, PP. 237–244

Life in the White House is described rather unsatisfactorily in Nicolay, *Our Capital on the Potomac;* Colman, *Seventy-five Years of White House Gossip;* Singleton, *Story of the White House;* Ellet, *Court Circles of the Republic;* Holloway, *Ladies of the White House;* Clay, *A Belle of the Fifties;* Pryor, *Reminiscences of Peace and War;* Bryan, *History of the National Capital;* Moore, *Picturesque Washington;* Ames, *Ten Years in Washington;* Keim, *Society in Washington.*

The physical arrangement of the White House in the Pierce administration is nowhere adequately described. *Gleason's Pictorial Drawing Room Companion* for Mar. 11, 1854, has the best account. See, also, Logan, *Thirty Years in Washington;* Stoddard, *Inside the White House; Bohn's Handbook of Washington; Mill's Guide to the Capital;* Force, *Picture of Washington and Vicinity.* The reports of the commissioners of public buildings, Wm. Easby, Benj. B. French and John B. Blake, give information about needed improvements. See *H. Ex. Doc. 79,* 32: 1 (641); *H. Mis. Doc. 66,* 32: 1

(652); *H. Mis. Doc. 20, 23, 32:* 2 (685); *H. Mis. Doc. 11,* 33: 1 (741); *S. Ex. Doc. 1,* 33: 2 (746), pp. 598–608; *H. Ex. Doc. 1,* 34: 1 (840), pp. 595–612; *H. Ex. Doc. 1,* 34: 3 (893), pp. 849–864; *H. Ex. Doc. 15,* 34: 3 (897); *H. Mis. Doc. 62, 64,* 34: 3 (911); *S. Ex. Doc. 11,* 35: 1 (919); *H. Ex. Doc. 84,* 35: 1 (956); *S. Doc. 197,* 57: 2 (4439).

Press items of interest are found in the Washington *Union,* Mar. 8, Apr. 20, 1853; Washington *Republic,* Mar. 14, 1853; Washington *Star,* Aug. 13, Sept. 3, 5, 1853; Baltimore *Sun,* Mar. 7–9, 12, 26, 31, Apr. 1, 1853. See also Lawrence to Giles Richards, Apr. 21, 1854, Lawrence to his brother, Apr. 24, 1854, Lawrence MSS.; Hawthorne, *Letters to Ticknor,* I, 7–9; Hawthorne, *Love Letters,* II, 225; Ticknor, *Hawthorne and his Publisher,* 35–47. Pierce's personal copy of Thornton, *Family Prayers,* as well as a number of handsome gift books presented to the President during his White House sojourn, are in the possession of the family at Hillsborough.

CHAPTER XXXIII, PP. 247–258

1. *American Secretaries of State,* VI, 167–168, 293–294; for a more extended treatment of the subject of this chapter see Nichols, *Democratic Machine, 1850–1854,* 183–196.
2. New Orleans *Weekly Delta,* Mar. 20, 1853; Washington *Union,* Mar. 8, 1853; Clay, *A Belle of the Fifties,* 70; Cotterill, "James Guthrie," *Ky. Hist. Soc. Reg.,* Sept., 1922.
3. *Proc. of Grafton and Coös Co. Bar Assoc.,* 1896, 311; Clay, *op. cit.,* 68; Dodd, *Jefferson Davis;* Eckenrode, *Jefferson Davis;* Winston, *High Stakes and Hair Trigger;* Cutting, *Jefferson Davis.*
4. Hawthorne, *French and Italian Notebooks,* entry for Mar. 23, 1859; Fuess, *Caleb Cushing.*
5. McClure, *Old Time Notes of Pennsylvania,* I, 193; *Proc. of Grafton and Coös Co. Bar Assoc.,* 1896, 311; *Records of Am. Cath. Hist. Soc.,* V, 265–303.
6. Washington *Union,* Mar. 8, 1853; Clay *op. cit.,* 65.
7. New Orleans *Weekly Delta,* Mar. 20, 1853; Baltimore *Sun,* July 9, 1853; Nevin, *Men of Mark of the Cumberland Valley, Pa.*
8. *Union,* Mar. 8, 1853; Baltimore *Sun,* Mar. 11, May 5, 12, 1853; H. F. French to B. B. French, Nov. 3, 1853, French MSS.; Parish, *Geo. W. Jones,* 186; *Life and Reminiscences of Jefferson Davis by distinguished men of his times,* 129; Guthrie to Joseph Holt, June, 1853, Holt MSS.
9. Connor, *John A. Campbell,* 17.
10. Everett Diary, Apr. 9, 1853.
11. Marcy MSS., Mar., 1853, *passim;* O'Conor to McClelland, Mar. 29, 1853, McClelland MSS.; John Van Buren to Marcy, Oct. 17, 1853, Marcy MSS.; Dix to Pierce, Mar. 14, Apr. 2, 26, 1853, Dix MSS.
12. O'Conor to McClelland, Apr. 13, 1853, McClelland MSS.; *Sen. Ex. Journal,* IX, 130; *Seward at Washington,* 202; Baltimore *Sun,* Apr. 4, 1853.
13. *Hunter Corr.,* 156; Buchanan to Wise, June 1, 1853, L. of C.; Wise to Buchanan, Mar. 19, Apr. 9, 24, May 2, 1853, Buchanan MSS.; *Times of the*

Tylers, II, 504; Mason to Marcy, Apr. 15, 1853, Marcy MSS.; Baltimore *Sun*, May 20, 1853.

14. Morris, *Rebellious Puritan*, 265; Ticknor, *Hawthorne and his Publisher*, 35–47, 124; Mrs. Means to A. A. Lawrence, Apr. 4, 1853, Lawrence MSS.; Slidell to Buchanan, Mar. 30, 1853, Sept. 25, 1852, Pierce to Buchanan, Mar. 30, 1853, Buchanan MSS.

15. Curtis, *Buchanan*, II, 76–79; Buchanan to Campbell, Apr. 3, 1853, L. of C.

16. N. Y. *Herald*, July 23, 1853; Baltimore *Sun*, June 23, 1853.

CHAPTER XXXIV, PP. 259–275

1. N. Y. *Times*, Nov. 9, 1857; Fuess, *Cushing*, II, 135–136; Tyler Dennett to the author, Nov. 1, 1929; Marcy to Pierce, Apr. 6, 1853, State Dept. MSS.

2. Curtis, *Buchanan*, II, 81.

3. *American Secretaries of State*, VI, article on "Wm. L. Marcy" by H. B. Learned, 217–219; Williams, *Anglo-American Isthmian Diplomacy*, 110–152; Baltimore *Sun*, Mar. 16, 1853.

4. Tansill, *Canadian Reciprocity Treaty of 1854*, 1–53.

5. Scroggs, *Filibusters and Financiers*, 71–81; Baltimore *Sun*, Apr. 1, 2, 5, 1853; *S. Ex. Doc. No. 8*, 33:1 (694); Marcy to Borland, June 17, 1853, Nicaragua Instructions, State Dept. MSS.

6. Marcy to Clayton, June 1, 1853, Clayton to Marcy, June 4, 11, July 1, 1853, Marcy MSS.; Marcy to Buchanan, June 1, 1853, Buchanan MSS.; Curtis, *Buchanan*, II, 81–91; *American Secretaries of State*, VI, 220–221.

7. Tansill, *op. cit.*, 54–62; *American Secretaries of State*, VI, 278; *H. Ex. Doc. No. 21*, 33: 1 (717); I. D. Andrews to Marcy, June 17, 1853, Marcy MSS.; *Sun*, May 10, 25–27, June 6, 21, 25, 27, 30, 1853.

8. Rippy, *United States and Mexico*, 15–147; Garber, *Gadsden Treaty*, 1–95; Scroggs, *op. cit.*, 18–35; Baltimore *Sun*, Mar. 24, Apr. 1, 8, 9, 15, 22, 26, 27, 28, May 13, June 1, 11, 1853.

9. *American Secretaries of State*, VI, 183–189; Washington *Union*, Apr. 7, 20, 1853; Ettinger, *Royal Hist. Soc. Trans., 1930*, 172–176.

10. Marcy to Trousdale, Aug. 8, 1853, Brazil Instructions; to Green, Aug. 15, 1853, Colombia Instructions; to White, Aug. 20, 1853, Ecuador Instructions; to Clay, Aug. 30, 1853, Peruvian Instructions; State Dept. MSS.; Washington *Union*, May 10, 1853; Baltimore *Sun*, May 20, 1853.

11. Marcy to Gregg, Sept. 22, 1853, Hawaiian Instructions, State Dept. MSS.

12. Marcy to Humphrey Marshall, June 7, 1853, Chinese Instructions, State Dept. MSS.; Baltimore *Sun*, June 14, 18–21, 1853; N. Y. *Herald*, June 23, 1853; Walker to Marcy, Feb. 2, 1854, Marcy MSS.; Pierce to Allen, Sept. 5, 1853, Allen MSS.; Marcy to McLane, Dec. 16, 1853, Chinese Instructions; Dennett, *Americans in Eastern Asia*, 226–324; Marcy to Mason, Dec. 16, 1853, French Instructions; Buchanan, *Works*, IX, 102; Marcy to Buchanan, Dec. 16, 1853, British Instructions, State Dept. MSS.

13. *American Secretaries of State*, VI, 262–268; Dix to Marcy, June 13, 1853, Marcy MSS.; Baltimore *Sun*, June 14, 1853.

14. *American Secretaries of State*, VI, 268–273; Baltimore *Sun*, July 25, Aug. 5, Sept. 30, 1853; Washington *Star*, Aug. 18, Sept. 30, 1853.

15. Washington *Union*, Mar. 11, 30, Apr. 23, May 12, 20, 1853; Baltimore *Sun*, Mar. 16, Apr. 13, 14, 18, May 17, 1853; Washington *Star*, Oct. 5, 1853.

16. Davis, *Works*, II, 199, 221, 228, 229; *Globe*, 33:1, 2109; *H. Ex. Doc. No. 1*, 33:1 (711), pt. 2, 55–63, 76; Richardson, *Messages and Papers of the Presidents*, V, 204; Washington *Union*, Apr. 5, 1853; Baltimore *Sun*, May 11, 1853.

17. Baltimore *Sun*, May 31; Washington *Union*, Mar. 19, May 24, 27, June 3, 1853.

18. Fuess, *Cushing*, II, 136–138.

19. Washington *Star*, Dec. 4, 1854; Washington *Union*, Apr. 27, 1853.

20. Washington *Union*, Mar. 10, 1853; Baltimore *Sun*, June 3, 8, July 2, 9, 1853; B. B. French to H. F. French, July 3, 1853, French MSS.

21. Baltimore *Sun*, July 12, 1853; New Hampshire *Patriot*, Oct. 17, 1855.

CHAPTER XXXV, PP. 276–284

1. London *Times*, Mar. 18, 1853.

2. Grund to Marcy, Apr. 9, 1853, Marcy MSS.; Grund to Burke, Aug. 17, 1853, Burke MSS.

3. New Hampshire *Patriot, New Hampshire State Capital Reporter*, June, 1853; Baltimore *Sun*, June 11, 13, 1853; N. Y. *Times*, July 1, 1853; N. Y. *Herald*, July 3, 1853; Washington *Star*, July 16, 1853. A number of items in Burke MSS., 1853, and Burke to Douglas, Jan. 16, 1853, Douglas MSS., show that Burke began to feel slighted immediately after the Convention of 1852.

4. Nichols, *Democratic Machine, 1850–1854*, 202–206.

5. Nicholson to Pierce, Apr. 12, 1853, N. Y. Hist. Soc.; N. Y. *Herald*, June 17, 25, July 1, 1853; Baltimore *Sun*, May 5, June 4, 25, July 8, 13, 1853; M. V. McKean to J. C. Breckinridge, June 17, 1853, Breckinridge MSS.; C. L. Ward to Buchanan, Oct. 23, 1853, Buchanan MSS.; Watterson, *Marse Henry*, I, 26–27.

6. Baltimore *Sun*, Apr. 16, June 9, 15, 16, 1853; Washington *Union*, July 10, 1853; London *Times*, July 4, 1853; Davis, *Memoir of Jefferson Davis*, I, 518; B. B. French to H. F. French, July 10, 1853, French MSS.; Egbert, *Kentucky's Interest in the Pacific Railroad Question from 1830 to 1865*.

7. Baltimore *Sun*, July 12, 1853; N. Y. *Herald*, July 13, 14, 15, 16, 1853; Phila. *Pennsylvanian*, July 13, 18, 20, 1853; Washington *Union*, July 17, 21, 29, 1853; Trenton *State Gazette*, July 14, 1853; Trenton *Weekly True American*, July 22, 1853; Newark *Daily Advertiser*, July 14, 1853; Washington *Star*, July 18, 19, 20, 1853; Washington *National Intelligencer*, July 16, 1853; Curtis, *Buchanan*, II, 91–93; Lyell, *Life, Letters, and Journals of Sir Charles Lyell, Bart.*, II, 187–189.

CHAPTER XXXVI, PP. 285–293

1. *Proc. of Grafton and Coös Co. Bar Assoc., 1896*, 311–312.

2. Washington *Star*, Sept. 19, 20, 1853; Dix to Wm. H. Ludlow, Aug. 27,

Ludlow to Marcy, Aug. 30, 1853, Marcy MSS.; Dix, *Memoirs*, I, 276; Dix to Pierce, Aug. 22, Sept. 7, 28, 1853, Dix MSS.; *Ga. Hist. Quart.*, VI, 48; N. Y. *Herald*, Sept. 13-29, 1853; John Y. Mason to Jefferson Davis, Oct. 2, 1853, Davis MSS.; Cole, *Whig Party in the South*, 277.

3. Nichols, *op. cit.*, 206-216, treats this episode more at length. See also Washington *Star*, Sept. 8-20, 26, Oct. 3, 22, 24, 1853; James G. Bennett to Pierce, Dec. 15, 1852, Pierce MSS. (L. of C.); Pierce to George, Oct. 11, 1853, N. H. Hist. Soc.; J. Glancy Jones to Buchanan, Oct. 3, 1853, Cave Johnson to Buchanan, Nov. 20, 1853, Buchanan MSS.; Marcy to Richmond, Aug. 29, 1853; J. C. Wright to Marcy, Sept. 11, 1853, Marcy MSS.; London *Times*, Aug. 30, 1853; N. H. *Statesman*, Oct. 29, 1853.

4. Fuess, *Cushing*, II, 139-143; *Sun*, Jan. 18, 1855; H. F. French to B. B. French, Nov. 3, 1853, French MSS.; Cushing to Thos. C. Reynolds, Nov. 26, 1853, L. of C.

5. Nichols, *op. cit.*, 201; Nicholson to Pierce, Oct. 29, 1853, N. Y. Hist. Soc.; Pierce to Atherton, Oct. 29, 1853, Pierce MSS. (Hillsborough); Arkansas (Little Rock) *Whig*, Dec. 1, 1853; Washington *Union*, Nov. 4, 13, 1853; N. Y. *Herald*, Nov. 2, 1853; Cole, *op. cit.*, 277-279.

6. Andrew Harvie and I. Cook to Douglas, Nov. 14, 1853, Douglas MSS.

CHAPTER XXXVII, pp. 294-301

1. The President's message and the reports of the secretaries of war, navy, interior and the postmaster general are found in *H. Ex. Doc. No. 1*, 33:1 (710-712), or *S. Ex. Doc. No. 2* (690-692); the report of the secretary of the treasury to Congress is found in *H. Ex. Doc. No. 3*, 33:1 (714).

2. *H. Ex. Doc. No. 1*, 33:1, pt. 2, 23-24.

3. *Ibid.*, pt. 3, 307.

4. *Ibid.*, pt. 1, 251.

5. *Ibid.*, pt. 1, 53.

6. *Ibid.*, pt. 1, 88.

7. *Ibid.*, pt. 1, 55.

8. Pierce to John L. O'Sullivan, Dec. 5, 1853, Mass. Hist. Soc.

CHAPTER XXXVIII, pp. 302-310

1. Article by Welles on N. Y. situation written Oct., 1853, Welles MSS.

2. *Star*, Dec. 16, 1853.

3. McLaughlin, *Cass*; Eckloff, *Memories of a Senate Page*; *Proc. Grafton and Coös Co. Bar Assoc., 1896*, 312.

4. Johnson, *Stephen A. Douglas*; Curti, "Young America," *Amer. Hist. Rev.*, XXXII, 34-55.

5. MSS. Diary of Laura Jones Crawford, Jan. 21, 1859, L. of C.; see letters in Corcoran and Breckinridge MSS., *passim*.

6. Pelzer, *Henry Dodge*; Pelzer, *A. C. Dodge*; Parish, *G. W. Jones*.

7. Gwin's MSS. memoirs are in the Bancroft library at the University of California.

8. Hamlin, *Hannibal Hamlin*.

9. Forney, *Anecdotes of Public Men,* 57–58; Ray, *Repeal of the Missouri Compromise, passim;* James C. Malin, "Pro Slavery Background of the Kansas Struggle," *Miss. Valley Hist. Rev.,* X, 285; Hunter, *Robert M. T. Hunter;* Ambler, "Correspondence of Robert M. T. Hunter"; Mason, *James M. Mason.*

10. Sears, *John Slidell;* Forney to Buchanan, Nov. 21, 1853, Buchanan MSS.

11. *Proc. Grafton & Coos Co. Bar Assoc., 1896,* 312.

12. James, *The Raven.*

13. Bayard to Marcy, July 12, 20, Marcy to Bayard, July 15, 1853, Marcy MSS.; Webster, "Mr. Marcy," *Pol. Sci. Quart.,* VIII, 14.

14. Clay, *A Belle of the Fifties, passim.*

15. Bancroft, *Seward;* Haynes, *Sumner;* Pierce, *Sumner;* Frothingham, *Everett;* Riddle, *Wade;* Hart, Shuckers, and Warden each have a life of Chase; Phillips, *Toombs;* Butler, *Benjamin.* Sketches of Clayton and Fish are found in *American Secretaries of State,* VI, VII.

16. *Star,* Nov. 17, 1853.

17. Slidell to Buchanan, Jan. 14, 1854, Buchanan MSS.; see also Ingersoll to Cobb, Jan. 20, 1854, "Toombs Corr.," 339, and Jones to Buchanan, Oct. 3, 1853, Buchanan MSS.

18. *Star,* Nov. 5, 7, Dec. 7, 14, 1853; *Sun,* Nov. 9, 1853; Blair to Van Buren, Nov. 27, 1853, Van Buren MSS.; report on lobby activity is found in *Rept. of Com. No. 1,* special session of Sen. 33d Cong. (688).

19. *Star,* Oct. 25; *Union,* Nov. 10, 1853.

CHAPTER XXXIX, PP. 311–314

1. *Star,* July 23, 28, Sept. 13, Oct. 1, Nov. 1, 18, 22, 1853; Baltimore *Sun,* July 11, 1853.

2. Mrs. Lawrence to Amos A. Lawrence, Apr. 4, 1854, Lawrence Journal, Apr. 13, 15, 1854, Lawrence MSS.

3. *Sun,* Dec. 29, 1854, Jan. 3, 23, 1854; *Star,* Jan. 16, 21, Mar. 9, 14, 18, Apr. 1, May 5, 8, July 5, 20, Aug. 24, Sept. 18, Oct. 6, 1854.

4. Clay, *Belle of the Fifties,* 27–28, 59–61; Davis, *Memoir of Jefferson Davis,* I, 540–541.

5. *Star,* Oct. 13, Nov. 7, 8, Dec. 16, 1853, Apr. 7, June 17, July 6, 11, 24, 1854.

CHAPTER XL, PP. 315–318

1. J. Glancy Jones to Buchanan, Oct. 3, 1853, Buchanan MSS.

2. *Ibid.,* David S. Jenks to Buchanan, Jan. 5, 1854, Buchanan MSS.; Marcy to John M. Daniel, Dec. 15, 1853, Marcy MSS.; Jos. Lane to Nesmith, Dec. 13, 1853, Oregon Hist. Soc.; *Star,* Dec. 13, 14, 1853; *Globe,* 33:1, 15, 28; Eastman to Sibley, Jan. 1, 1854, Sibley MSS.

3. Marcy to Redfield, Dec. 18, 29, 1853, Marcy MSS.; *Globe,* 33:1, 40, 56–61, 173.

4. *Globe,* 33:1, App. 45, 50, 52, regular debate, 72, 79, 90.

5. *Globe,* 33:1, 38, 42, 45; *House Journal,* 33:1, 69, 79, 80; *Star,* Dec. 17, 1853.

6. *Globe,* 33:1, 80, 113, 121, 190–192, App. 72, 86, 87, 106, 111, 117, 126.

7. Marcy to Redfield, Dec. 18, 29, 1853, Jan. 1, 1854; Redfield to Douglas, Dec. 10, to Campbell, Dec. 15, to Marcy, Dec. 14, 15, 16, 17, 19, 22, 30, 1853, Marcy MSS.

8. Pierce to George, Jan. 24, 1854, N. H. Hist. Soc.; Cochrane to Marcy, Jan. 23, 1854, Marcy MSS.

CHAPTER XLI, PP. 319–324

1. *Globe,* 32:2, 1117.

2. Ray, *Repeal of the Missouri Compromise, passim*; Hodder, "Genesis of the Kansas Nebraska Act," *Proc. State Hist. Soc. of Wis. for 1912,* 69–86; Ray, "Genesis of the Kansas Nebraska Act," *Am. Hist. Assoc. Rept. 1914,* I, 261–280; Hodder, "Railroad Background of the Kansas Nebraska Act," *Miss. Val. Hist. Rev.,* XII, 3–22; Johnson, *Stephen A. Douglas*; Foote, *Casket of Reminiscences*; Cutts, *Brief Treatise upon Constitutional and Party Questions,* 90; Wentworth, *Congressional Reminiscences,* 54–55; Moses, *Illinois,* II, 588–589; McMahon, "Stephen A. Douglas, 1850–1860," *Wash. Hist. Quart.,* II, 209–233; Dixon, *True History of the Missouri Compromise and its Repeal*; Du Bois and Mathews, *Galusha A. Grow,* 144–145; A Member of the Western Bar (Henry M. Flint), *Stephen A. Douglas,* 171–174; Burgess, *Middle Period,* 387; *Speeches and Writings of the Hon. T. L. Clingman,* 335; Cole, *Centennial History of Illinois,* III, 101–124; Blair to Allen, Feb. 10, 1854, Allen MSS.; Blair to Van Buren, Mar. 4, 1854, Van Buren MSS.; *Opinions of Atty. Gen.,* VII, 575–576.

3. *N. Y. Herald,* Jan. 24, 1854; Diary, June 29, 1855, Welles MSS.; John A. Parker to Buchanan, Mar. 29, 1854, Buchanan MSS.; Beveridge, *Abraham Lincoln,* II, 169–217.

4. *Ibid.*; account of the repeal by P. Phillips, in Phillips MSS.; Learned, "Relation of Philip Phillips to the Repeal of the Missouri Compromise in 1854," *Miss. Val. Hist. Rev.,* VIII, 303–317; Fuess, *Caleb Cushing,* II, 204; Webster, "Responsibility for the War of Secession," *Pol. Sci. Quart.,* VIII, 270–276; Davis, *Rise and Fall of the Confederate Government,* I, 27; Davis to John H. Parker, June 13, 1888, *Works,* IX, 459; Joseph Robinson to John H. George, Jan. 24, 1854, N. H. Hist. Soc.; John A. Parker to L. G. Tyler, June 1, 1889, Tyler MSS.; J. B. Bowlin to Buchanan, Apr. 21, 1854, Buchanan MSS.; Connelley, *Kansas,* I, 289–301; Chase to Hamlin, Jan. 23, 1854, *Am. Hist. Assoc. Rept., 1902,* II, 256; Greeley, *Recollections of a Busy Life,* 292; Bigelow, *Retrospections,* I, 171; Giddings, *History of the Rebellion,* 365; Wilson, *Rise and Fall of the Slave Power,* II, 382–383; Smith, *Political History of Slavery,* I, 169; Du Bois and Mathews, *Galusha A. Grow,* 139–140; *Opinions of Atty. Gen.,* VII, 575–576.

5. Hibbard to George, Jan. 25, 1854, N. H. Hist. Soc.; *S. Ex. Journal,* IX, 217.

CHAPTER XLII, PP. 325–330

1. Garber, *Gadsden Treaty,* 115–117; Rippy, *United States and Mexico,* 148.

2. Buchanan to Marcy, Nov. 12, 1853, Mar. 17, 1854, *Works,* IX, 88, 165; Marcy to Buchanan, Dec. 4, 1853, *Works,* IX, 102; Marcy to Buchanan, Dec. 16, 1853, Mar. 12, 1854, Marcy to Mason, Dec. 16, 1853, Marcy MSS.; *Hispanic Am. Hist. Rev.,* IX, 364.

3. Washington *Union* started featuring editorials on this subject in October, 1853, and continued regularly.

4. N. Y. *Herald,* Feb. 20, 1854; *Globe,* 33:1, 483–484; Phila. *Ledger,* Feb. 27, 1854; Campbell to Buchanan, Mar. 14, 1854, Buchanan MSS.; Buchanan to Marcy, Jan. 10, 1854, *Works,* IX, 130.

5. *H. Ex. Doc. No. 93,* 33:2 (790); Webster, "Mr. Marcy; the Cuban Question, and the Ostend Manifesto," *Pol. Sci. Quart.,* VIII, 1–32.

6. Marcy to Buchanan, Mar. 11, 1854, Great Britain Instructions, State Dept. MSS.

7. Campbell to Buchanan, Mar. 14, 1854, Buchanan MSS.

8. Golder, "Russian-American Relations during the Crimean War," *Am. Hist. Rev.,* XXXI, 462–476; Thomas, *Russo-American Relations, 1815–1867,* 111–118.

9. Marcy to Buchanan, Mar. 11, 1854, *loc. cit.,* Mar. 12, 1854, Pierce to Buchanan, Feb. 22–Mar. 13, 1854, Buchanan MSS.

10. Marcy to Chas. W. Davis, Mar. 15, 1854, Special Missions, III, State Dept. MSS.

11. Marcy to Soulé, Mar. 17, 1854, *H. Ex. Doc. No. 93* (790), 31; *H. Ex. Doc. No. 86,* 33:1 (724); *American Secretaries of State,* VI, 187–192.

12. Soulé to Marcy, Feb. 23, 1854, Spanish Despatches, State Dept. MSS.; Buchanan to Marcy, Mar. 17, 1854, *Works,* IX, 165; Mason to Marcy, Feb. 20, Mar. 14, 30, 1854, French Despatches, State Dept. MSS.

13. Golder, "Purchase of Alaska," *Am. Hist. Rev.,* XXV, 412. Many years later Gwin told a different story, probably incorrect, found in his MSS. memoirs, p. 262 G.

14. Marcy to Soulé, Apr. 3, 1854, Spanish Instructions, Marcy to Gregg, Apr. 4, 1854, Hawaiian Instructions, Mason to Marcy, Apr. 22, 1854, French Despatches, Marcy to Cazneau, June 17, 1854, Special Missions, III, State Dept. MSS.; *H. Ex. Doc. No. 43,* 41:3 (1453); *American Secretaries of State,* VI, 192–195.

CHAPTER XLIII, PP. 333–338

1. Hamlin, *Hannibal Hamlin,* 264–274.

2. *Globe,* 35:2, 1248.

3. *Globe,* 34:1, App. 103.

4. *Sun,* Feb. 23, 1854; *Ledger,* Mar. 10, 1854.

5. *Globe,* 33:1, 610, 614.

6. Plitt to Buchanan, Mar. 3, 1854, Jas. B. Bowlin to Buchanan, Apr. 21, 1854, Forney to Buchanan, Nov. 21, 1853, Mar. 19, 1854, Buchanan MSS.;

Union, Feb. 17, 24, Mar. 1, 2, 1854; *Star,* Feb. 17, Mar. 7, 1854; Articles of agreement between Forney and Nicholson, May 26, 1854, N. Y. Hist. Soc.

7. Marcy to Seymour, Feb. 25, 1855, to Miller, Mar. 30, 1855, to J. Van Buren, Apr. 8, 1855, Marcy MSS.

8. *Globe,* 33:1, 703, 759, 764, App. 439.

9. James Guthrie to J. W. Stevenson, Apr. 1, 1854, Stevenson MSS.

10. Campbell to Buchanan, Mar. 14, 1854, Buchanan MSS.

11. *Proc. Grafton and Coös Co. Bar Assoc., 1896,* 301.

12. *Star,* Mar. 25, 1854; Clay to Clay, Sr., Apr. 5, 1854, Clay MSS.; *Union,* Mar. 29, 1854.

13. *Globe,* 33:2, 47, 64, App. 31–37; Robbins to Buchanan, Mar. 13, 1854, Buchanan MSS.

14. Webster to George, June 5, 1854, N. H. Hist. Soc.

CHAPTER XLIV, PP. 339–347

1. Rippy, *United States and Mexico,* 148–167; Garber, *Gadsden Treaty,* 117–145.

2. *Globe,* 33:1, 647.

3. Clingman, *Speeches and Writings,* 375–376.

4. *Globe,* 33:1, 1194, 1260, 1298; Rhodes, II, 23–24; Claiborne, *John A. Quitman,* II, 194–209; *American Secretaries of State,* VI, 192–198. Consular Despatches, Havana, v. 26, Nov. 30, 1853 to May 14, 1854, *passim. Ibid.,* v. 29, reports of Charles W. Davis to Marcy, Washington, May 22, 1854, with inclosures, and May 29, 1854. Reference to Davis's report kindly supplied me by Dr. Amos A. Ettinger.

5. *American Secretaries of State,* VI, 199.

6. N. Y. *Herald,* June 6, 1854; Slidell to Buchanan, June 17, 1854, Buchanan MSS.

7. Marcy to Soulé, June 24, 1854, Special Missions, III, 60, State Dept. MSS.

8. Marcy to Mason, July 23, 1854, Marcy MSS.

9. Johnston and Browne, *Alex. H. Stephens,* 278.

10. Tansill, *Canadian Reciprocity Treaty of 1854,* 73–81; *American Secretaries of State,* VI, 276–280; Marcy Letter Book, 84, Marcy MSS.; Marcy to Woodbury, June 9, 1854, N. Y. Hist. Soc.; *Proc. Grafton and Coös Co. Bar Assoc., 1892,* 380.

11. Scroggs, *Filibusters and Financiers,* 74–77; Williams, *Anglo-American Isthmian Diplomacy,* 173–179; Buchanan to Marcy, May 5, 1854, *Works,* IX, 189.

12. Buchanan, *Works,* IX, 162, 165, 169; *H. Ex. Doc. No. 103,* 33:1 (725).

13. Malloy, *Treaties, etc.,* II, 1519; Marcy to Mason, July 23, 1854, Marcy MSS.; Marcy to Buchanan, Aug. 7, 1854, Instructions to Great Britain, State Dept. MSS.

14. MSS. Journal of Elihu Burritt, Library of the Institute, New Britain, Conn., item supplied through the kindness of Prof. M. E. Curti.

15. *Am. Hist. Rev.,* XXXI, 471–474; Crampton, July 2–17, Clarendon MSS.

16. Scroggs, 76–78; Williams, 179–182; *Star,* July 27, 1854; *Sun,* July 26,

1854; *Union,* Aug. 2, 1854; Marcy to Buchanan, Aug. 8, Sept. 11, 1854, Buchanan MSS.; Crampton, Aug. 13, Clarendon MSS.

17. *American Secretaries of State,* VI, 281–283.

18. *Am. Hist. Rev.,* XLII, 500; Crampton, Nov. 1853, Clarendon MSS.

CHAPTER XLV, PP. 348–356

1. Marcy to Mason, July 22, 1854, Marcy MSS.

2. *Globe,* 33:1, 1087; *Star,* May 4, 1854; Tiffany, *Dorothea L. Dix.*

3. *Globe,* 33:1, App. 630, 642, 648, 798, 803–808, 982, 1000.

4. *Globe,* 33:1, 2204, App. 1100, 1105, 1115, 1122.

5. *Globe,* 33:1, 664, 670–671, 679, 908, 951, 957, 960, App. 406.

6. *Globe,* 33:1, 839, 854, 1963, 2114–2116, 2129, 2138, 2180–2184, 2185–2186, 2204; for Cushing's plans see *S. Ex. Docs. Nos. 41, 55,* 33:1 (698).

7. *Globe,* 33:1, 2061–2062, 2066.

8. Slidell to Buchanan, Aug. 6, 1854, Buchanan MSS.; *Globe,* 33:1, 2040, 2178.

9. *Globe,* 33:1, 1656, 1690, 2221–2222, App. 1146, 1151, 1160, 1162, 1202, 1210; *S. Jour.,* 33:1, 617–618; *Globe,* 34:1, 1543; John A. Parker to Claiborne, July 19, 1854, Claiborne MSS.

10. *Star, Sun, Ledger,* Aug. 7, 1854.

CHAPTER XLVI, PP. 357–359

1. Sickles to Buchanan, Aug. 15, 1854, Slidell to Buchanan, Aug. 6, 1854, Forney to Buchanan, Aug. 18, 1854, Buchanan MSS.; Buchanan to Slidell, May 23, 1854, Buchanan to Marcy, July 11, 21, 1854, Pierce to Buchanan, Aug. 12, 1854, Buchanan, *Works,* IX, 201, 211, 214, 243; Marcy to P. D. Vroom, Nov. 4, 1854, Marcy MSS.; Mason to Marcy, July 20, 1854, Despatches from France, State Dept. MSS.; John A. Parker to J. F. H. Claiborne, July 7, 19, 1854, Claiborne MSS.; Lane to Nesmith, Aug. 13, 1854, Oregon Hist. Soc.; *Ledger,* Aug. 4, 5, 1854; *Sun,* July 20, 26, 29, Aug. 2, 3, 7, 8, 1854; *Union,* Mar. 10, 1855; *H. Ex. Doc. No. 93,* 33: 2 (790); Marcy to Soulé, Aug. 16, 1854, Spanish Instructions, State Dept. MSS.; *American Secretaries of State,* VI, 195–203; Sickles to Douglas, Apr. 26, 1854, Douglas MSS.; Horatio J. Perry, secretary of legation at Madrid, had reported on the influence and interest of the Queen Mother in a letter to Pierce of Jan. 10, 1853, Buchanan MSS., under cover of Perry to Buchanan, Jan. 7, 1857.

CHAPTER XLVII, PP. 360–365

1. Pierce to John Aiken, Aug. 19, 1854, private collection.

2. Mitchell to Alex. H. H. Stuart, June 20, 1854, L. of C.

3. *Star,* May 30, 1854; Davis, *Works* II, 360; *Globe,* 33:1, App. 1050; *Globe,* 34:1, App. 536; Lawrence to Wm. Appleton, Mar. 6, to Mrs. Lawrence, Mar. 30, 1854, Lawrence MSS.; B. B. French to H. F. French, June 4, 1854, French MSS.

4. H. F. French to B. B. French, June 16, 1854, French MSS.; Webster to George, July 3, 1854, N. H. Hist. Soc.; *Star,* June 19, 1854.

5. Shepard to Marcy, July 6, Seymour to Marcy, July 6, Marcy to Seymour, July 12, 1854, Marcy MSS.; *Star*, June 20, July 11, 1854.

6. *Union*, Sept. 6, 1854.

7. Seymour to Marcy, Sept. 9, 18, 29, 1854, St. John B. S. Skinner to Marcy, Sept. 28, 1854, Marcy MSS.

8. Edmund Burke to Wm. Prescott, Sept. 18, 1854, N. H. Hist. Soc.; *Star*, Oct. 16, 1854.

9. Forney to Breckinridge, Oct. 19, 1854, Breckinridge MSS.; Jenks to Buchanan, Oct. 17, 1854, Buchanan MSS.

CHAPTER XLVIII, PP. 366–371

1. Buchanan to Pierce, Sept. 1, 1854, to Marcy, Dec. 22, 1854, *Works*, IX, 252, 288; Marcy to Buchanan, to Mason, Oct. 19, 1854, Marcy to Cass, Apr. 2, 1855, Marcy MSS.; Buchanan to Marcy, Dec. 8, 1854, Mason to Buchanan, Dec. 26, 1854, Buchanan to Marcy, Sept. 4, 1854, Soulé to Buchanan, Sept. 23, 29, 1854, Mason to Buchanan, Sept. 24, 29, 1854, Buchanan to Soulé, Sept. 26, 1854, Buchanan MSS.; *Star*, Oct. 19, 1854; *Sun*, Nov. 4, 8, 1854; *H. Ex. Doc. No. 93*, 33:2 (790); *American Secretaries of State*, VI, 203–211; Curtis, *Buchanan*, II, 136–141; Buchanan's rough draft of the report is in his MSS.; Field, *Memories of Many Men*, 95–100; *Pol. Sci. Quart.*, VIII, 23–24; speech of Davis quoted in *Union*, Oct. 30, 1957. See also A. A. Ettinger, *Mission to Spain of Pierre Soulé, passim*. I do not subscribe to Ettinger's assignment to Soulé of the principal role at Ostend. Crampton to Clarendon, May 21, July 17, Nov. 17, 1854, Jan. 15, Dec. 11, 1855, Clarendon MSS.

CHAPTER XLIX, PP. 372–379

1. The second annual message and reports are found in *H. Ex. Doc. No. 1*, 33:2 (777–778), and *H. Ex. Doc. No. 3*, 33:2 (780).

2. Johnston and Browne, *Alexander H. Stephens*, 280.

3. *Globe*, 33:2, 826–833.

4. Nicholson to Pierce, Feb. 10, 1855, N. Y. Hist. Soc.

5. *Globe*, 33:2, 801–803, 816, 820–823; *Sun*, Jan. 30, 1855.

6. *Globe*, 33:2, 1156–1157, 1186; *Union*, Mar. 8, 1855.

7. Pierce to Stuart, Mar. 13, 1855, Pierce MSS., L. of C.; *Sun*, Mar. 6, 1855.

8. Upham to Buchanan, April 9, 1855, Buchanan MSS.

9. *American Secretaries of State*, VI, 171; Marcy to Buchanan, Feb. 20, June 18, to Mason, Mar. 5, June 3, to Eames, June 20, 1855, Marcy MSS.

10. *Globe*, 33:2, 1060, 1062, 1088.

11. *Miss. Val. Hist. Rev.*, XII, 17–18; *H. Ex. Doc. No. 91*, 33:2 (791).

CHAPTER L, PP. 380–387

1. *S. Ex. Journal*, IX, 65, 225; Lane to Deady, Feb. 3, June 18, 1854, Oregon Hist. Soc.

2, Pierce to George, June 25, 1856, N. H. Hist. Soc.

3. Pierce to Marcy, Aug. 8, 1855, Marcy MSS.

4. Pierce to Douglas, July 20, 1855, Horatio King MSS.

5. *Star*, Jan. 2, 1855.

6. B. B. French to H. F. French, Apr. 1, 1855, French MSS.; *Globe,* 34:1, 1333, 1847, 1883, 1901, 1980–1984.

7. *American Secretaries of State,* VI, 171; *Atty. Gen. Opinions,* May 25, June 2, 1855.

8. *S. Rept. No. 8,* 34:1 (836); Du Pont, *Rear Admiral Samuel F. Du Pont,* 63 *et seq.;* Charles O. Paullin, " Naval Administration 1842–1861," *Proc. U. S. Naval Institute,* XXXIII, 1468–1473.

9. Davis, *Works,* II, III, contain a long series of letters which passed between Davis and Scott.

CHAPTER LI, PP. 388–392

1. Johnston and Browne, *Alexander H. Stephens,* 286.

2. Webster to George, Dec. 30, 1854, Jan. 20, 1855, N. H. Hist. Soc.

3. Pierce to Marcy, Jan. 25 or Feb. 1, 1855, Seymour to Marcy, Feb. 21, 28, 1855, Marcy to Seymour, Feb. 25, 1855, Marcy MSS.; N. Y. *Herald,* Feb. 1, 10, 1855; *Sun,* Feb. 5, 1855; *Star,* Feb. 12, 1855.

4. Pierce to George, Jan. 22, 26, Mar. 7, Webster to George, Mar. 8, 1855, N. H. Hist. Soc.

5. Marcy to Vroom, May 14, 1855, Marcy MSS.

6. *Ibid.*

7. B. B. French to H. F. French, June 5, 30, 1855, B. B. French to Pierce, June 30, 1855, French MSS.; *Star,* June 28, 29, 1855; Mason Diary, June 27, 29, 1855.

8. Carroll, *Review of the Pierce Administration.*

CHAPTER LII, PP. 393–399

1. *Sun,* Mar. 7, 1855.

2. *Union,* Mar. 11, 1855.

3. *Ledger,* Mar. 15, 1855; *Pol. Sci. Quart.,* VIII, 26; *S. Ex. Doc. No. 1,* 35: Sp. Sess. (930).

4. Marcy to Shepard, Apr. 15, 1855, Marcy MSS.

5. Jas. L. Reynolds to Buchanan, Apr. 25, 1855, I. I. Seibels to Buchanan, May 17, July 2, 1855, Buchanan MSS.; *Pol. Sci. Quart.,* VIII, 27; *Union,* Apr. 19, 1855.

6. Soulé to Buchanan, June 26, 1855, Buchanan MSS.; Parish, *George W. Jones,* 139–141; Pelzer, *A. C. Dodge,* 220, 221; Instructions to Spain, May 1, 1855, State Dept. MSS.; Dodge to Marquis of Pidal, Nov. 24, 1856, Buchanan MSS.

7. Gregg to Marcy, July 26, Aug. 7, Sept. 15, with draft of treaty, Dec. 29, 1854, Jan. 24, 1855, Hawaiian Despatches, Marcy to Gregg, Jan. 31, 1855, Hawaiian Instructions, State Dept. MSS.; Hopkins, *Hawaii,* 323; Carpenter, *America in Hawaii,* 118–119; *Globe,* 33:2, 834; Marcy to Buchanan, Sept. 11, Oct. 19, 1854, Buchanan to Marcy, Oct. 31, 1854, Buchanan MSS.

8. Cazneau to Marcy, Aug. 19, Nov. 23, Dec. 6, 23, 1854, Reports of Special Missions; Marcy to Cazneau, Dec. 18, 1854, Jan. 12, 1855, Marcy to Jonathan Elliot, Oct. 5, 9, 1855, Special Missions, State Dept. MSS.; Marcy to Buchanan, Oct. 19, 1854, Buchanan to Marcy, Oct. 31, 1854, Buchanan MSS.; Claiborne, *John A. Quitman,* II, 364–365.

9. Scroggs, *Filibusters and Financiers*, 100–107; Williams, *Anglo-American Isthmian Diplomacy*, 186–193; *Ledger*, Dec. 7, 12, 28, 1854; *Union*, Feb. 7, 1855; *Globe*, 33:2, App. 111.

10. Cushing to McKeon, Mar. 23, to Van Dyke, Mar. 26, to Pierce, Mar. 26, 1855, Atty. Gen. MSS.; *Sun*, Mar. 22, 26, 29, 2855; *American Secretaries of State*, VI, 237–243, 249.

11. See note 9.

12. Buchanan to Marcy, Apr. 6, 7, 26, 1855, *Works*, IX, 335, 338, 346; Marcy to Buchanan, May 28, 1855, Buchanan MSS.; *S. Ex. Doc. No. 35*, 34: 1 (819), 7.

CHAPTER LIII, PP. 400–406

1. Bancroft, *Utah*, 468, 492–493; *H. Ex. Doc. No. 1*, 34:1, Pt. II (841), 152–168, 506; *H. Ex. Doc. No. 71*, 35:1 (956); *Ledger*, Dec. 15, 1854; *Sun*, Aug. 27, 1855; *Sentinel*, Oct. 11, 1855; *S. Ex. Journal*, IX, 392, 395; Thos. L. Kane to Black, Mar. 21, 1857, Black MSS.; J. F. Kinney to Cushing, Apr. 1, 1855, Atty. Gen. MSS.; Luther Griffing to Sec. of State, Mar. 29, 1857, State Dept. MSS.; MSS. Journal History, Dec. 22–31, 1854, Mar. 29, Apr. 3, 1855; *Millenial Star*, XVII, 110, 268; Young, *Journal of Discourses*, I, 187, II, 179–183. I am indebted to Mrs. Susa Young Gates and to Alvin F. Smith, Historical Librarian of the Church of the Latter Day Saints.

2. Folwell, *History of Minnesota*, I, 327–350; *History of Northern Wisconsin*, 268–269; *H. Ex. Doc. No. 35*, 33:2 (783); John E. Warren to Marcy, Jan. 12, 1855, Marcy MSS.; A. G. Chatfield to Black, Apr. 4, 1857, Black MSS.; Minnesota *Democrat*, Feb. 14, 21, 1855; *Globe*, 33:2, 903; Gorman to Pierce, Feb. 10, 1855, Robt. W. Lowber to Pierce, May 12, 1856, Atty. Gen. MSS.; Rice to Breckinridge, Mar. 18, 20, 24, 26, Apr. 1, 12, 15, 21, May 9, 1855, Blair to Breckinridge, Mar. 26, Guthrie to Breckinridge, Mar. 30, 31, 1855, Breckinridge MSS. Through a grant of funds made to me by the American Council of Learned Societies and the assistance of Dr. Grace Lee Nute and Miss Alice Fitch I was able to have search made of material in the Minnesota Historical Society. The manuscript collections of Henry H. Sibley and Alexander Ramsey in that society and the files of the *Daily Pioneer* and the *Daily Minnesotian* yielded the most valuable data.

3. Pierce wrote several cordial letters to Douglas that summer in one of which he says, "I think with satisfaction of our last interview and entertain no doubt that the feeling is reciprocated." It is possible that this refers to the interviews of April 11, Pierce to Douglas, May 3(?), 28, June 18, July 25, 1855, Douglas MSS.

CHAPTER LIV, PP. 407–415

1. *Globe*, 33:2, 367; *H. Ex. Doc. No. 50*, 33:2 (783); *Ledger*, Dec. 8, 1854; *Star*, Dec. 28, 1854, Apr. 24, June 5, Apr. 30, May 1, 5, 1855; *Kansas Hist. Coll.*, V, 225–232; *Union*, June 19, 1855; *S. Ex. Doc. No. 1*, 34:1 (810), 328, 420; Minor, *Story of the Democratic Party*, 245; Smith, *Pol. History of Slavery*, I, 189; McClelland to Marcy, May 28, 1855, Marcy MSS.; Davis to Clayton, *Davis Works*, II, 488; Forney to Buchanan, Feb. 23, May 12, 1855, Buchanan MSS.; Forney to Black, May 22, 1855, Black MSS.; Mc-

Kean to Breckinridge, May 23, 1855, Breckinridge MSS.; *H. Rept. No. 200*, 34:1 (869), 937–944; *Union*, July 24, 1856; draft in Pierce's handwriting, Pierce MSS. (L. of C.); Lawrence, *Amos A. Lawrence*, 92, 95; Lawrence to Pomeroy, Apr. 17, 18, or 19, 1855, Lawrence Journal, Apr. 19, May 1, June 3, 1855, Dec. 30, 1856, Lawrence to "George," June 11, to Packard, July 14, to Pierce, July 15, 1855, Reeder to Lawrence, Feb. 1, 8, 1856, Lawrence to Reeder, Feb. 5, 1856, Lawrence MSS.; *Atchison Squatter Sovereign*, Feb. 3, 6, 13, Apr. 3, May 22, 1855; McClelland to Marcy, Apr. 11, 1857, Marcy MSS. The following items in the archives of the Indian office, Department of the Interior, were found for me through the kindness of Dr. Newton D. Mereness: Manypenny to Cumming, Mar. 31, 1855, Commissioner's Letter Book, LI, 186–187, Manypenny to Reeder, Mar. 31, 1855, *ibid.*, 189, Apr. 27, *ibid.*, 325–329, May 23, *ibid.*, 435. Cumming to Manypenny, May 16, 1855, enclosing copy of Clarke to Cumming, May 8, letters received; Manypenny to McClelland, Jan. 13, 1855, Report Book VIII, 240 (printed in part in Ser. 783).

Several recent studies are pointing the way to a rational consideration of the territorial troubles in Kansas. James C. Malin, "The Pro-Slavery Background of the Kansas Struggle," *Miss. Val. Hist. Rev.*, X, 285–305, and Elmer L. Craik, "Southern Interest in Territorial Kansas, 1854–1858," *Kans. Hist. Coll.*, XV, 334–450, are of special importance. Most interesting and important are Beveridge's conclusions in his *Abraham Lincoln*, II, 299–312.

CHAPTER LV, PP. 416–421

1. *Star*, June 28, 29, July 9, 13, 25, Aug. 2, 1855.
2. *Kans. Hist. Coll.*, V, 227–234; Elmore to Cushing, July 11, Aug. 23, Cushing to Elmore, Aug. 6, 1855, Atty. Gen. MSS.; *S. Ex. Journal*, X, 3, 36; *War Dept. Gen. Orders No. 20*, Dec. 10, 1855; Pierce to Marcy, Aug. 2, 4, 1855, Marcy MSS.; *Star*, July 30, Aug. 4; *Union*, Aug. 5; *Sun*, Aug. 7, 23, 1855. Beveridge, *Abraham Lincoln*, II, 318, says: "The Pawnee town site charge was never satisfactorily answered . . . [Reeder] must have been dismissed for the Pawnee scheme, regardless of political pressure." Mix to McClelland, July 23, 1855, Rept. Book IX, 462–474, Indian Office, Dept. of Interior; *Old Pawnee Capitol*.
3. Dennett, *Americans in Eastern Asia*, 225–241, 279–282, 347–352; Marcy to Wetmore, Mar. 26, 1855, Townsend Harris to Marcy, Aug. 1, 3, 1855, Marcy MSS.; Marcy to Townsend Harris, Sept. 12, 13, 1855, Japanese Instructions, State Dept. MSS.; Marcy to McLane, Feb. 26, 1855, Marcy to Parker, Sept. 27, 1855, Chinese Instructions, State Dept. MSS.; Pierce to Marcy, Aug. 16 [1855], Marcy MSS.
4. McKeon to Cushing, Aug. 6, 1855, Atty. Gen. MSS.; Pierce to Cushing, Aug. 6, Cushing to Pierce, Aug. 9, 1855, *S. Ex. Doc. No. 35*, 34:1 (819), 68–80; Pierce to Marcy, Aug. 6, 7 (3 notes), Marcy to Buchanan, Sept. 2, 1855, *Diary*, Apr. 18, 1857, Marcy MSS.; Pierce to Campbell, Aug. 9, 1855, Gratz Coll., Hist. Soc. Pa.; *American Secretaries of State*, VI, 242–256.
5. *Sun*, Aug. 27, 1855; Pryor, *Reminiscences of Peace and War*, 27; Sidney Webster to Marcy, Aug. 18, 1855, Marcy MSS.

Chapter LVI, pp. 425–428

1. Forney to Buchanan, July 13, Aug. 12, 1855, Jenks to Buchanan, July 16, Robert Tyler to Buchanan, July 27, J. H. Houston to Buchanan, Aug. 6, 1855, Buchanan MSS.; Forney to Breckinridge, Aug. 8, 1855, Breckinridge MSS.; Forney to Nicholson, Aug. 26, 1855, N. Y. Hist. Soc.

2. B. B. French to H. F. French, Sept. 23, 1855, French MSS.

3. Campbell to Nevitt, Mar. 1, 1856, Pierce MSS. (L. of C.).

4. Minot to George, Sept. 25, 1855, N. H. Hist. Soc.; Jones, *J. Glancy Jones*, I, 255–257.

5. Smith, *Cass*, 776–777; Chicago *Times*, Dec. 12, 1855; Forney to Buchanan, Oct. 23, 1855, Gilmore to Buchanan, Feb. 26, 1856, Buchanan MSS.; B. Tucker to Douglas, Apr. 19, 1856, Atchison to Douglas, Feb. 28, 1856, Douglas MSS.

6. Jones to Buchanan, Nov. 18, Forney to Buchanan, Nov. 25, Randall to Buchanan, Nov. 5, 19, 1855, Buchanan MSS.; Jones to Nicholson, Nov. 18, S. R. Anderson to Nicholson, Nov. 21, 1855, N. Y. Hist. Soc.

7. Webster to George, Nov. 7, 20, 23, 1855, Minot to George, Nov. 9, 1855, N. H. Hist. Soc.; N. H. *Patriot*, Oct. 24, Nov. 21, 1855.

Chapter LVII, pp. 429–434

1. Appleton to Buchanan, Dec. 3, 1855, Buchanan MSS.; Buchanan, *Works*, IX, 437, 444, 449–457; *S. Ex. Doc. No. 35*, 34:1 (819), especially 43–65. The message and reports are found in *H. Ex. Doc. No. 1*, 34:1 (840–842), and *H. Ex. Doc. No. 10*, 34:1 (846).

2. Thomas, *Russo-American Relations, 1815–1867*, 115.

Chapter LVIII, pp. 435–437

1. Jones to Buchanan, Mar. 9, 1856, Parker to Buchanan, Dec. 14, 1855, Buchanan MSS.

2. *Kans. Hist. Coll.*, V, 243.

3. Johnston and Browne, *Alexander H. Stephens*, 300–301; *Ga. Hist. Quart.*, VI, 166, letter wrongly dated Feb. 1, 1856 by editor, it was written Jan. 1, 1856; *American Secretaries of State*, VI, 256–258; Clay to Clay, Sr., Jan. 3, 1856, Clay MSS.

Chapter LIX, pp. 438–440

1. *Globe*, 34:1, 134; Eckloff, *Memories of a Senate Page*, 5.

2. *Star*, Jan. 18, 25, 26, 29, Feb. 2, 1856; N. Y. *Herald*, Jan. 23, 1856; for Hale's career see Chandler, *Statue of John P. Hale*.

Chapter LX, pp. 441–445

1. N. Y. *Herald*, Jan. 26, 1856. Beveridge in comment on this message in *Abraham Lincoln*, II, 337, says, "It is hard to see what else the President could have said." Mason thought Pierce, "had better not have done so," Diary, Jan. 24, 1856.

2. *Union*, Apr. 26, 1856; Forney to Buchanan, Feb. 3, 1856, Buchanan MSS.; Rhodes, *History of the United States*, II, 114; McLaughlin, *Life of John Kelly*, 154–156; Biggs to Reid, Feb. 2, 185[6], Reid MSS.

3. Draft of Proclamation in Cushing's handwriting in Pierce MSS. (L. of C.); Carroll, *Twelve Americans*, 19; *Kansas Hist. Coll.*, V, 245–247, 259–261; *Star*, Feb. 14, 1856; N. Y. *Herald*, Feb. 16, 17, 19, 1856; Mason's Diary, Feb. 17, 1856.

4. *Globe*, 34:1, 438, 496, 587, 591, App. 105.

5. *Ibid.*, 639, App. 280–289; *S. Rept. No. 34*, 34:1 (836).

CHAPTER LXI, PP. 446–449

1. Crandall, *Early History of the Republican Party*, passim.

2. *Globe*, 34:1, App. 399–405, 481, 512–526.

3. Johnston and Browne, *Alexander H. Stephens*, 308.

CHAPTER LXII, PP. 450–456

1. *Herald*, Apr. 2, 1856; Mason Diary, Mar. 17, 18, May 2, 8, 1856.

2. *Star*, Jan. 2, 1856; *Herald*, Feb. 2, 16, Mar. 2, 1856; John Cochrane to George, Feb. 1, 4, Mar. 1, to Webster, Mar. 1, 1856, J. G. Brodhead to George, Feb. 12, I. V. Fowler to George, Feb. 29, Webster to George, Feb. 5, 9, Mar. 3, Pierce to George, Mar. 3, 1856, N. H. Hist. Soc.; H. F. French to B. B. French, Feb. 10, 1856, French MSS.

3. Pierce to Henry Pierce, Mar. 17, 1856, Pierce MSS. (Hillsborough); Webster to George, Mar. 21, 1856, N. H. Hist. Soc.

4. Toombs, *Corr.*, 367–368.

5. Atchison to Corbin, Mar. 16, 1856, Rutgers Univ. Lib.

6. N. Y. *Herald*, Jan. 27, 1856; *Star*, Feb. 7, 1856; Johnson, *Stephen A. Douglas*, 288; Sheahan, *Stephen A. Douglas*, 286.

7. Rice to Breckinridge, Feb. 12, 1856, Breckinridge MSS.; Douglas to Reid, Jan. 11, 1856, Reid to Mrs. Reid, Mar. 3, 1856, Reid MSS.; Clay to Clay, Sr., Mar. 10, 1856, Clay MSS.; D. T. Disney to Douglas, series of letters Feb. 26–Mar. 7, 1856; Jas. W. Singleton to Douglas, Mar. 5, 1856, Bev. Tucker to Douglas, Apr. 19, 1856, Douglas MSS.; Mason Diary, Mar. 18, 25, 1856.

8. N. Y. *Herald*, Feb. 16, 21, 1856.

9. Harris to Breckinridge, Apr. 7, 1856, Breckinridge MSS.

10. Forney to Breckinridge, Jan. 25, 1856, Breckinridge MSS.; Forney to Buchanan, Jan. 3, Feb. 3, 26, Jenks to Buchanan, Jan. 18, 26, 1856, Buchanan MSS.; *Union*, Mar. 28, 1856; *Herald*, Apr. 2, 1856; Biggs to Reid, Jan. 21, 1856, Reid MSS.; Everett Diary, Dec. 16, 1853.

11. Jones to Buchanan, Apr. 28, 29, 1856, Buchanan MSS.

12. Rice to Breckinridge, May 1, 1856, Breckinridge MSS.; Tyler to Buchanan, May 26, Corcoran to Buchanan, May 27, 1856, Buchanan MSS.; *Herald*, Apr. 2, 29, 1856; S. Treat to Douglas, Apr. 26, 1856, S. F. Butterworth to Douglas, Apr. 30, May 3, 1856, Brown to Douglas, May 3, 1856, Kimball to Douglas, May 10, 1856, Redfield to Douglas, May 31, 1856, T. M.

Ward to Douglas, June 1, 1856, Button to Douglas, June 1, 1856, Douglas MSS.

13. Upham to Benj. F. Butler, May 24, to Forney, May 24, 1856, Benj. F. Butler MSS.; Isaac O. Barnes to Buchanan, Jan. 29, Upham to Buchanan, May 24, 1856, Buchanan MSS.

CHAPTER LXIII, PP. 457–463

1. Marcy to Buchanan, Jan. 3, 28, 1856, Buchanan MSS.; *Herald,* Jan. 16, 1856.

2. Buchanan, *Works,* X, 12, 23, 31; *S. Ex. Doc. No. 35,* 34:1 (819), 246–251; *Union,* Feb. 26, 1856; *Star,* Feb. 25, 27, 1856; *Herald,* Feb. 19, 27, 28, 29, Mar. 1, 1856.

3. *Globe,* 34:1, 489, 507, 528, 539, 544, 618, 622, 697, 1676; Slidell to Buchanan, Mar. 11, 1856, Buchanan MSS.

4. Scroggs, *Filibusters and Financiers,* 126, 129–130; Williams, *Anglo-American Isthmian Diplomacy,* 210–212; N. Y. *Herald,* Apr. 30, May 1, 5, 6, 8, 9, 13, 1856; *Globe,* 34:1, 699, 1069, 1108, 1159, App. 440; Marcy to Amos B. Corwine, May 12, 1856, Special Missions, III, State Dept. MSS.; Elliot to Marcy, Mar. 22, 1856, San Domingo, Consular Reports, II, State Dept. MSS.; Mary Treudley, "United States and San Domingo, 1789–1866," *Journal of Race Development,* VII; *Pol. Sci. Quart.,* VIII, 15.

5. Pierce to Marcy, May 12, 1856, Marcy to Dallas, May 12, 1856, Marcy MSS.; Dallas to Marcy, Apr. 25, 1856, Dallas, *Letters,* 25; Marcy to Dallas, May 24, 1856; Great Britain, Instructions, XIII, State Dept. MSS.; *S. Ex. Doc. No. 40,* 34:1 (823); *American Secretaries of State,* VI, 258–262.

CHAPTER LXIV, PP. 464–465

1. Peaslee to George, Apr. 25, May 15, Webster to George, May 1, John C. Wilson to George, May 10, 1856, N. H. Hist. Soc.

2. N. Y. *Herald,* Apr. 30, May 15, 20, 22, 25, 1856.

3. *Globe,* 34:1, 1271, 1324, 1725.

CHAPTER LXV, PP. 466–469

1. Curtis, *Buchanan,* II, 170–173; Slidell to Buchanan, Mar. 11, May 26, 1856, Buchanan MSS.

2. Pre-convention tabulation of votes, Atty.-Gen. MSS.

3. N. Y. *Herald,* May 29, 1856; *Ledger,* June 2, 1856; G. H. Martin to Buchanan, June 3, Reynolds to Buchanan, June 1, Forney to Buchanan, Nov. 12, 1856, Buchanan MSS.; Martin to Black, Mar. 31, 1857, Black MSS.

4. *Official Proceedings of the National Democratic Convention, passim; Trinity Historical Papers,* VI, 89; *Yulee,* 16; *Speech of Benjamin F. Butler at Lowell,* Aug. 10, 1860; W. A. Richardson to Douglas, June 1, 1856, Peter Gorman to Douglas, June 5, 1856, Disney to Douglas, June 7, 1856, Preston to Douglas, June 7, 1856, Pettit to Douglas, June 10, 1856, Douglas MSS.; Curry to Clay, May 10, 1856, Clay to Clay, Sr., June 7, 1856, Clay MSS.

5. Marcy to Dallas, June 10, 1856, Marcy MSS.; N. Y. *Herald,* June 8, 1856; Clay to Clay, Sr., June 7, 1856, Clay MSS.

CHAPTER LXVI, PP. 473–477

1. *Kans. Hist. Coll.,* IV, 386, 414–421, 425, 434; Sumner to Cooper, May 12, 1856, 244S of 56, Adj. Gen. Office, War Dept. MSS.

2. Coleman, *Crittenden,* II, 129; Slidell to Buchanan, June 17, 1856, P. F. Smith to Buchanan, Feb. 3, 1857, Buchanan MSS.; Johnston and Browne, *Alexander H. Stephens,* 309; Cooper to Harney, May 7, 1856, Letters sent, Adj. Gen. Office, War Dept. MSS.; *Kans. Hist. Coll.,* IV, 422–423, 425, 429; *Globe,* 34:1, 1381–1382.

3. *Globe,* 34:1, 1506, 1519, 1520, 1525, 1572, 1574, App. 772, 805; Lawrence to Haven, July 28, 1856, Lawrence MSS.

CHAPTER LXVII, PP. 478–480

1. *Kans. Hist. Coll.,* IV, 422–423, 448–449, 429–430, 450–453, 457.

2. Pomeroy to Lawrence, July 24, 1856, Lawrence to Pomeroy, July 12, 1856, Lawrence MSS.

3. *Globe,* 34:1, 1913, 1929, 2091–2093.

4. When Pierce heard that Stevens had invoked military law to overthrow the Washington territorial courts, he removed Stevens and appointed Joe Lane as governor, August 14, but the Senate took no action upon it and Stevens was not disturbed. *S. Ex. Journal,* X, 147, *S. Ex. Doc. No. 98,* 34:1 (823), *S. Ex. Doc. No. 47,* 34:3 (881); *Globe,* 34:3, 524–526, 534; Marcy disallowed the proclamation of martial law, Sept. 12, Stevens, *Life of Gen. I. I. Stevens,* II, 250 (this large life makes no mention of the removal).

5. *Globe,* 34:2, 35, 51; *Sun,* Aug. 20, 22, 29; *Papers of Thomas Ruffin,* II, 518; Johnston and Browne, *Alexander H. Stephens,* 315–316; *Union,* Sept. 9, 1856.

CHAPTER LXVIII, PP. 481–483

1. *Sun,* Sept. 1, 2, 5, 1856.

2. *Kans. Hist. Coll.,* IV, 426–428; Lawrence to Pierce, Sept. 8, 1856, Lawrence MSS.

3. *Kans. Hist. Coll.,* IV, 428, 468–470, 527, 535; Holloway, *History of Kansas,* 394; Wilder, *Annals of Kansas,* 136, 164–165; Cushing to Isaacs, Sept. 2, Isaacs to Cushing, Oct. 11, 22, enclosing indictment of May 20, 1856, Atty.-Gen. MSS.; Lawrence to Robinson, Sept. 16, to Mrs. Robinson, Oct. 3, 1856, Lawrence MSS.; Lawrence, *Amos A. Lawrence,* 111; *Union,* Sept. 10, 1856.

CHAPTER LXIX, PP. 484–488

1. *N. H. State Capitol Reporter,* Sept. 26, 1856; *N. H. Patriot,* Oct. 1, 1856; Webster to George, Aug. 21, James L. Orr to George, Sept. 1, Pierce to Butterfield, Sept. 24, 1856, N. H. Hist. Soc.; *Sun,* Sept. 25, 1856.

2. N. G. Upham to Marcy, Mar. 3, 1854, Geo. Bancroft to Marcy, Sept. 24, 1856, Marcy MSS.; N. G. Upham to Buchanan, Apr. 9, 1855, May 24, 1856, Buchanan MSS.; *French Journal,* 100; B. B. French to H. F. French, May 29, July 15, Nov. 27, 1856, H. F. French to B. B. French; June 16, 22, 1854, June 30, 1855, French MSS.

3. *Kans. Hist. Coll.,* IV, 430–431, 498–499, 535–538, 573; *Union,* Sept. 27, 1856.

4. *N. H. State Capitol Reporter,* Oct. 3, 10, 1856; *N. H. Patriot,* Oct. 8, 15, 1856; *Star,* Sept. 30, Oct. 9, 17, 1856; *Sun,* Oct. 2, 1856; *Kans. Hist. Coll.,* IV, 572; *Union,* Oct. 8, 1856; Marcy to Dallas, Oct. 7, 1856, Marcy MSS.

5. Pierce to Breckinridge, July 22, 1856, Breckinridge MSS.; *Recollections of Christopher Andrews,* 101; Mason, *James Murray Mason,* 117; J. Barton Breckinridge to J. C. Breckinridge, Oct. 10, 1856, Breckinridge MSS.

6. Pierce to Buchanan, Nov. 20, 1856, Buchanan MSS.

CHAPTER LXX, PP. 489–495

1. McClelland to Grosvenor, Nov. 17, 1856, McClelland Letter Book, L. of C. The final message and reports are found in *H. Ex. Docs. No. 1, 2,* 34: 3 (893–894, 896).

2. Dallas to Marcy, June 13, 20, Aug. 27, 1856, British Despatches, Marcy to Dallas, Sept. 26, 1856, British Instructions, State Dept. MSS.; *Correspondence respecting Central America, 1856–1860, presented to both Houses of Parliament,* 24 ff.; *American Secretaries of State,* VI, 229–233, 283–285.

3. Upon receipt of the news of rioting at Panama, Amos B. Corwine had been commissioned to investigate. He had reported the almost ludicrous incident of a riot caused by a slice of watermelon and a dime. Out of an altercation between a drunken American and a negro vendor over the above articles there developed a fight which had been brewing because the Panama R. R. Co. had put into service a small tug to bring passengers from ship to shore and thus had deprived many of the negro boatmen of their livelihood. Several lives and much property, most of it belonging to the railroad, had been destroyed in the resulting melée. Corwine reported that the Colombian officials were utterly incapable of providing proper protection. This report plus the fact that news had lately arrived that the Colombian Congress had recently passed a law levying taxes upon our mail crossing the isthmus which were calculated to amount to $2,000,000 each year had caused Pierce and Marcy to send Isaac E. Morse of Louisiana to join our minister Bowlin in an attempt to get damages for the April outrage and relief from the new law. Marcy to Corwine, May 12, 1856, Special Missions, III, Marcy to Isaac E. Morse, Oct. 30, 1856, *ibid.;* Corwine to Marcy, July 18, 1856, Marcy to Bowlin, July 3, 1856, Colombian Instructions, XV, State Dept. MSS.

4. *An Autobiography of Abraham Lincoln,* 126. Mason of Iowa thought the message " calculated to inflame the angry feelings of the largest portion of the Union. . . . The President does not seem to be aware of that fact," Diary, Dec. 4, 1856.

5. Geary to Pierce, Sept. 19, 1856, State Dept. MSS.; *Kans. Hist. Coll.,* IV, 613; Guthrie to Breckinrdige, Nov. 27, Dec. 4, 1856, Breckinridge MSS.; J.

B. Donalson to McClelland, Nov. 4, 1856, Cushing to E. F. Whittlesey, Feb. 11, 1857, Atty.-Gen. MSS.; Geary to Pierce, Dec. 22, 1856, Jan. 12, 1857, Pierce MSS. (L. of C.); *S. Ex. Jour.*, X, 162, 188, 192, 199, 202–203, 209.

CHAPTER LXXI, PP. 496–503

1. *Globe*, 34:3, 10, 12, 14, 26, 30, 53, 71, 94, App. 63; P. R. George to George, Feb. 8, 1857, N. H. Hist. Soc.; Pierce to Buchanan, Feb. 19, 1857, Buchanan MSS.
2. Marcy to Dallas, Jan. 31, 1857, British Instructions, State Dept. MSS.; Marcy to Bowlin and Morse, Dec. 3, 1856, Colombian Instructions, State Dept. MSS.; Marcy to Parker, Feb. 2, 27, 1857, Chinese Instructions, State Dept. MSS.; Rippy, *United States and Mexico*, 213.
3. Cooper to Smith, Nov. 1, 1856, Jan. 8, 1857, Letters Sent, P. F. Smith to Cooper, Jan. 27, 1857, Adj. Gen. Office, War Dept. MSS.; *Kans. Hist. Coll.*, IV, 710, 731, 735–736; Gihon, *Gov. Geary's Administration in Kansas*, 284.
4. *Kans. Hist. Coll.*, IV, 661; Marcy to Geary, Jan. 6, 1857 (trial draft), Marcy MSS.; Marcy to Geary, Jan. 8, 1857, *Kans. Hist. Coll.*, IV, 688, 699. Geary to Buchanan, Jan. 16, 1857, Buchanan MSS.; *Kans. Hist. Coll.*, IV, 726; S. D. Lecompte to Cushing, Jan. 9, 1857, Atty.-Gen. MSS.; *S. Ex. Jour.*, X, 179–180, 182, 194, 197, 199, 202, 203; *Kans. Hist. Coll.*, IV, 729; Geary to Buchanan, Feb. 20, 1857, State Dept. MSS.
5. Mrs. Davis, *Memoir of Jefferson Davis*, I, 529; Clay, *Belle of the Fifties*, 63.
6. Morgan Library, N. Y. C.

CHAPTERS LXXII–LXXVI, PP. 507–539

These latter chapters are drawn almost entirely from the three manuscript collections at Washington, Concord, and Hillsborough, and from the files of the New Hampshire *Patriot* and other local papers. Sidney Webster, *Franklin Pierce and his Administration*, the various Hawthorne sources, and Irelan also contribute occasional items.

In this later period personal recollections have been of assistance. Mrs. Pierce's nieces and nephew, the late Mrs. George Ripley, through the kindness of her son, Alfred L. Ripley, Mrs. Jane A. Snow and Gen. Wm. A. Aiken, very courteously contributed data in retrospect and carefully answered my questions. William P. Fowler, whom I have mentioned before, supplied me with some family traditions and a description of Little Boar's Head which he now owns. At Concord Miss Edith P. Minot, Miss Lena Minot, Miss Almira Fletcher and William J. Ahern gave me their interesting recollections, and Judge William H. Sawyer recounted to me a number of local traditions. Hamilton Fish Webster sent me some of his father's printed memoirs. Rev. Arthur P. Phinney of Concord supplied me with the record of Pierce's confirmation at St. Paul's. Through the kindness of Charles Lyon Chandler, Miss Lucy T. Poor provided a helpful reminiscence.

The episode connected with the Knights of the Golden Circle and the correspondence with Seward is based upon data in *War of the Rebellion; Official Records of the Union and Confederate Armies*, Series II, v. II (no.

115), p. 1244 *et seq.* Material contained in the papers of Robert McClelland was supplied through the courtesy of the late Mrs. Robert M. Berry, C. M. Burton, and Milo M. Quaife of Detroit. Debate on subjects in this chapter is found in *Globe*, 37:2, March 26, 1862, Senate, with special reference to p. 1371.

The best account of Mrs. Pierce's life is found in Mrs. Holloway's *Ladies of the White House*. Mrs. Holloway corresponded with Gen. Pierce, Sidney Webster, and others who knew Mrs. Pierce well, and incorporated much that they told her in the sketch of Mrs. Pierce in that volume. Prof. Aiken prepared an obituary which appeared in the Boston *Recorder*, Jan. 8, 1864. A letter which Pierce wrote Mrs. Holloway about his wife, March 29, 1869, was sold at auction at Anderson's in N. Y., Dec. 12, 1918. Hardly any of Mrs. Pierce's letters to her husband have survived. The largest single group of her letters are in the Lawrence MSS. We may suspect that Pierce before his death destroyed what must have been a voluminous correspondence between himself and his wife.

The friendship of Pierce for Hawthorne, besides being a very rich experience for them both, has been of inestimable service to the former for it preserved the best in his nature. The relatively large amount of Hawthorne literature has contributed a great deal to this biography and the testimony of the famous author has been a most revealing source. Hawthorne's campaign biography of Pierce is rather disappointing; it was done under pressure and Hawthorne never was at his best when pressed. Much more revealing are other items of his. His letters found in his son's *Nathaniel Hawthorne and his Wife*, Bridge's *Personal Recollections of Nathaniel Hawthorne*, *Love Letters of Nathaniel Hawthorne*, *Letters of Hawthorne to Wm. D. Ticknor*, contain numerous references to Pierce and explain vividly his estimate of his friend's character. His dedication in *Our Old Home* and stray references in the *Passages* from his French and Italian, English and American note books which his wife published with some alterations after his death contain much of value. Julian Hawthorne published a second work, *Hawthorne and his Circle*, in which he recorded his boyish impressions of Gen. Pierce; and items are found in the work of Hawthorne's daughter and her husband, Rose Hawthorne Lathrop, *Memories of Hawthorne*, and Geo. P. Lathrop, *A Study of Hawthorne*. The accounts of Hawthorne's relations with his publishers preserve a number of anecdotes: James T. Fields published his *Hawthorne* in 1876 and it was later incorporated in his *Yesterdays with Authors*, M. A. De Wolfe Howe edited Mrs. Fields' *Memories of a Hostess*, and Mrs. Ticknor in her *Hawthorne and his Publisher* made the letters of Hawthorne to Ticknor more accessible than in the privately printed edition mentioned above, although she did not publish them entirely. F. P. Stearns, *Life and Genius of Nathaniel Hawthorne*, F. B. Sanborn, *Hawthorne and his Friends*, and Lloyd R. Morris, *Rebellious Puritan*, have made contributions to these pages. Sidney Webster, *Franklin Pierce and his Administration*, published Pierce's own account of Hawthorne's death. Most valuable have been the numerous letters from Hawthorne and Mrs. Hawthorne found in the various collections of Pierce MSS. Hawthorne could have performed no greater service for his friend.

BIBLIOGRAPHY

Manuscript Collections

William Allen, L. C.
Attorney General, L. C.
Albert Baker, private collection.
George Bancroft, Mass. Hist. Soc.
Jeremiah S. Black, L. C.
John C. Breckinridge, L. C.
James Buchanan, L. C.
    "   "   Hist. Soc. Pa.
Edmund Burke, L. C.
Elihu Burritt, Library of Institute, New Britain, Conn.
Benjamin F. Butler, L. C.
Lewis Cass, Burton Collection, Detroit Pub. Lib.
Salmon P. Chase, L. C.
  "   "   "   Hist. Soc. Pa.
John F. H. Claiborne, L. C.
Clement C. Clay, Duke Univ. Lib.
Abel R. Corbin, Rutgers Univ. Lib.
Laura Jones Crawford, L. C.
Jefferson Davis, L. C.
John A. Dix, private collection.
Stephen A. Douglas, University of Chicago.
Edward Everett, Mass. Hist. Soc.
John Fairfield, L. C.
Asa Fowler, private collection.
Benjamin B. French, L. C.
John W. Geary, private collection.
John H. George, N. H. Hist. Soc.
Gratz Collection, Hist. Soc. Pa.
William M. Gwin Memoirs, University of California.
John P. Hale, N. H. Hist. Soc.
Joseph Holt, L. C.
Interior Dept., Archives in Indian Office.
Andrew Jackson, L. C.
Journal History, Historical Library of the Latter Day Saints, Salt Lake
    City, Utah.
Horatio King, L. C.
Joseph Lane, Ore. Hist. Soc.
Amos A. Lawrence, Mass. Hist. Soc.
Amos Lawrence, Mass. Hist. Soc.

William L. Marcy, L. C.
Charles Mason (typewritten copy of Diary), L. C.
Robert McClelland, L. C.
"   "   private collection.
Marcus Morton, Mass. Hist. Soc.
Alfred O. P. Nicholson, N. Y. Hist. Soc.
Philip Phillips, L. C.
Franklin Pierce, N. H. Hist. Soc.
"   "   L. C.
"   "   private collection.
James K. Polk, L. C.
Alexander Ramsey, Minn. State Hist. Soc.
David S. Reid, N. C. Hist. Com.
John Sessford, L. C.
Henry H. Sibley, Minn. State Hist. Soc.
State Dept. Archives, State Dept.
John W. Stevenson, L. C.
Alexander H. H. Stuart, L. C.
Benjamin Tappan, L. C.
John Tyler, L. C.
Martin Van Buren, L. C.
War Dept. Archives, War. Dept.
Gideon Welles, L. C.
Levi Woodbury, L. C.

BIOGRAPHICAL MATERIAL

Adams, John Quincy:
   Memoirs of, Charles F. Adams, ed., Phila., 1876.
Allen, William:
   Decade of Addresses, Concord, Mass., 1830.
Andrews, Christopher C.:
   Recollections of, Alice E. Andrews, ed., Cleveland, 1928.
Benjamin, Judah P.:
   Life, Pierce Butler, Phila., 1907.
Benton, Thomas H.:
   Thirty Years View, N. Y., 1854.
   Life, Wm. M. Meigs, Phila., 1904.
Bigelow, John:
   Retrospections of an Active Life, N. Y., 1909.
Brown, Bedford:
   "Selections from the Correspondence of," ed. W. K. Boyd, *Hist. Papers
      of the Trinity College Hist. Soc.*, Series VI, 1906.
Buchanan, James:
   Works, John Bassett Moore, ed., Phila., 1908–1910.
   Life, Geo. T. Curtis, N. Y., 1883.
Butler, Benjamin F.:
   Speech . . . delivered at Lowell, Aug. 10, 1860.

Caldwell, Rev. Zenas A.:
> *Life in Earnest; or Memories and Remains of,* Stephen M. Vail, Boston, 1855.

Campbell, James:
> *Records of Am. Cath. Hist. Soc. of Phila.,* V. 265–303, article by John M. Campbell.

Campbell, John A.:
> *Life,* Henry G. Connor, Boston, 1920.

Cass, Lewis:
> *Life and Times of,* W. L. G. Smith, N. Y., 1856.
> *Life,* Andrew C. McLaughlin, Boston, 1891.

Chase, Salmon P.:
> "Diary and Correspondence of," *Annual Rept. of the Am. Hist. Assoc., 1902,* II.
> *Life,* Albert B. Hart, Boston, 1899.

Clay, Mrs. C. C.:
> *A Belle of the Fifties,* N. Y., 1905.

Clingman, Thomas L.:
> *Selections from the Speeches and Writings of,* Raleigh, 1877.

Crittenden, John J.:
> *Life,* Mrs. Chapman Coleman, Phila., 1877.

Cobb, Howell:
> "Correspondence of," *Annual Rept. of the Am. Hist. Assoc., 1911,* II.
> "Papers," *Ga. Hist. Quart.,* VI, Nos. 1, 2, 3.

Cushing, Caleb:
> *Life,* Claude M. Fuess, N. Y., 1923.

Dallas, George M.:
> *A Series of Letters from London,* Julia Dallas, ed., Phila., 1869.

Dana, Richard H.:
> *Life,* Charles F. Adams, Jr., Boston, 1890.

Davis, Jefferson:
> *Jefferson Davis, Constitutionalist, his letters, papers and speeches* (cited as *Works*), Dunbar Rowland, ed., N. Y., 1923.
> *A Memoir,* Varina H. Davis, N. Y., 1890.
> *Life and Reminiscences of . . . by distinguished men of his times,* Baltimore, 1890.
> *Life,* Wm. E. Dodd, Phila., 1907.
> *Life,* H. J. Eckenrode, N. Y., 1923.
> *Life,* Allen Tate, N. Y., 1929.
> *High Stakes and Hair Trigger,* Robert W. Winston, N. Y., 1930.
> *Life,* Elisabeth Cutting, N. Y., 1930.

Dix, Dorothea L.:
> *Life,* Francis Tiffany, Boston, 1890.

Dix, John A.:
> *Memoirs of,* Morgan Dix, N. Y., 1883.

Dobbin, James C.:
> *Portrait of Eminent Americans now living,* John Livingston, N. Y., 1853–1854.

Dodge, Augustus Caesar:
Life, Louis Pelzer, Iowa City, 1909.
Dodge, Henry:
Life, Louis Pelzer, Iowa City, 1911.
Douglas, Stephen A.:
Life, Henry M. Flint (sometimes A Member of the Western Bar), N. Y.,
1860.
Life, Allen Johnson, N. Y., 1908.
"Stephen A. Douglas, 1850–1860," Ed. McMahon, *Wash. Hist. Quart.,* II.
Life, James W. Sheaham, N. Y., 1860.
"Life," Frank E. Stevens, *Journal of the Ill. State Hist. Soc.,* XVI,
Nos. 3, 4.
Du Pont, Samuel F.:
Life, Henry A. Du Pont, N. Y., 1926.
Eckloff, Charles F.:
Memories of a Senate Page, N. Y., 1909.
Eddy, Mary B.:
According to the Flesh, Fleta C. Springer, N. Y., 1930.
Life, Sibyl C. Wilbur, Boston, 1907.
Everett, Edward:
Life, Paul R. Frothingham, Boston, 1925.
Fairfield, John:
Letters of, Arthur G. Staples, ed., Lewiston, Me., 1922.
Field, Maunsell B.:
Reminiscences of Many Men and of some Women, N. Y., 1874.
Foote, Henry S.:
Casket of Reminiscences, Washington, 1874.
Forney, John W.:
Anecdotes of Public Men, N. Y., 1873–81.
French, Benjamin B.:
From the Diary and Correspondence of, Amos T. French, ed., N. Y.,
1904.
Geary, John W.:
Gov. Geary's Administration in Kansas, John H. Gihon, Phila., 1857.
Greeley, Horace:
Recollections of a Busy Life, N. Y., 1868.
Grow, Galusha A.:
Life, James T. Du Bois and Gertrude L. Mathews, Boston, 1917.
Guthrie, James:
"James Guthrie—Kentuckian, 1782–1869," Robt. S. Cotterill, *Ky. Hist.
Soc. Reg.,* XX, Sept., 1922.
Hale, John P.:
The Statue of . . . an account of the unveiling ceremonies, Wm. E.
Chandler, Concord, N. H., 1892.
Hamlin, Hannibal:
Life and times of, Chas. E. Hamlin, Cambridge, 1899.
Twelve Americans, Howard Carroll, N. Y., 1883.

Hatch, Albert R.:
  Proc. of Southern N. H. Bar Assoc., 1894, sketch by Calvin Page.
Hawthorne, Nathaniel:
  Fanshawe, Boston, 1876.
  Our Old Home, Boston, 1863.
  Snow Image, N. Y., 1864.
  Letters of . . . to Wm. D. Ticknor, 1851–64, Newark, N. J., 1910.
  Love Letters of, Chicago, 1907.
  Passages from the American Note-Books, Boston, 1868.
  Passages from the English Note-Books, Boston, 1870.
  Passages from the French and Italian Note-Books, Boston, 1872.
  Personal Recollections of, Horatio Bridge, N. Y., 1893.
  Hawthorne, James T. Fields, Boston, 1876.
  Yesterdays with Authors, James T. Fields, Boston, 1883.
  Memories of a Hostess (Mrs. James T. Fields), M. A. De Wolfe Howe,
      ed., Boston, 1922.
  Nathaniel Hawthorne and his wife, Julian Hawthorne, Boston, 1884.
  Hawthorne and his Circle, Julian Hawthorne, N. Y., 1903.
  A Study of Hawthorne, Geo. P. Lathrop, Boston, 1876.
  Memories of Hawthorne, Rose Hawthorne Lathrop, Boston, 1897.
  Rebellious Puritan, Lloyd R. Morris, N. Y., 1927.
  Hawthorne and his Friends, Frank B. Sanborn, Cedar Rapids, Ia., 1908.
  Life and Genius of Nathaniel Hawthorne, Frank P. Stearns, Phila., 1906.
  Hawthorne and his Publisher, Caroline Ticknor, Boston, 1913.
Hibbard, Harry:
  Proc. of Grafton & Coös Co. Bar Assoc., 1895, sketch by Geo. S. Hale.
Hill, Isaac:
  Biography of, Cyrus P. Bradley, Concord, N. H., 1835.
Houston, Sam:
  The Raven, Marquis James, Indianapolis, 1929.
Hunter, Robert M. T.:
  " Correspondence of," *Annual Rept. of the Am. Hist. Assoc., 1916,* II.
  Memoir of, Martha T. Hunter, Washington, 1903.
Jones, George W.:
  Life, John C. Parish, Iowa City, 1912.
Jones, J. Glancy:
  Life and Public Services of, Charles H. Jones, Phila., 1910.
Kelly, John:
  Life and Times of, James F. McLaughlin, N. Y., 1885.
Lawrence, Amos:
  Extracts from the Diary and Correspondence of, Wm. R. Lawrence,
      Boston, 1855.
Lawrence, Amos A.:
  Life of, Wm. Lawrence, Boston, 1888.
Lincoln, Abraham:
  An Autobiography of Abraham Lincoln, compiled by N. W. Stephenson,
      Indianapolis, 1926.

Longfellow, Henry W.:
> *Life*, Geo. L. Austin, Boston, 1882.
> *Life*, Samuel Longfellow, Boston, 1886.

Lyell, Sir Charles:
> *Life, Letters and Journals of*, Katherine M. Lyell, London, 1881.

Marcy, Wm. L.:
> *American Secretaries of State and their Diplomacy*, VI, Samuel F.
> Bemis, ed., sketch by H. Barrett Learned, N. Y., 1928.

Mason, James M.:
> *Public Life and Diplomatic Correspondence of*, Virginia Mason, N. Y.,
> 1906.

Mason, Jeremiah:
> *Memoir and Correspondence of*, G. S. Hillard, Boston, 1873.

McClelland, Robert:
> *Men of Mark of the Cumberland Valley, Pa.*, Alfred Nevin, Phila., 1876.

Nicholson, Alfred O. P.:
> *Sketches of the Bench and Bar of Tennessee*, Joshua W. Caldwell,
> Knoxville, 1898.

Pierce, Franklin (see also Campaign bibliography):
> *Review of the Pierce Administration*, Anna E. Carroll, Boston, 1856.
> "Franklin Pierce the Lawyer," David Cross, *Proc. of the N. H. State
> Bar Assoc., 1900.*
> *The Republic: Life and Times of Franklin Pierce*, John R. Irelan, Chi-
> cago, 1888.
> *Pierce Genealogy, Descendants of Thomas Pierce*, Fred B. Pierce,
> Worcester, Mass., 1882.
> *Dedication of a Statue of Gen. Franklin Pierce*, Henry H. Metcalf, ed.,
> Concord, 1914.
> *Franklin Pierce and Edmund Burke*, Henry H. Metcalf, Concord, N. H.,
> 1930.
> "Franklin Pierce," Grace Agnes Thompson, *New England Magazine*,
> Dec., 1904.
> *Franklin Pierce and his Administration*, Sidney Webster, N. Y., 1892.
> *Frank Pierce. His Political Life*, anon., n.p. [1863].
> *New Hampshire Peace Democracy, Vallandigham and Frank Pierce*,
> anon., n.p., n.d.
> *Review of the Veto Message of President Pierce of Feb. 17, 1855, on the
> Bill relating to French Spoliations*, James H. Causten, n.p. [1855].
> *The Record of a Month*, anon., n.p. [1864].

Polk, James K.:
> *Diary*, Milo M. Quaife, ed., Chicago, 1910.
> *Life*, Eugene I. McCormac, Berkeley, Cal., 1922.

Pryor, Mrs. Roger A.:
> *Reminiscences of Peace and War*, N. Y., 1904.
> *My Day*, N. Y., 1909.

Quitman, John A.:
> *Life*, J. F. H. Claiborne, N. Y., 1860.

Rix, James Madison:
Proc. of Grafton and Coös Co. Bar Assoc. for 1896, 295–316, by Henry O. Kent.
Ruffin, Thomas:
Papers, ed. by J. G. de R. Hamilton, Raleigh, 1918.
Seward, Wm. H.:
Life, Frederic Bancroft, N. Y., 1900.
Seward at Washington, Fred W. Seward, N. Y., 1891.
Seymour, Horatio:
Twelve Americans, Howard Carroll, N. Y., 1883.
Slidell, John:
Life, Louis M. Sears, Durham, N. C., 1925.
Stanton, Henry B.:
Random Recollections, 2d ed., N. Y., 1886.
Stephens, Alexander H.:
Life, R. M. Johnston and W. A. Browne, Phila., 1878.
"Correspondence," *Annual Rept. of Am. Hist. Assoc., 1911,* II.
Stevens, Isaac I.:
Life, Hazard Stevens, Boston, 1900.
Sumner, Charles:
Life, Geo. H. Haynes, Phila., 1909.
Toombs, Robert:
Life, Ulrich B. Phillips, N. Y., 1913.
"Correspondence," *Annual Rept. of Am. Hist. Assoc., 1911,* II.
Tyler, John:
Letters and Times of the Tylers, Lyon G. Tyler, Richmond, Va., 1884–5.
Upham, Nathaniel C.:
Proc. Grafton and Coös Co. Bar Assoc., 1892, by Henry P. Rolfe.
Van Buren, Martin:
An Epoch and a Man, Dennis T. Lynch, N. Y., 1929.
Wade, Benjamin F.:
Life, Albert G. Riddle, Cleveland, O., 1887.
Watterson, Henry:
"Marse Henry," N. Y., 1919.
Wells, John Sullivan:
Proc. Grafton and Coös Co. Bar Assoc., 1896, by Fletcher Ladd.
Williams, Jared W.:
Proc. Grafton and Coös Co. Bar Assoc., 1896, by Charles R. Corning.
Wentworth, John:
Congressional Reminiscences, Chicago, 1882.
Young, Brigham:
Journal of Discourses, I–II, Salt Lake City, 1853–1855.
Yulee, David L.:
Senator Yulee of Florida, Charles W. Yulee, Jacksonville, 1909.

NEWSPAPERS

(from which citations have been made)

Arkansas:
  Whig, Little Rock.
District of Columbia:
  National Intelligencer.
  Sentinel.
  Star.
  Union.
Kansas:
  Squatter Sovereign, Atchison.
Louisiana:
  Weekly Delta, New Orleans.
Maine:
  Advocate, Hallowell.
Maryland:
  Sun, Baltimore.
Massachusetts:
  Atlas, Boston.
Minnesota:
  Democrat, Minneapolis.
  Daily Pioneer, St. Paul.
  Daily Minnesotian, St. Paul.
New Hampshire:
  Cabinet, Amherst.
  Argus and Spectator, Claremont.
  Herald of Freedom, Concord.
  Hill's Patriot, Concord.
  Patriot, Concord.
  Statesman, Concord.
  State Capitol Reporter, Concord.
  Times and Enquirer, Dover.
  Journal, Portsmouth.
New Jersey:
  True American, Trenton.
  State Gazette, Trenton.
  Daily Advertiser, Newark.
New York:
  Express, New York.
  Herald, New York.
  Times, New York.
Tennessee:
  Union, Nashville.
Utah:
  Millenial Star, Salt Lake City.
Virginia:
  Enquirer, Richmond.

Great Britain:
  Times, London.

OFFICIAL PUBLICATIONS

Catalogue of Bowdoin College, annual editions, 1820–1824.
Commencement Program, Bowdoin College, 1824.
Laws of Bowdoin, 1824 edition.
Journal of the House of Representatives of the State of New Hampshire,
  sessions 1829–1832.
*Laws of the State of New Hampshire passed in the June (or November)
  Session*, 1829–1853.
Manual for the General Court (N. H.), 1917 edition.
Congressional Globe, 23d–27th, 32d–34th Congresses.
Congressional Documents (Serial numbers), same period.
Senate Executive Journal, v. IX–X, 1853–1857.
Proceedings of the Democratic National Convention, 1852 (2 editions), 1856,
  manuscript original in Buchanan MSS.
*Correspondence respecting Central America presented to both Houses of
  Parliament*, London, 1860.

CAMPAIGN LITERATURE

A. Democratic

I. *Biography.*
  Hermitage (C. Edwards Lester), *The Life of Gen. Frank. Pierce, The
    Granite Statesman*, N. Y., 1852.
  [Greene, C. G.], *The Life of Gen. Frank Pierce*, Boston, 1852 (pamphlet).
  *The Democratic Text Book containing the Lives of Pierce and King
    with illustrations of the Whig and Democratic Principles and Candidates*, Philadelphia [1852].
  *National Democratic Executive Com., Sketches of the Lives of Pierce
    and King* (also a German edition, Washington, 1852).
  Anon., *Life of Gen. Franklin Pierce, the Democratic Candidate for
    President*, Trenton, 1852 (pamphlet).
  †Jeffersonian Union, *Life of Franklin Pierce (Papers of the People,
    No. 2)*, N. Y., 1852.
  Bartlett, D. W., *Life of Gen. Franklin Pierce*, Auburn, N. Y., 1852.
  Hawthorne, Nathaniel, *Life of Franklin Pierce*, Boston, 1852 (also an
    English edition published in London; parts of it in French
    translation appeared in Paris, 1853, *Revue Britannique*, 7 Ser., t.
    XIII, under title " Le général Franklin Pierce ").
II. *Miscellaneous Pamphlets.*
  Vindication of Military Character and Services of General Pierce by his
    companions in arms in Mexico.

  * Greene's sketch revised by George and Webster.
  † Prepared by B. B. French.

The Whig Charge of [Religious] Intolerance against the New Hampshire Democrats and General Franklin Pierce.

Letter of General Shields (and other documents to urge Catholics to vote for Pierce).

The Record, the best refutation of Whig slander.

"Franklin Pierce and his Abolition Allies."

The Abolitionist Attack. Abolitionists against General Pierce (2 editions).

The Crisis: Shall Sewardism rule?

Memoir of General Scott from records contemporaneous with events.

The Political Letters and Writings of General Scott Reviewed, Discussed and Compared.

General Scott's Correspondence with Hon. W. L. Marcy, Secretary of War under President Polk.

Whig Testimony against the election of General Scott to the Presidency of the United States.

Old Soldier's Letters to General Scott.

General Scott's Illegal and Unjust Demands upon the Public Treasury.

Southern Opinions of Scott and Pierce.

The Dangers of Electing an incompetent man President. The Galphin Case! Facts for the people of all parties.

Whig Falsehoods Exposed. Gen. Pierce and the Religious Test. Gen. Scott's insult to the Catholic Church.

Pierce and King Democratic Association of the city of Washington to the Laboring and Producing classes of the United States.

New York Evening Post Documents, ten numbers.

Papers for the People, at least eighteen numbers.

Base Slanders Refuted. A Reply to Cromwell Whipple's address (broadside).

The Slander Nailed. The testimony of four Ministers of the Gospel against Mr. Whipple's Slanders (broadside).

Campaign Scrapbook—kept by Sidney Webster—N. H. Hist. Soc.

B. Whig

Frank. Pierce and his Abolition Allies.

The Presidency: Winfield Scott—Franklin Pierce. Their qualifications and fitness for that High Office.

A History of the Wrongs inflicted on Winfield Scott by the supporters of Franklin Pierce.

The Presidential Canvass, or Why Southern Whigs should support the nominees of the Whig Convention.

The Contrast; The Whig and Democratic Platforms, the Whig and Democratic Candidates for the Presidency.

A Brief chapter in the Life of Gen'l Franklin Pierce.

Franklin Pierce and Catholic Persecution in New Hampshire.

Life of General Scott.

Speech in exposition of New Hampshire democracy in its relations to Catholic emancipation, including a scrutiny of the part taken with reference thereto, by Gen. Franklin Pierce, and an exposure of the false assertions of Geo. M. Dallas and others, respecting the action of the Whigs of New Hampshire. By Wm. E. Robinson.

New Hampshire History

Bouton, Nathaniel, *History of Concord,* Concord, 1856.

Browne, George W., *History of Hillsborough, N. H., 1735–1921,* Manchester, N. H., 1921.

Cochrane, Warren R., and George K. Wood, *History of Francestown, N. H.,* Nashua, N. H., 1895.

Cook, Howard M., *Wayside Jottings,* Concord, 1910.

Hayes, John L., *Reminiscence of the Free Soil Movement in New Hampshire in 1845,* Cambridge, 1885.

Hayward, William W., *History of Hancock, N. H.,* Lowell, Mass., 1889.

Hurd D. Hamilton, *History of Hillsborough County, N. H.,* Phila., 1885.

Lyford, James O., ed., *History of Concord, N. H.,* Concord, 1903.

McClintock, John N., *History of New Hampshire,* Boston, 1888.

McFarland, Henry, *Personal Recollections,* Concord, 1889.

Pillsbury, Hobart, *History of New Hampshire,* N. Y., 1927.

Plummer, William, "Constitution of New Hampshire," *Pub. of Bar Assoc. of N. H.,* New Series, pt. 2, II, 201–204, 1905.

Rolfe, Abial, *Reminiscences of Concord,* Penacook, 1901.

Sanborn, Edwin D., *History of New Hampshire,* Manchester, N. H., 1875.

Sanborn, Frank B., *New Hampshire,* Boston, 1904.

Saunterings about Concord, N. H. Hist. Soc.

Secomb, Daniel F., *History of the Town of Amherst, Hillsborough County, N. H.,* Concord, 1883.

Smith, Charles J., *Annals of the Town of Hillsborough,* Sanbornton, N. H., 1841.

Stackpole, Everett S., *History of New Hampshire,* N. Y., 1916.

Miscellaneous

Ames, Mary C., *Ten Years in Washington,* Hartford, 1874.

Andreas, Alfred T., *History of Northern Wisconsin,* Chicago, 1881.

Bancroft, Hubert H., *Utah,* San Francisco, 1889.

Bohn's Handbook of Washington, Washington, 1852, 1856.

Bryan, Wilhelmus B., *History of the National Capital,* N. Y., 1914–16.

Burgess, John W., *Middle Period,* N. Y., 1904.

Butt, Archie, *Taft and Roosevelt, The Intimate Letters of Archie Butt,* N. Y., 1930.

Carpenter, Edmund J., *America in Hawaii,* Boston, 1899.

Cleaveland, Nehemiah, and Alpheus S. Packard, *History of Bowdoin College,* Boston, 1882.

Cole, Arthur C., *Centennial History of Illinois,* III, Springfield, 1919. *Whig Party in the South,* Washington, 1913.

Colman, Edna M., *Seventy-five years of White House Gossip*, N. Y., 1925.

Connelley, William E., *History of Kansas*, Chicago, 1928.

Craik, Elmer L., "Southern Interest in Kansas, 1854–58," *Kans. Hist. Coll.*, XV, 334–450.

Crandall, *The Early History of the Republican Party*, Boston, 1930.

Cutts, J. Madison, *Brief Treatise upon Constitutional and Party Questions*, N. Y., 1866.

Darling, Arthur B., *Political Changes in Massachusetts, 1824–1848*, New Haven, 1925.

Davis, Jefferson, *Rise and Fall of the Confederate Government*, N. Y., 1881.

Dennett, Tyler, *Americans in Eastern Asia*, N. Y., 1922.

Dixon, Susan B., *True History of the Missouri Compromise and its Repeal*, Cincinnati, 1899.

Egbert, Ercell J., *Kentucky's Interest in the Pacific R. R. Question from 1830 to 1865*, unpublished M.A. thesis, Univ. of Pa.

Ellet, Elizabeth F., *Court Circles of the Republic*, Phila., n.d.

Folwell, William W., *History of Minnesota*, St. Paul, 1921.

Force William Q., *Picture of Washington and Vicinity*, Washington, 1845.

Garber, Paul N., *Gadsden Treaty*, Phila., 1924.

Giddings, Joshua R., *History of the Rebellion*, N. Y., 1864.

Hatch, Louis, *History of Bowdoin College*, Portland, Me., 1927.

Holloway, John N., *History of Kansas*, Lafayette, Ind., 1868.

Holloway, Laura C., *Ladies of the White House*, Phila., 1884.

Hopkins, Manley, *Hawaii*, London, 1862.

Kansas State Historical Society, *The Old Pawnee Capitol*, Topeka, 1928.

Keim, De Benneville R., *Society in Washington*, Washington, 1887.

Logan, Mary S., *Thirty Years in Washington*, Hartford, 1901.

McClure, Alexander K., *Old Time Notes of Pennsylvania*, Phila., 1905.

Minor, Henry, *Story of the Democratic Party*, N. Y., 1928.

Mills' Guide to the Capitol, Washington, 1842, 1848, 1854.

Minot, John C., *Under the Bowdoin Pines*, Boston, 1907.

Moore, Jos. W., *Picturesque Washington*, Providence, 1884.

Moses, John, *Illinois*, Chicago, 1889–92.

Nichols, Roy F., *Democratic Machine, 1850–1854*, N. Y., 1923.

Nicolay, Helen, *Our Capitol on the Potomac*, N. Y., 1924.

Northend, Mary H., *We Visit Old Inns*, Boston, 1925.

    Historic Homes of New England, Boston, 1914.

Norton, Clarence C., *Democratic Party in Ante-Bellum North Carolina, 1835–1861*, Chapel Hill, 1930.

Old Pawnee Capitol, Topeka, 1928.

Phelps, Christine, *Anglo-American Peace Movement in Mid-Nineteenth Century*, N. Y., 1930.

Ray, P. Orman, *Repeal of the Missouri Compromise*, Cleveland, 1909.

Rhodes, James F., *History of the United States from . . . 1850*, N. Y., 1892.

Rippy, J. Fred, *United States and Mexico*, N. Y., 1926.

Robinson, William A., *Jeffersonian Democracy in New England*, New Haven, 1916.

Scroggs, William O., *Filibusters and Financiers*, N. Y., 1916.

Singleton, Esther, *Story of the White House*, N. Y., 1907.

Smith, Justin H., *War with Mexico*, N. Y., 1919.

Smith, William H., *Political History of Slavery*, N. Y., 1903.

Stoddard, William O., *Inside the White House*, N. Y., 1890.

Tansill, Charles C., *Canadian Reciprocity Treaty of 1854*, Baltimore, 1922.

Thomas, Benjamin P., *Russo-American Relations, 1815–1867*, Baltimore, 1930.

Thornton, Henry, *Family Prayers*, N. Y., 1841.

Wilder, Daniel W., *Annals of Kansas*, Topeka, 1875.

Williams, Mary W., *Anglo-American Isthmian Diplomacy, 1815–1915*, Baltimore, 1916.

Wilson, Henry, *History of the Rise and Fall of the Slave Power in America*, Boston, 1872–7.

ARTICLES IN PERIODICALS

"Appointment of Gov. Marcy as Sec. of State," *Magazine of History*, XV, XVI.

Brebner, J. Bartlet, "Joseph Howe and the Crimean War enlistment controversy between Great Britain and the United States," *Canadian Hist. Rev.*, Dec. 1930.

Curti, Merle E., "Young America," *Am. Hist. Rev.*, XXXII, 34.

"Documentary History of Kansas during the Administrations of Reeder, Shannon and Geary," *Kans. Hist. Coll.*, V, 1896.

Eldridge, Shalor W., "Recollections of Early Days in Kansas," *Publications of Kans. State Hist. Soc.*, II, 1920.

Ettinger, Amos A., "Proposed Anglo-Franco-American Treaty of 1852 to Guarantee Cuba to Spain," *Royal Hist. Soc. Trans.*, 4th Series, vol. XIII (1930), 149–187.

"Executive Minutes of Reeder, Shannon and Geary," *Kans. Hist. Coll.*, III, IV, 1886 and 1890.

Foster, Wm. L., "Reminiscences of the Merrimack and Cheshire Bar," *Proc. of the Southern N. H. Bar Assoc.*, 1893.

Golder, Frank G., "Russian-American Relations during the Crimean War," *Am. Hist. Rev.*, XXXI, 462–476.

"Purchase of Alaska," *Am. Hist. Rev.*, XXV, 411.

Hodder, Frank H., "Genesis of the Kansas Nebraska Act," *Proc. of State Hist. Soc. of Wis.*, 1912.

"Railroad Background of the Kansas Nebraska Act," *Miss. Valley Hist. Rev.*, XII.

Janes, Henry L., "Black Warrior Affair," *Am. Hist. Rev.*, XII, 280.

Klem, Mary J., "Missourians in the Kansas Struggle," *Proc. Miss. Vall. Hist. Assoc.*, IX, 393–413.

Learned, H. B., "Relation of Philip Phillips to the Repeal of the Missouri Compromise in 1854," *Miss. Vall. Hist. Rev.*, VIII, 303–317.

"Letter from Alexander M. Clayton to J. F. H. Claiborne relative to Cuban Affairs," *Hispanic Am. Hist. Rev.*, IX, 364.

Little, George P., "Historical Sketch," *General Catalogue of Bowdoin College*, 1894.

Lynch, William O., "Popular Sovereignty and the Colonization of Kansas, 1854–60," *Proc. Miss. Vall. Hist. Assoc.*, IX, 380–392.

Malin, James C., "Pro-slavery background of the Kansas Struggle," *Miss. Vall. Hist. Rev.*, X, 285–305.

Packard, George T., "Bowdoin," *Scribners*, May, 1876.

Paullin, Charles O., "Naval Administration, 1842–1861," *Proc. U. S. Naval Inst.*, XXXIII, 1468–1473.

Ray, P. Orman, "Genesis of the Kansas Nebraska Act," *Annual Report of Am. Hist. Assoc.*, 1914, I, 261–280.

Sawyer, William H., "Law Regulating the Traffic in intoxicating liquors; a historical review," *Proc. of Grafton & Coös Co. Bar Assoc.*, 1896.

Treudley, Mary, "United States and San Domingo, 1789–1866," *Journal of Race Development*, VII.

Webster, Sidney, "Franklin Pierce and the Canadian Reciprocity Treaty of 1854," *Proc. Grafton and Coös Co. Bar Assoc.*, 1892.

"Mr. Marcy, the Cuban Question and the Ostend Manifesto," *Pol. Sci. Quart.*, VIII, 1–32.

"Responsibility for the War of Secession," *Ibid.*, VIII, 268–286.

SUPPLEMENTARY BIBLIOGRAPHY

MANUSCRIPTS

William A. Aiken, privately owned
William Bigler, Historical Society of Pennsylvania
Francis P. and Montgomery Blair, Library of Congress
Lewis Cass, University of Michigan
4th Earl of Clarendon, Bodleian Library, Oxford
Howell Cobb, privately owned
Caleb Cushing, Library of Congress
George M. Dallas, Huntington Library, Historical Society of Pennsylvania, University of Pennsylvania
James Guthrie, Filson Club
Diary of Abigail Atherton Kent Means, 1853, privately owned
John Bassett Moore, Library of Congress
John V. L. Pruyn Journal, New York State Library
John A. Quitman, Harvard University Library
Alexander H. Stephens, Library of Congress, Emory University, Manhattanville College of the Sacred Heart
Waller Diary, Filson Club
John H. Wheeler Scrapbook, Library of Congress
David L. Yulee, Florida Historical Society

BOOKS AND PERIODICALS

Alfred Hoyt Bill, *Rehearsal for Conflict: The War with Mexico*, New York, 1947
Ray A. Billington, *The Protestant Crusade*, New York, 1938
Arthur Charles Cole, *The Irrepressible Conflict, 1850 to 1865*, New York, 1934
Avery O. Craven, *The Growth of Southern Nationalism, 1848–1861*, Baton Rouge, 1953
Avery O. Craven, *The Repressible Conflict, 1830–1861*, Baton Rouge, 1939
Avery O. Craven, *Coming of the Civil War*, New York, 1942, 1957
A. A. Ettinger, *Mission to Spain of Pierre Soulé*, New Haven, 1932
Dorothy Ganfield Fowler, *The Cabinet Politician, The Postmaster General, 1829–1909*, New York, 1943
John Arthur Garraty, *Silas Wright*, New York, 1949
Paul Wallace Gates, *Fifty Million Acres: Conflicts over Kansas Land Policy, 1854–1890*, Ithaca, 1954
Paul W. Gates, "A Fragment of Kansas Land History," *Kansas Historical Quarterly*, VI, 227–240 (August, 1937)

591

Paul W. Gates, "Southern Investments in Northern Lands Before the Civil War," *Journal Southern History*, V, 155–185 (May, 1939)

Laurence Greene, *The Filibuster*, Indianapolis, 1937

Ralph Volney Harlow, "The Rise and Fall of the Kansas Aid Movement," *American Historical Review*, XLI, 1–25 (October, 1935)

Fred Harvey Harrington, *Fighting Politician. Major-General N. P. Banks*, Philadelphia, 1948

Sister M. Michael Catherine Hodgson, *Caleb Cushing: Attorney General of the United States, 1853–1857*, Washington, 1955

Alban W. Hoopes, *Indian Affairs and their Administration with Special Reference to the Far West, 1849–1860*, Philadelphia, 1932

Henry Clyde Hubbart, *The Older Middle West, 1840–1880*, New York, 1936

William Turrentine Jackson, *Wagon Roads West: A Study of Federal Road Surveys and Construction in the Trans-Mississippi West, 1846–1869*, Berkeley, 1952

Samuel A. Johnson, *The Battle Cry of Freedom: The New England Emigrant Aid Company in the Kansas Crusade*, Lawrence, 1954

John Haskell Kemble, *The Panama Route, 1848–1869*, Berkeley, 1943

Robert McElroy, *Jefferson Davis, the Unreal and the Real*, New York, 1937

Robert McLane, *Reminiscences, 1827–1897*, n.p., 1903 ,

James C. Malin, *The Grassland of North America: Prolegomena to the History with Addenda*, Lawrence, Kansas, 1956

James C. Malin, *John Brown and the Legend of Fifty-Six*, Philadelphia, 1942

James C. Malin, "Judge Lecompte and the 'Sack of Lawrence,' May 21, 1856," *Kansas Historical Quarterly*, XX, 465–494, 553–597 (1953)

James C. Malin, "Speaker Banks Courts the Free-Soilers," *New England Quarterly*, XII, 103–112 (March, 1939)

James C. Malin, *The Nebraska Question 1852–1854*, Lawrence, 1953

W. R. Manning, ed., *Diplomatic Correspondence of the U. S. Inter-American Affairs, 1831–1860*, 12 vols., Washington, 1932–1939

Donald C. Masters, *Reciprocity Treaty of 1854*, Toronto, 1937

Robert D. Meade, *Judah P. Benjamin*, New York, 1943

Annie M. Means, *Amherst and our Family Tree*, Boston, 1921

Hunter Miller, ed., *Treaties and Other International Acts of the United States of America, 1776–1863*, 8 vols., Washington, 1931–1948

George Fort Milton, *The Eve of Conflict*, Boston, 1934

Stewart Mitchell, *Horatio Seymour of New York*, Cambridge, 1938

Allan Nevins, *Ordeal of the Union*, New York, 1947

Roy F. Nichols, "The Kansas-Nebraska Act: A Century of Historiography," *Mississippi Valley Historical Review*, XLIII, 187–212 (September, 1956)

Russell B. Nye, *George Bancroft: Brahmin Rebel*, New York, 1944

Joseph Howard Parks, *John Bell of Tennessee*, Baton Rouge, 1950

Ulrich B. Phillips, *Course of South to Secession*, New York, 1939

Samuel Augustus Pleasants, *Fernando Wood of New York*, New York, 1948

James B. Ranck, *Albert Gallatin Brown*, New York, 1937

Basil Rauch, *American Interests in Cuba*, New York, 1948

Siert F. Riepma, "Young America": A Study in American Nationalism Before the Civil War, Western Reserve University Dissertation, 1939

Robert R. Russel, *Improvement of Communication with the Pacific Coast as an Issue in American Politics, 1783–1864*, Cedar Rapids, Iowa, 1948

Henry T. Shanks, *Secession Movement in Virginia, 1847–1861*, Richmond, 1934

Henry H. Simms, *Life of Robert M. T. Hunter*, Richmond, 1935

Henry H. Simms, *A Decade of Sectional Controversy, 1851–1861*, Chapel Hill, 1942

William E. Smith, *The Francis Preston Blair Family in Politics*, New York, 1933

Ivor D. Spencer, William L. Marcy, unpublished

Hudson Strode, *Jefferson Davis, American Patriot, 1808–1861*, New York 1955

W. A. Swanberg, *Sickles The Incredible*, New York, 1956

Lloyd C. Taylor, Jr., "A Wife for Mr. Pierce," *New England Quarterly*, XXVIII, 339–348 (September, 1955)

Territorial Kansas: Studies Commemorating the Centennial, Lawrence, 1954

Harry M. Tinkcom, *John White Geary*, Philadelphia, 1940

C. Stanley Urban, "The Ideology of Southern Imperialism: New Orleans and the Caribbean, 1845–1860," *Louisiana Historical Quarterly*, XXXIX, 48–73

C. Stanley Urban, "The Africanization of Cuba Scare, 1853–1855," *Hispanic American Historical Review*, XXXVII, 29–45 (February, 1957)

Richard W. Van Alstyne, *American Diplomacy in Action*, Stanford, California, 1944

Richard W. Van Alstyne, "Anglo-American Relations, 1853–1857," *American Historical Review*, XLII, 491–500 (April, 1937)

Richard W. Van Alstyne, "John F. Crampton, Conspirator or Dupe?" *American Historical Review*, XLI, 492–502 (April, 1936)

Richard W. Van Alstyne, "Great Britain, the United States, and Hawaiian Independence, 1850–1855," *Pacific Historical Review*, IV, 15–24 (March, 1935)

Richard W. Van Alstyne, "British Diplomacy and the Clayton-Bulwer Treaty, 1850–1860," Journal of Modern History, XI, 149–183 (June, 1939)

Glyndon G. Van Deusen, *Horace Greeley*, Philadelphia, 1953

Glyndon G. Van Deusen, *Thurlow Weed*, Boston, 1947

Rudolph Von Abele, *Alexander H. Stephens*, New York, 1946

Edward S. Wallace, *Destiny and Glory*, New York, 1957

Leonard D. White, *The Jacksonians*, New York, 1954

Frank B. Woodford, *Lewis Cass*, New Brunswick, 1950

APPENDIX: THE OSTEND REPORT

A Theory of Composition

The document here reproduced is the rough draft of the Ostend report from which the fair copy sent to the State Department was made. It is found among the papers of James Buchanan and is entirely in his handwriting.

The paper appears to bear out the contention that Soulé and Buchanan had different schemes for the acquisition of Cuba. Soulé wanted a strong statement, possibly a threat of seizure if the sale of the island were refused, with which he could return to Spain and enforce his demands. Buchanan, on the other hand, wanted to save what little he could of his scheme for economic pressure, and prepare a sensible and calculated document which would appeal to bankers and taxpayers so forcibly as to gain their influence with Spanish politicians. Mason presumably was more favorable to Buchanan's views than to Soulé's. At any rate Buchanan not Soulé was chosen to draft the document in spite of the fact that Soulé had acted as secretary of the conference and had taken notes of its discussions. Provided with Soulé's notes Buchanan set to work.

That he used these notes freely in the development of the first proposition, "The United States ought if practicable to purchase Cuba with as little delay as possible," seems to be indicated by the quotation marks on pages two and three. In these pages the original Soulé ideas as interpreted by Buchanan are much worked over, modified and shaded. Their tone as finally revised is not so brusque or direct but has been softened. Space which Buchanan left for Soulé to fill in has been used by Buchanan himself.

Beginning on the fifth page, however, Buchanan is in his own province and uses his own ideas to develop the second proposition which he originally phrased "The highest and best interests of Spain demand that she should sell this island for the price which the United States is willing to give." Through the

595

next four pages the copy is much cleaner and Buchanan's economic ideas stand as he originally planned them.

Beginning at the bottom of page nine, however, Buchanan had to deal with the most difficult part of the report " But if Spain . . . refuse to sell Cuba . . . what ought to be the course of the American government? " How should Soulé's threat be incorporated? The result is embodied in two pages of curious writing; long study of this masterpiece of circumlocution leaves doubts as to its precise meaning. It certainly is not a direct threat such as Soulé wanted and such as the Republicans claimed it to be. It is a laborious attempt at a guarded hint to Spain that, if she did not sell and did Africanize the island, then the United States ought to consider whether the law of self preservation required seizure, and if the law did require it, then Cuba ought to be seized. Buchanan intended it, as we may suspect, as a possible talking point for international bankers and as a warning to Spain not to Africanize the island. Thus while the final draft incorporated Soulé's ideas in subsidiary places, Buchanan gave them uncertain meanings and took care that the document should be Buchanan's.

Hon: William L. Marcy
&c &c

Aix La Chapelles, Prussia
October 18th 1854

Sir /

                              In compliance with the wish
The undersigned, in obedience to the instructions
expressed by the President in the several confidential Despatches
which you have addressed to us respectively to that effect have
the August last took town met in conference; first at Ostend
in Belgium, on the 9th 10th & 11th Instants & then at: Aix la
Chapelles in Prussia on the days next following up to the
date hereof for the purpose of suggesting to the
President, such measures as we might deem most advisable
d sentiments
There has been "a free & ope interchange of views
which we are most happy to inform you
Here there has resulted in a cordial coincidence of opinion
the   grave & important subjects submitted to our consideration.
have agreed at the conclusion & are thoroughly convinced
We are thoroughly convinced that an immediate &
earnest effort ought to should be made by the Government of the
United States to purchase Cuba from Spain at any price
for which it can be obtained, not exceeding the sum of
The proposal should be
$100.000.000.   in our opinion, be made
in such a manner as to be prevented above to assembles
receiving diplomatic forms to the Supreme Constituent Cortes.
to accomplish this object,

We firmly believe that in the progress of human events, the time has arrived when the real interests of

Spain are ~~not~~ deeply involved in the Sales, as those of the
United States are in the purchase of the Island.
Under these circumstances we cannot anticipate a
~~favorable~~ we cannot anticipate a
~~to accomplish the object~~ unless through the means
~~interference~~ of foreign Powers who possess no interest
~~who~~ to interfere in the matter ~~~~ who have brought us to this

We proceed to state the reasons for

Conclusion   1 for the sake of clearness we shall discuss this
under two distinct heads.   the
The United States ought if practicable to purchase Cuba with

as soon as possible.

Financial Condition of the Island.

It should be made in an emphatic

interests of the Spanish people.

Then 1. It must be clear to every reflecting mind that from
the Union can never enjoy ~~repose~~ nor possess reliable
security to its ~~great~~ political future & the considerations
~~demands~~ to take as Cuba is ~~~~
attendant on it   Cuba is as necessary to the ~~United States~~ as any of
its present members & that ~~~~ it belongs
to the great family of States of which the union is the Providence has
Nature.   On the numerous navigable streams measuring an
aggregate course of some thirty thousand miles which descend
~~~~ this magnificent river into the Gulf of Mexico

the increase of the population within the last ten years

amounts to more than that of the entire Union at the

time Louisiana was annexed to it. [~~Their population was~~ " entire

~~with that which produced it~~] within] The natural & ~~proper~~

outlet to the products of ~~their fields~~ the entire population, & the ~~high was~~

~~the~~ direct intercourse with the Atlantic & the Pacific

can never be secure but must ever be in danger whilst Cuba is

States, ~~in~~ the ~~possession~~ of a distant Power ~~which is~~ [x x x

~~interest~~ a source of constant annoyance & embarrassment

these interests." [~~Under the influence~~ of these considerations,

the most accredited of ~~Northern Statesmen~~ of the ~~General~~ ~~assembly~~

~~&c &c &c~~]

indeed "The Union can never enjoy ~~repose~~ nor ~~possess~~ reliable

security as long as Cuba is not embraced within its boundaries."

[Its immediate acquisition by our Government is of

paramount importance." ~~Then forced to state~~ ~~will~~ ~~as~~

a ~~conceded form~~ & there is ~~actually~~ ~~thousand~~ its old inhabitants]

The intercourse which its proximity to our coasts encourages

between ~~them~~ & the colonies of the United States has, ~~in the process~~

~~course of time~~ so united these interests & blended their fortunes

that they now look upon each other as if they were one

people & had but one destiny.

4.

Considerations exist which render delay in the acquisition of this Island exceedingly dangerous to the United States. ~~The~~ The system of immigration & labor lately organized ~~within its limits~~ ~~will~~ ~~soon~~ ~~render here state these consideration briefly~~ & ~~with~~ the tyranny & oppression which characters the ~~Government~~ ~~of~~ its rulers threaten ~~to our federal union~~ an insurrection at every moment which ~~to the American people~~ may result in direful consequences ~~to the peace & tranquility of~~

~~Cuba~~ ~~has thus been~~ ~~converted into~~ become to us ~~the people of the United States, to whom it is~~ an unceasing danger & a ~~constant~~ permanent cause of anxiety & alarm ~~to the people of~~ ~~the United States.~~

But we need not enlarge on these topics.

= It can scarcely be apprehended that ~~the foreign nations, in~~ Powers violation of international laws, would interpose their influence with Spain to prevent our acquisition of the Island. ~~Its~~ inhabitants are now suffering under the worst of all possible Governments, — that of absolute despotism delegated by a distant power to irresponsible agents who ~~voluntarily~~ are ~~constantly~~ changing ~~at brief intervals~~ ~~who~~ are tempted to ~~take~~ improve the brief opportunity afforded them to ~~wrest accumulate~~ ~~fortunes wrest from the people all their own practical~~ accumulate ~~by exorbitant means. As long as this system shall endure, the humans may in vain demand the~~ fortunes. ~~The~~ ~~Suspension~~ of the ~~African Slave~~ trade in the Island ~~is~~ ~~rendered impossible; because whilst that infamous traffic remains an invaluable temptation to a source of immense profit to needy & avaricious officials~~ ~~accumulation of profits to needy men violent upon securing these base vile~~ ~~fortunes at the expense of the rights which ought to be held~~ ~~the proprietors of the people~~ ~~who to attain their ends scruple not to trample the most sacred principles under foot. The Spanish Government at home may be well disposed, but experience has~~ ~~proved that they cannot control these remote depositories of their power.~~ ~~most sacred~~

Besides, the ~~powerful~~ Commercial nations of the ~~hereine's~~ advantages world ~~cannot~~ fail to appreciate the great ~~advantages~~ which would

result
to these people from a dissolution of the forced &
unnatural connection between Spain & Cuba & the
annexation of the latter to the United States. The
trade of England & France with Cuba would in
that event at once assume an important & profitable
character & rapidly extend with the increasing
population, cultivation & prosperity of the Island.

2. But if the United States & every Commercial Nation
would be benefited by this transfer, the
interest of Spain would also be greatly & essentially promoted
. We cannot but see what such a sum as we
are willing to pay for the Island would effect in the development
of her vast natural resources. Two thirds of this sum
if employed in the construction of a System of Rail
Roads would ultimately prove a source of greater
wealth to the Spanish people than that opened to their
vision by Cortes. Their prosperity would date from the
ratification of the Treaty of Cession.

France has already constructed continuous lines

of rail-ways from Havre, Marseilles, Bâle, Valenciennes _Strasburg & Strasburg_
via Paris to the Spanish frontier & anxiously awaits
the day when Spain ~~will~~ _shall_ find herself in a condition
to extend these roads through her Northern Provinces &
to Madrid, Seville, Cadiz, Malaga & the frontiers of
Portugal. This object once accomplished, Spain would
become a center of attraction for the travelling world
& ~~there~~ ~~would~~ _secure_ a ~~certain~~ _permanent_ & profitable home market for
her various productions. Her fields, under the stimulus
given to industry by remunerating prices would teem
with cereal grain & her vineyards would bring forth
a vastly increased quantity of ~~luxurious~~ ~~the choicest~~ wines. Spain
would speedily become what a bountiful Providence
intended she should be, — one of the first _nations_ ~~countries~~ of
Continental Europe, — rich, powerful & contented.

Whilst two thirds of the price of the Island
would be ample for the completion of her most important
public improvements, she might with the remaining third
Millions, satisfy the demands ~~which~~ _now_ pressing so heavily
upon her credit & create a sinking fund which

would gradually relieve her from the overwhelming
debt which now paralyzing her energies.

Such is her present wretched financial condition,
that her best Bonds are sold upon her own Bourse, at about
one third of their par value; whilst another class,
on which she pays no interest, have but a nominal
value & are quoted at about one sixth of the amount
for which they were issued. These latter are held
principally by British Creditors, who may from day to day
obtain the absolute interposition of their own Government, for the purpose of
coercing payment. Intimations to that effect have
already been thrown out from high quarters; & unless some new source
of revenue shall enable Spain to provide for such exigencies, it is not improbable
that they may be waived. Should Spain reject the present golden opportunity
for developing her resources & removing her financial
embarassments, it may never again return. Cuba, in its
palmiest days, never yielded her Exchequer, after deducting
the expenses of its Government, a clear annual income of
more than a Million & a half of dollars; These expenses have increased to such a degree as to leave
a deficit chargeable on the Treasury of Spain to the amount of
Six hundred thousand dollars.
In a pecuniary point of view therefore the proposition of the

Island is an incumbrance instead of a source of
to the mother country
profit. Under no probable circumstances, can Cuba
amount
ever yield to Spain one per cent on the large sum
acquisition
which the United States are willing to pay for its ~~purchase~~.

But Spain is in emminent danger of losing the
Cuba
~~Island~~ without ~~any~~ renumeration.
now universally
Extreme oppression, it is admitted, justifies
any people in endeavouring to relieve themselves from the yoke
arbitrary
the corrupt & unrelenting
of their oppressors. The sufferings which ~~an consideration of~~
local administration necessarily
~~distant desputism~~ enlists ~~every day~~ upon the inhabitants
keep alive
of Cuba cannot fail to stimulate & ~~develope~~ that spirit
against Spain of late years
of resistance & revolution, which has been so often manifested.
In this condition of affairs
~~Under these circumstances~~ it is vain to expect, that the
sympathies of the people of the United States will not be
warmly enlisted in favor of their oppressed neighbours.

We know that the President is justly inflexible in
his determination to execute the Neutrality laws; but should
the Cubans themselves rise in revolt against the oppressions
which they suffer, no human power could prevent the
~~ardent persons~~ of
citizens of the United States & liberal minded men from
other
~~the~~ countries from rushing to their assistance. Besides the
present

is an age of adventure in which restless & daring spirits abound in every portion of the world.

It is not improbable, therefore, that Cuba may be wrested from Spain by a successful revolution; & in that event she will lose both the Island & the price which we are now willing to pay for it; — a price far beyond what was ever paid by one people to another for any province.

It may also be remarked that the return of Cuba to the United States settlement of this vexed question by the purchase would forever prevent the dangerous complications between nations to which it may otherwise give birth. It is certain that should the Cubans organize themselves an insurrection against the Spanish Government & other independent nations should come to the aid of Spain in the contest, — no human power could, in our opinion, prevent the people & Government of the United States from taking part in such a civil war in support of their neighbours & friends.

But if Spain deaf to the voice of her own interest & actuated by a false sense of honor should refuse to sell Cuba to the United States, then the question will arise, what ought to be the course of the American Government under such circumstances.

Self preservation is the first law of nature with

States as well as with individuals. All nations have at different periods acted upon this maxim. Although that it has been made the pretext for committing flagrant injustice; as in the partition of Poland & other similar cases which history records; Yet the principle itself though often has been abused, has always been recognized. The United States have never acquired a foot of territory except by fair purchase, upon the case of Mexico or as in the case of Texas, by the free & voluntary application of the people of that independent State who desired to blend their destinies with our own. Even our acquisitions from Mexico are no exception to this rule; because, although we ought have claimed them by the right of conquest, in a just war, we purchased them for what was then considered by both parties a full & ample equivalent. Our past history forbids that we should acquire the Island of Cuba without the consent of Spain, unless justified by the great law of self preservation. We must in any event preserve our own conscious rectitude & our own self respect. Whilst pursuing this course we can afford to disregard the censures of the world, to which we have so often & so unjustly been exposed.

After we shall have offered Spain a price for Cuba far beyond its present value & this shall have been refused, it will then be time to consider the question — does Cuba in the possession of Spain seriously endanger our internal peace & the existence of our cherished Union? Should this question be answered in the affirmative, then by every law human shall be justified in wresting it from Spain if

I adverse, we ~~are~~ to ~~ourselves~~ to ~~wrest it~~ of we possess the power. ~~from the possession of Spain~~. Under such circumstances we ought neither to count the cost nor regard the odds ~~against us~~ which Spain might ~~may~~ enlist against us. We forbear to enter into the question, whether the present condition of the Island ~~demanded our interference~~ would justify such a measure. We should however be recreant to our duty ~~sentiments~~, be unworthy of our gallant forefathers, & commit base treason against our posterity, should we ~~suffer~~ permit Cuba to be Africanized & become a second S. Domingo & a Black Government with all its attendant horrors to the White race & suffer the flames ~~a Black~~ actually to extend to our own neighbouring shores ~~there~~ seriously to endanger or to consume ~~Government to be established within sight of our shores~~ the fair fabric of our Union. We fear that the course & current of events, ~~& the interference~~ are rapidly tending towards such a catastrophe. We, however, hope for the best, though we ought certainly to be prepared for the worst.

And this upon the very same principle that an individual would justify ~~would be justified~~ in leaving down the burning house of his neighbour, if ~~there~~ there were no other means of preventing the flames from destroying his own home.

We, also, forbear to investigate the present condition of the
questions at issue between ~~Spain~~ & Spain the United States.
A long ~~list~~ series of injuries to our people have been committed in
Cuba by Spanish officials & are unredressed. But recently,
a most flagrant outrage on the rights of American citizens &
on the flag of the United States ~~occurred~~ was perpetrated in the harbor of
Havanna, under circumstances which, without immediate notice would have justified ~~~~
~~an immediate~~ a resort to measures of war in vindication of national honor.
That outrage is not only unatoned but the Spanish Government
has deliberately ~~justified~~ sanctioned the acts of its subordinates & assumed
the responsibility which attaches to ~~them~~. Nothing could more
impressively teach us the danger to which those peaceful relations
it has ever been the policy of the United States to cherish with
foreign Nations are constantly exposed than the circumstances of
that case. Situated as Spain & the United States are, the latter
have forborne to resort to ~~extreme~~ measures. But this course cannot
with due regard to their own dignity as an independent nation, continue;
& our recommendations now submitted are dictated by the firm belief
that the Cession of Cuba to the United States with stipulations as
beneficial to Spain as those suggested is ~~only~~ the only effectual mode
of settling all past differences & ~~of~~ securing the two countries
against future collisions.
We have already indulged seen the happy results for both countries
which followed a similar arrangement in regard to Florida.
Yours very respectfully
James Buchanan
John Y. Mason
Pierre Soulé

INDEX

* It has been thought unnecessary to refer in the index to all the important events of Pierce's career. The references given here simply amplify the table of contents for the convenience of the reader.